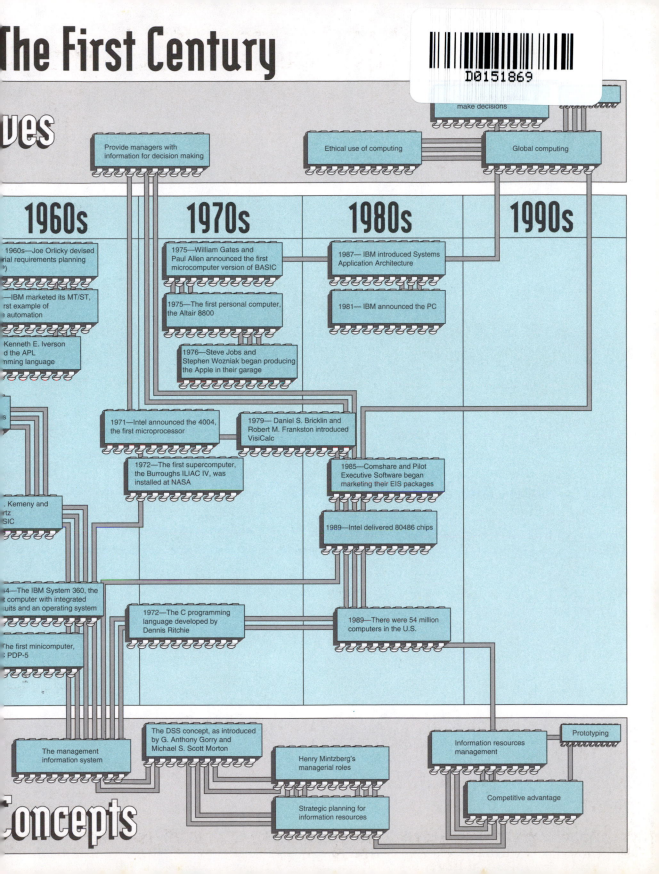

MANAGEMENT INFORMATION SYSTEMS

fifth edition

MANAGEMENT INFORMATION SYSTEMS

A Study of Computer-based Information Systems

Raymond McLeod, Jr.
Texas A & M University

Macmillan Publishing Company
New York

Maxwell Macmillan Canada
Toronto

Editor: Charles E. Stewart
Assistant Editor: Linda Ludewig
Production Supervisor: GTS Graphics
Production Manager: Aliza Greenblatt
Text Designer: GTS Graphics
Cover art: Richard Diebenkorn, *Ocean Park 115*. 1979. Oil on canvas, 8′4″ x 6′9″. Collection,
  The Museum of Modern Art, New York, Mrs. Charles G. Stachelberg Fund.
Photo Researcher: Diane Kraut
Illustrations: GTS Graphics

This book was set in Times Roman and Newtext Regular and Book by GTS Graphics
Company, and printed and bound by R. R. Donnelley & Sons. The cover was printed by
Lehigh Press, Inc.

Macmillan Publishing Company
866 Third Avenue, New York, New York 10022

Macmillan Publishing Company is part of the Maxwell Communication Group of Companies.

Maxwell Macmillan Canada, Inc.
1200 Eglinton Avenue East
Suite 200
Don Mills, Ontario M3C 3N1

Library of Congress Cataloging-in-Publication Data

McLeod, Raymond.
    Management information systems : a study of computer-base
    information systems / Raymond McLeod. Jr.—5th ed.
        p.   cm.
    Includes bibliographical references and index.
    ISBN 0-02-379481-X
    1. Management information systems.   I. Title.
HD30.213.M38   1993
658.4′038—DC20   92-41221
                                                              CIP

Printing: 2 3 4 5 6 7   Year: 3 4 5 6 7 8 9

DEDICATION

The dedication of a computer book to Thomas J. Watson, Jr., president of IBM during its early computer years, would be justified based on that fact alone. I have another, more personal reason. I was an IBM sales trainee in the San Antonio office when Mr. Watson paid a visit and addressed the employees. He was asked about the progress of a contest to sell punched card machines, and he replied that he "didn't know" about the contest, explaining his concern at the top level with problems of a longer-term nature. At first, I was surprised that this man I so admired didn't know everything. I later came to appreciate the courage that it took to admit a lack of knowledge when it would have been so easy to say "Oh, it's going quite well." That has been one of the important lessons of my life—that when you don't have the answer it is a sign of intelligence, not ignorance, to say "I don't know." I owe that lesson to Mr. Watson.

PREFACE

Two key ingredients go into the writing of any textbook. They are the selection of topics and their organization. These ingredients have always received top priority in *Management Information Systems,* but the task becomes more difficult with each edition. The reason is the dynamic nature of the computer field. Each year there are many new topics, and decisions must be made concerning where to put them and what old topics, if any, to delete.

Although these decisions present challenges to the author, two situations make the job easier. First, there are many more sources of material today than there were in the past. When the first edition of *Management Information Systems* was published in 1979, one good reference on a topic was considered a gold mine. For some topics there were no references at all. Fortunately that situation has changed. Today there are many excellent sources of material on each topic, making it possible to provide you the reader with complete descriptions from several points of view.

The second situation that simplifies the job of writing a computer text is the fact that the underlying theory really does not change that much. The theory provides the framework for the technology, and is relatively stable. So, when you set out to write a new edition it is not like starting out with a clean slate, wondering what the first word should be.

Management Information Systems has always enjoyed a strong brand loyalty among the instructors who select and use it. There are probably quite a few reasons for this support because textbook selection is a complex decision. However, the main reason must be the fact that students like it. They appreciate the logical organization and the clear descriptions. These features are possible in large part because of the solid theoretical base.

- **Logical Textbook Organization** You will find this Fifth Edition well organized, with the topics flowing logically from beginning to end. Terms are not used without first defining them.
- **Thorough Explanations** This edition also upholds the tradition of providing thorough descriptions of each topic. Emphasis has never been on the number of topics covered but on the number covered *well*.
- **Solid Theoretical Base** The framework for the text consists of many illustrations in the form of diagrams. The diagrams make it easier for you to learn the material in this course and will guide you to innovative solutions when you pursue a business career.

A MANAGEMENT ORIENTATION

As with earlier editions, the Fifth Edition views the computer through the eyes of the manager. The management orientation has always seemed appropriate, but the case is even stronger today in light of the movement to end-user computing.

When you become a manager and make use of the computer you will have many opportunities to apply the text material. Perhaps, however, you are not aiming at a career in management but in information systems. Even so, you will apply the material as you work with managers in developing their systems. Regardless of your position in the organization, it will benefit you to see problems from the management viewpoint. This text will give you that perspective.

A NEW EMPHASIS

When the first computers were applied to business problems in the 1950s there were so few users that they had almost total influence over their systems. If a user needed information and no file existed to provide the data, a special file was created. That situation changed during the 1960s and 1970s as the number of users grew. It then became necessary to consider the combined needs of all users so that the systems could function in an efficient manner. During the 1980s the situation became even tighter when a new player entered the picture—the organization. Today systems are developed in an organizational context.

As a user you will most certainly be able to use the computer as a problem-solving tool. However, this use will occur within an overall organizational framework. *Management Information Systems,* Fifth Edition, will prepare you for this environment, which is likely to be the dominant influence on business computing throughout your career.

OVERVIEW OF THE CHAPTERS

The text consists of twenty-one chapters that are organized into six parts.

Part One—The Computer As an Organizational Information System

Part One consists of the first two chapters. Chapter 1 provides an overview of the entire text, introducing all major topics and providing a foundation for the following material. Chapter 2 addresses the subject of organizational computing by describing the topics that are receiving the most attention today—strategic planning for information resources, end-user computing, the chief information officer, and information resources management.

Part Two—Information Methodologies and Tools

Chapters 3 through 7 provide you with the technology that you will need to apply the computer to your problems. Chapters 3 through 5 present methodologies, or recommended ways of doing things. Chapter 3 describes the general systems model of the firm, which regards all organizations as systems. Chapter 4 explains the systems approach—a systematic way to solve problems of all kinds. Chapter 5 describes the system life cycle, the evolutionary pattern followed by all computer-based systems.

Chapters 6 and 7 consist of the tools that you will use to apply the methodologies. *Management Information Systems* is unique in that it devotes thorough coverage to all of the important tools such as data flow diagrams, structured English, entity-relationship diagrams, Warnier-Orr diagrams, flowcharting, and CASE (computer-aided software engineering).

After completing Part Two, you will have the resources that you need to solve problems—a good set of blueprints (the methodologies) and a good kit of tools.

Part Three—The Computer As a Problem-Solving Tool

Three chapters convey the material that describes current computing technology. Chapter 8 addresses the fundamentals, Chapter 9 is devoted to the database, and Chapter 10 to data communications. These chapters do not simply rehash material learned in the introductory computer course but present the technology in the context of business problem solving.

Part Four—the Computer-Based Information System

This part of the text organizes and explains the major business applications. You have heard of many of these terms—data processing systems, management information systems, decision support systems, office automation systems, and a subset of artificial intelligence—expert systems. All of these systems comprise the computer-based information system, or CBIS. This part of the text provides you with an appreciation of the variety of ways that organizations are applying the computer.

Part Five—Organizational Information Systems

In Part Five we slice the CBIS pie a different way—according to where the users are located in the organization. Chapter 16 describes executive information systems, and Chapters 17 through 20 describe computer use in the major functional areas—marketing, manufacturing, finance, and human resources. As the trend to end-user computing intensifies, these organizational areas provide the settings for many of the innovative computer applications.

Part Six—Forces that Are Influencing the Future

Part Six consists of Chapter 21 and examines major computer-related issues facing organizations today. Firms are considering strategies aimed at making their computer installations more profitable—strategies with exotic names such as outsourcing, insourcing, and downsizing. Firms are also faced with decisions about what to do with old systems that drain resources, and they are considering strategies such as the "three Rs"—reverse engineering, restructuring, and reengineering. Computer security is also receiving more attention than ever before in the face of high-grade risks—individuals, groups, and even governments who may seek to destroy or cripple computer facilities as terrorist acts. Finally, the subject of ethics is more important in computing than ever before. Firms must use their computers in a manner that protects everyone's rights to privacy. These issues are the subject of Part Six.

MODULAR FORMAT

Although the material has a logical organization, with the topics unfolding in a manner that facilitates learning and application, it is not a rigid format that allows no deviation. One instructor may not want to cover all of the topics, and another may want to cover them in a sequence that is different from the one in the text. The material is packaged to permit such flexibility.

Unless there is some compelling reason, all courses should begin with Part One—the overview and organizational influence. But from this point on both the parts and the chapters in each part can be studied in any sequence. It is neither necessary to include all of the parts nor all of the chapters in a part. The instructor can pick and choose those chapters that represent the desired focus of the course. The package that is presented to the student will be one that is tailored to the student's needs.

PROVEN CHAPTER PEDAGOGY

With one exception, the same chapter organization of previous editions is retained. Each chapter begins with learning objectives and an introduction, and ends with key terms, key concepts, questions, problems, one or two case problems, and a selected bibliography. The new ingredient is *Topics for Discussion*—issues that are yet unresolved and lend themselves to a variety of views.

This chapter format has proven successful for thousands of students around the world for approximately fifteen years. By taking advantage of the pedagogy that is incorporated in the text and its ancillary items, you *will* learn management information sytems.

AN EXTENSIVE GLOSSARY

As each key term is presented in the chapters, it is printed in boldface and accompanied with a complete definition. In the event that you want an *additional definition,* using *different words,* you will likely find one in the glossary. It is not a complete computer dictionary, as it does not contain terms that you should have learned in an introductory computer course—terms such as bit and byte. Rather it is a *glossary of management information systems.* It includes descriptions of *all* of the important terms—almost 550 of them—that contribute to not only your computer literacy but also your information literacy—an understanding of how to use information as a problem-solving resource.

STRONG TIES TO THE LITERATURE

Footnotes and the bibliographies at the end of the chapters tie the material to the literature. Sources are not included simply because they have a current date. Many references are "classics" that provide the solid theoretical framework. However, many references focus on the ever-changing technology. As a student, you are provided not only with a look at the field today but an appreciation for how we reached this point. This appreciation enables you to predict where the field might be headed in the future.

A COMPLETE PACKAGE

As a student or instructor you have available a complete set of materials that will contribute to a successful course.

Material to Help the Student

- **Study Guide.** The study guide prepares the student for lectures by identifying the more important topics and suggesting the best ways to learn the material. The study guide also prepares the student for exams by providing sample exam questions.

Materials to Help the Instructor

- **Instructor's Manual (IM).** The IM includes suggestions for designing the course and presenting the material. Each chapter is supported by lecture notes and transparency masters (many of which are not in the text), as well as answers to end-of-chapter questions and problems, and suggestions concerning the discussion topics and cases. The *IM* also includes suggestions for integrating the *MIS Case Book* and using the *Solve It!* software and the videotape package, as well as teaching tips and sample course syllabi.
- **Test Bank: Paperback.** The paperback version of the test bank consists of true-false and multiple-choice questions plus a 10-point mini quiz for each chapter. All of these questions are written by the author, and many were used in classes during the Summer and Fall 1992 semesters.
- **Test Bank: Computer Version.** The computer version of the test bank includes the same questions as the paperback version, only in diskette form. The *Macmillan Test Generating System* enables the instructor to select questions and assemble customized exams.

Materials to Enrich Classroom Use

- **Transparencies.** A set of transparency acetates illustrate the major textbook concepts and are produced in two colors.
- **Management Information Systems Case Book.** The *MIS Case Book,* Fifth Edition, is written by George Schell, an MIS professor at the University of North Carolina at Wilmington. It provides case problems in addition to those in the text. The cases are ideal for teaching the systems approach and lend themselves to classroom discussion.
- **Solve It!** The *Solve It!* software package, a product of Azimuth Corporation, enables students to use spreadsheets and databases in solving management problems.
- **Video Tape Package.** The video package includes a selection of video tapes prepared by firms to describe their computer applications. The tapes are all professionally made and provide insights into computer use, which can only come from the firms themselves. Each video is keyed to the chapters in the text where they best apply, and mini quiz questions are included in the IM for each video.

This is the most complete set of materials ever offered with an MIS textook and provides both students and instructor with a variety of options in terms of course support.

A TEAM EFFORT

Throughout the text I use the term *we*. Although there is only one author, it has been a group effort. Playing key roles have been the people at Macmillan—my editor Charles E. Stewart, Jr., assistant editor Linda Ludewig, and freelance manager Aliza Greenblatt.

Another organization, GTS Graphics of Commerce, California, also has played a key role. Rebecca Lipshultz and Sherrie Beyen were my main contacts during manuscript preparation, coordinating the typesetting and preparation of the artwork. And midway between the coasts, in Chicago, is Timothy Taylor, my copyeditor. I have worked with Tim in the past, and we make a good team.

At other times when I say *we* I am including my students. I used the manuscript in a senior-level MIS course during the Summer 1992 and Fall 1992 semesters, and owe a debt to those students.

TECHNICAL CONSULTANTS

Several experts in certain technical areas were retained to serve as consultants, making suggestions concerning content and in many instances providing new material. These consultants were Wayne Headrick of New Mexico State University (computer fundamentals), Craig Fisher of Marist College (database), Michael Chung of Texas A & M University (data communications), Joey F. George of the University of Arizona (organizational information systems), Milam Aiken of the University of Mississippi (GDSS), and John D. Johnson of the University of Mississippi (GDSS and expert systems). The contributions of these consultants makes possible a level of competence in leading-edge technologies, which would otherwise be impossible.

ACKNOWLEDGEMENTS

I also want to thank others who provided support. Valuable suggestions concerning chapter content have been provided by the following persons, who reviewed the detailed outline: Gary Armstrong, *Shippensburg University;* Louise Boyer Burky, *Indiana University of Pennsylvania;* Jason Chen, *Gonzaga University;* Craig Fisher, *Marist College;* Joey F. George, *University of Arizona;* Jane Whitney Gibson, *Nova University;* Robert L. Heckman, *Duquesne University;* Timothy J. Hoffman, *Georgia State University;* Jim Kraushaar, *University of Vermont;* Kenneth R. Laird, *Southern Connecticut State University;* Bruce A. Lawson, *The Hartford Graduate Center;* R. Ryan Nelson, *McIntire School of Commerce;* Beverly Oswalt, *University of Central Arkansas;* David Barton Smith, *Temple University;* David Sullivan, *Oregon State University;* William J. Viereck, *St. Joseph's University;* Thomas W. Voight, *Franklin University.*

Other reviewers addressed specific portions of the manuscript: Michael Carrigg of Science Research Associates (DB2), David Dietzel of Federal Express (SUPER TRACKER), and Joobin Choobineh of Texas A & M University (Entity-relationship diagrams).

Several people from industry also contributed valuable material. This support was received from Bonnie Zelter of DIALOG Information Systems (DIALOG OnDisc), Burch Mollett of Infodata Systems (INQUIRE/Text), Shelly Cagner of Arbitron Ratings (ScanAmerica), Donald H. Bender of Government Personnel Mutual Life of San Antonio (strategic planning for information resources), Lanning P. Forrest of Strategic Mapping Inc. (graphic output), and Walter Viali of Texaco (business process redesign).

Finally, I would like to recognize the support from my family—my wife Martha and children Sharlotte and Glenn. Now that this edition is completed, I can give them the attention that they deserve.

Even though I have received much help along the way, I alone am responsible for the manner in which the material is presented. In some cases I was advised to do one thing and elected to do another. Therefore, any shortcomings are my own doing.

One final note: when I wrote the Third Edition I included a dedication to Mr. Thomas J. Watson, Jr., former president and chief executive officer of IBM. A couple of years later I met an instructor who used that text and required his students to read the dedication. When a student asked why the dedication was assigned, the instructor replied, "Because it is an important lesson." Since the lesson is just as appropriate today as it was in 1986, we had better leave it in.

Raymond McLeod, Jr.
Department of Business Analysis and Research
College of Business Administration
Texas A & M University
College Station, Texas 77843

Brief Contents

CONTENTS

Part II   INFORMATION METHODOLOGIES AND TOOLS   71

Part III   THE COMPUTER AS A PROBLEM-SOLVING TOOL   271

■ **Chapter 8** Fundamentals of Computer Processing   273

■ **Chapter 9** The Database and Database Management System   312

■ **Chapter 10** **Data Communications**   352

Part IV   THE COMPUTER-BASED INFORMATION SYSTEM   387

■ Chapter 11   The Data Processing System   389

■ Chapter 12   Management Information System   423

■ Chapter 15 Expert Systems   528

Part V ORGANIZATIONAL INFORMATION SYSTEMS 567

■ Chapter 16 Executive Information Systems   571

■ Chapter 18   Manufacturing Information Systems 642

■ Chapter 19   Financial Information Systems   677

■ Chapter 20   Human Resource Information Systems   **711**

Part VI   FORCES THAT ARE INFLUENCING THE FUTURE   741

THE MACMILLAN SERIES IN INFORMATION TECHNOLOGY

BIDGOLI

Information Systems Literacy and Software Productivity Tools: DOS, WordPerfect, Lotus 1-2-3 and dBASE III Plus, 0-02-309421-4, 1991

Information Systems Literacy and Software Productivity Tools: DOS, WordStar, Lotus 1-2-3, and dBASE III Plus, 0-02-309431-1, 1991

Information Systems Literacy and Software Productivity Tools: Introductory Concepts, 0-02-309474-5, 1991

Information Systems Literacy and Software Productivity Tools: DOS, 0-02-309427-3, 1991

Information Systems Literacy and Software Productivity Tools: dBASE III Plus, 0-02-309428-1, 1991

Information Systems Literacy and Software Productivity Tools: WordPerfect 5.1, 0-02-309429-X, 1991

Information Systems Literacy and Software Productivity Tools: Goldspread, 0-02-309461-3, 1991

Information Systems Literacy and Software Productivity Tools: WordStar 5.5, 0-02-309451-6, 1991

Information Systems Literacy and Software Productivity Tools: Quattro, 0-02-309455-9, 1991

Information Systems Literacy and Software Productivity Tools: IBM Basic, 0-02-309465-6, 1991

Information Systems Literacy: Concepts, DOS 5.0, WordPerfect 5.1, Lotus 1-2-3 Rel. 2.3, dBASE IV Rel. 1.1 and 1.5, 0-02-309481-8, 1993

Information Systems Literacy: Concepts, 0-02-309501-6, 1993

Information Systems Literacy: dBASE IV Rel. 1.1 and 1.5, 0-02-309491-5, 1993

Information Systems Literacy: DOS 5.0, 0-02-309521-0, 1993

Information Systems Literacy: Lotus 1-2-3 Rel. 2.3, 0-02-309511-3, 1993

Information Systems Literacy: Paradox 3.5, 0-02-309541-5, 1993

Information Systems Literacy: Quattro Pro Rel. 3.0, 0-02-309499-0, 1993

Information Systems Literacy: Windows 3.1, 0-02-309533-4, 1993

Information Systems Literacy: WordPerfect 5.1, 0-02-309531-8, 1993

BOHL/RYNN   **Tools for Structured Design, Third Edition,** 0-02-311861-X, 1993

DOLOGITE   **Developing Knowledge-Based Systems Using VP-Expert,** 0-02-381886-7, 1993

DUGGAL   **Business Programming Using dBASE IV,** 0-02-330588-6, 1992

ELIASON   **Online Business Computer Applications, Third Edition,** 0-02-332481-3, 1991

ERICKSON/VONK   **Easy PageMaker: A Guide to Learning PageMaker for the IBM PC,** 0-675-21305-3, 1991

Easy PageMaker: A Guide to Learning PageMaker for the Macintosh Featuring Version 4.0, 0-675-21382-7, 1992

HOBART/ OCTERNAUD/ SYTSMA

Hands-On Computing Using DOS, 0-675-22386-5, 1991

Hands-On Computing Using Procomm, 0-675-22368-7, 1991

Hands-On Computing Using Microsoft Word, 0-675-22370-9, 1991

Hands-On Computing Using WordStar 5.5, 0-675-22372-5, 1991

Hands-On Computing Using WordPerfect 5.1, 0-675-22374-1, 1991

Hands-On Computing Using FoxPro, 0-675-22376-8, 1991

Hands-On Computing Using Paradox 3, 0-675-22378-4, 1991

Hands-On Computing Using dBASE IV, 0-675-22384-9, 1991

Hands-On Computing Using Lotus 1-2-3 Release 2.2, 0-675-22380-6, 1991

INGALSBE

Business Applications Software for IBM and Compatible Microcomputers: Alternate Edition with WordStar 5.5, dBASE III+, and Lotus 1-2-3 (with Software Disks), 0-675-22389-X, 1991

FoxPro for IBM and Compatible Microcomputers (with Software Disk), 0-675-22394-6, 1991

Using Computers and Application Software, Second Edition, 0-02-359640-6, 1992

Computing Fundamentals, 0-02-359712-7, 1992

Application Software Fundamentals, 0-02-359702-X, 1992

JESSUP/VALACICH   **Group Support Systems,** 0-02-360625-8, 1993 (out already)

KROENKE	**Database Processing: Fundamentals, Design, Implementation, Fourth Edition,** 0-02-366875-X, 1992
LAUDON/LAUDON	**Management Information Systems: A Contemporary Perspective, Second Edition,** 0-02-368101-2, 1991
MARTIN, M.	**Analysis and Design of Business Information Systems,** 0-675-20852-1, 1991
MARTIN/DEHAYES/ HOFFER/PERKINS	**Managing Information Technology: What Managers Need to Know,** 0-02-328231-2, 1991
MCLEOD	**Management Information Systems, Fifth Edition,** 0-02-379841-X, 1993
MOCKLER	**Computer Software to Support Strategic Management Decision Making,** 0-02-381895-6, 1992
	Developing Knowledge-Based Systems Using an Expert System Shell, 0-02-381875-1, 1992
MOCKLER/ DOLOGITE	**Knowledge-Based Systems: An Introduction to Expert Systems,** 0-02-381897-2, 1992
NEWCOMER	**Select...SQL: The Relational Database Language,** 0-02-386693-4, 1992
OLSON/COURTNEY	**Decision Support Models and Expert Systems,** 0-02-389340-0, 1992
ORMAN	**Elements of Information Systems,** 0-02-389475-X, 1991
RAMOS/ SCHROEDER/ SIMPSON	**Data Communication and Networking Fundamentals Using Novell NetWare,** 0-02-407791-7, 1992
RAMOS/ SCHROEDER	**Contemporary Data Communications,** 0-02-408021-7, 1993
ROCHE	**Managing Information Technology in Multinational Corporations,** 0-02-402690-5, 1992
ROWE	**Business Telecommunications, Second Edition,** 0-02-404104-1, 1991
SALKIND	**Applying Macintosh: Solutions, Ideas, and Tools,** 0-675-22133-1, 1992
	Using Windows, 0-02-405345-7, 1993
	Using Lotus for Windows, 0-02-405287-6, 1993
	Using WordPerfect for Windows, 0-02-405346-5, 1993
SCHROEDER/ RAMOS	**Introduction to Microsoft Works: A Problem Solving Approach,** 0-02-408015-2, 1991
	Introduction to Microsoft Works: A Problem Solving Approach, Macintosh Version, 0-02-407771-2, 1992
SPRANKLE	**Problem Solving and Programming Concepts, Second Edition,** 0-02-415340-0, 1992
SZYMANSKI/ SZYMANSKI/ MORRIS/ PULSCHEN	**Introduction to Computers and Information Systems, Second Edition,** 0-0-675-21272-3, 1991
	Introduction to Computers and Information Systems with Hands-On Software Tutorials, 0-672-22184-6, 1991
	Computers and Applications Software, Second Edition, 0-675-21269-3, 1991
TRAUTH/KAHN/ WARDEN	**Information Literacy: An Introduction to Information Systems,** 0-675-20841-6, 1991
TURBAN	**Expert Systems and Applied Artificial Intelligence,** 0-02-421665-8, 1992
	Decision Support and Expert Systems: Management Support Systems, Third Edition, 0-02-421691-7, 1993
WENIG	**Introduction to C.A.S.E. Technology Using Visible Analyst Workbench,** 0-675-21367-3, 1991

THE COMPUTER AS AN ORGANIZATIONAL INFORMATION SYSTEM

Managers have always used information to perform their tasks, so the subject of management information is nothing new. What *is* new is the ease with which accurate and current information can be obtained. The innovation that makes this capability possible is the electronic computer. Organizations are becoming increasingly aware that information is a resource of strategic importance, and that the computer can cultivate that resource.

In Chapter 1 we trace the evolution of the computer as it has been applied to an expanded scope of business applications. The first application involved the handling of accounting transactions and was called *data processing*. Then, managers and computer scientists recognized that far greater potential existed in the form of information support for decision making. The first application of the computer as an information system was called the *management information system*, and was followed by more specialized applications such as *decision support systems*, *office automation*, and *expert systems*. We use the term *computer-based information system (CBIS)* to describe all of these business applications of the computer. The objective of Chapter 1 is to introduce the CBIS as an information management tool.

Chapter 2 expands upon the topic of information management by explaining a concept that is currently stimulating much attention in business computing. The concept is called *information resources management (IRM)*. IRM recognizes the strategic value of information as a resource and provides the vehicle for achieving a more competitive position in the marketplace.

The two chapters in Part One provide the important setting within which the subject of computer-based information systems will be studied.

Chapter 1

Introduction to the Computer-based Information System

LEARNING OBJECTIVES

After studying this chapter, you should:

- Know the main types of resources that are available to a firm
- Appreciate that information needs to be managed just like any other resource
- Understand why there is so much interest in managing information
- Know who the users of computers are
- Know where managers are located within an organization, what they do, and what basic skills and knowledge they should possess
- Have an introductory understanding of systems concepts
- Know the difference between data and information
- Know the elements of the computer-based information system (CBIS) and how they evolved
- Be familiar with the types of information specialists who can assist the user in developing information systems
- Understand that users are doing more and more of their application development, and how this trend affects information specialists
- Appreciate the difficulty in economically justifying the cost of a computer system
- Understand how a computer system evolves through a life cycle and recognize the roles played by the manager and information specialists
- Understand that information systems belong to their users—not to the information specialists

3

INTRODUCTION

Information is one of the main types of resources that are available to the manager. Information can be managed just as any other resource, and interest in this topic stems from two influences. First, business has become more complex, and second, the computer has achieved improved capabilities.

The information output of computers is used by managers, nonmanagers, and persons and organizations within the firm's environment. Managers are found on all organizational levels of the firm, and in all functional areas. Managers perform functions and play roles, and need skills in communications and problem solving in order to be successful. Managers should be computer literate, but, more importantly, they should be information literate.

It is helpful if the manager has an ability to see his or her unit as a system comprised of subsystems and existing in a larger supersystem. The firm is a physical system, but it is managed through the use of a conceptual system, which consists of an information processor that transforms data into information and represents the physical resources.

The first major computer application was data processing. It has been followed by four others: management information systems, decision support systems, office automation, and expert systems. All five of these applications comprise the computer-based information system (CBIS).

Firms establish an information services organization of information specialists to provide expertise in the development of computer-based systems. These specialists include systems analysts, database administrators, network specialists, programmers, and operators. During the past few years users have begun doing much of the work of the specialists—a phenomenon called end-user computing.

It is very difficult to prove the economic value of a computer application, but much analysis goes into justifying each potential project. Once underway, the project evolves through five life-cycle phases. Information specialists can participate in varying degrees, but the entire cycle, including both development and use, is managed by the manager.

INFORMATION MANAGEMENT

The manager of a small newsstand in the lobby of a hotel can manage by observing the tangible assets—the merchandise, the cash register, the room, and the customer flow. As the scale of operation increases to a firm with several hundred or several thousand employees, with operations scattered over a wide area, the manager relies less on observation and more on information.[1] The manager uses many reports or information displays to reflect the physical condition of the firm. It is easy to imagine the almost complete reliance that the president of Wal-Mart or Texaco or Sears

---

[1] We use the term **firm** in this text to describe any type of organization. The text material applies to nonprofit and governmental organizations as well as those of a profit-seeking nature.

must place on information. These executives could very well regard information as their most valuable resource.

Main Types of Resources

The manager manages five main types of resources:

- Personnel
- Material
- Machines (including facilities and energy)
- Money
- Information (including data)

The number of types is intentionally small in order to make the classification easy to use.[2] The task of the manager is to manage these resources in order to use them in the most effective way.

The first four resource types are tangible; they exist physically and can be touched. We use the term **physical resource** to describe them. The fifth resource type, information, is not valuable for its tangible form but for what it represents. We use the term **conceptual resource** to describe information and data. Managers use conceptual resources to manage physical resources.

Management of the Resources

Resources are acquired and assembled to be available for use when needed. Very often the assembly process entails converting an essentially raw material into a refined form, such as training an employee or constructing a piece of special machinery. Once these resources have been assembled, the manager strives to maximize their use. He or she minimizes their idle time and keeps them functioning at peak efficiency. Finally, the manager replaces these resources at a critical time— before they become inefficient or obsolete.

How Information Is Managed

It is easy to see how the manager manages the physical resources, but the concept is a little more difficult to envision for the conceptual resources. However, it can be done. The manager ensures that the necessary raw data is gathered and then processed into usable information. He or she then assures that appropriate individuals within the organization receive the information in the proper form at the proper time so that it can be used. Finally, the manager discards information that has outlived its usefulness and replaces it with information that is current and accurate.

---

[2]This classification is from Richard J. Hopeman, *Systems Analysis and Operations Management* (Columbus, OH: Charles E. Merrill, 1969), 125–30.

All of this activity, acquiring information, using it in the most effective way, and discarding it at the proper time, is called **information management**.

INTEREST IN INFORMATION MANAGEMENT

Managers have paid an increasing amount of attention to information management during recent years for two main reasons. First, business activity has become increasingly complex. Second, the computer has acquired improved capabilities.

Increasing Complexity of Business Activity

Business has always been complex, but it is more so today than ever before. All firms are subject to international economic influences and compete in a worldwide marketplace, the technology of business is becoming more complex, the time frame for taking action is shrinking, and there are social constraints.

International Economic Influences Firms of all sizes are subject to economic influences that can originate anywhere in the world. Such influence can be seen in the relative values of the currencies of each nation. Buyers make purchases in those countries where their currencies have the greatest value. For example, when Mexico devalued its peso during the late 1980s, tourists decided to take their vacations south of the border rather than in other places, such as Hawaii.

Worldwide Competition Firms no longer compete in only their own geographic area. Rather, competition exists on a worldwide scale. The effects of this competition can be seen in the imports from foreign countries. The decision by General Motors in late 1991 to close many of its plants indicates that even industry giants are not insulated from the effects of competition, which can originate anywhere in the world.

Increasing Complexity of Technology We see examples of technology in business every day—bar code scanners in supermarkets, computer-based airline reservation systems, automated teller machines, and closed-circuit television in parking garages. There is also much behind-the-scenes technology that we do not see—factory robots and automated merchandise storage and handling equipment, for example. Firms invest in this technology so that they may perform their necessary operations. Just think what would happen if Federal Express, L. L. Bean, or AT&T could no longer use their computers!

Shrinking Time Frames All phases of business operations are performed more rapidly today than ever before. Sales representatives engage in telemarketing to contact their customers within seconds by telephone, sales orders are transmitted electronically from one computer to another, and manufacturers schedule raw material deliveries to arrive "just in time."

Social Constraints   Oddly enough, not all pressures favor production; some favor *non*production. This is true in the case of products and services that society finds undesirable. Business decisions must be based on economic factors, but social costs and payoffs must be considered as well. Plant expansion, new products, new sales outlets, and similar actions must all be weighed in terms of their environmental impacts.

Each of these influences contribute to the complexity of business.

Improved Computer Capabilities

Compared to today's computers, the first models were dinosaurs in terms of their size and speed. The giant computers of the 1950s and 60s were located down the hall, to be touched only by the firm's computer specialists. Users never came in direct contact with the hardware, but this arrangement suited the users just fine. In most cases, users did not know how to use the computers, and many were afraid to learn.

Today's users, on the other hand, most likely have either keyboard terminals or microcomputers in their offices. Many of the micros are connected to other computers in a network. Not only are the computers available, the users know how to use them.

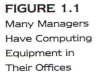

FIGURE 1.1
Many Managers
Have Computing
Equipment in
Their Offices

Courtesy International Business Machines Corporation

Today's user does not regard the computer as something special but as a necessary piece of office equipment, just like a filing cabinet, a copying machine, or a telephone.

WHO ARE USERS?

The first users of computer output were clerical employees in the accounting area, where the computer performed applications such as payroll, inventory, and billing. Some information was also made available to managers but as a byproduct of the accounting applications.

The idea of using the computer as a management information system (MIS), was a major breakthrough in that it recognized the needs of managers for problem-solving information. When firms embraced the MIS concept, they began to develop applications specifically aimed at management support.

But managers were not the only beneficiaries of MIS. Nonmanagers and staff specialists used the output as well. Users also existed outside the firm. Customers received invoices and statements, stockholders received dividend checks, and the federal government received tax reports. So, the term MIS really did not tell the whole story. The MIS was not a system for producing *management* information, but *problem-solving* information.

We recognize that the users of computer output include:

- Managers
- Nonmanagers
- Persons and organizations in the firm's environment

However, in this text, we will emphasize use by the managers. The reason for this approach is that before long you will be a manager, and the purpose of the text is to prepare you to use the firm's computer resources as a step toward becoming a successful manager.

Where Managers Are Found

Managers can be found everywhere, but it is helpful to recognize that they exist on various levels and within various functional areas of the firm.

Management Levels   Managers at the top of the organizational hierarchy, such as the president and vice presidents, are often referred to as being on the **strategic planning level**.[3] This term recognizes the impact that decisions have on the entire organization for years to come. Middle-level managers include regional managers, product directors, and division heads. Their level has been called the

---

[3] The names for the levels are attributed to Robert N. Anthony. For more detail, *see* his 1965 book, *Planning and Control Systems: A Framework for Analysis,* published by Harvard University.

management control level, recognizing the responsibility to put plans into action and to ensure that goals are met. Lower-level managers include department heads, supervisors, and project leaders, who are responsible for accomplishing the plans specified by managers on upper levels. This lowest level has been called the **operational control level,** as it is where the operations of the firm occur.

The term **executive** is often used to describe a manager on the strategic planning level. In some firms, the president and vice presidents comprise an **executive committee** that addresses the major issues facing the firm.

When designing information systems, it is important to take into consideration the manager's level, as this can influence both the source of information and how it is presented. The top graphic of Figure 1.2 shows that managers on the strategic planning level place greater emphasis on environmental information than do managers on the lower levels, and that managers on the operational control level regard internal information as most vital. The bottom graphic shows that strategic-planning-level managers prefer information in a summary format, whereas operational-control-level managers prefer detail.

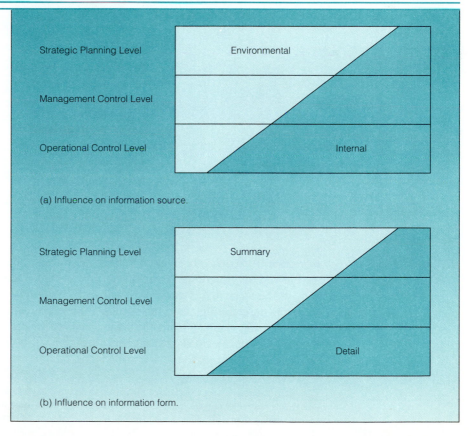

FIGURE 1.2
Management Level Can Influence both the Source and Presentation Form of Information

Strategic Planning Level   Environmental

Management Control Level

Operational Control Level   Internal

(a) Influence on information source.

Strategic Planning Level   Summary

Management Control Level

Operational Control Level   Detail

(b) Influence on information form.

FIGURE 1.3
Managers Can Be Found on All Levels and in All Functional Areas of
the Firm

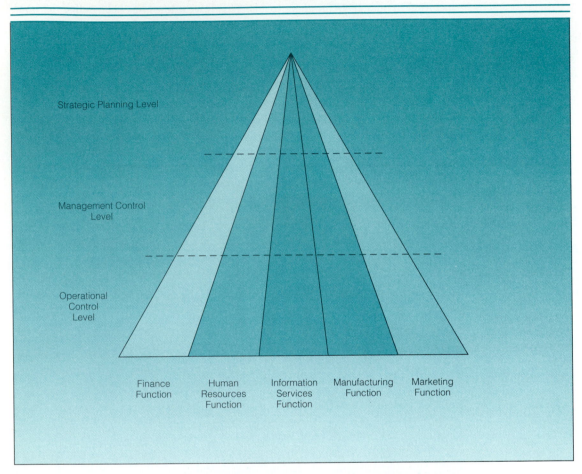

Functional Areas   In addition to these organizational levels, managers can be found in various **functional areas** of the firm, where resources are segregated according to the work that is performed. The three traditional functional areas are marketing, manufacturing, and finance. Recently, two additional areas have assumed major importance—human resources and information services.[4]

Figure 1.3 illustrates how managers can be grouped by level and functional area in a manufacturing firm.

[4]The term **information services** is used in this text to describe the organizational unit of the firm, which has the responsibility to manage the firm's information resources. **IS** is also used, but it can also mean **information systems.** You often see the letters **IT,** which means **information technology.**

What Managers Do

Even in light of obvious differences that exist between the management levels and functional areas, all managers perform the same functions and play the same roles.

Management Functions   Early in this century, around 1914, the French management theorist, Henri Fayol, recognized that managers perform five major **management functions**. First, managers *plan* what they are to do. Then, they *organize* to meet the plan. Next, they *staff* their organization with the necessary resources. With the resources in place, they *direct* them to execute the plan. Finally, they *control* the resouces—keeping them on course.

All managers, regardless of their level or functional area, perform these functions to some degree, although perhaps with varying emphasis. Figure 1.4 illustrates how management level can influence the emphasis on the various management functions.[5]

Managerial Roles   Within the past twenty years the idea of managerial roles has become popular. Henry Mintzberg, a professor at McGill University in Canada, decided that Fayol's functions did not tell the whole story. He developed

FIGURE 1.4

Management Level Can Influence the Relative Emphasis on the
Management Functions

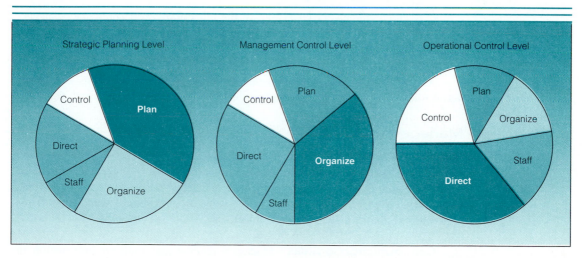

[5]Figure 1.4 is a *conceptual representation* of a condition that is *believed* to exist, but for which there is very litle supporting evidence. Other diagrams in this text, such as Figure 1.2, are of this type. The diagrams provide useful guidelines, but you must remember that each manager has unique information needs, and it is important to identify those needs when designing information systems.

TABLE 1.1 Mintzberg's Managerial Roles	*Interpersonal Roles*	*Figurehead* The manager performs ceremonial duties, such as giving visiting dignitaries tours of the facilities. *Leader* The manager maintains the unit by hiring and training the staff and providing motivation and encouragement. *Liaison* The manager makes contacts with persons outside the manager's own unit—peers and others in the unit's environment—for the purpose of attending to business matters.
	Informational Roles	*Monitor* The manager constantly looks for information bearing on the performance of the unit. The manager's sensory perceptors scan both the internal activity of the unit and its environment. *Disseminator* The manager passes valuable information along to others in the unit. *Spokesperson* The manager passes valuable information along to those outside the unit—superiors and persons in the environment.
	Decisional Roles	*Entrepreneur* The manager makes rather permanent improvements to the unit, such as changing the organizational structure. *Disturbance handler* The manager reacts to unanticipated events, such as the devaluation of the dollar in a foreign country where the firm has operations. *Resource allocator* The manager controls the purse strings of the unit, determining which subsidiary units get which resources. *Negotiator* The manager resolves disputes both within the unit and between the unit and its environment.

a more detailed framework consisting of the ten **managerial roles** that managers play, involving interpersonal, informational, and decisional activities. Table 1.1 lists the roles and provides brief definitions.

As you design information systems, these management functions and managerial roles will provide useful ways to classify the work that managers do.

Management Skills

Many skills can be listed that a successful manager should possess but two stand out as being basic—communications and problem solving. Managers communicate with their subordinates, their superiors, other managers on the same level, and persons outside the firm. They also solve problems by making changes to the firm's operations so that it can achieve its objectives.

Communications Skills   Managers receive and transmit information in both an oral and a written form. Oral communications occur in meetings, while touring facilities, in the process of enagaging in telephone conversations, and during business meals and social activities. Written communications include reports, memos, letters, and periodicals. Figure 1.5 shows how these media can originate

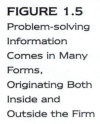

FIGURE 1.5

Problem-solving Information Comes in Many Forms, Originating Both Inside and Outside the Firm

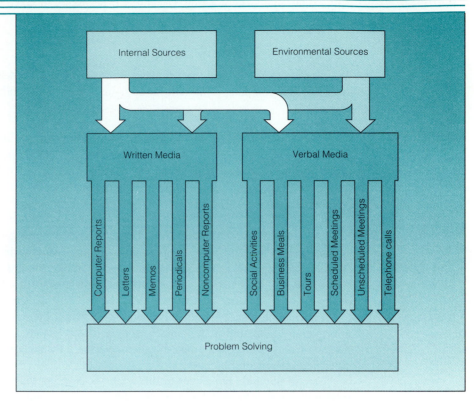

either internally or in the environment and how the manager uses the information in problem solving.

Individual managers have their own media preferences. One manager may favor telephone conversations over computer reports, whereas another may feel just the opposite. Managers assemble a mix of communications media to fit their particular management style.

Problem Solving Skills   We define **problem solving** as all of the activities that lead to the solution of a problem. Much attention is currently being given to problem solving, with the concept and selected techniques being introduced at the elementary school level. However, it is easy to get the idea that a problem is always something bad because the subject of opportunity seizing receives relatively little attention. We incorporate opportunity seizing into problem solving by defining a **problem** as a condition or event that is harmful or potentially harmful to a firm in a negative way, *or is beneficial or potentially beneficial in a positive way.* The outcome of the problem solving activity is a solution.

During the process of solving problems, managers engage in **decision making,** which is the act of selecting from alternate courses of action. A **decision** is a particular selected course of action. Usually, it is necessary to make multiple decisions in the process of solving a single problem.

Management Knowledge

The term literacy has been used to describe two types of knowledge that are key to use of the computer. One term is computer literacy; the other is information literacy.

Computer Literacy
The knowledge of the computer that is necessary to function in today's world is called **computer literacy**. This knowledge includes an understanding of computer terminology, a recognition of the strengths and weaknesses of the computer, an ability to use the computer (although not necessarily by being a programmer), and so on.

Information Literacy
In addition to understanding the computer, the modern manager should have an information literacy. **Information literacy** consists of understanding how to use information at each step of the problem-solving process, where that information can be obtained, and how to share information with others.

Information literacy is not dependent on computer literacy. A manager can be information literate but not computer literate. In fact, if one had to choose, information literacy is more important. Ideally, however, a manager should be both computer *and* information literate.

One of the main objectives of this textbook is to lay the foundation for information literacy. You will build on this foundation as you gain experience as a manager.

THE MANAGER AND SYSTEMS

Management experts often say that a manager should view his or her organization as a system.

What Is a System?

A **system** is a group of elements that are integrated with the common purpose of achieving an objective. An organization such as a firm or a functional area fits this definition. The organization consists of the resources that we identified earlier, and they work toward achieving particular objectives that are specified by the owners or management.

System Elements

All systems do not have the same combination of elements, but a basic configuration is illustrated in Figure 1.6. Input resources are transformed into output

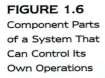

FIGURE 1.6

Component Parts
of a System That
Can Control Its
Own Operations

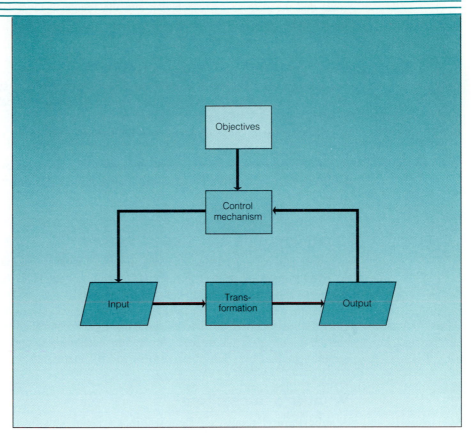

resources. The resources flow from the *input element*, through the *transformation element*, and to the *output element*. A *control mechanism* monitors the transformation process to ensure that the system meets its *objectives*. The control mechanism is connected to the resource flow by means of a *feedback loop,* which obtains information from the system output and makes it available to the control mechanism. The control mechanism compares the feedback signals to the objectives and directs signals to the input element when it is necessary to change the system operation.

When this arrangement of elements is used to explain a heating system, for example, the input represents the fuel, such as natural gas or coal. The heating process transforms the fuel into heat—the output. The control mechanism is the thermostat, the feedback loop is the wiring that connects the thermostat to the heater, and the objective is the temperature that is dialed into the thermostat. When the system elements represent a manufacturer, the input resources are the raw materials, which are transformed into finished products or services by the manufacturing process. The control mechanism is the firm's management, the objectives are the goals that the firm seeks to achieve, and the feedback loop is the flow of information both to and from management.

Open-loop and Closed-loop Systems

Not all systems are able to control their own operations. A system without the control mechanism, feedback loop, and objective elements is called an **open-loop system**. Figure 1.7 illustrates an open-loop system. An example of such a system is a small electric space heater that is plugged in, turned on, and gives out heat until it is turned off. There is no way to control its output.

A system *with* the three control elements (objectives, control mechanism, and feedback loop) is called a **closed-loop system**. Figure 1.6 illustrates a closed-loop system.

Open Systems and Closed Systems

A system that is connected to its environment by means of resource flows is called an **open system**. A heating system, for example, obtains its input from a utility company, and makes its heat available to the building or room that it is heating.

Using the same logic, a system that is not connected to its environment is a **closed system**. Closed systems exist only in tightly controlled laboratory situations and are not of interest to us here. We are interested only in open systems; for, those are the type that best describes the firm and its operations.

What Is a Subsystem?

A **subsystem** is simply a system within a system. This means that systems exist on more than one level.

An automobile is a system composed of subsidiary systems such as the engine system, body system, and frame system. Each of these systems is composed of lower-level systems. For example, the engine system is a combination of a carburetor system, a generator system, a fuel system, and so on. These systems may be subdivided into still lower-level systems or elemental parts. The parts of a sys-

FIGURE 1.7
An Open-loop
System

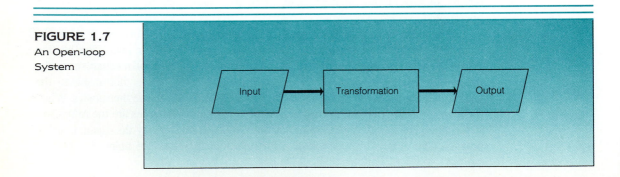

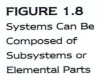

FIGURE 1.8

Systems Can Be
Composed of
Subsystems or
Elemental Parts

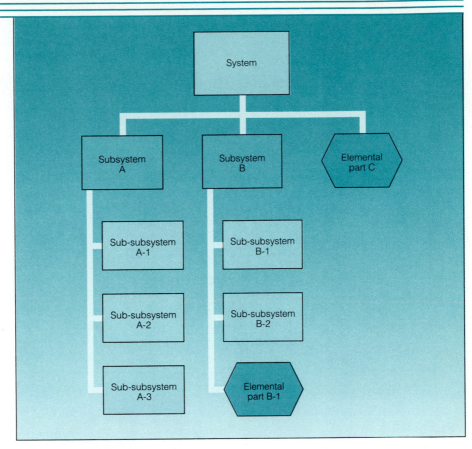

tem therefore may be either lower-level systems or elemental parts. Figure 1.8 illustrates this relationship.

What Is a Supersystem?

Although the term supersystem is not often used, they do exist. When a system is a part of a larger system, the larger system is the **supersystem**. For example, the Marine Corps is a system, but it is also part of a larger system—the Department of Defense. The DOD is a supersystem of the Marine Corps and is also a subsystem of the federal government.

The Business System

The manager's major responsibility is to assure that the firm meets its objectives. Efforts are aimed at making the various parts of the firm work together as they should. The manager is the control element in the system, keeping it on course as it moves toward its objectives.

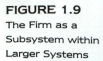

FIGURE 1.9

The Firm as a
Subsystem within
Larger Systems

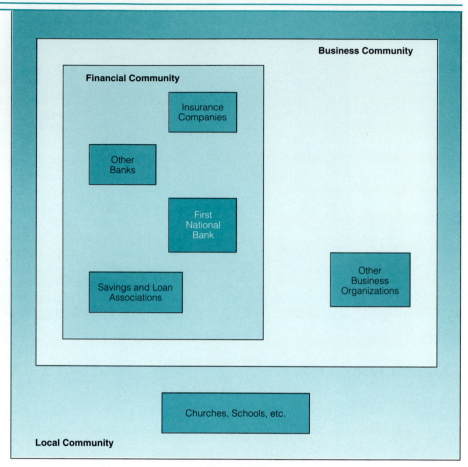

As with all systems, the system of the firm exists in one or more larger environmental systems or supersystems. If the firm is a bank, for example, it is part of the financial community. It is also part of both the business community and the local community as shown in Figure 1.9.

The system of the firm also includes smaller systems, or subsystems. The subsystems of the bank may be such departments as savings, demand deposit (checking accounts), and installment loan. Although each of these subsystems has its own objectives, these subsidiary objectives support and contribute to the overall objectives of the firm (the bank).

Physical Systems and Conceptual Systems

The business firm is a **physical system**. It is composed of physical resources. A **conceptual system,** on the other hand, is a system that uses conceptual resources, information and data, to represent a physical system. A conceptual system commonly exists as mental images in the manager's mind, as figures or lines on a sheet of paper, or as magnetized areas of the computer's storage.

The computer is a physical system, but the data and information stored in it can be viewed as a conceptual system. The data and information represent one or more physical systems. *How* the data and information is stored is unimportant. What *is* important is what the data and information represents. The physical system is important for what it is; the conceptual system is important for its representation of the physical system. For example, if the computer storage indicates that there are seventy widgets in the warehouse, an inspection of the warehouse should reveal those seventy widgets.

A good example of the importance of the conceptual system is provided by Lee Iacocca, describing the situation at Chrysler when he became chairman in 1978:

> A couple of months after I arrived, something hit me like a ton of bricks. We were running out of cash! Gradually, I was finding out that Chrysler had no overall system of financial controls—nobody in the whole place seemed to fully understand what was going on when it came to financial planning and projecting. I couldn't find out *anything*. This was probably the greatest jolt I've ever had in my business career. I already knew about the lousy cars, the bad morale and the deteriorating factories. But I simply had no idea that I wouldn't even be able to get hold of the right numbers so that we could begin to attack some basic problems.[6]

Iacocca could handle the poor state of Chrysler's physical system, but he was unprepared for the poor state of the conceptual system.

The Importance of a Systems View

A **systems view** regards business operations as systems embedded within a larger environmental setting. This is an abstract way of thinking, but it has potential value to the manager. The systems view:

1. Prevents the manager from getting lost in the complexity of the organizational structure and details of the job,
2. Recognizes the necessity of having good objectives,
3. Emphasizes the importance of all of the parts of the organization working together,
4. Acknowledges the interconnections of the organization with its environment,
5. Places a high value on feedback information that can only be achieved by means of a closed-loop system.

If you ask managers whether they have a systems view, you may get a negative answer, or an: "I don't know. I never thought about it." However, they most likely recognize the five points above.

[6] "Iacocca: An Autobiography," *Newsweek,* October 8, 1984, 62.

DATA VERSUS INFORMATION

We have combined data and information in our classification resource types, however, they are not the same. **Data** consists of facts and figures that are relatively meaningless to the user. For example, data may be the number of hours worked for each employee in the company. When this data is processed, it can be converted into information. When the hours worked by each employee are multiplied by the hourly rate, the product is the gross earnings. When the figures for each employee's gross earnings are added, the sum is the total payroll amount for the entire firm. This payroll amount would be information to the owner of the firm. **Information** is processed data, or meaningful data.

Antique dealers and fleamarket operators are fond of saying, "One person's junk is another person's treasure." Applying the same logic to data and information, we could say, "One person's data is another person's information." The gross earnings figures for a firm's employees provide an illustration. The separate figures are information to each employee—each figure tells them how much money they earned last week. But to the company's owner, these figures are data. The owner wants to know the total payroll for the firm, and the individual figures (the data) must be processed to produce this amount. The transformation of data into information is performed by an **information processor**. *The information processor is one of the key elements in the conceptual system.* The information processor can include computer elements, noncomputer elements, or some combination.

THE EVOLUTION OF COMPUTER-BASED INFORMATION SYSTEMS

The initial efforts to apply the computer in the business area focused on data. Then came emphasis on information and decision support. Today, communication and consultation are receiving the most attention.

The Initial Focus on Data

During the first half of the twentieth century, when punched card and keydriven bookkeeping machines were in their heyday, firms generally ignored the information needs of managers. This practice was continued with the first computers as they were restricted to accounting applications.

The name given to these computer-based accounting applications was **electronic data processing** (**EDP**). The term EDP is no longer popular, having been shortened to **data processing** (**DP**). DP produces *some* information, as a byproduct of the accounting processes.

The New Focus on Information

In 1964, a new generation of computing equipment was introduced that exerted a strong influence on the manner in which computers were employed. The new computers were the first to use silicon chip circuitry, and they offered opportunities for more processing power per dollar. The concept of using the computer as a management information system, or MIS, was promoted by the computer manufacturers to justify the new equipment. The MIS concept recognized that computer applications should be implemented for the *primary* purpose of producing management information. The concept was quickly adopted by many larger firms.

The road traveled by these pioneers was rocky. Actual accomplishments seldom matched those initially envisioned. There were several reasons for this shortfall—a general lack of computer literacy among users, a general lack of business literacy and an ignorance of the management role by information specialists, computing equipment that was both expensive and limited by today's standards, and so on. But one error in particular characterized the early systems. They were too ambitious. Firms believed that they could build giant information systems to support *all* managers. System designs snowballed, and the task became unmanageable. Some firms stuck it out, invested more resources, and eventually developed workable systems—although more modest in size than originally projected.[7] Other firms decided to scrap the entire MIS idea and retreated to DP.

The Revised Focus on Decision Support

While many watched from the sidelines as firms grappled with their giant MISs, some information scientists at the Massachusetts Institute of Technology (MIT) formulated a different approach. These scientists were Michael S. Scott Morton, G. Anthony Gorry, and Peter G. W. Keen, and their concept was named the **decision support system** (**DSS**). A DSS is an information-producing system aimed at a particular problem that a manager must solve and decisions that the manager must make. The manager can be located anywhere in the organization—on any level and in any functional area.

For the first few years of the DSS era, there was considerable argument concerning DSS and MIS. Did the DSS offer a new approach to computer use and if so, how? Those arguments were never really settled, but the issue does not seem to be as critical today as it once was.

This text holds the view that the MIS is an organizational resource. The MIS is intended to provide problem-solving information to a group of managers in a general way, whereas the DSS is intended to support a single manager in a specific way. We regard the **management information system** (**MIS**) as an information-producing system that is intended to support a group of managers who represent an organizational unit such as a management level or a functional area.

The Current Focus on Communication

During the time that the DSS evolved, interest was also focused on another computer application—**office automation** (**OA**). OA facilitates communication and increases productivity among managers and office workers through the use of electronic devices.

---

[7]For a good description of an early MIS design, *see* George W. Gershefski, "Building a Corporate Financial Model," *Harvard Business Review* 47 (July–August 1969), 61–72.

OA got its start in 1964 when IBM announced its Magnetic Tape/Selectric Typewriter (MT/ST)—a typewriter that could type words that had been recorded on magnetic tape. This automatic typing operation led to the OA application that is called word processing.

Office automation has grown to include such applications as teleconferencing, voice mail, electronic mail, electronic calendaring, facsimile transmission, and desktop publishing.

The Potential Focus on Consultation

There is a movement presently under way to apply **artificial intelligence** (**AI**) to business problems. The basic idea is that the computer can be programmed to perform some of the same logical reasoning as a human. A special subclass of AI, expert systems, is receiving the most attention. An **expert system** is one that functions as a specialist in an area. For example, an expert system can provide some of the same assistance to a manager as would come from a management consultant. Expect expert systems to play a greater role during the decade of the 90s, as firms continue to pioneer these innovative applications.

A MODEL OF A COMPUTER-BASED INFORMATION SYSTEM

Managers make decisions to solve problems, and information is used in making the decisions. Information is presented in both an oral and written form by an information processor. The computer portion of the information processor contains each of the computer-based application areas—DP, MIS, DSS, OA, and ES. We use the term **computer-based information system** (**CBIS**) to describe the five subsystems that utilize the computer. Figure 1.10 shows the model of the CBIS. All of the CBIS subsystems provide information for problem solving.

AN EXAMPLE OF A MANAGEMENT INFORMATION SYSTEM

The marketing division of a life insurance company in San Antonio, Texas uses an information system that consists of a notebook of computer printouts prepared each month. Some of the printouts are intended to help marketing managers plan future personnel hiring programs.

One of the reports is illustrated in Figure 1.11. The report is a projection of sales for the next forty-eight months, along with corresponding personnel needs. Reading from left to right, the report identifies the month, the sales goal for the month, the portion of the sales to be made by sales agents currently employed by the company, and the portion to be made by new agents. New agents will be needed to meet the increasing sales goals and to replace agents who are promoted or leave for greener pastures. The number of agents needed to meet the sales goals are identified in the center columns of the report. The *To hire* column identifies the number

FIGURE 1.10

The Model of the
Computer-based
Information
System

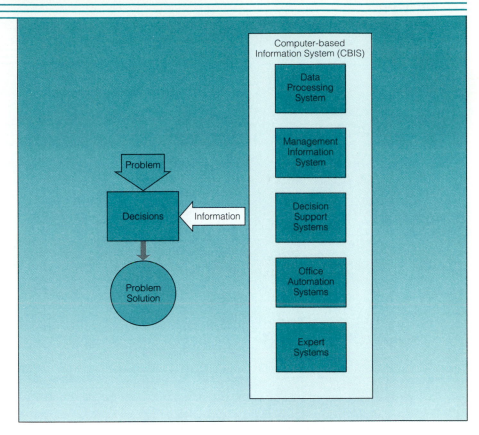

of agents to be hired that month. The right-hand columns identify the number of full-time recruiters that will be needed to hire the new agents. The report is a good example of how a firm's objectives can provide the basis for determining the human resources needed to meet those objectives.

Figure 1.12 is a graph that the insurance company prepares to supplement the tabular report. The graph shows the proportion of sales to be made by current and future sales agents.

The computer programs that prepare these outputs are an example of a management information system. The MIS assists marketing management in solving the problem of building a sales force to accomplish the firm's sales objectives.

THE INFORMATION SERVICES ORGANIZATION

The first computer-using firms recognized the necessity of establishing separate organizational units of specialists who were responsible for implementing the systems. The first data processing departments were a part of the financial function

FIGURE 1.11

A Report of Personnel Projections Prepared by a Life Insurance
Company

2/19/92

REPORT 1.10
SUMMARY PROJECTIONS REPORT
ASSUMED GROWTH RATE 110

MO	DATE	PRODUCTION POINTS			ACTIVE AGENTS				RECRUITERS			
		GOAL	CURRENT AGENTS	NEW AGENTS	ALL	CURRENT AGENTS	NEW AGENTS	TO HIRE	ALL	CURRENT	NEW	TO HIRE
1	2-92	367500	367500	0	158	158	0	18	9	9	0	0
2	3-92	425000	350000	75000	182	150	32	18	9	8	1	1
3	4-92	428000	339500	88500	183	146	37	18	9	8	1	0
4	5-92	432000	322000	110000	185	138	47	18	9	8	1	0
5	6-92	435000	301000	134000	186	129	57	18	9	8	1	0
6	7-92	438000	294000	144000	188	126	62	16	8	7	1	0
7	8-92	442000	280000	162000	189	120	69	16	8	7	1	0
8	9-92	445000	269500	175500	191	116	75	16	8	7	1	0
9	10-92	449000	266000	183000	192	114	78	16	8	7	1	0
10	11-92	452000	255500	196500	194	110	84	14	7	6	1	0
11	12-92	456000	245000	211000	195	105	90	14	7	6	1	0
12	1-93	459000	238000	221000	197	102	95	14	7	6	1	0
13	2-93	463000	234500	228500	198	101	97	14	7	6	1	0
14	3-93	467000	227500	239500	200	98	102	12	6	6	0	0
15	4-93	470000	220500	249500	201	95	106	12	6	6	0	0
16	5-93	474000	213500	260500	203	92	111	10	5	5	0	0
17	6-93	478000	206500	271500	205	89	116	10	5	5	0	0
18	7-93	481000	203000	278000	206	87	119	10	5	5	0	0
19	8-93	485000	196000	289000	208	84	124	10	5	5	0	0
20	9-93	489000	192500	296500	210	83	127	10	5	5	0	0
21	10-93	493000	189000	304000	211	81	130	10	5	5	0	0
22	11-93	496000	178500	317500	213	77	136	10	5	5	0	0
23	12-93	500000	178500	321500	214	77	137	10	5	5	0	0
24	1-94	504000	178500	325500	216	77	139	10	5	5	0	0
25	2-94	508000	175000	333000	218	75	143	10	5	4	1	1
26	3-94	512000	171500	340500	219	74	145	12	6	4	2	1
27	4-94	516000	171500	344500	221	74	147	12	6	4	2	0
28	5-94	520000	168000	352000	223	72	151	12	6	4	2	0
29	6-94	524000	164500	359500	225	71	154	12	6	4	2	0
30	7-94	528000	161000	367000	226	69	157	12	6	4	2	0
31	8-94	532000	161000	371000	228	69	159	12	6	4	2	0
32	9-94	536000	157500	378500	230	68	162	12	6	4	2	0
33	10-94	540000	157500	382500	231	68	163	10	5	4	1	0
34	11-94	544000	157500	386500	233	68	165	10	5	4	1	0
35	12-94	548000	154000	394000	235	66	169	12	6	4	2	1
36	1-95	552000	154000	398000	237	66	171	14	7	4	3	1
37	2-95	557000	154000	403000	239	66	173	14	7	4	3	0
38	3-95	561000	143500	417500	240	62	178	14	7	4	3	0
39	4-95	565000	147000	418000	242	63	179	14	7	4	3	0
40	5-95	569000	147000	422000	244	63	181	14	7	4	3	0
41	6-95	574000	140000	434000	246	60	186	14	7	4	3	1
42	7-95	578000	140000	438000	248	60	188	14	7	4	3	0
43	8-95	582000	129500	452500	249	56	193	14	7	4	3	0
44	9-95	587000	129500	457500	252	56	196	16	8	4	4	1
45	10-95	591000	129500	461500	253	56	197	16	8	4	4	0
46	11-95	595000	122500	472500	255	53	202	12	6	3	3	0
47	12-95	600000	136500	463500	257	59	198	12	6	3	3	0
48	1-96	604000	129500	474500	259	56	203	12	6	3	3	0
TOTAL								630				7

POINTS PER PRIMARY COMPANY AGENT (YRS 1-5+) = 3500 3500 3500 3500 3500
ACTIVE/P C A RATIO = 1.65/1 (1989 ACTUAL)
NEW ACTIVE PER MONTH PER RECRUITER = 2
ESTIMATE OF COST FROM REPORT 1.9 IS 2409200 DOLLARS
RT:BASERT...FN:SUMREPORT

FIGURE 1.12

A Graphic Display of Sales Projections for the Life Insurance
Company

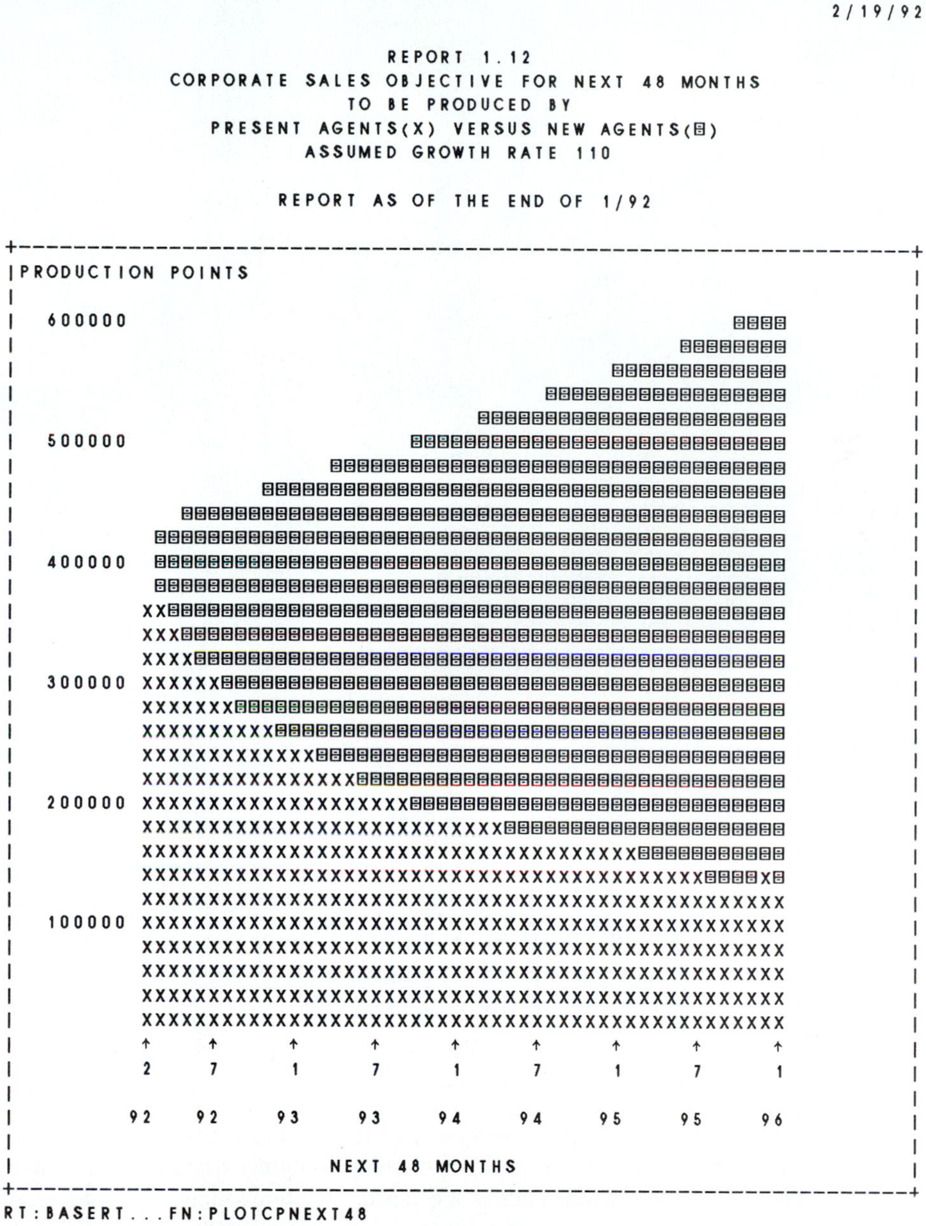

2/19/92

```
                         REPORT 1.12
       CORPORATE SALES OBJECTIVE FOR NEXT 48 MONTHS
                       TO BE PRODUCED BY
         PRESENT AGENTS(X) VERSUS NEW AGENTS(☐)
                  ASSUMED GROWTH RATE 110

              REPORT AS OF THE END OF 1/92

+-------------------------------------------------------------------+
|PRODUCTION POINTS                                                  |
|                                                                   |
|   600000                                        ☐☐☐☐              |
|                                               ☐☐☐☐☐☐☐☐            |
|                                             ☐☐☐☐☐☐☐☐☐☐☐☐          |
|                                           ☐☐☐☐☐☐☐☐☐☐☐☐☐☐☐☐        |
|                                         ☐☐☐☐☐☐☐☐☐☐☐☐☐☐☐☐☐☐☐☐      |
|   500000                              ☐☐☐☐☐☐☐☐☐☐☐☐☐☐☐☐☐☐☐☐☐☐☐☐    |
|                                     ☐☐☐☐☐☐☐☐☐☐☐☐☐☐☐☐☐☐☐☐☐☐☐☐☐☐☐☐  |
|                                   ☐☐☐☐☐☐☐☐☐☐☐☐☐☐☐☐☐☐☐☐☐☐☐☐☐☐☐☐☐☐☐☐|
|                                 ☐☐☐☐☐☐☐☐☐☐☐☐☐☐☐☐☐☐☐☐☐☐☐☐☐☐☐☐☐☐☐☐☐☐|
|                               ☐☐☐☐☐☐☐☐☐☐☐☐☐☐☐☐☐☐☐☐☐☐☐☐☐☐☐☐☐☐☐☐☐☐☐☐|
|   400000                    ☐☐☐☐☐☐☐☐☐☐☐☐☐☐☐☐☐☐☐☐☐☐☐☐☐☐☐☐☐☐☐☐☐☐☐☐☐☐|
|                             ☐☐☐☐☐☐☐☐☐☐☐☐☐☐☐☐☐☐☐☐☐☐☐☐☐☐☐☐☐☐☐☐☐☐☐☐☐☐|
|               XX☐☐☐☐☐☐☐☐☐☐☐☐☐☐☐☐☐☐☐☐☐☐☐☐☐☐☐☐☐☐☐☐☐☐☐☐☐☐☐☐☐☐☐☐☐☐☐☐|
|               XXX☐☐☐☐☐☐☐☐☐☐☐☐☐☐☐☐☐☐☐☐☐☐☐☐☐☐☐☐☐☐☐☐☐☐☐☐☐☐☐☐☐☐☐☐☐☐☐|
|               XXXX☐☐☐☐☐☐☐☐☐☐☐☐☐☐☐☐☐☐☐☐☐☐☐☐☐☐☐☐☐☐☐☐☐☐☐☐☐☐☐☐☐☐☐☐☐☐|
|   300000      XXXXXX☐☐☐☐☐☐☐☐☐☐☐☐☐☐☐☐☐☐☐☐☐☐☐☐☐☐☐☐☐☐☐☐☐☐☐☐☐☐☐☐☐☐☐☐|
|               XXXXXXX☐☐☐☐☐☐☐☐☐☐☐☐☐☐☐☐☐☐☐☐☐☐☐☐☐☐☐☐☐☐☐☐☐☐☐☐☐☐☐☐☐☐☐|
|               XXXXXXXXX☐☐☐☐☐☐☐☐☐☐☐☐☐☐☐☐☐☐☐☐☐☐☐☐☐☐☐☐☐☐☐☐☐☐☐☐☐☐☐☐|
|               XXXXXXXXXXX☐☐☐☐☐☐☐☐☐☐☐☐☐☐☐☐☐☐☐☐☐☐☐☐☐☐☐☐☐☐☐☐☐☐☐☐☐☐|
|               XXXXXXXXXXXXX☐☐☐☐☐☐☐☐☐☐☐☐☐☐☐☐☐☐☐☐☐☐☐☐☐☐☐☐☐☐☐☐☐☐☐|
|   200000      XXXXXXXXXXXXXXXXX☐☐☐☐☐☐☐☐☐☐☐☐☐☐☐☐☐☐☐☐☐☐☐☐☐☐☐☐☐☐☐☐|
|               XXXXXXXXXXXXXXXXXXXXXX☐☐☐☐☐☐☐☐☐☐☐☐☐☐☐☐☐☐☐☐☐☐☐☐☐☐|
|               XXXXXXXXXXXXXXXXXXXXXXXXXXX☐☐☐☐☐☐☐☐☐☐☐☐☐☐☐☐☐☐|
|               XXXXXXXXXXXXXXXXXXXXXXXXXXXXXXXXXXXX☐☐☐☐X☐☐|
|               XXXXXXXXXXXXXXXXXXXXXXXXXXXXXXXXXXXXXXXXXXXXXX|
|   100000      XXXXXXXXXXXXXXXXXXXXXXXXXXXXXXXXXXXXXXXXXXXXXX|
|               XXXXXXXXXXXXXXXXXXXXXXXXXXXXXXXXXXXXXXXXXXXXXX|
|               XXXXXXXXXXXXXXXXXXXXXXXXXXXXXXXXXXXXXXXXXXXXXX|
|               XXXXXXXXXXXXXXXXXXXXXXXXXXXXXXXXXXXXXXXXXXXXXX|
|               XXXXXXXXXXXXXXXXXXXXXXXXXXXXXXXXXXXXXXXXXXXXXX|
|                ↑      ↑      ↑      ↑      ↑      ↑      ↑      ↑      ↑  |
|                2      7      1      7      1      7      1      7      1  |
|                                                                   |
|               92     92     93     93     94     94     95     95     96 |
|                                                                   |
|                       NEXT 48 MONTHS                              |
+-------------------------------------------------------------------+
RT:BASERT...FN:PLOTCPNEXT48
```

FIGURE 1.13

The Traditional Communication Chain

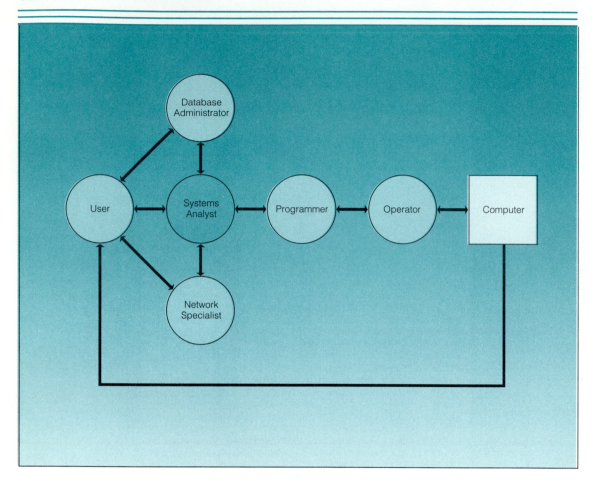

and were under the direction of one of the firm's financial officers, such as the controller. Today, the practice is to establish computing as a separate, major organizational entity, led by a vice president.

Information Specialists

We use the term **information specialist** to describe any of a firm's employees who have the full-time responsibility to develop computer-based systems. There are five main categories of information specialists—systems analysts, database administrators, network specialists, programmers, and operators. Figure 1.13 shows how these specialists work together and with the user in developing computer-based systems. The arrows represent communication flows, including the ultimate flow of information from the computer to the user. The figure illustrates the **traditional communication chain** that connects the user, the information specialists, and the computer. The user can be a manager, a nonmanager, or an individual or organization in the firm's environment.

Systems analysts work with the users in developing new systems and in improving existing systems. Systems analysts are expert at defining problems and in preparing written documentation of how the computer will assist in solving the problems.

Database administrators work with users and systems analysts in creating the database that contains the data needed to produce the user's information. A **database** is an integrated collection of computer data, organized and stored in a manner that facilitates easy retrieval. Once the database is created, database administrators manage this important resource.

Network specialists work with systems analysts and users in establishing the data communications network that ties together widespread computing resources. Network specialists combine expertise from the fields of computing and telecommunications.

Programmers use the documentation prepared by the systems analysts to code the instructions that cause the computer to transform the data into information that is needed by the user.

Operators operate the large-scale computing equipment such as mainframe computers and minicomputers. The operators monitor the consoles, change paper forms in the printers, manage libraries of tape and disk storage, and perform other similar duties.

We will provide more information on these information specialists later in the text.

THE TREND TO END-USER COMPUTING

Information specialists do not always participate in the development of computer-based systems as illustrated in Figure 1.13. That is the traditional approach, which was the way that all systems were developed during the 1950s, 60s, and early 70s.

However, during the late 1970s a trend began, which had a big influence on computer use. The trend was growing interest on the part of the users in developing their own computer applications. The name that has been applied to this situation is end-user computing. **End user** is synonymous with user; he or she uses the end product of a computer-based system. **End-user computing** (**EUC**), therefore, is the development by users of all or part of their computer-based systems.

What Stimulated End-user Computing?

End-user computing evolved because of four main influences—users became more computer literate, information services became less capable of keeping up with demand, low-cost hardware came onto the scene, and prewritten software made custom programming an option rather than a requirement.

Increase in Computer Literacy During the early 1980s, the impact of good computer education programs at both the college and precollege level made themselves felt. Management ranks, especially on the lower levels, began to be filled with persons having good computer skills.

The Information Services Backlog Information specialists have always had more work than they can handle. This situation became critical during the early 1980s when the managers began making demands on information services for additional systems support. Information services could not respond fast enough, and backlogs built up of jobs waiting to go on the computer. Some managers had to wait two or three years for their jobs to work their way through the backlog.

Low-Cost Hardware During this same period, the market became flooded with low-cost microcomputers. Users could obtain their own hardware by placing an order at the local computer store by telephone and making payment from the petty cash fund.

Prewritten Software Both hardware and software firms produced software that would perform basic accounting tasks as well as provide information for decision making. This prewritten software offered enhanced support and ease of use, and enabled firms and individual users with little or no computer expertise to implement computer-based systems.

The combination of these four influences accounted for the explosion of end-user computing.

The Role of the Information Specialists in End-user Computing

It is not necessary that users assume total responsibility for systems development, but they must do some portion. In many cases the user will work with information specialists in jointly developing systems. Therefore, the EUC concept does not mean that there will be no more need for information specialists. Rather, it means that information specialists will assume more of a consulting role than they have in the past.

Figure 1.14 pictures an end-user computing scenario where the user relies on the information specialists for some degree of support. We call this the **end-user computing communication chain**.

JUSTIFYING THE CBIS

Regardless of whether information specialists or users develop the applications, the CBIS should be justified in the same manner as any other large investment of the firm. During the EDP era, firms attempted to justify their computers based on dis-

FIGURE 1.14

The End-user Computing Communication Chain

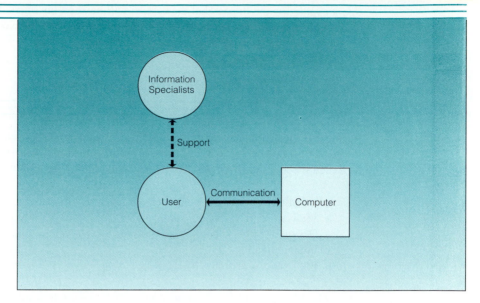

placed clerical costs. As things worked out, few of the clerical workers lost their jobs. Faced with the task of firing employees who had been replaced by the computer, management usually opted to assign them to other jobs. Many of the jobs had never before been performed due to a lack of available personnel.

Although the computer did not cut clerical costs as planned, substantially more success was achieved in doing things better—achieving increased efficiency or reduced investment. The time that was devoted to designing the computer systems made them more efficient than their manual predecessors. One of the first computer applications was inventory control, and firms often reduced their inventory investment by computerizing their inventory records. If EDP could reduce a $10 million inventory by 3 percent, then $300,000 was available to invest elsewhere.

Computer justification became more difficult with the emergence of information-oriented systems. An MIS or a DSS can produce a valuable report, but how valuable is it? The same question can be asked of an electronic mail message or the consultation provided by an expert system.

The value of a piece of information is difficult to assess. One approach would be for a firm to implement a new report and then compare the profit for the period during which the report was used with the profit during a prior period. However, for this comparison to be valid, the report would have to be the only change in the firm's operations. This is hardly feasible in the dynamic world of business. There are usually many factors that contribute to profit, and singling out one is almost impossible.

Because of the difficulty of measuring CBIS value, firms approach the decision to implement such systems very cautiously. Much manager and staff time is spent evaluating the impact that the system will have on the organization. Justifying a CBIS, using a combination of quantitative and subjective measures, is a key step in achieving this valuable resource and is reviewed in Chapter 5.

ACHIEVING THE CBIS

In some respects, each subsystem of the CBIS is like a living organism—it is born, it grows and matures, it functions, and eventually it dies. This evolutionary process is called the **system life cycle (SLC)**, and consists of the following phases:

- Planning
- Analysis
- Design
- Implementation
- Use

The life cycle of a particular computer-based system might last only a few months, or it might last several years. The MIS that projects the agent and recruiter figures for the insurance company has been in use since the mid-1980s. Sooner or later, the dynamic nature of business will catch up with the information systems, and they will have to be updated.

Figure 1.15 illustrates how the life cycle phases fit into a circular pattern. When a system outlives its usefulness and must be replaced, a new life cycle is initiated, beginning with the planning phase.

MANAGING THE CBIS

Even though many people may contribute their specialized skills to the development of a computer-based system, it is the user who is responsible for the system life cycle. In keeping with our emphasis on the manager as the user, we assign the manager the responsibility for managing the CBIS. As the CBIS evolves, the manager plans the life cycle and controls the information specialists who are involved. After implementation, the manager controls the CBIS to ensure that it continues to provide the desired support. The manager's overall responsibility and the phase-by-phase support provided by information specialists are illustrated in Figure 1.16.

When the manager elects to make use of the support of information specialists, both parties follow this procedure to identify and define the problem, identify and evaluate alternate solutions, select the best solution, assemble appropriate hardware and software, create the database, and keep the system current. When the manager elects to pursue end-user computing in its purest form, the manager performs all of these tasks.

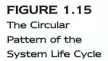

FIGURE 1.15
The Circular
Pattern of the
System Life Cycle

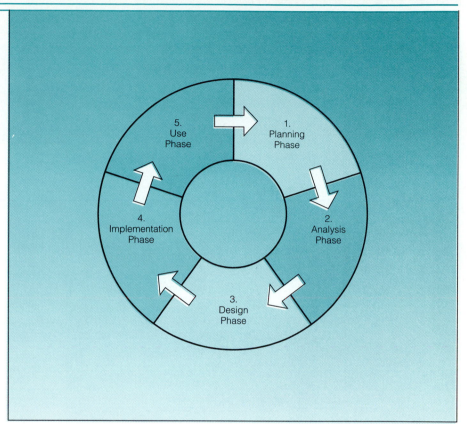

PUTTING THE CBIS IN CONTEXT

During the early years of the computer, firms had a choice as to whether they used the electronic device. The managers of the early computer-using firms were visionaries, recognizing that the computer gave them some edge over their competitors. As the cost of computing hardware and software decreased, the applications pioneered by the early firms became available to practically all firms—even the very smallest.

Today's manager really does not have much choice concerning computer use. The question is not whether to use it but, rather, how extensively to use it. As a minimum, the computer processes the firm's accounting data. Most firms have become completely dependent on their computer-based data processing systems and could not handle a day's transactions without them. Some firms have also achieved systems that provide problem-solving information, speed the flow of communications, and make available expertise of the richest sort.

As you embark on your career in a business or nonbusiness organization, you

FIGURE 1.16
The Cooperative System Development Process

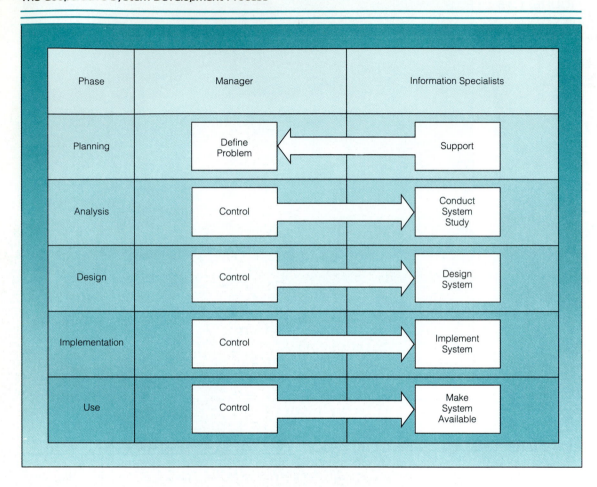

Phase	Manager	Information Specialists
Planning	Define Problem	Support
Analysis	Control	Conduct System Study
Design	Control	Design System
Implementation	Control	Implement System
Use	Control	Make System Available

will find yourself in a computer environment. In the remaining chapters of the text, we describe this environment, not simply so that you can fit in but so that you can contribute to improved computer use.

SUMMARY

Information is one of five main types of resources that the manager has at her or his disposal. All of the resources, including information, can be managed. The importance of information management increases as business becomes more complex and computer capabilities expand.

Computer output is used by managers, nonmanagers, and persons and organizations in the firm's environment. Managers are found on all levels and in all functional areas. As managers perform their functions and play their roles, they augment their basic communications and problem-solving skills with computer and information literacy.

A system is an integration of elements, all working toward an objective. All systems include three primary elements—input, transformation, and output. Some systems can control their own operations, and they are called closed-loop systems. Closed-loop systems include a control mechanism, objectives, and a feedback loop in addition to the three primary elements. Systems that do not have a control capability are called open-loop systems. All of the systems that we study in this text are open systems, in that they interface with their environment.

The manager manages a physical system composed of facilities, people, equipment, and materials. The manager monitors the physical system by using a conceptual system. The conceptual system provides information that describes the physical system of the firm in its environment.

Managers should take a systems view of their organizational units. Such a view enables managers to more easily focus the system elements on the organizational objectives.

There is a difference between information and data. Data includes relatively meaningless facts and figures that are transformed into information by an information processor. Information is meaningful to the user. An information processor provides information in both an oral and written form. The information comes from both internal and environmental sources and is used in making decisions to solve problems.

Computers were initially used for data processing but then were recognized to have potential value as a management information system, or MIS. Subsequently, interest expanded into areas such as decision support systems (DSS), office automation (OA), and expert systems (ES). All five of these application areas comprise the computer-based information system (CBIS).

The first computer-using firms established computer departments and gave them the responsibility for systems development. This practice continues, with the units including information specialists such as systems analysts, database administrators, network specialists, programmers, and operators. We use the name information services to describe these units.

During recent years, many users have taken the initiative to develop their own applications rather than rely entirely on information specialists. This approach has been named end-user computing, or EUC. When a user is completely dedicated to EUC, there is no need for information specialists. However, the user can use information specialists to perform a portion of the development work or to serve as consultants.

Early computer-using firms attempted to justify their data processing systems based on displaced clerical costs, but failed to carry through with the termination of unneeded employees. More success was achieved in striving for increased efficiency or reduced investment. Today, it is extremely difficult to place a dollar value on the output of the information-oriented CBIS subsystems such as MIS, DSS, and ES. Instead, more weight is placed on subjective measures.

A CBIS is developed in stages—planning, analysis, design, implementation, and use. These stages are called the system life cycle (SLC) and can be taken by the user alone, or the user working with information specialists. Even when systems are developed jointly, it is the manager who is responsible for each life cycle phase.

This first chapter has provided an overview of the CBIS. In the next chapter, we recognize that top-level management can use the CBIS as a strategic tool by following a philosophy of information resources management.

KEY TERMS

information management
executive
executive committee
problem
problem solving
decision
decision making
computer literacy

information literacy
systems view
data
information
information processor
information services
information specialist
end-user computing

KEY CONCEPTS

Physical and conceptual resources
Information as a resource to be managed
How managers can be segregated based on organizational levels
How managers can be segregated based on functional areas
How management work can be classified in terms of functions and roles
Systems orientation
A system as a combination of elements all working toward an overall objective

How a system can control its own operations
How a system is connected to its environment by resource flows
Levels of systems
How a conceptual system can represent a physical system
The computer-based information system as a composite of five subsystems, each with its own unique characteristics
The system life cycle

QUESTIONS

1. List the steps that the manager takes in managing physical resources.

2. List the steps that the manager takes in managing information.

3. What was the first computer application to recognize the information needs of managers?

4. What are the three classes of computer users?

5. What are the three management levels as identified by Anthony?

6. What is the difference between a functional area and a management function?

7. What are the three categories of managerial roles that Mintzberg identified?

8. The text identifies two basic skills that a manager should possess. What are they?

9. Explain the difference between problem solving and decision making.

10. An ad for a razor with a replaceable double blade referred to it as a shaving system. Is the razor really a system? What are its elements? What is the objective?

11. List the elements to be found in a closed-loop system. Place an asterisk next to those elements that are also found in an open-loop system.

12. Can you identify a firm that does not transform an input into an output? If so, explain.

13. What is the control mechanism in a firm?

14. Each day, a large metropolitan telephone company prints thousands of bills. Are the bills data or information? Explain.

15. What are the five subsystems of the CBIS? Match each one with one of the following terms: data, consultation, communication, information, semistructured problem.

16. Name the information specialists who work directly with the user.

17. A manager in the finance function obtains a PC and Lotus, learns how to use them by using the tutorials, and produces the firm's monthly income statement. Is this an example of EUC? Explain your answer.

18. Do you think that the manager in Question 16 has a computer literacy? An information literacy? Explain.

19. Name three approaches that were used in justifying EDP systems. Which two were the most successful?

20. Why is it difficult to justify an information-oriented CBIS subsystem such as the MIS or DSS?

21. What are the five phases of the SLC? What is the role of the information specialist in the first phase? The role of the manager in the last four?

TOPICS FOR DISCUSSION

1. In January of 1992 President Bush traveled to Japan in an effort to convice the Japanese to accept more U.S. imports. Assuming that he was successful, did he decrease the complexity of business for U.S. managers, increase it, or both? Explain.

2. How is modern information technology contributing to the shrinking time frames of business transactions? For example, what equipment is available for use with the telephone? Pick a type of equipment and give an example of its impact.

3. The text states that an information literacy is more important than a computer literacy. Do you agree? Explain why or why not.

4. Explain why your college or university is a system. Explain why it is a supersystem. A subsytem.

5. Is a computer a physical system, a conceptual system, or both?

6. In order to print the report of personnel projections shown in Figure 1.12, the insurance company has to know how much insurance, on the average, an agent can sell in a month. What other things does the company need to know? Where will this information come from?

7. Explain why a system does not belong to the information specialists even though they may do most of the work in developing it.

PROBLEMS

Go to the library and examine recent copies of *The Wall Street Journal*. Find an article that deals with worldwide competition. Read the article and write a one-page summary.

Go to the library and locate the earliest article containing the term *end-user computing* in its title, which you can find. Read the article and summarize it in a written report.

A new insurance company wants to plan its sales expenses for its first twelve months of operation. They want to sell $100,000 of insurance in the first month and increase that by $20,000 each month. One agent can sell $10,000 per month. An agent's salary is $2,000 per month, and each month an agent incurs the following expenses: $50 telephone, $100 travel, $10 entertainment. Use an electronic spreadsheet to produce an expense report, showing the various expenses as vertical columns and the twelve months as horizontal rows. Include both row and column totals.

CASE PROBLEM

King Furniture

You are a sales representative for Furniture Software, Inc., a national firm that markets a computer-based system for use by furniture stores. The system, called FLAIR (Furniture Location And Information Retrieval), consists of both the hardware and software.

One day while you are talking with Alton Fox, the sales manager for King Furniture, you learn that he has an inventory problem. King has never seen fit to acquire a computer and uses a manual bookkeeping system. A local college student, Alisa Stack, works each weekday afternoon and updates the inventory records from the written copies of the sales slips and receiving reports.

Fox says that the inventory records are practically useless since they do not accurately reflect the inventory status—the types and quantities of furniture items in the warehouse. For example, a customer comes in and wants to buy a certain style of coffee table. According to the inventory records there is one in stock, but when the warehouse clerk goes to get it, it is not there. Most likely, when it was sold, someone failed to fill out a sales slip, the slip became lost, or Alisa failed to post the transaction properly.

Other errors also occur when new stock arrives from the furniture manufacturers. Alisa only updates the records with the receipts on Wednesdays—when she has the least number of sales to handle. A salesperson might have a customer who wants a particular furniture item, and perhaps the item has just been received and is in the warehouse, but the salesperson will never know it. A sale is lost because of poor information.

You know that your system can solve the problem. Once a store gets FLAIR, and the computer records are updated as soon as a shipment arrives or a sale is made, the computer storage will always reflect exactly what is in the warehouse. This capability can be achieved at a very reasonable cost. The overall cost, including a full-time operator, is well within the reach of even the smallest furniture stores.

Fox tells you that the person who makes all decisions concerning the bookkeeping operation is the vice president of finance, Phil King, the owner's son. You call on Phil and begin your sales pitch. He interrupts you and says: "Hey, hold the phone. I'm new on the job. I just received my MBA last month, with a major in systems theory. If you could just explain how your product will help us, in systems terms, I think I can understand. Better yet, why don't you put in a memo. I can look it over and then we can talk."

Assignment

Prepare the memo that Phil King requests. Assume that he is familiar with taking a systems view of his operation. Your instructor will advise you on the memo's specifications.

SELECTED BIBLIOGRAPHY

Ackoff, Russell L. "Management Misinformation Systems." *Management Science* 14 (December 1967): B147–B156.

Alter, Steven L. "How Effective Managers Use Information Systems." *Harvard Business Review* 54 (November–December 1976): 97–104.

Aron, Joel. D. "Information Systems in Perspective." *Computing Surveys* 1 (December 1969): 213–36.

Dearden, John. "MIS is a Mirage." *Harvard Business Review* 50 (January–February 1972): 90–99.

Durand, Douglas; Floyd, Steven; and Kublanow, Samuel. "How Do 'Real' Managers Use Office Systems?" *Journal of Information Technology Management* 1 (Number 2, 1990): 25–32.

Edelman, Franz. "The Management of Information Resources—A Challenge for American Business." *MIS Quarterly* 5 (March 1981): 17–27.

Franz, Charles R. "User Leadership in the Systems Development Life Cycle: A Contingency Model." *Journal of Management Information Systems* 2 (Fall 1985): 5–25.

Gorry, G. Anthony, and Scott Morton, Michael S. "A Framework for Management Information Systems." *Sloan Management Review* 13 (Fall 1971): 55–70.

Kerr, Susan. "The New IS Force." *Datamation* 35 (August 1, 1989): 18*ff*.

Leitheiser, Robert L., and Wetherbe, James C. "Service Support Levels: An Organized Approach to End-User Computing." *MIS Quarterly* 10 (December 1986): 337–49.

Lucas, Henry C., Jr. "Utilizing Information Technology: Guidelines for Managers." *Sloan Management Review* 27 (Fall 1986): 39–47.

McLeod, Raymond, Jr., and Jones, Jack William. "A Framework for Office Automation." *MIS Quarterly* 11 (March 1987): 87–104.

Meyer, Marc H., and Curley, Kathleen Foley. "Putting Expert Systems Technology to Work." *Sloan Management Review* 32 (Winter 1991): 21–31.

Munro, Malcolm C.; Huff, Sid L.; and Moore, Gary. "Expansion and Control of End-User Computing." *Journal of Management Information Systems* 4 (Winter 1987–88): 5–27.

Nadkarni, Ashok R., and Kenny, Graham K. "Expert Systems and Organizational Decision Making." *Journal of General Management* 13 (Autumn 1987): 60–68.

Olson, Margrethe H., and Lucas, Henry C., Jr. "The Impact of Office Automation on the Organization: Some Implications for Research and Practice." *Communications of the ACM* 25 (November 1982): 838–47.

Sprague, Ralph H., Jr. "A Framework for the Development of Decision Support Systems." *MIS Quarterly* 4 (December 1980): 1–26.

Sviokla, John J. "An Examination of the Impact of Expert Systems on the Firm: The Case of XCON." *MIS Quarterly* 14 (June 1990): 127–40.

Weitzel, John R., and Kerschberg, Larry. "Developing Knowledge-based Systems: Reorganizing the System Development Life Cycle." *Communications of the ACM* 32 (April 1989): 482–88.

Zani, William M. "Blueprint for MIS." *Harvard Business Review* 48 (November– December 1970): 95–100.

Chapter 2

Using Information Technology for Competitive Advantage

 LEARNING OBJECTIVES

After studying this chapter, you should:

- Understand the relationship between a firm and its environment
- Recognize that a firm can control its environment to a certain extent
- Appreciate that competitive advantage can be achieved by managing the information flows that connect the firm to all environmental elements
- Know what the information resources are, and who manages them
- Understand the meaning of the chief information officer concept
- Be aware that the firm's executives chart its course through its competitive environment by engaging in long-range, strategic planning
- Appreciate why it is so important that the top-level managers in each functional area cooperate when developing their own strategic plans
- Be aware of the activity called strategic planning for information resources
- Have an idea of the content of a firm's strategic plan for its information resources
- Know the ingredients that comprise the modern concept of information resources management

INTRODUCTION

The firm exists in an environment consisting of elements that can be either individuals or organizations. Resources flow between the firm and each of the elements. The firm's management can exert some influence on the environment by following certain strategies.

In seeking success in its marketplace, managers are especially aware of the influence of the firm's customers and competitors. They attempt to gain a competitive advantage by managing the flow of information. First efforts concentrate on the information flow to and from the firm's customers. A broader view encompasses other environmental elements, such as suppliers. Electronic linkages between the computers of the firm and those of the environmental elements enable all of the organizations to function as an interorganizational information system.

The firm's information resources include more than the information. They also include hardware, facilities, software, data, information specialists, and users of the information.

Managers on all levels engage in planning, but the plans of the top-level managers extend far into the future. These strategic plans identify what the firm is to achieve five, ten, or more years in the future, and spell out how those objectives are to be met. After the executives prepare the strategic plan for the firm, similar plans are made for each of its functional areas. Functional strategic plans describe how each of these areas will contribute to the achievement of the firm's objectives.

The activity of identifying the information resources that the firm will need in the future, acquiring those resources, and managing them is called strategic planning for information resources, or SPIR. SPIR is a responsiblity of all managers, but the manager of the information services organization plays the key role. The title CIO, for chief information officer, has become increasingly popular to describe the information services manager.

Of all the recent innovations in computer use, none has had a greater impact than has end-user computing. End users are now developing many of their own applications. This trend will continue, and will produce overall benefits for the firm, although not without some serious risks. The risks can be eliminated or minimized through proper management controls.

When the firm's managers recognize information as a strategic resource, establish policies that apply information in a strategic way, and follow up to ensure that those policies are carried out, the activity is called information resources management, or IRM. IRM is a concept that integrates the other concepts of competitive advantage, CIO, SPIR, and end-user computing. As such, IRM provides a framework for effective computer use.

THE FIRM IN ITS ENVIRONMENT

In Chapter 1, we saw that a firm is a physical system, managed through the use of a conceptual system. It consists of a combination of physical and conceptual resources. The physical system of the firm is a closed-loop system in that it is controlled by management, using feedback information to ensure that the objectives are met. The firm is also an open system in that it interfaces with its environment. A firm takes resources from its environment, transforms those resources into products and services, and returns the transformed resources to its environment.

It is important to recognize the importance of the environment to the firm. The environment is the very reason for the firm's existence. The firm's owners see a need to provide products and services to meet specific environmental needs, and invest money so that the firm can perform this activity. The environment then provides the resources that are required to produce the products and services.

The Eight Environmental Elements

The environment of one firm is not exactly the same as the environment of another. A bank has a different environment than does a sporting goods store or a church, for example. However, we can lend some order to this variablility by identifying eight major *types* of elements that exist in the environments of *all* firms.[1] These **environmental elements** are organizations and individuals that exist outside the firm and have either a direct or indirect influence on the firm. These eight elements exist in a larger system called **society**. Figure 2.1 depicts the firm in its environmental context.

Suppliers, also called vendors, supply materials, machines, services, and information that are used by the firm to produce its products and services. These products and services are marketed to the firm's **customers,** which include both current and prospective users. **Labor unions** are the organizations of both skilled and unskilled workers. The **financial community** consists of institutions that influence the money resources that are available to the firm. Examples of members of the financial community include banks and other lending institutions and investment firms. **Stockholders** or **owners** are the persons who invest money in the firm and represent the highest level of management. The **competitors** include all of the organizations that compete with the firm in its marketplace. The **government,** on the federal, state, and local levels, provides constraints in the form of laws and regulations but also provides assistance in the form of purchases, information, and funds. The **local community** is the geographic area where the firm performs its operations and in recent years has assumed global proportions. The firm demonstrates its responsibility to the local community by using antipollution devices, adhering to safety practices, supporting charitable and civic programs, and so on.

Environmental Resource Flows

The firm is connected to these environmental elements by means of resource flows. You recall from Chapter 1 that the resources include personnel, material, machines, money, and information. Resources flow to the firm from the elements, through the

[1] Richard J. Hopeman, *Systems Analysis and Operations Management* (Columbus, OH: Charles E. Merrill, 1969), 79–103.

FIGURE 2.1

Eight
Environmental
Elements

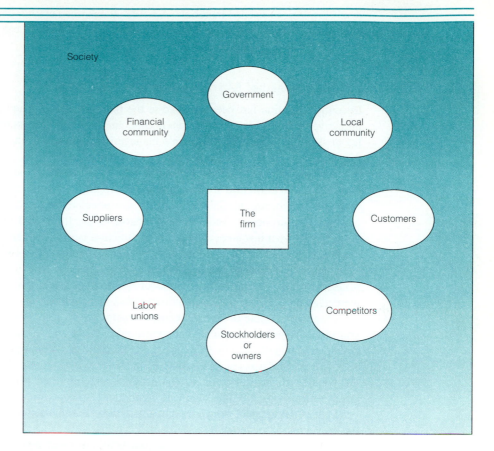

firm, and back to the elements. *All* resources that enter the firm from the environment eventually return to the environment.

Some of the resources flow more frequently than do others. Very common flows include information flow from customers, material flow to customers, money flow to stockholders, machine flow from suppliers, and personnel flow from labor unions. Less frequent flows include money flow from the government (for research, for example), material flow to suppliers (returned merchandise), and personnel flow to competitors (employees "pirated" by other firms).

Not *all* resources flow between the firm and *all* environmental elements. For example, machines normally do not flow from the firm to stockholders, money should not flow to competitors, and material should not flow to labor unions. The only resource that connects the firm with all of the elements is information.

Indirect Environmental Influences

Resource flows are made more complicated by the influence that one environmental element can have on another. An example is a strike by a labor union against a supplier. The supplier might have to shut down its manufacturing process. The result is a lack of needed materials. A strike against the supplier can have the same effect as a strike against the firm. Similar indirect influences can involve any of the other environmental elements.

Environmental Management

Recently, attention has been directed at the benefits to be gained from adopting a proactive, rather than a reactive, environmental attitude. A **proactive environmental attitude** is a belief by the firm's management that they can execute strategies that alter the environment to a certain extent.

Jay R. Galbraith, a management professor at the Wharton School, calls this approach **environmental management**—changing the context in which the firm operates.[2] According to Galbraith, a firm can adopt three basic strategies in influencing its environment. **Independent strategies** are those that the firm can carry out using its own resources, so that it can function better in its environment. **Cooperative strategies** involve working with other elements in the environment for the same purpose. **Strategic maneuvering** enables the firm to actually alter its environment. Table 2.1 contains examples of specific strategies that firms have implemented in an effort to achieve environmental management.

A good example of an independent strategy is the competitive advertising that you see on television, such as that sponsored by Visa and Master Card to compare their products with American Express. An example of a cooperative strategy is the arrangement that was reached between Mrs. Fields Cookies and "TCBY", enabling the yogurt firm to sell cookies. The arrangement provided Mrs. Fields with new retail outlets, and "TCBY" with new products. An example of strategic maneuvering was the entry of brewing companies such as Anheuser-Busch and Stroh into the nonalcoholic beverage market.

By taking actions such as these, the firm can exert some degree of control over the environment in which it operates.

COMPETITIVE ADVANTAGE

An environment-related term that began to receive widespread attention during the late 1980s is competitive advantage. Competitive advantage can be achieved in many ways, such as by providing products and services at a low price, providing products and services that are better than those of the competitors, and meeting the special needs of certain market segments.[3] As applied in the computer field, **competitive advantage** refers to the use of information to gain leverage in the marketplace. The idea is that the firm does not have to rely entirely on superior physical

---

[2] Jay R. Galbraith, *Organization Design* (Reading, MA: Addison-Wesley, 1977), 204–21.

[3] For more information on competitive advantage, *see* Michael E. Porter, "How Competitive Forces Shape Strategy," *Harvard Business Review* 57 (March–April 1979), 137–45, and Michael E. Porter, *Competitive Advantage* (New York: Free Press, 1985).

TABLE 2.1
Environmental
Management
Strategies

Basic Strategy	Specific Strategy	Example
Independent Strategies	Competitive Aggression	Product differentiation. Aggressive pricing. Comparative advertising.
	Legal action	Private antitrust suits brought against competitors.
	Political Action	Issue advertising. Lobbying.
Cooperative Strategies	Co-optation	Consumer representatives, women, and bankers on boards of directors.
	Coalition	Industry association. Political initiatives of the Business Roundtable and the U.S. Chamber of Commerce.
Strategic Maneuvering	Domain Selection	IBM's entry into the personal computer market. Miller Brewing Company's entry into the light beer market.
	Diversification	General Electric's wide product mix.
	Merger and acquisition	Merger between Pan American and National Airlines.

Source: Carl P. Zeithaml and Valarie A. Zeithaml, "Environmental Management: Revising the Marketing Perspective," *Journal of Marketing* 48 (Spring 1984), 50–51. Reprinted with permission.

resources when engaged in competition. Rather, superior conceptual resources—data and information—can be used as well. The firm's managers use conceptual as well as physical resources in meeting the strategic objectives of the firm.

The Initial View of Competitive Advantage

A number of firms have received widespread publicity from their use of information to achieve competitive advantage. Among the first were American Airlines with its airline reservation system called Sabre, American Hospital Supply with its EDI (electronic data interchange) network, and McKesson Drug with its distribution system called Economost.

American Airlines   The first airline to install a computer-based reservation system was American. The Sabre system, in use more than thirty years, provides

FIGURE 2.2
American Airlines
Has Achieved a
Competitive
Advantage with
Its Sabre
Reservation
System

Courtesy of American Airlines

an up-to-the-minute conceptual representation of the status of American's future flights. Not only do American reservation agents use the system, but it is used by many travel agents as well. The ease with which a reservation can be made on an American flight has played a large role in the leadership that American has achieved in the airlines industry.

American Hospital Supply   American Hospital Supply sells a wide range of products to hospitals. Traditionally, the hospitals placed orders by mail, telephone, or personal contact with the firm's sales representatives. Management decided that the liklihood of the hospitals ordering from American Hospital would be increased if the ordering process was made more convenient. American Hospital management decided to let the hospitals place orders electronically, by keying the order data into terminals located in the hospitals, and transmitting the data directly to the American Hospital computer.

The electronic transmission of computer data from one firm to another is called **electronic data interchange** (**EDI**). EDI eliminates many paper forms and achieves a level of speed and accuracy that is beyond written and oral media.

EDI makes it possible for multiple firms to link their separate computer-based systems to form a single interorganizational information system. An **interorganizational information system** (**IOS**) is a combination of multiple firms that are integrated through information flows. Although it is not necessary that the flows be computer based, the electronic medium is preferred. When a firm establishes an IOS link with its customers, using EDI, it is extremely difficult for other firms to compete for the business. The most widely publicized examples of IOSs are the airlines' reservations systems, but other industries have applied the same strategy. First Boston, for example, uses a system called Shelternet to provide information on home loans to real estate firms. The realtors are provided with a line of credit so that they can close loans on a local basis and then sell the loans to First Boston.[4]

McKesson Drug   McKesson Drug is a large wholesaler of pharmaceutical supplies that are sold to drug stores. McKesson has achieved an IOS that is very similar to that of American Hosptial Supply. McKesson's system, called Economost, enables drug stores to enter order data into the McKesson computer. The arrangement benefits both McKesson and its customers. McKesson has been able to streamline its order entry process, eliminating the manual order entry activity of 250 clerical employees. The drug stores have been able to enjoy a higher level of service. For example, Economost prints labels that bear the particular prices that each of the drug stores charge. The labels are enclosed with the items when they are shipped, saving the customers the expense of performing the printing task themselves.

There are two key points concerning these three examples of competitive advantage. First, none of the firms were content to rely entirely on their physical resources in being tough competitors. Rather, they supplemented the physical resources with those of a conceptual nature—their computer-based information systems. Second, all three firms focused their information resources on their customers. This was the initial thrust of the competitive advantage strategy, and, although it can be effective, it is possible to achieve more by taking a broader view.

A Broad View of Competitive Advantage   As a way of achieving the maximum value from the use of information as a competitive resource, firms should

---

[4]For more information on EDI and IOS, *see* H. Russell Johnstone and Michael R. Vitale, "Creating Competitive Advantage with Interorganizational Information Systems," *MIS Quarterly* 12 (June 1988): 153–65.

build IOSs that provide links with *all* eight environmental elements. All of the information linkages should be two-way, with the exception of the one relating to competitors, which is incoming only. Management seeks to stimulate information flows *from,* but suppress flows *to,* competitors.

A firm can exploit information flows to and from its suppliers by establishing an EDI network that permits the transmissions illustrated in Figure 2.3. The firm transmits a request for quotation (RFQ) to a supplier's computer. The supplier responds with a price quote in an electronic form, and the firm transmits a purchase order (P.O.) the same way. The supplier electronically acknowledges receipt of the P.O., and sends an invoice in an electronic form when the merchandise is shipped. Standard formats have been devised by pioneering EDI firms for each of these types of transactions, making it easy for firms to form IOSs with their suppliers.

The government has established similar standards for the transmission of tax data. Firms can submit their tax reports in an electronic, rather than paper, form.

Transmission standards do not exist for electronic linkages with the financial community, but can be custom tailored to the specific needs of the firms. For example, a firm that frequently borrows money can electronically transmit its financial statement to banks and other lending agencies when applying for a loan. In a similar fashion, banks can make information available concerning economic projections, changes in the interest rates, and so on.

The environmental elements that offer the greatest opportunity for two-way EDI linkages are the customers, suppliers, government, and financial community. Other elements—local community, labor unions, and stockholders or owners—are much more difficult to establish, but should not be ignored. In these latter cases, IOS linkages can consist of noncomputer media.

WHAT ARE THE INFORMATION RESOURCES?

In Chapter 1, we introduced the topic of information management and explained why it is receiving so much attention. We also distinguished between data and information, identifying data as the raw material of information.

The first efforts to engage in information management focused on the data. These efforts were in conjunction with the widespread adoption of database management systems (DBMSs) during the 1970s and 1980s. Firms reasoned that if they managed their data by implementing the computer-based DBMSs, they would, in effect, manage their information. The view that data and information are resources to be managed like any other resource is still prevalent and represents a positive approach to computer use.

Another, supplementary view has emerged, however, and that is the view that you can manage information by managing the *resources* that produce the information. In other words, rather than concentrate on the input (the data) and the output (the information), attention should also be given to the information processor

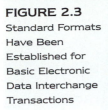

FIGURE 2.3
Standard Formats
Have Been
Established for
Basic Electronic
Data Interchange
Transactions

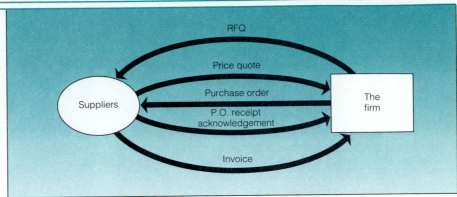

that transforms the input into the output. This processor includes the hardware and software, as well as the persons who develop, operate, and use the systems. Also included are the facilities that house the resources.

Types of Information Resources

A firm's information resources therefore consist of:

- Computer hardware
- Computer software
- Information specialists
- Users
- Facilities
- The database
- Information

When a firm's managers decide to use information to achieve competitive advantage, they must recognize each of these elements as information resources. For example, the managers must understand that personnel who are capable of applying the computer to business problems are a valuable resource, as are environmental users. Then, the firm must manage these resources in order to achieve the desired results.

WHO MANAGES THE INFORMATION RESOURCES?

As we saw in Chapter 1, the first computer-using firms placed the responsibility for managing the information resources in the hands of a special unit of computer specialists. This unit, which we call information services, is managed by a manager

FIGURE 2.4
Computer Users
Are Information
Resources

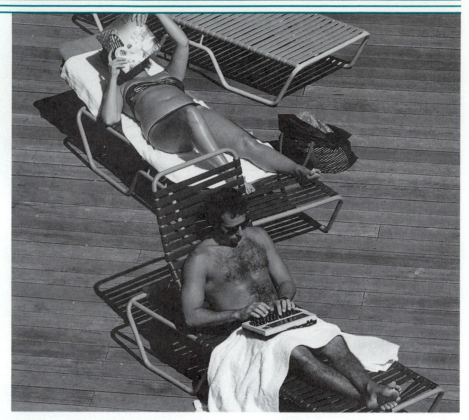

© Miro Vintoniv/The Picture Cube

who can have vice-presidential status. The trend today is toward establishing information services as a major functional area and including its top manager in the select group of executives, such as the executive committee, who make the key decisions of the firm.

The Chief Information Officer

The term *CEO* is firmly implanted in the vocabulary of business; everyone knows that the CEO is the person who exerts the strongest influence on the firm's operations, and usually has the title of president or chairperson of the board. Terms such as *CFO,* for chief financial officer, and *COO,* for chief operating officer, have been coined as well. The 1980s saw similar terminology created for the information services manager. The term is CIO, for chief information officer.

The fact of the matter is that the term CIO does not always evoke a positive reaction. Some information services managers feel uncomfortable with the title, perhaps thinking that it calls for a level of performance that they cannot provide. For this and other reasons, the title has not been widely adopted. A 1988 study conducted by the accounting firm Coopers & Lybrand, in conjunction with *Datamation* magazine, revealed that only 14 percent of the top information services managers

FIGURE 2.5

Most Managers of the Firm's Information Resources Do Not Have
the CIO Title

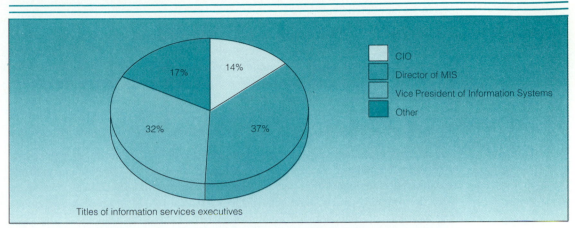

Source: Ralph Emmett Carlyle, "CIO: Misfit or Misnomer?"
Datamation 34 (August 1, 1988), 51. Used with permission.

had the CIO title. Figure 2.5 shows the survey results.[5] The most popular title was director of MIS, with vice president of information systems close behind.

CIO—More than a Title

A point that is often overlooked is the fact that the term CIO implies more than simply a title. It implies a recommended role that the top information services manager should play. As intended by the concept, the **chief information officer (CIO)**, is the manager of information services who contributes managerial skills to solving not only problems relating to the information resources but to other areas of the firm's operations as well.

This attitude has not always prevailed. Many of the first computer managers were seen by their superiors and peers as technicians who came up short when it came to their strategic management skills. Unfortunately, that image has persisted, often without basis, in many companies throughout the years.

Such a situation does not exist in those firms where top management recognizes the value of information resources, and where the information services managers work aggressively to achieve executive status. An information services manager can perform as a chief information officer by taking the following advice:[6]

- Spend time with the business and in business training. Learn the business, not just the technology.
- Build partnerships with business units and line management; don't wait to be invited.

[5] Ralph Emmett Carlyle, "CIO: Misfit or Misnomer?" *Datamation* 34 (August 1, 1988), 50*ff.*
[6] Jeff Moad, "Why You Should Be Making IS Allies," *Datamation* 36 (May 1, 1990), 26*ff.*

- ■ Focus on improving basic business processes.
- ■ Explain IS costs in business terms.
- ■ Build credibility by delivering reliable IS services.
- ■ Be nondefensive.

For the firm that has embraced the CIO concept, the top information services manager, whatever her or his title, works with executives from the other functional areas in jointly solving the firm's strategic problems. From this point on in the text, we will use the term CIO when describing the top-level manager of information services. We will assume that this person performs as intended by the CIO concept.

The Increasing Complexity of Information Management

For the first ten or so years of the computer era, *all* of the information resources were centrally located in the firm's information services unit. Beginning with the installation of keyboard terminals in user areas in the mid-1960s, and continuing with the spread of microcomputers in the 1980s, more and more of the hardware has been located outside of information services. If the disbursement trend continues, the day may come when practically all of the resources are managed by users.[7]

As firms acquire more information resources, and those resources are disbursed throughout the organization, the task of information resource management becomes more complex. The management responsibility falls on the shoulders of not only the CIO, but on *all* managers in the firm.

STRATEGIC PLANNING

In Chapter 1, we discussed Henri Fayol's management functions—plan, organize, staff, direct, and control. These functions are performed in the order given, with the plan providing the basis for all of the subsequent activity. We also saw in Chapter 1 that managers are located on levels of the organizational hierarchy.

One way to distinguish between the levels is to use the managers' planning horizons. A **planning horizon** is the future time period for which a manager has a planning responsibility. Executives on the strategic planning level have the longest planning horizon, stretching from a period of five to ten or so years into the future. Management control level managers typically plan for a period one to five years into the future, and managers on the operational control level plan for the current year.

The fact that executives have the most distant planning horizon does not mean that they are unconcerned with what is currently happening in the firm. *All* managers, even very senior executives, stay on top of current events. This fact is borne out by the way that the President of the United States reacts immediately to crises that occur anywhere in the world. The distant planning horizon of the executives simply means that they are the only ones who are responsible for taking a long-range view of the firm's future.

[7] For more information on this view, *see* John J. Donovan, "Beyond Chief Information Officer to Network Manager," *Harvard Business Review* 66 (September–October 1988), 134–40.

Long-range planning is also known as **strategic planning** since it identifies objectives that are intended to give the firm the most favorable position in its environment and specifies the strategies for achieving those objectives. The importance of strategic planning on the upper-management level is no doubt the reason why Robert Anthony named the level the strategic planning level.

When a firm organizes its executives into an executive committee, this group invariably assumes responsibility for strategic planning.

Functional Strategic Planning

Once the strategic plan for the firm has been established, it becomes the responsibility of each functional area to develop its own strategic plan. The functional plans detail how those areas will support the firm as it works toward its strategic objectives.

One approach to functional strategic planning would be for each area to establish its own plan independently of the others. However, that approach does not ensure that the areas will work together as synchronized subsystems. Figure 2.6

FIGURE 2.6

The Functional Areas Should Cooperate in Developing Their Strategic Plans

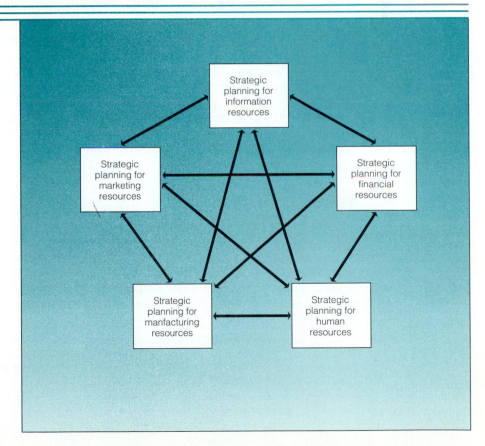

shows how all of the functional areas should cooperate in their strategic planning processes. The arrows represent flows of information and influence.

STRATEGIC PLANNING FOR INFORMATION RESOURCES

During the past few years, information services has probably devoted more attention to strategic planning than have most of the other areas. The first term used to describe this activity was strategy set transformation. More recently the term strategic planning for information resources has become popular.

Strategy Set Transformation

When information services began to develop strategic plans, the recommended approach was to base them entirely on the firm's strategic objectives, which were termed the **organizational strategy set**. As a second, separate step an information services plan was devised to support the firm's objectives. The information services plan was called the **MIS strategy set,** and it consisted of objectives, constraints, and strategies. This approach, called **strategy set transformation,** is illustrated in Figure 2.7.[8]

There was a basic flaw in strategy set transformation, and it was the fact that the functional areas did not always have the resources to ensure the accomplishment of the firm's strategic objectives. For example, the firm might plan to add a new product line, but the marketing division did not have enough sales reps to sell the new products, and information services did not have the programmers to write the necessary new code.

The SPIR Approach

The solution to the problem was **strategic planning for information resources (SPIR)**. When a firm embraces SPIR, the strategic plan for information services and the strategic plan for the firm are developed *concurrently*. The firm's plan reflects the support that can be provided by information services, and the information services plan reflects future demands for systems support. Figure 2.8 illustrates the manner in which each planning process influences the other.[9]

---

[8] The terminology of strategic set transformation is attributed to MIS professor William R. King of the University of Pittsburgh, who is regarded as the premier expert on strategic information planning. For more details, *see* William R. King, "Strategic Planning for Management Information Systems," *MIS Quarterly* 2 (March 1978), 27–37.

[9] William R. King, "Strategic Planning for Information Resources: The Evolution of Concepts and Practice," *Information Resources Management Journal* 1 (Fall 1988), 1–8.

FIGURE 2.7
Strategy Set
Transformation

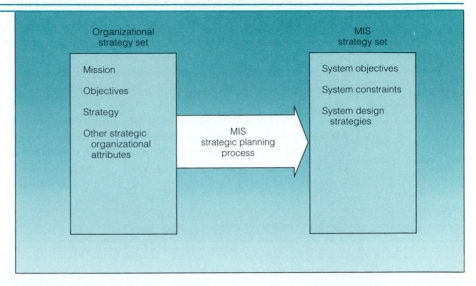

Source: William R. King, ''Strategic Planning for Management Information Systems,''
MIS Quarterly 2 (March 1978), 28. Reprinted with permission.

FIGURE 2.8
Strategic Planning
for Information
Resources

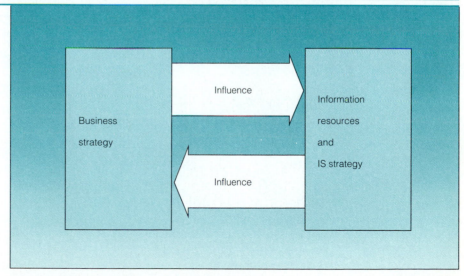

Source: William R. King, ''Strategic Planning for Information Resources: The
Evolution of Concepts and Practice,'' *Information Resources Management Journal* 1
(Fall 1988), 3. Reprinted with permission.

Content of a Strategic Plan for Information Resources

Each firm will develop a strategic plan for information resources, which meets its own particular needs. However, we can identify some major topics that should be included. Essentially, the plan should specify: (1) the objectives to be achieved by each CBIS subsystem during the period defined by the planning horizon, and (2) the information resources necessary to meet the objectives. This content is illustrated in Figure 2.9.

As an example of how the plan can consider the needs of a particular CBIS subsystem, assume that an inventory system is to be modified to allow customer orders to be filled more quickly. Increased speed can be achieved by locating the inventory items in the warehouse in such a fashion that the order fillers pick the

FIGURE 2.9

Basic Framework of a Strategic Plan for Information Resources

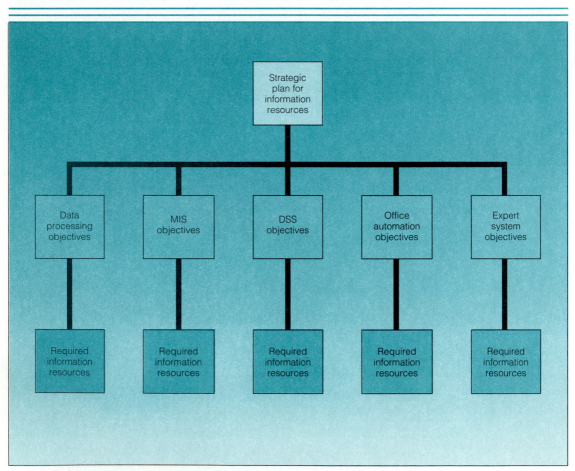

items from the shelves in the most efficient sequence. The next step in the planning process is to identify the information resources that will be necessary to accomplish the objective. Figure 2.10 provides a sample of the manner in which the objectives and resource requirements can be spelled out.

Attention is carefully paid to the role that the users will play in the project. This attention is especially important when the users are expected to do some or all of the developmental work.

FIGURE 2.10

Example of a Strategic Plan for an Inventory System

System: Inventory

Subsystem: Warehouse Layout

Objective: Implement a program on October 1st of next year, which determines the location of items in the warehouse that best facilitates order filling. The program will be run quarterly.

Resource Requirements

Hardware: Approximately two hours of mainframe time per quarter, including program maintenance and testing. Mainframe configuration requires approximately 20 MB of disk space, one keyboard terminal, a line printer, and a plotter.

Facilities: Use existing facilities.

Software: Modified linear programming program that provides for both graphic and tabular interface. Estimated coding requirement is 1,000 lines.

Database: Use existing inventory master file.

Information Specialists: Approximately 18 person months of development time by information services personnel are allocated as follows: systems analyst (6), database administrator (4), programmer (6), console operator (2). In addition, the warehouse systems staff will contribute approximately two person months.

Information: Warehouse stock clerks require warehouse location code on picking tickets. The code is included in the inventory master record.

Users: Warehouse systems staff will provide information services with layouts of all screens, plus a statement of the objective function and a list of all constraints in mathematical notation. The warehouse manager will require two days of hands-on training in use of system, administered by a member of the warehouse systems staff. Information services will provide a user manual.

END-USER COMPUTING AS A STRATEGIC ISSUE

In Chapter 1 we introduced the topic of end-user computing, or EUC. It was triggered by four forces—an increase in computer literacy, the information services backlog, low-priced hardware, and prewritten software. In order to better understand the importance of EUC to SPIR, we must explain in greater detail its effect on computer use in the firm.

Levels of End-user Computing

All of the persons who engage in EUC do not have the same level of computer literacy. It is possible to classify end-users into four categories, based on their computer capabilities: menu-level end users, command-level end-users, end-user programmers, and functional support personnel.[10]

Menu-level end-users Some end users are unable to create their own software, but can communicate with prewritten software by means of menus such as those featured by Lotus, dBASE, and WordPerfect.

Command-level end users Some end users have capabilities for using prewritten software that go beyond menu selection. These end users can use the command language of the software to perform arithmetic and logical operations on the data. For example, users of the dBASE database management system (DBMS) can use special commands to accomplish processes not possible through the use of the menus.

End-user Programmers Some end users can use programming languages such as BASIC or the dBASE programming language contained within that DBMS, and develop custom programs to meet their own needs.

Functional Support Personnel In some firms, information specialists are members of functional units rather than information services. These functional support personnel are information specialists in every sense of the word, but they owe their allegiance to their particular user areas and report to their functional managers. This decentralization of information specialists is one of the major trends occurring in firms today.

Two key ingredients characterize all four levels of end-user capability. First, all levels have an ability to develop applications, and second, none are members of the information services organization.

---

[10] This classification is a modification of one described in John F. Rockart and Lauren S. Flannery, "The Management of End User Computing," *Communications of the ACM* 26 (October 1983), 776–84.

Types of End-user Applications

Thus far, EUC has impacted the major CBIS subsystems in varying degrees. Most end-user computing applications have been restricted to:

- Relatively simple DSSs
- Office automation applications that meet individual needs

This leaves the information specialists with the responsibility for working with users in developing:

- Complex DSSs
- Data processing and management information systems
- Office automation applications that meet organizational needs
- Expert systems

As long as this variability in the impact of EUC continues, which it should, there will always be a need for information specialists.

Benefits of End-user Computing

EUC benefits the firm in two primary ways; it shifts some of the systems development workload to the user, and it eliminates or reduces the communications gap between the user and the information specialist.

Workload Shift   The shift in the workload for systems development to user areas frees up the specialists to concentrate on the organizational and complex systems, doing a better job in those areas. The specialists also have more time to devote to maintaining existing systems—an important, and growing, area of responsibility.

The Communications Gap   A difficulty that has plagued systems development since the first days of computing has been the communications between the user and the information specialist. The user understands the problem area but not the computing technology. The specialist, on the other hand, is expert in the technology but not the problem area. The two speak different languages. By letting the users develop their own applications, there is no communications gap because there is no need for communication. Likewise, when users develop a portion of their systems, the gap is reduced.

Both of these benefits result in the development of better systems than when the information specialists try to do the majority of the work themselves.

Risks of End-user Computing

The benefits of EUC do not come without their price. When end users develop their own systems, they expose the firm to risks of poorly aimed systems, poorly designed and documented systems, inefficient use of hardware and software resources, loss of data integrity, and loss of security.

Poorly Aimed Systems   End users may apply the computer to applications that should be performed some other way, such as manually.

Poorly Designed and Documented Systems   End users, although they may have high levels of computer literacy, cannot match the professionalism of the information specialists when it comes to designing systems. Also, in the rush to get the systems on the air, end users tend to overlook the need to document their designs so that the systems can be maintained, perhaps by other users.

Inefficient Use of Information Resources   When there is no central control over acquisition of hardware and software, the firm can end up with hardware that is incompatible and redundant software. For example, different brands of personal computers are acquired that cannot be linked to form a network, and multiple copies of software are purchased when a single copy could be shared. Also, end users may "reinvent the wheel" by developing systems that have already been developed—by information specialists or by other end users.

Loss of Data Integrity   End users may not exercise the necessary care in entering data into the firm's database. Other users use this erroneous data, assuming it is accurate. The result is contaminated output that can cause managers to make the wrong decisions.

Loss of Security   In a similar fashion, end users may not safeguard their data and software. Diskettes are left lying on desktops, printouts are tossed in wastebaskets, doors to computer rooms are left unlocked, and so on. Computer criminals can gain access to the system and harm the firm in many ways.

None of these risks are as great when information services develops systems because that organization can establish centralized controls.

A Unique End-user Computing Strategy—the Information Center

When the firm's management became aware of the increasing interest among their users in end-user computing, there was often a reluctance to approve the requests for support. Management was not certain that the users really needed their own hardware and software. Some firms devised a strategy that was intended to provide the resources, but not on an individual basis. They established central locations, called **information centers,** where the resources were made available to everyone. When a user wanted to engage in EUC, he or she went to the information center and used the resources there. The resources typically included microcomputers, keyboard terminals connected to the firm's mainframe, plotters capable of produc-

FIGURE 2.11
An Information
Center

© Spencer Grant/Stock, Boston

ing hardcopy graphics, the necessary software such as DBMSs and electronic spreadsheets, plus support personnel. The task of the support personnel was not to do the work for the users but to provide the help that the users needed to become self sufficient. Figure 2.11 shows a typical information center.

Some firms used their information centers as only an interim measure—until users could be supplied with their own resources. Other firms have retained their centers as a special form of user support.

Putting End-user Computing In Perspective

End-user computing is a phenomenon that is not going to go away. If anything, its influence will only increase. Because of the potential benefits, the firm must develop a strategic plan for information resources that allows EUC to grow and flourish. As far as the risks are concerned, the same types of controls must be applied to user areas that have worked so well in information services.

THE INFORMATION RESOURCES
MANAGEMENT CONCEPT

Viewing information as a resource is nothing new. What has happened in the past decade is the realization that a firm's information resources go far beyond the information itself. The topics that we have discussed in this chapter form the basis for managing all of the information resources. **Information resources management**

(**IRM**) is an activity that is pursued by managers on all levels of the firm for the purpose of identifying the information resources needed to meet user needs, acquiring the resources, and managing the resources.

Required IRM Elements

In order for a firm to fully achieve IRM, it is necessary that a set of conditions exist. These conditions include:

- **A recognition that competitive advantage can be achieved by means of superior information resources.** The firm's executives and other managers who engage in strategic planning must appreciate that the firm can achieve superiority over competitors by managing information flows.
- **A recognition that information services is a major functional area.** The firm's organizational structure should reflect that information services has an importance equal to other major functional areas, such as finance and marketing.
- **A recognition that the CIO is a top-level executive.** The CIO should contribute, when appropriate, to decision making that affects the entire firm's operations, not just those of information services. This recognition is most easily demonstrated by including the CIO on the executive committee.
- **A consideration of the firm's information resources when engaging in strategic planning** When executives engage in strategic planning for the firm, they should consider the information resources necessary to achieve the strategic objectives.
- **A formal strategic plan for information resources.** A formal plan should exist for acquiring and managing information resources. The resources should include those in user areas as well as information services.
- **A strategy for stimulating and managing end-user computing**. The strategic plan for information resources should address the issue of making information resources available to end users, yet maintaining control over those resources.

IRM reflects an appreciation for the value of information and those resources that produce the information. Managers on all levels contribute to IRM, but the attitude of top executives, such as the CEO and other members of the executive committee, is the key. Unless these leaders recognize that conceptual resources are just as important as physical resources, IRM will never occur.

The IRM Model

The required IRM conditions do not exist separately but work together in a coordinated way, as is shown in Figure 2.12. The numbers in the figure correspond to the numbered sections below.

1. **The environment of the firm**. The eight environmental elements provide the setting for achieving competitive advantage. Executives are aware of

FIGURE 2.12
The IRM Model

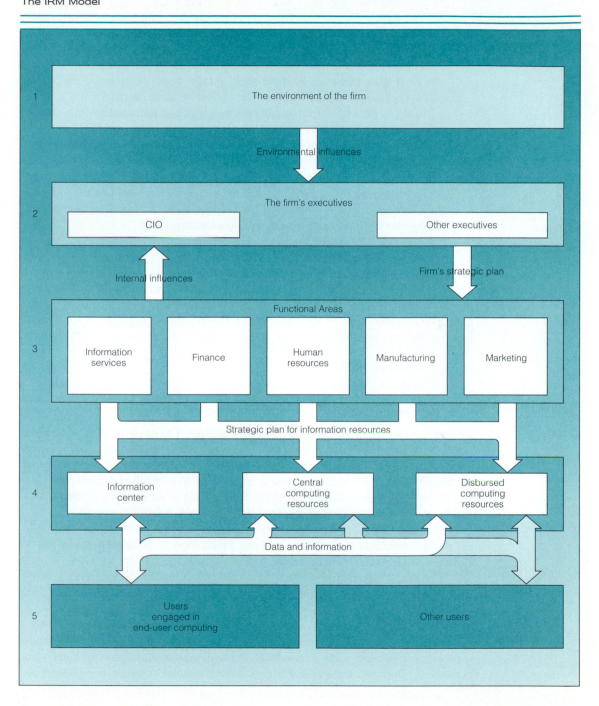

the need to manage resource flows as a means of meeting the needs of the environmental elements in a competitive market.

2. **The firm's executives**. The CIO is included among the group of executives who guide the firm toward its objectives. One of the key activities of this group is strategic planning.

3. **The functional areas**. Information services is included as a major functional area, and each of these areas jointly develops strategic plans that support the strategic plan of the firm. One of these functional plans is the strategic plan for information resources, which is prepared by information services working with the other functional areas.

4. **The information resources**. The strategic plan for information resources describes how all information resources will be acquired and managed. Some of these resources are centralized in information services, and some are disbursed throughout the firm in information centers and user areas.

5. **Users**. Data and information flow between the information resources and the users. Some users engage in end-user computing.

The figure illustrates how levels of systems influence information resources management. The environment forms the supersystem of the firm. The firm's managers on the top level plan the strategy that enables the firm as a system to achieve its objectives. The functional areas represent the firm's subsystems, and their strategic plans support that of the firm. All of the functional strategic plans specify how information resources are to be made available to users on all levels.

SUMMARY

The environment of a firm consists of eight elements. The elements represent organizations or individuals and include suppliers, customers, labor unions, the financial community, stockholders or owners, competitors, the government, and the local community. These elements comprise a larger supersystem called society. The five main types of resources flow between the firm and the environmental elements, and the flows create both direct and indirect influences on the firm's operations.

The firm is able to control its environment to some extent. This control is called environmental management and can be attained by following any of three strategies—independent, cooperative, and strategic maneuvering.

The first efforts of firms to use information as a means of achieving a competitive advantage have featured computer links with customers. Electronic data interchange, or EDI, provides the technological base for firms banding together so as to form interorganizational systems, or IOSs. The current, broader view of competitive advantage recognizes the importance of information flows with all environmental elements. EDI can handle electronic transmissions to and from customers, suppliers, the government, and the financial community. Information flows with other environmental elements are more difficult to achieve electronically, and may utilize noncomputer links.

Information resources include hardware, facilities, software, the database, information specialists, information, and users. The resources that are located in information services are managed by the CIO. The CIO concept recognizes the information services manager as an executive. The information resources located outside of information services are managed by managers of the user areas.

All managers plan, and executives engage in long-range, strategic planning. The first efforts to develop a strategic plan for information services were called strategy set transformation. In many cases the required information resources were not present. This problem was solved by concurrently developing the strategic plans for the firm and information services. This approach has been given the name strategic planning for information resources, or SPIR. The product of SPIR is a plan that identifies the information resource needs for each of the CBIS subsystems for the period covered by the strategic planning horizon.

The SPIR task has been complicated by the boom in end-user computing, or EUC. EUC was triggered by an increasing computer literacy on the part of users, a growing information services backlog, and the availability of low-cost hardware and prewritten software. Some firms enabled users to engage in EUC by erecting information centers.

All end users do not possess the same capabilities. Some can only use menus, some can use command languages, and some have programming skills. Still others are information specialists located in user areas. Although more and more systems are being developed by end users, the systems tend to be relatively simple DSSs and OA systems intended for individual support. The remaining systems continue to be developed jointly by users working with information specialists.

EUC is here to stay; it benefits the firm by shifting part of the system development workload to the users and by bridging the communications gap. The risks that are inherent in EUC deal with poorly aimed systems, poorly designed and documented systems, inefficient use of hardware and software resources, loss of data integrity, and loss of security. These risks can be minimized or even eliminated by management control.

The idea that all of the firm's managers should engage in information management is a recent revelation, and is called information resources management, or IRM. IRM flourishes when: (1) the firm strives to use information to achieve competitive advantage, (2) executives recognize information services as a major functional area, (3) executives admit the CIO to their elite circle, (4) executives consider information resources when conducting strategic planning, (5) a formal strategic plan for information resources exists, and (6) the plan addresses the issue of end-user computing.

IRM is an integrating concept that ties together the environment, the levels of management, the functional areas, the information resources, and the users. The achievement of IRM will be the charge of executives of the 1990s and is the underlying theme of this book.

KEY TERMS

electronic data interchange (EDI)
interorganizational information system (IOS)
planning horizon

strategic planning
strategy set transformation
information center

KEY CONCEPTS

The firm's environment, comprised of eight
    elements existing in society
How the environmental elements are connected
    to the firm by means of resource flows
Environmental management
Competitive advantage

The broad range of information resources
The chief information officer (CIO)
Strategic planning for information resources
    (SPIR)
Levels of end-user capabilities
Information resources management (IRM)

QUESTIONS

1. How does the firm interact with its environment?

2. What are the eight environmental elements?

3. What are the three strategies that a firm can use to influence its environment?

4. What distinguishes the initial view of competitive advantage from the broader view?

5. What two factors do the competitive advantage efforts of American Airlines, American Hospital Supply, and McKesson have in common?

6. Is EDI a necessary requirement for IOS? Explain.

7. Which of the environmental elements can most easily be linked with the firm by means of electronic transmissions?

8. List the seven types of information resources. Place an asterisk next to those that are always located in information services.

9. Could a manager be a CIO even though he or she does not have that title? Explain your reasoning.

10. Would a degree in business administration help a CIO? Explain.

11. Has information management become more or less complex during the past decade? Explain.

12. How can the management levels be distinguished?

13. Which management levels are concerned with the firm's current activity?

14. Why might executives come up with an unworkable plan when they engage in top-down strategic planning?

15. Why might the lower-level managers come up with a plan that is unacceptable to the executives when a bottom-up planning approach is followed?

16. Name a major weakness of strategy set transformation.

17. What are the two elements that should be included in a strategic plan for information resources?

18. What four conditiions triggered EUC?

19. What was the logic underlying the establishment of information centers?

20. What are the four classes of end users?

21. The text states that end users are not likely to develop complex DSSs. Would there be any limitations on the systems that functional support personnel develop? If so, explain.

22. What are the main benefits of EUC? What are the main risks? How can the risks be minimized?

23. How could an inspection of the firm's organization chart provide an indication that the firm is striving to achieve IRM?

24. If the top manager in the information services area has the title of CIO, does this mean that the firm is practicing IRM? Explain.

25. Where are the information resources located that are the subject of the strategic plan for information resources?

TOPICS FOR DISCUSSION

1. Give examples of information that flows between a firm and its stockholders. How can information technology be used to facilitate this flow?

2. Does the size of the organization have any influence on the ability of the firm to engage in environmental management?

3. The text says that McKesson eliminated the work of 250 clerical employees with its Economost system. If you had been the McKesson CEO at the time, would you have terminated those employees' employment, or assigned them to other jobs? Explain.

4. Why are a firm's computer users considered to be an information resource? Does the value of this resource increase or decrease when the users engage in end-user computing?

PROBLEMS

1. Draw a diagram, similar in layout to Figure 2.1, which shows the physical resources that flow most frequently between the firm and its environment. Use arrows to show the flows.

2. Draw a diagram, similar to Figure 2.1, which shows the flows of data and information between the firm and each of the environmental elements. The arrows should show the direction of the flows—one-way or two-way.

3. Draw a diagram, similar to Figure 2.1, which shows the indirect influences when:

(1) a strike at a supplier's plant shuts off the firm's incoming material flow, and (2) the Federal Reserve Board increases the prime interest rate, making it more difficult for the firm to secure loans. Show the influences with arrows labeled "Influence."

4. Go to the library and find a recent reference (within the past two years) on one of the following topics: information centers, the CIO, IRM, EDI, or IOS. Read the article and write a brief summary. Your instructor will advise you concerning the required length and format.

Polybac Equipment Service Company of Mexico

Polybac Equipment Service Company (PESCO) is a Philadelphia-based manufacturer of industrial wastewater treatment systems. They have plants around the world, including Mexico City. Emilio Chavez is the president of PESCO Mexico, and has recently decided to implement SPIR. PESCO Mexico has a large mainframe computing operation but has never had a strategic information plan. Chavez sent E-mail messages to the other members of the executive committee, advising them of his intentions, and asking for their ideas. He has received replies from all three members—Benito Flores, the vice president of manufacturing and sales; Juan Alvarez, the vice president of finance; and Betty Wilson, the vice president of information systems. President Chavez reads the E-mail replies:

From: Benito

I have given the subject of SPIR a great deal of thought since we discussed it in the last executive committee meeting. I would like to see manufacturing and sales develop our own strategic plan, independently of the rest of the organization—including IS. We have a large amount of computing equipment that we use for our own applications, and we should have the freedom to plan how that equipment, plus additional equipment, will be used in the future. Let Betty and Juan do the same thing—develop their own strategic plans as they see fit.

From: Juan

Thanks for the opportunity to voice my views. I think that all three vice presidents should work together in developing a single strategic plan. We have a good working relationship and cooperate on many other activities. There is no reason why a joint approach to SPIR would not work.

From: Betty

Emilio, you know my views since I have voiced them many times. Since information systems is my only responsibility, IS should be able to prepare the strategic information resources plan for all of Polybac Mexico. Juan and Benito have enough responsibility in their own areas to waste their time on IS problems. Give IS the total strategic planning responsibility.

After Chavez has read all three replies, he leans back in his chair and says: "Our next executive committee meeting should really be exciting."

Assignment

Assume that you are a consultant, and that president Chavez has retained you to advise him on the SPIR approach. Write a memo to him that includes:

- A list of the advantgages and disadvantages of each of the three approaches.
- A recommendation of the approach that you believe should be implemented. Briefly summarize your reason for the selection.

SELECTED BIBLIOGRAPHY

Alavi, Maryam; Nelson, R. Ryan; and Weiss, Ira R. "Strategies for End-User Computing: An Integrative Framework." *Journal of Management Information Systems* 4 (Winter 1987–88): 29–49.

Blanton, J. Ellis, and Hubona, Geoffrey S. "Forging the Link: Information Systems to Enable Business Strategy." *Journal of Information Technology Management* 1 (Number 2, 1990): 33–38.

Carlyle, Ralph. "The Out of Touch CIO" *Datamation* 36 (August 15, 1990): 30*ff.*

Clemons, Eric K. "Evaluation of Strategic Investments in Information Technology." *Communications of the ACM* 34 (January 1991): 22–36.

Clemons, Eric K., and Row, Michael C. "Sustaining IT Advantage: The Role of Structural Differences." *MIS Quarterly* 15 (September 1991): 275–92.

Durand, Douglas; Floyd, Steven; and Kublanow, Samuel. "How Do 'Real' Managers Use Office Systems?" *Journal of Information Technology Management* 1 (Number 2, 1990): 25–32.

Fleck, Robert A. "Information as a Competitive Weapon." *Information Executive* 3 (Spring 1990): 42–46.

Frolick, Mark N., and Carr, Houston H. "The Role of Management Information Systems in Environmental Scanning: A Strategic Issue." *Journal of Information Technology Management* 2 (Number 3, 1991): 33–37.

Ghani, Jawaid A., and Chacko, Cherackal. "End User Dependence on Computer Technology." *Journal of Information Technology Management* 2 (Number 3, 1991): 9–15.

Grant, Robert M. "The Resource-Based Theory of Competitive Advantage: Implications for Strategy Formulation." *California Management Review* 33 (Spring 1991): 114–135.

Gurbaxani, Vijay, and Whang, Seungjin. "The Impact of Information Systems on Organizations and Markets." *Communications of the ACM* 34 (January 1991): 59–73.

Henderson, John C. "Plugging into Strategic Partnerships: The Critical IS Connection." *Sloan Management Review* 31 (Spring 1990): 7–18.

Henderson, John C., and Treacy, Michael E. "Managing End-User Computing for Competitive Advantage." *Sloan Management Review* 27 (Winter 1986): 3–14.

Hershey, Gerald L., and Eatman, John L. "Why IS Execs Feel Left Out Of Big Decisions." *Datamation* 36 (May 15, 1990): 97–99.

Lederer, Albert L., and Sethi, Vijay. "Critical Dimensions of Strategic Information Systems Planning." *Decision Sciences* 22 (Winter 1991): 104–19.

Lee, Yang W.; Madnick, Stuart E.; and Wang, Y. Richard. "Beyond the Globalization of Information Technology: The Life of an Organization and the Role of Information Technology." *Journal of Information Technology Management* 2 (Number 1, 1991): 1–10.

Miller, Frederick W. "Managing Information for International Success." *EDGE* 3 (November/December 1990): 37–44.

Moad, Jeff. "Why You Should Be Making IS Allies." *Datamation* 36 (May 1, 1990): 26*ff.*

Moynihan, Tony. "What Chief Executives and Senior Managers Want from Their IT Departments." *MIS Quarterly* 14 (March 1990): 15–25.

Neeley, Lynn, and Lauer, Joachim (Jim). "Strategic Information Systems Planning in Practice." *Journal of Information Technology Management* 2 (Number 1, 1990): 25–30.

Newman, William A., and Brock, Floyd J. "A Framework for Designing Competitive Information Systems." *Information Executive* 3 (Spring 1990): 33–36.

Pike, Bill. "Nurturing the Help Desk." *Datacenter Manager* 3 (July/August 1991): 53–56.

Porter, Michael E., and Millar, Victor E. "How Information Gives You Competitive Advantage." *Harvard Business Review* 63 (July–August 1985): 149–60.

Reid, Richard A., and Bullers, William I., Jr. "Strategic Information Systems Help Create Competitive Advantage." *Information Executive* 3 (Spring 1990): 51–54.

Rockart, John F., and Short, James E. "IT in the 1990s: Managing Organizational Interdependence." *Sloan Management Review* 30 (Winter 1989): 7–17.

Shah, Joe, and Leja, Christine. "Businesses Triumph with IRM." *Information Executive* 4 (Fall 1991): 31–34.

Simmons, Laurette Poulos; Burbridge, John J.; Harris, William L.; and Ames, Kenneth E. "The Impact of Information Centers on End-User Computing." *Information Resources Management Journal* 2 (Spring 1989): 13–21.

Snapp, Cheryl D. "EDI Aims High for Global Growth." *Datamation* 36 (March 1, 1990): 77*ff.*

Watson, Richard T. "Influences on the IS Manager's Perceptions of Key Issues: Information Scanning and the Relationship with the CEO." *MIS Quarterly* 14 (June 1990): 217–31.

Winkler, Connie. "An Illumunating CEO-CIO Alliance." *Datamation* 36 (August 15, 1990): 79*ff.*

Part II

INFORMATION METHODOLOGIES AND TOOLS

The task of creating a computer-based information system is similar to the construction of a house. Architects create blueprints to guide the efforts of the construction workers, who use various tools to perform the carpentry, electrical work, plumbing, and so on. The work of the developers of computer-based systems is guided by blueprints that are called methodologies, and the developers also use an assortment of tools. Part Two is devoted to a description of the more popular methodologies and tools.

Chapter 3 illustrates and describes how systems theory can be applied to any type of organization, such as a business firm. The end product of this application is called the general systems model of the firm.

Chapter 4 describes the basic systems methodology—the systems approach. Managers can follow the systems approach in solving the multitude of problems that they face, and information specialists can follow the same general pattern in solving problems relating to systems development and use.

Chapter 5 is an application of the systems approach to the life cycle of a computer-based system. We see that such a system is born, matures, and eventually dies. However, unlike living organisms, the computer-based system is invariably replaced by a newer system—a type of reincarnation. Chapter 5 explains the many steps that are taken from the inception of a system until the time comes for replacement.

Chapters 3, 4, and 5 deal with methodologies, leaving the tools for Chapter 6, which describes tools that are used in systems planning and analysis, and Chapter 7, which describes tools that are used in systems design, implementation, audit, and control.

Traditionally, these methodologies and tools were the exclusive bailiwick of the information specialists. With the advent of end-user computing, however, a strong case can be made for users acquiring the same knowledge and skills. With an understanding of the material in Part Two, you can begin to develop computer-based systems, either as an information specialist or a user.

Chapter 3

The General Systems Model of the Firm

LEARNING OBJECTIVES

After studying this chapter, you should:

- Know what a model is, what types exist, and how they are used in business
- Appreciate the value of a general model
- Feel comfortable with the concept that the firm is a network of resource flows
- Understand what a system must contain in order for it to control itself
- Know the four dimensions of information that give it value
- Understand the concept of management by exception
- Be able to use the general systems model as the basis for understanding and evaluating any type of organization

INTRODUCTION

Managers use models to solve problems, and there are four basic model types—physical, narrative, graphic, and mathematical. They all facilitate both understanding and communication, and the mathematical model can also be used to predict the future.

Some models represent their entities in a very specific way, whereas others do so in a general fashion. A general model has the advantage of applying to a wide variety of situations. We present a general model of a firm that consists of both a physical system and a conceptual system. The physical system includes an input element, a transformation element, and an output element, and provides a pathway for the flow of physical resources. The conceptual system consists of data and information that represent the physical system.

The integral parts of the conceptual system are a feedback loop and a control mechanism. The control mechanism in a business firm is represented by management, and the feedback loop by information flow. Data is gathered from the physical system and is transformed into information by an information processor.

There are four dimensions of information, which contribute to its value. Information should be relevant to the problem being solved, it should be accurate, it should be timely, and it should be complete.

Managers compare the information from the information processor to standards that specify acceptable levels or ranges of performance. Managers may elect to only become involved when performance falls outside the acceptable range. The performance may be better than expected, or worse. This concept of only attending to activities that merit the manager's attention is called management by exception. A similar concept is called critical success factors. It involves the monitoring of a few select actions that contribute to the firm's success.

Once management determines that changes should be made in the physical system, those decisions are communicated to the appropriate system elements.

Because the general systems model of the firm represents all types of organizations and shows how information is used in managing the organizations, it is a useful tool for problem solvers.

MODELS

A **model** is an abstraction of something. It represents some object or activity, which is called an **entity**.

Managers use models to represent problems to be solved. The objects or activities that cause problems are the entities.

Types of Models

There are four basic types of models:

1. Physical models
2. Narrative models

FIGURE 3.1
A Physical Model

Courtesy of Rockwell International Corporation.

3. Graphic models

4. Mathematical models

Physical Models   A **physical model** is a three-dimensional representation of its entity. Physical models used in the business world include scale models of shopping centers, and prototypes of new automobiles.

The physical model serves a purpose that cannot be fulfilled by the real thing. For example, it is much less expensive for the shopping center investors and automakers to make changes in the designs of their physical models than the final products.

Of the four model types, the physical model probably has the least value to the business manager. It is usually not necessary for a manager to see something in a three-dimensional form in order to understand it or use it in problem solving.

Narrative Models   One type of model that managers use daily is seldom recognized as a model. This is the **narrative model,** which describes its entity with spoken or written words. The listener or reader can understand the entity from the narrative. All business communications are narrative models, making it the most popular model type.

Graphic Models   Another type of model in constant use is the graphic model. A **graphic model** represents its entity with an abstraction of lines, symbols, or shapes. Graphic models are used in business to communicate information. Many corporations' annual reports to their stockholders contain colorful graphs to convey

FIGURE 3.2

A Graphic Model
of the Economic
Order Quantity
Concept

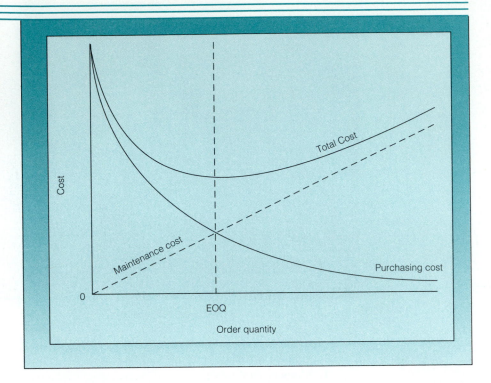

FIGURE 3.2

A Graphic Model of the Economic Order Quantity Concept

the financial condition of the firm. Graphs are also used to communicate information to managers.

The graphic model in Figure 3.2 illustrates one of the most popular concepts in business—economic order quantity. The **economic order quantity (EOQ)** is the optimum quantity of replenishment stock to order from a supplier. The EOQ balances the costs of purchasing the stock and of maintaining it. The line that slopes down from the left represents the unit purchasing cost that decreases as the order quantity increases. The dotted line that increases from left to right represents how the maintenance cost increases in a linear fashion as the order quantity increases. Both costs are added together, and the low point in the total cost curve represents the EOQ.

Graphic models are also used in the design of information systems. Many of the tools used by the systems analyst and programmer are graphic in nature. Flowcharts and data flow diagrams are examples, and are illustrated in Figure 3.3. We describe these graphic tools in Chapter 6.

Mathematical Models   The mathematical model accounts for most of the current interest in business modeling. Any mathematical formula or equation is a

FIGURE 3.3

Graphic Models Are Used to Document Information Systems

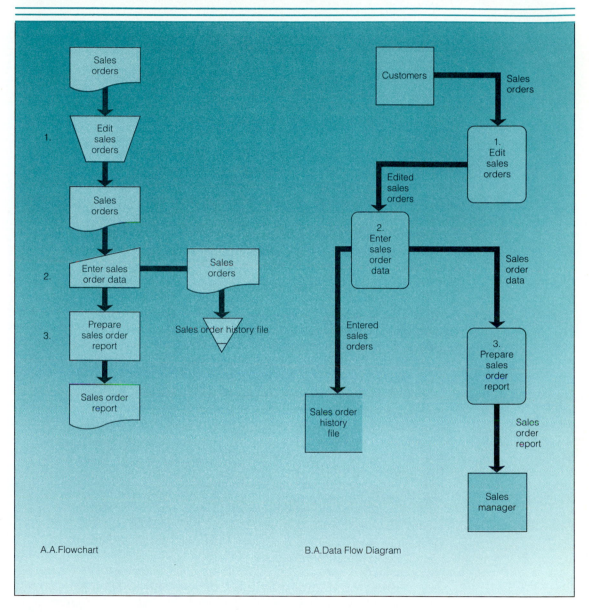

A.A.Flowchart   B.A.Data Flow Diagram

mathematical model. Many of the mathematical models that business managers use are no more complex than the one used to compute the EOQ:

$$EOQ = \sqrt{\frac{2PS}{M}}$$

where P is the unit purchasing cost (in dollars), S is the annual sales (in units), and M is the annual maintenance cost per unit (in dollars). The maintenance cost includes all of the costs involved with storing the item, such as insurance, spoilage, and theft.

Figure 3.4 shows a computer program module written in BASIC, which computes the EOQ. The module is a mathematical model, representing the calculations in a programming language. Once the EOQ formula is programmed, the computer can determine the best order quantity, relieving the manager of the time-consuming calculations.

Figure 3.5 is the screen display that shows the dialog between the EOQ model and the user. Assuming that the preparation cost of a purchase order is $20, the annual sales of the item are 1,000, and it costs $0.16 a year to maintain it, the EOQ is 500 units.

The EOQ model uses only one equation. Some mathematical models use hundreds or even thousands. For example, a financial planning model developed by the Sun Oil Company during the early years of its MIS used approximately 2000 equations.[1] Experience with such large models has shown that they tend to be cum-

FIGURE 3.4

A BASIC Program Module that Computes the EOQ

```
200 REM COMPUTE EOQ
210 WHILE RESPONSE$ = "Y"
220     PRINT "ENTER PURCHASING COST"
230     INPUT PUR.COST
240     PRINT "ENTER ANNUAL SALES UNITS"
250     INPUT ANNUAL.SALES
260     PRINT "ENTER UNIT MAINTENANCE COST"
270     INPUT MAINT.COST
280     LET EOQ = SQR(2 * PUR.COST * ANNUAL.SALES / MAINT.COST)
290     PRINT "EOQ IS "; EOQ
300     PRINT
310     PRINT "DO YOU WANT TO COMPUTE ANOTHER EOQ? ENTER Y OR N"
320     INPUT RESPONSE$
330 WEND
340 RETURN
```

[1] George W. Gershefski, "Building a Corporate Financial Model," *Harvard Business Review* 47 (July–August 1969), 39.

FIGURE 3.5
Output from the
EOQ Model

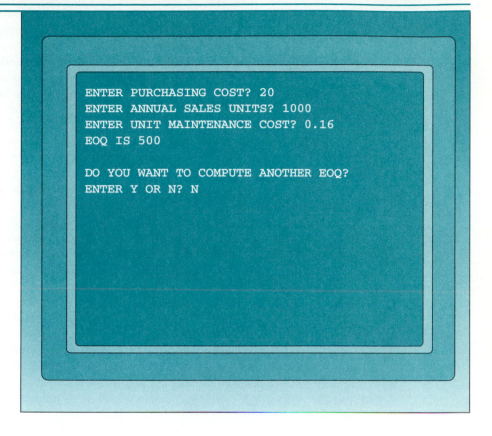

```
ENTER PURCHASING COST? 20
ENTER ANNUAL SALES UNITS? 1000
ENTER UNIT MAINTENANCE COST? 0.16
EOQ IS 500

DO YOU WANT TO COMPUTE ANOTHER EOQ?
ENTER Y OR N? N
```

bersome and difficult to use. The trend today is toward smaller models aimed at helping particular managers solve specific problems.

Another advantage is the precision with which the relationships among the parts of an object can be described. Mathematics can handle relationships expressed in more than the two dimensions of the graphic model or the three of the physical model. To the mathematician, and to the manager who recognizes the complexity of business systems, the multidimensional ability of the mathematical model is a great asset.

Use of Models

All four types of models facilitate both understanding and communication. Mathematical models, in addition, offer a predictive capability.

Facilitate Understanding   A model is typically more simple than its entity. It is easier to understand the entity when its elements and their relationships are presented in a simplified way.

Each of the four types of models can vary in detail. A physical model can represent only features of interest, a narrative can be boiled down to a summary, a diagram can show only the main relationships, and a mathematical equation can contain only primary ingredients. In each case, an effort is made to present the model in a simplified form. Once these simple models are understood, they can gradually be made more complex so as to more accurately represent their entities. However, the models still only *represent* their entities and *never match them exactly.*

Facilitate Communication   Once the problem solver understands the entity, it is often necessary to communicate that understanding to others. Perhaps the systems analyst must communicate to the manager or to the programmer. Or, perhaps one manager must communicate to other members of a problem-solving team.

All four types of models can communicate information quickly and accurately to those persons who understand the meaning of the shapes, words, graphics, and mathematics. We mentioned that mathematics represents an international language. The symbols used in flowcharts and data flow diagrams have this same high degree of universal understanding.

Predict the Future   The precision with which the mathematical model can represent its entity enables it to offer a capability that is not available from the other model types. The mathematical model can predict what might happen in the future, but it is not 100 percent accurate. No model is that good. Because assumptions usually must be made concerning much of the data that is fed into the model, the manager must always combine the output with much judgment and intuition.

THE GENERAL SYSTEMS MODEL

This book takes a general approach in describing computer use in business, enabling you to apply the principles to any type of information system in any type of organization. The vehicle that we use as the main basis of our description is called the **general systems model of the firm**. It is a graphic diagram with an accompanying narrative that depicts all organizations in a general way, using a systems framework.

The Physical System

In Chapter 1, we distinguished between open and closed systems. You recall that open systems interface with their environments, and closed systems do not. Our main concern is with open systems. This concept can be used to study business organizations and their environments, managers, employees, and information systems.

FIGURE 3.6

The Physical System of the Firm

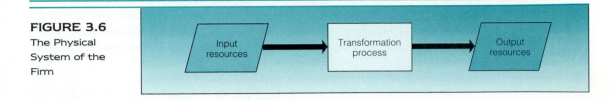

Figure 3.6 shows the physical system of the firm that transforms input resources into output resources. The input resources come from the firm's environment, a transformation occurs, and the output resources are returned to the same environment. The physical system of the firm is therefore an open system, interacting with its environment by means of physical resource flows.

Although Figure 3.6 can represent any type of firm, it is especially easy to see how it fits a manufacturing operation where raw materials are transformed into finished products. The three other physical resources flow as well.

Material Flow Input materials are received from suppliers of raw materials, parts, and assembled components. These materials are held in a storage area until they are required for the transformation process. Then, they are released to the manufacturing activity. At the conclusion of the transformation, the materials, now in a finished form, are placed in a storage area until they are shipped to customers.

In a manufacturing firm, two functional areas are involved with this material flow. The manufacturing function transforms the raw materials into finished products, and the marketing function distributes the finished products to the customers. These two areas must work together to facilitate the material flow.

Personnel Flow Personnel input originates in the environment. Prospective employees come from the local community and perhaps from labor unions and competitors. This personnel input is usually processed by the human resources function and then assigned to different functional areas. While in those areas, the employees are involved in the transformation process, either directly or indirectly. Some of the employees leave the firm shortly after joining it. Others remain until retirement. The human resources function processes the termination, and the resource is returned to the environment.

Machine Flow Machines are obtained from suppliers. The machines usually remain in the firm for a long period—from three to twenty years or so. Ultimately, however, all machines return to the environment in the form of trade-ins on new models, or as scrap.

While in the firm, machines are seldom stored. Rather, they are continually available—either as delivery trucks in the marketing division, desktop calculators in the accounting department, or drill presses in the manufacturing division. Because of special supply sources, the lack of in-firm storage, and special disposal outlets, the machine flow is the most straightforward of the physical resource flows. However, control of the machine flow is diffused among all functional areas using the machines.

Money Flow Money is obtained primarily from the owners, who provide investment capital, and from the firm's customers who provide sales revenue. Other sources include financial institutions, which make loans and pay interest on investments, and the government, which provides money in the form of loans and grants.

Whereas several sources provide money, the responsibility for controlling the money flow lies with the finance function.

The flow of money through the firm is unusual in one respect. Physical money is seldom involved. Rather, there is a flow of something representing money— checks, credit card slips, and even transactions in an electronic form. Only on the retail level does cash actually change hands, and even there it is giving way to other means of payment.

The money flow, therefore, connects the firm to its financial institutions, customers, suppliers, stockholders, and employees. In some cases, the firm holds specific funds for a long time. An example is a five-year CD. In other cases, there is a quick turnover of money, as when sales revenue is quickly converted into checks payable to suppliers and employees.

The Conceptual System

Some open systems can control their own operations, and some cannot. Control is achieved by means of a loop that is built into the system. The loop, called a **feedback loop,** provides a pathway for signals from the system to a control mechanism, and from the control mechanism back to the system. The **control mechanism** is a device of some type that uses the feedback signals to evaluate system performance and determine whether corrective action is necessary.

Open-loop Systems We noted in Chapter 1 that a system with no feedback loop or control mechanism is called an **open-loop system**. The system in Figure 3.6, in addition to being an open system, is an open-loop system. There is no feedback from the system to affect necessary changes in the system.

There are probably a few business firms of the open-loop variety. They are open systems, but the feedback and control mechanism do not work as they should. The firms set off on a particular course and never change direction. If they get out of control, nothing is done to restore equilibrium. The result is system destruction (bankruptcy).

Closed-loop Systems Figure 3.7 shows a **closed-loop system**—one with a feedback loop and control mechanism. Such a system can control its output by making adjustments to its input.

FIGURE 3.7
A Closed-loop
System

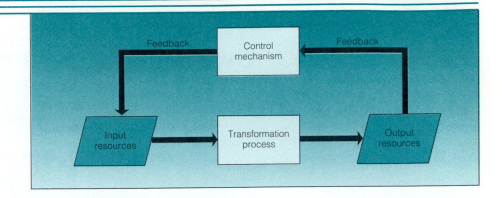

Figure 3.8 shows a business firm as a closed-loop system. The feedback loop consists of information. The control mechanism is the firm's management. Management uses the information as a basis for making changes in the physical system.

Management Control   As shown in Figure 3.8, management receives information that describes the system's output. Many management reports include this type of information—production volume, distribution costs, sales analyses, and so on. Since the main purpose of the firm is to produce some type of output, a measure of the output is an integral part of system control.

Figure 3.9 is an example of a report of system output—a sales report of fast-moving products. The report calls the manager's attention to the products that are selling the best. The manager then determines why these products are selling well and uses the findings to increase the sales of other products.

Output feedback is valuable to the manager, but the manager also must know the status of the inputs and transformation processes. For example, the manager wants information describing how well suppliers are meeting the firm's needs for input material, and the production efficiency of the manufacturing operation. Figure

FIGURE 3.8
The Physical
System of the
Firm as a
Controlled
System

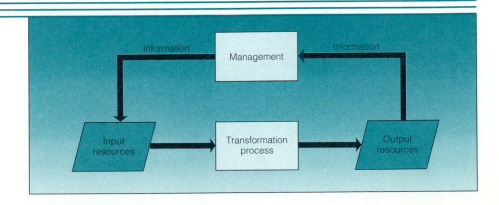

FIGURE 3.9

A Sales Report of Fast-moving Products

```
--------------------------------------------------------------------
                                YEAR-TO-DATE    PERCENT OF TOTAL
ITEM NUMBER    ITEM DESCRIPTION  SALES VOLUME  YEAR-TO-DATE SALES*
--------------------------------------------------------------------
   400293      BRAKE PIPE          $1,702.93          .068
   319421      DOOR HANDLE GASKET   1,624.00          .065
   786402      CLUTCH DRIVEN PLATE  1,403.97          .056
   190796      CARPET SNAP          1,102.00          .044
   001007      SPARK PLUG           1,010.79          .040
   739792      HOSE CLIP              949.20          .038
   722210      RUBBER PLUG            946.73          .038
   410615      UPPER DOOR HINGE       938.40          .038
   963214      REAR TUBE SHOCK        922.19          .037
   000123      NEEDLE VALVE           919.26          .037

               TOTALS              $11,519.47          .461

--------------------------------------------------------------------
*BASED ON YEAR-TO-DATE SALES OF $24,988.00
```

3.10 reflects the addition of information-gathering activities to the input and processing parts of the physical system.

Figure 3.11 is a report that describes an aspect of the system's input. This supplier analysis compares the suppliers of a particular type of raw material in terms of price, delivery, and quality. A buyer in the purchasing department can request such a report before deciding who the supplier will be.

Figure 3.12 illustrates how the status of transformation processing can be reported to management. In this example, a production manager wants to know some details about a particular job that is in progress. The job number is keyed

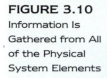

FIGURE 3.10

Information Is Gathered from All of the Physical System Elements

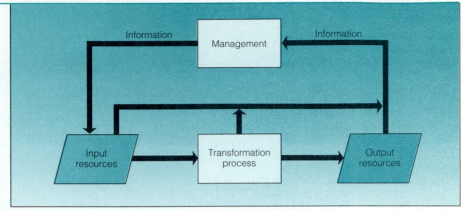

into a terminal, and the terminal displays the information. The manager sees that the job has reached Step 4 in Department 410, that the step was begun on October 8 at 10:15 A.M., and that the job should be completed on October 14 by 9:30 A.M. This example shows how the conceptual system can keep the manager up-to-date on the status of the physical system.

The Information Processor   Information does not always travel directly from the physical system to the manager. Most managers are usually located some distance from the physical activity. This is especially true of upper-level managers. These managers must obtain information from a system or procedure that produces

FIGURE 3.11

A Supplier Analysis Report

| ITEM NUMBER | | | 410615 | | | | | |
| ITEM DESCRIPTION | | | UPPER DOOR HINGE | | | | | |

	SUPPLIER		LAST TRANSACTION			UNIT	DAYS TO	PCT.
NUMBER		NAME	DATE	P.O. NO.	QTY	PRICE	RECEIPT	REJECTS
3062	CARTER AND SONS		7/12	1048–10	360	$8.75	12	.00
4189	PACIFIC MACHINING		4/13	962–10	350	9.10	8	.02
0140	A.B. MERRIL & CO.		1/04	550–10	350	8.12	3	.00
2111	BAY AREA METALS		8/19	1196–10	360	11.60	19	.04

FIGURE 3.12

A Job Status Report Provides Information about the Transformation Process

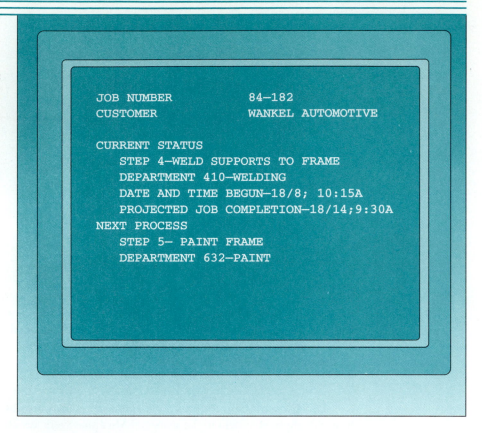

```
JOB NUMBER              84—182
CUSTOMER                WANKEL AUTOMOTIVE

CURRENT STATUS
    STEP 4—WELD SUPPORTS TO FRAME
    DEPARTMENT 410—WELDING
    DATE AND TIME BEGUN—18/8; 10:15A
    PROJECTED JOB COMPLETION—18/14;9:30A
NEXT PROCESS
    STEP 5— PAINT FRAME
    DEPARTMENT 632—PAINT
```

the information from gathered data. We call the information-producing mechanism the **information processor**.

Figure 3.13 includes the addition of the information processor, which, in this discussion, we assume to be a computer. However, a noncomputer mechanism, such as a manual or keydriven system, could easily do the job in certain situations.

Dimensions of Information

As managers define the output that the information processor is to provide, they consider four basic dimensions of information.[2] These dimensions contribute to information value.

1. **Relevancy** Information has **relevancy** when it pertains specifically to the problem at hand. The manager should be able to select information that is needed without wading through a volume of information on other subjects.

[2] For the classic description of information value, *see* Robert W. Zmud, "An Empirical Investigation of the Dimensionality of the Concept of Information," *Decision Sciences* 9 (April 1978), 187–95.

FIGURE 3.13

The Information
Processor
Transforms Data
into Information

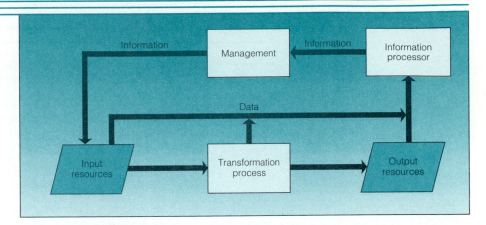

2. **Accuracy**   Ideally, all information should be accurate, but features that contribute to system accuracy add to the cost. For that reason, managers often settle for less than perfect accuracy. Applications involving money, such as payroll, billing, and accounts receivable, demand 100 percent accuracy. Other applications, such as long-range economic forecasts and statistical reports, often can be just as useful when the data contains a few errors.

3. **Timeliness**   Information should be available for problem solving before crisis situations get out of hand or opportunities are lost. The manager should be able to obtain information that describes what is happening now, in addition to what happened in the past.

4. **Completeness**   The manager should be able to obtain information that presents a complete picture of a problem or a solution. However, systems should not be designed that drown the manager in a sea of information. The term **information overload** recognizes the harm that can come from too much information. The manager should be able to determine the amount of detail that is needed.

The manager is the best person to specify the dimensions of the information that he or she needs. When necessary, the systems analyst can help the manager approach this task in a logical manner.

Standards   In order for the manager to exercise control over her or his area of responsibility, two ingredients must exist. First, there must be information that describes what the area *is* accomplishing. Second, there must be performance standards that reflect what the area *should* accomplish.

In Chapter 1, we defined a system as a group of elements that are integrated with the common purpose of achieving an objective. We can define an **objective** as the overall goal that a system is to attain. A system must have at least one objective, but multiple objectives are not uncommon. Objectives tend to be stated in a

TABLE 3.1	Objectives	Standards of Performance
A Comparison of Objectives and Standards	*Satisfy customer needs*	Achieve an annual sales volume of at least $25 million Maintain a 20% share of the market Maintain an annual growth rate of 15%
	Produce a return on investment for the owners	Pay dividends to stockholders each quarter Maintain the price of the firm's common stock above $85 per share
	Operate efficiently	Realize an after-tax profit of 15% of sales Maintain a record of accident-free days Keep employee turnover below 10%
	Invest in the future	Invest a minimum of 15% of sales in research and development
	Develop sources of supply	Achieve stockouts on no more than 2% of the items in inventory during the year Keep the number of backorders to less than 5% of all orders processed Have no plant shutdowns due to unavailable raw materials
	Operate ethically	Successfully defend the firm against legal actions filed by cutomers, suppliers, and the government
	Take advantage of modern methods	Invest no less than 10% of sales revenue in automation, computerization, and mechanization

general manner. In order for the managers to control the system, they need something more specific than the objectives, and this is accomplished with standards. A **standard** is a measure of acceptable performance, ideally stated in specific terms. Table 3.1 illustrates the difference between the general nature of objectives and the specific nature of standards.

The manager uses standards to control the physical system by comparing actual performance, as reported by the information processor, with the standards. The results of the comparison determine whether action is necessary. Figure 3.14 illustrates the addition of the required standards to the general model. *The conceptual system that controls the physical system therefore consists of three key elements—management, the information processor, and standards.*

It is important to note in the figure that the standards are made available to the information processor as well as the manager. This arrangement enables the information processor to relieve the manager of much of the monitoring activity. The information processor can tell the manager when actual performance varies too much from the standards.

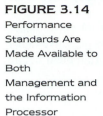

FIGURE 3.14

Performance
Standards Are
Made Available to
Both
Management and
the Information
Processor

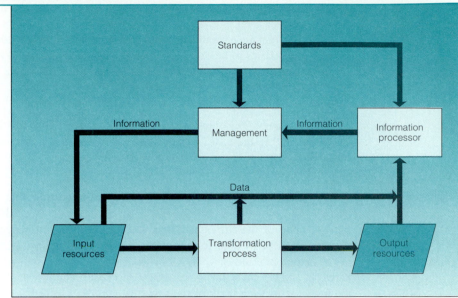

Management by Exception   Standards, combined with the information output of the information processor, enable the manager to engage in management by exception. **Management by exception** is a style that the manager follows by only becoming involved in activity when it falls outside the range of acceptable performance. Management by exception can be caused, in part, by information overload. Managers can receive so much information that it is difficult to focus on the important issues. In order for the manager to practice management by exception, standards in the form of both upper and lower boundaries of acceptable performance must be established. For example, when a manager decides that shoe production should range from 1,000 to 1,250 pairs per day, the manager only follows up on variances outside that range.

Management by exception offers three basic *advantages*:

1. The manager does not waste time monitoring activity that is progressing in a normal manner.
2. Since fewer decisions are made, each one can receive more thorough attention.
3. Attention is focused on opportunities, as well as things going wrong.

There are some *constraints,* however, that must be recognized:

1. It is not always easy to quantify certain types of business performance so that standards can be set.

2. An information system that accurately monitors performance is essential.
3. Attention must continually be directed at the standards to keep them at the correct level.
4. The manager should not grow passive and simply wait for performance boundaries to be exceeded. Ideally, the manager should be proactive rather than reactive. That is, the manager should act to solve a problem before the situation gets out of hand.

Management by exception is a fundamental capability that is provided by the CBIS. By letting the CBIS assume some of the responsibility for monitoring the physical system, the manager's time is used in the most effective way.

Critical Success Factors   A management concept that is similar to management by exception is called critical success factors. A **critical success factor (CSF)** is one of the firm's activities that has a strong influence on the ability of the firm to meet its objectives. Firms typically have multiple CSFs. For example, in the automobile industry, the CSFs are believed to be styling, an efficient dealer network, and tight control of manufacturing cost.[3] The information system enables the manager to keep track of the CSFs by reporting information on them.

The CSF concept is similar to management by exception in that it focuses attention on a portion of the firm's operations rather than the whole. The two concepts differ in that the CSFs are relatively stable, whereas the exception items can vary from one time period to the next.

Decision Flow   Another addition to the general model is necessary to reflect how management decisions can change the physical system. Just as the manager must gather data from all three elements in the physical system—input, processing, and output—it is important that the manager also be able to make changes in the performance of all three elements.

In the model drawn in Figure 3.14, the manager can only make changes to the input element. If information indicates that activity in either the transformation or the output area requires adjustment, the manager must be able to make such change directly.

This modification is made in Figure 3.15. The feedback from the manager to the physical system is relabeled *decisions* to reflect the manner in which the manager changes the system's performance.

The basic feedback loop as drawn initially in Figure 3.6 still represents signals from the physical system, but the signals are in three different forms—data, information, and decisions. *Data is transformed into information by the information processor, and information is transformed into decisions by the manager. The*

---

[3] These CSFs are from John F. Rockart, "Chief Executives Define Their Own Data Needs," *Harvard Business Review* 57 (March–April 1979), 85.

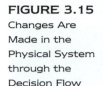

FIGURE 3.15
Changes Are
Made in the
Physical System
through the
Decision Flow

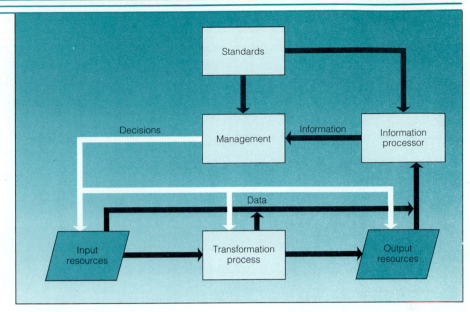

information processor and the manager work together to transform data into decisions.

The Environment

We studied the firm's environment in Chapter 2. The final form of the general model recognizes that resources flow into the firm from the environment and from the firm back into the environment. This addition is made in Figure 3.16, completing the model.

Physical resources flow through the physical system at the bottom of the model. *Conceptual* resources (information and data) enter the information processor, where they are either stored or made available to the manager. Information and data also flow from the information processor to the environment.

USE OF THE GENERAL SYSTEMS MODEL

The flow of materials through a manufacturing firm and the control exercised by the managers, as illustrated by the general systems model, are very clear. It is not quite so easy to relate the model to other types of organizations. In the sections below, the model is used to describe a retailer and an organization that provides a service. Our objective is to show that the model can provide a basic structure for the analysis of any type of organization.

FIGURE 3.16

The General Systems Model of the Firm

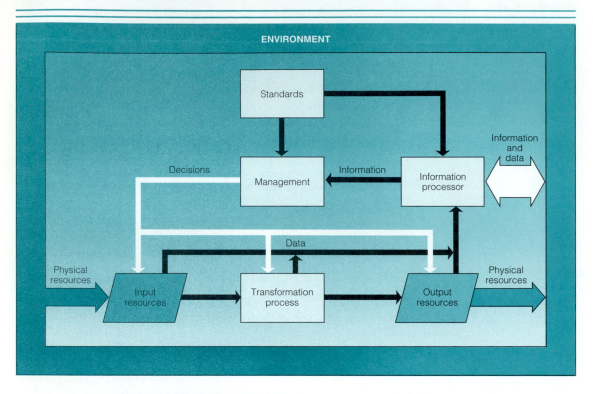

A Supermarket

All of the physical resources flow through the physical system of a supermarket. The primary flow is materials—groceries and other items that are sold. The personnel flow consists of the store managers, the checkout clerks, stock clerks, and so on who are hired, work for a period of time, and eventually leave. A few machines are used in a supermarket. The bar code readers at the checkout counters are the most obvious, but there are others behind the scenes, such as a minicomputer, desk calculators and telephones. Additionally, machines include the refrigerated coolers, display cases, and shelves that are used to store the merchandise awaiting sale. The flow of money into the supermarket is provided by customers, and the flow out is primarily in the form of payments to suppliers, employees, and owners.

The transformation process includes opening cartons of merchandise and arranging the items on the shelves. It also consists of preparing fresh vegetables and fruit for display, cutting meat, and perhaps baking pastries and preparing deli items. All activity that makes the products conveniently and attractively available for sale can be considered transformation.

The management element in the conceptual system consists of the store manager and assistant managers. The information processor is the store minicomputer, which controls the bar code readers and provides the prices of the various items. The minicomputer also transmits data to the headquarters that specifies items to be ordered, provides sales statistics, and so on. The standards of performance for the supermarket are jointly established by headquarters and the store management.

Standards in the form of sales quotas and operating budgets give managers guidelines concerning the level of performance that is to be achieved. Managers use observation and the information processor to monitor actual performance and compare it with the standards. Managers receive reports that show which items are selling well and which are not. The managers respond to these reports by taking such action as adjusting order quantities, reallocating shelf space, putting items on sale, and adding promotional signs and displays. The reports can also show the times during the day and the days during the week when sales are very high and very low. This information is useful in hiring and scheduling employees to provide the necessary level of customer service.

The supermarket manager uses information from the information processor, plus the standards, as bases for making changes in the physical system so that the supermarket continually works toward its objectives.

A Law Firm

There are several obvious differences between a law firm and a supermarket. A law firm usually consists of a small number of professional people who have been specially educated and certified to perform their jobs. Their work emphasizes mental, rather than physical activity. The flow of materials through the law firm is minimal, consisting primarily of bookkeeping supplies such as legal pads and pencils.

Even with these basic differences, a law firm can be described by the same general model used for the supermarket. Each law firm is a controlled physical system. In a large firm the control is exercised by several persons called partners.

The main responsibility of the partners is to ensure that the firm meets its objectives. The performance standards most likely are not as specific as those of the supermarket. A law firm probably does not strive to handle a certain number of cases or win a certain percentage of jury trials. However, we can assume a profit objective since the partners understand that profit is the key to continued operation.

The transformation process in the law firm is one of converting the raw materials (clients with legal problems) into finished products (clients whose legal problems have been solved). This transformation is accomplished by the lawyers, who represent the most important resource available to the firm. One could argue that information is the most important resource. Everyone has seen pictures of attorneys' offices with bookshelves filled with law books. Any lawyer will tell you, however, that the key to success is not the books, but knowing where to look in the books.

Even though formal standards might not exist, the partners know what level of performance is necessary in order for the firm to be successful. When these intuitive standards are not being met, decisions are made to alter the physical system. If too few legal problems are being converted into solutions (the firm is losing too many cases), additional lawyers can be hired, existing lawyers can be replaced, college students can work part time to do library research, and so forth.

The general model provides a structure for the basic elements of any law firm. A new lawyer fresh out of law school expects to find these elements even though he or she has never before served in the firm and has no previous knowledge of its people or history. The new lawyer expects to find standards that he or she will be expected to meet, an information system that provides a legal database, and a personnel resource capable of performing the transformation process in a manner acceptable to the managing partners and the clients.

PUTTING THE GENERAL SYSTEMS MODEL IN CONTEXT

The real value of the general systems model will become apparent when you graduate and begin your career. The model will help you to adjust to your firm. In the beginning, everything will be new to you—new faces, new facilities, new terminology. The model will provide a sense of stability as you learn about your firm. Nothing that you see will surprise you because the model will provide you with a mental picture that tells you what to expect.

However, you will continue to benefit from the model throughout your career. As you progress up the management ranks, you will use the model as a constant reminder of the elements that are necessary for the firm and its subsidiary units to meet their objectives.

SUMMARY

A model is an abstraction of something called an entity. There are four types of models—physical, narrative, graphic, and mathematical. All types permit the user to better understand the entity, and to communicate that understanding to others. Mathematical models also enable the user to predict the future, although with something less than perfect accuracy.

A general model has wide applicability but does not address any particular situation in an exact way. The general systems model of the firm can be used to analyze an organization of any type but not as precisely as a model designed to fit a particular organization.

The physical system consists of three elements—input, transformation, and output. Physical resources flow through the physical system.

The conceptual system includes a feedback loop and a control mechanism. A firm is an example of such a closed-loop system, with the management serving as the control mechanism. The feedback flow originates as data, is transformed into information by the information processor, and is then used by management in problem solving.

The information processor may or may not be a computer-based system. The manager, perhaps aided by a systems analyst, specifies the information that the information processor is to provide, in terms of relevancy, accuracy, timeliness, and completeness.

Information that describes the actual performance of the physical system is only one ingredient that enables the manager to achieve control. Also necessary are standards that specify the desired performance. Management, the information processor, and standards comprise the conceptual system.

Management can practice management by exception by using the information processor to monitor the physical system. By making the standards available to the information processor, the processor can determine whether management attention is warranted. The information processor can also provide information on the status of critical success factors.

When actual performance does not measure up to standards, management makes decisions that produce changes. The decisions are communicated to all three elements in the physical system.

This chapter serves only to introduce the general systems model. Each part of the model will be analyzed in more detail in the remainder of the book. The beauty of the general systems model is its simplicity; it is useful to anybody in any situation. It is also a basic ingredient of the systems approach to problem solving, which we describe in the next chapter.

KEY TERMS

economic order quantity (EOQ)
feedback loop
control mechanism
open-loop system

closed-loop system
information processor
information overload
environment

KEY CONCEPTS

A model as an abstraction of its entity
Different types of models
The main uses of models
Comparative advantages of general and specific
    models
The general systems model of the firm
The dimensions of information
The relationship between objectives and
    standards

Management by exceptionp
Critical success factors
The three different media that comprise the
    feedback loop—data, information, and
    decisions
How the elements of the conceptual system—
    management, the information processor,
    and standards—work together to enable
    the firm to operate as a closed-loop system

QUESTIONS

1. Name the four basic types of models. Which one does a manager use the least? The most?

2. Give an example of each of the four model types. For each example, identify the entity.

3. What capabilities do all models provide? What capability does only the mathematical model provide?

4. What are the four physical resource flows?

5. What is the difference between an open-loop and a closed-loop system? Which of these types describes a business firm?

6. Of the three reports in Figures 3.9, 3.11, and 3.12, one incorporates both information and standards. Identify which one, and explain how the standards are incorporated.

7. What is the role of the information processor?

8. Name four dimensions of information that the manager should consider.

9. Comment on the following statements:
   a. Information produced by the information processor should contain no errors.
   b. An information processor should provide the manager with as much information as possible.

10. Since a system is intended to meet objectives, why are they not included in the general systems model?

11. Why are standards provided to the information processor?

12. What three types of media flow through the feedback loop in a firm? List them in the order of their flow.

13. What two elements exist in the conceptual system to transform one feedback medium into another?

14. By what route through the model does information gathered from the environment travel to the manager?

TOPICS FOR DISCUSSION

1. Which of the physical resource flows should the manager try to speed up? Which should the manager try to slow down? Explain your reasoning.

2. Why would a manager want her or his daily routine to be interrrupted by a signal that something is going better than planned?

PROBLEMS

1. Write a paper describing how a fast-food restaurant fits the general systems model. Your instructor will tell you how long the paper should be and its format.

2. Repeat problem 1, using a hospital.

3. Assume that you are a buyer in the purchasing department analyzing the supplier analysis report in Figure 3.11. Which supplier would you select for your next purchase? Why?

Bargain City

Your career is moving along faster than you expected. You thought that your MIS degree would result in an initial break-in period as a programmer for Bargain City. Bargain City is a retail chain modeled along the lines of Wal-Mart. But, the resignation of three systems analysts changed all that. The analysts left to form their own consulting firm.

Knowing that you had a strong dose of systems analysis in college, your boss, Alisa Ernst, decided to let you begin as a systems analyst. And, it didn't take her long to give you your first assignment. Alisa made arrangements for you to visit an area store for the purpose of becoming familiar with activity at the store level. She expects you to prepare a written report that might serve as the basis for future systems projects.

You arrive at the West Alameda store at 9 A.M., and are amazed at how many people are already shopping. The lot is full, and you have to wait ten minutes—it seems like thirty—to get a parking place. Inside, the conditions are no better. The store is huge, with fifteen checkout counters, but only four are open. Each of the four, one of which is the express lane, has a long line of shoppers waiting to check out. It's a good thing that you are not buying anything. Since you are only conducting a systems study, you will be able to get out sooner.

You watch the action—or inaction—for a while and then wander back to the storeroom where three stock clerks are opening boxes. You hear one of them say: "Have you found it yet?" Curious, you introduce yourself and ask what they are looking for. One of the clerks tells you that the store has a special on cookout items, but ran out of charcoal starter fluid. The truck that was supposed to bring additional stock broke down in Tuba City. The lack of starter fluid is one reason the lines up front are so long; the checkout clerks are having to give out rain checks. You can understand why the stock clerks are having such difficulty; the storeroom is a real mess. Boxes are stacked everywhere. There seems to be no rhyme or reason to anything.

You ask where the store computer is, and are directed to a small room in the corner. There it is, humming away. Automation in action.

With a good grasp of the back-room operation, you return to the front for the purpose of checking out the office. There's a big line there as well—people waiting to cash checks and return purchases. Most of the returns seem to be glassware items that the customers found to be broken when they opened their shopping bags at home. The sackers had not packed the items properly.

When you finally reach the head of the line, you are surprised to learn that the cashier is really the store manager. He asks you to come back when he has more time. He explains that he had to "let a lot of people go" in order to stay within the budget that headquarters imposed. You can tell by the way he snarls his explanation that he is not very happy about the whole situation. You decide not to stick around, or you might find yourself looking for starter fluid. You say good-bye and head for your office to write your report while everything is fresh on your mind.

Assignment

Prepare a memo to Alisa. She is the manager of systems analysis. First, list problems with the physical system of the West Alameda store. For each problem, identify a possible corrective action. Then, do the same for the conceptual system. Go ahead and use the systems terminology from the chapter. Alisa had MIS in college, too.

SELECTED BIBLIOGRAPHY

Boulding, Kenneth E. "General Systems Theory—the Skeleton of Science." *Management Science* 2 (April 1956): 197–208.

Brewer, Stanley H., and Rosenzweig, James. "Rhochrematics and Organizational Adjustments." *California Management Review* 3 (Spring 1961): 72–81.

Debons, Anthony; Horne, Esther; and Cronenweth, Scott. *Information Science: An Integrated View*. Boston: G. K. Hall & Co, 1988.

Duncan, Otis Dudley. "Social Organization and the Ecosystem." In *Handbook of Modern Sociology*, edited by Robert E. L. Faris, 36–45. Chicago: Rand McNally, 1964.

Edelman, Franz. "The Management of Information Resources—A Challenge for American Business." *MIS Quarterly* 5 (March 1981): 17–27.

Fuerst, William L., and Martin, Merle P. "Effective Design and Use of Computer Decision Models." *MIS Quarterly* 8 (March 1984): 17–26.

Hopeman, Richard J. *Systems Analysis and Operations Management*. Columbus, OH: Charles E. Merrill, 1969, 125–50.

Ives, Blake. "Graphical User Interfaces for Business Information Systems." *MIS Quarterly* (Special Issue 1982): 15–47.

Jarvenpaa, Sirkka L., and Dickson, Gary W. "Graphics and Managerial Decision Making: Research Based Guidelines." *Communications of the ACM* 31 (June 1988): 764–74.

Johnson, Richard A.; Kast, Fremont E.; and Rosenzweig, James E. *The Theory and Management of Systems*. 2d ed. New York: McGraw-Hill, 1967.

Kador, John. "Modeling: New Ways to Make the Future Happen." *EDGE* 1 (November–December 1988): 46–49.

Miller, Jeffrey G., and Gilmour, Peter. "Materials Managers: Who Needs Them?" *Harvard Business Review* 57 (July–August 1979): 143–53.

Schoderbek, Peter P.; Schoderbek, Charles G.; and Kefalas, Asterios G. *Management Systems: Conceptual Considerations.* 4th ed. Homewood, IL: BPI/Irwin, 1990.

von Bertalanffy, Ludwig. "General System Theory: A New Approach to the Unity of Science." *Human Biology* 23 (December 1951): 302–61.

von Bertalanffy, Ludwig. "General System Theory: A Critical Review." *General Systems* 7 (1962): 1–20.

Weinberg, Gerald M. *An Introduction to General Systems Thinking.* New York: John Wiley & Sons, 1975.

Chapter 4

The Systems Approach

LEARNING OBJECTIVES

After studying this chapter, you should:

- Appreciate the importance of problem solving
- Understand the relationship between problem solving and decision making
- Know which elements must be present to solve a problem
- Understand the difference between problems and symptoms
- Know how problem structure can affect problem solving
- Understand the steps of the systems approach and how they form a powerful problem-solving tool
- Appreciate individual differences in problem-solving styles and how they can affect CBIS design

INTRODUCTION

Managers solve problems so that the firm can meet its objectives. During the course of solving a problem, the manager makes multiple decisions, and several problem-solving elements must be present. As the problem solving process unfolds, the manager is careful to distinguish symptoms from the cause.

The problem structure influences how problems are solved. Problems that are unstructured must be solved by the manager, but problems that are structured can be solved by the computer. Manager and computer can work together to solve semi-structured problems.

A systematic approach to problem solving has been devised, and it is called the systems approach. The systems approach consists of three types of effort— preparation, definition, and solution. In preparing to solve a problem, the manager views the firm as a system, understands the environment of the firm, and identifies the subsystems within the firm. In defining the problem the manager proceeds from a system to a subsystem level, and analyzes the system parts in a particular sequence. In solving the problem the manager identifies alternate solutions, evaluates them, selects the best one, implements it, and follows up to make certain that the solution works.

Factors that are unique to the manager can influence problem solving. These factors include different styles of problem sensing, information gathering, and information using.

Just as the general systems model of the firm fits all types of organizations, the systems approach fits all types of problems. Together, the general model and the systems approach provide a solid foundation upon which to build computer-based problem-solving systems.

PROBLEM SOLVING

The term problem solving brings to mind the correction of things that are going bad. There is no doubt that managers respond quickly to harmful influences, seeking to prevent or minimize the damage. However, managers also respond to things that are going better than expected. When managers spot performance that is going exceptionally well, they act to make it even better or to achieve the same good performance in other areas.

With these facts in mind, we define a **problem** as a condition that has the potential to cause exceptional harm or produce exceptional benefit. **Problem solving** then becomes the act of responding to problems so as to suppress their harmful effects or capitalize on the opportunity for benefit.

The Importance of Problem Solving

Managers do things other than solve problems. In fact, problem solving might account for only a small portion of a manager's time. However, the importance of problem solving is not based on the amount of time spent doing it but rather on the consequences. A set of decisions to solve a problem might require only a few hours but could affect the firm's profits to the tune of thousands or even millions of dollars.

Decision Making and Problem Solving

In the course of solving a problem, a manager will make many decisions. A **decision** is a selection of a strategy or action. **Decision making** is the act of selecting the strategy or action that the manager believes offers the best solution to the problem. Usually there are several strategies or actions that the manager can consider. One of the keys to problem solving is the identification of decision alternatives.

Elements of a Problem-Solving Process

Several elements must be present if a manager is to successfuly engage in problem solving. Naturally, there must be a *problem* and a *problem solver* (the manager). The other elements are less obvious, but if any are absent the end results are likely to be poor. All of these elements are pictured in Figure 4.1.

The solution to a problem must best enable the system to meet its objectives, as reflected in the system's performance standards. These standards describe the **desired state**—what the system should achieve. In addition, the manager must have available *information* that describes the **current state**—what the system is now achieving. If the current state and the desired state are the same, there is no problem and the manager takes no action. If the two states are different, some problem is the cause and must be solved.

The figure indicates that the problem-solving elements—manager, standards, and information—are also the elements of the conceptual system portion of the general systems model. The conceptual system is therefore a problem-solving system.

The difference between the current state and the desired state represents the **solution criterion**—what it will take to bring the current state to the desired state. For example, if the standard is to sell a minimum of 125 ski jackets a day, and sales are averaging 75 jackets, the solution to the problem is one that will increase sales by at least 50 jackets. The 50 jackets are the solution criterion.

Of course, if the current state happens to represent a *higher* level of performance than the desired state, the task is *not* to bring the current state in line. Rather, the task is to keep the current state at the higher level. If the higher-level performance can be maintained, then the desired state should be raised.

It is the manager's responsibility to identify *alternate solutions,* which always exist. This is one step of the problem-solving process where computers have been of little help. The manager typically relies on her or his own experience, or obtains help from the noncomputer portion of the information system, such as input from others both inside and outside the organization.

Once the alternatives have been identified, the information system can be used to evaluate each one. This evaluation should consider any possible *constraints,*

FIGURE 4.1
The Problem-solving Elements

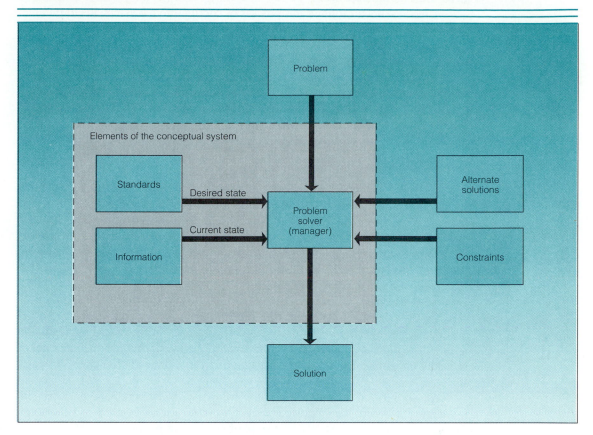

which can be either internal or environmental. **Internal constraints** take the form of limited resources. **Environmental constraints** take the form of pressures from various environmental elements, such as the government or competitors, to act in a particular way.

When all of these elements exist and the manager understands them, a *solution* to the problem is possible.

Problems Versus Symptoms

It is important to recognize the distinction between problems and symptoms. **Symptoms** are conditions produced by the problem. Very often the manager sees the symptoms rather than the problem. The symptoms are called to the manager's attention by the feedback loop. However, symptoms do not tell the entire story. They are like the tip of the iceberg; the manager must look beneath the symptoms to locate the real problem cause.

A medical doctor follows this process of sorting through symptoms to find the cause of an ailment. The patient complains of constant headaches, but something is causing the headaches, and the doctor must identify what it is. Perhaps the problem is nervous tension, poor vision, poor diet, or something else.

A manager faces the same task when confronted with a symptom, such as low profits. Something is causing the low profits. The problem is the *cause* of the low profits. In fact, it is good to think of a problem as the *cause of the trouble,* or the *cause of the opportunity*.

Problem Structure

A manager may understand some problems better than others. The problem of how much replenishment stock to reorder is an example of a problem that a manager may understand very well. In fact, as we saw in in Chapter 3, a mathematical model called the EOQ formula prescribes how the problem is to be solved. Such a problem is called a **structured problem** because it consists of elements and relationships between elements, which are all understood by the problem solver. When such a high level of understanding exists, it is often possible to express the problem in the form of a mathematical model.

On the other hand, there may be problems that are not understood at all by the manager, which are called unstructured problems. An **unstructured problem** is one that contains no elements or relationships between elements that are understood by the problem solver. Quantification of an unstructured problem is difficult, if not impossible.

An example of an unstructured problem is a personnel problem that exists in a department, where the employees cannot work as a team because of behavioral differences. The employees clash because of conflicting personalities, different cultures, different social classes, and so on. The business manager is usually ill equipped to define such problems in a structured way.

Actually, there are very few completely structured and completely unstructured problems in an organization. Most problems are of the type where the manager has a less than perfect understanding of the elements and their relationships, and are called semistructured problems. A **semistructured problem** is one that contains *some* elements or relationships that are understood by the problem solver. An example is the selection of a location to build a new plant. Some of the elements, such as land cost, taxes, and the costs of shipping in raw materials, can be measured with a high degree of precision. Other elements, however, such as natural hazards and local culture, are difficult to identify and measure.

Once procedures have been devised, computers can solve structured problems without the need for manager involvement. On the other hand, the manager has to do most of the work in solving unstructured problems. In the vast middle ground of semistructured problems, the manager and the computer can jointly work toward solution.

THE SYSTEMS APPROACH

A search for the origin of a systematic problem-solving process leads to John Dewey, a philosophy professor at Columbia University around the turn of the century. In a 1910 book he identified three series of judgments involved in adequately resolving a controversy:[1]

1. Recognize the controversy
2. Weigh alternative claims
3. Form a judgment.

Dewey did not use the term systems approach, but he recognized the sequential nature of problem solving—beginning with a problem, considering different ways to solve it, and selecting the solution that appears best.

Dewey's framework essentially lay dormant for many years, but during the late 1960s and early 1970s, interest in systematic problem solving reached new heights. Computer manufacturers, management scientists, and information specialists were all searching for ways to use the computer in solving the manager's problems. The recommended framework for using the computer became known as the **systems approach**—a series of problem-solving steps that ensure the problem is first understood, alternate solutions are considered, and the selected solution works.

A Series of Steps

The number of steps in the systems approach can vary, depending on the source. We use ten steps, grouped in three phases, as illustrated in Figure 4.2. Each phase consists of a particular type of effort, which the manager must expend—preparation effort, definition effort, and solution effort.

Preparation effort prepares the manager for problem solving by providing a systems orientation. **Definition effort** consists of identifying a problem to be solved and then understanding it. **Solution effort** involves the identification of the alternate solutions, their evaluation, the selection of the one that appears best, its implementation, and follow-up activity to ensure that the problem is solved.

The Systems Approach, Problem Solving, and Decision Making

The steps of the systems approach provide a good way to categorize the multiple decisions that must be made in the process of solving a single problem. Each step of definition effort and solution effort requires at least one decision, as shown in Table 4.1.

---

[1] John Dewey, *How We Think* (New York: D. C. Heath & Company, 1910), 101–107.

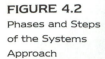

FIGURE 4.2

Phases and Steps
of the Systems
Approach

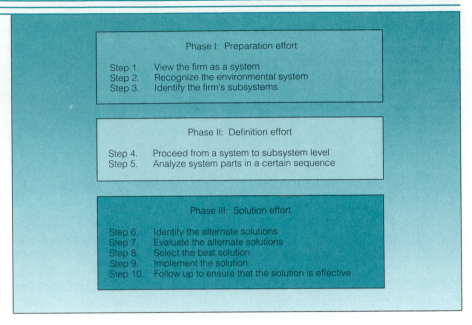

The Systems Approach and the CBIS

The CBIS can be used as a support system while applying the systems approach. A CBIS subsystem, such as a DSS, expert system, or office automation application, can provide support to a separate decision, as illustrated in Figure 4.3. It is also possible for a CBIS subsystem to support several decisions—perhaps all that are required to solve the problem. The systems approach serves as a bridge between the problem and the CBIS, providing a framework for the various decisions.

With this introduction to the systems approach, we will describe each step in more detail.

PREPARATION EFFORT

The three preparatory steps do not have to be taken in order, as they jointly produce the desired frame of mind for addressing problems. And, the steps can be taken over a long period of time—beginning now, in this course.

Step One—View the Firm as a System.

You must be able to see your firm as a system. This can be accomplished with the use of the general systems model that was described in Chapter 3. You must be able to see how the firm fits the model.

TABLE 4.1
The Systems Approach Requires Decision Making

Phase	Step	Decisions
Definition Effort	4. Proceed from a system to a subsystem level.	Where is the problem? Does new data need to be gathered, or does data already exist?
	5. Analyze system parts in a certain sequence.	How will the data be gathered? What is causing the problem?
Solution Effort	6. Identify alternate solutions.	How many alternatives should be identified? Are these alternatives feasible?
	7. Evaluate the alternate solutions.	Which criteria should be used? How does each alternative measure up to each criterion? Do all criteria have equal weight?
	8. Select the best solution.	Is there enough information to make a selection? Which alternative measures up best to the criteria?
	9. Implement the solution.	When should this solution be implemented? How should this solution be implemented?
	10. Follow up to ensure that the solution is effective.	Who should perform the evaluation? How well is the solution meeting the objectives?

Step Two—Recognize the Environmental System.

The firm's relationship to its environment is also important. The eight environmental elements that we discussed in Chapter 2 provide an effective way of positioning the firm as a system in its environment.

Step Three—Identify the Firm's Subsystems.

It is also necessary to identify the major subsystems of the firm, and they can take several forms. The easiest for the manager to see are the *functional areas*. Each can be regarded as a separate system, existing on the same hierarchical level within the firm as shown in Figure 4.4. The process of identifying these functional subsystems within the firm is called **functional decomposition**. The system of the firm is decomposed, or subdivided, into its lower-level subsystems.

The manager also can regard the *levels of management* as subsystems, as illustrated in Figure 4.5. Here the subsystems have a superior-subordinate relationship

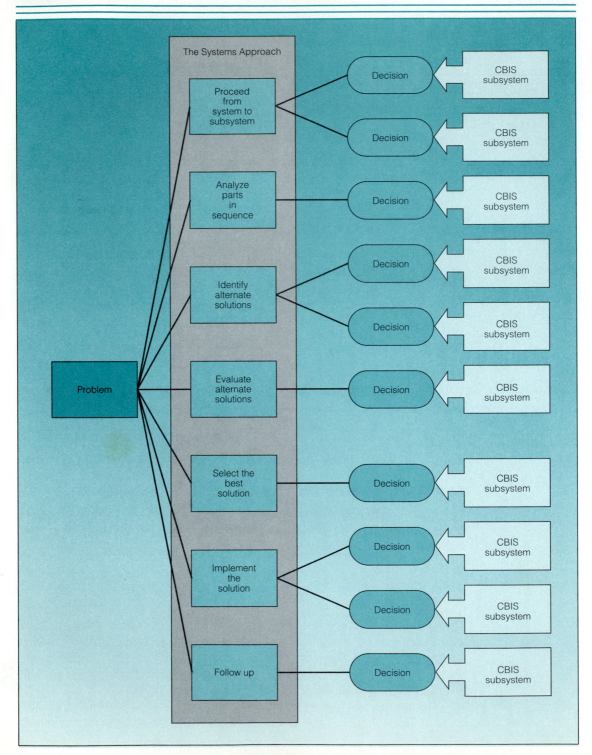

FIGURE 4.4
Each Functional Area Is a Subsystem

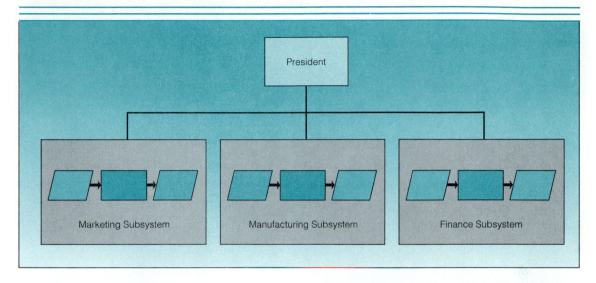

and are connected by both information and decision flows. Top management makes decisions that filter down through the organization. The firm creates the products and services on the lower level, and information describing that activity flows up through the organization. When the manager sees the firm in this manner, the importance of information flows is clear. Without these flows, upper-level management is cut off from the physical system of the firm.

The manager can also use *resource flows* as a basis for dividing the firm into subsystems. The functional form of organization accomplishes this to a certain degree. The finance function specializes in the money flow, and the human resources function specializes in the personnel flow.

Some manufacturing firms have added a separate materials management function to handle the material flow through the manufacturing and marketing functions. But, even in these firms, the manager must look beyond the functional structure in order to isolate all of the flows.

When a manager can see the firm as a system of subsystems existing within an environment, a systems orientation has been achieved. The manager has completed the preparation effort and is now ready to use the systems approach in problem solving.

DEFINITION EFFORT

The definition effort consists of first becoming aware that a problem exists or is about to exist (**problem identification**) and then understanding it well enough to pursue a solution (**problem understanding**).

FIGURE 4.5

Each Management Level Is a Subsystem

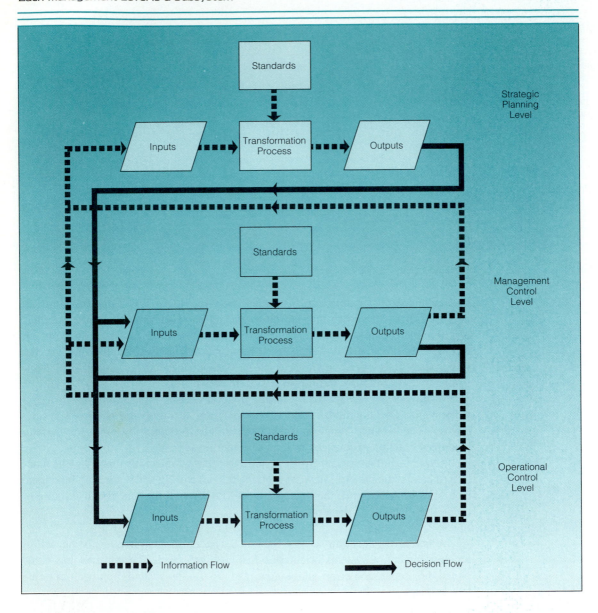

The definition effort is stimulated by some feedback signal that indicates things are going better or worse than planned. The signal can originate from within the firm or its environment and serves as a **problem trigger** by initiating a problem-solving process.

The manager or someone in the manager's unit usually identifies the problem or a symptom. These persons are on the scene and understand the system. Consequently, they are in a better position to detect difficulties or opportunities than is an outsider, such as the systems analyst.

Once the problem is identified, the manager can call upon the analyst to assist in problem understanding. The analyst is skilled in converting an ill-defined problem into the specifications of a new or revised system. The manager and the analyst use a combination of information-gathering methods to understand the problem. The findings are documented using the tools described later in the text—flowcharts, data flow diagrams, and the like.

The definition effort consists of two steps—proceed from a system to a subsystem level and analyze system parts in a certain sequence.

Step Four—Proceed from a System to a Subsystem Level.

As the manager seeks to understand the problem, the analysis begins with the system for which the manager is responsible. The system can be the firm or one of its units. The analysis then proceeds down the system hierarchy—level by level.

The manager first studies the position of the *system* in relation to its environment. Is the system in equilibrium with its environment? Are resources flowing between the system and its environment in the desired manner? Is the system meeting its objectives of providing products and services to the environment?

It is important to understand that the system can exist on any level. It is not necessary to begin with the firm as a system. The analysis can be directed at any subsystem in the firm.

Next, the manager analyzes the system in terms of its *subsystems.* Are the subsystems integrated into a smoothly functioning unit? Are all of the subsystems working toward the system objectives?

The purpose of this top-down analysis is to identify the system *level* where the cause of the problem exists.

Step Five—Analyze System Parts in a Certain Sequence.

The manager studies each element of her or his system in sequence. For example, the president asks whether the *firm* is meeting its responsibilities to the environment. If not, which of the elements pictured in Figure 4.6 is defective? The vice president of marketing asks the same questions about the marketing function, and so on down the line. The analysis of each system level proceeds in the sequence shown in the figure. The sequence reflects the priority of each element in the problem-solving process. For example, a problem in element four cannot be solved if there is a problem in element three.

Element One—Evaluate Standards   The performance standards for the firm or one of its organizational units are usually stated in the form of plans, budgets, and quotas.

FIGURE 4.6

Each Part of the System Is Analyzed in Sequence

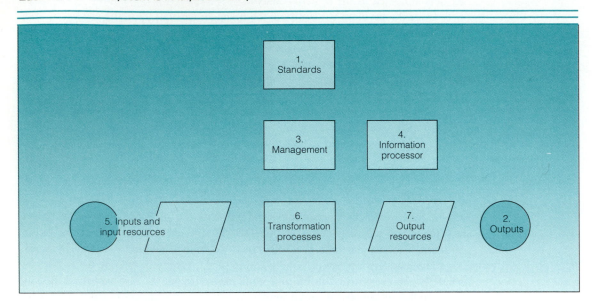

Management sets the standards, and must ensure that they have certain characteristics. The standards must be *valid*. That is, they must be a good measure of system performance. For example, a certain high sales volume may not be a valid standard, if the objective is to achieve a certain level of profitability. The standards also must be *realistic*. A 20 percent increase in sales is not very realistic if it has never before been achieved and there is nothing to warrant such optimism. Standards must be *understandable* to those who are expected to meet them, and they should be *measurable*. If the standard is "maximum profits," the manager never knows whether the standard has been achieved. "Realize a profit of 10 percent of sales" is the type of standard that leaves little doubt.

Element Two—Compare System Outputs with Standards   Once the manager is satisfied with the standards, he or she next evaluates the outputs of the system by comparing them with the standards.

If the system is meeting its standards, there is no need to continue with the systems approach to problem solving. There is no problem to solve *on this particular system level.* Rather, the manager should reevaluate the standards in the light of the good current performance. Perhaps the standards should be increased.

If the system is not meeting its standards, the manager must identify the cause. A problem exists, which must be solved. In some cases, the problem will be a system that is performing better than anticipated.

The remaining system elements are possible locations of the problem or problems.

Element Three—Evaluate Management   A critical appraisal is made of the system's management *and organizational structure*. Does a management team exist in terms of both the required quantity and quality? Are there enough managers, and do they have the right skills and abilities? The signals that indicate this to be a problem are (1) managers working excessively long hours and (2) decisions that prove to be faulty.

Does the organizational structure help or hinder the problem-solving process? In some cases, the establishment of a new unit is in order. For example, a corporate intelligence department is formed to gather information from the environment.

As a general rule, if the problem can be solved with the present management team and structure, then the management element is not the problem.

Element Four—Evaluate the Information Processor   It is possible that a good management team is present, but the team is simply not getting the information that it needs. If this is the case, the needs must be identified, and an adequate information system must be designed and implemented.

You might ask: "Doesn't a poor information processor indicate poor management?" It is possible that the managers simply have not had time to devote to their information processor. Perhaps things have been going so well that the information processor has been continually shoved to the background. This is a healthier situation than one of poor management. The problem of an inadequate information processor is easier to solve than one of poor management.

Element Five—Evaluate the Inputs and the Input Resources   When this level of the system analysis is reached, the conceptual system is no longer a concern, and the problem is known to exist within the physical system. An analysis is made of both the physical resources in the input element of the system, and the resources flowing through that element from the environment. For example, is the firm's receiving dock adequately staffed, and do materials ordered from suppliers arrive on time?

Element Six—Evaluate the Transformation Processes   Inefficient procedures and practices might be causing difficulties in transforming the inputs into outputs. Automation, robotics, computer-aided design and computer-aided manufacturing (CAD/CAM), and computer integrated manufacturing (CIM) are modern-day examples of efforts to solve transformation problems.

Element Seven—Evaluate the Output Resources   In Step 2, we paid attention to the outputs produced by the system. Here, we consider the physical resources in the output element of the system. Examples of such resources are a finished goods storeroom; the shipping dock, its personnel, and machines; and the fleet of delivery trucks.

Let us pause and review our progress. After adopting a systems way of thinking, something triggered a problem-solving process. We defined the problem by starting at the system level and working down. On each level, we studied the elements of that system in a certain sequence. Figure 4.7 shows this process. In this example, the analysis starts with the level of the firm and proceeds from one system element to another. This is the approach that the firm's president would take. If necessary, the analysis drops to the next lower system level. That level is analyzed, element by element, and the problem element on that level is identified. Again, if necessary, the analysis drops to still lower system levels.

As Figure 4.7 shows, it is unnecessary to analyze all seven elements on each level. As soon as the problem element is identified, attention is focused on that element by studying it on a lower system level. For example, assume that the president is alerted to the fact that the firm is not meeting its sales quota each month. Hence, the output of the firm is not up to standard. The next system element, management, is studied and determined to be deficient. There is no need at this point to continue with the analysis on the firm level, since the remaining elements are of a lower priority. We follow the priority sequence on each level, studying the most important elements first.

The problem element (in this case, management) must be understood once it is identified. The nature of a management deficiency must be explored. Perhaps the president learns that a high turnover of managers in the marketing division has kept the firm from meeting its standards.

The president's attention now shifts from the system of the firm to the marketing division. In analyzing the marketing system, the president learns that managers have been leaving the firm because they felt that the annual sales quotas were unreasonable. The problem lies within the standards established for marketing management. Continued study reveals that the reason for the unrealistic quotas is a poorly functioning marketing research department. The department is not doing a good job of measuring the market potential that the managers should be expected to achieve.

The president's attention now shifts from the marketing division to the marketing research department. The president learns that the problem in marketing research is an inadequate information processor. The firm has a computer, but the marketing research routines need improving. The president can now direct attention toward solving the problem.

The signals received at the higher system levels—low sales, deficient management, high management turnover, and poor quotas—were only symptoms of the problem: a poor marketing research information processor.

One of the most important tasks facing the manager is problem definition. Once this is achieved, the problem can be solved.

SOLUTION EFFORT

Solution effort involves a consideration of the feasible alternatives, a selection of the best, and its implementation.

FIGURE 4.7

The Systems Approach Provides the Path to Problem Definition

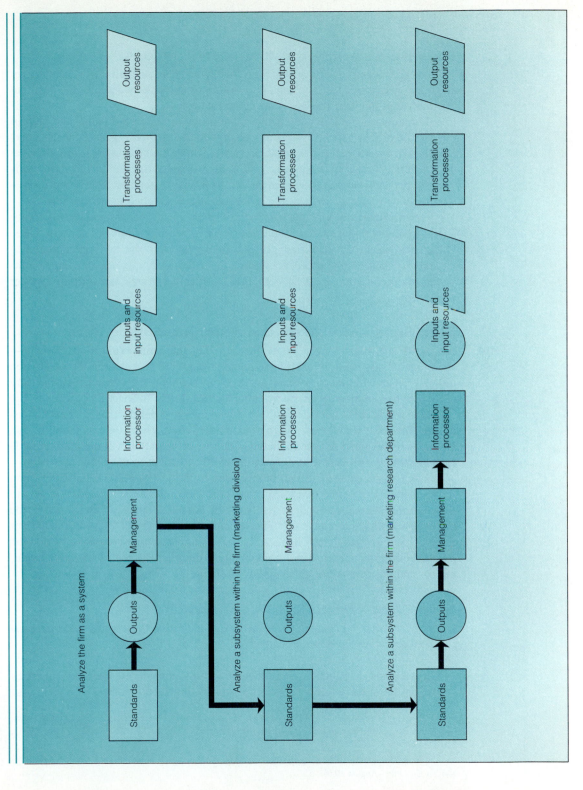

Step Six—Identify the Alternate Solutions

The manager identifies *different* ways to solve the *same* problem. This is easier for an experienced manager, who can apply solutions that have worked in the past, but creativity and intuition can also play important roles.

The manager seldom attempts to solve problems alone but enlists the help of others. The problem solvers frequently engage in **brainstorming,** an informal activity where the participants present their views, which are discussed. A more formal approach is called a **JAD session.** JAD stands for **joint application design** and is a group decision support system approach to problem solution. The group discussion is guided by a leader, and the proceedings are recorded in written form.[2]

As an example of how alternate solutions are identified, assume that the problem is a computer that cannot handle the firm's increasing volume of activity. Three alternate solutions are identified: (1) add more devices to the existing computer to increase its capacity and speed, (2) replace the existing computer with a larger computer, (3) replace the existing computer with a local area network of smaller computers.

Step Seven—Evaluate the Alternate Solutions

All of the alternatives must be evaluated using the same **evaluation criteria**—measures of how well an alternative solves the problem. Although the evaluation criteria can provide many avenues to problem solution, the fundamental measure is the extent to which an alternative enables the system to meet its objectives.

It is necessary to consider both the advantages and disadvantages of each alternative. Table 4.2 shows how the three computer alternatives are compared. In this example, the evaluation criteria include (1) cost of operation, (2) user training, (3) responsiveness, (4) data security, and (5) ability to adapt to changing user needs.

You should understand two points relative to the example in the table. First, the evaluation criteria will vary from one problem to the next. Second, it is best to evaluate the alternatives quantitatively when possible. For example, it would be better to state for alternative 1: "The operating costs will not exceed $60,000 per month" than to state "small increase." The quantitative measure makes evaluation easier. You must, of course, have good supporting data for the quantitative evaluations, and the data is not always easy to obtain.

Step Eight—Select the Best Solution

Henry Mintzberg, a management theorist, has identified three ways that managers go about selecting the best alternative:[3]

- **Analysis**—systematic evaluation of options, considering their consequences on the organization's goals. An example might be members of a JAD ses-

---

[2] For a good description of JAD, *see* Per O. Flaatten, Donald J. McCubbrey, P. Declan O'Riordan, and Keith Burgesss, *Foundations of Business Analysis,* (Fort Worth, TX: The Dryden Press, 1991), 210–18.

[3] Henry Mintzberg, "Planning on the Left Side and Managing on the Right," *Harvard Business Review* 54 (July–August 1976), 55.

TABLE 4.2
Evaluation of
Alternatives

	Alternative 1: Upgrade Existing System	Alternative 2: Install Larger System	Alternative 3: Install Microcomputer Network
Advantages	1. Small increase in cost of operation 2. No user training required 3. Provides maximum data security	1. Very responsive to information requests 2. Good data security 3. Easily adaptable to changing user needs	1. Slight decrease in cost of operation 2. Slightly adaptable to changing user needs
Disadvantages	1. Moderately responsive to information requests 2. Not easily adaptable to changing user needs	1. Large increase in cost of operation 2. Much user training required	1. Some user training required 2. Moderately responsive to information requests 3. Presents data security problems

sion, who are deciding which approach to take in implementing an executive information system (EIS), elect to purchase EIS software.

- **Judgment**—the mental process of a single manager. For example, a manufacturing manager applies experience and intuition in evaluating the layout of a new plant proposed by a mathematical model.
- **Bargaining**—negotiations between several managers. An example is the give and take that goes on among members of the executive committee concerning which functional information system to implement first.

Although emphasis here is on analysis, judgment and bargaining should not be ignored. All three ways would probably be involved in the selection of the best of the three computer alternatives.

Step Nine—Implement the Solution

The problem is not solved simply by selecting the best solution. It is necessary to implement the solution. In our example, it would be necessary to install the required computing equipment.

Step Ten—Follow Up to Ensure that the Solution Is Effective

The manager should follow up to make certain that the solution achieves the planned performance. When the solution falls short of expectations, it is necessary to retrace the problem-solving steps to determine what went wrong. Then, another try is made. This process is repeated until the manager is satisfied that the problem has been solved.

REVIEW OF THE SYSTEMS APPROACH

Although it is not difficult to understand each step of the systems approach separately, fitting them together into a single process requires effort. Managers develop this integrative skill through experience.

A good starting point is the *preparation effort* that the manager should expend before problem solving begins. The manager should view her or his organizational unit as a system residing within a larger environmental supersystem and consisting of several subsystems. This orientation represents the outer ring in Figure 4.8 Now the manager is ready to look for a problem or respond to one that appears.

The manager engages in functional decomposition by proceeding from system to subsystem, and by analyzing system parts in a certain sequence. Together these activities constitute *definition effort* in the upper circle of the figure.

Once the problem has been defined, it can be solved by following the remaining five steps in the lower circle—the *solution effort.*

AN EXAMPLE OF THE SYSTEMS APPROACH

Now that we understand what the systems approach is, let us apply it to a sample problem. Assume that you are a Houston management consultant and that you are invited by the Armadillo Motors (AM) executive committee to determine why their market share has been declining. AM management might regard the declining market share as the problem, but you suspect it to be a symptom.

Preparation Effort

Step One—View the Firm as a System It is easy for you to see AM as a system. Its Houston assembly plant performs the transformation process. Input raw materials, parts, and subassemblies are supplied by hundreds of firms. The AM dealerships distribute the output to government, business, and individual buyers around the world. Hundreds of managers on different levels perform the control function, using information from computers of all sizes as well as other types of information processors.

Step Two—Recognize the Environmental System With this view of AM as a system, you study the worldwide automobile market—reading articles that have appeared in business publications. You review government legislation that affects AM's operations and study the more important court cases in which AM

FIGURE 4.8

An Integrative
Model of the
Systems
Approach

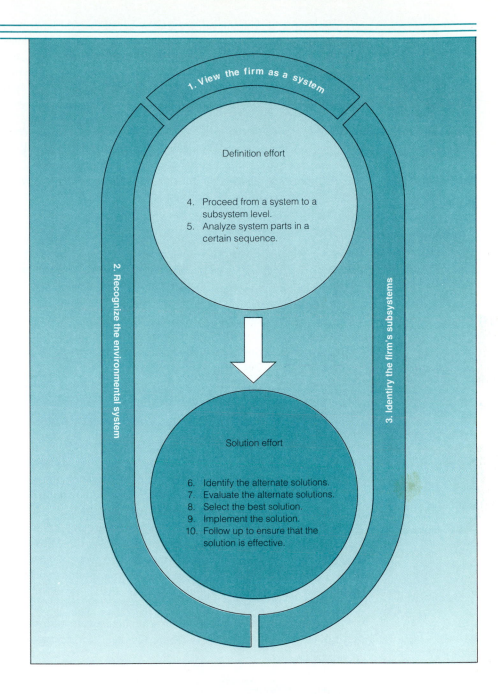

1. View the firm as a system

Definition effort

4. Proceed from a system to a subsystem level.
5. Analyze system parts in a certain sequence.

2. Recognize the environmental system

3. Identiry the firm's subsystems

Solution effort

6. Identify the alternate solutions.
7. Evaluate the alternate solutions.
8. Select the best solution.
9. Implement the solution.
10. Follow up to ensure that the solution is effective.

has been involved. You interview the manager of the AM labor relations department to learn about AM's relationships with organized labor. You also obtain statistics from the federal government, which address the issue of imports and exports, and review the most recent AM annual reports to study the company's financial condition. As a final step, you visit several automobile dealerships in the Houston area. You feel that you have a good feeling for the environment in which AM operates.

Step Three—Identify the Firm's Subsystems As a last step before searching for the cause of the declining market share, you ask the director of the AM human resources division to supply you with copies of organization charts and the policy manual. From this information you can identify the subsystems within AM and understand their relationships.

Definition Effort

Steps Four and Five—Proceed from a System to Subsystem Level and Analyze System Parts in a Certain Sequence Now you are ready to define the problem. You begin by interviewing top-level managers. You first ask to see copies of their objectives and performance standards. Next, you obtain computer printouts that show how well the standards are being met. You notice that the division that is having the most difficulty in meeting its market share objectives is the MiniVan Division. You shift your focus from AM as a system to the MiniVan Division subsystem.

You obtain more detailed information concerning the MiniVan standards and outputs. For example, you learn which models are selling well and which are not. The least-expensive models are having the greatest difficulties since that market segment is the most competitive.

You interview several top MiniVan managers and obtain information concerning their mangement team. You are permitted to examine copies of their annual performance reviews, and conclude that the management resource is there. It exists in adequate numbers and possesses the required knowledge and skills.

You next turn to the information processors that are available to the MiniVan Division. The hardware and software resources are impressive, and the information specialists use leading-edge techniques. Even so, the MiniVan managers are not receiving all of the information that they need. Specifically, not enough information is available on government and business organizations that buy competitive automobiles. Without this information, AM is unable to tap those particular market segments.

You have identified the problem as an inadequate information processor within the MiniVan subsystem of AM. There is a need for management information that is not being met.

Solution Effort

Step Six—Identify the Alternate Solutions The task is to create a system that will provide MiniVan management with the needed information and keep it current. Two basic alternatives are identified. One involves beefing up the

MIS by giving the marketing research department the responsibility of gathering information from government publications and entering it into the MiniVan mainframe. The other is an office automation application establishing an office of corporate intelligence that would obtain information from commercial databases of government information.

Step Seven—Evaluate the Alternate Solutions The relative advantages and disadvantages of the two alternatives are weighed.

Step Eight—Select the Best Solution The executive committee decides to let marketing research do the work. The vice president of marketing believes that the control achieved by gathering the data in-house would be worth the extra cost. The other executives concur.

Step Nine—Implement the Solution A system is implemented that automatically notifies marketing research when it is time to gather new data and provides the system output in the form of periodic reports. In addition, MiniVan management can obtain special reports from the database upon demand.

Step Ten—Follow Up to Ensure that the Solution Is Effective
As a control to ensure that the system continues to function, the MiniVan executive committee establishes a schedule of quarterly reviews that include user suggestions.

In this example, a top-down approach is followed in defining the problem—focusing first on AM as a system and then on the MiniVan Division as a subsystem. On each system level the system elements are studied in sequence. Once the problem is identified as the MiniVan information processor, it is solved by considering the possible alternatives, evaluating each, implementing the one that appears best, and following up.

PERSONAL FACTORS INFLUENCING PROBLEM SOLVING

Despite the picture we have painted so far of a manager who seeks out problems to solve, in actual practice, however, all managers are not so proactive. It may not be their nature, or they may not have time.

Each manager has a unique problem-solving style. The three dimensions of this style provide the opportunity to classify managers according to their individual differences. These deal with problem sensing, information gathering, and information using.[4]

[4] The information-gathering and information-using styles were first presented by James L. McKenney and Peter G. W. Keen, "How Managers' Minds Work," *Harvard Business Review* 52 (May–June 1974), 79–90. Andrew D. Szilagyi, Jr. added the problem-sensing style in *Management and Performance* (Santa Monica, CA: Goodyear Publishing Co, 1981), 220–25.

Problem Sensing

Managers fall into three basic categories in terms of their **problem-sensing styles**—how they confront problems.

- **Problem avoider**   This manager takes a positive attitude and assumes that everything is fine. An effort is made to block out the possibility of problems by ignoring information or avoiding thorough planning.
- **Problem solver**   This manager neither looks for problems nor blocks them out. If a problem arises, it is solved.
- **Problem seeker**   This manager enjoys solving problems and seeks them out.

Information Gathering

There are also differences in how managers develop and evaluate alternatives once problems have been sensed. Managers can exhibit one of two **information-gathering styles** or attitudes toward the total volume of information available to them:

- **Preceptive style**   This type of manager clings to management by exception and screens out everything that is not relative to his or her area of interest.
- **Receptive style**   This type of manager wants to look at everything and then determines whether it has value to himself or herself, or to anyone else in the organization.

Information Using

Managers also tend to favor one of two different **information-using styles,** ways of using information to solve a problem:

- **Systematic style**   The manager pays particular attention to following a prescribed method of problem solving, such as the systems approach.
- **Intuitive style**   The manager does not favor any certain method but tailors the approach to the situation.

It is important to recognize these individual differences. All too often the CBIS is described with statements that supposedly apply to all managers. Statements such as "Upper-level managers use summarized information" probably hold true *most* but not all of the time. The critical element in the CBIS is the manager, and each uses the CBIS in a different way.

It is also important to keep in mind the point that we made earlier in the chapter that managers seldom attempt to solve problems alone. Group problem solving is the order of the day, but, within the groups, personal differences exert a strong influence.

PUTTING THE SYSTEMS APPROACH IN PERSPECTIVE

Before we conclude our discussion of the systems approach, three comments are in order.

1. **The systems approach is really just common sense.** Although the technique involves many separate steps, and is never completely mastered, the underlying logic is quite simple. You seek to understand a problem before attempting to solve it, and you consider possible solutions.

2. **The systems approach is only one way to solve problems.** If you were to observe managers as they develop solutions, you would see that all of the steps we have described are not always followed, or they are not followed in sequence. This is what Harvard professor Daniel J. Isenberg learned when he studied the problem-solving behavior of a dozen executives. He found that:

   > "... they seldom think in ways that one might simplistically view as 'rational,' i.e., they rarely systematically formulate goals, assess their worth, evaluate the probabilities of alternative ways of reaching them, and choose the path that maximizes expected return. Rather, managers frequently bypass rigorous, analytical planning altogether, particularly when they face difficult, novel, or extremely entangled problems. When they do use analysis for a prolonged time, it is always in conjunction with intuition."[5]

   The systems approach provides a framework for understanding the processes that go into solving a problem, regardless of whether the processes are followed in a systematic or an intuitive fashion. Without such a framework, it would be difficult to define the areas where support from the CBIS can be applied.

3. **The systems approach is the basic systems methodology.** You hear the word methodology quite often in the computer field these days. A **methodology** is a prescribed way of doing something. A methodology is like a recommended way to go about selecting a college, or a procedure for coding a structured computer program.

   The systems approach is a methodology. In fact, the systems approach is *the basic* methodology in the computer field. All other methodologies are derivatives, to some degree, of the systems approach.

In this chapter, we described how the systems approach is used by the manager. In the next chapter, when we describe how managers and information specialists jointly develop the CBIS, we will see that the systems approach provides the basis for the system life cycle.

---

[5]Daniel J. Isenberg, "How Senior Managers Think," *Harvard Business Review* 62 (November–December 1984), 82.

SUMMARY

Managers engage in problem solving to solve problems that may be potentially harmful or beneficial. The problem-solving process requires that multiple decisions be made.

The conceptual system is a problem-solving system consisting of the manager, information, and standards. Two other elements enter into the process of transforming a problem into a solution. These elements are alternate solutions and constraints. It is critical that the manager separate the problem from its symptoms.

A popular way to classify problems is to place them on a continuum ranging from structured to unstructured. Most problems fall in between; they are semistructured in that the manager understands some of the elements and relationships, but not all.

The systems approach is a step-by-step procedure used in solving business problems. Each step involves one or more decisions, and information is required for each. The CBIS can support the manager by providing information for each decision. The steps of the systems approach provide a bridge between a single problem and the multiple decisions needed to solve it.

The systems approach requires that the manager regard the firm as a system, recognize the environmental system, and identify subsystems in the firm. These are all orientations that the manager should adopt before attempting to define a problem. While looking for the source of a problem and understanding it, the manager proceeds from system to subsystem level and analyzes the parts in a certain sequence. Once the problem has been defined, the manager identifies alternate solutions, evaluates them, selects and implements the one that appears to be the best, and follows up to ensure that the solution is effective.

Descriptions of decision making and decision makers frequently overlook exceptions to the rule. Personal factors create three basic problem-sensing styles (problem avoiders, problem solvers, and problem seekers). Managers also differ in how they gather information (preceptive and receptive), and how they use the information to solve problems (systematic and intuitive).

Although all managers do not follow the systems approach in solving problems, it serves as the basic systems methodology.

KEY TERMS

problem solving
decision making
preparation effort
definition effort
solution effort
functional decomposition

problem identification
problem understanding
problem trigger
brainstorming
joint application design (JAD)
evaluation criteria

KEY CONCEPTS

How a problem can be something good as well
as something bad

How multiple decisions are made to solve a
single problem

Problem-solving elements

How the difference between the desired state
and the current state is the solution
criterion

Problems versus symptoms

Problem structure

The systems approach

The relationship between a problem, the
systems approach, decisions, and the CBIS

Problem-sensing styles

Information-gathering styles

Information-using styles

The systems approach as the basic systems
methodology

QUESTIONS

1. Should a manager be happy or sad that a
problem exists? Explain.

2. Which of the problem-solving elements
also appear in the general systems model of
the firm?

3. What element of the general systems model
would provide the desired state? The current state?

4. What happens when the current state is
below the desired state? Above the desired
state?

5. In order for a problem to be structured,
what must the manager know about it?

6. Who, or what, solves a structured problem?
What about an unstructured one? A semistructured one?

7. What name did Dewey use for *problem*?
For *decision*?

8. What are the three phases of effort in applying the systems approach?

9. How many CBIS subsystems are required
to solve a problem?

10. What did we study in Chapter 3 that
enables the manager to view her or his firm
as a system?

11. What did we study in Chapter 2 that
enables the manager to recognize the environmental system?

12. Name three ways to subdivide a firm into
its subsystems.

13. Distinguish between problem identification
and problem understanding.

14. Who is in the best position to recognize the
problem trigger?

15. What are the four desired characteristics of
standards.

16. What is the difference, if any, between the
solution criterion and the evaluation
criteria?

17. What are the three ways of selecting the
best alternative, according to Mintzberg?

18. There are three offices side-by-side. In the
first, there is no evidence of computing
equipment or output. In the second there is
a stack of computer reports on the desk. In
the third there is a terminal. Which office
belongs to the problem seeker? The problem solver? The problem avoider?

19. In what ways is the systems approach just
common sense?

TOPICS FOR DISCUSSION

1. Which system elements are analyzed first— those representing the physical system or the conceptual system? Can you explain why?

2. Could a good CBIS conceivably change a problem solver into a problem seeker? Explain your reasoning.

3. How could a CBIS support a manager who has a preceptive style of information gathering?

4. Can you see any relationship between information-using style (systematic versus intuitive) and degree of managerial experience? Explain.

PROBLEMS

1. Assume that you are going to use the systems approach in buying a car. Make a list of the evaluation criteria that you would use. Pick three cars that interest you, and list the advantages and disadvantages of each criterion for each car.

2. Make three lists of questions that you would ask a manager in order to categorize her or him as a (1) problem avoider, problem solver, problem seeker; (2) preceptive gatherer or receptive gatherer; and (3) systematic user or intuitive user.

Albatross Industries, Inc.

Albatross is a manufacturer of small, gasoline-powered engines, which are sold to manufacturers of lawn mowers, chain saws, and the like. The manufacturing facilities are very impressive, with some 2,500 workers and much specialized machinery. In addition to the typical applications, their mainframe computer is used for CAD/CAM, and they are in the process of automating the assembly line with robots.

Alfred Brantley is a systems analysis in the information services division and has been assigned the task of studying the feasibility of implementing a materials management system. Albatross president, Kelly McCann, came up with the idea in response to difficulties that have been experienced in tracking the material flow through the plant.

Data collection terminals are installed in key locations—on the receiving dock, in the raw-materials storeroom, at each work station on the plant floor, in the finished-goods storeroom, and on the shipping dock. As the material moves from one location to another, the employees key identifying data into their terminals so that the database will reflect the current material location. Too often, however, the employees have either not keyed the data in at all—they say they forgot, or they have keyed in the wrong data. The result has been an unusable database.

McCann felt that one way to solve the problem would be to create an entirely new organization—a materials management division. As a way to get acquainted with the overall situation, Alfred plans to interview Biff Landrum, the vice president of manufacturing, Donna Crum, the vice president of marketing, and Frank Winfield, the transportation manager who will have the responsibility for materials management should the reorganization take place. After the interviews, Alfred is to report to McCann with his recommendation.

Biff Landrum Interview

ALFRED: How do you feel about the possibility of forming a materials management division?

BIFF LANDRUM, Vice President of Manufacturing: Personally, I think it stinks. It's going to result in me losing control over a big portion of the production process. Now don't get me wrong. I have nothing against Frank. He's worked for me for years, and I think he's a great guy. But, his expertise is limited to transportation. He knows how to get the finished goods to our customers the best and cheapest way, but he knows absolutely nothing about the flow of material through the plant or the receipt of raw materials from the suppliers.

ALFRED: So, he's only been involved with the flow of materials out of the plant.

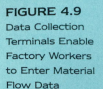

FIGURE 4.9
Data Collection
Terminals Enable
Factory Workers
to Enter Material
Flow Data

Stock, Boston

BIFF: That's right. And the people who will be working for him have the same limited knowledge. I'm not about to let him have my people in receiving and in the raw-materials and finished goods storerooms. I need those people to make sure that my production workers get their materials on time.

ALFRED: So, Frank will have only a handful of transportation specialists working for him. How will he get his job done?

BIFF: He'll essentially maintain a database. He'll rely on other people throughout the plant to key the data into the computer, and his group will have the responsibility for tracking the flow so that everything goes smoothly. For example, if a supplier calls in and says that their plant is on strike, Frank will have to work with the people in purchasing to get material from an alternate source. Or, if a piece of machinery breaks down on the plant floor and slows down production, Frank will have to reschedule the shipping.

ALFRED: But, it seems to me that the data will be no better than it is now. Why can't the workers keep the database accurate?

BIFF: It's because they have better things to do. That's why. They have responsibilities to receive the materials, to give it quality control inspections, to use it in the production process, to inspect it after production, to store it, and to ship it. If they spend all their time keying data into the computer, they never will get their work done. I've been sympathetic to them. I haven't pushed them in that regard.

ALFRED: Well, what do you think the solution is?

BIFF: I think that each division should have their own computing operation. We should have our own mainframe. Marketing should have their's and so on. Give me my own hardware and the people to run it, and we'll do just fine. Everybody else can worry about their own problems.

ALFRED: But, won't it be difficult for manufacturing to go it alone? You're tied in so closely with other areas—purchasing, marketing, and so on.

BIFF: We'll manage. Believe me.

Donna Crum Interview

ALFRED: Well, thanks for the rundown on marketing's responsibility in getting the finished goods to the customers. I always thought that was entirely Frank Winfield's responsibility in transportation. It's interesting that marketing has the overall responsibility for the customers. Frank is only concerned with getting the products there. It sounds like Frank should have been working for you rather than Biff.

DONNA CRUM, Vice president of Marketing: I've felt that way all along. We do all the selling, take the orders, coordinate the shipping with Frank to meet the customers' needs, and follow up to make sure the goods arrive on time and in good condition. We provide an ongoing service to the accounts so that when the time comes for them to order more, we get the business.

ALFRED: So, I guess you're somewhat unhappy about the fact that the materials database is not too reliable.

DONNA: That's putting it mildly. I lay most of the blame on Biff, but that's no secret. I've told him that to his face. Biff doesn't care whether his people do the data entry or not, and that's absurd. We give all of our sales reps laptops and they use them to enter data describing the orders and the shipments. Much of the data is entered while they are in the customers' offices. You can imagine how that impresses the customers. It's a real sales aid. We stress to our people the importance of clean data, and they do the job. I don't know why Biff can't expect the same from his people.

ALFRED: Biff would like to have his own computing operation—mainframe and all. What do you think about that?

DONNA: That's Biff. He's generally uncooperative. How long do you think that would last? Manufacturing is no island. It's connected to every other operation in the company. He can't exist alone. He has to use data flows from everybody else to survive. And, everybody else depends on data flows from him. I'm surprised he can't see that. If he goes his own way, it will not only be very expensive and inefficient, but will probably ruin the company.

ALFRED: Well, what do you recommend?

DONNA: I don't think we should go the materials management route. Frank really is not qualified to take it on. What Biff told you about Frank is true. By the time he learns about the material flow that occurs prior to transportation, we'll have lost every customer and supplier that we have. Personally, I would like to see manufacturing and marketing work together. I can't see adding another organizational unit. To me, that will only muddy the water.

Frank Winfield Interview

ALFRED: I guess you're pretty excited about the possibilities of the material management function?

FRANK WINFIELD, Transportation Manager: You bet. Most of the progressive manufacturers have gone that way. It's the systems approach.

ALFRED: It's my understanding that you have never had such broad-reaching responsibility. How do you feel about that?

FRANK: It's true that all of my jobs have been in transportation. But, I've worked with people in purchasing, receiving, production, and so on. I know what goes on in those areas. Material flow is material flow. The job of getting it out of the plant is really no different from getting it in, and getting it through the production area.

ALFRED: So you believe strongly in yourself and the need for a materials management unit?

FRANK: Exactly. Finance has the responsibility for the money flow. Materials are just as important as money, but look who all has their fingers in the pie—purchasing, manufacturing, transportation, and marketing. It's no wonder things have been fouled up.

ALFRED: Do you think that you can unfoul them, so to speak?

FRANK: No doubt about it. Having a unit that has all of the material flow responsibility will solve the problem.

ALFRED: But, your people will not be keying the data into the computer. That will be done by people in those other units. You won't have any control over that. How can you expect that to go any better?

FRANK: Good point.

Assignment

Prepare a memo to the Albatross president, defining the problem and identifying three alternate solutions. Give the advantages and disadvantages of each alternative and recommend one to be implemented.

SELECTED BIBLIOGRAPHY

Ahn, Taesik, and Grudnitski, Gary. "Conceptual Perspectives on Key Factors in DSS Development: A Systems Approach.: *Journal of Management Information Systems* 2 (Summer 1985): 18–32.

Cerveny, Robert P.; Garrity, Edward J.; and Sanders, G. Lawrence. "A Problem-Solving Perspective on Systems Development." *Journal of Management Information Systems* 6 (Spring 1990): 103–22.

Einhorn, Hillel J., and Hogarth, Robin M. "Decision Making: Going Forward in Reverse." *Harvard Business Review* 65 (January–February 1987): 66–70.

Floyd, Barry, and Ronen, Boaz. "Where Best to System Invest." *Datamation* 35 (November 15, 1989): 111*ff.*

Hogarth, Robin M. *Judgement and Choice.* New York: John Wiley & Sons, 1980, 130–54.

Johnson, Richard A.; Kast, Fremont E.; and Rosenzweig, James E. *The Theory and Management of Systems.* 2d ed. New York: McGraw-Hill, 1967, 280–82.

Lederer, Albert L., and Smith, George L., Jr. "Individual Differences and Decision-Making Using Various Levels of Aggregation of Information." *Journal of Management Information Systems* 5 (Winter 1988–89): 53–69.

Martin, Merle P. "Problem Identification." *Journal of Systems Management* 28 (December 1977): 10–15.

Martin, Merle P. "Problem Identification Indicators." *Journal of Systems Management* 29 (September 1978): 36– 39.

Mosard, Gil. "Problem Definition: Tasks and Techniques." *Journal of Systems Management* 34 (June 1983): 16–21.

Sabherwal, Rajiv, and Grover, Varun. "Computer Support for Strategic Decision-Making Processes: Review and Analysis." *Decision Sciences* 20 (Winter 1989): 54–76.

Simon, Herbert A. *The New Science of Management Decision.* New York: Harper & Brothers, 1960: 54*ff.*

Wedberg, George H. "But First, Understand the Problem." *Journal of Systems Management* 41 (June 1990): 20–28.

Yadav, Surya B. "Classifying an Organization to Identify Its Information Requirements: A Comprehensive Framework." *Journal of Management Information Systems* 2 (Summer 1985): 39–60.

Chapter 5

The System Life Cycle

LEARNING OBJECTIVES

After studying this chapter, you should:

- Realize that the development and use of a computer-based system progresses through a life cycle, and that users and information specialists play key roles in each phase
- Understand that life cycle management can originate from several organizational levels
- Be aware of the MIS steering committee, the functions that it performs, and the advantages that accrue from its participation in the life cycle
- Be aware of the team approach to systems development
- Know the benefits that can be expected from planning the system life cycle
- Know the steps that are taken for each of the life cycle phases
- Know the six dimensions of CBIS feasibility
- Realize that the manager can exercise a go/no go control over each life cycle phase
- Be familiar with one way to identify information needs
- Have an introductory understanding of structured design
- Understand the logical way that a computer configuration is determined
- Be familiar with the process of requesting and evaluating hardware and software proposals of suppliers
- Understand three approaches for cutting over to the new system
- Know the main reasons for performing systems maintenance

■ Understand what rapid application development is, and how CASE and prototyping are involved

INTRODUCTION

The concept of a life cycle fits anything that originates, matures over time, and eventually dies. This pattern applies to a computer-based system such as a data processing subsystem or a DSS.

The system life cycle consists of five phases, with the first four devoted to development and the fifth to use. Each phase of the system life cycle requires the participation and cooperation of users and information specialists. The activities of these people are managed from several vantage points within the firm. The president can provide top-level leadership, as can other executives, perhaps functioning as an executive committee. On a slightly lower level, a special committee called the MIS steering committee can manage all life cycles in the firm. As each of the life cycles go through the developmental phases, the project leaders supervise the team members.

The planning phase begins with a problem definition and continues by identifying system objectives and constraints. The systems analyst conducts a feasibility study and proposes to the manager that a system study be launched. When the manager approves the study, a control mechanism is established.

The analysis phase has the important task of identifying the users' information needs and determining the level of system performance that will be necessary to satisfy those needs. When the system study indicates that a new system may solve the manager's problem, the analyst prepares a proposal, recommending that the new system be designed.

The design phase involves the determination of the processing and data required by the new system, and the selection of the best configuration of hardware to carry out the design. An implementation proposal allows the manager to determine whether the implementation phase should be taken.

The implementation phase involves many additional information specialists who convert the design from its paper form to one consisting of hardware, software, and data. Facilities are prepared, users are educated, and the cutover to the new system occurs.

During the use phase, audits are conducted to ensure that the system is doing what it is supposed to do, and maintenance is performed so that the system provides the desired support.

The system life cycle is an application of the systems approach to the task of developing and using a computer-based system. As such, the system life cycle is a methodology, but its pattern is being influenced by the need to develop systems more quickly, and with less human effort. Two innovations make rapid application development possible—computer-aided software engineering (CASE), and prototyping. In this chapter, we first describe the system life cycle and then we discuss how rapid application development alters that traditional life cycle pattern.

THE SYSTEM LIFE CYCLE

The **system life cycle** (**SLC**) is the evolutionary process that is followed in implementing a computer-based information system or subsystem. This has been the traditional implementation approach throughout the computer era, and there is general agreement among computer scientists concerning the tasks to be performed. The only disagreement comes in the number of steps and their names. Each authority tends to describe the process in a slightly different manner. A close inspection reveals, however, that all of the descriptions follow the same general pattern, and that the pattern closely follows the systems approach.

Many SLCs exist within a computer-using firm. There may be a hundred or more. There is one SLC for each system being used or developed. For example, there is a payroll SLC, a cash flow model SLC, a sales reporting SLC, and so on. Each of the SLCs is an expression of the firm's strategic plan for information resources. In fact, the SLCs are the vehicles by which management carries out the strategic plan.

Life Cycle Phases

Our interpretation of the system life cycle is summarized in Figure 5.1. There are five phases: (1) planning, (2) analysis, (3) design, (4) implementation, and (5) use. The first four phases are devoted to system development, and the term **system development life cycle** (**SDLC**) is often used to describe that overall process. System development can span many months or years, involve many people, and incur great cost. This effort is expended with the intention of using the system, in stage five, for a long period of time. Some systems have been in use for twenty-five or thirty years, whereas others have not been quite so lucky—having been scrapped after a few weeks or months. During the use phase, the system must be maintained to keep it operational. At some point, however, it becomes impractical to continue the maintenance, and management decides that it is time to develop a new, improved system. At this point, the SLC is repeated.

Life Cycle Participants

When users develop their own systems, end-user computing, all of the work is performed by the users. When users take advantage of the knowledge and skills of information specialists, both parties share the work.

Information specialists include those persons who communicate directly with the user, such as the systems analyst, the database administrator (DBA), and the network specialist. Other information specialists include the programmer and operations personnel, who make their contributions during the implementation phase. All information specialists participate in maintaining the system during the use phase.

Although most of the firm's SLC efforts have historically been carried out by members of the information services staff, this situation is changing. More and more firms are contracting out a portion or all of the SLC effort to external orga-

FIGURE 5.1

The Five Phases
of the System
Life Cycle

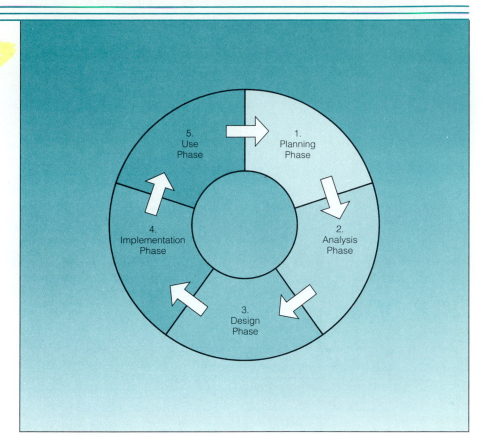

nizations, an activity called **outsourcing**. We describe outsourcing in Chapter 21 when we address current issues and trends.

Life Cycle Management

The first system life cycles were managed by the manager of the information services unit, assisted by the managers of systems analysis, programming, and operations. In many firms, the responsibility still resides at that level. However, the recent trend has been to also place responsibility at both higher and lower levels. Today, it is possible for life cycle management to span several organizational levels and to involve managers outside of information services. Figure 5.2 shows the hierarchical nature of life cycle management.

Executive Responsibility   When the system has potential strategic value or affects the entire organization, the president or the executive committee may decide to oversee the development project. As the system scope narrows and the focus is more operational, the likelihood increases that lower-level executives will

FIGURE 5.2

Managers of Systems Life Cycles Are Arranged in a Hierarchy

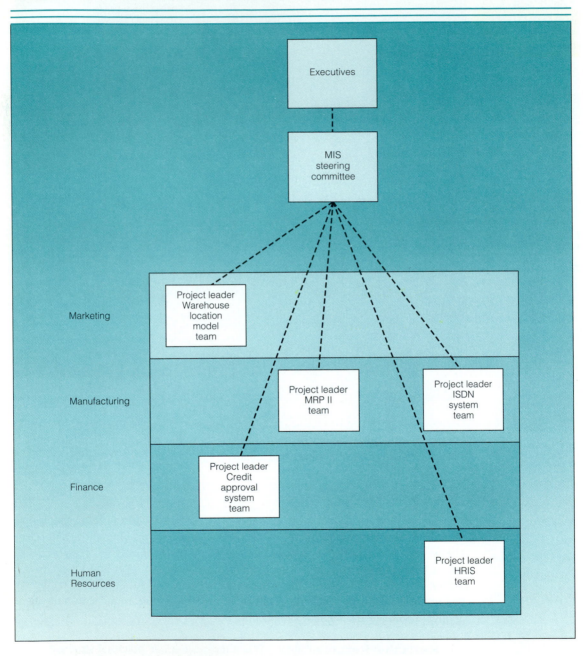

provide the overall leadership. Management positions that lend themselves to this type of direction are the executive vice president, the vice president of administration, and the CIO.

The MIS Steering Committee Many firms establish a special committee, below the level of the executive committee, which assumes responsibility for overseeing all of the systems projects. When the purpose of a committee is to provide ongoing guidance, direction, and control, it is called a **steering committee**. When a firm establishes a steering committee for the purpose of directing the use of the firm's computing resources, the name **MIS steering committee** is used.

The MIS steering committee is ongoing. That means that its membership is relatively stable, with members serving until the president decides that a change is in order. Permanent members invariably include the top executives from each functional area, including the CIO. It is not uncommon for the president to also belong. Temporary members include lower-level managers and consultants who are involved when their expertise is needed.

The MIS steering committee performs three main functions.[1] It:

- **Establishes policies** that ensure computer support for achieving the strategic objectives of the firm.
- **Provides fiscal control** by serving as the approval authority for all requests for computer-related funds.
- **Resolves conflicts** that arise concerning priorities for computer use.

In effect, the task of the MIS steering committee is to carry out the strategy that is established by the executive committee and the strategic plan for information resources.

By centralizing the management of system life cycles within the steering committee, two main advantages accrue:[2]

- The liklihood is increased that the computer will be used to support users throughout the firm.
- The liklihood is increased that computer projects will be characterized by good planning and control.

The MIS steering committee is the most visible evidence that the firm intends to make information resources available to all users who have a genuine need.

Project Leadership

Although the MIS steering committee makes the main decisions concerning systems development, it seldom gets directly involved with the details of the work. That responsibility goes to project teams. A **project team** includes users, infor-

---

[1] Taken from D. H. Drury, "An Evaluation of Data Processing Steering Committees," *MIS Quarterly* 8 (December 1984), 259.

[2] *Ibid,* 260.

mation specialists from the information services unit, and perhaps an internal auditor from the firm's internal auditing unit. These team members perform the tasks necessary to develop a computer-based system. The team activity is directed by a **project leader** who provides leadership throughout the life of the project. Unlike the MIS steering committee, the project team is not ongoing in that it is usually disbanded when implementation is completed. In some cases, one or more members are given maintenance responsibility.

In our description, we will assume that the system life cycle is controlled by an MIS steering committee working in conjunction with project teams. The steering committee maintains the focus of the teams on the strategic objectives, and the project leader sees to it that the work is done.

THE PLANNING PHASE

Development of a CBIS subsystem should receive the same degree of planning as the introduction of a new product or the construction of a new plant.

Benefits from Planning the CBIS Project

The MIS steering committee and the project teams anticipate that planning will yield the following benefits:

- **Define the scope of the project**   Which organizational units, activities, or systems are involved? Which are not? This information provides an initial estimate of the scale of resources required.
- **Recognize potential problem areas**   Planning will point out things that might go wrong so that they may be prevented.
- **Arrange a sequence of tasks**   Many separate tasks will be necessary to achieve the system. These tasks are arranged in a logical sequence based on information priorities and the need for efficiency.
- **Provide a basis for control**   Certain levels of performance and methods of measurement should be specified in advance.

Management invests time in planning with the anticipation that it will pay dividends later in the life cycle.

STEPS OF THE PLANNING PHASE

Figure 5.3 is a graphic model of the planning phase. It shows each of the steps to be taken and identifies the responsibilities of the MIS steering committee, the manager of the user area, and the systems analyst.

FIGURE 5.3

The Planning
Phase

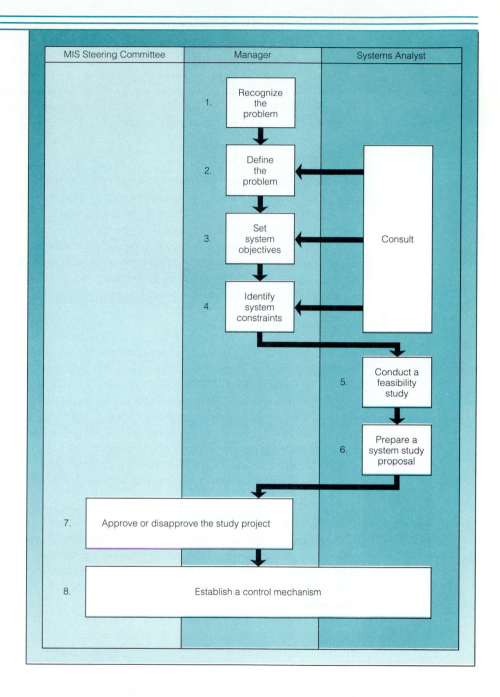

1. Recognize the Problem

The need for a CBIS project is usually recognized by the firm's managers, non-managers, and elements in the firm's environment. Only rarely will information specialists from the information services unit initiate a CBIS project, because they are not always on the scene to notice the problem symptoms. However, in those firms that distribute their information resources to user areas, the functional specialists *are* in a position to recognize problems.

2. Define the Problem

Once the manager realizes that a problem exists, he or she must understand it well enough to pursue a solution. However, the manager does not attempt to gather *all* of the information at this point. Instead, the manager seeks only to identify *where* the problem exists and what the *cause* might be.

If the firm has policies that encourage end-user computing, and the manager wants to pursue that approach to system development, then she or he solicits the assistance of the systems analyst in formulating the problem definition. We will assume that the manager and the analyst work together.

3. Set System Objectives

The manager and the systems analyst develop a list of system objectives that the system must meet in order to satisfy the users. For example, the marketing function might have an objective of $25 million in sales revenue with operating expenses under $1.2 million. In order to meet these marketing objectives, the vice president of marketing might require a monthly expense report. A project is initiated to develop such a reporting system. Later in the life cycle, the report requirements will be made more specific. At this point, however, the objectives are stated in only general terms, such as: "Provide a monthly expense report that compares actual expenses with budgeted expenses for each operating unit."

4. Identify System Constraints

The new system will not operate free from constraints. Some are imposed by the environment, such as the government's demand for tax reports and the customers' need for billing information. Others are imposed by the firm's management, such as the requirement to use existing hardware, or to have the system up and running on a certain date.

It is important that these constraints be identified before work on the system actually begins. In this way, both the system design and the project activity will fall within the constraints.

5. Conduct a Feasibility Study

The systems analyst initially serves as a consultant to the manager, and then uses the gathered information as a guideline for conducting a feasibility study. A **feas-**

ibility study is a brief look at the major factors that will influence the ability of the system to achieve the desired objectives. It is not a full-scale study effort; that study will come later after the project feasibility has been demonstrated.

There are six dimensions of feasibility:[3]

- **Technical**   Is there hardware and software available to perform the necessary processing?
- **Economic return**   Can the proposed system be justified monetarily by comparing its benefits and its costs?
- **Noneconomic return**   Can the proposed system be justified based on benefits that cannot be measured in monetary terms?
- **Legal**   Will the proposed system operate within legal and ethical boundaries?
  Operational   Is the system design such that it can and will receive the support of the people who must make it work?
- **Schedule**   Will it be possible to implement the system within the imposed time constraints?

The systems analyst gathers the information necessary to answer these questions primarily by interviewing key employees in the user area. The intent is to gather the needed information in the shortest time, at the least cost, and with the least disruption to the daily routine.

6. Prepare a System Study Proposal

If the feasibility study indicates that the project should continue, it will be necessary to conduct a full-blown system study. The **system study** will provide the *detailed* basis for the design of the new system in terms of what it should do and how it should do it. The system study will be conducted by the analyst, perhaps with the support of the database administrator and network specialist, and will represent a considerable expense. The analyst prepares a **system study proposal** that provides the manager with a basis for deciding whether to incur the analysis expense.

Figure 5.4 is a sample outline of the system study proposal. The executive summary (Section 1) distills the entire report for the MIS steering committee, and the introduction (Section 2) states the reason for initiating the project. The system objectives and constraints (Section 3) are the result of the first four steps of the planning phase.

Sections 4 through 7 are the product of the feasibility study. Section 4 briefly describes possible system solutions. The analyst determines which alternative appears to be best suited for the particular situation, and that alternative is described in Section 5, along with a brief explanation of the resources needed for implementation.

---

[3] This list is derived from John G. Burch, Jr., Felix R. Strater, and Gary Grudnitski, *Information Systems: Theory and Practice,* 3d ed. (New York: John Wiley & Sons, 1983), 341–42.

FIGURE 5.4

Outline of a
System Study
Proposal

1. Executive summary
2. Introduction
3. System objectives and constraints
4. Possible system alternatives
5. The recommended system study project
   5.1 Tasks to be performed
   5.2 Human resource requirements
   5.3 Schedule of work
   5.4 Estimated cost
6. Expected impact of the system
   6.1 Impact on the firm's organization structure
   6.2 Impact on the firm's operations
   6.3 Impact on the firm's resources
7. General development plan (analysis, design, and implementation phases)
8. Summary

Section 6 describes the effects, both positive and negative, on the firm and its operations of implementing the recommended system.

The first six sections relate to the system that will be achieved. Section 7 relates to the study project leading to the system. In this section, the analyst identifies the tasks involved in carrying out the analysis, design, and implementation phases.

The important point to understand concerning the system study proposal is that, at this early stage in the SLC, much of the content is based on the informed estimates of both the manager and the systems analyst. As the life cycle unfolds, more will be learned. But, at this point, the estimates are the best information available.

Written copies of the study project proposal are given to the MIS steering committee. The systems analyst may also be invited to supplement the written report with an oral presentation.

7. Approve or Disapprove the Study Project

The manager and the steering committee weigh the pros and cons of the proposed project and system design, and decide whether to proceed—a **go/no go decision**.

As the committee makes its decision, two key questions are asked:

1. Will the proposed system accomplish its objectives?
2. Is the proposed study project the best way to conduct the systems analysis?

In order for the committee to answer these questions, they must have confidence in the ability of the manager and the systems analyst to establish the planning base for the project.

If the decision is *go*, the project continues to the study phase. If the decision is *no go*, all of the parties turn their attention to other matters.[4]

8. Establish a Control Mechanism

Before the study begins, the MIS steering committee must establish control over the project. Project control involves the specification of what needs to be done, who will do it, and when will it be done.

Table 5.1 provides an example of how these questions are answered. The example lists the tasks that might be required to develop a mathematical model to be used by marketing management in deciding whether to delete a product from the line. The amount of time required for each task is listed in person months.

A **person month** is the amount of time for *one person,* working for an entire calendar month, to accomplish some task. For example, it might be projected that it will take 176 hours (twenty-two working days times eight hours a day) to define a manager's information needs. We would say that the task requires one person month.

By assigning multiple persons to a task, it is possible to reduce the number of *calendar* months, although not necessarily in a linear fashion. For example, if a task is expected to require six person months, the assignment of six persons might not permit the task to be completed in one calendar month. One reason is the time that must be spent on coordination when multiple people work together.

The person month estimates that are incorporated in the control mechanism are based on the combined experience of the information specialists in developing similar systems.

Monitoring Project Progress   Once the project schedule has been established, it is next necessary to document it in a form that will facilitate control. Various documentation techniques can be used, including graphs and network diagrams.

A **network diagram** uses arrows to represent the tasks, and links the arrows to show their interrelationships. Figure 5.5 is an example of the activities required to develop the product deletion model. Each arrow in the diagram represents work to be done, and is called an **activity**. Each activity is labeled and the estimated time is shown.

Network diagrams and graphs can be prepared by **project management software** that is designed to help the manager control projects such as development of computer-based systems. There are over one hundred such packages, with versions

---

[4]For a description of the considerations that comprise the project abandonment decision, *see* Kweku Ewusi-Mensah and Zbigniew H. Przasnyski, "On Information Systems Project Abandonment: An Exploratory Study of Organizational Practices, *MIS Quarterly* 15 (March 1991), 67–86.

TABLE 5.1
A Project
Schedule

Functional System:	Marketing
Subsystem:	Product
Model:	Product Deletion

Subtask	Responsibility	Time Estimate (Person Months)
1. Identify deletion criteria	Systems analyst Product manager	0.75
2. Identify output information requirements	Systems analyst Network specialist Product manager	0.25
3. Identify input data requirements	Systems analyst DBA	0.50
4. Prepare new system documentation	Systems analyst	2.00
5. Design network	Network specialist	1.50
6. Design database	DBA	0.50
7. Review design	Product manager Systems analyst	0.25
8. Prepare program documentation	Programmer	1.00
9. Code program	Programmer	1.25
10. Test program	Programmer Operations staff	0.75
11. Approve program	Product manager VP of marketing	0.50
12. Prepare database	DBA	2.00
13. Educate users	Systems analyst	0.50
14. Cutover to model	Operations staff	0.75

available for both microcomputers and mainframes.[5] The network diagram in Figure 5.5 was prepared by the Harvard Project Manager from Software Publishing Corporation of Mountain View, California.

[5]For a brief description of some of the more popular project management packages, *see* Tom McCusker, "Tools To Manage Big Projects," *Datamation* 37 (January 15, 1991), 71*ff*.

THE ANALYSIS PHASE

With the planning completed and the control mechanism in place, the participants' attention turns to analysis of the existing system. An understanding of the existing system forms the basis of the design of a new system. **Systems analysis** is the study of an existing system for the purpose of designing a new or improved system.

During the analysis phase, the systems analyst continues to work with the manager, and the MIS steering committee is involved at crucial points as shown in Figure 5.6.

1. Announce the System Study

When a firm implements a new computer application, management must do everything possible to ensure the cooperation of the employees. An initial concern is the employees' fears of how the computer might affect their jobs. The best way to combat these fears is to discuss with the employees (1) the firm's reasons for the project and (2) how the new system will benefit the firm *and the employees*. If the company is small, the president can conduct a meeting. In larger organizations, lower-level managers can address the employees in smaller groups. These oral presentations can be supplemented with written communications such as memos and articles in the company newspaper.

2. Organize the Project Team

The project team that will conduct the system study is assembled. At this stage, the team consists of users, one or more systems analysts, and perhaps a DBA, a network specialist, and an internal auditor. The project leader is designated, and in some cases a user plays this role. It is crucial to the success of the project that users actively participate.

3. Define Information Needs

Analysts learn about the users' information needs by engaging in a variety of information-gathering activities: personal interviews, observations, record searches, and surveys. Of all these methods, the personal interview is preferred for the following reasons:

- It provides the opportunity for two-way communication and the observation of body language.
- It can stimulate enthusiasm for the project on the part of both the information specialists and the users.
- It can establish a common bond of trust between the users and the information specialists.
- It provides the opportunity for the participants in the project to express alternate views.

FIGURE 5.5

A Network Diagram of the Product Deletion Model Project

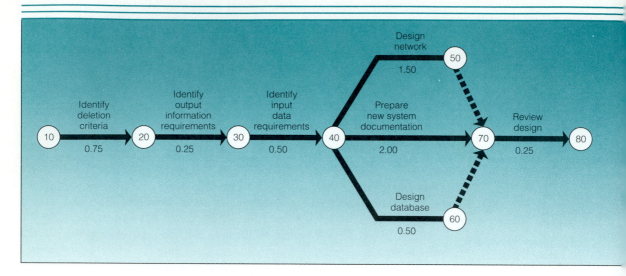

As the analyst conducts an interview, he or she might pursue a line of questioning similar to the following:[6]

1. What decisions do you regularly make?
2. What information do you need to make these decisions?
3. What information do you currently receive?
4. What information would you like to receive?
5. What specialized studies do you request?
6. What magazines and trade reports would you like to have routed to you
   on a regular basis?
7. Of what specific topics would you like to be informed?
8. What are the four most helpful improvements that could be made in the
   present information system?

Very often, it is difficult for the manager to answer the questions, and several
interviews may be necessary. Also, the analyst may have to take a more indirect
approach. For example, a prototype system may be prepared to provide a basis for
identifying specific information preferences or needs.

This is the point in the SLC where the analyst assembles the documentation
of the existing system. The analyst reviews documentation that may have been prepared when the current system was originally developed and adds new documentation when necessary. The documentation includes flowcharts, data flow diagrams,
and other graphic and narrative descriptions of processes and data.

[6]Adapted from Philip Kotler, *Marketing Management: Analysis, Planning, and Control,* 3d ed.
(Englewood Cliffs, NJ: Prentice-Hall, 1976), 423.

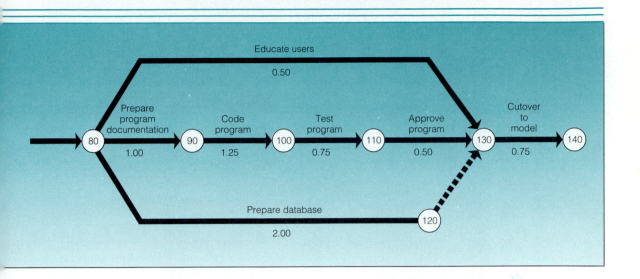

4. Define System Performance Criteria

With the manager's information needs defined, it is now possible to specify in exact terms what the system should accomplish—its **performance criteria**. These performance criteria are expansions on the system objectives that were stated in general terms during the planning phase.

For example, the marketing manager, who needs a monthly expense report in order to meet sales revenue and expense objectives, may insist on the following performance criteria:

- ■ The report should be prepared in both a hardcopy and displayed form.
- ■ The report must be available no later than three days after the end of the month.
- ■ The report is to compare actual and budgeted revenue and expenses for both the recent month and year to date.

Of course, these specifications are adopted as the performance criteria only when the project team agrees that they are achievable.

5. Prepare the Design Proposal

The systems analyst provides the manager with the opportunity to make a go/no go decision concerning the next life cycle phase, just as was done at the end of the planning phase. Here, the manager must approve the design phase, and the support for that decision is included in the design proposal. A sample format for this document is included in Figure 5.7.

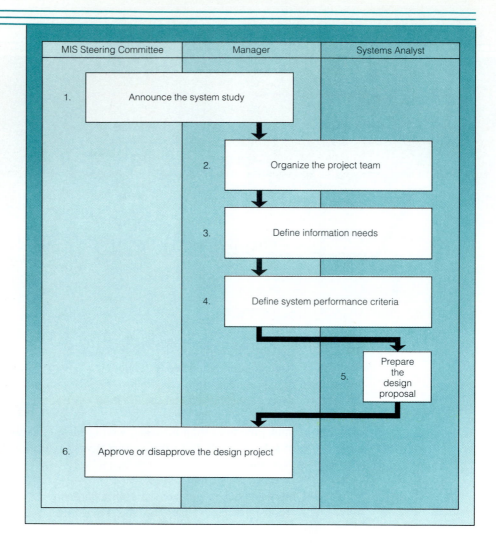

FIGURE 5.6

The Analysis Phase

proposal. Section 7 specifies the required design work, and estimates the necessary resources and their costs. Section 8 expands on the anticipated impact of the system as originally described in the study proposal. Section 9 offers a general plan for executing the two remaining development phases.

6. Approve or Disapprove the Design Project

The manager and the MIS steering committee evaluate the design proposal and determine whether to grant approval. In some cases, approval will not be granted. The team may be asked to conduct another analysis and resubmit, or the project

FIGURE 5.7

Outline of a
Design Proposal

1. Executive summary
2. Introduction
3. Problem definition
4. System objectives and constraints
5. Performance criteria
6. Possible system alternatives
7. The recommended design project
    7.1 Tasks to be performed
    7.2 Human resource requirements
    7.3 Schedule of work
    7.4 Estimated cost
8. Expected impact of the system
    8.1 Impact on the firm's organization structure
    8.2 Impact on the firm's operations
    8.3 Impact on the firm's resources
9. General development plan (design and implementation phases)
10. Summary

may be abandoned. When approval is granted, the project moves to the design phase.

THE DESIGN PHASE

With an understanding of the existing system and the requirements for the new system, the project team can address the design of the new system. **Systems design** is the determination of the processes and data that are required by a new system. When the system is computer-based, the design can include a specification of the types of equipment to be used. The steps of the design phase are pictured in Figure 5.8.

1. Prepare the Detailed System Design

The analyst works with the user, and documents the new system design with the tools that are described in Chapters 6 and 7. Table 5.2 list the more popular tools.

Some of the tools enable the analyst to prepare the documentation in a top-down manner, beginning with the big picture and gradually cranking in more detail. This top-down approach is a characteristic of **structured design**, where the design proceeds from a system to a subsystem level.

Figures 5.9 and 5.10 illustrate this top-down process. Figure 5.9 is a data flow diagram, or DFD, that shows how four data processing systems are linked by data flows—the arrows. The systems are represented by the upright rectangles. Three of these systems are also linked to the customer element in the environment.

FIGURE 5.8

The Design Phase

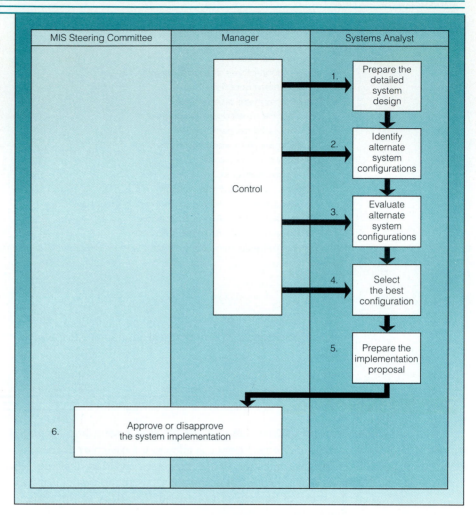

MIS Steering Committee	Manager	Systems Analyst

Control

1. Prepare the detailed system design

2. Identify alternate system configurations

3. Evaluate alternate system configurations

4. Select the best configuration

5. Prepare the implementation proposal

6. Approve or disapprove the system implementation

TABLE 5.2

Popular Documentation Tools

	Document Processes	Document Data
Graphic Tools	System Flowchart Data Flow Diagram Warnier-Orr Diagram	Entity Relationship Diagram Printer Spacing Chart Record Layout Chart Data Structure Diagram
Narrative tools	Structured English Decision Logic Table	Data Dictionary

FIGURE 5.9

A Data Flow Diagram of Four Data Processing Subsystems

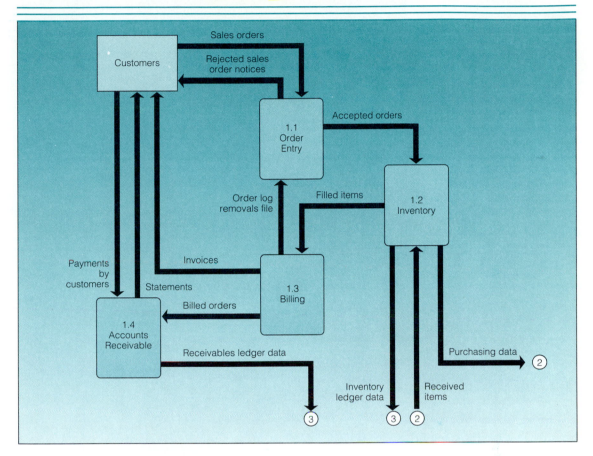

Figure 5.10 shows how one of the subsystems, order entry, is documented in greater detail. The order entry system consists of four subsystems, numbered 1.1.1 through 1.1.4. Each of these subsystems could be documented on still lower system levels.

Each of the arrows in the figures represents a data flow, and can be documented with an entry in the data dictionary. The **data dictionary** is the formal description of the contents of the firm's database. The data dictionary provides a common language for all project teams to use in describing the firm's data resource. Figure 5.11 is a data flow dictionary entry for the Sales orders data flow in Figure 5.10.

This documentation of processes and data can provide the basis for either a computer or noncomputer system. We will assume that a computer is to be used, and attention to the hardware begins in the next step.

FIGURE 5.10

A Data Flow Diagram of the Order Entry System

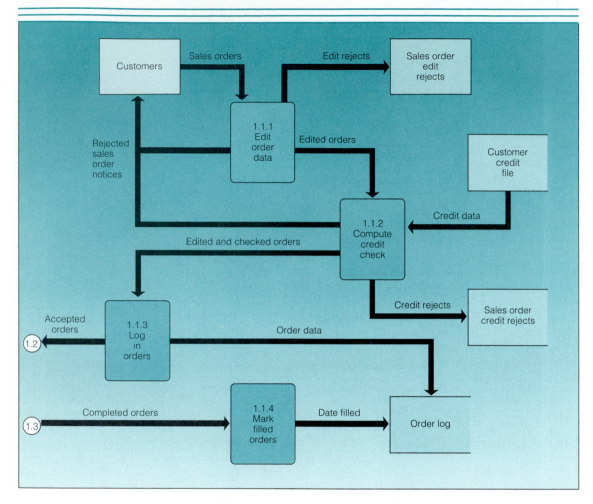

2. Identify Alternate System Configurations

The analyst now must identify the *configuration*—not the brand or model—of computing equipment that will best enable the system to accomplish the processing. The identification is a sequential process, starting with the identification of various combinations that can accomplish each task. Some combinations that might be considered for the order entry system are listed in Table 5.3.

The analyst eliminates combinations of equipment that are obviously incompatible or unacceptable. For example, a CRT terminal would not be feasible for preparing the rejected order notice since that notice is to be mailed to the customer. The analyst can thus reduce the alternatives to a reasonable number, say three or four. Table 5.4 identifies three alternatives for detailed study.

FIGURE 5.11
A Data Flow Dictionary Entry

DATA FLOW DICTIONARY ENTRY

Use: To describe each data flow in a data flow diagram.

DATA FLOW NAME: Sales orders

DESCRIPTION: The documents that are filled out by the customers to
identify the products, and the quantities of each, that
they wish to purchase.

FROM: Customers

TO: 1.1.1 Edit order data

DATA STRUCTURES: Sales order record

COMMENTS:

TABLE 5.3
Hardware Choices Make Possible Multiple System Configurations

System Elements	Alternatives
Input	CRT terminal Hardcopy terminal OCR
Order log	Magnetic tape DASD
Customer credit file	Magnetic tape DASD
Rejected orders file	Magnetic tape DASD
Accepted orders file	Magnetic tape DASD
Completed orders file	Magnetic tape DASD
Rejected orders notice	Printer CRT terminal Hardcopy terminal
Processing	Batch Online

TABLE 5.4
Alternatives Selected for Detailed Study

Alternative	Input	Order Log	Customer Credit File	Accepted and Rejected Orders Files	Completed Orders File	Rejected Orders Notice
1	CRT	Magnetic tape	DASD	Magnetic tape	Magnetic tape	Printer
2	Hardcopy terminal	DASD	DASD	Magnetic tape	Magnetic tape	Printer
3	Hardcopy terminal	DASD	DASD	DASD	Magnetic tape	Hardcopy terminal

3. Evaluate Alternate System Configurations

The analyst, working closely with the manager, evaluates the three alternatives for the order entry subsystem. The one is selected that best enables the subsystem to satisfy the performance criteria, given the constraints. Assume that the choice is Alternative 3.

The other three subsystems in Figure 5.9—inventory, billing, and accounts receivable—are evaluated in the same manner. For each, the analyst and manager identify the best configuration. Table 5.5 illustrates the possible configurations of the four subsystems.

4. Select the Best Configuration

The analyst evaluates all subsystem configurations and adjusts the device mix so that all subsystems conform to a single configuration. For example, OCR input might be replaced with CRT input for the inventory and accounts receivable subsystems. When done, the analyst presents the recommendation to the manager for approval. If the configuration is unacceptable, the analyst continues to work with the manager until agreement is reached. When the manager approves the configuration, approval by the MIS steering committee is sought.

The result of this design process is an equipment configuration, such as the one in Figure 5.12, which best enables the system to meet its objectives within its constraints. The analyst considers the needs of each subsystem, and then optimizes the configuration for the system as a whole. This system specification will be

TABLE 5.5
Comparison of Subsystem Configurations

Subsystem	Input Devices			Secondary Storage			Output Devices			
	Hardcopy Terminal	CRT Terminal	OCR	Magnetic Tape	DASD	Printer	Hardcopy Terminal	CRT Terminal	Plotter	COM
Order Entry	X			X	X		X			
Inventory	X		X		X	X	X			X
Billing				X	X					
Accounts Receivable			X		X	X		X		

FIGURE 5.12
The Selected Equipment Configuration

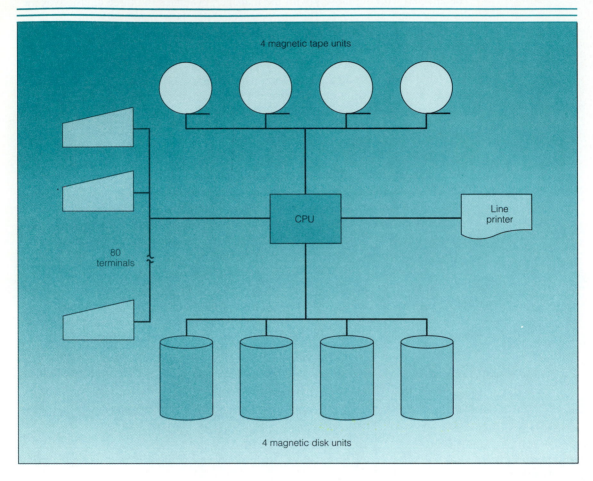

imposed in a top-down fashion when the subsystems are implemented in the implementation phase.

5. Prepare the Implementation Proposal

The analyst prepares an **implementation proposal** outlining the implementation work to be done, the expected benefits, and the costs. The format of this proposal is shown in Figure 5.13.

6. Approve or Disapprove the System Implementation

The go-ahead decision for the implementation phase is especially important, as this effort will greatly expand the number of participants to include the remaining infor-

FIGURE 5.13

Outline of an
Implementation
Proposal

1. Executive summary
2. Introduction
3. Problem definition
4. System objectives and constraints
5. Performance criteria
6. System design
   6.1 Summary description
   6.2 Equipment configuration
7. The recommended implementation project
   7.1 Tasks to be performed
   7.2 Human resource requirements
   7.3 Schedule of work
   7.4 Estimated cost
8. Expected impact of the system
   8.1 Impact on the firm's organization structure
   8.2 Impact on the firm's operations
   8.3 Impact on the firm's resources
9. General implementation plan
10. Summary

mation specialists and users. If the expected benefits from the system exceed the costs, the implementation will be approved.

THE IMPLEMENTATION PHASE

At this point, the design exists only in the form of graphic and narrative descriptions—in a hardcopy form or in the computer's storage. The name **project dictionary** is used to describe all of the documentation that is prepared during the development phases. Table 5.6 shows the contents of the project dictionary at this point. Additional documentation will be added during implementation.

Implementation is the acquisition and integration of the physical and conceptual resources that produce a working system. The tasks are shown in Figure 5.14. The two-headed arrows that connect Steps 3 through 7 show that those tasks can be carried out at the same time.

1. Plan the Implementation

At the end of the planning phase, a control mechanism was established, but it was necessarily general in nature because few details were known about the project. Now, only one development phase remains before the new system is put into use, and the managers and information specialists have a specific knowledge of the sys-

TABLE 5.6
Contents of the Project Dictionary at the End of the Design Phase

1. Problem definition
2. System objectives and constraints
3. Documentation of the current system
   3.1 Process documentation (some combination of the following)
       3.1.1 System flowchart
       3.1.2 Program flowcharts
       3.1.3 Data flow diagrams
       3.1.4 Hierarchy diagrams
       3.1.5 Warnier-Orr diagrams
       3.1.6 Structured English (Process dictionary entries)
       3.1.7 Other process documentation tools
   3.2 Data documentation
       3.2.1 Entity-relationship diagram
       3.2.1 Data dictionary entries
4. Performance criteria
5. Documentation of the new system
   5.1 Alternate feasible system configurations
   5.2 The recommended system configuration
   5.3 Process documentation (same types of documentation as section 3.1 above with the exception of program flowcharts and possibly structured English)
   5.4 Data documentation (same types of documentation as section 3.2 above)
6. General implementation plan
7. Appendix
   7.1 Transcripts of interview tapes
   7.2 Working papers
   7.3 Joint application design (JAD) session transcript

tem design. They can use this knowledge to develop a very detailed implementation plan.

2. Announce the Implementation

The implementation project is announced to the employees in much the same way as the system study. The purpose of the announcement is to inform the employees of the decision to implement the new system and to ask for their cooperation.

Some companies take an elaborate approach. For example, when Federal Express implemented the system that enables its carriers to use hand-held wands to optically scan bar codes on packages, the president announced the system by means of a videotape. The tape was shown to Federal Express employees around the world.

3. Obtain the Hardware Resources

The system design is made available to the suppliers of the types of computing equipment contained in the approved configuration. Each supplier is provided with a **request for proposal** (**RFP**), which is outlined in Figure 5.15. The RFP describes the system in a summary fashion, inviting the supplier to submit a bid.

FIGURE 5.14
The Implementation Phase

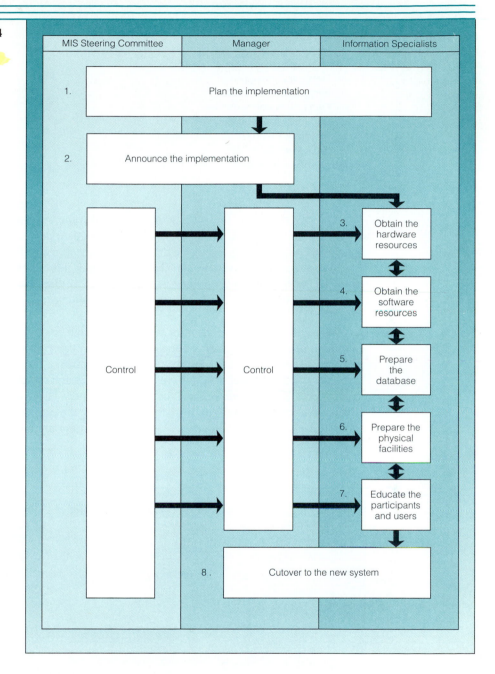

MIS Steering Committee	Manager	Information Specialists

1. Plan the implementation

2. Announce the implementation

Control

Control

3. Obtain the hardware resources

4. Obtain the software resources

5. Prepare the database

6. Prepare the physical facilities

7. Educate the participants and users

8. Cutover to the new system

FIGURE 5.15

Outline of a
Request for
Proposal

1. Letter of transmittal
2. System objectives and applicable constraints
3. System design
   a. Summary description
   b. Performance criteria
   c. Equipment configuration
   d. Summary system documentation
   e. Estimated transaction volume
   f. Estimated file sizes
4. Installation schedule

The description of the systems design enables the suppliers to select those computing units that will do the best job. The installation schedule tells the suppliers when the equipment must be delivered and made ready for use.

When suppliers choose to compete for the order, they each prepare a written **proposal**, such as the one outlined in Figure 5.16. An important section explains how the proposed equipment will enable the system to satisfy its performance criteria.

When all of the proposals have been received and analyzed, the MIS steering committee selects the supplier or suppliers. The information specialists provide support for this decision by studying the proposals and making recommendations. This is the relationship between the information specialists and the managers; the information specialists *recommend*, and the managers *decide*. If the decision is one that affects the strategic plan of the firm, the approval by the president or the executive committee might also be required. With the acquisition approved, the firm places the orders.

FIGURE 5.16

Outline of a
Supplier Proposal

1. Letter of transmittal

2. Summary of recommendations

3. Advantages

4. Equipment configuration

5. Equipment specifications
   5.1 Performance data
   5.2 Prices

6. Satisfaction of performance criteria

7. Delivery schedule

4. Obtain the Software Resources

When a firm decides to create its own application software, the programmer uses the documentation prepared by the systems analyst as the starting point. The programmer may prepare more detailed documentation, such as structured English or program flowcharts. The coding is performed, and the programs are tested. The end product is a software library of application programs.

When prewritten application software is purchased, the selection of the software supplier can involve an RFP. The selection can also come *before* the selection of the hardware supplier. This is the case when a small firm decides to implement a microcomputer to be driven entirely, or primarily, by prewritten software. The best software is selected, and then the hardware that runs the software is obtained.

5. Prepare the Database

The DBA is responsible for all data-related activity, and this includes the preparation of the database.

In some cases, it will be necessary to gather new data, and in other cases, it will be necessary to reformat existing data so that it conforms to the new system design. Those tasks are performed, and the data is entered into the database.

If the firm is not already using a database management system (DBMS), the DBA will play a key role in selecting that software. DBMS software is described in Chapter 9.

6. Prepare the Physical Facilities

When the new system requires equipment that cannot fit into existing facilities, it is necessary to engage in new contruction or remodeling. A computer room that houses a mainframe or large-scale mini is a complex combination of raised flooring, special temperature and humidity controls, security measures, fire detection and extinguishing equipment, and so on. Construction of such facilities can be a large operation and must be scheduled so that it coincides with the overall project plan.

7. Educate Participants and Users

The new system will most likely affect many people. Some will make the system work, and others will use its output. All must be educated about (1) their role in the system and (2) how the system will benefit them. This education can be aimed at members of the firm's environment, as well as the firm's own employees. It can be provided by systems analysts, personnel in other departments, or outsiders such as consultants.

The educational requirements should be specified early in the life cycle so that programs can be scheduled at the appropriate time—just before the learned material is applied.

FIGURE 5.17

Cutover
Approaches

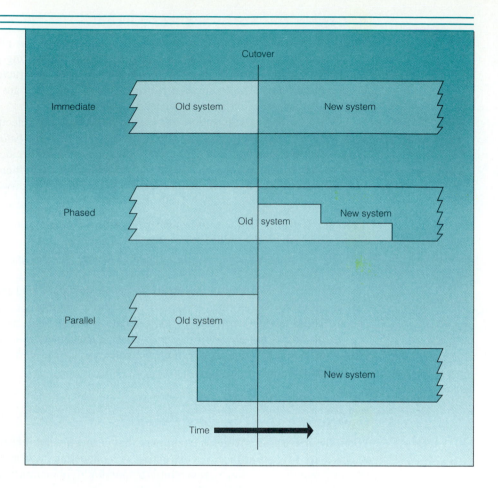

8. Cutover to the New System

The process of halting use of the old system and starting use of the new one is called **cutover**. There are three basic approaches: immediate, phased, and parallel. These approaches are illustrated in Figure 5.17.

1. **Immediate**   The simplest approach is to convert from the old system to the new one on a given day. However, this approach is feasible for only small firms or small systems, since the timing problems become greater as the scale of operation increases.

2. **Phased**   A phased cutover consists of the new system being put into use one part at a time. For example, the firm can cutover to the order entry system, followed by the inventory system, and so on. Or, cutover for all of the systems can be accomplished at one geographic location, followed

by another location, and so on. Phased cutover is popular for large-scale systems.[7]

3. **Parallel**   A parallel cutover requires that the old system be maintained until the new one is fully checked out. This approach offers the greatest security against failure, but is the most expensive, as two sets of resources must be maintained.

The cutover signals the end of the development phases, the system development life cycle. System use can now begin.

THE USE PHASE

The use phase includes the fewest number of steps, three, as shown in Figure 5.18.

1. Use the System

Users use the system to meet the objectives that were identified in the planning phase.

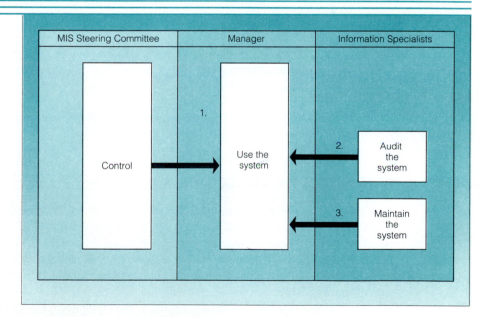

FIGURE 5.18

The Use Phase

[7] The term **pilot** is used to describe a trial system. If the trial succeeds, the system is implemented on an overall basis. Some persons regard the pilot as a fourth type of cutover. We regard it as the first phase of a phased cutover.

2. Audit the System

After the new system has had a chance to settle down, a formal study is conducted to determine how well it is satisfying the performance criteria. Such a study is called a **postimplementation review** and can be conducted by someone from information services or by an internal auditor. In some cases both will conduct separate reviews. The results of the audit are reported to the CIO, to the MIS steering committee, and to the user. This process is repeated, perhaps on a yearly basis, for as long as system use continues.

3. Maintain the System

During the time the manager uses the system, modifications are made so that the system continues to provide the needed support. These modifications are called **systems maintenance** and can account for a large portion of the information services staff time. Systems maintenance is performed for three reasons:

1. **To correct errors** System use uncovers bugs in the programs or weakneses in the design, which were not detected in system testing. These errors are corrected.
2. **To keep systems current** Over time, changes occur in the system's environment, which require modifications in the design or software. For example, the federal government changes the formula for computing social security tax.
3. **To improve the systems** As managers use the systems, they see ways to make improvements. These suggestions are passed along to the information specialists, who modify the systems accordingly.

At some point, modifications to a system will be such that it is best to start over. Then, the life cycle is repeated.

RAPID APPLICATION DEVELOPMENT

The system life cycle represents the classical way to implement computer-based systems and has provided the basic guideline for thousands of systems projects. However, it is becoming more and more difficult for firms to follow the deliberate, sequential pattern. Information specialists are spread thin, with demands for both the development of new systems and the maintenance of an ever-increasing volume of existing systems.

Information specialists have turned to the computer for help in solving workload problems. Two innovations hold special promise that future demands for systems development and maintenance can be met. Those innovations are CASE and prototyping, and they can be implemented separately, jointly, or as elements in a comprehensive approach called rapid application development.

CASE Tools

The acronym **CASE** stands for **computer-aided software engineering**, and includes software products that are used in developing and maintaining computer-based systems.

The original goal of CASE was to relieve information specialists of much of the time-consuming work that is involved in design, implementation, and maintenance. This goal has been accomplished by tools that are used in preparing documentation of systems processes and data, and in generating computer code. The data flow diagrams in Figures 5.9 and 5.10 were drawn with the Excelerator CASE tool.

More recently, CASE tools have been developed, which can be used in the planning and analysis phases. Today, it is possible for the entire SLC to be supported by CASE. The term **I-CASE**, for **integrated CASE tool** describes a tool that supports the entire SLC. An important feature of an I-CASE tool is its ability to generate executable computer code from the documentation. Texas Instrument's Information Engineering Facility (IEF), and Andersen Consulting's DESIGN-1 are examples of I-CASE tools.

With the entire SLC supported by CASE, some of the implementation and maintenance workload is shifted forward in the life cycle to the planning, analysis, and design phases. This shift is shown in Figure 5.19.

Prototyping

System developers are now using the same approach in creating computer-based systems, which has been followed by design engineers of products such as automobiles. This approach is called **prototyping** and involves the use of a working model of the final product to aid in the design process. The working model, or **prototype**, is shown to the user for the purpose of obtaining feedback. The user makes suggestions for improvement, and the designers incorporate those suggestions into an improved prototype. This cycle is repeated until the system is acceptable to the user.

Prototyping is made possible by a variety of software tools that enable the information specialists to quickly prepare systems models. Examples of such tools are fourth-generation languages such as FOCUS and SQL, database management systems such as Rbase, code generators such as Telon, and certain CASE tools such as Excelerator.

Rapid Application Development and Its Enterprise Framework[8]

Rapid application development (**RAD**) is the term coined by James Martin, computer consultant and author, for a development life cycle designed to give much faster development and higher-quality results than with the traditional SLC.

[8] This section is based on James Martin, *Rapid Application Development* (New York: Macmillan, 1991).

FIGURE 5.19
CASE Can Change the Distribution of the SLC Workload

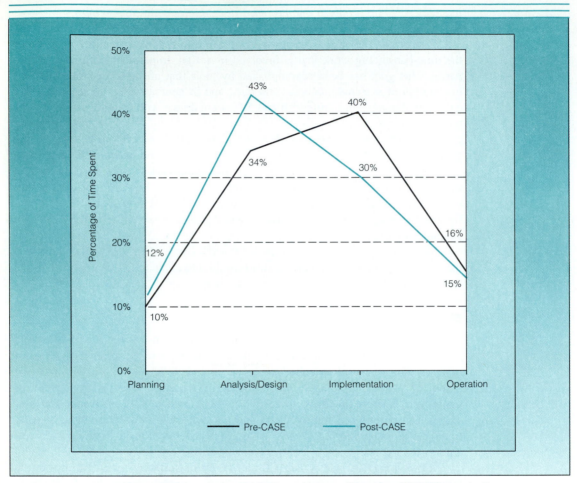

Source: Marcus Loh, and R. Ryan Nelson, "Reaping CASE Harvests,"
Datamation 35 (July 1, 1989): 31.

RAD is an integrated set of strategies, methodologies, and tools, which exist within an overall framework called information engineering. **Information engineering (IE)** is another one of Martin's concepts, which treats systems development as a firm-wide activity. The term **enterprise** is used to describe the entire firm. In IE, computer-based tools such as I-CASE are used to develop systems, and the documentation is maintained in the computer in the form of a repository.

IE begins at the executive level, with strategic information resources planning applied to the entire enterprise. Martin uses the term **information strategy planning (ISP)** to describe SPIR. Next, each business unit within the firm is subjected

FIGURE 5.20

Rapid Application Development Is an Integral Part of Information Engineering

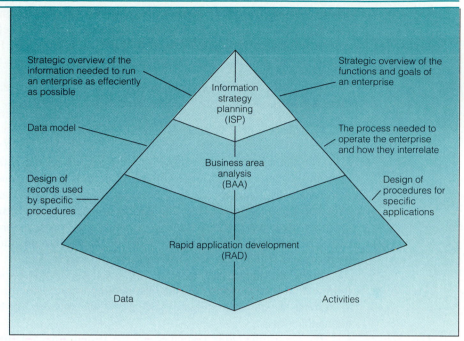

to what Martin calls **business area analysis** (**BAA**) to define the activities or processes and data that are necessary for the unit to function as intended. With the BAA completed, rapid application development can proceed. Figure 5.20 shows the relationships among ISP, BAA, and RAD in terms of both data and activities.

The Essential Ingredients of RAD

RAD requires four essential ingredients—management, people, methodologies, and tools.

Management   Ideally, management, especially top management, should be **experimenters,** who like to do things a new way, or **early adapters,** who quickly learn how to use new methodologies. Management should exude excitement concerning RAD, and should provide a work environment that makes the RAD activity as enjoyable as possible.

People   Rather than utilize a single team to perform all SLC activities, RAD recognizes the efficiencies that can be achieved through the use of several specialized teams. There can be teams for requirements planning, user design, construction, user review, and cutover. Members of these teams are masters of the methodologies and tools that are required to perform their specialized tasks.

Methodologies The basic RAD methodology is the RAD life cycle that consists of four phases: (1) requirements planning, (2) user design, (3) construction, and (4) cutover. These phases, like the traditional SLC, reflect the systems approach. Users play key roles in each phase, participating in JAD sessions with information specialists.

Tools RAD tools consist mainly of I-CASE and fourth-generation languages that facilitate prototyping and code generation.

Putting IE, RAD, and the SLC in Perspective

RAD, or a similar concept, is obviously the desired approach to system development in the future. The growing volume of systems development and maintenance work demands computer-based techniques. At present, RAD and IE are leading edge approaches but are being followed by a relatively few firms. Most firms do not have the necessary resources. Overcoming this resources problem will not be easy. The methodologies and tools can be bought and learned, but enlightened management and skilled personnel will be more difficult to acquire.

In the meantime, the traditional SLC provides the framework that most firms follow. Both RAD and the SLC are methodologies that apply the systems approach to systems development. Figure 5.21 shows the relationship between the three methodologies.

For almost the entire computer era, the system life cycle has been one of the fundamental types of knowledge that all information specialists should possess. Managers who become involved in end-user computing should also possess that same knowledge. As the use of computer-based development tools become more commonplace, a knowledge of the RAD life cycle and an ability to function within that cycle will also become critical.

SUMMARY

The evolution of a computer system follows a pattern that is called the system life cycle. The first four phases include planning, analysis, design, and implementation, and are devoted to development. The term system development life cycle is often used for these four phases. The fifth phase is the use phase.

Users can perform all of the life cycle tasks when they engage in end-user computing, but information specialists can do a lion's share of the work when their special skills are required. Users are represented by their manager, and an internal auditor often lends additional, specialized assistance.

Responsibility for life cycle management can reside on several organizational levels, beginning with the president, and including other executives, the executive committee, the MIS steering committee, and project leaders.

The manager engages in planning with the intent of achieving benefits later in the project. The systems analyst helps the manager define the problem, set objectives, and recognize constraints, and then conducts a feasibility study. When appropriate, the DBA and network specialist are members of the team. The feasibility

FIGURE 5.21

The SLC and RAD Are Both Applications of the Systems Approach

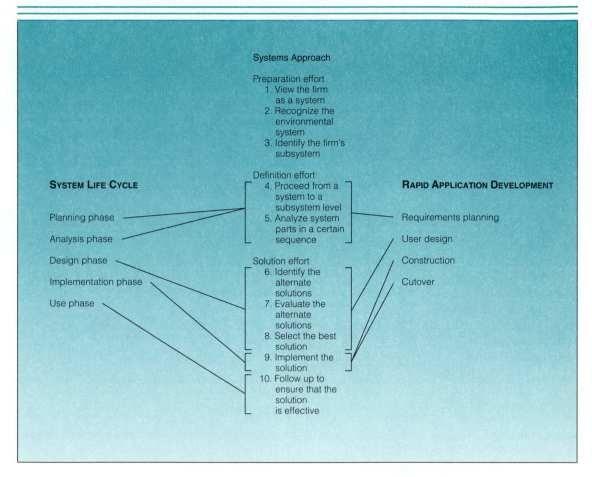

study provides the basis for a proposal to continue. The MIS steering committee and manager decide whether the project merits continuation. This go/no go decision is made at the end of each life cycle phase. A decision to proceed signals the need for the participants to establish a control mechanism.

The analysis phase is inaugurated by an announcement to the employees, and the formation of a project team. The next steps are crucial—where the users define their information needs and specify the performance criteria. The analyst prepares a design proposal, which provides the justification for designing the new system.

The design phase begins with the analyst engaging in detailed system design, using structured techniques and tools that document both processes and data. Alternate system configurations are identified and evaluated, and the best one is selected. An implementation proposal gives management the basis for creating a working system from the design documentation.

The implementation phase involves the remaining information specialists, additional users, and perhaps outsiders such as consultants and contractors. After detailed planning and an announcement, hardware and software are obtained, and the database is created. When the physical facilities are ready and the necessary education has been conducted, cutover to the new system can occur.

Shortly after the beginning of the use phase, the systems analyst and internal auditor conduct postimplementation reviews, which are repeated on a periodic basis throughout the life of the system. Information specialists also perform maintenance.

Although the system life cycle represents the basic format of systems work, it is being subjected to change by other methodologies that stress the use of computer-based development tools. Rapid application development is one such methodology, and it incorporates both CASE and prototyping.

KEY TERMS

MIS steering committee	systems design
project leader	implementation
feasibility study	request for proposal (RFP)
system study	cutover
go/no go decision	postimplementation review
person month	systems maintenance
network diagram	computer-aided software engineering (CASE)
systems analysis	prototyping
performance criteria	

KEY CONCEPTS

System life cycle (SLC)

System development life cycle (SDLC)

The joint involvement of managers, users, and information specialists in SLC activity and management

The opportunity for management to make a go/no go decision at the conclusion of each SLC phase

The way that the general estimates made early in the life cycle are made more detailed as additional information is learned

Structured design

How serial activity characterizes all of the phases except implementation, where many jobs are being done at the same time

Information engineering (IE)

Rapid application development (RAD)

The SLC and RAD as applications of the systems approach

QUESTIONS

1. What is the difference between the SLC and the SDLC?

2. Why do people other than the information specialists make the important decisions during the SLC?

3. What functions does the MIS steering committee perform?

4. Why do managers plan?

5. Who typically recognizes problems?

6. Where do system constraints originate?

7. What is the difference between a feasibility study and a system study?

8. What are the six types of feasibility? Place an asterisk next to the one that relates to the project rather than the system.

9. When the MIS steering committee decides whether to authorize the analysis phase, what two questions do they ask?

10. Which SLC phases include announcements to employees? What is the purpose of each announcement?

11. What has proven to be the most effective way for the analyst to determine the users' information needs?

12. What is the relationship between structured design and levels of systems?

13. How does the selection of the best system configuration relate to the systems approach?

14. How can the decision to purchase prewritten software affect the order in which decisions relating to hardware and software are made?

15. Which of the following activities can go on at the same time: Programming, database preparation, construction of physical facilities, education?

16. Name the three types of cutover. Which is feasible only for a small system or organization? Which offers the greatest security against failure?

17. Who conducts postimplementation reviews? Exactly when are they conducted?

18. What creates a need for systems maintenance?

19. What effect is CASE having on the SLC?

20. Explain how prototyping is used in defining the user's information needs.

21. What is the relationship between SPIR and IE?

22. What are the essential ingredients of RAD?

TOPICS FOR DISCUSSION

1. What is the relationship between the MIS steering committee and IRM?

2. At what points in the SLC does the manager have an opportunity to make a go/no go decision?

3. What does a network diagram tell you that a simple list of the activities does not? Use Table 5.1 and Figure 5.5 as examples.

4. Explain the connection between system objectives and performance criteria.

PROBLEMS

1. Assume that you have been asked by your boss to prepare a list of suppliers of printers for microcomputers. Your boss will send each one an RFP. Go to the library and conduct a review of popular microcomputer publications, identifying the names and addresses of the companies that appear to be good sources. The publications often have special issues or articles on certain categories of hardware and software. Report your findings in a memo. Your instructor will advise you concerning the format.

2. Repeat Problem 1, only assume that your boss wants to obtain a graphics package for an IBM PC.

CASE PROBLEM

Epic Publications

Karen and Alice became close friends at Epic, a company that publishes trade magazines. Karen works in the finance department, and Alice in information systems. One day, they are having a Coke in the snack bar.

KAREN: Did you ever finish that project you were working on in advertising?

ALICE: We finally wrapped that up last week. It was a long one; we were on it for over a year.

KAREN: I know it was a long time. Why does it take so long to implement a computer system?

ALICE: Well, there is just so much to do, and so many people are involved. We call it the system life cycle, or SLC. Sometimes they last much longer. Why do you ask?

KAREN: Well, I've been thinking. You know, I learned Lotus in school but never used it since. We have it on the hard disk of the computer that is in my section. I've been thinking about using it to develop the budget.

ALICE: Oh, I think that's a great idea. Do you want me to help out?

KAREN: No, I would like to try it myself—end-user computing. I do remember that term. But, I am a little fuzzy on how to go about it. Could you give me a hand in planning what steps I should take? Will my SLC, as you call it, be any different from the one that you followed with advertising?

ALICE: Sure. Let me make some notes and I'll get back with you at break tomorrow.

Assignment

Prepare a list of steps that Karen should take. Subdivide the list into the SDLC phases and number each step. Keep in mind that Karen will do all of the work herself and knows Lotus and how to use the computer.

SELECTED BIBLIOGRAPHY

Bersoff, Edward H., and Davis, Alan M. "Impacts of Life Cycle Models on Software Configuration Management." *Communications of the ACM* 34 (August 1991): 104–18.

Chandra, Satish, and Menezes, Dennis. "An Examination of the Software Development Backlog Problem." *Journal of Information Technology Management* 2 (Number 3, 1991): 1–7.

Doll, William J., and Torkzadeh, Golamreza. "The Relationship of MIS Steering Committees to Size of Firm and Formalization of MIS Planning." *Communications of the ACM* 30 (November 1987): 972–78.

"EDGE's Guide to Project Management Software." *EDGE* 3 (January/February 1990): 40–43.

Forte, Gene, and Norman, Ronald J. "CASE: A Self-Assessment by the Software Engineering Community." *Communications of the ACM* 35 (April 1992): 28–32.

Gavurin, Stuart L. "Where Does Prototyping Fit In IS Development?" *Journal of Systems Management* 42 (February 1991): 13–17.

Gerlach, James H., and Kuo, Feng-Yang. "Understanding Human Computer Interaction for Information Systems Design." *MIS Quarterly* 15 (December 1991), 527–49.

Gupta, Yash P., and Raghunathan, T. S. "Impact of Information Systems (IS) Steering Committees on IS Planning." *Decision Sciences* 20 (Fall, 1989): 777–93.

Henderson, John C. "Managing the IS Design Environment." *Sloan School of Management Working Paper No. 1897–87*. Cambridge, MA: Massachusetts Institute of Technolgy, May 1987.

Hollist, Pen, and Utterback, Jon. "The CASE-Project Management Connection." *System Builder* 4 (April/May 1991): 39–42.

Klein, Gary, and Beck, Philip O. "A Decision Aid for Selecting Among Information System Alternatives." *MIS Quarterly* 11 (June 1987): 177–85.

Li, Eldon Y. "Software Testing In a System Development Process: A Life Cycle Perspective." *Journal of Systems Management* 41 (August 1990): 23–31.

Loh, Marcus, and Nelson, R. Ryan. "Reaping CASE Harvests." *Datamation* 35 (July 1, 1989): 31*ff.*

Marks, William W. "Successful Project Management Means Business Management." *System Builder* 4 (April/May 1991): 45*ff.*

Mashaw, Bijan, and Casey, Salley D. 1990. "An Assessment of the Phases of the System Life Cycle." In *Proceedings 1990 Annual Meeting Decision Sciences Institute,* ed. Betty Whitten and James Gilbert, 1026–29. San Diego, CA.

McCusker, Tom. "Tools to Manage Big Projects." *Datamation* 37 (January 15, 1991): 71*ff.*

Nolan, Richard L. "Managing Information Systems by Committee." *Harvard Business Review* 60 (July–August 1982): 72–79.

Palvia, Prashant, and Nosek, John T. "An Empirical Evaluation of System Development Methodologies." *Information Resources Management Journal* 3 (Summer 1990): 23–32.

Palvia, Shailendra, and Palvia, Prashant. "Timing Strategies for Feasibility Studies in Information Systems Development." *Information Resources Management Journal* 3 (Winter 1990): 15–27.

Stevens, W. P.; Myers, G. J.; and Constantine, L. L. "Structured Design." *IBM Systems Journal* 2 (Number 2, 1974): 115–39.

Vessey, Iris; Jarvenpaa, Sirkka L.; and Tractinsky, Noam. "Evaluation of Vendor Products: CASE Tools as Methodology Companions." *Communications of the ACM* 35 (April 1992): 90–105.

Wedberg, George H. "But First, Understand the Problem." *Journal of Systems Management* 41 (June 1990): 20–28.

Willis, T. Hillman, and Tesch, Debbie B. "An Assessment of Systems Development Methodologies." *Journal of Information Technology Management* 2 (Number 2, 1991): 39–45.

Winkler, Connie. "Better Project Management in Uncertain Times." *Datamation* 36 (June 1, 1990): 95–98.

Yourdon, Edward, and Constantine, Larry L. *Structured Design: Fundamentals of a Discipline of Computer Program and Systems Design.* Englewood Cliffs, NJ: Prentice-Hall, 1979.

Chapter 6

Tools of Systems Planning and Analysis

 LEARNING OBJECTIVES

After studying this chapter, you should:

- Know how to prepare a network diagram that can be used to plan and control a system development project
- Know how to document the processes of a system using data flow diagrams and structured English
- Know how to document the data of a system using a set of data dictionary forms
- Be familiar with how a popular CASE tool, Excelerator, can be used in system documentation

INTRODUCTION

The system life cycle provides the main framework for systems development projects. Within those projects, developers use a variety of tools. The tools can be used in all four developmental phases and also in the use phase when the system is maintained.

The last step of the planning phase consists of the building of a control mechanism. One of the most effective tools for planning and controlling a complex project such as system development is the network diagram. The network diagram shows the interrelationships among the activities and identifies the path through the network that is most crucial to meeting the completion date for the project. Network diagrams come in two varieties—critical path method (or CPM), and program evaluation and review technique (or PERT). Software-based project management systems can be used to draw and maintain the network diagrams.

During the analysis phase, the task is to learn about the current system—its processes and data. As the analyst acquires this knowledge, the processes can be documented using a series of data flow diagrams, or DFDs, plus structured English. In a like manner, the data can be documented using data dictionary entry forms.

Computer-aided software enginnering, or CASE, tools can be used to prepare and maintain documentation of all system life cycle phases.

NETWORK ANALYSIS

Henri Fayol's management functions begin with planning and end with controlling. Planning is the key to all the other functions, including controlling. In fact, the planning provides the basis for the controlling. A manager cannot control unless there is a standard of desired performance, and the plan provides this standard.

Planning and controlling also play a big role in the development and use of a computer-based information system. As the final step of the planning phase of the system life cycle, the MIS steering committee, the manager, and the systems analyst establish a control mechanism that can be used for the remainder of the project.

Elements of a Control Mechanism

Most likely, the mechanism that management uses to control a computer system project will include multiple elements such as:

- A *plan* that identifies what is to be done, who will do it, and when it will be done.
- *Weekly progress reports* prepared by the systems analyst or project leader, and made available to the manager of the user area and the MIS steering committee
- *Scheduled weekly meetings* of the participants to discuss progress during the previous week and objectives for the coming week

FIGURE 6.1

A Gantt Chart of a System Study

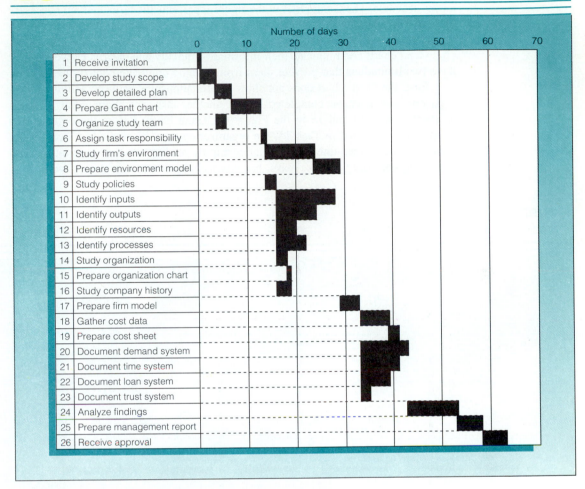

■ *Presentation graphics* that are used in group meetings to communicate project status, and serve as a guide of the discussion

A well-controlled project will contain all of these elements.

Gantt Charts

The basic task in preparing a graphic description of a project is to show how the activities will be performed over time. This can be accomplished quite simply with a type of bar chart called a Gantt chart. Figure 6.1 is an example of a Gantt chart, named after Harry L. Gantt, a management scientist, who plied his trade around the turn of this century.

In a **Gantt chart** the tasks to be performed are listed down the left-hand side, and the activity is depicted as horizontal bars. The bars are arranged according to a time schedule. The Gantt chart in the figure represents the tasks that are necessary to study the operations of a bank and prepare a management report. According to the chart, the project will require over sixty days to complete.

Gantt charts communicate their information quickly and clearly. However, they have two limitations that prevent them from being a complete control mechanism.

First, the Gantt chart does not show interrelationships between activities. Perhaps one task must be completed before another task can begin. That situation exists for Tasks 14 and 15 in the Figure 6.1 Gantt chart. Before the organization chart can be prepared in Task 15, the organization must be studied in Task 14. Of course, you could assume such a relationship by reading the task descriptions and examining the bars for those tasks, but this technique does not always work.

FIGURE 6.2

A Network Diagram of a System Study

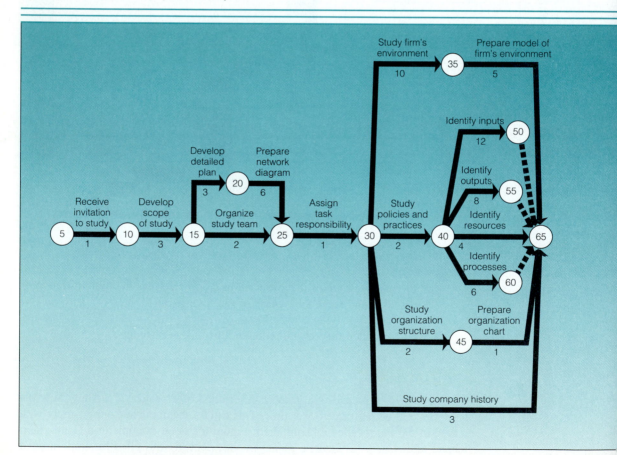

The second limitation is that the Gantt chart does not identify those tasks that are especially critical to the accomplishment of the project schedule. In a project consisting of a large number of tasks, there are usually a few that are key. They must be done when they are supposed to be done, otherwise the whole schedule is thrown off.

Network Diagrams

Both limitations of the Gantt chart are overcome in a network diagram. A **network diagram** is a drawing that uses arrows to represent tasks, and the arrows are linked to show the relationships between the tasks. Figure 6.2 is a network diagram of the same tasks that are illustrated with the Gantt chart.

Activities   The name **activity** is used to describe each task. Each activity is labeled with a brief description of the work to be done (above the arrow), and an

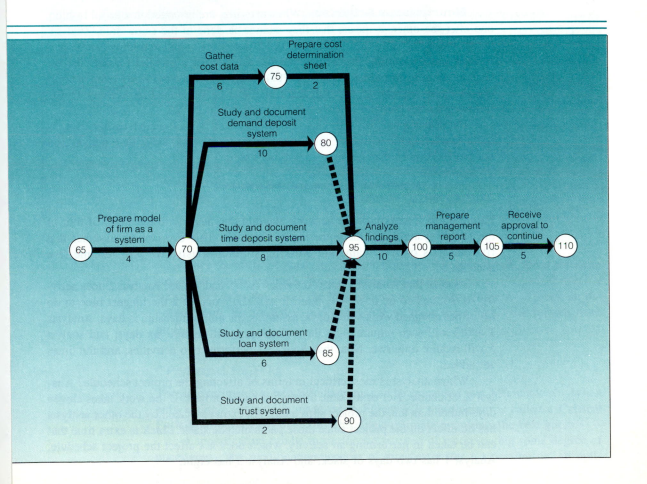

FIGURE 6.4

The Critical Path for the System Study

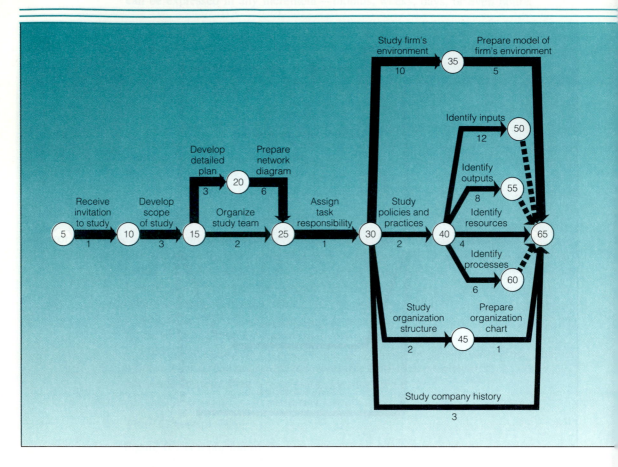

mistic, and a most likely. With this modification, the diagram becomes a **PERT**, **Program Evaluation and Review Technique**, chart. Figure 6.5 shows the earlier network diagram in PERT chart form.

Any formula can be used to incorporate the three PERT chart estimates, but the one below is very popular:

$$\text{Activity time} = \frac{P + 4L + O}{6}$$

$$\text{Where: } P = \text{Pessimistic time}$$
$$L = \text{Most likely time}$$
$$O = \text{Optimistic time}$$

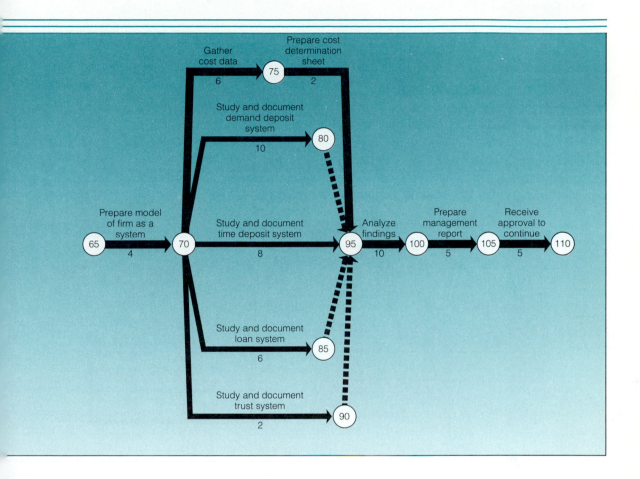

For example, if the pessimistic time is 2 days, the most likely is 5, and the optimistic is 6, the PERT time is 4.7 days. The PERT time is slightly less than the most likely time, reflecting the influence of the pessimistic time.

Putting the Network Diagram in Perspective

When management decides to use a network diagram to control a project, it is first necessary to identify the tasks to be performed and to estimate the time required for each. Then, the data is entered into a software system that prepares the diagram and determines the critical path.

Each week, the MIS steering committee meets to review the project progress,

FIGURE 6.5
A PERT Chart

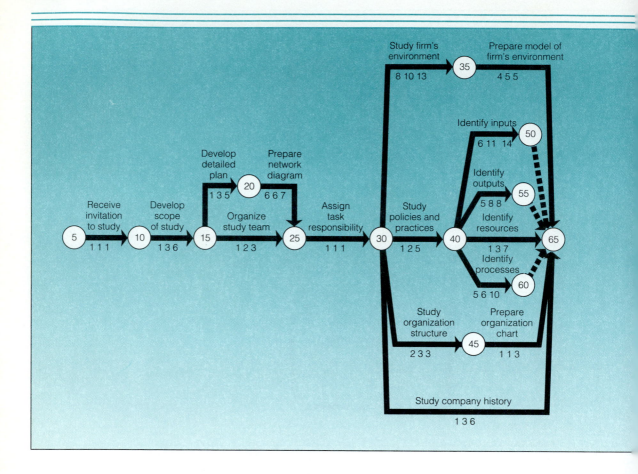

and the network diagram provides the basis for the discussion. The analyst and manager report actual time that has been taken, and this time is compared with the estimated time. Management can see when activities take more time than planned, or less, and can see the effect on the project schedule. New estimates can be made to reflect the changes, and a new diagram can be prepared.

As the project unfolds, new activities may be added, reflecting the more detailed knowledge of the work to be done. For example, as the project enters the implementation phase, activities may be arrayed in a much more detailed manner than when the diagram was first prepared.

The network diagram provides the project leader with an effective way to communicate project status to mangement and to the members of the project team.

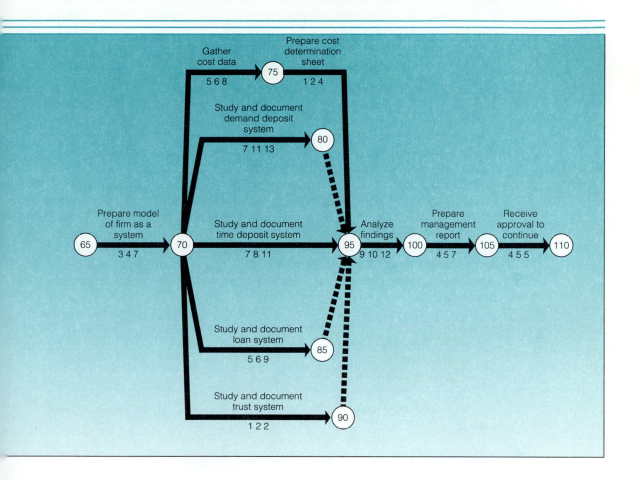

DATA FLOW DIAGRAMS[1]

A **data flow diagram (DFD)** is a graphic documentation tool that uses a small number of symbols to illustrate how data flows through interconnected processes. Although the name implies an emphasis on the data, the situation is just the opposite; the emphasis is on the processes.

A DFD is perhaps the most natural way to document processes. If you were interviewing someone to learn about a system, you would likely sketch the details

[1] This description is derived from Edward Yourdon, *Modern Structured Analysis* (Englewood Cliffs, NJ: Yourdon Press, 1989), 139–87.

on a note pad as the person talked. You would draw circles to represent processing steps, and enter a brief description of each. You would link the circles with arrows to show how the output from one process provides the input for another. This is essentially the form of a DFD.

A Part of a Top-down Tool Set

In Chapter 5, we summarized structured design by illustrating its top-down format. A point that we did not make was the fact that systems design is not the only activity that can be accomplished in a top-down manner. In fact, structured programming was the first application of the technique. Structured programming was accepted so well that it was followed by structured analysis, structured design, structured testing, and structured implementation.

In **structured analysis**, attention is initially focused on understanding the overall system, and then on successively lower systems levels. At each system level, the analyst documents both the processes and the data.

Data flow diagramming is best suited for documenting system processes at the higher and middle levels of the systems hierarchy. Other tools must be used to document both the processes and data on the lower, detail level. Structured English serves this purpose in terms of the processes, and the data dictionary is effective for the data.

Therefore, a popular combination of documentation tools consists of:

- Data flow diagramming
- Structured English
- Data dictionary

With these three tools, you can completely document a system's processes and data.

The Role of DFDs in Analysis and Design

DFDs are excellent for documenting existing systems during systems analysis, but they are also just as good for documenting new systems during systems design. In fact, *all* of the systems documentation tools can be used in *both* systems analysis *and* systems design. That capability is not clear in the organization of this text. We discuss some tools dealing with analysis in this chapter, and dealing with design in the next. Some tools are more suitable for one life cycle activity than another, and such suitability differences have influenced the content of these two chapters. However, the tools are flexible enough to be used at any point in the SLC.

DFD Symbols

DFDs consist of only four symbols. The symbols are used to represent: (1) environmental elements with which the system interfaces, (2) processes, (3) data flows, and (4) storage of data.

Environmental Elements   Environmental elements exist outside the boundary of the system. These elements provide the system with data input and receive its data output. In a DFD, no distinction is made between data and information. All of the flows are regarded as data.

The name **terminator** is used to describe the environmental elements, as they mark the points where the system terminates. A terminator is represented in a DFD with a square or a rectangle. Each terminator symbol is labeled with the name of the environmental element.

A terminator can be:

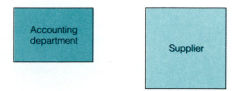

- A *person*, such as a manager, who receives a report from the system
- An *organization*, such as another department within the company, or another company
- *Another system* with which our system interfaces

An important task in systems analysis and design is the definition of the system boundary. The terminators serve this purpose. The problem solver works within the boundary and establishes linkages with the system's environment in the form of data flows.

Processes   A **process** is something that transforms input into output. It can be illustrated with a circle, a rectangle, or a rectangle with rounded corners. Each process symbol is identified with a label. The most common labeling technique is to use a *verb and an object*, but you can also use the name of a *computer program*.

Data Flows   A **data flow** consists of a group of data elements that travel from one point or process to another. Think of a data flow as *data on the move*. The arrow symbol is used to illustrate the data flows in a DFD; the arrows can be drawn with either straight or curved lines.

The amount of data represented by a single data flow can vary from a single data element to one or more files. An example of a data flow consisting of a single element is a response to a manager's query of the database to obtain last month's total profit figure.

A data flow consists of one or more data structures. A **structure** is a group of data elements that describe a particular item or transaction. It is easiest to think of a structure as the arrangement of data elements that comprise a *record*, or as a line of elements printed on a document.

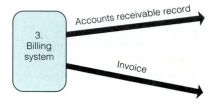

Data flows can *diverge* when the same data travels to multiple locations in the system.

Data flows can also *converge* to show several identical data flows that travel to a single location.

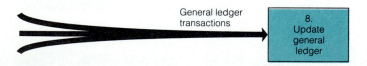

Sometimes, the system design will call for a *two-way flow*. Perhaps a manager enters a query to obtain an order status, and the system responds with the requested information. This can be illustrated with a single, two-headed arrow.

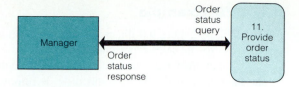

Or, two arrows can be used.

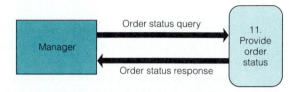

The term *data in motion* is a good way to describe a data flow, since the data moves from one point in the system to another.

Data Storage   When it becomes necessary to hold data for some reason, a data store is used. In DFD terminology, a **data store is a repository of data.** Think of a data store as *data at rest*.

You have the choice of illustrating a data store with a set of parallel lines, an open-ended rectangle, or an oval.

Data stores are incorporated into systems for two purposes. First, they satisfy a *user requirement*. The user specifies that a certain store be maintained. For example, a manager says: "I want to keep the sales orders on file for three years."

The second purpose of a store is to satisfy an *implementation requirement*. You use a store in order to implement the system. For example, assume that a manager specifies that a monthly payroll report is to summarize all of the weekly transactions. You realize that you must create a store of weekly payroll files. Records are added to the store as the weekly payrolls are computed. At the end of the month, the store provides the data for the monthly report.

The process of drawing a DFD is simply one of identifying the processes, linking them with data flows to show relationships, identifying the terminators that provide input and receive output, and adding data stores where needed.

A DFD Example

The DFD in Figure 6.6 illustrates a system that a firm might use to compute commissions for its sales representatives.

A customer fills out a sales order and mails it to the company. In Process 1 the mail is opened, and the sales order is removed. The data from the sales order is entered into the information processor in Process 2. After the data has been entered, the sales order forms are filed away for safekeeping in the Sales Order Form file. In Process 3, the sales order data is sorted into a particular sequence. The sorted records are then used in Process 4 to prepare a sales commission report for the sales manager.

The sales commission system has two terminators. The first, the customer, is a person or an organization outside the firm. The second, the sales manager, is a person within the firm.

There is one feature of Figure 6.6 that you should note. The output from Process 3 is a file of sorted records. Even though it is a file, the data store symbol is not used. In this situation, the file is not data at rest. Rather, it is data in motion. It connects Process 3 to Process 4. For this reason, the file is diagrammed as a data flow.

The DFD Does Not Show Processing Technology

You cannot determine from a DFD whether it describes a manual system or one that includes some type of labor-saving device, such as a computer. For example, a computer may be used in Process 4 of Figure 6.6, but you cannot be certain. In recognizing this characteristic to treat both processes and data in a generic way, we say that the DFD is **nonhardware specific**.

This characteristic makes the DFD an excellent tool for documenting an existing system. In performing this task, the analyst is more concerned with *what* the system does than *how* it does it.

The DFD Documents Processes and Data in Nondetailed Way

In the same fashion, The DFD does not reveal the detailed computations and logic that are included within the processes, nor the records and data elements that are included in files. As an example, you do not know exactly what data is entered from the sales order in Process 2 of Figure 6.6.

Structured English or some other tool provides the processing detail, and the data dictionary provides the data detail.

Leveled Data Flow Diagrams

Figure 6.6 identifies the major processes of the system, and it is called a **Figure 0 diagram**. Each of the processes is labeled with a single-digit number in addition to its name.

FIGURE 6.6

A Data Flow
Diagram of a
Sales Commission
System

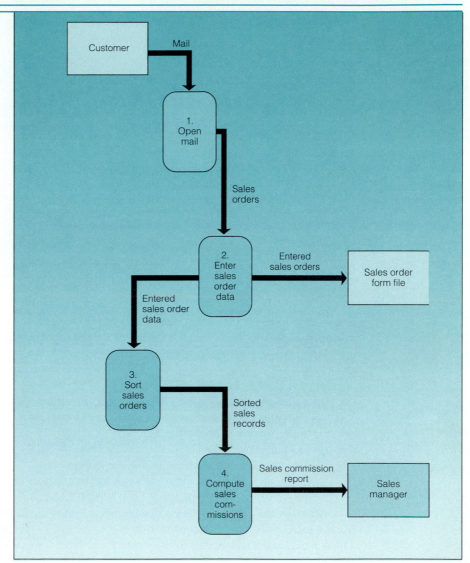

It is possible to use additional DFDs to achieve documentation at both a more summary and a more detail level. A diagram that documents the system at a more summary level is called a context diagram, and a diagram that provides more detail is called a Figure *n* diagram.

The Context Diagram The **context diagram** positions the system in an environmental context. The diagram consists of a single process symbol that rep-

FIGURE 6.7

Context Diagram
of a Sales
Commission
System

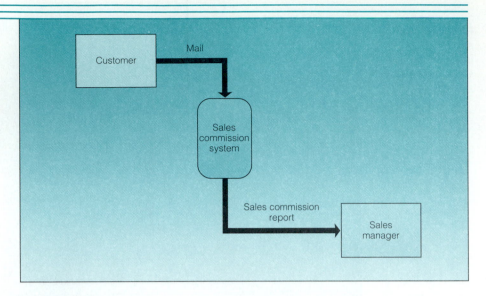

resents the entire system, and it shows the data flows leading to and from the terminators. Figure 6.7 is a context diagram of the sales commission system.

When drawing a context diagram, you:

1. Use only a single process symbol.
2. Label the process symbol to represent the entire system. You can use a verb plus object such as "Process sales commissions," or you can use the system name as in the figure.
3. Do not number the single process symbol.
4. Include all of the terminators for the system.
5. Show all of the data flows between the terminators and the system.

Although the context diagram documents a system at the highest level, it is usually easier to begin the documentation at a lower level—say, the Figure 0 level. The context diagram is easiest to draw when you have a specific idea of what the system does.

Figure *n* Diagrams When it is necessary to document the system in greater detail than the Figure 0 diagram, you use one or more Figure *n* diagrams. A **Figure *n* diagram** documents a single process of a DFD in a greater amount of detail. The *n* represents the process number. Take the sales commission system in Figure 6.6, for example. Processes 1, 2, and 3 are documented in sufficient detail, however, Process 4 represents two processes—compute the commission amounts and accumulate the totals. You may want to show that detail in a lower-level DFD.

Figure 6.8 shows a **Figure 4 diagram**. It explodes process 4 of the Figure 0 diagram, making it a Figure 4 diagram. If you document process 4.1 in still more

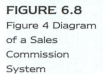

FIGURE 6.8

Figure 4 Diagram of a Sales Commission System

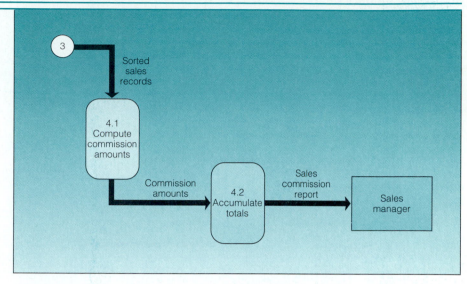

detail, you draw another Figure n diagram, called a Figure 4.1 diagram. As you continue to document lower levels, you use names such as Figure 4.1.1, Figure 4.1.1.1, and so on.

You notice that the data flow into process 4.1 has a small circle at one end. The circle, called a **connector**, contains the number of the process that provides the data flow. This is the way that the processes of one DFD are linked to the processes of another.

The term **leveled DFDs** is used to describe the hierarchy of diagrams, ranging from the context diagram to the lowest-level Figure *n* diagram, which are used to document a system.

How Much Detail to Show

The Figure 4 diagram in Figure 6.8 represents the lowest level of detail that should be attempted when documenting the sales commission system using the DFD technique. Any remaining detail is best suited to another tool.

There are two rules of thumb to follow when deciding how many levels of DFDs to use. One, restrict a single DFD to no more than six processes. Two, use another tool to document the lowest level of detail, but use no more than a single page. If more space is required, you stopped using data flow diagramming too soon.

Data Flow Diagramming Guidelines

In addition to the rules and techniques that are discussed above, there are several guidelines that will increase the effectiveness of your DFDs.

FIGURE 6.9
Deleted Records
are Removed
From a File and
Retained

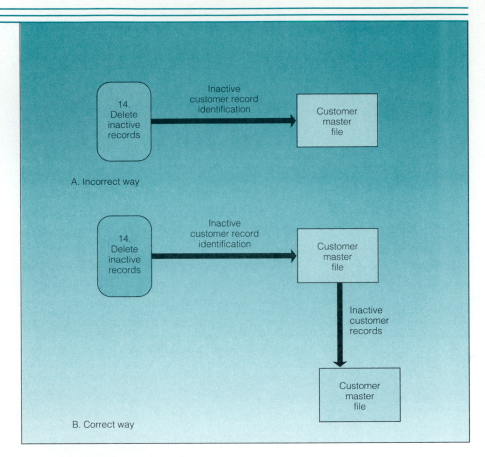

A. Incorrect way

B. Correct way

1. **Label each data flow with a unique name.** By using a unique label, each data flow is represented in the data dictionary by a data flow dictionary entry.
2. **Keep data flow names constant from one level to the next.** The data flows provide a continuity from level to level. For example, if you use the name "Mail" for the data flow from the customer in the context diagram, use the same name when that flow appears on lower levels. DFDs that have this characteristic are called **balanced DFDs.**
3. **Show proper disposition of records deleted from a data store.** It is common practice to retain the records deleted from a data store in a history file in the event that they are later needed. Figure 6.9 shows the proper technique. A process symbol is not needed between the two data store symbols since no transformation takes place.
4. **When documenting a computer program, do not include reads and writes.** Only include steps that transform data in some manner. The reads and writes can be assumed from the incoming and outgoing data flows. *See* Figure 6.8 for an example.

5. **Avoid read-only processes.** If a system contains a process with only data inflows and no outflows, something is wrong. Such a process has been given exotic names such as **black hole** and **infinite sink**.

6. **Write-only processes are permissable when time serves as the trigger.** Processes can be initiated by either an action or a passage of time. Receipt of a source document such as a sales order is an example of an action. The end of a time period such as a month is an example of a passage of time. The illustration below shows how a policy of taking a physical inventory at the end of the year initiates an inventory system.

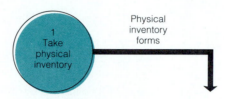

These are only a few guidelines to get you started. As you gain experience with data flow diagramming, you will add to the list.

Putting Data Flow Diagramming in Perspective

Data flow diagramming is a natural way to document a system. The few symbols and the rules for keeping each DFD as simple as possible make the DFD an effective communication medium. When the systems analyst draws the DFDs, the manager can easily understand them. When the manager wishes to engage in end-user computing, he or she can draw the DFDs when designing the system. Of all the structured tools for documenting processes, the DFD is the most popular, and its popularity should increase. DFDs are supported by practically all CASE tools.

STRUCTURED ENGLISH

When end-user computing became popular during the mid-1970s, many of the users were not interested in following the rigid documentation rules that had been established by the information specialists. The users were content to simply sketch out the logic using their own abbreviated narrative that consisted primarily of key words and phrases. This narrative form was called **pseudocode**.

Pseudocode became so popular that information specialists recognized it as a good way to document processes in detail. Over a period of time, the information services organizations have established some basic guidelines. The end product of this effort to formalize pseudocode to a certain degree has been given name structured English. **Structured English** is an abbreviated narrative in a particular format that looks like computer code but is not. Figure 6.10 is an example of the logic that a firm would employ in paying commissions to its salespersons.

FIGURE 6.10

Structured English Documentation of a Salesperson Commission
Program

```
START

Initialize storage
     TOTAL.SALES, TOTAL.COM = 0

Process sales data
     DO WHILE (more records)
        PERFORM Read data
        PERFORM Process data
        PERFORM Print data
     END DO

Final totals
     PRINT TOTAL.SALES, TOTAL.COM

STOP

Read data
     READ SALES.RECORD

Process data
     IF (SALES.AMT > 1000)
        THEN
              COMMISSION = 100 + (SALES.AMT - 1000) * .15
        ELSE
              COMMISSION = SALES.AMT * .10
     END IF
     Accumulate TOTAL.SALES, TOTAL.COM

Print data
     PRINT detail line
```

The Objective of Structured English

The objective of structured English is to document processes in a detail fashion. Used in conjunction with DFDs, structured English takes over where the DFDs leave off. It shows the arithmetic operations and logic that are incorporated into a computer program. As a general rule, each program will be documented with structured English or some equivalent.

Structured English Guidelines

Structured English is not a standardized tool. There are no conventions that users around the world are expected to follow. However, a number of guidelines have emerged, which differentiate structured English from pseudocode.

1. Use a verb when describing each processing step.
2. Supplement the verb with one or more objects when necessary.
3. Use only the three constructs of structured programming: (1) sequence, (2) selection, (3) and repetition.
4. Use only data names that are defined in the data dictionary. These names can describe data flows, data stores, data structures, or data elements.
5. Use uppercase for all data names and "computer" syntax, such as START, STOP, IF, THEN, and ELSE.
6. Indent to show hierarchical system structure. Words on the same hierarchical level should be indented the same number of spaces.
7. When the documentation is subdivided into modules, use the first line of each module for an identifying label and leave blank lines between modules.
8. Restrict each module to only a single entry point and a single exit point.

Here are a few examples of how the guidelines can be implemented.

Verbs and Objects   Most entries will begin with a verb such as READ, COMPUTE, or WRITE.

Two entries will consist of only a verb and will not require an object. These are:

```
START
STOP
```

Use START at the beginning of the system documentation, and STOP at the logical end. The logical end might not be the same as the physical end as illustrated in Figure 6.10.

Some entries will include a single object. An example is:

```
READ PAYROLL-RECORD
```

Some entries will include multiple objects, such as:

```
COMPUTE   REGULAR-EARNINGS,   OVERTIME-EARNINGS,   GROSS-
EARNINGS
```

In these examples, hyphens are included in the data names, reflecting how the names are defined in the data dictionary. Other characters such as periods or underline marks can be used.

Structured Programming Constructs   Specific formats are recommended when using the three structured programming constructs.

When documenting the *sequence construct*, the entries are aligned on the same margin, one after the other:

```
READ _____
COMPUTE _____
WRITE _____
```

When documenting the *selection construct*, use the following format for an IF-THEN situation:

```
IF (condition)
      THEN
                action when the condition is true
END IF
```

Notice that IF and END are aligned on the same margin. An example is:

```
IF (HOURS = or < 40)
      THEN
                COMPUTE GROSS-PAY = RATE * HOURS
END IF
```

Notice that the condition is enclosed in parentheses.
Use the following format for an IF-THEN-ELSE situation:

```
IF (condition)
      THEN
                action when the condition is true
      ELSE
                action when the condition is not true
END IF
```

Notice that THEN and ELSE, and the true and false actions are aligned on the same margins. An example is:

```
IF (HOURS = or < 40)
        THEN
                COMPUTE GROSS-PAY = RATE * HOURS
        ELSE
                COMPUTE GROSS-PAY = (RATE * 40) + ((HOURS - 40) *
                RATE * 1.5)
    END IF
```

You will notice the use of the asterisk to indicate multiplication. It is not necessary that programming syntax be followed that closely.

When documenting the *repetition construct*, the DO WHILE format will handle the majority of cases. It appears as:

```
    DO WHILE (condition)
            action
    END DO
```

An example is a process that is executed a variable number of times, depending on the number of records in a file.

```
    DO WHILE (there are payroll records)
            COMPUTE CURRENT.GROSS.PAY
            COMPUTE CURRENT.INCOME.TAX
            COMPUTE CURRENT.NET.PAY
    END DO
```

Use Uppercase for Data Names and Computer Syntax   You will notice that in the above examples most of the words are uppercase. This is because most of them are the names of data records or elements, or words that typically comprise the syntax of a programming language.

Identify Each Module   In most cases, it will be necessary to subdivide the system into modules. Figure 6.10 illustrates the technique of devoting the first line of each module to a label and leaving a blank line between modules.

The Process Dictionary Entry

It is possible to write the structured English on ordinary paper, however, a special form can be designed to link the narrative to other tools. A form that accomplishes this purpose appears in Figure 6.11 and is named the process dictionary entry.[2] This sample contains entries that link the structured English to a DFD and the data dic-

---

[2] This form and the data dictionary forms in the next section are based on formats from James Senn, *Analysis and Design of Information Systems* (New York: McGraw-Hill, 1984), 125–34, 132–33.

FIGURE 6.11
Process Dictionary Entry

PROCESS DICTIONARY ENTRY

Use: To describe each process in a data flow diagram.

PROCESS: 2. Enter sales order data

INPUT: Sales orders

OUTPUT: Entered sales order data

Entered sales orders

LOGIC SUMMARY

Data - entry - process

DO WHILE (there are sales orders)

Enter CUSTOMER.NUMBER, CUSTOMER.ORDER.NUMBER, CUSTOMER.ORDER.DATE

DO WHILE (there are ordered items)

Enter ITEM.NUMBER, ITEM.QUANTITY, ITEM.UNIT.PRICE

END DO

END DO

File - entered - sales - orders - process

Files sales orders in SALES.ORDER.FORM.FILE

tionary. The same type of form can be used to establish linkages to other tools such as system flowcharts and Warnier-Orr diagrams.

The field labeled *Process* contains the number and name from the DFD. There is one process dictionary entry for each process in the DFD. The *Input* field identifies the data flows that enter the process, and the *Output* field identifies the data flows created by the process.

The *Logic Summary* area is where the structured English appears. When the process documentation is too lengthy to fit on the front of the form, it can be continued on the back.

Putting Structured English in Perspective

The manager can use structured English while engaged in end-user computing. When information specialists become involved with more complex systems, it is the programmer rather than the systems analyst who is the likely user. The systems analyst will document the systems in a summary fashion, and the programmer can use structured English to provide the additional detail.

Structured English closely resembles computer code, and for that reason it is not ideal for communicating system detail to a user who has little or no understanding of computing. In that situation, it is better to use graphic media such as program flowcharts or Warnier-Orr diagrams, both of which we describe in the next chapter.

DATA DICTIONARY

The **data dictionary** is a written description of the data contained in the database. Some dictionaries are *computer based*—they are maintained in the computer's secondary storage. Other dictionaries are *document based*—they are maintained in a printed form.

Even when the data dictionary is computer based, much thought must go into the identification of the data elements and their description before those specifications are entered into the computer. The specifications are recorded in a written form to serve as source documents for the data entry. Therefore, a document-based data dictionary can be the desired end product, or it can be a step toward developing a computer-based dictionary. In this appendix, we describe how to develop a document-based data dictionary.

Data Dictionary Forms

The system presented here consists of a set of four dictionary forms that describe the database contents in the hierarchy illustrated in Figure 6.12.

This set of forms enables the data dictionary to provide a complete documentation of the firm's data resource—from a high-level summary in terms of the flows

FIGURE 6.12

The Hierarchy of
the Data
Dictionary Forms

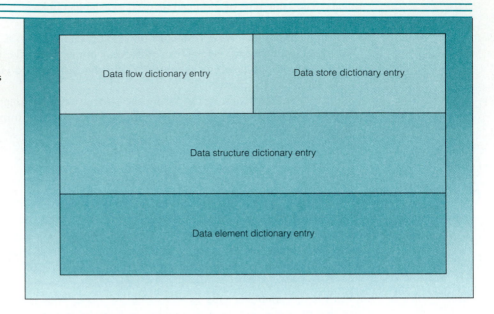

and stores to a detail description of each data element. The data dictionary is there-fore a top-down, structured tool.

Data Flow Dictionary Entry   A data flow dictionary entry describes each data flow on a DFD. A completed entry is illustrated in Figure 6.13. This is the "Sales orders" data flow for the Figure 0 diagram of the sales commission system illustrated in Figure 6.6.

The *Data Flow Name* is the one used on the DFD, and the *Description* briefly explains the role of the flow in the system. The *From* field identifies where the data flow originates. It can include one or more processes, data stores, or termi-nators. The *To* field identifies the processes, stores, or terminators to which the data flow is directed. When identifying processes, use both the process number and label that appear on the DFD. When the flow originates or terminates with a data store or terminator, simply enter the name of the store or terminator. The *Data Structures* field lists each structure that is included in the flow. You can add any necessary explanations in the *Comments* section.

The data flow dictionary entry contains only summary data. For additional detail, you refer to the data structure dictionary entry.

Data Store Dictionary Entry

The data store dictionary entry describes each unique data store in a DFD. If the same data store appears more than once, only a single entry form is used. Figure 6.14 contains a completed sample. This is the Sales Order Form file in the sales commission system (*see* Figure 6.6). The *Data Store Name* is the same one that appears on the DFD. The *Description* briefly explains what kind of data is con-

FIGURE 6.13
Data Flow Dictionary Entry

DATA FLOW DICTIONARY ENTRY

Use: To describe each data flow in a data flow diagram.

DATA FLOW NAME: Sales orders

DESCRIPTION: The documents that are filled out by the customers to
identify the products, and the quantities of each, that
they wish to purchase.

FROM: 1. Open mail

TO: 2. Enter sales order data

DATA STRUCTURES: Sales order record

COMMENTS:

FIGURE 6.14
Data Store Dictionary Entry

DATA STORE DICTIONARY ENTRY

Use: To describe each unique data store in a data flow diagram.

DATA STORE NAME: Sales order form file

DESCRIPTION: The history file of sales order forms, after the data
has been entered into the sales commission system.

DATA STRUCTURES: Sales order record

VOLUME: Approximately 140 per day

ACTIVITY:

ACCESS: Order department personnel

COMMENTS:

tained within the store and perhaps how the data is used. The *Data Structures* field lists those structures that comprise the store. Most files have only one *type* of record. For example, a payroll consists of payroll records—all of which have the same format. For that reason, a data store will typically contain only a single structure.

Some indication of the size of the store is entered in the *Volume* area. This is the number of times that the structures *occur* in the store. For example, in describing a data store named the Inventory Master file, you might want to describe the volume as:

"Varies from 18,000 to 20,000 records, with an average of 18,750. Growing at the rate of approximately 5% per year."

In the *Activity* area, you include any information relative to how active the individual records are in the file. This information is pertinent only for master files that are maintained in an up-to-date condition. For example, in the inventory file of 18,750 records, perhaps only 20 percent are active each day. This means that on a given day you can expect about 3,700 to be involved in some type of inventory transaction.

If the firm has established any restrictions on data availability, they are explained in the *Access* field. The contents of this field are used in designing database security measures. Any necessary *Comments* are recorded at the bottom of the form.

As with the data flow dictionary entry, the data store dictionary entry contains only summary data. You must refer to the data structure dictionary entry for additional detail.

Data Structure Dictionary Entry

A data structure dictionary entry is completed for each structure listed on the data store and data flow forms. The sample in Figure 6.15 is the Sales Order record from the sales commission system. The *Structure Name* field contains the same name used on the data store or data flow forms. The *Description* field describes how the structure is used. The *Data Elements* field lists each data element contained in the structure. The bottom of the form includes a *Comments* field for explanations such as the one in the sample.

Data Element Dictionary Entry

A data element dictionary entry form is used for each data element included in all of the structures—structures that exist in data flows and data stores. However, only a single form is used for each data element even though it might appear at several points in the system.

A completed data element dictionary entry appears in Figure 6.16. It is the Salesperson Number field on the sales order. The *Type* of data is indicated—alphabetic, numeric, or alphanumeric (combined alphabetic and numeric). The *Length* specifies the element size, in number of positions or bytes. If the element is numeric, you can specify the *Number of Decimal Positions*.

FIGURE 6.15
Data Structure Dictionary Entry

DATA STRUCTURE DICTIONARY ENTRY

Use: To describe each unique data structure that exists in (1) data flows and (2) data stores:

STRUCTURE NAME: Sales order record

DESCRIPTION: The sales order form that the customer uses to order

merchandise.

DATA ELEMENTS: CUSTOMER.NUMBER

CUSTOMER.ORDER.NUMBER

SALESPERSON.NUMBER

CUSTOMER.ORDER.DATE

*ITEM.NUMBER

*ITEM.DESCRIPTION

*ITEM.QUANTITY

*ITEM.UNIT.PRICE

*ITEM.EXTENDED.PRICE

COMMENTS: Elements marked with asterisks occur for each item record.

FIGURE 6.16
Data Element Dictionary Entry

DATA ELEMENT DICTIONARY ENTRY

Use: To describe each unique data element contained in a data structure.

DATA ELEMENT NAME: SALESPERSON.NUMBER

DESCRIPTION: The number that identifies the salesperson.

TYPE: Numeric

LENGTH: 4

NO. DECIMAL POS:

ALIASES: Salesman Number, Sales Rep Number

RANGE OF VALUES: 0001-9999

TYPICAL VALUE:

SPECIFIC VALUES:

OTHER EDITING
DETAILS:

If the data element is also identified by other names, or *Aliases*, they are listed. Perhaps an invoice is also called a bill, and a purchase order is also called a P.O.

When appropriate, the *Range of Values* is specified. This information is useful to programmers who code editing routines to detect data errors. The same logic underlies the inclusion of a *Typical Value*, and any *Specific Values* when they are appropriate. The Specific Values field is completed in a situation such as a data element that identifies a sales region. Perhaps a digit 1 represents the Eastern region, a 2 represents the Midwestern region, and so on. The Range of Values, Typical Value, and Specific Values fields are completed only when necessary.

If there are any *Other Editing Details*, they are listed at the bottom. For example, perhaps a data element named Employee Age can be verified by using the Date of Birth data element.

You can see how the detail of the database unfolds in a gradual manner. With the data flow and data store forms, you describe files and identify records. With the data structure form, you provide more detail about the records and identify the data elements. With the data element forms, you provide the detail for each data element.

Complementary Nature of the Forms

The four data dictionary forms work together as a set, as illustrated in Figure 6.17. The data flow form identifies the structures within the data flow. The data store form identifies the structures within the store. The structure and element forms specify lower levels of the data hierarchy in both the data flow and the data store.

Responsibility for the Data Dictionary

The DBA is responsibile for the database and the data dictionary. The DBA must see to it that all of the entries are (1) filled out, and (2) maintained in a current status, either in a paper or a computer form.

Some firms even designate certain persons as having responsibility for particular data elements. These persons are, in effect, data managers. They are responsible not only for the forms but for the data itself—ensuring that it is kept current and secure.

Putting the Data Dictionary in Perspective

The manager will not actually create the dictionary, but can provide valuable input to its development. The manager benefits from the data dictionary, but in an indirect way. The data dictionary is a necessary step toward providing the manager with the information that is needed for problem solving.

FIGURE 6.17

The Entry Forms Provide a Complete Description of Data Flows and Stores

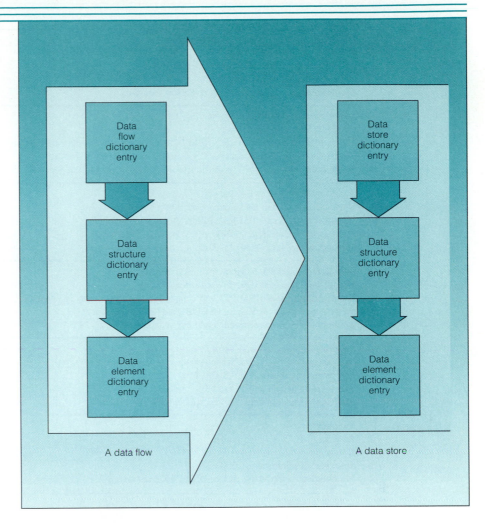

A data flow

A data store

COMPUTER-ASSISTED SOFTWARE ENGINEERING (CASE)

The objective of CASE is to transfer some of the systems development workload from the human developers to the computer. Today, there are CASE products being marketed by over fifty software and hardware suppliers that accomplish this objective to various degrees. Table 6.1 lists some of the tools to give you an idea of the range of their capabilities.

TABLE 6.1
Some Popular
CASE Tools

Supplier: Computer Systems Advisers, Inc.
Product: Pose
Hardware required: IBM PCs and compatibles
Source code generated: COBOL
Methodologies supported: Gane & Sarson, Yourdon

Supplier: Iconix Software Engineering, Inc.
Product: Powertools
Hardware required: Macintosh, IBM PCs, and compatibles, Sun Sparcstation
Source code generated: Ada, C, C++, COBOL, FORTRAN, Pascal
Methodologies supported: Buhr/Booch, Chen, DeMarco, Martin, Shlaer/Mellor, Yourdon

Supplier: Knowledgeware, Inc.
Product: Application Development Workbench
Hardware required: IBM PS/2 Model 70 or 80
Source code generated: COBOL
Methodologies supported: Methodology independent

Supplier: Scandura Intelligent Systems
Product: Prodoc RE/NU Sys Workbench
Hardware required: IBM PCs and compatibles, RS/6000, Sun Sparcstation
Source code generated: Ada, C, COBOL, FORTRAN, Pascal
Methodologies supported: Methodology independent

Supplier: System Software Associates
Product: As/Set ADK, As/Set Integrator
Hardware required: IBM AS/400, PS/2
Source code generated: RPG/400
Methodologies supported: Information engineering

Supplier: Unisys Corp.
Product: The Linc Environment
Hardware required: Unisys U, A, V, 1100/2200 series, PW2
Source code generated: COBOL
Methodologies supported: Linc, DFDs, ER diagrams

The range of a particular tool's capabilities can be expressed in terms of where it can be used in the SLC. Four categories have been defined:

- An **upper CASE tool** can be used by the firm's executives when they engage in strategic planning. The output of this activity, the strategic plan for information resources, lays the foundation for the planning phase of each system life cycle. Examples of upper-CASE tools are IEW/Planning Workstation from KnowledgeWare, and Develop-Mate from IBM.
- A **middle CASE tool** can be used during the analysis and design phases to document the processes and data of both the existing system and the new

system. Examples are Visible Analyst from Visible Systems, and Excelerator from Index Technology.

■ A **lower CASE tool** is used during the implementation and use phases to help the programmer develop, test, and maintain code. These tools are often referred to as **code generators**. A popular example is Telon from Pansophic Systems, which generates executable COBOL or PL/I code.

■ An **integrated CASE tool (I-CASE tool)** offers the combined coverage of the upper, middle, and lower CASE tools. Well-known examples include Information Engineering Facility, or IEF, from Texas Instruments, and DESIGN-1 from Andersen Consulting.

Most of the activity has been concentrated on the middle CASE level, where the need was initially recognized to free systems analysts from the drudgery of documenting existing and new system designs. Subsequently, interest in SPIR and systems maintenance exanded the scope of CASE to enclose the entire SLC.

Excelerator—An Example of CASE

Excelerator from Index Technology is one of the most popular CASE tools. It can document processes with DFDs, flowcharts, and structured English, and can document data with entity-relationship diagrams (ERDs) and a data dictionary. Excelerator, therefore, offers the capability of documenting *all* of the processes and data of a system. In addition, it can check the documentation for completeness and consistency, and can develop prototypes of input screens and reports.

Drawing a Context Diagram with Excelerator

To document your system with DFDs using Excelerator, you obtain the **Graphics Drawing Screen** illustrated in Figure 6.18. The large area is the drawing area, and a menu of commands appears in the upper-left-hand area. The Excelerator menus work in the same way as those of Lotus, dBASE, or WordPerfect; they exist in a hierarchy. When you make a menu selection, a lower-level menu appears. Menu selection can be accomplished by either pressing the appropriate keys on the keyboard, or by using the mouse. To use the mouse, you move the cursor to the proper area of the screen and then press the Enter button on the mouse. This action is called *clicking on* the mouse.

Draw the Terminators   To draw a terminator, you:

1. Select OBJECT from the command menu. This action displays a lower submenu.
2. Select X ENTITY from the submenu. Excelerator uses the term **external entity** instead of terminator.
3. Move the arrow to the location where the terminator is to appear, and click on the mouse.

FIGURE 6.18

The Excelerator
Graphics Drawing
Screen

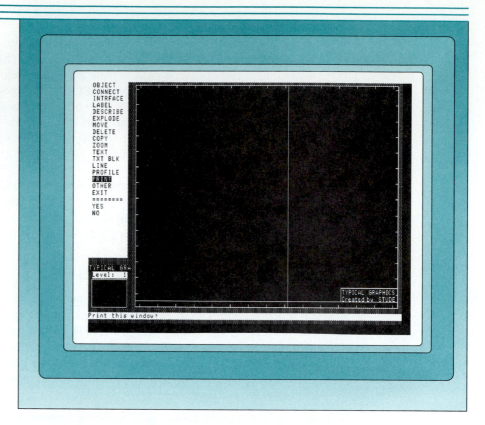

You repeat steps 2 and 3 to add each remaining terminator. Your context diagram should now have the same general appearance as the one in Figure 6.19A.

Draw the Process Symbol To draw the single process symbol of the context diagram, you repeat the procedure that you followed for the terminators, only select PROCESS from the submenu. Figure 6.19B shows the result.

Draw the Data Stores You draw data stores by selecting STORE from the submenu and following the same procedure as for the other symbols. In most cases, a context diagram will not include data stores.

Draw the Data Flows To draw an arrow, select CONNECT from the submenu. Position the cursor arrow on the symbol to which the *tail* of the data flow arrow will be connected and click. Then, position the cursor arrow on the symbol to which the *head* will be connected and click. The data flow arrow is drawn. Repeat this procedure for each data flow. Your context diagram should now have the appearance of Figure 6.19C.

FIGURE 6.19
The Context
Diagram Evolves
Step by Step

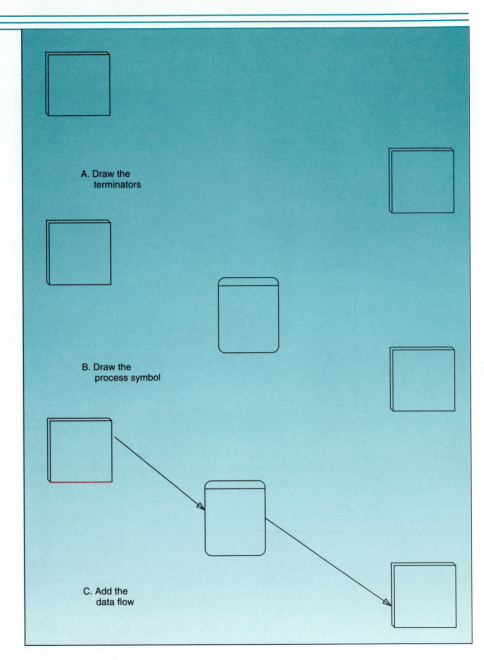

A. Draw the
   terminators

B. Draw the
   process symbol

C. Add the
   data flow

FIGURE 6.20

The External
Entity Description
Screen Allows
You to Describe
the Terminators

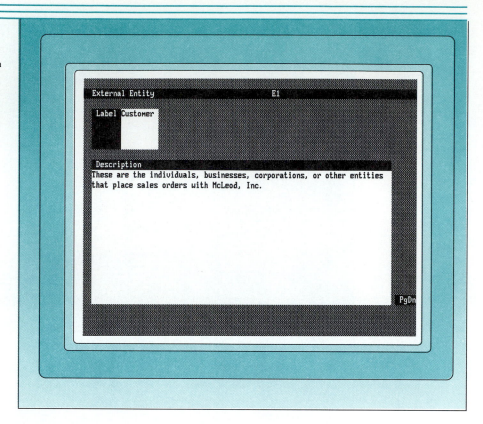

Label the Terminators With the symbols drawn, you next enter the labels. Take these steps to label a terminator:

1. Select DESCRIBE from the command menu.
2. Use the mouse to position the cursor on the symbol to be labeled.
3. You will then be prompted to key in the ID.
4. Excelerator will then display the **External Entity Description Screen** shown in Figure 6.20. The white rectangle at the top represents the labeling area. You can key in as many as four lines. Then, you key in a description.
5. You press the F3 function key to add the label to the symbol, and to save the dictionary description on the hard disk or diskette.

Repeat the procedure for the remaining labels.

Label the Process You specify that a label is to be added to the single process symbol of the context diagram by repeating the first three steps for labeling

FIGURE 6.21
The Process
Description
Screen

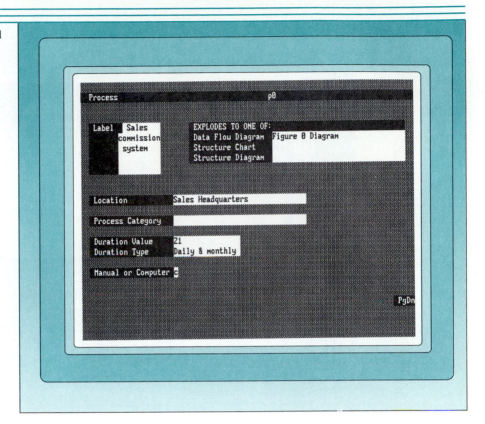

the terminators. Then, you obtain the **Process Description Screen** in Figure 6.21. Take the steps:

1. Enter the label.
2. Enter the name of the next-lower-level DFD in the window titled **EXPLODES TO ONE OF: Data Flow Diagram.** For example, when drawing a context diagram, you enter *Figure 0 diagram.* By establishing this linkage now, you will be able to use it later.
3. You may provide additional information by using the mouse to move the cursor to the lower windows, and keying in the data.
4. Use the PgDn key to move to the next screen to describe the process. Figure 6.22 shows a completed sample. The Description area can contain a structured English documentation of the lowest-level processes.
5. Save with F3.

Label the Data Stores and Data Flows   You follow generally the same procedure in labeling data stores and data flows as you use for the terminators.

FIGURE 6.22
The Second Page of the Process Description Screen Permits a Detailed Description Using Structured English

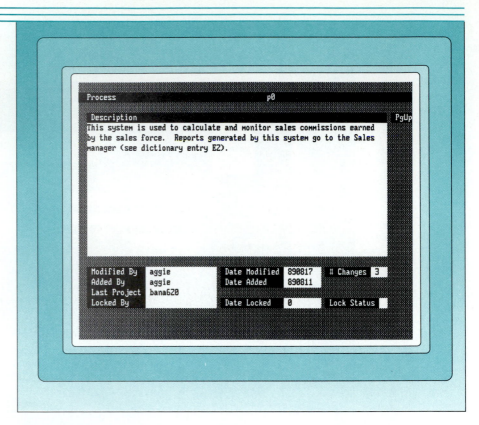

FIGURE 6.23
A Context Diagram Printed by Excelerator

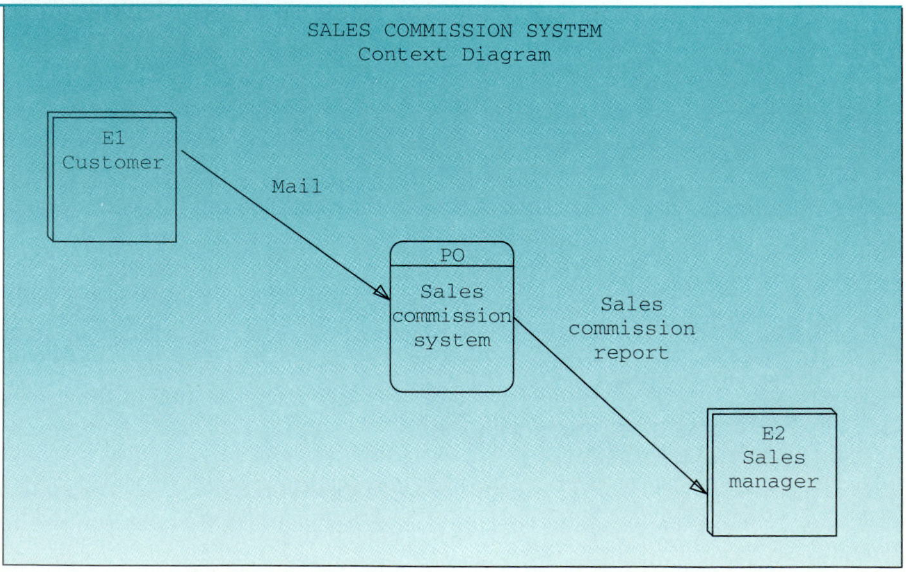

Save and Print the Context Diagram   A completed context diagram appears in Figure 6.23. It can be saved on the diskette and printed at this point.

Draw the Figure 0 Diagram   With the context diagram displayed, select **EXPLODE** from the command menu. Move the arrow to the process symbol and click. A blank Graphics Drawing Screen will be displayed. Draw the Figure 0 diagram, following the same procedure as for the context diagram, only enter multiple process symbols and data stores. When you label each process step, you establish the explosion path if you plan to continue the documentation with a lower-level DFD. You save and print your Figure 0 diagram when you are satisfied with the layout. Figure 6.24 shows a sample.

Draw Lower-level DFDs   Repeat the same procedure for each lower-level DFD. First **EXPLODE** a process and draw each lower-level DFD on the new screen. Save and print.

Print the Dictionary   As you produced your DFDs and used the **DESCRIBE** command, Excelerator created corresponding dictionary entries. You can now print copies of the:

- Data store dictionary
- Data flow dictionary
- Process dictionary
- Terminator dictionary

A sample of the data store dictionary entry appears in Figure 6.25.

This dictionary form does not have exactly the same appearance as the one described earlier and illustrated in Figure 6.14. However, both forms serve the same purpose.

Putting CASE in Perspective

CASE can be used by the firm's executives when they engage in strategic planning and by the information specialists when they develop systems. Most managers who are engaged in end-user computing will elect not to use CASE. They will perceive the system design as being so simple that it does not warrant the time of preparing the documentation. Some managers, however, will be exceptions.

Although CASE can make real contributions throughout the SLC, its work is limited to the monotonous, mechanical tasks. Executives, members of the MIS steering committee, managers, and information specialists still must do the creative work of planning, analysis, design, and programming. The human developers, rather than the development software, remain the key ingredient in the process of achieving large and complex computer-based information systems.

FIGURE 6.24
A Figure 0
Diagram Printed
by Excelerator

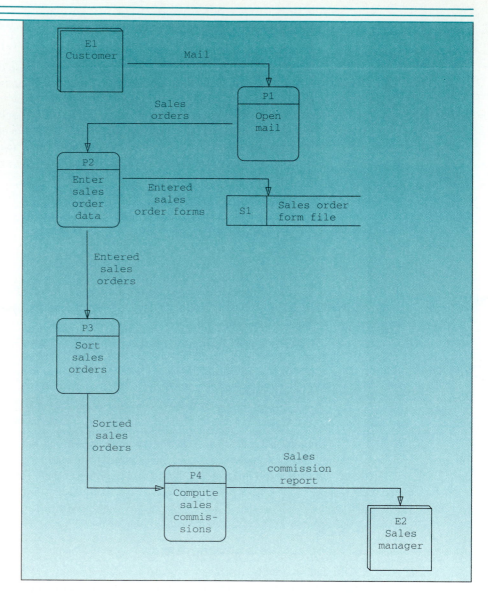

SUMMARY

Management uses a control mechanism that includes elements such as a plan, weekly reports, weekly meetings, and presentation graphics. Two popular forms of graphics are Gantt charts and network diagrams. Network diagrams overcome the limitations of Gantt charts by showing relationships among activities and identi-

FIGURE 6.25
A Data Store
Dictionary Entry
Printed by
Excelerator

```
DATE: 16-AUG-89       DATA STORE - OUTPUT                    PAGE    1
TIME: 15:52           NAME: S1                        EXCELERATOR 1.8

TYPE Data Store                                NAME S1

                                EXPLODES TO ONE OF:
        Label Sales order       Record
              form file         Data Model Diagram
                                ERA Diagram


                     Location
                     Manual or Computer M
                     Number of records  0

                     Index Elements

     Description
     This file is used to retain the sales order forms after the data has
     been entered into the computer.  The forms are filed according to the
     day they were entered.


     Modified By    aggie          Date Modified  890816   # Changes  3
     Added By       aggie          Date Added     890811
     Last Project   bana620
     Locked By                     Date Locked    0         Lock Status
```

fying the critical path. Network diagrams can take the form of Critical Path Method (CPM) diagrams or Program Evaluation and Review Technique (PERT) charts. CPM expresses activity times in a single estimate, whereas PERT uses pessimistic, most likely, and optimistic estimates.

Data flow diagrams, or DFDs, are part of a top-down tool set. DFDs document system processes and data in a summary fashion, and are supplemented by structured English and the data dictionary.

DFDs use only four types of symbols and show neither technology nor detail. A set of DFDs is required to document a system, beginning with the context diagram on the top level, followed by a Figure 0 diagram and possibly one or more Figure *n* diagrams. These diagrams are called level DFDs.

DFDs are so user friendly that they can be used by the user when involved in end-user computing, as well as by the information specialist.

Structured English provides the detail processing documentation that is not included in DFDs. A derivative of pseudocode, structured English consists of a set of guidelines that closely parallel those of structured programming. Structured

English can be documented in the form of a process dictionary entry to establish formal connections to other documentation such as DFDs and the data dictionary. The most likely users of structured English are users engaged in end-user computing, and programmers. It is not a good way to communicate processing detail to users who rely on the information specialists for support.

The data dictionary is a top-down tool for use in documenting data. A set of four forms document data flows, data stores, data structures, and data elements. These forms can comprise a paper-based documentation system or be used as source documents for preparing a computer-based system. The person most likely to create and maintain the data dictionary forms is the DBA.

The task of documenting a system with DFDs, structured English, and the data dictionary is a gigantic one. In an effort to relieve the developers from the time-consuming mechanical tasks, computer-aided software engineeering, or CASE, tools were developed. Upper CASE tools can be used for systems planning, middle CASE tools can be used for analysis and design, and lower CASE tools can be used for implementation and maintenance. Integrated CASE tools can provide support beginning with strategic planning and continuing through the use phase. CASE can free executives, managers, and information specialists from redundant tasks related to systems development so that they can concentrate on the more creative tasks.

KEY TERMS

Gantt chart
network diagram
critical path
Critical Path Method (CPM) diagram
Program Evaluation and Review Technique
      (PERT) chart
data flow diagram (DFD)

structured analysis
figure 0 diagram
context diagram
figure n diagram
structured English
data dictionary

KEY CONCEPTS

How the bars of a Gantt chart are represented
      in a network diagram in the form of
      interconnected arrows
How leveled DFDs document system processes
      in a top-down manner

How DFDs relate to both structured English
      and the data dictionary
How the data dictionary entries document
      system data in a top-down manner
The relationship between the various CASE
      tools and the SLC

QUESTIONS

1. Name four elements in the control mechanism of a system project.

2. What distinguishes a Gantt chart from an ordinary bar chart?

3. What are the two limitations of a Gantt chart that are overcome by the network diagram?

4. Define: activity, node, dummy activity, slack, critical path.

5. Distinguish between CPM and PERT.

6. How do DFDs and structured English work together to document a system?

7. How do DFDs and the data dictionary work together to document a system?

8. Are DFDs, structured English, and the data dictionary used in systems analysis or systems design? Explain.

9. Define: terminator, process, data flow, data store.

10. What is the name of the top-level DFD? How does it differ from other DFDs?

11. What is the name of the DFD just below the context diagram in the hierarchy?

12. Keeping in mind that a Figure 4 diagram documents the number 4 process of the system level just above, can you guess how the term "Figure 0 diagram" originated? Explain.

13. What are the two ways that a process in a DFD can be triggered?

14. Is structured English just another name for pseudocode? Explain.

15. What types of words appear in uppercase in structured English?

16. Two of the data dictionary entry forms are represented by symbols on a DFD. What are they?

17. Explain the relationship between data flow, data structure, and data element forms. Do the same for the data store, data structure, and data element forms.

18. Assume that a DFD contains six processes, ten data flows, and one data store that appears at three different points in the system, how many process dictionary entries will you have? Data flow dictionary entries? Data store dictionary entries?

19. Would an executive be most interested in an upper CASE tool, a middle CASE tool, or a lower CASE tool? What about a programmer? What about a systems analyst?

TOPICS FOR DISCUSSION

1. Why would a manager not want to use any of the documentation tools described in this chapter?

2. Should a manager use the tools?

PROBLEMS

1. Draw a CPM diagram of the implementation phase illustrated in Figure 5.14. Steps 3 through 7 can be performed simultaneously. The estimated times for performing the steps are: (1) 2 weeks, (2) .2 weeks, (3) 12 weeks, (4) 14 weeks, (5) 8 weeks, (6) 4 weeks, (7) 2 weeks, (8) 3 weeks. Identify the critical path with a heavy line.

2. Using the data in Problem 1, how long will the project take?

3. Compute the time required for each activity in the PERT chart in Figure 6.5. Use the formula in the chapter. List each activity, along with the computed times. Add the activity times to produce the project time.

4. The president of Bryan's Department Store has asked to receive a report at the end of each month summarizing the payroll expenses. The report is prepared by the computer from a Current Earnings file, an output of the monthly payroll system. Regard that system as an environmental element. One program distills the Current Earnings file data into a summary form, and creates a Monthly Earnings file. A second program uses this file to prepare the president's report.

Tasks:

A. Prepare a Figure 0 diagram.

B. Prepare a context diagram.

5. Eagle Mailorder Services customers fill out sales order forms that are enclosed in the mailorder catalogs. The forms are mailed to the Eagle office in New York City. Upon receipt, a clerk opens the envelopes and removes the sales order forms. The clerk gives the forms to a data entry operator who keys the data onto a diskette using a microcomputer. After data entry, the sales orders are filed in a Sales Order History file. The diskette containing all of the sales order data is then read by a minicomputer. For each ordered item, the Inventory Master record is retrieved from the Inventory Master file and the Balance on Hand is reduced by the ordered amount. The updated Inventory Master record is written back to the file. The same program prints picking tickets and writes a Daily Sales Report file. The picking tickets are input to the order filling system where they are used by warehouse personnel in picking the merchandise from the shelves for shipment to the customers. Another minicomputer program reads the Daily Sales Report file and prepares a daily sales report that goes to the sales manager.

Tasks:

A. Prepare a Figure 0 diagram. Regard the order filling system as a part of the environment.

B. Prepare a context diagram.

C. Prepare a Figure n diagram of the first minicomputer program. Begin and end the diagram with connector symbols. Connect the two processes with a data flow named *Sales data*.

6. Top management of Newcastle Coal Company has become concerned about the increased losses from bad debts. They feel that too many customers are allowed to buy on credit and then do not pay for a variety of reasons. The credit manager, Phil Jordan, is considering two approaches to conducting a customer credit check. He has asked you to document both approaches using structured English so that he can review the logic with top management. One approach, called the *credit code approach*, involves the use of customer credit codes. The codes will be contained in each customer record, and will be retrieved upon receipt of an order. A code 1 customer can make unlimited purchases on credit, and a code 2 customer must pay cash. Only codes 1 and 2 are to be used; any other character represents an error. The other approach, called the *credit limit approach*, involves setting a credit limit. All customers are eligible to receive credit, but the total amount of any customer's accounts receivable cannot exceed $5,000. The total amount is com-

puted by adding the sales order amount to the current accounts receivable amount. When the limit is exceeded, the customer must pay cash. Both approaches will be performed by the computer, and will produce a detail report.

Task:

Prepare the two sets of documentation. Use Figure 6.10 as a guide. The first diagram will require nested IF statements.

7. After graduating from college, you took a job as a systems analyst trainee for Bayside Auto Supply Company (BASCO). The manager of systems analysis, Fred Dorn, has asked you to document a data flow in the new inventory system. The data flow that you are to document is labeled *Sales order transactions*, and it includes only the minimum amount of data necessary to update the Balance on Hand field in the Inventory Master file. The updating involves reducing the Balance on Hand by the sales quantity. Your task is to prepare the data flow dictionary entry, the data structure dictionary entry, and each of the data element dictionary entries that are needed. Use Figures 6.13, 6.15, and 6.16 as examples. You are to provide the names of the structure and the elements. Also, let your imagination run wild and make entries that you feel would be appropriate in the various fields of the forms.

8. You did such a good job on the BASCO data flow assignment that Fred has asked you to do some of the documentation of the Inventory Master file used by the same process. Fred wants you to prepare the data store dictionary entry, the data structure dictionary entry, and three data element dictionary entries. Use Figure 6.14 as an example of the data store form. The data elements to be documented include the Item Number, Item Description, and Balance on Hand.

Rhinegold Chemicals (A)

Rhinegold manufactures the chemicals that are used in making artificial fingernails. Most of the operations are conducted in Pittsburgh, and this is where information services is located. A disk-oriented minicomputer is used primarily for data processing and is linked to twenty keyboard terminals scattered throughout the company. Most of the terminals are in the accounting department, but some are in managers' offices.

Of the 125 employees who work in the Pittsburgh factory, 100 are paid an hourly rate. The regular rate applies to the first forty hours of work each week and the overtime rate of one-and-one-half times the regular rate applies to the hours over forty.

Each employee has a Payroll Master record (on magnetic disk) that contains the following data elements: Employee Name, Employee Number, Social Security Number, Department Number, Work Shift, Job Classification Code, Date of Birth, Sex, Date of Employment, Effective Date of Current Job Classification, Regular Hourly Rate, Year-to-Date Gross Earnings, Year-to-Date Income Tax, Year-to-Date Social Security Tax, and Year-to-Date Net Earnings (take-home pay).

Daily Attendance Recording

As the hourly employees report for work, they remove their time cards from the rack, insert them in the time clock to record the time of day, and then return the cards to the rack. The same procedure is repeated when the employees leave at the end of their shifts. Ringold has gone to three shifts in some departments in order to keep up with the increasing volume of business.

After the employees clock off at the end of the week, they calculate the number of hours worked each day (using pencil and paper), and record the number (in tenths) on the time cards for each day. Then the employees add up the number of daily hours to determine the total hours, which are written on the time cards.

Weekly Payroll Processing

The employees give their time cards to the departmental secretary, who verifies that all of the fields have been filled in, counts the cards to make certain that they are all there, and gives all of the cards for the week to the department head. The department head scans each card to verify that both the daily hours and the weekly hours are correct (the department heads usually know when their employees must work overtime each day and approximately how much).

If the department head encounters any situation that cannot be approved (such as an employee reporting overtime work when none was scheduled for that day), the department head writes a big "40" on the card and signs it. In that case, the employee is paid for forty hours that week. If the employee is, in fact, due overtime pay, an additional payroll check is issued the following week. After scanning each card, the department head signs it at the bottom.

When finished with all of the cards, the department head places them in an envelope and sends them through the company mail to the computer department. When the envelopes arrive at the computer department, the data from each card is entered on a keyboard terminal, and the computer writes a Weekly Time Card file on magnetic disk. A prewritten sort program then sorts the disk records into employee number sequence within department. The output from the sort is the Sorted Weekly Time Card file, on magnetic disk.

The computer then uses the Sorted Weekly Time Card file and the Employee Payroll Master file to compute the weekly payroll data—Number of Overtime Hours Worked (if any), Regular Earnings, Overtime Earnings, Gross Earnings, Income Tax, Social Security Tax, and Net Earnings (Gross Earnings less the tax amounts). The Employee Payroll Master file resides on magnetic disk. When the payroll computations for an employee have been made, the appropriate fields are updated in the Employee Payroll Master record, and a Weekly Payroll Earnings record is written to disk.

The Weekly Payroll Earnings file is used as input to another program that prints the payroll checks, which are sent directly to the employees through the company mail. After the printing process, the Weekly Payroll Earnings file is retained for use at the end of the month.

Monthly Payroll Processing

Carl Rhinegold, the president, has asked to receive a monthly payroll summary report that contains the monthly totals for each department and overall totals for the company. The report is prepared by combining data from the Weekly Payroll Earnings files for that month. First, the files are merged, and then a second program prints the report. Rhinegold uses the report as a control to ensure that overtime pay does not get out of hand.

Assignments

Hint: You may find it easier to work Assignments 3 and 4 before you begin work on 1 and 2.

1. Prepare a context diagram of the entire system (weekly and monthly). Do not include the daily processing performed by the employees or the processing when special overtime checks must be printed. Regard the employees as members of the environment.

2. Prepare a Figure 0 diagram of the entire system. The diagram should contain two processes—one for the weekly procedure and one for the monthly procedure.

3. Prepare a Figure 1 diagram of the weekly procedure. Your diagram should include one diverging flow.

4. Prepare a Figure 2 diagram of the monthly procedure. A data store named *This month's payroll earnings files* connects the weekly and monthly procedures.

5. Prepare a Figure *n* diagram of the portion of the weekly procedure that computes the weekly data and updates the Payroll Master file. Begin and end with connector symbols.

6. Use structured English to document the tasks performed by a department head. Use Figure 6.10 as a guide.

7. Document the data flow that represents the payroll checks. Prepare all of the dictionary entries—data flow, structure, and element. Name the structure the *Payroll check record.* The data elements include Employee Name, Employee Number, Pay Period Ending Date, Payroll Check Number, Payroll Check Date, and Payroll Check Amount. Use Figures 6.13, 6.15, and 6.16 as guides. Document only two data elements; one must be the Payroll Check Amount.

8. Document the data store named the Employee Payroll Master file. Prepare the data store and structure forms, but only five data element forms. You can select the data elements to document. Approximately 98 percent of the records are active weekly, and access is provided only to members of the payroll section of the accounting department. Use Figure 6.14 as a guide.

SELECTED BIBLIOGRAPHY

Appleton, Daniel S. "The Modern Data Dictionary." *Datamation* 33 (March 1, 1987): 66–68.

Forte, Gene, and Norman, Ronald J. "A Self-Assessment by the Software Engineering Community." *Communications of the ACM* 35 (April 1992): 28–32.

Gibson, Michael Lucas. "The CASE Philosophy." *BYTE* 14 (April 1989): 209*ff.*

Hollist, Pen, and Utterback, Jon. "The CASE-Project Management Connection." *System Builder* 4 (April/May 1991): 39–42.

Holton, John B. "Data, Process and Logic (DPL) Flow Diagramming: An Integrated Approach to CIS Development." *Information Executive* 3 (Winter 1990): 57–63.

Huff, Clifford C. "Elements of a Realistic CASE Tool Adoption Budget." *Communications of the ACM* 35 (April 1992): 45–54.

Hughes, Cary T., and Clark, Jon D. "The Stages of CASE Usage." *Datamation* 36 (February 1, 1990): 41–44.

Kievit, KarenAnn. "Software Review: EXCELERATOR 1.9." *Journal of Management Systems* 3 (Number 1, 1991): 83–90.

Kuehn, Ralph R., and Fleck, Jr., Robert A. "Data Flow Diagrams for Managerial Problem Analysis." *Information Executive* 3 (Winter 1990): 11–15.

Lindholm, Elizabeth. "A World of CASE Tools." *Datamation* 38 (March 1, 1992): 75ff.

Loh, Marcus, and Nelson, R. Ryan. "Reaping CASE Harvests." *Datamation* 35 (July 1, 1989): 31*ff.*

McCusker, Tom. "Tools to Manage Big Projects." *Datamation* 37 (January 15, 1991): 71ff.

McMullen, John. "CASE Tackles Software Maintenance." *Datamation* 37 (January 1, 1991): 65–66.

Moran, Robert. "The Case Against CASE." *InformationWeek* (February 17, 1992), 28*ff.*

Norman, Ronald J., and Nunamaker, Jr., Jay F. "CASE Productivity Perceptions of Software Engineering Professionals." *Communications of the ACM* 32 (September 1989): 1102–1108.

Prakash, Jay. "How Europe Is Using CASE." *Datamation* 36 (August 1, 1990): 79ff.

Ricciuti, Mike. "Database Vendors Make Their CASE." *Datamation* 38 (March 1, 1992): 59–60.

Statland, Norman. "Payoffs Down the Pike: A CASE Study." *Datamation* 35 (April 1, 1989): 32*ff.*

Sullivan-Trainor, Michael L. "TI's IEF Scores High for Integration, Benefits Delivery." *ComputerWorld* 25 (April 22, 1991): 72–73.

Vessey, Iris; Jarvenpaa, Sirkka L.; and Tractinsky, Noam. "Evaluation of Vendor Products: CASE Tools as Methodology Companions." *Communications of the ACM* 35 (April 1992): 90–105.

Winkler, Connie. "Better Project Management in Uncertain Times." *Datamation* 36 (June 1, 1990): 95–98.

Winsberg, Paul. "CASE: Getting the Big Picture." *Database Programming & Design* 1 (March 1988): 54–57.

Yourdon, Edward. "What Ever Happened to Structured Analysis?" *Datamation* 32 (June 1, 1986): 133ff.

Chapter 7

Tools of Systems Design, Implementation, and Use

LEARNING OBJECTIVES

After studying this chapter, you should:

- Understand how the definition of the firm's data resource can begin with an entity-relationship diagram, and be able to draw such a diagram
- Be able to draw Warnier-Orr diagrams to document systems processes on all levels—from the highest summary to the lowest detail
- Be able to draw system flowcharts to document the technology that is incorporated into systems designs
- Know more about the impact that prototyping is having on the system life cycle

INTRODUCTION

When the firm's executives engage in strategic planning, one of the outputs can be an enterprise data model that describes future data needs for the entire organization. One form of the enterprise data model is an entity-relationship diagram that identifies the data entities and shows their relationships.

We saw in the previous chapter that some tools of analysis and design are suited for documenting systems processes in a summary fashion, whereas other tools are better suited to the detail. However, there is one tool that does not have this limitation. It is Warnier-Orr, which can handle all documentation levels. You can completely document systems processes with only Warnier-Orr diagrams.

Most of the documentation tools do not reveal the technology that is used in processing and storing the data. A tool that does show technology is the one that has been around the longest—the flowchart. System flowcharts document systems at a summary level, and program flowcharts capture the detail.

All of the documentation tools are applied within the framework of one or more methodologies. The SLC is the traditional methodology, but this pattern is being impacted by a newer methodology called prototyping. Systems developers can prepare prototypes of the final system as a means of determining user information needs and characteristics of systems design. The prototypes improve the communications between the information specialists and the manager, and reduce the time required to deliver operational systems.

This chapter concludes our discussion of methodologies and tools. These topics assume greater importance as systems become more complex, and as the scope of systems projects expands to include users who are expected to actively contribute to the developmental effort.

THE DETERMINATION OF DATA NEEDS

Data plays the central role in a firm's CBIS. In fact, you could say that all of the firm's computer processing revolves around the database. The processing transforms the data into the information that is needed by the various users. Therefore, the definition of data needs is a key step in achieving a CBIS that supports the users in the way that they expect.

A Problem-oriented Approach

Firms first defined their data needs separately for each system, following a series of logical steps. For example, when information specialists were developing a particular system such as a DSS, they would follow the sequence illustrated in Figure 7.1. First the *problem* would be defined. Then, the *decisions* required to solve the problem would be identified, and for each decision the required *information* would be described. Next, the *processing* necessary to produce the information would be determined, and finally the *data* required by the processing would be specified.

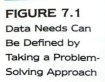

FIGURE 7.1

Data Needs Can
Be Defined by
Taking a Problem-
Solving Approach

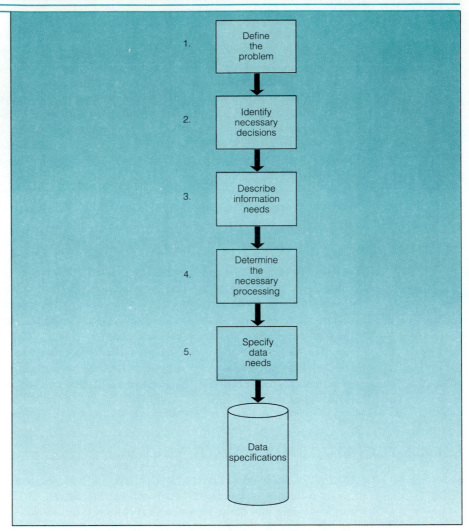

1. Define the problem
2. Identify necessary decisions
3. Describe information needs
4. Determine the necessary processing
5. Specify data needs

Data specifications

An Enterprise Modeling Approach

Although the approach of keying on the users' problems enabled the data needs of each system to be defined in a logical manner, a weakness was the difficulty of linking the data of one system to that of another. Systems could not easily share data. This weakness was overcome by the database management systems, or DBMSs, which became popular during the 1970s.

The DBMSs made the contents of the database easier to use, but the contents were still determined in a system-by-system manner. Very frequently, when designing a new system, data would be required, which had not previously been identified and would have to be added to the database.

A solution to this difficulty was seen to be a formal effort to determine the firm's entire data needs and then the storage of that data in the database. Subsequent systems development efforts would then draw on the data already in the database. It was a *proactive strategy* of anticipating needs in advance of systems development, rather than a *reactive strategy* of waiting for individual users to express their needs.

This is essentially the idea behind enterprise data modeling. During strategic planning, when the firm's executives define the future role of the firm in its environment, the firm's data is documented. The name that has been given to the description of all of the firm's data is **enterprise data model**. This top-down process of determining data needs is illustrated in Figure 7.2.

A good way to document the enterprise data model is by means of an entity-relationship diagram. The entity-relationship diagram provides the basis for all subsequent database documentation, including the data dictionary.

FIGURE 7.2

Data Needs Can Be Defined by Creating an Enterprise Data Model

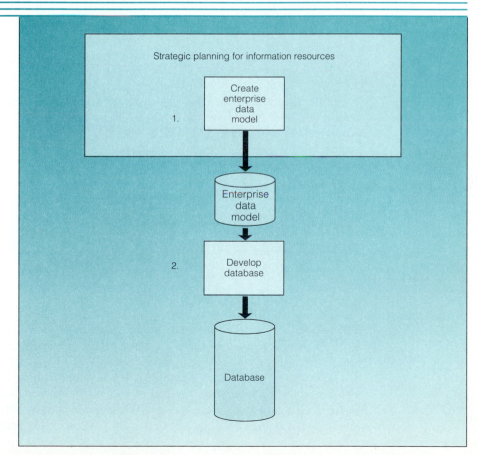

THE ENTITY-RELATIONSHIP DIAGRAM

An **entity-relationship diagram (ER diagram)** documents the firm's data by identifying the data entities and showing the relationships that exist between the entities.

Entities

An **entity** can be (1) an environmental element, (2) a resource, or (3) a transaction, which is of such importance to the firm that it is documented with data. The entities are documented in the ER diagram with rectangles, as shown below. Each rectangle is labeled with the name of the entity, which is usually a singular noun. Although an entity is labeled with a singular noun, this entity can occur multiple times. For example, there are multiple employees, time cards, and customers.

Relationships

A **relationship** is an association that exists between two entities and is illustrated with a diamond. Each diamond is labeled with a verb. In the example below an employee *fills out* a time card. This relationship can also be read in the reverse sequence: time card *is filled out by* employee.

Connectivity

The number of times that one entity occurs in relation to another entity is referred to as its **connectivity**, and there are three types: one-to-one, one-to-many, and many-to-many. A common way to show connectivity is to use the Characters 1 and *M*, as shown in Figure 7.3. In Figure 7.3A one invoice produces one picking ticket, which enables the warehouse workers to pull the items listed on the invoice. In Figure 7.3B a customer's accounts receivable contains charges reflected by multiple invoices, and in Figure 7.3C many customers purchase many products.

FIGURE 7.3

Types of
Connectivity

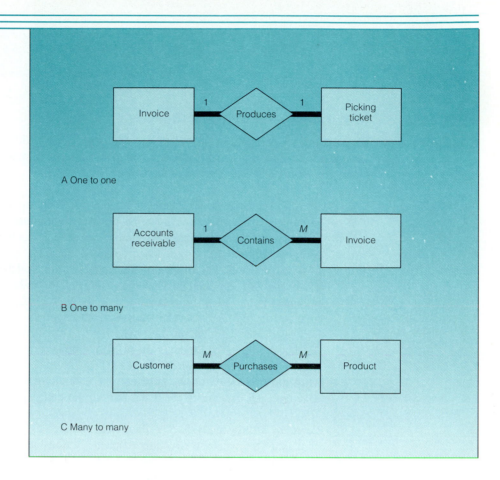

A One to one

B One to many

C Many to many

Identification of Entities

It is necessary to identify each occurrence of each entity, and this is accomplished
by means of attributes. An **attribute** is a characteristic of an entity. As an example,
the attributes of a customer include customer number, customer name, and sales
territory. The attributes are actually data elements, and each is given a single value,
called the **attribute value**. For example, the customer number 8790331 is assigned
to the Acme Company, which is located in sales territory 66.

Some attributes serve to identify the entity, and they are called **identifiers**. An
example is customer number. No two customers have the same number. Other
attributes describe the entity, and they are called **descriptors**. Examples are customer name and territory. Several customers might have the same name, and several
most certainly would be located in the same territory. Identifiers are often shown
in the ER diagram as underlined entries, next to their entities.

Preparation of an ER Diagram

ER diagrams are prepared by information specialists, working with users. The users can include executives, the MIS steering committee, user area managers, and non-managers. The specialists take seven steps:

1. **Identify the entities.** Management decides which environmental elements, resources, and transactions are to be described with data.
2. **Identify the relationships.** Each entity is related to another by means of some type of action.
3. **Prepare a rough ER diagram.** The symbols are sketched out so that, when possible, the relationships read from left to right, or from top to bottom. Figure 7.4 is an example of a rough ER diagram of the data involved in the purchase of materials from suppliers. A supplier fills a purchase order that contains raw materials that the firm needs for its production process. The amounts of all of a supplier's purchase orders represent its accounts payable.
4. **Map data elements to the entities.** The data elements that identify and describe each data entity are listed next to the entity, as shown in Figure 7.5.
5. **Perform a data analysis.** The data elements are studied for the purpose of making the database structure efficient. Actions such as the following are taken:

   ■ **Eliminate repeating elements in an entity.** For example, a purchase order record should not contain multiple ordered items. Note the *occurs n times* entries. This problem is eliminated by creating a new entity, such as a *Purchase order line item*, as shown below. In this example, the new entity contains two identifier attributes—Purchase order number and line item number. Such multiple identifier attributes are called **composite keys**.

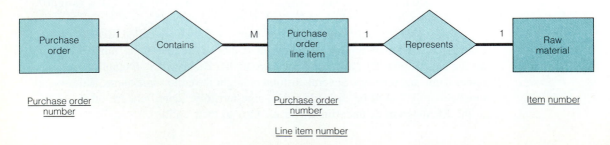

FIGURE 7.4

A Rough Entity-
Relationship
Diagram

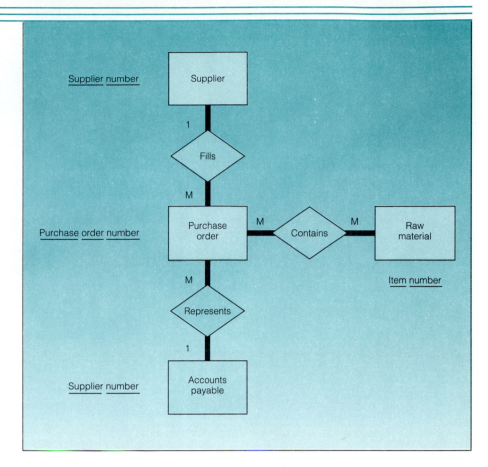

- **Ensure that descriptor keys rely on the entire composite key for identification.** For example, in the *Purchase order line item* entity, values can be assigned to descriptor elements only when both the purchase order number and the line item number are known.
- **Ensure that the values of attributes do not rely on the values of other attributes in the same entity.** For example, you would not want to include *Item extended price* if it could be computed by multiplying *Item unit price* times *Item quantity ordered.*

6. **Prepare a modified ER diagram.** The results of the data analysis are incorporated into a new ER diagram as shown in Figure 7.6.
7. **Review the ER diagram with managers and refine.** The systems analyst reviews the diagram with management and refines it when necessary.

   The ER diagram can then provide the basis for the development of the data dictionary. Each attribute on the ER diagram can be documented with a data element dictionary entry.

FIGURE 7.5

Data Elements Are Mapped to the Entity-Relationship Diagram

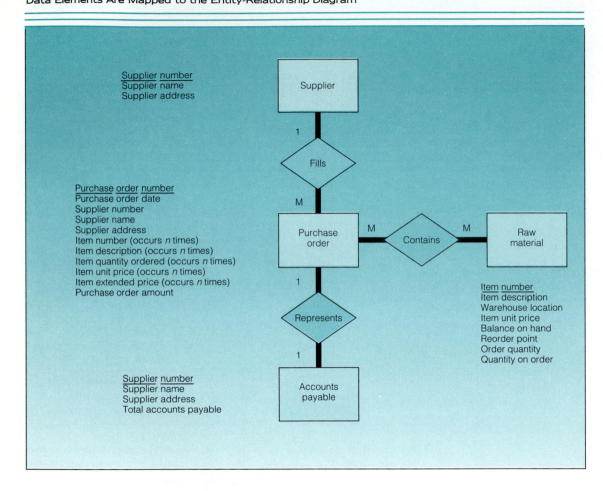

The ER Diagram Shows Relationships, Not Flows

An important point to keep in mind is the fact that the ER diagram does not show data flow. The ER diagram is a static model. It is a snapshot of entities and relationships between them.

Putting the ER Diagram in Perspective

The ER diagram is a recent innovation, only having been introduced in 1976.[1] It is a useful tool for conceptualizing the contents of a database. Enterprise data modeling is no doubt the way to go, but it requires the firm's executives to engage in

[1] Peter Chen, "The Entity-Relationship Model—Toward a Unified View of Data," *ACM Transactions on Database Systems* 1 (March 1976), 9–36.

FIGURE 7.6

A Modified Entity-Relationship Diagram

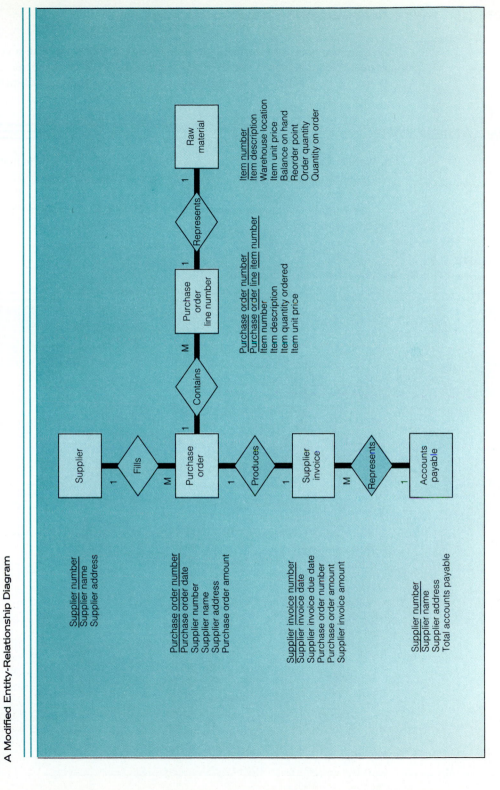

strategic planning for information resources and to follow up with a commitment to create a comprehensive database. As support for SPIR gains momentum, the use of the ER diagram as the starting point for database definition will increase.

WARNIER-ORR

A Warnier-Orr diagram represents the structure of a system in a form that resembles an organization chart. Figure 7.7A shows such a chart, and Figure 7.7B shows the Warnier-Orr equivalent.

A Warnier-Orr diagram uses brackets, or braces, to show hierarchy. The upper level is at the left, and the lowest level is at the right. In Figure 7.7B, the large

FIGURE 7.7
A Warnier-Orr Diagram Shows Hierarchical Structure

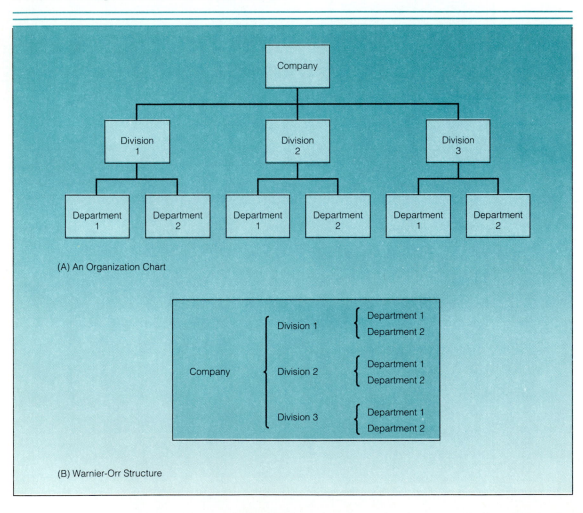

(A) An Organization Chart

(B) Warnier-Orr Structure

bracket in the center shows that there are multiple divisions in the company. The three brackets on the right show that each division is subdivided into multiple departments.

The Three Basic Contructs

Like structured English, Warnier-Orr illustrates a system using the three structured programming constructs: (1) sequence, (2) selection, and (3) repetition.

The Sequence Construct   Sequential processes are enclosed in a bracket and are executed from top to bottom. Figure 7.8 shows how the process of printing a detail line consists of three steps. First, Data Element 1 is moved. Then, Data Element 2 is moved. Finally, the line is printed.

The Selection Construct   The selection construct is used to choose between two or more alternatives, based on a particular condition. In a programming language, this is accomplished by one or more **IF** statements. In Warnier-Orr, the different alternatives are separated by a special symbol—a circle containing a plus sign.

$$\oplus$$

The symbol is called an **exclusive**, or an **exclusive or**, and it means that the alternatives are mutually exclusive. That is, you perform one *or* the other—you do not perform them in combination. For example, if you prepare a summary report only at the end of the month, you could illustrate this with the pattern in Figure 7.9.

The word **Skip** means that no action is taken when the corresponding condition exists. The word **Null** is also used. This is an example of the **IF-THEN** structure.

The (0,1) beneath each condition is a **subscript** that identifies how many times the condition exists. The 0 means that the condition may exist zero times, and the 1 means that it may exist one time.

FIGURE 7.8
The Sequence
Contruct

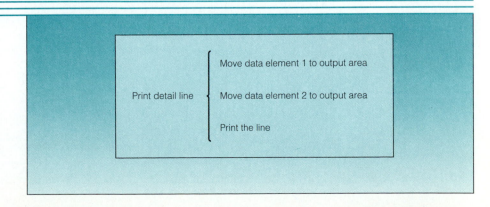

FIGURE 7.9
The Selection
Contruct

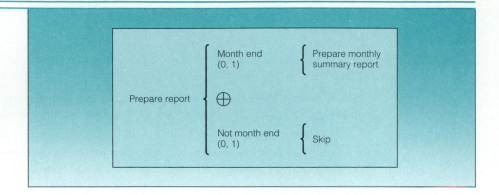

You will notice in this example that the right-hand brackets contain only single entries. Multiple entries are also acceptable. The entries in the right-hand brackets are the *actions* that correspond to the *conditions* in the center bracket.

We can easily modify the above example to reflect the IF–THEN–ELSE structure by replacing the word Skip with an action. Assume that when it is not the end of the month you want to prepare a daily detail listing. This design is illustrated in Figure 7.10.

Another modification in the figure is important. Instead of the second condition reading *Not month end*, it reads *Month end* with a bar above it. The bar is called a **negation**, and means that the condition stated immediately below does *not* exist.

The conditions are not restricted to binary choices between two alternatives. You can have multiple alternatives. Figure 7.11 is an example of three possible customer discounts based on the dollar amount of the order.

Notice that you still use the (0, 1) subscript for each condition even though there are more than two. When multiple conditions are linked with exclusives, only *one* condition can exist at a time.

FIGURE 7.10
The IF–THEN–
ELSE Selection
Construct

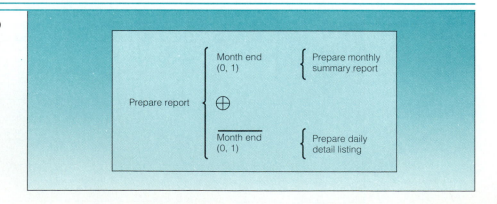

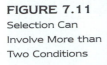

FIGURE 7.11

Selection Can
Involve More than
Two Conditions

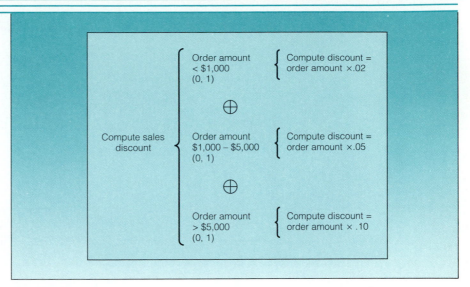

The Repetition Construct   When a routine is repeated, indicate this by using numbers and letters for the subscript to represent a particular number or a range of iterations.

When a process is performed a known number of times, use that number for the subscript. For example, if the process is performed only one time, use a (1). Perhaps you are documenting an order entry system and you want to show that you enter certain order identification data only one time. That procedure is diagrammed in Figure 7.12.

In those situations where you are not certain how many times a process is to be repeated, you use (n). Let us continue with the order entry example to illustrate this technique. A data entry operator enters sales order data into a keyboard terminal. Figure 7.13 documents this portion of the system. The (n) subscript for the *Enter sales order* process means that the exact number of orders is not certain; it

FIGURE 7.12

Subscripts Can
Show that a
Process is
Performed Only
One Time

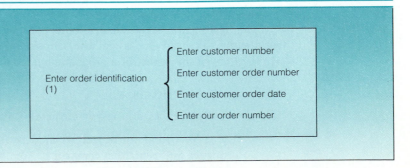

FIGURE 7.13
Example of the
Repetition
Construct

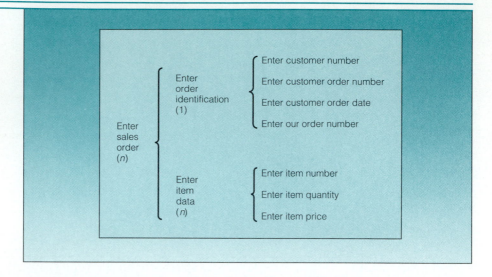

varies with sales activity. The (*n*) subscript for the *Enter item data* process means that the item data is entered a variable number of times *per order* depending on the number of items that each customer orders.

Notice that subscripts are not included for the processes contained in the right-hand brackets. This is because the brackets reflect the sequence construct.

A Warnier-Orr Example

Figure 7.14 is a Warnier-Orr diagram of a salesperson commission system.

A subscript is not used for the *Compute salesperson commissions* process, as it represents the entire system; the system is performed one time.

The first step of the processing is to initialize storage, and it is done once. Next, a variable number of sales transactions are processed. For each transaction, it is necessary to read a record, determine the commission amount, accumulate totals, and print a detail line. After all of the transaction records have been processed, final totals are printed.

A selection construct shows how the commission amount is determined. When the sales amount is greater than $1,000, a bonus is added to the commission.

The right-hand brackets contain the data elements and arithmetic expressions that describe the detail processing. They are similar to structured English, and can take the form of the syntax of a programming language.

Warnier-Orr Guidelines

Here are some guidelines to help you create effective Warnier-Orr diagrams:

1. **Use a verb and an object when describing the processing of both sequence and repetition constructs. For the selection construct, simply state the conditions.**

FIGURE 7.14

A Warnier-Orr Diagram of the Salesperson Commission System

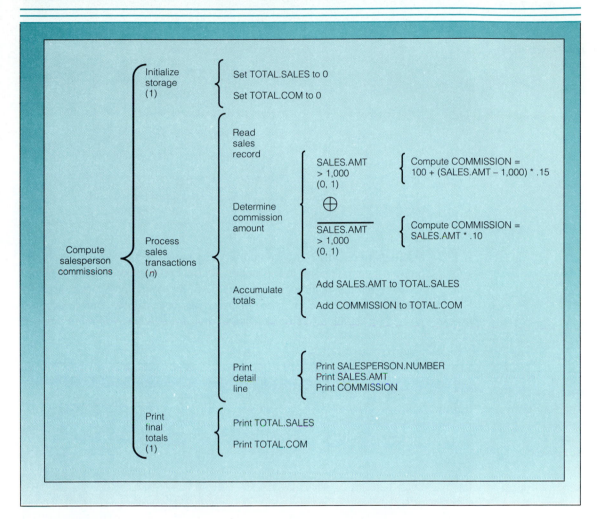

2. **Use a series of Warnier-Orr diagrams to document large systems.** Figure 7.15 shows how a system named the distribution system consists of eight subsystems.

Figure 7.16 shows how the first subsystem, order entry, can be documented in terms of its four major processes.

Figure 7.17 shows how the second order entry process, *Compute credit check*, can be documented.

Here we used three diagrams to document the three systems levels. The process names on the diagrams provide the linkage between the systems levels.

FIGURE 7.15

The Eight
Subsystems of
the Distribution
System

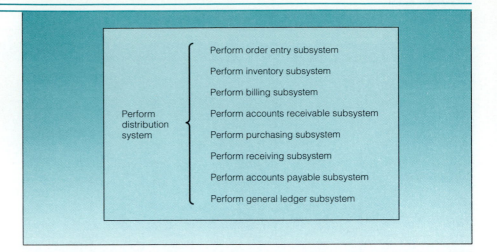

Perform distribution system

Perform order entry subsystem

Perform inventory subsystem

Perform billing subsystem

Perform accounts receivable subsystem

Perform purchasing subsystem

Perform receiving subsystem

Perform accounts payable subsystem

Perform general ledger subsystem

3. **Set flags to establish logical connections between diagrams.** Very often processing at one point in a system will affect processing at another point. Take the reorder-point logic in Figure 7.18, for example. We only want to check the reorder point when an order has been filled. This is accomplished by setting a filled-order flag in the *Check balance on hand* process

FIGURE 7.16

The Four Main
Processes of the
Order Entry
Subsystem

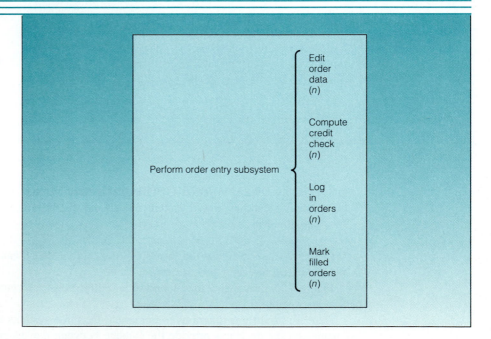

Perform order entry subsystem

Edit order data (*n*)

Compute credit check (*n*)

Log in orders (*n*)

Mark filled orders (*n*)

FIGURE 7.17

The Process of Computing a Credit Check

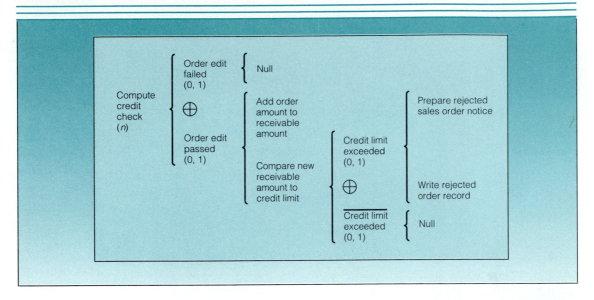

and then testing the flag in the *Check reorder point* process. In a computer-based system, a **flag** is a character (such as a 1) that is stored in a certain storage location. The term **switch** is also used. A flag can also establish a logical connection between separate systems. The purchase flag that is set in the lower-right-hand corner of Figure 7.18 can be checked by the purchasing system to determine when a purchase order is to be prepared.

4. **Do not mix constructs within a bracket.** A bracket should contain only a sequence, a selection, or a repetition construct—not a combination.

Reasons to Use Warnier-Orr

All things considered, Warnier-Orr is probably the best of the process documentation tools. The reasons are:

1. Warnier-Orr is very user friendly. Its few symbols and rules make it easy to learn and to understand. The manager can use it when engaged in end-user computing, and the systems analyst can use it to communicate the design when developing a system for the manager.

2. Warnier-Orr can be used to document any level of system structure—from a top-level overview to the detail logic of a program module. This feature, combined with user friendliness, means a manager can work with the systems analyst for a longer period of the system development process. The extended involvement increases the likelihood that the system will meet the manager's needs.

FIGURE 7.18

Flags Enable Logical Connections between System Components

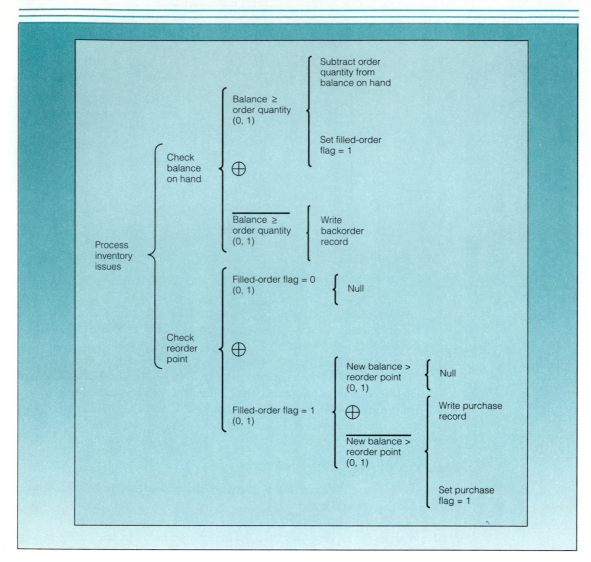

3. The left-to-right pattern of the Warnier-Orr documentation forces a top-down, structured approach. It is virtually impossible to develop a system design in other than a top-down manner.

4. A Warnier-Orr diagram can be very **machine readable**. This does not mean that the diagram can be read by the computer. Rather, it means that very little effort is required to convert the diagram to program code. The overall structure is very similar to that of a structured program. The entries

within the Warnier-Orr brackets can be regarded as program modules, and can be stated in the syntax of the programming language to be used.

A Reason Not to Use Warnier-Orr

A major reason *not* to use Warnier-Orr is that it is not well supported by CASE tools. Most of the tools elect, instead, to document processes with DFDs. That means that if a firm decides to use Warnier-Orr and CASE, there is a limited selection of CASE products from which to choose.

Putting Warnier-Orr in Perspective

When a systems tool is evaluated in terms of its ability to assist the manager in problem solving, two key considerations are important. First, the tool should be structurally sound, yet sufficiently user friendly for the manager to use it personally when engaged in end-user computing. Second, the tool should be usable by the systems analyst to create the design and then communicate that design to the manager or other information specialists. In both of these respects, Warnier-Orr is excellent.

FLOWCHARTING

Flowcharting was the only analysis and design tool during the punched card era. When computers replaced punched card machines, information specialists continued to rely on flowcharting. Many of the flowchart symbols were intended to illustrate punched card processes and data, and are not ordinarily used with computer-based systems. In addition, the flowchart symbols have not been updated to reflect innovations in computing technology and systems designs. For these reasons, flowcharting was better suited to the systems of the 1960s than the systems of today. However, flowcharting continues to be one of the primary documentation tools.

Flowcharting Fundamentals

There are two basic types of flowcharts. One is used to illustrate how separate processes are linked to form a system. This type of flowchart is the big picture of the system and is called a **system flowchart**. The other type is used to show the steps executed by a single computer program, and is called a **program flowchart**.

Both types of flowcharts are drawn using symbols that have been standardized on an international scale. Flowcharting, therefore, represents a common language of problem solvers around the world.

System Flowcharts

The system flowchart symbols illustrate both processes and data.

Process Symbols   There are three primary ways to process data: manually, with a keydriven device, and with a computer.

- **Manual Processes** A manual process does not employ any type of mechanical, electromechanical, or electronic equipment. The work is performed by hand or with the use of pencil and paper. A manual process is illustrated with this symbol:

In choosing the process label, be as specific as possible. For example, do not simply say *Make calculations*. Specify the type of calculations, such as *Make weekly payroll calculations*.

- **Keydriven Device Processes** Keydriven devices are operated by pressing keys on a keyboard. There are two basic types—offline and online. An **offline keydriven device** is not connected directly to the computer. Examples are a typewriter, a cash register, and a pocket calculator. A process performed with this type of device is represented by:

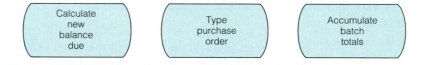

An **online keydriven device** is connected directly to the computer. Good examples are a cathode-ray tube (CRT) terminal, and a microcomputer keyboard. Processes performed by operating an online keydriven device are represented by:

- **Computer Processes** Each computer program is illustrated with a rectangle:

The label describes what the program does or identifies its name.

Data symbols   Figure 7.19 illustrates some data symbols that can be used. Standard symbols do not exist for all types of media. For example, there is no standard symbol for the magnetic diskette. In cases such as this, the organization creates its own symbol, as we did for the figure.

A Sample System Flowchart   A flowchart usually consists of alternating process and data symbols. The data output from one process is the input to the next. This rule does not always apply, but it is a good way to think of the flowchart pattern. Figure 7.20 is a system flowchart of a sales commission system. The steps below correspond to the numbered steps in the flowchart.

1. The mail is opened, and the sales orders are removed.
2. The sales order data is entered into an online keyboard device, and the sales order forms are filed in a Sales Order Form file. A manual process symbol could have been used for the filing process but in this particular instance is not necessary. The manual process can be assumed.
3. The computer sorts the records, and the output file is written onto a mag-, netic disk. The bracket at the right is an **annotation symbol**, and it is used to add comments that do not fit within the symbols. In this case the comment identifies the sort key.
4. The sorted sales records serve as input to a program that computes the sales commissions and prints a sales commission report.

The process flow should be from top to bottom and from left to right when the page layout permits. As long as the flow is in this direction, there is no need to put arrowheads on the lines. However, if arrowheads are used, they should be used only on lines that: (1) enter process symbols or (2) enter data symbols at the end of a flow. Examine Figure 7.20 to see how this guideline is followed. The only data symbols with arrowheads leading into them are the Sales Order Form file and the sales commission report—both at ends of flows.

Three Primary System Flowcharting Processes   Although there is practically an infinite number of possible symbol arrangements, three basic processes are very common. These processes are data input, sorting, and file maintenance.

1. **Data Input**   Most systems are triggered by the receipt of some type of source document. In the system illustrated in Figure 7.20, the source document is the sales order.

   The most popular way to enter the source document data is with an online keydriven device. This operation is diagrammed as:

FIGURE 7.19
Data Symbols

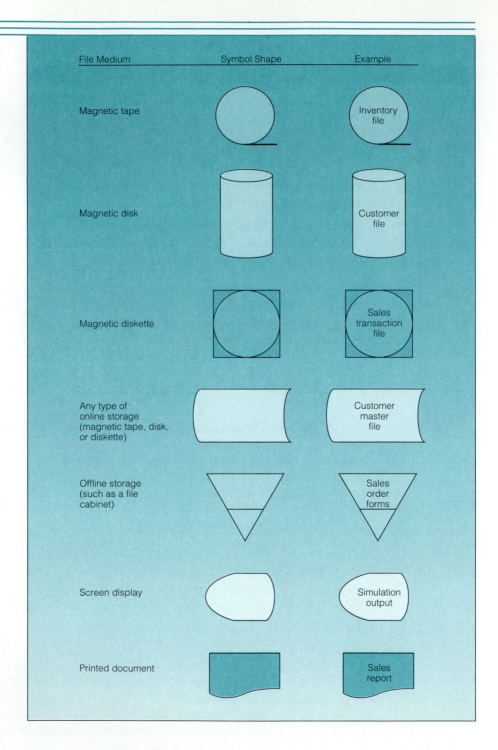

File Medium	Symbol Shape	Example
Magnetic tape		Inventory file
Magnetic disk		Customer file
Magnetic diskette		Sales transaction file
Any type of online storage (magnetic tape, disk, or diskette)		Customer master file
Offline storage (such as a file cabinet)		Sales order forms
Screen display		Simulation output
Printed document		Sales report

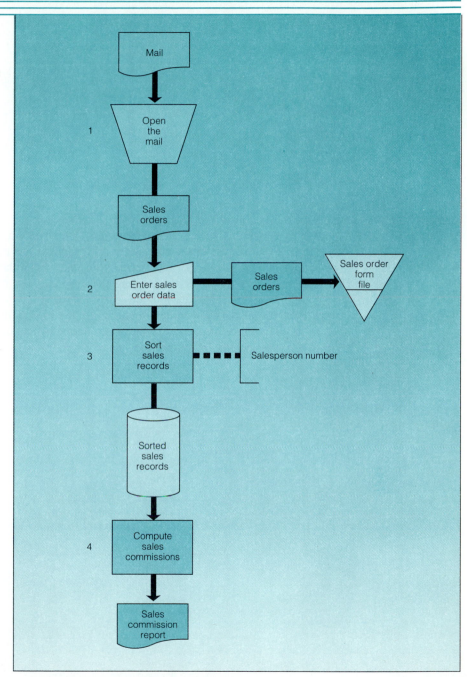

FIGURE 7.20
A System
Flowchart of a
Sales Commission
System

The online keydriven device symbol is connected directly to a rectangle that represents the computer's CPU. This is one instance when two process symbols are not separated by an intervening data symbol. Think of the two symbols as representing the keyboard and the computer, and the line as the cable that provides the connection.

2. **Sorting** When a sort program rearranges the records in a file, you show the file both before and after the sort. Notice the use of the word *Sorted* below to identify the output file.

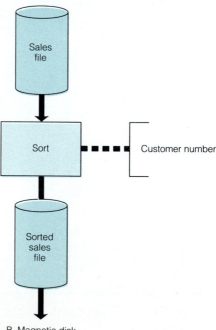

B. Magnetic disk

3. **File Maintenance**   When a master file is updated with transaction data, the process is called **file maintenance**. The transactions cause new master records to be added, master records that are no longer needed to be deleted, and changes to be made to master record fields. When the records of the master file are arranged sequentially and each must be processed in sequence, it is necessary to create a completely new master file:

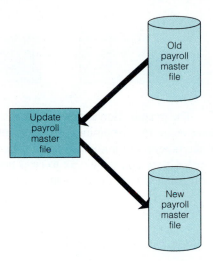

Notice the use of the words *Old* and *New* to identify the two files.

When the master file is organized for direct access, changes are made directly to the existing file. Notice the use of the two-headed arrow to illustrate how old records are read from the master file and new records are written to it.

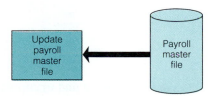

These three system flowcharting patterns (data entry, sorting, and file maintenance) account for a large portion of system processes.

Program Flowcharts

Since a system flowchart documents a system at a summary level, it is necessary to supplement it with more detailed documentation. Program flowcharts can serve this purpose.

Unlike the system flowchart, the program flowchart does not document data. It documents only processes, which fall into five categories: (1) predefined processes, (2) preparation, (3) input and output, (4) data movement and manipulation, and (5) logic.

The **predefined process symbol** represents program statements that refer to other program modules. The driver module of a structured program consists primarily of predefined process statements, which are illustrated with this symbol:

The **preparation symbol** represents statements that are used to make the computer ready for processing. These statements usually are included at the beginning of the program to initialize certain data values, to set flags or switches that can be tested with program logic, or to clear primary storage areas. Preparation statements are illustrated with the hexagon:

The **input and output symbol** is used to illustrate statements such as READ, WRITE, and PRINT.

The **data movement and manipulation symbol** represents the statements that perform the different types of arithmetic processes and move data elements from one primary storage location to another.

The **logic symbol** represents the statements that enable the the computer to select between alternatives. In most cases, the computer makes a binary decision, deciding whether the answer to a question is *yes or no* or *true or false*.

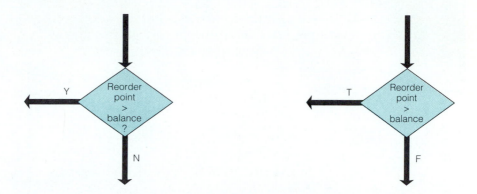

One arrow leads into the diamond, and two arrows exit from it. Any points on the diamond can be used, but entry is usually from the top. Take care to always label both exits.

In addition to the process symbols, the **terminal symbol** is used in *program flowcharts only* to identify the beginning and end of program modules.

The terminal symbols that mark the beginning and end of the driver module are usually labeled with the words *Start* and *End*, respectively. The symbol at the beginning of a subsidiary module contains the module name, and the one at the end contains the word *Return*.

Program Flowchart Example   Figure 7.21 illustrates a program that performs the salesperson commission processing in Step 4 of the system flowchart in Figure 7.20.

Lengthy Flowcharts

Do not try to put an entire system or program flowchart on a single page if it will not easily fit. Rather, use multiple pages. The process flow from one page to another can be accomplished with a special symbol called the **off-page connector**. It has the appearance of home plate on a baseball diamond and is always positioned upright as shown. The same letter or number is entered in the pair of symbols to show the relationship.

FIGURE 7.21
A Program Flowchart Example

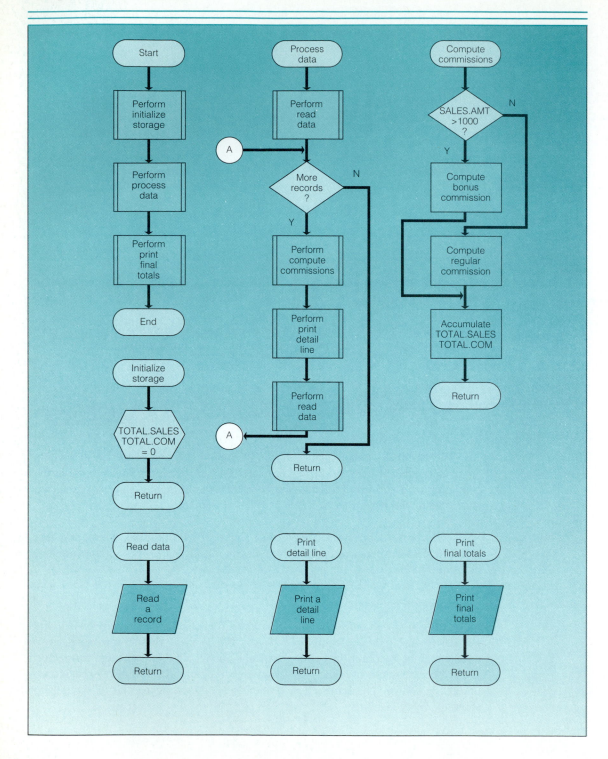

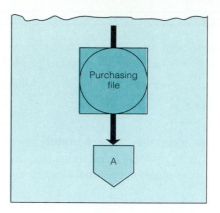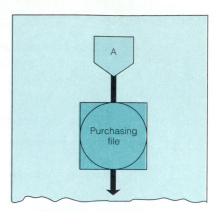

When using off-page connectors in a *system* flowchart, always repeat the file symbol on the succeeding page as shown. This technique enables the reader to know which file is being used on the succeeding page without having to refer back to the preceeding page.

Another connector eliminates long lines on a single page and is called the **on-page connector**. The symbol is a small circle. We used this technique in Figure 7.21.

Either letters or numbers are entered in sets of related connector symbols. If letters are used for off-page connectors, numbers can be used for on-page, or vice versa.

Putting Flowcharting in Perspective

System flowcharts are the only documentation tool that shows computing technology. At a glance, you can see how the computer is being used in the system. The standardized symbol shapes of both the system and program flowchart make them effective media for communicating system design and logic.

The big disadvantage of flowcharting is that detail cannot be gradually cranked into the structure. Structured tools such as DFDs and Warnier-Orr enable the structure to unfold gradually, like using a rheostat to gradually brighten a light. Using the same analogy, flowcharting is like an ordinary on-off switch. Just as the light is either off or on, you either use the system flowchart to show a summary or the program flowchart to show detail. There are no intermediate levels.

Although the program flowchart can be used in structured programming, the system flowchart is not adaptable to structured design. This limitation has diminished the popularity of flowcharts but not eliminated them. Information specialists are slow to reject tools that they have mastered and have used with success. For this reason flowcharts are likely to be around for some time.

PROTOTYPING

A **prototype** provides developers and potential users with an idea of how the system in its completed form will function. The process of producing a prototype is called **prototyping**.

Types of Prototypes[2]

There are two types of prototypes. A **Type I prototype** eventually becomes the operational system. A **Type II prototype** is a throwaway model that serves as the blueprint for the development of the operational system.

Development of a Type I Prototype   Figure 7.22 shows the steps involved in developing a Type I prototype.

1. **Identify user needs.** The systems analyst interviews the user to obtain an idea of what the user wants out of the system.
2. **Develop a prototype.** The systems analyst, perhaps working with other information specialists, uses one or more prototyping tools to develop a prototype. Examples of prototyping tools are integrated application generatators and prototyping toolkits. An **integrated application generator** is a prewritten software system that is capable of producing *all* of the desired features in the new system—menus, reports, screens, a database, and so on. Examples of integrated tools are R:base 5000 and NOMAD2. A **prototyping toolkit** includes separate software systems, each capable of producing a *portion* of the desired system features. Examples of toolkit contents are electronic spreadsheets, DBMSs, report generators, and screen generators. Some CASE tools offer some of these features.
3. **Determine if the prototype is acceptable.** The analyst educates the user in prototype use and gives the user an opportunity to become familiar with the system. The user advises the analyst whether the prototype is satisfactory. If so, Step 4 is taken; if not, the prototype is revised by repeating Steps 1, 2, and 3 with a better understanding of the user needs.
4. **Use the prototype.** The prototype becomes the operational system.

This approach is possible only when the prototyping tools enable the prototype to contain *all* of the essential elements of the new system.

Development of a Type II Prototype   Figure 7.23 shows the steps involved in developing a Type II prototype.

The first three steps are the same as for a Type I prototype.

---

[2]This discussion is based on Jane M. Carey, "Prototyping: Alternative Systems Development Methodology," *Information and Software Technology* 32 (March 1990), 120–21.

FIGURE 7.22

Development of a
Type I Prototype

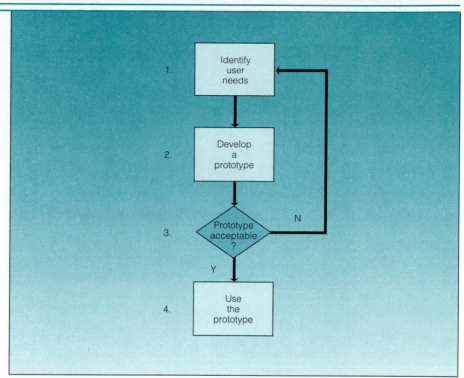

5. **Code the operational system.** The programmer uses the prototype as the basis for coding the operational system.
6. **Test the operational system.** The programmer tests the system.
7. **Determine if the operational system is acceptable.** The user advises the analyst whether the system is acceptable. If so, Step 7 is taken; if not, Steps 4 and 5 are repeated.
8. **Use the operational system.**

This approach is popular when the prototype only has the *appearance* of an operational system and does not contain all of the essential system elements.

Prototyping and the System Development Life Cycle

For small-scale systems, prototyping can replace the system development life cycle. However, for large-scale systems or those that affect large organizational units, prototyping is incorporated into the SDLC. Table 7.1 shows that prototyping can be used in all four of the developmental phases. In addition, it can be used in the use phase to serve as the basis for systems maintenance.

FIGURE 7.23

Development of a
Type II Prototype

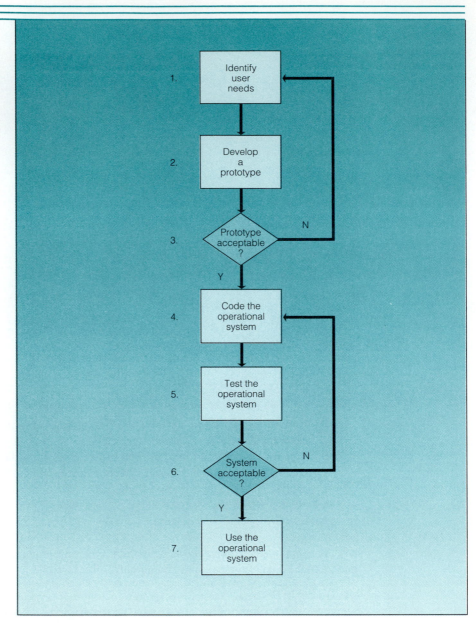

TABLE 7.1
Points in the
System Life
Cycle where
Prototyping
Can Be Used

Life cycle phase	Step
Planning	Define the problem
	Set system objectives
Analysis	Define information needs
Design	Prepare the detailed system design
	Evaluate alternate system configurations
Implementation	Specify the hardware resources
	Obtain the software resources
Use	Maintain the system

The Attraction of Prototyping[3]

Both users and information specialists like prototyping for the following reasons:

- Communications between the systems analyst and user are improved.
- The analyst can do a better job of determining the user's needs.
- The user plays a more active role in system development.
- The information specialists and user spend less time and effort in developing the system.
- Implementation is much easier because the user knows what to expect.

These advantages enable prototyping to cut developmental costs and increase user satisfaction with the delivered system.

Potential Pitfalls of Prototyping

Prototyping is not without its potential pitfalls:

- The haste to deliver the prototype may produce shortcuts in problem definition, alternative evaluation, and documentation. The term "quick and dirty" has been used to describe some prototyping efforts.
- The users may get so excited about the prototype that they have unrealistic expectations of the operational system.

[3] This and the next section are from Carey, "Prototyping," 121–22.

- Type I prototypes might not be as efficient as systems coded in a programming language.
- The computer-human interface provided by certain prototyping tools may not reflect good design techniques.

Both the user and the information specialists should be aware of these potential pitfalls when they elect to pursue the prototyping approach. If the warnings are not heeded, the results of the prototyping effort may be poor.

Applications That Are Good Prospects for Prototyping[4]

Prototyping works best for applications characterized by:

- **High risk** The problem is not well structured, there is a high rate of change over time, and the data requirements are uncertain.
- **Considerable user interaction** The system features online dialog between the user and a micro or a terminal.
- **Large number of users** Agreement on design details is difficult to achieve without hands-on experience.
- **A need for quick delivery**
- **An expected short use phase of the system**
- **An innovative system** The system is on the cutting edge, either in the way that it solves the problem or its use of hardware.
- **The user's behavior is unpredictable** The user has had no previous experience with such a system.

Applications that do not reflect these characteristics can be developed by following the SDLC in the traditional manner.

Putting Prototyping and Structured Development in Perspective

During the past decade prototyping and the structured approach to systems development have received much attention. Of the two, prototyping has fared better. The truth of the matter is that the structured approach was slow to catch on. Senior information specialists were so wedded to the traditional approach that they were hesitant to change. It took years for newer specialists to finally establish the validity of structured development.

Prototyping caught on much faster—too fast, perhaps. The above list of potential prototyping pitfalls is based on the experiences of firms that became too enthusiastic, and implemented prototype-based systems without giving adequate thought

[4]David Avison, and David Wilson, "Controls for Effective Prototyping," *Journal of Management Controls* 3 (Number 1, 1991), 45.

to planning, training, and control. Today's users are much more cautious and are more likely to achieve the potential advantages.

Structured development, using prototyping, represents the modern approach for implementing systems and will become more widespread in the future.

SUMMARY

When defining the content of the database, you can take either a problem-solving or a data modeling approach. The problem-solving approach begins with an identification of a problem to be solved, then successively identifies the decisions, the information, the processes, and, finally, the data. The data modeling approach involves the development of an enterprise data model as a part of SPIR. The model is a description of future data needs and can be represented by an ER diagram.

The preparation of an ER diagram is a step-by-step process that begins with an identification of the entities and their relationships, which are incorporated into a rough ER diagram. Data elements are mapped to the entitites, and a data analysis improves the efficiency of the data structure. In its final form the ER diagram must receive the approval of the managers. As more executives support SPIR, the popularity of ER diagramming will increase.

Warnier-Orr is unique in that it can document processes on all systems levels, using a series of brackets to represent the three structured programming constructs. The brackets on the left provide the summary documentation, and the brackets on the right provide the detail. Large systems are documented with a series of Warnier-Orr diagrams, and flags can be used to establish linkages within a single diagram or between multiple diagrams. Warnier-Orr is very user friendly, yet it can produce documentation that can be described as machine readable. When systems developers use Warnier-Orr, it forces them to take a top-down, structured approach. The main limitation of Warnier-Orr is the fact that relatively few CASE tools support it.

The documentation tool that has been around the longest, the flowchart, can indicate how computing technology is used in a system. However, the flowcharting symbols have not been kept current in terms of that technology. The two main types of flowcharts are system and program.

System flowcharts document entire systems with symbols for both processes and data. Special process symbols exist for manual, offline keydriven, online keydriven, and computer processes. These symbols are combined with data symbols that indicate the file media such as magnetic disk, document, and display. There are many possible symbol patterns, but three basic processes account for a large portion of systems designs. The processes are data input, sorting, and file maintenance.

Program flowcharts show the detail processing and logic of computer programs. Five symbol categories are used to show predefined processes, preparation, input and output, data movement and manipulation, and logic. Other symbols are used to show program terminal points, link system points on separate pages, and eliminate long lines on a page. The big limitation of flowcharting is that it does not lend itself to structured design. In spite of this deficiency, flowcharts remain popular, due, in part, to the fact that information specialists are hesitant to discard proven techniques.

Plagued with an inability to always accurately identify user needs, information specialists have adopted the prototyping approach. Type I prototypes eventually become operational systems, but Type II prototypes only serve as blueprints for custom programming efforts. Prototyping is made possible by modern prototyping tools. Integrated application generators contain all of the desired system elements. Prototyping toolkits contain software systems such as screen generators and DBMSs that treat system elements in an individual fashion. Prototypes can either replace the system life cycle or be inserted during any of the phases. The response of users and information specialists to prototyping has been excellent, in spite of some potential pitfalls. These pitfalls can be avoided through proper planning, training, and control. The prototyping methodology is a key ingredient in structured development and will become the standard way to develop systems in the future.

KEY TERMS

Entity
Relationship
Connectivity
Attribute
Attribute value
Exclusive, exclusive or
Negation

System flowchart
Program flowchart
Type I prototype
Type II prototype
Integrated application generator
Prototyping toolkit

KEY CONCEPTS

The two routes to data definition—a problem orientation and the enterprise data model
How mapping data elements to the ER diagram establishes a linkage with the data dictionary
How Warnier-Orr brackets handle levels and types of system structure, and contents of

brackets can provide both summary and detail descriptions
Machine readability
The hardware specific nature of system flowcharts
The relationship of prototyping to the system life cycle

QUESTIONS

1. What are the two basic approaches that a firm can take to the definition of its data needs?

2. Which documentation tool is well suited to the enterprise data model?

3. What are the three phenomena that entities represent?

4. Name the three types of connectivity.

5. What are the two types of attributes? Give one example of each for an employee.

6. When data elements are mapped to the ER diagram, some elements are underlined. What are they?

7. What is a composite key?

8. How do you eliminate repeating elements in an entity?

9. Why would you not want to include a data element such as Gross pay in an hourly employee's weekly payroll record?

10. How can you identify a sequence construct in a Warnier-Orr diagram? A selection construct? A repetition construct?

11. What word or words would indicate that a selection construct in a Warnier-Orr diagram expresses an IF-THEN logic?

12. How do you indicate that conditions in a Warnier-Orr diagram are mutually exclusive?

13. How do you show repetition in a Warnier-Orr diagram?

14. Name two uses of flags in Warnier-Orr diagrams.

15. What are the two main types of flowcharts?

16. What are the four process symbols used in a system flowchart?

17. Which of the three basic flowcharting pro-

cesses is represented by two process symbols with no intervening data symbol? What does the connecting line represent?

18. How does file maintenance of a direct access file differ from that of a sequential file?

19. What does a parallelogram represent in a program flowchart? What about a rectangle? A diamond? A hexagon?

20. What name is given to a small circle on a flowchart? To a symbol that looks like home plate?

21. What is the difference between a Type I and a Type II prototype?

22. What are the two categories of software that can be used to develop a prototype?

23. How can prototyping be used during the planning phase of the SLC? The analysis phase? The design phase? The implementation phase? The use phase?

24. Does the term "quick and dirty" reflect the prototyping philosophy? Explain.

25. List the characteristics of systems that are *not* good prospects of prototyping. Hint: Just reverse the prototyping characteristics.

TOPICS FOR DISCUSSION

1. Do you think that enterprise data modeling will become the most popular approach to developing a database?

2. Which of the documentation tools that we have described in Chapters 6 and 7 do you think is the most user friendly?

3. If you were a systems analyst, which tools would you select to document a system?

4. If you were a programmer, which tools would you prefer that the analyst use?

PROBLEMS

1. Draw a rough ER diagram of the data entities and relationships that are involved when a customer orders products from our firm. The customer places a sales order.

Each order contains one or more inventory items and represents an addition to the accounts receivable. When drawing the diagram, keep in mind that we are our supplier's customer and use Figure 7.4 as an example.

2. Now, map data elements to your rough ER diagram. Use Figure 7.5 as a basis.

3. Modify your rough ER diagram to eliminate data elements that occur multiple times within an entity and data elements that can be computed from other elements within the same entity. Use Figure 7.6 as a basis.

4. Do you remember Bryan's Department Store from Chapter 6? The president just returned from a seminar where Warnier-Orr was discussed. Your new task is to redocument the system described in Problem 4 at the end of Chapter 6, using, you guessed it, Warnier-Orr.

5. Prepare a Warnier-Orr diagram that documents the Eagle Mailorder Services processes described in Problem 5 at the end of Chapter 6.

6. As manager of the accounts receivable section at Tampa Linen Supply, you are always on the alert for ways to improve your procedures. You have just completed a college course in Warnier-Orr, and decide to use it to document a batch balancing procedure. Prepare a Warnier-Orr diagram that shows the following:
   a. Data is entered on a keyboard terminal from batched source documents. The source documents are then filed in a Batch Suspense file. The computer accumulates a batch total for each batch and writes the entered data onto a diskette file named the Transaction file.
   b. After all of the batches have been processed, batch totals are printed.
   c. A clerk compares the batch totals printed by the computer with batch totals that have been recorded on special paper forms by departmental supervisors. The forms are called batch control sheets.
   d. For each out-of-balance condition, the appropriate batch is removed from the

Batch Suspense file, and the error is corrected. The corrected data is entered into the computer using a keyboard terminal. The computer uses the corrected data to update the Transaction file. No action is taken when the batches are in balance.

Use Figures 7.14 and 7.18 as examples. Hint: Set a switch when an out-of-balance condition exists.

7. Draw a system flowchart of the following procedure:
   a. Open the mail.
   b. Separate the mail contents into two groups—sales orders and payments.
   c. File the payments in the Today's Payments file.
   d. Enter the sales order data into a keyboard terminal. After entering the data, file the sales orders in the Today's Sales Orders file.
   e. Use the entered sales order data to print a sales order listing.

8. Draw a system flowchart of the following procedure:
   a. The Sales Statistics file resides on a disk.
   b. Sort the file in salesperson number sequence.
   c. Use the sorted file to prepare a sales analysis by salesperson report.

9. Draw a system flowchart, showing how a file of Sales transaction records, on magnetic tape, are used to update the Inventory Master file, also on tape. The sales transaction records must be sorted into item number sequence before the master file is updated. Magnetic tape is a sequential storage medium. The same program that performs the file maintenance also prints a detail report of all activity.

10. Draw a system flowchart that shows:
    a. Data is entered on a keyboard terminal from batched source documents. The source documents are then filed in a Batch Suspense file.

b. The computer writes the entered data onto a diskette file named the Transaction file, accumulates totals for each batch, and prints the totals.

c. A clerk compares the batch totals printed by the computer with batch totals that have been recorded on special paper forms by departmental supervisors. The forms are called batch control sheets.

d. When an out-of-balance condition is detected, the appropriate batches are removed from the Batch Suspense file, and the errors are corrected. The corrected data is entered into the computer using a keyboard terminal. The computer uses the corrected data to update the Transaction file. No action is taken when the batches are in balance.

When the same file is used at different points in the system, you can simply repeat the symbol. Hint: Do not use a diamond to show the IF-THEN logic of the comparison of the batch totals. Simply label the arrow connecting that manual process with the next one of removing the error batches. Use the label "Out-of-balance condition."

Rhinegold Chemicals (B)

Assignments

Prepare the following documentation, using the procedure described in the Rhinegold Chemicals (A) case at the end of Chapter 6.

1. Prepare an ER diagram that includes the following entities: Employee, Time card, and Payroll data. The employee completes a time card, which is used to update the payroll data (represented by the Payroll Master file).

2. Prepare a Warnier-Orr diagram of the weekly procedure. Do not include the logic contained in any of the computer programs. Note that the procedure does not include any processing by the departmental secretary to correct error conditions.

3. Prepare a system flowchart of the weekly procedure. Begin the procedure with the receipt of the Time cards by the departmental secretary. Do not include the processing when special overtime checks are printed the following week.

4. Prepare a system flowchart of the monthly procedure. Represent the Weekly Payroll Earnings files with four disk symbols, labeled Week 1, 2, 3, and 4.

SELECTED BIBLIOGRAPHY

Alavi, Maryam. "An Assessment of the Prototyping Approach to Information Systems Development." *Communications of the ACM* 27 (June 1984): 556–63.

Cerveny, Robert P.; Garrity, Edward J.; and Sanders, G. Lawrence. "The Application of Prototyping to Systems Development: A Rationale and Model." *Journal of Management Information Systems* 3 (Fall 1986): 52–62.

Choobineh, Joobin; Mannino, Michael V.; and Tseng, Veronica P. "A Form-Based Approach for Database Analysis and Design." *Communications of the ACM* 35 (February 1992): 108–20.

Foss, W. Burry. "Early Wins Are Key to System Success." *Datamation* 36 (January 15, 1990): 79–82.

Gavurin, Stuart L. "Where Does Prototyping Fit In IS Development?" *Journal of Systems Management* 42 (February 1991): 13–17.

Gorman, Kevin, and Choobineh, Joobin. "The Object-Oriented Entity-Relationship Model." *Journal of Management Information Systems* 7 (Winter 1990/91): 41–65.

Hamilton, Robert, and Hamilton, Dennis. "On-Line Documentation Delivers." *Datamation* 36 (July 1, 1990): 45ff.

Hix, Deborah, and Schulman, Robert S. "Humam-Computer Interface Development Tools: A Methodology for their Evaluation." *Communications of the ACM* 34 (March 1991): 74–87.

Jain, Hemant K., and Bu-Hulaiga, Mohammed I. "E-R Approach to Distributed Heterogeneous Database Systems for Integrated Manufacturing." *Information Resources Management Journal* 3 (Winter 1990): 29–40.

Naumann, Justus D., and Jenkins, A Milton. "Prototyping: The New Paradigm for Systems Development." *MIS Quarterly* 6 (September 1982): 29–44.

Orr, Ken; Gane, Chris; Yourdon, Edward; Chen, Peter P.; and Constantine, Larry L. "Methodology: The Experts Speak." *BYTE* 14 (April 1989): 221*ff*.

Swift, Michael K. "Prototyping in IS Design and Development." *Journal of Systems Management* 40 (July 1989): 14–20.

Te'eni, Dov. "Determinants and Consequences of Perceived Complexity in Human-Computer Interaction." *Decision Sciences* 20 (Winter 1989): 166–81.

Teorey, Toby J.; Wei, Guangping; Bolton, Deborah L.; and Koenig, John A. "ER Model Clustering as an Aid for User Communication and Documentation in Database Design." *Communications of the ACM* 32 (August 1989), 975–87.

Voltmer, John G. "Selling Management on the Prototyping Approach." *Journal of Systems Management* 40 (July 1989): 24–25.

Warnier, Jean-Dominique. *Logical Construction of Systems* (New York: Van Nostrand Reinhold, 1981).

Part III

THE COMPUTER AS A PROBLEM-SOLVING TOOL

In Chapter 1 we recognized that managers use an information system to solve the firm's problems. When the computer is included in this system, the computerized portion is called the computer-based information system, or CBIS.

The purpose of this part of the text is to provide an understanding of the information technology that is incorporated in the CBIS. In Chapter 8 we describe the units that can be found in all computers—the central processing unit, or CPU, and the input and output units. We discuss the various types of software that have evolved and methods that make it user friendly and reduce errors.

Chapters 9 and 10 round out Part Three. Chapter 9 deals with secondary storage, how storage affects the type of processing that can be performed, the database, and the database management system (DBMS). Chapter 10 introduces you to the fundamentals of data communications—the hardware and software that are used to link widespread computing resources, the types of networks that are possible, standard network architectures and protocols, and the role of data communications in problem solving.

An understanding of the material contained in this part of the text contributes to your computer literacy. However, we present the material in the context of business problem solving, so that it also contributes to your information literacy. An information literacy and its supporting computer literacy are the prime ingredients in building and using a CBIS.

Chapter 8

Fundamentals of Computer Processing

LEARNING OBJECTIVES

After studying this chapter, you should:

- Know the basic architecture of all computer systems
- Understand the role that primary storage plays in computer use
- Have an appreciation for the variety of input devices that can be used to enter data into a CBIS, as well as the different output devices that can provide the results of the processing
- Understand the role that the input and output devices play in problem solving
- Know the main features of system and application software, including how each is used in problem solving
- Know how to achieve user friendliness in software
- Know the basic ways to minimize input errors

INTRODUCTION

Although today's computers bear little resemblance to the early models, all computers reflect the same basic architecture. Control is provided by both hardware and software, making the computer a closed-loop system.

Computer storage exists in two fundamental forms—primary and secondary. Primary storage employs integrated circuit technology to provide for random access memory (RAM), read-only memory (ROM), and cache memory.

The keyboard is the most popular computer input unit, and its efficiency has been enhanced by pointing devices. However, a greater contribution has been made toward reducing the input bottleneck by source data automation. Although once regarded as the potential solution to input problems, voice input has not lived up to expectations.

Users love displayed output, but printed documents can be prepared by a variety of printers and plotters. More specialized output is provided in the form of audio response and microform.

Software can be subdivided into two main categories—system and application. System software includes operating systems, utility programs, and translators. Application software comes in four major varieties—general business, industry-specific, organizational productivity, and personal productivity.

One reason for the popularity of end-user computing is the user friendliness of much application software. Such a characteristic can be achieved through the use of techniques such as menus and graphic user interfaces.

The accuracy of computer processing depends to a great extent on the quality of the input data. Input errors can be reduced but not completely eliminated by incorporating error prevention, detection, and correction into systems designs.

THE COMPUTER AS AN ELEMENT IN AN INFORMATION SYSTEM

When a firm decides to incorporate a computer into its information system, a long-term project is begun, which affects the entire organization and many of its environmental elements. Since there are so many types of computers and they can be used in so many ways, the firm's managers are faced with many choices. Information specialists help the managers assemble the proper configuration.

Evolution in Size

Computers come in all sizes. Large ones are called **mainframes**, and they have been around the longest. Mainframes are the backbone of data processing in the larger organizations such as the federal government and *Fortune 500* firms. Even larger and more powerful than the mainframes are the **supercomputers**. The supercomputers are so powerful that they are found in only the very largest organizations, where they are used mainly for scientific calculations.

FIGURE 8.1

The IBM AS/400
Is an Example of
a Minicomputer

Courtesy of International Business Machines Corporation

The recent trend has not been to larger computers, however, but to smaller ones. In the 1970s, this trend got its start with **minicomputers**, or **minis**. These computers were smaller than the mainframes but in many cases outperformed the larger units. A good example of a minicomputer is the IBM AS/400, which is shown in Figure 8.1.

The minis were received so well that computer manufacturers produced even smaller designs—called **microcomputers** or **micros**. Most of the microcomputer's main circuitry is in the form of a silicon integrated circuit chip, smaller than your fingernail. The chip is called a **microprocessor**.

You also hear terms like small business computer and personal computer. A **small business computer** is a multiuser mini or micro that is usually found in smaller firms, providing the computational support for the entire organization. A **personal computer (PC)** is a micro that is used by only a single person, or perhaps a few people working in the same area.

COMPUTER ARCHITECTURE

Figure 8.2 is a diagram of the basic units that are found in all computers. It is called **the computer schematic** and has been around since the early days of computing. The computer units, called **hardware**, are usually packaged in separate cabinets,

FIGURE 8.2

The Computer Schematic

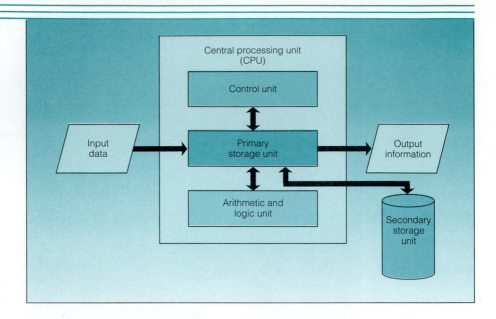

interconnected with electrical cables. The flow of data through the system is represented by the arrows in the figure.

The most important unit is the **central processing unit (CPU)**, which controls all of the other units of the computer system and transforms the input into output. The CPU includes a storage unit called **primary storage**, often called **main memory**.[1] Primary storage contains both the data being processed and the **program**— the list of instructions that process the data. The term **software** is used to describe one or more programs. The **control unit** causes all of the units to work together as a system, and the **arithmetic and logic unit (ALU)** is where the calculations and logical operations take place. The name **processor** is used to describe the control unit and ALU; they process the contents of primary storage.

One or more **input units** enter data into primary storage. Since primary storage is limited in its capacity, an additional storage area, called secondary storage, is needed. **Secondary storage** provides a place to keep programs and data while they are not being used. The stored programs are called the **software library** and the stored data is called the **database**.

The results of the processing are recorded by the **output units**. Printed output is called **hard copy**, but the advent of the microcomputer has made displayed output popular.

We explain each of these computer units in more detail later in the chapter.

---

[1] Not all computer scientists include primary storage in the CPU. Their contention is that its circuitry is separate from that of the other CPU components. Since our view is more logical than physical, we include it as one of the three main CPU elements.

THE COMPUTER AS A CLOSED-LOOP SYSTEM

In Chapter 1 we introduced systems concepts and described an open-loop system. The diagram of the closed-loop system in Figure 1.6 is very similar to the computer schematic. The computer input units provide the *system input*, the CPU performs the *transformation* of the input into the output, and the computer output units provide the *system output*. The control unit of the CPU serves as the *control mechanism*, and the program stored in the primary storage provides the *objectives*. The control mechanism and the program enable the computer to control its own operations so that the objectives are achieved. The computer is a closed-loop system.

THE EXPANDING SCOPE OF COMPUTER USE

The federal government has always been a leader in the use of data processing devices. The first punched card tabulating machines were developed by a Buffalo, New York statistician named Herman Hollerith and installed in the Bureau of the Census in 1890. Figure 8.3 shows an early punched card machine.

FIGURE 8.3
An Early IBM
Punched Card
Machine

Courtesy of International Business Machines Corporation

FIGURE 8.4

The First Mass-Produced Computer—the UNIVAC I

The Bettmann Archives

The first mass-produced computer, the Remington Rand UNIVAC I pictured in Figure 8.4 was installed by the same federal agency in 1951. Large scale operations such as compiling and analyzing census data were a primary reason for the government's early interest in computers. Private business in America got into the computer game with the installation of a UNIVAC I by General Electric in 1954.

Because early computers were very expensive by today's standards, their use was restricted to only the largest organizations. In fact, the systems were so expensive that they were usually leased rather than purchased. The monthly lease price of a small computer could be as much as $5,000, with a large computer leasing for $25,000 to $75,000 per month.

The introduction of minicomputers and microcomputers in the 1970s has revolutionized the use of computing. With the advent of the smaller systems, even one-person organizations can enjoy the benefits of computerized data processing at an affordable cost. No longer do organizations ask the question: "Can we afford a computer?" The question today is: "Do we need a computer?" The answer is usually "Yes."

PRIMARY STORAGE

The first computers used magnetic drums and magnetic cores for primary storage. The cores were tiny doughnut-shaped pieces of ferrite material about the size of the head of a pin that could easily be magnetized. Wires running through the cores changed the direction of the magnetic field and determined the magnetic state. Beginning in 1964 the drums and cores began to be replaced by storage constructed of integrated circuits.

Bits and Bytes

Today, integrated circuits each have the capacity to store up to 4 Mb (megabits, or million bits) of data. A **bit** is an electronic storage position that is either on or off. A combination of bits comprise a **byte**, or character. Eight circuit chips grouped together form 4 megabytes of storage. The size of primary storage is normally measured in terms of some multiple of bytes, or characters. A **kilobyte** (abbreviated as **KB**) is actually 1,024, not 1,000, bytes. And, a **megabyte**, **MB**, is really not one million bytes but rather 1,024 times 1,024, or 1,048,576 bytes.

Different Forms of Primary Storage

Primary storage comes in different forms, which provide varying capabilities in terms of operations and speed. The forms are random access memory, read-only memory, and cache memory.

Random Access Memory When reading microcomputer literature, you run across the terms RAM and ROM. **RAM** stands for **random access memory** and is the name given to the integrated circuits that serve as the portion of primary storage used to store software and data. RAM allows both read and write operations but is also said to be **volatile** because the contents are lost when the power is turned off.

Read-Only Memory A special type of primary storage permits reading but not writing. It is called **ROM**, for **read-only memory**. You can read instructions and data that previously have been stored in ROM but you cannot change those contents by writing over them. The computer manufacturer uses ROM to store material such as the instructions that tell your computer what to do when you turn it on. ROM is **nonvolatile** in that its contents are not erased when the system power is turned off.

Cache Memory The movement of program instructions and data between primary storage and the processor (the control unit and the ALU) is accomplished at very high speeds. Such operations require as little as 50 nanoseconds. A **nanosecond** is one-billionth of a second. Although this seems quite fast, some computers are able to achieve even faster speeds by including a limited amount of very high-speed and very expensive RAM between the regular RAM and the processor. Known as **cache memory**, its contents are checked by the processor prior to looking for a needed program instruction or data in regular RAM. If cache memory has the needed contents, the retrieval is accomplished much more quickly than if regular RAM is involved.

The capacity of primary storage has continually increased throughout the computer era. The first mainframe computers had as little as 4 KB of storage; today's microcomputers that are used as small business systems can accept as much as 96 MB of storage.

INPUT DEVICES

There are five basic ways of entering data into a computer, as illustrated in Figure 8.5. You can operate a keyboard device, you can use a pointing device, the data can be read optically or magnetically, and you can speak to the computer.

Keyboard Devices

The most popular input unit is the keyboard of a terminal or microcomputer. The keyboard allows you to input data by pressing the appropriate keys. Similar in many ways to the typewriter, most computer keyboards are equipped with a number of extra keys. An example is the **numeric keypad** that includes keys arranged in the same pattern as a pocket calculator to facilitate entry of numeric data. Other special purpose keys include **arrow** or **cursor control keys** that are used to move the cursor around on the screen, and **function keys** that accomplish particular tasks for the user, depending on the software.

The Ergonomics of Computer Use

Ergonomics is the study of the physical and behavioral influences of objects such as computers and office equipment on their users. The terms **human engineering** and **human factors considerations** are especially appropriate when computer use is involved.

One of the first ergonomics studies was that of August Dvorak, who addressed the task of keying data into a keyboard. The standard keyboard layout is known as the **QWERTY keyboard** because of the first six letters on the top row of letter keys. QWERTY was designed nearly 100 years ago to prevent skilled typists from typing faster than the equipment would allow.

As a result of his ergonomic studies, Dvorak invented a new key arrangement called the **Dvorak keyboard** that significantly increased the speed and accuracy of even the best typists. Although it has been proven quite superior, acceptance of the Dvorak keyboard has been slowed by the fact that most users initially learn QWERTY, and, until recently, it was difficult to obtain a computer keyboard in the Dvorak arrangement.

Both the QWERTY and Dvorak keyboards are pictured in Figure 8.6.

Today, the subject of ergonomics is receiving much attention. Persons who work with computers for long periods of time are subject to a variety of physical and behavioral ailments as a result. One such ailment is **carpal tunnel syndrome**, an injury to a person's wrists that can be incurred by typing for long periods with the hands in an unnatural position.

FIGURE 8.5
Means of
Entering Input
Data Into the
Computer

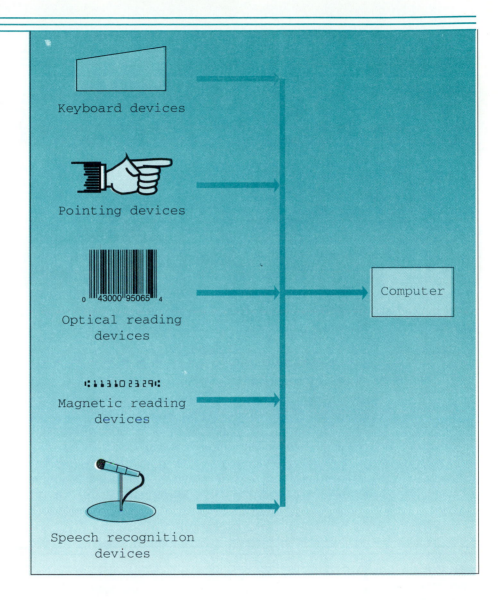

Ergonomics can affect anyone who works with computers in any capacity, but most attention is focused on persons who use the input and output devices.[2] Some computer manufacturers enclose brochures with their equipment, which warn of harmful effects that can occur from improper use and suggest ways to minimize

[2] The Association for Computing Machinery (ACM) has a special interest group called SIGCHI, which stands for Special Interest Group for Computer and Human Interaction. SIGCHI specializes in the issues relating to computer use. They sponsor conferences and publish a newsletter. For more information, contact ACM, 1515 Broadway, New York, NY 10036–9998.

FIGURE 8.6

Two Approaches to Keyboard Layout

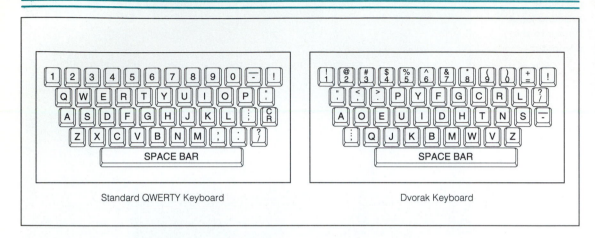

Standard QWERTY Keyboard   Dvorak Keyboard

these effects. Table 8.1 lists some suggestions from Apple for purchasers of its Macintosh computers.

Pointing Devices

Even though the arrow keys enable the user to move the cursor around the screen, much modern software has been designed to take advantage of the unique pointing capabilities of devices such as the mouse, trackball, touch screen, light pen, and remote control unit. These devices allow the user to move the cursor from one point on the screen to another quickly and easily.

■ **Mouse** The **mouse** is a small, lightweight device approximately the size of a deck of cards that fits into the palm of your hand. Attached to the

TABLE 8.1

Ergonomic Suggestions for Computer Use

■ Adjust your chair height so your feet are flat on the floor.
■ Position your keyboard so your elbows are at the same height as the keyboard and your wrists have little or no tilt.
■ Position your mouse at the same height as your keyboard.
■ Set up your display so the top of the screen is at or slightly below eye level.
■ Position your screen so it doesn't reflect glare into your eyes.
■ Keep your screen clean.
■ Make sure your display's brightness and contrast controls are properly adjusted.
■ Place your laser printer in a well-ventilated area and make sure it receives regular maintenance.
■ Alternate working at the computer with tasks that use different muscles.
■ Take frequent breaks to rest your eyes and move your body.
■ Visit a qualified health professional if persistent pain develops while using your computer.

FIGURE 8.7
A Trackball
Pointing Device

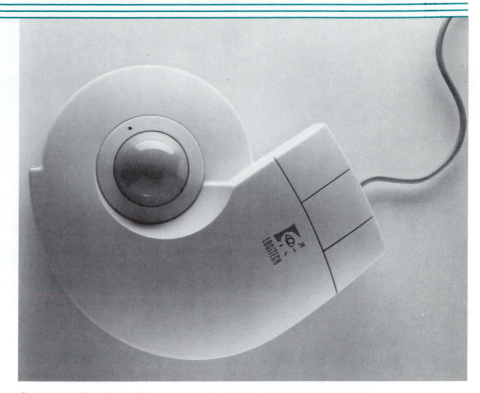

Courtesy of Logitech, Inc.

computer by a thin cable, it has a small ball on its underside and one, two or three buttons on the top. Moving it around on a flat surface causes the ball to rotate. That rotation is interpreted by the computer, and the cursor is moved on the screen to match the pattern followed by the mouse.

■ **Trackball**   The **trackball** is a pointing device similar to the mouse, except that the ball is on the top instead of the bottom. Figure 8.7 provides a photograph of the Trackman, from Logitech. Because of the ball location, the user can move the cursor by simply rotating the ball without moving the entire device. For those of us who always seem to end up with cluttered desks, the trackball offers the advantage over the mouse of not requiring much clean space.

■ **Touch Screen**   Some screens have a **touch screen** capability that allows you to enter data or instructions by simply touching a location on the screen using your finger or any other nontransparent object. The most common way for the computer to identify the touched location is through the use of infrared light beams. The beams are projected across the screen surface in a grid pattern. Your finger interrupts the grid and tells the computer where the touch occurred.

■ **Light Pen**   The **light pen** is used to point at the screen in a manner that is similar to pointing at a touch screen with your finger. When the pen is

FIGURE 8.8

A Light Pen
Lends Itself to
Applications Such
as Computer-
Aided Design and
Drawing
Animated
Cartoons

© Spencer Grant/Monkmeyer Press Photo Service

placed against the screen, it senses the light being emitted from the screen and sends an electronic signal through a thin cable to the computer so that the signal can be interpreted by the program. Light pens are popular with CAD/CAM systems—**computer-aided design (CAD)**, and **computer-aided manufacturing (CAM)**. Figure 8.8 shows a design engineer using a light pen to accomplish CAD.

▪ **Remote Control Unit** It is possible to communicate with the computer in much the same way that you control a TV by using a hand-held **remote control unit**. Comshare originally offered such an input device with their executive information system called Executive Edge. The executives did not respond to the unit as well as expected, and now the system emphasizes the use of a mouse.

Most of the pointing devices are designed to ease the process of moving the cursor or identifying a particular screen object. They are not designed to enter data. That job is best performed by the keyboard.

Source Data Automation Input Devices

Although computer input can be accomplished quite rapidly when experienced operators use the keyboard and pointing devices, the speeds are slow compared to those of the computer. Human input speeds are measured in the number of characters per second (CPS), or words per minute (WPM), whereas the internal processing speeds of the computer are measured in millions of instructions per second (MIPS).

The relatively slow input speeds can create an **input bottleneck** of data awaiting entry into the computer. Some firms have reduced their input bottlenecks through the use of source data automation. **Source data automation (SDA)** refers to the reading of data directly from documents or objects. There are two basic technologies—optical reading and magnetic reading.

Optical Reading Devices   The input devices that read data by shining a bright light on it and then capturing the reflected image on a matrix of photoelectric cells are called **optical reading units**. The terms **optical scanners** and **scanners** are also used. This approach to computer input is called **OCR**, for **optical character recognition**.

There are several classes of optical reading units. **Optical mark readers** can only detect the presence or absence of marks on paper. The test scoring machines that grade your true-false and multiple-choice exams are examples. **Barcode readers** are capable of deciphering the meaning of data that is recorded in the form of bar codes. The scanners at checkout counters of supermarkets are good examples. Those scanners are unique in that they read bar codes printed on objects—the food and other items—rather than paper documents. **Optical character readers** are capable of reading numeric, alphabetic, and special character data from paper. Such data is usually prerecorded on the documents, often in a special OCR font. A **font** is simply a type style. **Handprint readers** are capable of reading characters that are written on documents by hand. Much technical development remains for the handprint readers to reach the same level of accuracy that the other types of OCR input enjoy.

Magnetic Reading Devices   The first successful form of SDA was **magnetic ink character recognition (MICR)**, which was originated in the late 1950s by the American Banking Association. The ABA decreed that special characters be printed in a special ink on the bottom of checks. The special ink contains properties that can be magnetically charged immediately prior to the reading. The combination of the ink and the unusual shape of the characters facilitates the reading process.

Although the use of MICR has enabled banks to handle the ever-increasing volume of checks, a new approach to handling monetary transactions gained popularity in the 1980s. This approach is called **electronic funds transfer (EFT)**. Examples of EFT include the automatic deposit of your paycheck in your bank account, the automatic transfer of funds from your checking account to make your house or car payment, and automated teller machines, or ATMs. As EFT transactions such as these become more common, check volume, and the use of MICR, may begin to decrease.

Speech Recognition Input Devices

It is also possible to enter commands and data into the computer by simply speaking into a microphone that is connected to a speech recognition unit. The **speech rec-**

ognition unit analyzes analog speech patterns and converts them to a digital form for processing.

Although prototype models of speech recognition units were built in the late 1950s, it was not until the 1970s that the units began to be mass produced. Most units require a particular user to train the system to recognize the user's voice by speaking the words of a limited vocabulary. As the words are spoken, they are coded in a digital form by the system and, after each word has been spoken several times, a digital pattern is stored for later reference. This type of system is commonly called a **speaker-dependent system** because the vocabulary is tailored to a particular user or selected group of users.

It is easy to see that a speaker-dependent system has its drawbacks. The system must be retrained when a new user wants to enter data, or an existing user has a cold or spent the previous evening cheering for the home team. In an attempt to overcome such problems, an entirely different **speaker-independent system** of speech recognition is being developed. Basing the recognition process on *how* we speak rather than *what*, this technique holds the promise of being able to recognize any user, speaking in any language for which the speech modeling process has been accomplished.

Up to this point, speech recognition has not been accepted by CBIS users as quickly as was originally anticipated. As the technology continues to improve, it is quite possible that someday speech might provide a primary means for communicating with the computer.

OUTPUT DEVICES

The end product of all computer processing is some form of output. Figure 8.9 illustrates the basic options—displayed, printed, and spoken—as well as specialized options such as plotters and computer output microform.

Displayed Output Devices

The output device that is most popular with end-users is the **display screen**, also often referred to as the **monitor**, **cathode ray tube (CRT)**, or **video display terminal (VDT)**. The display screen is used with all sizes of computers, and is almost always packaged with a keyboard.

Display screens vary in their size, resolution, and color capability. Unless the screen has been designed for some specialized function, its *size* is determined by measuring diagonally across the screen surface. The *resolution*, or clarity, of the display depends on the number of individual dots that can be projected on the screen. These dots, or **pixels**, are individually illuminated to produce the character or graphic pattern. As the number of pixels is increased, the resolution improves. If you have a **monochrome display**, the display will typically consist of white, green, or amber characters on a black background, or gray characters on a white

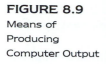

FIGURE 8.9

Means of
Producing
Computer Output

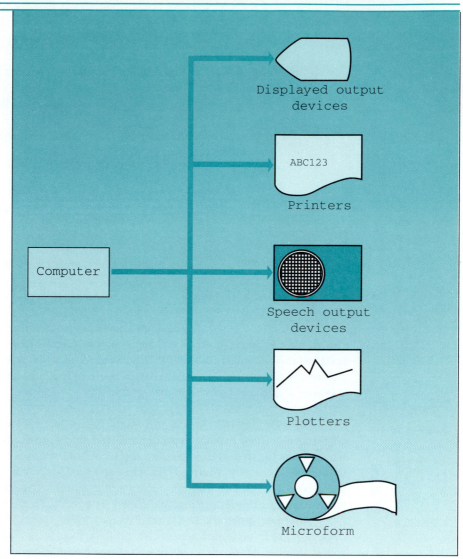

background. If you have a **color display**, or **color monitor**, you may have as many as 262,144 colors from which to choose.

Although most display screens use the CRT technology, a growing number of portable microcomputers, such as laptops, notebooks, and palmtops use a flat panel. The **flat-panel technogy** consists of a liquid crystal or plasma display that requires only a relatively thin package, such as the hinged cover of the portables.

Printed Output Devices

The major disadvantage of the display screen is its inability to produce a paper copy, or **hard copy,** of the output. Hard copy is preferred or even necessary when:

1. Information must be sent through the mail (such as an invoice or bill that must be mailed to a customer).
2. A historical record is required (such as a listing of the month's payroll checks).
3. The volume of output is relatively large (such as a management report that extends over several pages).
4. Several people must use the same information at the same time (such as in a conference).

Output devices called **printers** produce hard copy output. There are three basic types of printers—line, character, and page.

Line Printers   The first computer printers were called **line printers** because they printed so rapidly that it appeared as if they were printing a line at a time. Line printers are still included in mainframe configurations and operate at speeds ranging from 300 to 3,000 lines per minute.

Line printers are an example of an impact printer. An **impact printer** transfers characters onto paper by striking a metallic object that is embossed with the characters against an inked ribbon that is positioned over the paper. This is the same technology that is used in a typewriter. Because of the impact technology, multiple copies of a document can be printed at one time.

Character Printers   As you might expect, **character printers** print one character at a time. Popular impact character printers are the **dot matrix printer**, which prints the characters in the form of a matrix of ink dots, and the **daisy wheel printer**, which uses full-formed characters arranged in the configuration illustrated in Figure 8.10. Because they are impact printers, dot-matrix and daisy-wheel printers are capable of printing multiple copies of a report at one time.

Nonimpact printers do not involve the striking of an object against an ink ribbon. Popular non-impact character printers include the **ink jet printer** that sprays droplets of ink onto the paper to form the character shapes, and the **laser printer** that causes characters to adhere to the paper by means of an electrostatic process. Since there is no impact, nonimpact printers cannot print multiple copies in a single process.

Page Printers   The fastest printers are called **page printers** because they appear to print a page at a time. Ranging from desktop printers that can produce from four to ten pages per minute to large systems that produce as many as 500 pages per minute, they are all nonimpact printers that operate in a manner similar to a copying machine. Figure 8.11 shows a page printer.

FIGURE 8.10
A Daisy Wheel
Printing Element

Courtesy of Mark McKenna.

Speech Output Devices

Although speech input has been slow to catch on, spoken computer output has been in use for some time. A **speech output unit**, or **audio response unit**, can select a series of digitized words to form an audible computer output that can be transmitted directly or over a communications channel. When you dial a telephone number and receive the message "I'm sorry, the number you dialed is no longer in service. The new number is . . ." it is being generated by a speech output device.

Audio response permits the use of the computer as an information system when the only means of communication is a push-button telephone. For example, a salesperson in a customer's office can use the customer's phone to determine the

FIGURE 8.11
A Page Printer

Courtesy of International Business Machines Corporation

inventory level of an item that the customer wants to buy, or check on the status of an order that was previously placed.

Plotters

Some of the first computer users were engineers and scientists who recognized the need to produce graphic output. Special output devices called **plotters** were designed to meet this need. Plotters come in various sizes. Small desktop models produce drawings on 8 1/2 by 11 inch paper, and large models print on rolls of paper that can be up to four feet wide.

The two basic types of plotters are flatbed plotters and drum plotters. **Flatbed plotters** hold the paper in one place on a flat surface while one or more ink pens move over the paper surface under computer control. **Drum plotters**, on the other hand, use a rotating cylinder over which the paper is placed and the pens are mounted. In this configuration the pens move back and forth along the length of the cylinder as it rotates.

Microform

Firms with large document files often maintain them in a miniature form on photographic film. The name **microform** is given to all such technologies, with the term **microfilm** describing the film in reel form, and **microfiche** describing the film in sheet form. Using microforms, it is possible to record the images of a room full of paper documents on a few reels or sheets that can fit into a desk drawer. When connected directly to a computer, a **computer output microform (COM) device** prints documents on microfilm or microfiche. Special **microfilm viewers** that are offline to the computer are used to display the document images, and **microfilm printers** produce full-sized hard copies. Many microform applications are being replaced by optical disk. We will describe optical disk storage in Chapter 14.

THE ROLE OF INPUT AND OUTPUT DEVICES IN PROBLEM SOLVING

It is easy to see how a manager might use a keyboard and display screen, and perhaps a printer and plotter in solving problems. The keyboard can be supplemented by a pointing device that allows easy cursor movement. These input and output devices provide the communications link between the manager and the computer and therefore play a direct role in problem solving.

What about the other devices? Source data automation devices provide for rapid and accurate data entry, which, in turn, makes available an accurate and up-to-date database. These input devices play an indirect role in problem solving. In a similar fashion, many of the output devices affect problem solving indirectly. For example, a manager might ask a staff member to glean information from some microfilmed reports and present a summary in the form of a plotted graph.

All of the input and output devices can contribute to problem solving in either direct or indirect ways.

SOFTWARE

The computer is directed to accomplish a particular task by following the instructions in the program. The program must reside in primary storage before the CPU can execute it.

Although there seems to be a practically unexhaustible number of program types, computer software can be classified as either system software or application software.

System Software

System software performs certain fundamental tasks that all users of a particular computer require. These are tasks that relate to the hardware, and not to the applications that the firm performs. It is impossible to use a modern computer without using at least some of its system software. System software is usually prepared by the manufacturer of the hardware (the hardware vendor, or supplier) or by a firm that specializes in producing software (a software vendor, or supplier).

There are three basic types of system software—operating systems, language translators, and utility programs.

Operating Systems The **operating system** manages the computer's processes, functioning as an interface between the user, the software that processes the firm's data (the application software), and the hardware. An operating system consists of a number of component routines. The **supervisor** (also known as the **monitor** or **executive**) manages all of the operating system activities. The supervisor is said to be **main memory resident** in that it remains in primary storage at all times. Other operating system routines are called **transient routines** because they are maintained in secondary storage and brought into primary storage only when needed.

There are six basic functions that an operating system *can* perform.

- **Schedule Jobs** Determine the sequence in which jobs are executed, using priorities established by the firm.
- **Manage Hardware and Software Resources** Cause the user's application program to be executed by loading it into primary storage, and then cause the various hardware units to perform as specified by the application.
- **Maintain Systems Security** Require users to enter a **password**—a group of characters that identify users as being authorized to have access to the system.
- **Enable Multiple User Resource Sharing** Handle the scheduling and execution of the application programs for many users at the same time—a feature called **multiprogramming**.
- **Handle Interrupts** An **interrupt** is a mechanism used by the operating system to temporarily suspend the processing of one program in order to allow another program to be executed. Interrupts are issued when a program requests an operation that does not require the CPU, such as input or output, or when the program exceeds some predetermined time limit.
- **Maintain Usage Records** Keep track of the amount of time used by each user for each system unit—the CPU, secondary storage, and input and output devices. Such information is usually maintained for the purpose of charging users' departments for their use of the firm's computing resources.

All computers have operating systems, but the systems vary in the number of basic functions and how they are performed. The operating system of a mainframe is much more complex than that of a single-user micro because the mainframe must coordinate the operations of many input and output devices, as well as handle many simultaneous users. The operating systems of local area networks (LANs) and minicomputers can be as complex as those of mainframe computers.

Utility Programs There are several "workhorse" tasks that every user requires, regardless of the application. Those tasks are handled by systems software in the form of utility programs. A **utility program**, often simply called a **utility**, is a routine that enables the user to perform certain basic data processing operations that are not unique to the user's applications. Utilities enable users to copy files, erase files, sort the contents of files, merge two or more files together, and prepare removable storage media for use. Other utilities allow the computer operations manager to recover lost or bad files, monitor the performance of the system, and even control the flow of data between users and computers.

Language Translators

Computer hardware has evolved through several generations. In the first generation the electronic circuitry was provided by vacuum tubes. In the second it was transistors, and in the third it was integrated circuits. After this point, the generations became less distinct, and computer scientists lost interest in the subject. Software is another matter. It can also be categorized in terms of generations, and there is still an interest in doing so. For this reason, we include such a classification here.

First-Generation Languages—Machine Language   The early computers were programmed in **machine language**, or **first-generation language**—a series of zeros and ones that the CPU can interpret and execute. Machine language is important because it is the only language that the computer understands. However, it quickly became obvious to the early programmers that machine language was difficult to use, and so they set out to develop programming languages that were more in keeping with human communication.

The basic idea was that the program written in the programmer's language would be translated into machine language before it was run. The program written by the programmer is known as the **source program**. The system software that translates the source program is called the **translator**, and the machine language is called the **object program**. The translation process is illustrated in Figure 8.12.

FIGURE 8.12
The Program Is Translated Before the Data Is Processed

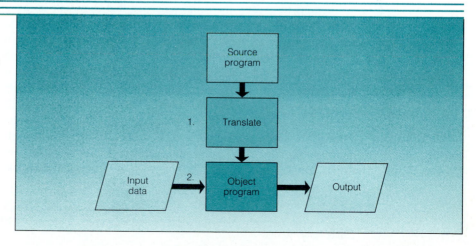

Second-Generation Languages—the Assemblers The first translators were called **assemblers**, and they permitted the programmer to code programs in **assembly language**, or **second-generation language**. An assembly language uses *mnemonic names* (such as DIV for divide) for the operations that are to be performed, and *symbolic names* (such as PAYRATE) for the data that is processed. Also, there is generally a one-for-one relationship between source instructions written by the programmer and the object instructions that are generated. This means that if the object program requires 500 instructions, the programmer has to code almost that many.

Although assembly language was a big improvement over machine language from the programmer's point of view, it had its down side. The assembly language programs tended to be lengthy and were difficult for the programmers to read. Another disadvantage was the fact that the assembly languages were different for every model of CPU. This meant that when one firm wanted to replace its computer with a newer model, all of the programs had to be rewritten. This requirement got old after a while and led to the development of a new generation of translators.[3]

Third-Generation Languages—the Compilers and Interpreters Unlike assembly languages, a **third-generation language** can produce multiple object program instructions from a single source program instruction. This means that programmers have to produce fewer lines of code. And, the syntax of the third-generation languages is more like the language that the user uses. Popular third-generation languages are COBOL, FORTRAN, PL/I, and BASIC.

COBOL, FORTRAN, and PL/I are compiler languages. A **compiler** produces a complete object program in one process. Then, the object program is executed. An **interpreter**, on the other hand, translates a source language instruction and executes it before going on to the next instruction. There is no complete object program as such. BASIC programs are most often translated by an interpreter.

The terms procedure-oriented and problem-oriented are also associated with third-generation languages. In a **procedure-oriented language** you must code the instructions in exactly the same sequence that they will be executed by the computer. The computer is not very forgiving in this respect. Although procedure-oriented languages are usually classified as business, scientific, or multipurpose, they are flexible enough to permit a programmer to model almost any procedure.

A **problem-oriented language** is designed to address the needs of a specific application or set of problems. COBOL, for example, was designed to solve business problems, and FORTRAN was aimed at problems faced by mathematicians and scientists. The problem-oriented languages allow the programmer to concentrate on the input and output activities because the majority of the processing is built into the language. Simulation languages such as GPSS and Siman, and statistical analysis languages like SAS and SPSS are also examples of problem-oriented languages.

---

[3] We use past tense when describing assembly language. Some firms still use it, but they are getting harder to find.

FIGURE 8.13

Fourth-generation Languages as DSS Tools

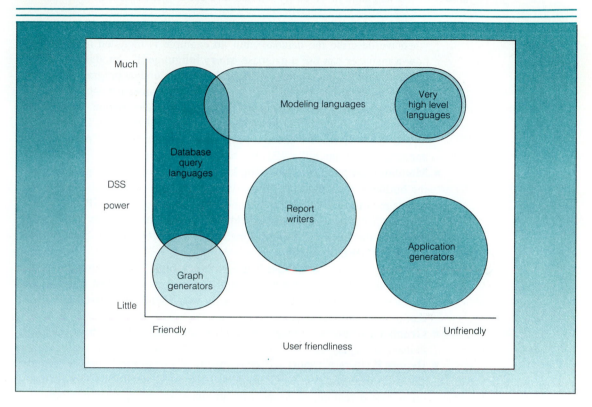

The third-generation languages are sufficiently standardized that, with minor modifications, they are portable. A program is **portable** if it can be executed on a variety of computers.

Fourth-Generation Languages—the Natural Languages   The term **fourth generation language**, abbreviated **4GL**, refers to a language that allows a programmer or user to instruct the computer on *what* to do rather than *how* to do it. The term **nonprocedural language** is often used because the sequence of the instructions is not as critical as with the third-generation languages. The term **natural language** is also used because the syntax of the 4GL can be very similar to our everyday speech.

The 4GLs include the wide variety of software types that are graphed in Figure 8.13.[4] The types are positioned in the graph based on their decision-support power and user friendliness. By power we mean their capability to provide support for

[4]This classification is from Dipankar Basu, "Cleaning Up the Language," *ICP Data Processing Management* 9 (Winter 1984); 44*ff*.

each step of the problem solving process, and by user friendliness we mean the ability of the language to be easily learned and used.

■ **Database Query Languages** We will discuss query language in Chapter 9 when we describe the database, but an example is included here to show how a manager can use a database **query language** that produces a special report from database contents without the need to code a program. The 4GL used in the example is FOCUS. Assume that a manager wants a report of the sales for each of the company's products by sales region. Figure 8.14 shows the instructions that the manager enters, and Figure 8.15 shows the report. If you have ever coded a program to prepare such a report, you can appreciate how much the 4GL has simplified the process.

■ **Modeling Languages** A **modeling language** is especially designed to make the building of mathematical models easier than when a problem-oriented language is used. One of the first modeling languages was GPSS (General Purpose Simulation System) developed by IBM in the early 1960s. The more popular ones that followed include DYNAMO, SLAM, SIMSCRIPT, GASP, MODEL, and IFPS.

■ **Very High Level Languages** The term **very high level language** is often used to describe a programming language, such as APL, that offers a succinctness and power (but not necessarily user friendliness) over and above that of conventional languages.

■ **Graph Generators** A **graph generator**, also called a **graphics package**, is used to display or print data in a variety of graphic forms.

■ **Report Writers** A **report writer** is specifically designed to prepare reports. The first example was RPG (Report Program Generator). COBOL has a report writer feature, as do most of the database management systems.

■ **Application Generators** An **application generator** produces an application

FIGURE 8.14

Example of the FOCUS Query Language

```
DEFINE FILE SALES
REGION/A12=DECODE REGION (NE 'NORTH EAST'
            SE 'SOUTH EAST' MW 'MID WEST'
            MA 'MID-ATLANTIC');
END
TABLE FILE SALES
HEADING CENTER
''PRODUCT UNIT SALES ANALYSIS </1 ''
SUM UNITS AND ROW-TOTAL AND COLUMN-TOTAL
ACROSS REGION
BY PRODNUM AS 'PRODUCT,NUMBER'
END
```

FIGURE 8.15

A Special Report Produced with FOCUS

PAGE 1

PRODUCT UNIT SALES ANALYSIS

PRODUCT NUMBER	REGION MIDWEST	MID-ATLANTIC	NORTH EAST	SOUTH EAST	TOTAL
10524	164	181	184	115	644
10526	40	126	150	45	361
11275	189	219	133	168	709
11302	179	130	288	172	769
11303	99	121	220	30	470
11537	90	260	110	124	584
11563	297	245	520	371	1433
11567	86	80	.	20	186
12275	.	.	.	30	30
12345	.	10	.	.	10
13737	.	.	29	.	29
13797	110	160	65	389	724
13938	324	186	441	164	1115
13979	.	12	.	.	12
14156	200	538	120	169	1027
15016	94	257	156	245	752
16394	252	210	187	40	689
16436	.	132	52	20	204
16934	.	50	.	.	50
17434	166	378	84	174	802
17905	164	70	108	199	541
34562	25	.	.	.	25
34567	100	.	.	.	100
56267	146	190	910	255	1501
TOTAL	2725	3555	3757	2730	12767

program, such as inventory or payroll, without programming. Examples are MANTIS and MARK V.

Most managers could be expected to use the 4GL types classified as friendly in Figure 8.13. An important point to recognize, however, is that there are 4GLs in the upper-left-hand corner of the figure that offer substantial DSS power in combination with friendliness. These are the 4GLs that are likely to be used by information specialists.

Application Software

Just as system software was developed to accomplish the tasks related to managing the computer, application software was developed to assist in managing the firm's physical and conceptual resources. Over time, four basic categories of application software have emerged—general business packages, industry-specific packages, organizational productivity packages, and personal productivity packages. The term **application development software** is often used to describe both the personal and organizational productivity package.

Although this discussion concentrates on prewritten software, you should remember that organizations with their own programming staffs create many of their own applications.

General Business Packages

Nearly all organizations have employees who must be paid, inventory that must be maintained, customers who must be tracked, and accounts receivables that must be collected. Because these and other such activities are performed by most organizations, a great variety of application packages have been written to accomplish the necessary processing on the computer. This situation is particularly true for small businesses who use microcomputers.

General business packages are examples of the data processing subsystem of the CBIS.

Industry-Specific Packages

Application packages have also been created to meet the specific needs of such industries as ranching and agriculture, real estate, trucking, and health care. Many industry-specific packages are simply highly tailored versions of general business packages, which are geared toward the business practices and terminology of a particular industry.

Other industry-specific packages, however, include features that aid the user in problem solving and decision making. One example is the pharmacy system that not only handles inventory, prints prescription bottle labels, and prepares customer statements, but also checks for possible adverse reactions between medications when the patient has multiple prescriptions.

Industry-specific programs with such problem-solving capabilities are examples of the MIS and DSS subsystems of the CBIS.

Organizational Productivity Packages

This rather general category includes software that is aimed at meeting the needs of the organization rather than individual problem solvers. The term **productivity** means that the software provides the user with the power to accomplish more, expend less effort, or both, when performing a particular task. *Group decision support systems* enable groups of problem solvers working together to solve problems by means of reports or mathematical modeling. *Electronic mail* enables problem solvers to use their networked terminals or micros to send communications back and forth. *Project management packages* facilitate the control of large projects such as the development of computer applications. *Forecasting and statistical analysis packages* permit the projection of future firm activity and the interpretation of large volumes of data in the database. These are only a few examples, but, in each case, the software improves the productivity of the problem solvers in addressing organizational problems.

Organizational productivity packages are examples of the MIS, DSS, OA, and expert systems subsystems of the CIBS.

Personal Productivity Packages   Because the microcomputer is generally considered to be a personal tool, most personal productivity packages have been developed to run on micros. Problem solvers use *word processing* to send and receive written communications that bear on problems. *Electronic spreadsheet systems* represent easy-to-use mathematical modeling tools, and *graphics packages* provide an additional dimension to problem-solving information. Members of the problem solver's staff use *desktop publishing* software to prepare written communications that have a professional appearance. An important feature of all these examples is that individual problem solvers can tailor each one to their own particular needs.

Personal productivity packages are examples of the DSS, OA, and expert systems subsystems of the CIBS.

THE ROLE OF SOFTWARE IN PROBLEM SOLVING

Software can play either a direct or indirect role in problem solving. System software, because it is not geared to the user's particular operations, always plays an indirect role. The management of the system by the operating system, the performance of workhorse activities by the utility programs, and the translation of source programs by the translators all provide indirect support.

Application software, on the other hand, can play either a direct or indirect role. Most general business and industry-specific packages are designed to play an indirect role by creating and maintaining the database that provides the basis for the information-oriented CBIS subsystems. Industry-specific packages, of course, often go beyond data processing, providing components that directly contribute to problem-solving.

As with general business and industry-specific software, some organizational and personal productivity software only indirectly affects problem-solving by simplifying the creation and transmission of data that is used. However, other productivity software such as electronic spreadsheet, project management, and forecasting and statistical analysis packages provide direct support.

ACHIEVING USER FRIENDLINESS IN SOFTWARE

Software that is to be used in end-user computing should be as easy to learn and use, or **user-friendly**, as possible. To achieve user friendliness, software designers make use of a variety of tools and techniques in various hardware environments.

In the mainframe and minicomputer environments, menus, context sensitive help, and guided dialog all contribute to ease of use by the user. In the microcomputer environment, the graphic user interface, with its mouse- or trackball-driven icons, windows, and pull-down menus, has emerged as the unofficial standard.

Menus

In the language of computing, a **menu** is a list of choices from which the user makes a selection, enabling the user to specify what is to be done. The choices can be arranged in either a horizontal or vertical format, and the user makes a selection by entering the number of the item, or by moving the cursor to the item and pressing the Enter key. An alternative method is to type the first character of the choice.

When the application requires that the user select from a large number of choices, menus are arranged in a hierarchy. The selection made on the first menu causes a second menu to be displayed, the selection made on the second menu causes a third menu to be displayed, and so on until the desired activity is finally selected. Figure 8.16 illustrates the top-down selection from four menus arranged in a hierarchy to reach the desired action of sorting a particular file. The term **navigation** is used to describe the user's movement up and down through the menu hierarchy.

A system that bases user interaction on menus is called a **menu-driven system**. It is important to remember that when designing such a system the presentation of menu choices and the process by which the user makes a selection should be standardized throughout the system. This technique ensures that the menus make the maximum contribution to user friendliness.

Context Sensitive Help

When a user encounters difficulty or is unsure of the options available while using software, the user should be able to request a display that explains how to overcome the difficulty or indicates the valid options. Such a display is called a **help screen** or **help message**, and is **context sensitive help** because it addresses only the problem at hand. Figure 8.17 illustrates a help screen that explains a particular data element that is being entered into a mathematical model. Also included in the screen are instructions for returning to the data entry process after the help screen has been viewed.

Guided Dialog

When the user interacts with an application program, it is necessary to enter certain information. Rather than require the user to memorize the entry routine, the program specifies to the user what information to enter, where to enter it, and when to enter it. This exchange between the computer and the user is called a **guided dialog**. The computer is said to be in the **interactive mode** when the computer and the user converse with each other.

FIGURE 8.16

Menus in a
Hierarchy

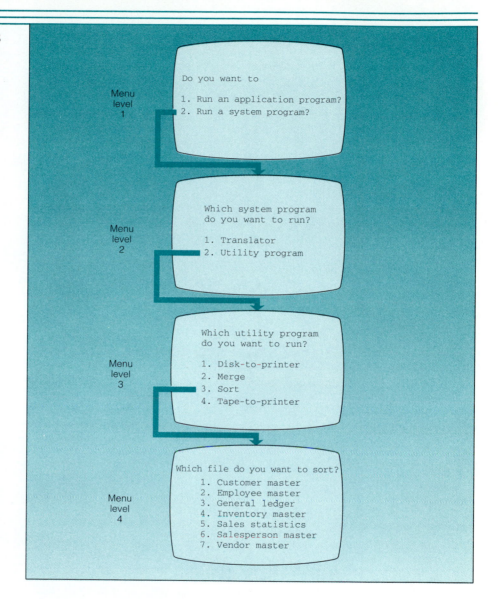

Three techniques can be used to achieve guided dialog. They include menus, the question-and-answer technique, and form filling.

When the application program requires an input from the user, a question or instruction can be displayed on the screen. The question or instruction is called a **prompt**. The user responds by keying in the response. This is called the **question-and-answer technique**. Figure 8.18 is an example of how the user might use this technique to enter six data elements into a mathematical model.

FIGURE 8.17
A Help Screen

```
D A T A   I T E M   H E L P
LEAD TIME PROBABILITY
This is the probability that a certain number of days will elapse from
the time the reorder point is reached until the receipt of the replenish-
ment merchandise. the exact value is determined by the model using the
Monte Carlo method. The Lead time varies from purchase to purchase in a
random fashion using the times included in the lead time probability
distribution. You may use the default probability distribution or enter
a different one. When entering a probability distribution, the probabil-
ities can range from .01 through .99. Enter one or two digits with no
decimal point. Rightmost zeros are not required.




PRESS <ESC> TO END PROGRAM OR ANY OTHER KEY FOR DATA ENTRY SCREEN
```

FIGURE 8.18
The Question-
and-answer
Technique

```
ENTER DATA DESCRIBING THE FIRM'S ACTIVITIES LAST QUARTER
     WHAT WAS THE PRICE? 30
     WHAT WAS THE MARKETING BUDGET? 550000
     HOW MUCH WAS SPENT FOR RESEARCH & DEVELOPMENT? 0
     WHAT WAS THE PLANT INVESTMENT? 0
     HOW MANY UNITS REMAINED IN INVENTORY? 500
     WHAT WAS THE VALUE OF THE REMAINING RAW MATERIALS? 225000
DO YOU WANT A DETAILED LISTING? (Y/N)_
```

FIGURE 8.19
The Form-filling
Technique

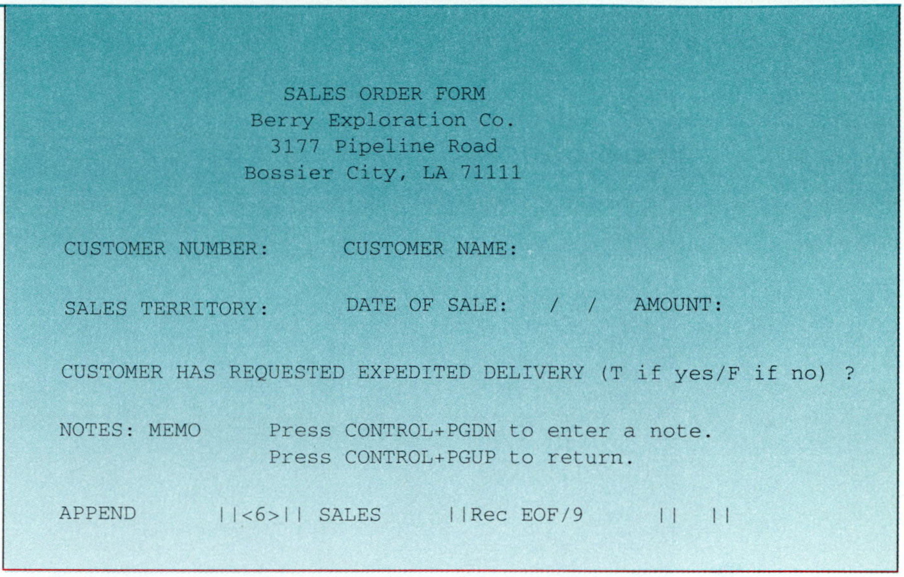

```
                        SALES ORDER FORM
                     Berry Exploration Co.
                       3177 Pipeline Road
                     Bossier City, LA 71111


      CUSTOMER NUMBER:       CUSTOMER NAME:


      SALES TERRITORY:       DATE OF SALE:   /  /   AMOUNT:


      CUSTOMER HAS REQUESTED EXPEDITED DELIVERY (T if yes/F if no) ?


      NOTES: MEMO        Press CONTROL+PGDN to enter a note.
                         Press CONTROL+PGUP to return.


      APPEND       ||<6>|| SALES       ||Rec EOF/9      ||   ||
```

It is also possible to display a form, or **template**, on the screen with blanks to be filled in by the user. The **form-filling technique** is used by moving the cursor from one blank to another and entering the appropriate data. Figure 8.19 shows how the template for entering a sales order might appear. Because the size of each blank is the exact size of the applicable field in the database and the prompt indicates the field, the user is not likely to attempt to enter the wrong data.

Graphic User Interface

In research done in the 1970s at the Xerox Palo Alto Research Center, it was found that the use of **icons**, or graphic images, to represent data files or processing options made it easier to teach novices to use a computer. This feature of software to communicate with the user by means of graphics is called a **graphic user interface (GUI)**, which is pronounced "gooey." The user moves the cursor around the screen with a mouse or trackball to select the desired icon. When the cursor is properly positioned, that data file or processing option can be activated by pressing the appropriate mouse button.

Executive information systems tend to incorporate GUI, and this feature has contributed to their acceptance by executives with little computer background. The main menu of the Commander EIS from Comshare, illustrated in Figure 8.20, provides an example of the technique.

Because GUI is easy to use and takes a relatively short time to learn, most microcomputer software that is being written today incorporates as many GUI features as possible.

FIGURE 8.20
The Graphic User Interface of the Commander Executive Information System from Comshare

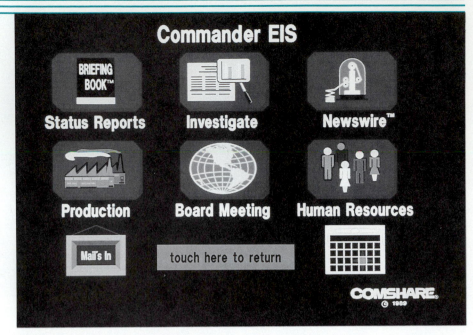

The Comshare Commander™ EIS Menu.

KEEPING INPUT ERRORS TO A MINIMUM

Even with all the techniques that have been devised to assist the user with data entry, it is still possible to make errors. Typographical errors are just as easy to make with a computer as with a typewriter. In other cases, the user simply enters the incorrect data.

Software can be designed to reduce the opportunity for errors by providing for their prevention, detection, and correction.

Error Prevention

An input screen can be designed so that certain displayed data cannot be changed inadvertently by the user. Data fields into which the user cannot move the cursor are said to have a **protected format**. Another error prevention technique is to allow the user to back out of possible trouble by pressing a particular key such as the Escape key found on microcomputer keyboards.

Error Detection

The best time to detect an error is when the data is being entered, before the data has had the opportunity to impact the system. To achieve this objective, most application software includes **edit routines** that detect the entry of the wrong type of data. For example, if you try to enter an alphabetic character in a numeric field, an **error message** is displayed that tells you what type of error you have made, along with an explanation of how to make a correction.

Error Correction

Most software provides the capability to edit the contents of a data record by allowing the user to move the cursor to the error field and rekey all or a part of the entry.

Putting Error Handling in Perspective

Through the use of the basic error reduction techniques described above, the opportunity for accurate input data is maximized. You should realize, however, that regardless of how diligently you follow these techniques, errors will still be made.

Because error controls that are built into a system add to its cost, a system designed to be completely error free would be so expensive that few firms could afford it. Therefore, rather than attempt to eliminate errors completely, you should concentrate on eliminating those errors that would, if uncorrected, have a devastating effect on your organization, and then strive to keep other errors to an acceptable minimum.

SUMMARY

Although computer technology has changed significantly over the years, all systems include a CPU, one or more input devices and output devices, and secondary storage. The CPU contains the control unit, the ALU, and primary storage.

Primary storage is constructed of integrated circuit chips and comes in three types. RAM permits reading and writing, but ROM permits only reading. Cache memory resides between the processor and regular RAM to speed up the retrieval of instructions and data.

Input devices include the keyboard, pointing devices such as the mouse and the trackball, source data automation technologies such as OCR and MICR, and speech recognition devices. The variety of output devices is also large, including display screens, printers, speech output devices, and special purpose devices, such as plotters and COM. The manager personally uses some of the input and output devices in problem solving, while others play an indirect role.

The computer accomplishes its work by following the instructions of computer software. One of the two basic types of software, system software, includes the computer's operating system, utility programs, and language translators. The other type, application software, includes general business, industry-specific, organizational productivity, and personal productivity packages.

System software supports problem solving in an indirect way. Application software can provide direct or indirect support, depending on the type. General business packages are the least likely to provide direct support.

User friendliness in software is accomplished by providing the user with menus, context sensitive help, guided dialog, and, in the microcomputer environment, GUI.

Although computer-based systems are not immune to errors, high levels of accuracy can be achieved by incorporating measures aimed at error prevention, error detection, and error correction.

This chapter lays the groundwork for our study of the computer. In the next chapter, we concentrate on the database, and then in Chapter 10 we address data communications.

KEY TERMS

random access memory (RAM)
read-only memory (ROM)
cache memory
ergonomics, human engineering, human factors
    considerations
trackball
touch screen
light pen
source data automation (SDA)
optical reading unit, scanner
optical character recognition (OCR)
font
magnetic ink character recognition (MICR)
electronic funds transfer (EFT)
speaker-dependent system
speaker-independent system
display screen, monitor, cathode ray tube
    (CRT), video display terminal (VDT)
monochrome display
color display, color monitor
line printer
character printer
page printer
speech output unit, audio response unit
computer output microform (COM)
system software

operating system
supervisor, monitor, executive
utility program, utility
machine language
source program
translator
object program
assembler
assembly language
compiler
interpreter
procedure-oriented language
problem-oriented language
fourth generation language (4GL),
    nonprocedural language, natural language
menu
navigation
context sensitive help
guided dialogue
prompt
question-and-answer technique
form-filling technique
icon
graphic user interface (GUI)
protected format

KEY CONCEPTS

How the computer schematic reflects the basic
    architecture of all computers
The computer as a closed-loop system

How input and output devices play direct and
    indirect roles in problem solving
Multiprogramming

Generations of computer languages

How software plays direct and indirect roles in problem solving

User friendliness

The importance of reducing errors at the point of input

QUESTIONS

1. Name the four categories of computers in terms of their size. Which category was the first that evolved? Which was the last? In which category, or categories, would you find a small business computer?

2. What are the three main components of the CPU?

3. What are the two types of material that are kept in secondary storage?

4. Which hardware unit enables the computer to be a closed-loop system? Does anything else contribute? If so, what?

5. Name the organization that installed the first punched card machines. Do the same for the first mass-produced computer. What was the first business organization, what was the computer, and when was it installed?

6. Since RAM is volatile, how do you prevent loss of its contents when the power is shut off?

7. Would a firm likely keep its database in cache memory? Explain why or why not.

8. Why is keyboard design an example of ergonomics?

9. What is the major distinction between a mouse and a trackball?

10. What is a similarity between touch screen and light pen technologies? What is a difference?

11. What is the main difference between OCR and MICR in terms of how the data is read?

12. Which technology has enjoyed the greatest success in business systems—speech input or speech output? Why?

13. What are the four conditions that demand printed output?

14. What is one major reason why you might choose a line printer over a page printer to produce a particular report?

15. Name three output devices that can produce graphics.

16. Which technology is replacing COM?

17. Name the input and output devices that play direct roles in problem solving.

18. What are the three types of system software?

19. What is a basic difference between an assembler and a compiler? Between a compiler and an interpreter?

20. Is BASIC a procedure-oriented language? Why or why not?

21. Which type of 4GL would offer the user the most power, yet be the most difficult to learn and use?

22. Which types of application software perform data processing functions?

23. Which type of software plays only an indirect role in problem solving?

24. What two characteristics should software have in order to be user friendly?

25. What three techniques can be used to achieve guided dialog?

26. Which input error minimization technique is least likely to be computerized?

TOPICS FOR DISCUSSION

1. What are some examples of ergonomic design that we see in our everyday lives?

2. The chapter does not elaborate on why users prefer displayed output over hard copy? Why do you think that is so?

3. Describe how the four reasons for hard copy output could be satisfied with electronic transmission and display.

4. Which of the six operating system functions would be performed by DOS? Which utilities does DOS provide?

5. What are some examples of icons that we see in our everyday lives?

PROBLEMS

1. Draw a diagram that tailors the computer schematic to a Macintosh computer with a GUI, a hard drive, and a laser printer.

2. Go to the library and read a magazine or journal article on one of the following topics:

   - Pointing devices
   - Optical character recognition
   - Speech recognition
   - Display screens
   - Printers
   - Plotters
   - Ergonomics

Summarize your findings on two double-spaced pages. At the top of the first page, identify the source on six lines: (1) author or authors, (2) title, (3) publication name, (4) volume number and issue number, (5) date, and (6) page numbers.

Northwest Camping Products, Inc.

Dear Lynn,

Welcome aboard. We are looking forward to benefitting from your college education in computing. As one of the nation's leading manufacturers of camping supplies, we feel that we are in the right position to maintain our leadership in a growing industry. And, an important part of that growth will be our implementation of a computer!

Yes, your recommendation has been approved. The top-management committee met yesterday and decided to install a computer to perform data processing, office automation, and decision-support applications. However, your recommendation of a networked mini was not approved. Instead, the decision was made to go with a single micro. The micro will include 5 MB of RAM, an 80 MB hard drive, a high-resolution color monitor, and a laser printer. In addition, it was decided that we use prewritten programs entirely. There are no plans to hire programmers or systems analysts, but we will have one full-time operator. It will be your responsibility to get the applications "on the air."

The committee has requested that you provide them with a list of the *types* of software that we will need. We want a computerized accounting system and want our managers to be able to do a better job of forecasting the future and engage in mathematical modeling. You recall that none of our managers have strong mathematical skills. The managers also would like to be able to retrieve information from the company database and produce graphs. Finally, we want to get into electronic mail.

As soon as you prepare the list, let us get together and discuss it before we take it to the committee.

Sincerely,

Alex Weston
Administrative Vice President

Assignments

1. Provide the list that the committee has requested.
2. Write a memo to Mr. Weston, addressing the decision to go with a single micro instead of a networked mini. List any constraints that the decision will cause in achieving the full capabilities in each application area.

SELECTED BIBLIOGRAPHY

Armero, Marcy Bruch. "Computer Furniture and Worker Comfort." *The Office* 113 (March 1991): 69*ff.*

Davis, Stephen G. "FORTRAN at 30: Formula for Success." *Datamation* 33 (April 1, 1987): 47*ff.*

Ditlea, Steve. "In Support of Laptops." *Datamation* 36 (July 1, 1990): 70*ff.*

Drummond, Marshall E., and Reitsch, Arthur R. "Selection Criteria for Fourth Generation Languages." *Journal of Systems Management* 41 (September 1990): 24–27.

Esters, Stephanie D. "486 Computers: Revved to Go." *Black Enterprise* 21 (April 1991): 35–36.

Fitzgerald, Michael. "GUI Revs PCs at Big Six Firm." *Computerworld* 26 (January 13, 1992): 1*ff.*

Gerlach, James H., and Kuo, Feng-Yang. "Understanding Human-Computer Interaction for Information Systems Design." *MIS Quarterly* 15 (December 1991): 527–549.

Gibson, Steve. "Static RAM Caching Provides Superior Memory Performance." *InfoWorld* 13 (February 11, 1991): 30.

Hardie, Hugh. "Getting Ready for a GUI." *CA Magazine* 124 (June 1991): 47–48.

IBM Application System/400 Global Review. Publication G360-2060-00. Somers, NY: International Business Machines Corporation. 1991.

Kagan, Albert; Lau, Kinnam; and Nusgart, Keith R. "Information System Usage Within Small Business Firms." *Entrepreneurship Theory & Practice* 14 (Spring 1990): 25–37.

Keen, Peter G. W., and Woodman, Lynda A. "What To Do with All Those Micros." *Harvard Business Review* 62 (September-October 1984): 142–150.

Ketler, Karen, and Smith, Robert D. "Differences Between Third and Fourth Generation Programmers: A Human Factor Analysis." *Information Resources Management Journal* 5 (Spring 1992): 25–35.

Kirkpatrick, David. "Here Comes the Payoff from PCs." *Fortune* 125 (March 23, 1992): 93*ff.*

Martin, James. "IBM's AS/400 Holds Key to the Future of Computing." *PC Week* 6 (May 15, 1989): 54.

Moad, Jeff. "Large Systems Are Hot!" *Datamation* 36 (May 15, 1990): 24*ff.*

Nath, Ravinder. "Are Frequent Computer Users More Satisfied?" *Information Processing & Management* 25 (Number 5, 1989): 557–562.

Necco, Charles R.; Tsai, Nancy W.; and Smith, Barbara. "Structured Documentation for a Specific Type of Fourth Generation Language: Electronic Spreadsheets." *Journal of Information Technology Management* 2 (Number 1, 1991): 31–42.

Philips, Roger. "Productivity Tools Sit Idle." *Computerworld* 22 (February 1, 1988): 53–55.

Radding, Alan. "Speech Recognition." *Bank Management* 66 (March 1990): 42*ff.*

Verity, John W., Lewis, Geoff. "Computers: The New Look." *Business Week* (November 30, 1987): 112*ff.*

"Voice Response: Lower-Cost POS Alternative." *Chain Store Age Executive* 66 (October 1990): 72.

Chapter 9

The Database and Database Management System

LEARNING OBJECTIVES

After studying this chapter, you should:

- Be familiar with the ingredients of data management—how data is organized, stored, accessed, and used
- Understand that the applications determine the type of processing, which, in turn, determines the type of secondary storage
- Be familiar with how the database concept evolved and its influence on computer processing
- Know what a database management system (DBMS) is—its functions, and how it is used
- Have a better understanding of the role of the database administrator
- Have an introductory understanding of how a manager uses a popular mainframe DBMS—DB2
- Appreciate the advantages and disadvantages of using a DBMS to manage the database

INTRODUCTION

Data management is a subset of information resources management and ensures that the firm's data resource accurately reflects the physical system that it represents. The data resource is maintained in secondary storage, which can take a sequential or direct access form. Magnetic tape is the most popular sequential storage medium, and magnetic disk has been the dominant means of achieving direct access. However, a new direct access technology, the optical disk, is gaining popularity.

Prior to the database era firms were restricted in their data management because of the ways that the data was arranged in the secondary storage media. Early efforts to overcome these constraints included file sorting and merging, extensive computer programming to search and match file records, and file indexes and links built into data records. The database concept builds on these indexes and links to achieve a logical relationship between files.

The software that manages the database is called the database management system, or DBMS. All DBMSs have a database desciption language processor that is used to create the database, and a database manager that makes the database contents available to users. Users use data manipulation and query languages. The person who has responsibility for the database and the DBMS is the database administrator, or DBA.

The DBMS offers real advantages to firms as they use their computer as an information system. However, the DBMS adds some real costs in the form of hardware, software, and information specialists.

THE HIERARCHY OF DATA

Firms have traditionally organized their data in a hierarchy that consists of elements, records, and files.

- A **data element** is the smallest unit of data—it cannot be subdivided into meaningful units. In a payroll record you find such data elements as name, employee number, social security number, hourly rate of pay, and number of dependents.
- The next step up the hierarchy is the record. A **record** consists of all of the data elements relating to a particular object or activity. For example, there are records that describe each inventory item and each sale.
- All of the records of the same type are organized into a file. A **file** is a collection of data records that relate to a particular subject. For example, an Outstanding Purchase Order file describes the purchase orders that have been sent to suppliers but not yet filled.

The traditional data hierarchy, therefore, is:

- ■ File
  - ■ Record
    - ■ Data element

The file is the highest level and the data element is the lowest.

DATA MANAGEMENT

In Chapter 2, we saw that information resources management, or IRM, is the overall effort of the firm to create and maintain the information resources. Since data is one of the resources it must be managed and this process is called data management. **Data management** is a subset of information resources management, which includes all of the activities involved in making certain that the firm's data resources are accurate, current, safe from harm, and available to users.

Data Management Activities

The data management activities include:

- ■ **Data collection**   The necessary data is gathered and recorded on a form called a **source document** that serves as input to the system. For example, data describing a sale is entered on a sales order form.
- ■ **Integrity and verification**   The data is examined to assure its consistency and accuracy based on prespecified constraints and rules.
- ■ **Storage**   The data is stored on some medium such as magnetic tape or magnetic disk.
- ■ **Maintenance**   New data is added, existing data is changed, and data no longer needed is deleted for the purpose of keeping the data resource current.
- ■ **Security**   The data is safeguarded to prevent destruction, damage, or misuse.
- ■ **Organization**   The data is arranged in such a way as to meet the information needs of users.
- ■ **Retrieval**   The data is made available to users.

Prior to the computer era, all of these activities were performed by clerical employees, supported by the primitive punched-card and keydriven machines. Today, people are still required for much data collection and verification, but the computer has assumed most of the data management responsibility.

SECONDARY STORAGE

All computers include some type of secondary storage to supplement the primary storage that is housed in the CPU. The two main types of secondary storage are sequential and direct access.

Sequential Storage

Sequential storage is an organization or arrangement of data on a storage medium that consists of one record following another in a particular order. For example, employee records are arranged in employee number sequence. When sequential storage is used the first record must be processed first, the second record second, and so on until the end of the file is reached.

Some computer storage media can only process data that is arranged sequentially. The punched card and magnetic tape files used by early computers were sequential. The punched card files have all disappeared, but magnetic tape is still in use.

Magnetic Tape Storage

The magnetic tape that is used to store computer data has the same physical properties as audio tape. The tape consists of a plastic material that is coated with a substance that facilitates the recording. In the case of the computer tape, the data is recorded in the form of magnetized bits. The bits that represent each character are arranged across the width of the tape. Recording densities as great as 1600 bits per inch (bpi) are common.

The first magnetic tape media consisted of large reels, but now cartridges are preferred because they can store more data and require less storage space. Most mainframe computer systems include one or more **tape units** or **tape drives** that read and write the tape data in either a reel or cartridge form. The cartridges have not changed the way that magnetic tape is used; the same principles apply to both reels and cartridges.

Magnetic Tape Records

All of the data elements that are included in a record are recorded along the length of the tape as shown in Figure 9.1. All of the records comprise the file, as shown in Figure 9.2. Blank gaps separate the records.

FIGURE 9.1
A Magnetic Tape Record

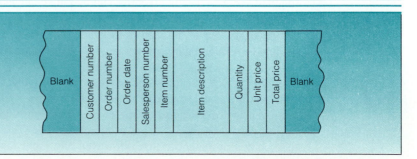

FIGURE 9.2

A Magnetic Tape File

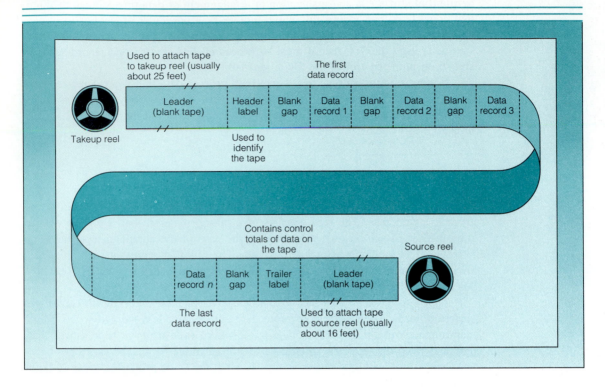

Updating a Magnetic Tape File

The files that provide the conceptual representation of the firm are called **master files.** There are Inventory Master files, Customer Master files, Employee Master files, and so on. Each master file contains data about its particular subject. The master files are updated with data from transaction files. A **transaction file** contains data describing activities of the firm such as sales, purchases, and employee hours worked.

The process of updating a file is called **file maintenance,** and it involves adding new records, deleting records, and making changes to records. When a magnetic tape master file is maintained, it is not practical to write the updated record back to the same area of the tape from which the record was read. The updated record should be written onto another tape. For that reason, file maintenance of a magnetic tape file produces a second, updated tape.

Figure 9.3 illustrates the process. The original file is called the **old master file,** and the updated file is called the **new master file.** When performing the file maintenance of a sequential master file, the records in the transaction file must be in the same sequence as those in the master file. The transaction file in the figure is recorded on magnetic tape. However, any input medium can be used.

FIGURE 9.3

Updating a
Magnetic Tape
File

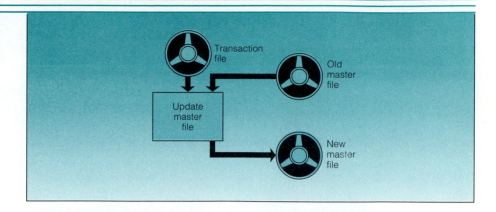

Uses of Magnetic Tape

Magnetic tape is best suited for use as a **historical storage medium.** The firm can store data on tape and retain the tape as a record of business activity. A similar use of magnetic tape is as a **backup file** for a master file on a direct access storage device. The backup file can be used if something happens to the direct access master file.

Magnetic tape can also serve as an **input medium.** Some cash registers in retail stores include a magnetic tape unit that records data as sales are made. After the store closes, a central computer, perhaps in another city, automatically retrieves the data from the tape.

Finally, magnetic tape can serve as a **communications medium** that can be sent through the mail. Larger firms are required to submit their tax data to the IRS in this manner.

Direct Access Storage

Direct access storage is a way to organize data that allows records to be written and read without a sequential search. The hardware unit that makes this possible is called a **direct access storage device (DASD).** The DASD contains a reading and writing mechanism that can be directed to any particular location in the storage medium. Although several DASD technologies have been devised, the most popular is the magnetic disk.

Magnetic Disk Storage

The disks that are used to record computer data are usually made of metal and are covered with the same recording material that is used on magnetic tape. Multiple disks can be mounted in a vertical **disk stack** as shown in Figure 9.4. All of the disks are attached to a single spindle, and they rotate past an access mechanism that contains access arms. Located at the end of each arm are read/write heads that

FIGURE 9.4
A Disk Stack

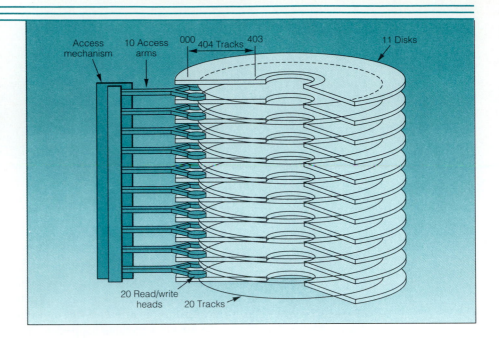

read data from the disk and write data to it. As shown in the figure, the data is recorded on the disk surfaces in the form of tracks. A **track** is a circular pattern of data bits. You can think of the tracks as serving the same purpose as the grooves on a phonograph record. The access mechanism is positioned on a track and can read data from the track or write data to it as the disk rotates.

The disk stack is housed in a **disk drive** or **disk unit.** Large mainframe or minicomputer configurations include multiple disk drives to provide adequate capacity. It is not uncommon to find installations with 100 or more disk drives providing trillions of bytes of data. In microcomputer configurations the disk drives take the form of diskette drives and hard disks.

Reading and Writing Disk Data

When data is to be read from or written to a disk, it is first necessary to position the access mechanism on the proper track and then activate the proper read/write head. The access mechanism must be given the address where the record is located on the disk. The **disk address** specifies the track number, the read/write head number, and usually the record number on the track—Record 1, Record 2, and so on. Figure 9.5 illustrates a DASD address.

Record Addressing

There are three basic approaches to producing the address that the DASD requires to access a record. The approaches are direct, hashing, and indexed sequential.

FIGURE 9.5
A DASD Address

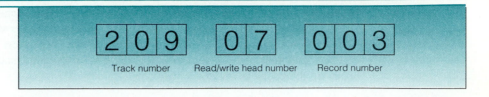

Track number   Read/write head number   Record number

Direct Addressing   In **direct addressing** the record key serves as the address. The **key** is the data element that identifies the records of a file. For example, the key of an Employee Master file is employee number. If direct addressing had been used to produce the DASD address in Figure 9.5, the employee number would have been 20907003. The number is simply subdivided to produce the required address components.

This direct translation of a file key into a disk storage address is highly unusual in business applications. There are not many files with keys that are suitable for translation.

Hashing   It is possible to compute the address from the key. The address is transformed by an algorithm called a **hashing scheme** or **randomizing formula** to produce the address.

Although hashing performs a valuable service, it has its problems. The hashing algorithm and the set of file keys seldom yield a set of disk addresses that uniformly fill the disk. There may be many unused or unfilled tracks. Also, the algorithm may yield the same disk address for more than one key. The event of two or more keys receiving the same address is called a **collision.** Collisions are handled by means of an overflow area. An **overflow area** is a part of the DASD that is reserved for the storage of records with keys that have already been assigned. Such duplicate keys are called **synonyms.** Retrieving records from the overflow area adds to the access time.

Indexed Sequential   When a file is organized indexed sequential the records are recorded on the disk in sequence. The system remembers the actual disk address where a subset (such as every 100th record) of the file is loaded. Then these record keys and their disk addresses are placed in a separate file or table called an **index.** The subset of records may be predetermined by percentage; for example, every hundredth record will be included in the index. To locate the 745th record requires searching to the seventh record in the index and then searching the disk by starting with the 700th record and continuing until the forty-fifth record is reached. This is basically the way you use the Yellow Pages to get the number of a pizza restaurant. You look at the table of contents, see that the pizza listings begin on page 80, and skip over pages 1 through 79.

Accessing the data file by means of the index provides faster access than sequential processing but somewhat slower processing than direct addressing or hashing. However, there is minimal wasted space. The disadvantage of indexed sequential comes when adding and deleting records. Such operations can require a modification of the index or changes to linkage fields in the database.

In the predatabase era, systems analysts and programmers were preoccupied with establishing optimal file addressing and index structures. Today only the DBAs spend their time on such issues, freeing the other information specialists to focus on the business issues.

Updating a DASD File

Figure 9.6 illustrates how file maintenance is performed on a DASD file. The transaction data is shown being entered using an online keydriven device such as a CRT terminal but could take the form of any input medium. Further, it is not necessary that the transaction data be in any particular sequence. Since the access mechanism can be directed to any record for reading or writing at that location, it is not necessary to create a second file, as with magnetic tape. Updated records are rewritten in their original location.

Uses of DASD

DASD is a good **master file medium.** The files can be updated as transactions occur, producing a current record of the firm's activity. Another popular use is as an **intermediate storage medium** to contain semiprocessed data. For example, data can be transferred from one program to another in a disk form. DASD can also be used as an **input medium** in the same manner as magnetic tape. DASD is not good for historical storage since the disk stacks are much more expensive than tape reels or cartridges.

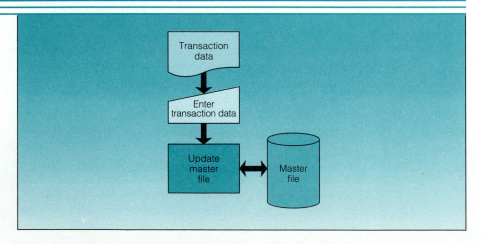

FIGURE 9.6
Updating a DASD File

Optical Disks

For most of the computer era, magnetic disks have proven to be unbeatable as a DASD. Other technologies have been tried—magnetic drums, bins of magnetic tape loops, magnetic cards, magnetic bubbles, and silicon chips. Only the drums have had any real impact, being used for fast access by mainframes.

The new DASD technology that has the best chance of becoming established as a secondary storage medium is the optical disk. An **optical disk,** also called a **laser disk** and **compact disk (CD),** is one that represents data by combinations of tiny blemishes on the disk surface that are created by a laser beam. The blemishes take the form of pits, bubbles, or changed crystalline states. A lower-intensity laser beam is used to read the blemishes.

The main advantage of optical disks is their large capacity. A 5¼-inch optical disk can contain between 440 megabytes (MB), or million bytes, and 1 gigabyte (GB), or billion bytes, with 650 MB being the average. This is about 540 times as much data as can be stored on a microcomputer diskette, assuming a diskette capacity of 1.5 MB. This single-disk capacity can be increased even more by mounting the disks in a multiplatter automated disk library called a **jukebox.**

The first optical disks had a write-once capability—termed **WORM (write-once, read-many).** You could record data on the disk only one time, but you could read the data as many times as you liked. The term **CD-ROM (compact disk—read-only memory)** is used to describe the WORM technology that is becoming a popular device for use with microcomputers. WORM is ideal for historical storage, where data cannot be changed once it is recorded.

During the late 1980s optical disks became available, which can be erased and rewritten an unlimited number of times. These disks are called **rewritable disks.** Rewritable disks can be used in the same way as magnetic disks, only the access time is much slower. Some optical disk suppliers are now offering drives that can handle both WORM and rewritable disks. These drives are called **multifunction drives.**

In time the optical disk will replace magnetic tape as the preferred historical storage medium. The key to the optical disk replacing the magnetic disk is the access time. Until that increase in speed is achieved, firms will use optical disks in conjunction with magnetic disks. Less-active data will be housed in optical disk units, and more-active data will be maintained in magnetic disk storage for fast access.

THE RELATIONSHIP OF SECONDARY STORAGE TO PROCESSING

There are two principal ways to process data—batch and online. **Batch processing** involves holding transactions and processing them all at once, in batches. **Online processing** involves processing the transactions individually, often at the time they occur. Since the online processing is transaction oriented the term **transaction pro-**

cessing is often used. We will use online processing, as transaction processing can also mean data processing.

What determines the type of processing? It is the firm's applications. If the processing does not have to be done when transactions occur, batch processing can be performed, and either magnetic tape or magnetic disk can be used. Payroll systems are good examples of applications that lend themselves to batch processing. On the other hand, if there is reason to process transactions individually, online processing is the choice and some type of DASD is required.

Batch Processing

Figure 9.7 is a system flowchart that illustrates batch processing. The objective of this system is to update three master files—Inventory, Accounts Receivable, and Sales Analysis. Firms typically update their batch files on a daily basis, called a **daily cycle.**

The first file to be updated is the Inventory file, which is arranged in item-number sequence. Item number is the **sort key,** the data element that determines the sequence.

Since the transaction records must be in the same sequence as the master file they are sorted in Step 1, and the Inventory file is updated in Step 2. Steps 3 and 4 accomplish the updating of the Accounts Receivable file, and Steps 5 and 6 do the same for the Sales Analysis file.

Batch processing is the most efficient way to use the computing hardware since it is an assembly-line process. There is little wasted motion and storage space. The main shortcoming of batch processing is the fact that the file is only current immediately following the cycle update. This means that management does not always have available current information describing the physical system.

Online Processing

Online processing was developed to overcome the problem of out-of-date files. The technological breakthrough that made online processing possible was magnetic disk storage.

Figure 9.8 illustrates the online approach to updating the same three files as in the batch example. *Each* transaction is processed against *all* of the applicable master files while the transaction data is in primary storage. The appropriate Inventory record is read into primary storage, updated with the transaction data, and then rewritten to the DASD. Then the Accounts Receivable record is updated in the same manner, followed by the Sales Analysis record. All three DASD files are updated before the next transaction is entered.

Realtime Systems

The term *realtime* is often used in conjunction with a computer system. You hear someone say, "We have a realtime system," or "Our system operates in realtime."

FIGURE 9.7

Batch Processing

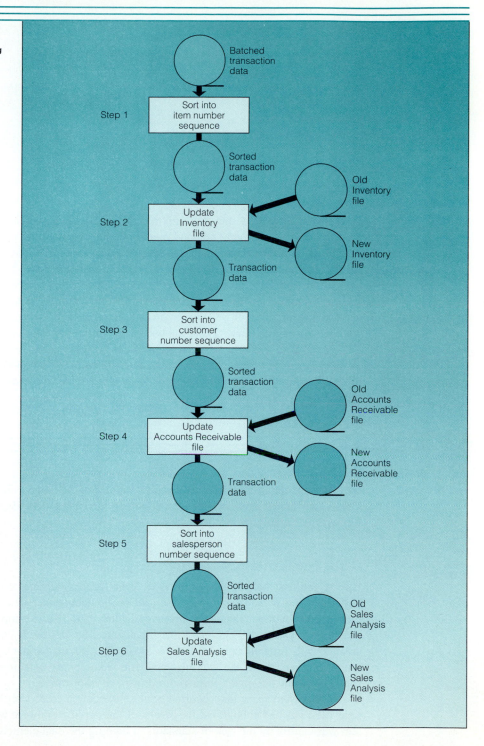

FIGURE 9.8
Online Processing

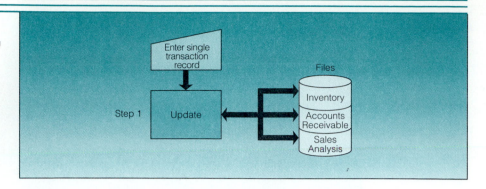

A **realtime system** is one that controls the physical system in some way. This requires that the computer respond quickly to the status of the physical system.

Assume, for example, that you want to write a check to pay for a department store purchase and the clerk asks to see your driver's license. The clerk keys the license number into the cash register terminal that is connected to the computer, and the computer conducts a credit check. If your credit is O.K., you are allowed to make the purchase; if not, you go away empty handed. The computer determines whether the sale is made. The computer controls the physical system.

A realtime system is a special form of online system. The online system makes available a current conceptual resource, and the realtime system extends that capability by using the conceptual resource to determine the operations of the physical system.

THE PREDATABASE ERA

The era of computer use that existed prior to the database concept was characterized by excessive data redundancy and tight coupling of data and computer programs. These two conditions contributed to something called data dependence, which limited the capabilities of the systems.

Data Redundancy

During the first half of this century, as firms processed data manually and with keydriven and punched card machines, all of the data-related decisions were made individually, without regard to any overall data plan. For example, as each data processing system was designed, the input data files needed by that system were created with little thought as to how those files affected other systems. Perhaps much, or even all, of the data in a new file was already contained in an existing file. The result was much **data redundancy,** or duplication.

The wasted space that occurred because the data records were repeated in multiple files was bad enough but the results of the duplication were worse. One problem was caused by the lack of standards in naming the data elements. For example, consider the situation where *Stock-on-hand* in one inventory system refers to stock located in the storeroom. Another system in the same firm defines *Stock-on-hand* to mean all available stock, including new arrivals on the receiving dock. A manager who requests information could get different answers depending on which system is used to generate the report.

Another problem was the lack of synchronization in updating the duplicate data. Multiple copies of data were often updated on different frequencies. One file would be updated daily, another weekly, and a third monthly. Reports based on one file could conflict with reports based on another, with the user being unaware of the differences.

Data Dependence

Data dependence refers to the tight coupling of data specifications and computer programs. Data characteristics such as field length, record length, and so on were coded into each program that accessed the data. This situation meant that every time a file changed in any way, all of the programs that accessed the file had to be modified. In some cases all of the programs that accessed a changed file were not even identified until they began to fail because of their inability to handle the new format.

Diffused Data Ownership

The interaction of data redundancy and data dependence also increased the data problems during the predatabase era. To avoid changing multiple programs due to one "simple field change," a programmer would create an entirely new file. Effectively, each programmer owned the data that his or her program accessed.

It was extremely difficult to agree on ownership and standardization of data for an information system. This situation of the 1950s and early 1960s may have been the seed that gave the first MISs a bad name. Information specialists appeared unable to deliver systems that provided consistent, accurate, and reliable information.

THE DAWN OF THE DATABASE ERA

Information specialists sought ways to solve the problems caused by the way the data was organized physically, and their efforts led to the concept of logical organization. **Logical organization** integrates data from several different physical locations and is how the *user* sees the data. For example, a manager sees all of the information on a report as having a logical integration even though the data might have been retrieved from physically separate files. The **physical organization,** on the other hand, is how the *computer* sees the data—as separate files.

The task of information specialists was to provide the logical organization required by the user within the constraints of the physical organization. Users often want data from a single file to be arranged in a sequence other than its order in the storage medium, and want to assemble data from multiple files. Techniques were developed to meet these needs by means of logical integration.

Logical Integration within a Single File

Two approaches enable the selection of records from a single file based on characteristics other than the key. These approaches are called inverted files and linked lists. Both require a DASD.

Inverted Files An **inverted file** is a file maintained in a particular sequence, but an accompanying index enables records from the file to be selected in another sequence.

The type of problem that the inverted file was designed to solve was the request by a manager for a report listing only certain records in a file. For example, a sales manager might want to see a listing of the sales made by Salesperson 23. Each record in the file had to be examined by the computer to determine if it was a Salesperson 23 record. If so, it was selected and used to print the report. A file containing thousands of records might include only a dozen or so records for Salesperson 23, but *every* record in the file had to be scanned. The approach was very inefficient.

The information specialists realized they could create an index for the Salesperson Master file that identified all of the records for each salesperson. Such an **inverted file index,** often called a **secondary index,** is illustrated in Figure 9.9. When the index is needed, it is read into primary storage and the program scans the salesperson number column looking for Salesperson 23. When that row is found the program can scan across to the right and pick up the needed record numbers. In the example there is a record for each of Salesperson 23's customers who has made a purchase. The needed records can be selected without searching the entire file.

FIGURE 9.9

An Inverted File Index

Salesperson number	Salesperson name	Customer 1	Customer 2	Customer 3	Customer n
16		17042	21096		
20		41854			
23		23694	25410	30102	30111
31		31002			
56		34107	13109		
92		20842			
98		61634			
104		10974			
110		16342	64210	51263	41782

FIGURE 9.10

A Linked List

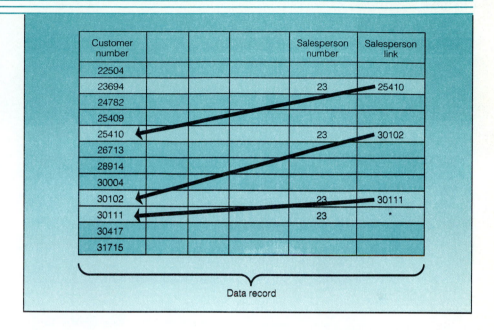

Data record

Linked Lists   Another technique can achieve the same results. Assume that the same manager wants the same report but the information specialist wants to avoid use of an index to achieve faster access. A separate field, the salesperson link, is added to each record in the Salesperson Master file as pictured in Figure 9.10. The field contains a **link,** or **pointer,** that ties together all of the records for each salesperson. A file containing such link fields is called a **linked list.**

Only the links for Salesperson 23 are shown in the figure. The program selects the records by scanning each record in the file until the first record for Salesperson 23 is found. The link field in the first record is called the **head,** and it identifies the *next* record for Salesperson 23. The next record is retrieved, and its link field identifies the third record. This process is continued until the last record is retrieved. The link field in the last record contains a special code that identifies it as the **tail.**

Inverted files and linked lists provide a way to logically integrate records that are physically scattered throughout a single file. A need also exists to achieve the same results between multiple files.

Logical Integration between Files

In the mid-1960s General Electric modified COBOL to allow data to be retrieved from multiple files. Links were used to interconnect the records in one *file* to the logically related records in *other files.* GE's system was named IDS, for Integrated Data Store, and it was the first step toward an integrated database of multiple files.

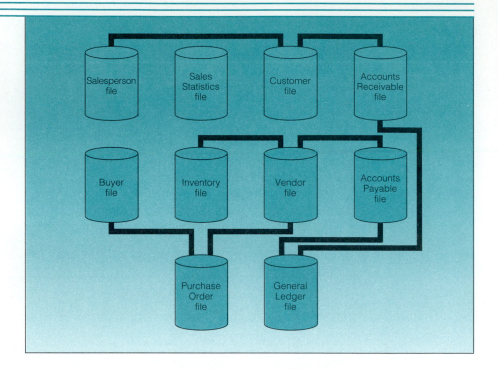

FIGURE 9.11
A Database
Consists of One
or More Files

THE DATABASE CONCEPT

A **database** is an integrated collection of computer data, organized and stored in a manner that facilitates easy retrieval. Direct access storage devices must be used. Figure 9.11 shows that many of the firm's files can be logically integrated. This logical integration of records in multiple files is called the **database concept.** The lines in the figure represent the logical integration.

Two primary goals of the database concept are to minimize redundancy and achieve data independence. **Data independence** is the ability to make changes in data structure without making changes to the programs that process the data. Data independence is accomplished by the placement of data specifications in tables and dictionaries that are physically separate from the programs. The programs reference the tables in order to access the data. Changes to data structure are made only once—in the tables.

When a firm adopts the database concept, the hierarchy of data becomes:

- Database
    - File
        - Record
            - Data element

Separate files can still exist, representing the major components of the database, however the physical organization of the data does not constrain the user. Means are provided to integrate the contents of the files that have logical relationships.

DATABASE STRUCTURES

The logical integration of files can be achieved explicitly or implicitly.

Explicit Relationships

The inverted indexes and link fields establish **explicit relationships** between logically integrated data. The indexes and fields exist physically and must be incorporated into the files when they are created. If they are not, the manager's request for logically integrated information can only be met by time-consuming and expensive special programming and sorting.

Hierarchical Structure   Figure 9.12 shows how the records of four separate files can be integrated using explicit relationships. Each salesperson has a *single* salesperson record that contains data such as that listed in the figure. Each salesperson has *multiple* sales statistics records—one record for each item sold to a customer. Each salesperson also has *multiple* customer records that provide information about each customer in the salesperson's territory. Finally, each of the salesperson's customers can have *multiple* accounts receivable records—one for each unpaid purchase.

The records in the figure are arranged in a hierarchy. Each record on one level can be related to multiple records on the next-lower level. When such a logical relationship exists between the records in different files it is called a **hierarchical structure.** A record on one level that has subsidiary records is called the **parent.** The records on the next-lower level are called **children.** In a hierarchical structure, a child can have only a single parent.

Another important feature of Figure 9.12 is the link fields that establish the explicit relationships. Once you retrieve a salesperson record (say for Salesperson 23), the link in that record can lead you to another record *in another file* that is logically related to that salesperson. A link field in the second record leads to a third record, and so on, creating a chain reaction through an entire set of files.

Network Structure   The other popular database structure that uses explicit relationships is the network structure. The main difference between the network and hierarchical structures is that in the **network structure** a child can have more than one parent.

Figure 9.13 shows a network structure. In this example, each buyer in the purchasing department is represented by a record. Each buyer is responsible for purchasing multiple inventory items, and each item is represented by a record. Each inventory item can be acquired from multiple suppliers, and there is a supplier rec-

FIGURE 9.12

Explicit
Relationships
between Files

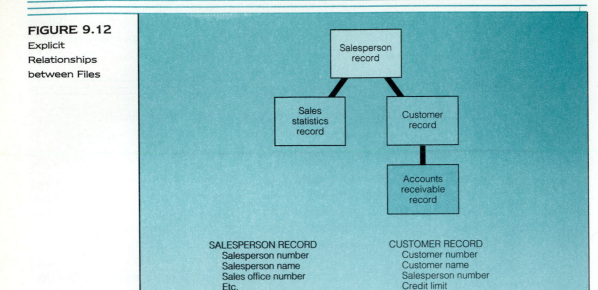

ord for each. Multiple purchase order records exist for each buyer and each inventory item. The purchase order records have two parents—buyer records and inventory records.

The Limitation of Explicit Relationships   While the hierarchical and network structures represented a giant step toward eliminating physical constraints, the use of explicit relationships has its disadvantages. It is necessary to identify the groups of files that must be logically integrated *before* the database is created. This restricts the manager from making **ad hoc requests**—special requests for combinations of information not previously specified.

Implicit Relationships

In the early 1970s Edgar F. Codd and C. J. Date, both of IBM but working separately, developed an approach to establishing relationships between records, which do not have to be stated explicitly. Special link fields do not have to be included in the records. The Codd and Date approach has been named the **relational struc-**

FIGURE 9.13

The Network
Structure

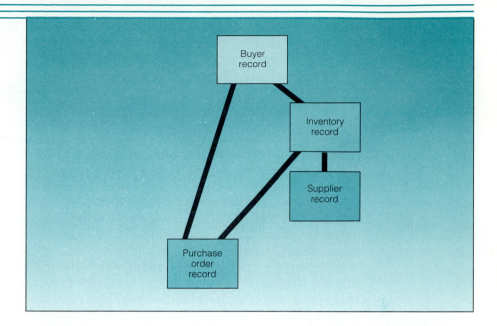

ture, and it uses **implicit relationships**— relationships that can be implied from the existing record data.

Assume we want to use two data tables to prepare a report. The data in a relational database is in the form of tables called flat files. A **flat file** is a two-dimensional arrangement of data in columns and rows.

The two data tables appear in Table 9.1. We want the report to list the salespersons in Territory 1, showing their salesperson numbers and their names. Both tables are needed; Table A provides the means of identifying the records for Territory 1, and Table B provides the salesperson names. The implicit relationship is established by the salesperson number field in both tables, tying together the territory numbers in Table A and the salesperson names in Table B.

TABLE 9.1

An Example of
Two Flat Files

Table A	
SALESNO	TERR
112	1
128	3
153	2
159	1
162	1
166	2

Table B	
SALESNO	NAME
112	ADAMS
128	WINKLER
153	HOUSE
159	FRANCIS
162	WILLIS
166	GROVETON

The big advantage of the relational structure to the CBIS is the flexibility it offers in design and use of the database. Users and information specialists are freed from the need to identify all of the information needs prior to database creation.

DATABASE SOFTWARE

The software that establishes and maintains the logical integration between files, whether it be explicit or implicit, is called the **database management system (DBMS).** GE's IDS was the first example, and it was followed by similar efforts of other hardware and software suppliers. The packages that enjoyed the widest acceptance were IBM's IMS (for Information Management System), Cincom's TOTAL, Software AG's ADABAS, Intel's SYSTEM 2000, and Cullinet's IDMS. IMS and SYSTEM 2000 are examples of the hierarchical structure. TOTAL and ADABAS use the network structure. These systems, still in use, were very expensive, costing $100,000 or so.

The next wave of DBMS innovation featured relational software, and the first packages were aimed at mainframe users. SQL/DS (Structured Query Language/ Data System) and QBE (Query By Example) from IBM, and ORACLE from Relational Software, Inc. all enjoyed acceptance. At about the same time, around 1980, software suppliers began developing scaled-down DBMS packages for the microcomputer market. The first micro-based DBMS to make a big impression was dBASE II, marketed by Ashton-Tate (now a part of Borland International, Inc.).

During recent years, DBMS development has focused on the microcomputer market and has applied the relational structure.[1]

CREATING A DATABASE

The process of creating a database includes three main steps. First, you determine the data that you need. Second, you describe the data. Third, you enter the data into the database.

Determine the Data Needs

In Chapter 7, we identified two basic approaches to determining data needs. One is the problem-oriented approach, and the other is the enterprise modeling approach.

Problem-solving Approach   In the problem-solving approach, the user (1) defines the *problem* to be solved, (2) specifies the *decisions* necessary to solve the problem, (3) specifies the *information* necessary to make the decisions, (4) spec-

---

[1] The best source for additional information concerning DBMSs are the various computing reference sets such as *Datapro Computer Systems Series,* published by the Datapro Information Systems Group of Delran New Jersey. See also database textbooks such as David M. Kroenke, *Database Processing: Fundamentals, Design, Implementation* 4th ed (New York, NY: Macmillan), 1992.

ifies the *processing* necessary to produce the information, and (5) specifies the *data* required by the processing. A chain reaction begins with the problem, and ends with the specification of individual data elements.

Enterprise Modeling Approach   In the enterprise modeling approach the information specialists, working with executives, create an enterprise data model. The model specifies the data that is to be maintained in order for the firm to meet the objectives contained in its strategic plan for information resources.

Normalize the Data   In Chapter 7 we described how data analysis is conducted to make the database structure efficient. This is a process called **normalization.**[2] First it is necessary to prepare a rough entity-relationship diagram. We illustrated the diagram in Figure 7.5. The analysis then involves converting the structure to a series of normal forms:

- **First normal form**   In the first normal form any repeating elements in an entity are eliminated. This can result in adding new entities, identified with composite keys. A **composite key** is one with multiple elements. For example a combination of invoice number and line item number would identify any data elements in the body of an invoice.
- **Second normal form**   In the **second normal form** the elements that describe an entity rely on the entire composite key for identification.
- **Third normal form**   In the third normal form a value of one element cannot be produced from other elements in the same entity. For example, *Extended item price* is not included as an element if *Unit price* and *Quantity* are in the same entity.

With the data analysis complete a new entity-relationship diagram is drawn. See Figure 7.6 for an example.

Describe the Data

Once the individual data elements are identified, following either of the two basic approaches, they are described in the form of a data dictionary. The **data dictionary** is an encyclopedia of information concerning each data element. We described the data dictionary in Chapter 6 and recognized that it can exist as either a notebook of paper forms or as a computer file.

The Data Dictionary System   When the data dictionary exists as a computer file, special software is necessary to create and maintain the dictionary and make it available for use. Such software is called a **data dictionary system (DDS).** DDSs can be acquired as separate software packages or as modules within systems such as DBMSs and CASE tools.

---

[2] A detailed description of normalization usually can be found in database textbooks. Systems analysis and design texts also often provide good coverage.

FIGURE 9.14

Describing the
Database
Contents

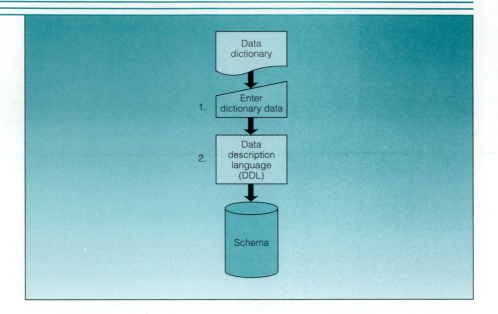

The Data Description Language Once the data dictionary has been created, its descriptions must be entered into the DBMS. The DBMS includes a **data description language (DDL),** used to describe the data. Figure 9.14 shows how the contents of a paper-based data dictionary are entered into the computer and the DDL produces the schema.

The **schema** is not the data itself, but is the *description* of the data. The schema usually specifies the attributes or characteristics of the data such as:

- The data element name
- Aliases (other names used for the same data element)
- The type of data (numeric, alphabetic, and so on)
- The number of positions
- The number of decimal positions (for numeric data only)
- Various integrity rules

The term **subschema** is used for a subset of the overall description that relates to a particular user. Each user has specific data needs, and the descriptions of those data elements are represented by one or more subschemas. For example, a credit manager might have a subschema that includes customer number, customer name, customer address, invoice number, invoice date, invoice amount, and so on. That subschema is used in preparing a report of past-due receivables.

The combination of the schema, subschema, and data dictionary prepare the system for data independence and reduce redundancy by pointing all database users to views of the central database. There is no need to create new individual files.

Enter the Data

Once the schema and subschema have been created, the data can be entered into the database. This can be accomplished by keying the data directly into the DBMS, reading the data from tape or disk, or optically scanning the data. With the data in the database, it is available for use.

USING A DATABASE

A **database user** can be a *person* or an *application program*. A person usually uses the database from a terminal and retrieves data and information by using a query language. A **query** is a request for information from a database, and a **query language** is a special, user-friendly language that enables the computer to respond to the query.

When an application program, such as a payroll program, retrieves data from the database or stores data in it, a special **data manipulation language (DML)** is used. The DML statements are embedded in the application program at the points where they are needed.

So, a human user accesses the database by means of a query language, and a program uses a DML. There is no need to know the technical specifications of the data. The users only need to name the data elements and the DBMS does the rest. This is a major step toward data independence.

DBMS Events

The events that take place when an application program retrieves data from the database are illustrated in Figure 9.15. In Step 1 the DML specifies to the DBMS what data is needed. In Step 2 the DBMS checks the schema and subschema to verify that the data exists in the database and the application program is entitled to use it. In Step 3 the DBMS passes along the data request to the operating system, which retrieves the data in Step 4 and enters it in a special buffer storage area in primary storage. The data then is transferred into the application program's input area in Step 5. The DBMS returns control to the application program in Step 6, and the application program uses the data in Step 7.

The same series of events occur when a query language is used. In that case the query language is a subset of the DBMS and the retrieved information is displayed on the user's output device.

A MODEL OF A DBMS

A model that shows the major DBMS elements is pictured in Figure 9.16. The elements include a data description language processor, a performance statistics processor, a backup/recovery module, and a database manager.

FIGURE 9.15

DBMS Events

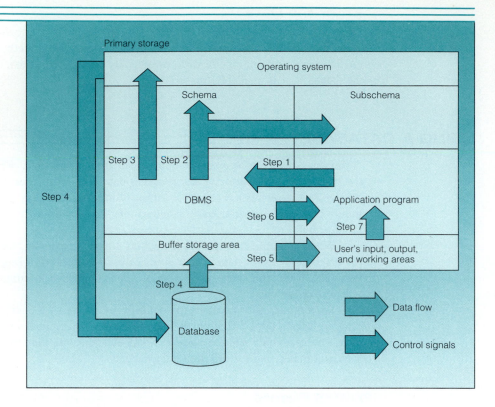

Data Description Language Processor

The **data description language processor** transforms the data dictionary into the database schema. This is the DDL described earlier. All DBMSs have a DDL.

Performance Statistics Processor

The **performance statistics processor** maintains statistics that identify what data is being used, who is using it, when it is being used, and so forth. The statistics are used in managing the database. Microcomputer-based DBMSs typically do not include this element.

Backup/Recovery Module

Periodically, such as daily, a backup copy of the database is made. As subsequent transactions are processed against the master files, a **transaction log** keeps a record of all changes. Then, when a disaster occurs, the transaction log is processed against the backup database to reconstruct the database. The backup/recovery module accomplishes this reconstruction, but is not usually found in microcomputer DBMSs.

FIGURE 9.16

A DBMS Model

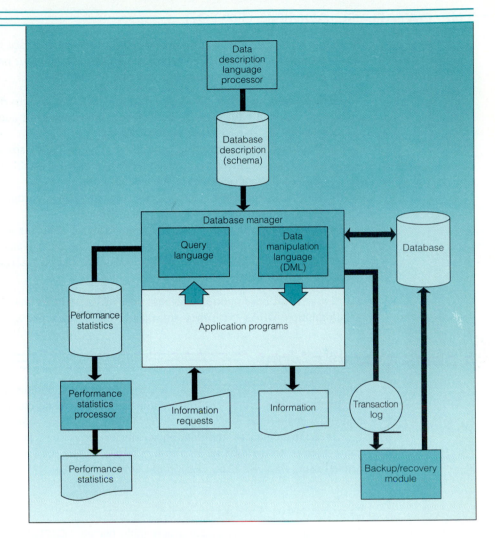

Database Manager

The **database manager** is the most important element in that it handles the users' data requests. The query language and the DML are a part of the database manager. The database manager also produces the performance statistics processed by the performance statistics processor, and the transaction log processed by the backup/ recovery module. All DBMSs include this element.

The database manager is the only DBMS element that is **main-memory res-ident**. That is, it remains in primary storage at all times. The other elements are **transient routines,** being kept in secondary storage and brought into primary stor-age when they are needed.

THE DATABASE ADMINISTRATOR

An information specialist who has responsibility for the database is called a **database administrator (DBA)**. The duties of the DBA fall into four major areas: planning, implementation, operation, and security.

- **Database planning** involves working with executives to define the firm's schema, and with users to define their subschemas. In addition, the DBA plays a key role in selecting the DBMS.
- **Database implementation** consists of creating the database to conform to the specifications of the selected DBMS, as well as establishing and enforcing policies and procedures for database use.
- **Database operation** includes offering educational programs to database users, and providing assistance when needed.
- **Database security** includes the monitoring of database activity using statistics provided by the DBMS. In addition, the DBA ensures that the database remains secure. We will address the important issue of database security in Chapter 21.

Large firms have multiple database specialists, and they may be called DBAs. When multiple DBAs exist, they are managed by a DBA manager.

A DBMS EXAMPLE—DB2

DB2 is a relational DBMS that is used with larger IBM computers. Its statements can be executed interactively from terminals or they can be embedded in application programs written in COBOL, PL/I, FORTRAN, C, or Assembler.

In a DB2 database, the data physically exists as files, but it is manipulated and presented to the user in the form of tables. Tables are created, changed, and deleted using the DB2 Data Definition Language (DDL).

Create New Tables

Assume that you want to create a new table named `TEMPL` to contain three data elements relating to employees—`EMPNO` (employee number), `NAME` (employee name), and `DEPT` (department). You use the following DB2 `CREATE` statement:

```
CREATE TABLE TEMPL
    (EMPNO CHAR (5) NOT NULL,
     NAME VARCHAR (28) NOT NULL,
     DEPT CHAR(3) NOT NULL);
```

The syntax of the DB2 statements is very similar to that of a programming language. The definition of the three data elements is bounded by parentheses, and the semicolon signals the end of the statement. Commas separate items in a list—the specifications for each element. Lines are indented for readability, and the number of spaces that separate words is not critical.

CHAR means that the data element is character data—it can contain any letter, number, or special character. The number in parentheses is the size of the field. Employee number is 5 positions and department number is 3. Employee name is also character data, but it can vary in size up to 28 positions. The NOT NULL clause means that when data is loaded into the table in a separate operation, those fields must contain data. They cannot have zero or blank values. The table, complete with data, appears in Table 9.2a.

DB2 allows for data types in addition to numeric and character. For example, if you define a date field, you do not have to specify the number of positions. DB2 assumes that it is eight—in the format YYYYMMDD. If you create a table to contain the dates that employees were hired, you would code:

```
CREATE TABLE TEMPHIRE
      (EMPNO CHAR (5), NOT NULL,
       HIREDATE DATE, NOT NULL);
```

Microcomputer DBMSs also enable you to define date fields in this manner.

Make Changes to Tables

Assume that you later decide to add a new column to the TEMPL table. You want to add salary, which is a six-position decimal field. It can contain only the decimal digits. You use the ALTER statement:

```
ALTER TABLE TEMPL
      ADD SALARY DECIMAL (6);
```

Table 9.2
A DB2 Table Can
Be Modified by
Adding Columns

TEMPL

EMPNO	NAME	DEPT
15962	LEE	280
11704	MARTINEZ	126
12386	SMITH	430
21596	COLLINS	430
01047	LEHNERT	280
15635	MCCULLIN	126
18217	FOX	126
20324	GARCIA	110
12492	MAREK	430
15965	HUDSON	280

A A DB2 table

TEMPL

EMPNO	NAME	DEPT	SALARY
15962	LEE	280	
11704	MARTINEZ	126	
12386	SMITH	430	
21596	COLLINS	430	
01047	LEHNERT	280	
15635	MCCULLIN	126	
18217	FOX	126	
20324	GARCIA	110	
12492	MAREK	430	
15965	HUDSON	280	

B A modified table

The ALTER statement permits you to add only a single column at a time, and it is always added to the right-hand side of the table.

The altered table now appears as shown in Table 9.2b. The fourth column has been added, but data has not yet been loaded into it.

Delete Tables

When it comes time to delete a table, you use the DROP statement:

```
DROP TABLE TEMPL;
```

This deletes the entire table from the database.

Making Database Queries

Once the structure of the DB2 database has been established with the DDL, you can retrieve the data and make changes to it using the Structured Query Language (SQL). SQL provides for four basic operations—select, update, insert, and delete. You use the SELECT statement to query the database, you make changes to data elements with the UPDATE statement, you add new rows of data to a table with the INSERT statement, and you delete data rows with the DELETE statement.

Retrieving Specified Columns   Let us see how a manager would use the SELECT statement to make queries. If the manager wants a display of all three columns from the TEMPL table, the statement below is used:

```
SELECT EMPNO, NAME, SALARY
     FROM TEMPL;
```

The three columns are displayed on the manager's output device in the same left-to-right sequence as the data element names appear in the SELECT statement.

Retrieving Specified Rows   If the manager wants to select only certain rows, say for employees in Department 430, a WHERE clause is added:

```
SELECT EMPNO, NAME, SALARY
     FROM TEMPL
          WHERE DEPT = '430';
```

The 430 is enclosed in quote marks since it is a constant rather than a variable.

Sequencing Retrieved Data   When the data is retrieved, it is displayed in no particular sequence. If the manager wants the records displayed by employee number within department number, for example, an ORDER BY clause is used:

```
SELECT DEPT, EMPNO, NAME, SALARY
    FROM TEMPL
            ORDER BY DEPT, EMPNO;
```

The first data element name that is entered (DEPT) is the major sort key, and the last one (EMPNO) is the minor key.

Retrieving Data from Multiple Tables

One of the main advantages of a relational database is the ability to select data from multiple tables without first having to incorporate explicit linkages. In order to accomplish this, the user only has to specify the implicit linkages that tie the tables together, and this is done at execution time.

Assume that the manager wants to retrieve four data elements from three tables. Figure 9.17 shows the implicit relationships (the dotted arrows) and the extraction of the four elements from the three tables (the solid arrows). The manager enters:

```
SELECT EMPNO, NAME, SALARY, DEPTNAME
    FROM TEMPL, TSAL, TDEPT
            WHERE EMPNO = EMPNUM
                AND DEPT = DEPTNO
            ORDER BY EMPNO
```

The first line specifies the four data elements to be retrieved, and the second line identifies the tables. The third and fourth lines establish the implicit relationships between the tables. WHERE EMPNO = EMPNUM tells DB2 to regard rows in those two columns with the same values as being logically related. In other words, a row in the TEMPL table with an EMPNO of 12386 is logically related to a row in the TSAL table with an EMPNUM of the same value. The DEPT = DEPTNO establishes the same type of relationship between the TEMPL and TDEPT tables. The fifth line specifies that the records are to be displayed in sequence by employee number.

This is only an introduction to DB2. We have explained the main operations that are of interest to the manager—being able to create tables and retrieve their contents. DB2 is much more powerful than these examples indicate. That power, combined with its user friendliness that is obvious from the above examples, contributes to its widespread acceptance.

PUTTING THE DATABASE AND DBMS IN PERSPECTIVE

The DBMS makes it possible to create a database in the computer's direct access storage, maintain its contents, and make the contents available to users without costly custom programming.

FIGURE 9.17

Retrieving
Information from
Multiple Tables

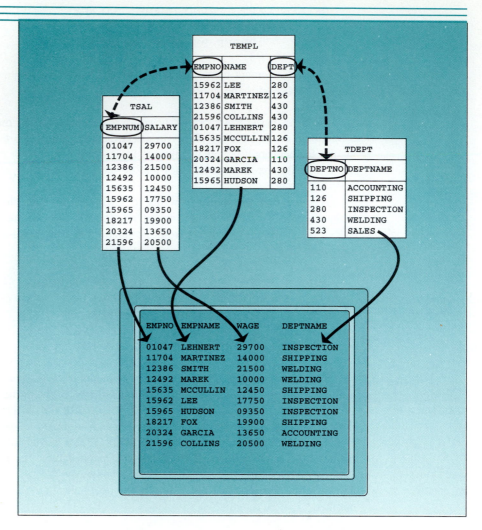

When firms or individual users decide whether to use a DBMS they must weigh the advantages and the disadvantages.

DBMS Advantages

The DBMS enables both firms and individual users to:

- **Reduce data redundancy**   The total number of files are reduced by deleting duplicate files. There is also a minimum of common data among files.
- **Data independence**   The specifications of the data are maintained in schemas in tables and in the data dictionary rather than in each application pro-

gram. Changes may be made to the data structure without impacting the programs that access the data.

- **Integrate data from multiple files**   When the files are constructed so as to provide the logical linkages, the physical organization no longer provides a constraint.
- **Retrieve data and information rapidly**   Both the logical relationships and the DML and query language enable users to retrieve in seconds or minutes what otherwise might require hours or days.
- **Improve security**   Both mainframe and microcomputer DBMSs can include multiple levels of security precautions such as passwords, user directories, and encryption. The data managed by these DBMSs is more secure than other data in the firm.

These are the conditions that favor use of a DBMS.

DBMS Disadvantages

A decision to use a DBMS commits a firm or user to:

- **Obtain expensive software**   The mainframe DBMSs remain very expensive. The microcomputer-based DBMSs, while costing only a few hundred dollars, can represent a substantial outlay for a small organization.
- **Obtain a large hardware configuration**   The DBMSs often require larger primary and secondary storage capacities than are required by the application programs. Also, the ease with which the DBMS can retrieve information encourages the inclusion of more user terminals in the configuration than would otherwise be the case.
- **Hire and maintain a DBA staff**   The DBMS requires specialized knowledge in order to make full use of its capabilities. This specialized knowledge is best provided by DBAs.

Neither a computerized databases nor a DBMS is an absolute prerequisite to problem solving. However, they provide information specialists and users with the raw materials that enable the firm to use its computer as an information system.

SUMMARY

Data is organized into files, each file contains records, and each record contains data elements. This hierarchy exists within the database when a firm adopts the database concept.

Data management is the subset of IRM that performs the functions of data collection, integrity and verification, storage, maintenance, security, organization, and retrieval.

Secondary storage devices are of two types—sequential and direct access. Magnetic tape is an example of sequential storage. When a magnetic tape master file is updated, it is necessary to create a new, complete file. Magnetic tape is excellent for historical storage and also serves as a backup file to one maintained on a DASD. Magnetic tape can also be used as input and communications media.

The most popular type of DASD is magnetic disk. Mainframe and minicomputer configurations include disk drives, or units. Microcomputers have diskette drives and hard disks. The DASD access mechanism can be directed to any record in the file by providing an address that specifies where the record is located. The address can be produced directly from the record key, by an algorithm called a hashing scheme or randomizing formula, or by means of an index. Updated DASD records are written to the same location from where they were read. DASD is ideal for use as a master file medium and can also serve as intermediate storage and as an input medium.

Optical disks with a WORM capability have been used for several years in place of magnetic tape for historical storage. Rewritable optical disks can be used for master files. Future use of optical disks as a replacement for magnetic disks will require continued improvements in access speed.

The user application determines whether batch or online processing is used. Batch processing can be performed using either sequential or direct access storage media. Online processing requires direct access. The name realtime is used to describe a type of online system that reacts to activity within the physical system quickly enough to control that system.

During the predatabase era, system performance suffered because of data redundancy, data dependence, and diffused data ownership. These difficulties were partially overcome by using inverted files and linked lists but programmers had to become experts in these complicated techniques. GE used links to logically integrate multiple files—the first example of the database concept. Logical integration can be achieved explicitly in hierarchical or network structures, and implicitly in relational structures.

The data in the database is managed by the database management system, or DBMS. The first systems were designed for mainframes, but most recent activity has been in the area of microcomputer versions.

The first step in creating a database is to determine the data needs by following either a problem-oriented or enterprise-modeling approach. Next the data is normalized by converting it to first, second, and third normal forms. The purpose of the normalization is to reduce redundancy and make the structure as efficient as possible. The normalized data is then described in a data dictionary, and this description is communicated to the computer by means of the data description language, which produces the schema. Subschemas reflect individual users' needs. With the schema and subschemas specified, the data can be entered.

Either a person or an application program can be a database user. The person uses a query language and the program uses a DML. The DBMS works in conjunction with the operating system to make database contents available to users.

All DBMSs have a DDL processor and a database manager, but micro versions usually do not include a performance statistics processor or a backup/recovery module.

The information specialists who have responsibility for the firm's data resource are called DBAs. A DBA has four areas of responsibility relating to the database—planning, implementation, operation, and security.

DB2 is an example of a relational database that logically organizes data into tables. Tables are created, modified, and deleted using a DDL. Data can be selectively retrieved from one or more tables by using SQL.

The combination of the data dictionary, DDL, schemas, subschemas, DML, and related DBMS functions provide a high degree of data independence with minimal data redundancy. The database administrator is responsible for making this a reality.

Conditions that indicate a possible need for a DBMS include: (1) redundant data in the form of duplicate files and duplicate data within single files, (2) tightly coupled data and programs, (3) a need to integrate data from multiple files, (4) a need to obtain data or information quickly, and (5) a need to make the data more secure. A DBMS can satisfy these conditions, but at a cost in terms additional hardware, software, and information specialists.

Although a logically integrated database and a DBMS are not absolute requirements of a CBIS, they can represent a valuable resource in problem solving.

KEY TERMS

data element

record

file

sequential storage

master file

transaction file

file maintenance

direct access storage

direct access storage device (DASD)

direct addressing

key

hashing scheme, randomizing formula

collision

index

optical disk, laser disk, compact disk (CD)

write-once, read-many (WORM)

compact disk—read-only memory (CD-ROM)

batch processing

online processing

realtime system

database

ad hoc request

database management system (DBMS)

normalization

data dictionary

data description language (DDL)

schema

subschema

query

query language

data manipulation language (DML)

database manager

database administrator (DBA)

KEY CONCEPTS

Data management

The relationship between applications, basic ways to process data, and secondary storage media

Physical and logical organizations of data

How inverted files and linked lists facilitate selective retrieval of database contents

The database concept

Data independence

How explicit relationships enable hierarchical and network structures to achieve logical organization

How implicit relationships enable relational structure to achieve logical integration

The database user as a person or a program

QUESTIONS

1. Which data management activity uses source documents?

2. Name a sequential storage medium in use today.

3. What is the operation called that updates a master file from a transaction file?

4. What is the most popular DASD medium?

5. How does the access mechanism know where to position itself in a DASD file so as to read or write a record?

6. Name three ways to generate a DASD address.

7. Why is magnetic disk not a good historical storage medium?

8. What is the main advantage of the optical disk?

9. What type of optical disk is well suited for use as a historical storage medium? Explain why.

10. What are the two principal ways to process data?

11. Would you use the sort utility more often with batch processing or online? Why is this so?

12. What distinguishes a realtime system from an online system?

13. How did data dependence contribute to data redundancy?

14. What is meant by the physical organization of data? The logical organization?

15. Name two predatabase techniques used to select records from a file without the need to scan the entire file.

16. What is an explicit relationship? What is its serious drawback?

17. What is an implicit relationship? Which database structure uses it?

18. What are the two basic approaches to determining data needs?

19. Why is data normalized?

20. Where do you find a data dictionary?

21. Who are the database users? What languages do they use to obtain data from the database?

22. What is the title of the person who specializes in solving database problems?

TOPICS FOR DISCUSSION

1. Do inverted file indexes and link fields establish explicit or implicit relationships between data?

2. Does data have to be stored in a computer to be considered a database?

3. What is the relationship between the entity-relationship diagram, the data dictionary, the DDL, and the schema?

4. Why do microcomputer DBMSs not normally have a performance statistics processor? Why do they not have a backup/recovery module?

PROBLEMS

1. Assume that the following records comprise the entire Customer Master file and that a user needs information by salesperson. Enter the link fields.

Customer Number	Year-to-Date Sales	Salesperson Number	Salesperson Link
104	25,000	33	
109	17,500	17	
111	12,500	33	
118	6,000	33	
124	12,000	49	
127	300	14	
132	18,000	49	
138	24,000	33	
142	26,500	14	
149	120	17	
151	8,000	14	

2. Construct an inverted file index in salesperson number sequence for the above file.

3. Use the DB2 DDL to create a table named ORDLOG. This is an order log that will include a record of each sales order that the firm receives. It includes the following fields:

- Today's date (ORDDATE)
- Our order number (OURORDNO), a five-position numeric field
- Customer number (CUSTNO), a six-position numeric field
- The customer's order number (CUSTORDNO), a character field that can be up to twelve positions
- The order amount (ORDAMT), a seven-position decimal field that contains whole-dollar amounts
- Date filled (FILLDATE)

The first five fields must contain data. The sixth field will remain blank until the order is filled.

4. You decide that it would be a good idea to add another field to the order log created in Problem 3. The field will contain the date that the customer prepared the purchase order. Add the field, and name it CUSTDATE.

5. As manager of the order department, you want to know how many orders have been received from customer 334200. Code the

query, using SQL, to display the customer order date, customer order number, and the order amount. Specify that the records are to be in sequence by customer order number (minor) within customer order date (major).

6. List the steps that would be required for a firm to put a DBMS into use. Regard the DBMS as a solution to a problem, and follow the system life cycle procedure described in Chapter 5. Assume that the firm has a computer, but no DBA staff.

Acadia Data Consultants, Inc.

Jim Ford and Hardy Roberts founded Acadia Data Consultants after graduating from college. They rented a small office in Bar Harbor, Maine, and began marketing their services along the seacoast. Their services consist of serving as DBAs to small firms that cannot afford their own staff. The firms invariably use microcomputers, and Jim and Hardy specialize in DBMSs for those systems.

When Jim and Hardy determine that a firm needs a DBMS, they recommend the one that is best suited to the firm's needs. Then, they conduct training classes that show the company's employees how to use the DBMS. This activity requires that Jim and Hardy each spend about sixteen hours with each client company, spread over a period of about a month. They typically charge a flat fee of one thousand dollars.

Hardy and Jim have been able to obtain enough work to pay the bills, but that is about all. Since business has been slow, they have plenty of time to discuss strategy. That is what they are doing one April morning, waiting for the spring thaw.

JIM: The main problem with selling to small companies is that you waste a lot of time making sales calls that don't amount to anything.

HARDY: That's for sure. If we just had a way to screen our prospects, we could concentrate our efforts where they would do the most good.

JIM: Maybe you've hit on something. We could design a mail questionnaire that asked a company a few key questions to determine whether they need a DBMS. They return the questionnaire, and we follow up with a call when they look like a good prospect.

HARDY: I like that. The questionnaire should be easy to fill out—no more than a single sheet of paper. Some fill-in-the-blank questions, some yes-no questions, maybe a scale or two. We could enclose a stamped envelope to encourage return.

JIM: And, even when we decide that a company doesn't need a DBMS, we should write them a letter, advising them of that fact. We can keep the questionnaires on file, and, who knows, some of the companies might turn into good prospects some day.

HARDY: It sounds like a good long-term sales promotion strategy. Let's do it. Boot up the word processor, Jim, and let's get started.

Assignments

1. Write a letter that can be sent to prospects, asking them to fill out the questionnaire. Explain that by filling out and returning the form, the respondent will receive a free evaluation of their database needs from computer professionals.

2. Design a one-page questionnaire that can be easily filled out. Include a couple of questions that relate to the hardware and software currently in use. Then ask some questions that determine whether a DBMS is needed.

SELECTED BIBLIOGRAPHY

Appleton, Daniel S. "The Modern Data Dictionary." *Datamation* 33 (March 1, 1987): 66–68.

Choobineh, Joobin; Mannino, Michael V.; and Tseng, Veronica P. "A Form-Based Approach for Database Analysis and Design." *Communications of the ACM* 35 (February 1992): 108–120.

Cohen, Edward I.; King, Gary M.; and Brady, James. T. "Storage Hierarchies." *IBM Systems Journal* 28 (Number 1 1989): 62–76.

Davis, Lelia. "On-Line Applications Grow Up." *Datamation* 36 (January 1, 1990): 61–63.

Davis, Leila. "New Uses For Optical Storage." *Datamation* 38 (March 15, 1992): 78*ff.*

DeLoach, Allan. "The Path to Writing Efficient Queries in SQL/DS." *Database Programming & Design* 1 (1987): 26–32.

DeWitt, David, and Gray, Jim. "Parallel Database Systems: The Future of High Performance Database Systems." *Communications of the ACM* 35 (June 1992): 85–98.

Garcia-Rose, Linda, and Fosdick, Howard. "The Maturation of DB2." *Datamation* 36 (March 15, 1990): 75*ff.*

Gelb, Jack P. "System-managed Storage." *IBM Systems Journal* 28 (Number 1, 1989): 77–103.

Goodhue, Dale L.; Kirsch, Laurie J.; Quillard, Judith A.; and Wybo, Michael D. "Strategic Data Planning: Lessons From the Field." *MIS Quarterly* 16 (March 1992): 11–34.

Kintisch, Larry. "Strategies for Improved SQL Performance." *Database Programming & Design* 1 (February 1988): 42–47.

Madnick, Stuart E., and Wang, Y. Richard. "Evolution towards Strategic Applications of Databases through Composite Information Systems." *Journal of Management Information Systems* 5 (Fall 1988): 5–22.

Myers, Edith D. "The Long Shadow of DB2." *Datamation* 33 (October 1, 1987): 110*ff.*

Orli, Richard J. "Modeling Data for the Summary Database." *DATA BASE* 21 (Spring 1990): 11–19.

Rapaport, Matthew. "Interview: Dr. Edgar F. Codd." *Database Programming & Design* 1 (February 1988): 60–65.

Ricciuti, Mike. "Universal Database Access!" *Datamation* 37 (November 1, 1991): 30*ff.*

Snell, Ned. "New Ways To Distribute Mainframe Storage." *Datamation* 37 (December 1, 1991): 67*ff.*

The', Lee. "CD-ROM Reaches For Critical Mass." *Datamation* 38 (April 15, 1992): 47*ff.*

Vassiliou, Yannis. "On the Interactive Use of Databases: Query Languages." *Journal of Management Information Systems* 1 (Winter 1984-85): 33–48.

Chapter 10

Data Communications

LEARNING OBJECTIVES

After studying this chapter, you should:

- Have an understanding of the fundamental data communications terminology that is necessary to work with specialists in developing communications-based CBISs
- See how the basic communication model that describes human communications also applies to data communications using computing equipment
- Know the difference between a WAN and a LAN
- Know the different types of terminals that are available
- Become acquainted with the hardware and software used in a typical business data communications network
- Know the basic approaches to network processing— timesharing, distributed processing, and client/server computing
- Become familiar with some of the products and services that common carriers provide, such as ISDN
- Know the basic network topologies—star, ring, tree, and hybrid
- Have a good understanding of the network type that is creating the most interest—the local area network, or LAN
- Gain a fundamental understanding of standard data communications protocols and architectures
- Understand the significance of network management and the responsibilities of data communications specialists in a firm.
- Appreciate the effect that data communications is having on problem solving at both the organization and the individual levels

INTRODUCTION

As the scale of business operations grows, it becomes necessary to gather data and disseminate decisions over geographically dispersed areas. Data communications enables the computer to perform this task. The basic model that depicts communications between humans can also serve as the basis of data communications.

There are many variations in data communications network arrangements, but the basic types are the wide area network, or WAN, and the local area network, or LAN. These networks include both hardware and software. The hardware includes various types of terminals, cluster control units, modems, multiplexers, one or more front-end processors, one or more host computers, and channels. Most of the software resides in the host and the front-end processor.

The first WANs were established to provide timesharing services, and then, with the introduction of microcomputers, the networks facilitated the distribution of computing resources throughout the firm. Today, both WANs and LANs are being used for client/server computing.

In a LAN all of the hardware and circuitry are owned by the firm, but in a WAN the channel is provided by a common carrier. Common carriers provide a variety of products and services. A product that is in the process of revolutionizing how data and information are communicated is the integrated services digital network, or ISDN.

The pattern of hardware in a network is called its topology. The main topologies are the star, the ring, the tree, and the hybrid.

One of the problems with using a LAN is achieving control over the many users that can share its facilities. Two means have been devised—a contention based control that reflects a "first come, first served" philosophy, and a token-passing control that is more orderly.

The wide variety of data communications hardware has prompted equipment manufacturers to establish standard network architectures. IBM has received an impressive response to its SNA, but the quest for international standards has culminated in the OSI model.

Data communications are so important to firms that a sound network management program based on planning and control is a must. The network manager is a key element in this program.

Data communications helps managers by removing the geographical barriers to computer use. Data communications helps firms by enabling a strategy of either centralized or decentralized decision making.

THE BASIC COMMUNICATION MODEL

The most common form of human communication is when one person speaks to another. This process can be illustrated with the diagram in Figure 10.1. The diagram is called the **basic communication model,** and the two most important elements are the **sender** and the **receiver.** When one person speaks to another the

FIGURE 10.1

The Basic
Communication
Model

sender uses his or her brain and voice as a **coder** to put the communication, or **message,** into a form that can be transmitted. The message must travel along some type of pathway, called a **channel,** to reach the receiver. A verbal message communicated in face-to-face conversation travels in the form of sound waves through the air. When the message reaches the receiver, it must be decoded. The receiver's ears and brain serve as the **decoder.**

When one person talks to another person over the telephone, the sender's telephone performs the coding, the telephone lines serve as the channel, and the receiver's telephone performs the decoding. Telephone communication fits the model in Figure 10.1 as do announcements made by pilots to passengers, and the Six O'Clock News. The basic communication model represents *any* type of communication from a sender to one or more receivers.

COMPUTER-BASED DATA
COMMUNICATIONS

The basic communication model can also serve as the basis for a diagram that shows how data is communicated by computer. **Data communications** is the movement of coded data and information from one point to another by means of electrical or electromagnetic devices, fiber-optical cables, or microwave signals. Other terms used are **teleprocessing, telecommunications, telecom,** and **datacom.** We will use datacom.

Figure 10.2 shows the **basic data communications schematic.** This is the simplest form of computer communication. A single terminal is linked to a computer. This diagram differs from the basic communication model in that the communication can flow in either direction. The terminal can be the sender and the computer can be the receiver, or vice versa.

FIGURE 10.2

The Basic Data
Communication
Schematic

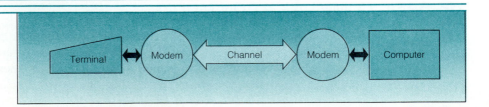

As with communication between humans, computer messages must travel along a channel. Many technologies are used in datacom channels, but the most common is the same telephone circuit used for voice communication. A **circuit** or **line** is the transmission facility that provides one or more channels. For example, a standard telephone line can provide twenty-four channels.

In order to use the telephone circuit, a special device must be included at each end. The device is called a **modem,** which stands for *mo*dulator-*dem*odulator. The modems convert the electronic signals of the computing equipment (the terminal and the computer) to the electronic signals of the telephone circuit, and vice versa. The engineers who design the computing and the telephone equipment use different approaches to code the data. Data is represented in a computer system in a *digital* form. The characters are coded using combinations of bits that have only two possible states—*on* and *off.* The telephone equipment, on the other hand, typically uses an *analog* form of signal that represents the characters with electrical waves of varying frequencies. The different tones you hear when you press the buttons of a push-button telephone are the sound frequencies of the various digits.

The modem on the sender end of the channel converts the digital computer signals to the analog telephone signals. The modem on the receiver end converts the signal back into its original form.

Types of Networks

All of the interconnected datacom devices are called the **network.** The devices are *networked* to achieve the communication. A datacom network can be a wide area network, a local area network, or a combination.

Wide Area Networks   A **wide area network (WAN)** covers a large geographic area with various communications facilities such as long distance telephone service, satellite transmission, and undersea cables. The WAN typically involves host computers and many different types of communications hardware and software. Examples of WANs include interstate banking networks and airline reservation systems.

Local Area Networks   By contrast a **local area network (LAN)** covers a limited area. This distinction, however, is changing as the scope of LAN coverage becomes increasingly broader. A typical LAN connects as many as a hundred or so microcomputers that are all located in a relatively close space, such as a single floor of a building. Firms have been attracted to LANs because they enable multiple users to share software, data, and devices, and enable applications such as office automation.

COMMUNICATIONS HARDWARE

Figure 10.3 illustrates an expanded datacom network. These are not all of the hardware devices that can be included, but they provide a good idea of how a network might appear in a business organization.

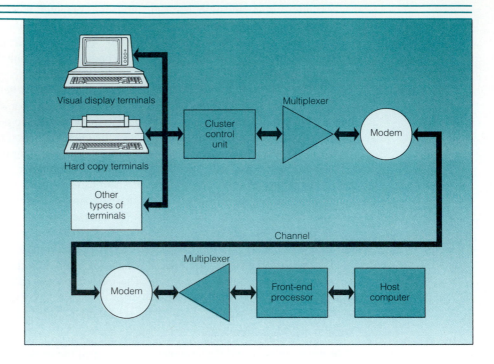

FIGURE 10.3

An Expanded
Data
Communications
Network

One end of the channel includes terminals that users use to access the network resources. The other end includes two computers; one is called the host computer, and the other is called the front-end processor. We will begin at the user's end of the network and describe each of the units.

Terminals

In Chapter 8 we recognized the keyboard terminal as the most popular input device. Actually, the keyboard unit is one of six terminal types.

Keyboard Terminals   Keyboard terminals come in two varieties—those that display output on a screen and those that print the output on paper. The terminal that utilizes the screen display is the CRT, or VDT. The terminal that produces the output in a paper form is called a **hard copy terminal,** or **teleprinter terminal.** Hard copy terminals were very popular during the 1970s but have largely given way to the CRTs. Users found that they would rather do without the hard copy so that they could enjoy the greater speed, color, and graphics of the CRTs.

Keyboard terminals are popular with managers. The pointing devices that we explained in Chapter 8 help overcome many managers' dislike of keyboarding. Managers can use terminals in their offices to receive periodic reports, request special reports, engage in dialog with mathematical models and expert systems, and send and receive communications such as electronic mail.

Push-button Telephones   In Chapter 8 we explained how a computer equipped with an audio response device can transmit messages that the user can hear on a push-button telephone. The push buttons are used to transmit data and instructions to the computer. For example, a manager might be driving home from work and decide to check on the status of a raw material that has been in short supply. The manager can use a cellular telephone to query the database to determine the stock status. The telephone is the most readily available and lowest-priced terminal type.

Point of Sale (POS) Terminals   In Chapter 5 we also saw how OCR readers are used in supermarkets. These terminals provide a means of entering transaction data into the database at the point of the sale. For this reason, they are called **POS terminals,** and they can be found in all types of retail operations. They are especially popular in department stores where sales clerks scan price tags using an OCR wand. The terminals make possible a database that reflects the current status of the firm.

Data Collection Terminals   A special type of terminal has been designed for use by factory employees. It is called a **data collection terminal** and it is used to collect data that describes employee attendance and job performance. **Attendance reporting** is accomplished by punching in when you come to work and punching out when you leave. The attendance data provides the input to the hourly

FIGURE 10.4
A Point of Sale
Terminal

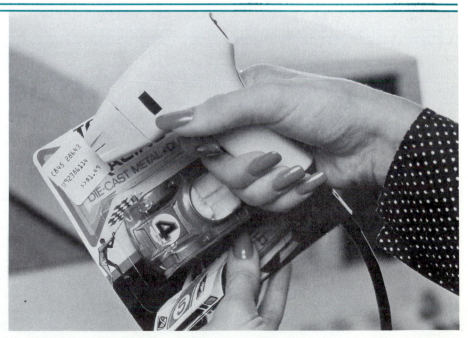

PhotoEdit

payroll system. **Job reporting** involves clocking on a production job when it is begun and clocking off when it is completed. The job data provides the basis for production control.

Data collection terminals, such as the one pictured in Figure 10.5, feature an OCR wand, a badge reader, and a keyboard. The OCR wand can be used to read characters from documents that travel with the job through the plant, facilitating job reporting. The badge reader reads data recorded on the workers' badges either as punched holes or as bits on a magnetic strip, facilitating attendance reporting.

Remote Job Entry Terminals   When there is a need to print a large volume of data at one location, a special terminal called a **remote job entry terminal,** shortened to **RJE terminal,** can be used. RJE terminals are perfect for printing copies of students' programs that have been run on the college's central computer. The printer uses a line-printer technology that permits several hundred lines of printing per minute. As with all of the other devices that are geared to batch production of hard copy output, RJE terminals are not as popular as they once were.

Special Purpose Terminals   Perhaps you have noticed special cash-register-like terminals in places like McDonald's, donut shops, and cafeterias. The terminals usually feature a large bank of keys—one key for each sales item. You purchase a Happy Meal and the salesperson presses one key. Such terminals are **special purpose terminals** in that they have been designed for a particular use.

A good example of a special purpose terminal is the Federal Express FED EX SUPER TRACKER Plus hand-held terminal shown in Figure 10.6. When the cour-

FIGURE 10.5
A Data Collection
Terminal

© Spencer Grant/The Picture Cube

FIGURE 10.6
SUPERTRACKER
Even Code
Scanner used by
the Federal
Express
Corporation

ier picks up a package, SUPER TRACKER is used to gather data to be used in tracking the package through the Federal Express system. Some of the data is optically scanned by SUPER TRACKER, and some is entered by the courier by means of the SUPER TRACKER keyboard. SUPER TRACKER then uses its microprocessor and ROM to determine the best route to the destination. The courier inserts SUPER TRACKER into a portable Astra printer, which prints a label that is attached to the package. The Astra label contains a barcode that identifies the destination, the type of service to be provided, and the routing.

When the Federal Express courier delivers a package, SUPER TRACKER optically scans the Astra label on the package. The courier then keys in the first initial and last name of the recipient. When the courier gets back to the truck, SUPER TRACKER is inserted into another terminal, which adds the date and time. The truck terminal then transmits the data by microwave to an area computer (there are about 150 across the United States and also in London and Hong Kong). The area computer transmits the data to the main computer center in Memphis. Within two minutes after the package is delivered, the Memphis computer has a record of the transaction. The Federal Express system is an excellent example of how a firm can track resource flows on a global basis—in realtime.

OTHER COMMUNICATIONS HARDWARE

Even though the choice of terminal is an important element in the network configuration, the other elements are important as well. These other elements include cluster control units, modems, multiplexers, the channel, the front-end processor, and the host computer.

Cluster Control Unit

The **cluster control unit** establishes the connection between the terminals that it controls (usually thirty-two or less) and other devices and channels. It enables the terminals to share a printer or access multiple computers via different channels. The cluster control unit can also perform error checking and code conversion.

Modem

The older communications technologies represent data in the analog fashion described earlier. The newer technologies use a digital approach. However, even when a digital signal is used, a modem is still required to shape the signal for transmission. The only time that a modem is not required is when a push-button telephone is used as a terminal. All other datacom channels include a modem of some type on each end.

Modems are designed to operate at certain speeds—usually 300, 1200, 2400, 4800, or 9600 bits per second, and up. The modem speed determines the rate at which messages are transmitted.

If you want to use your personal computer to access your college's main computer or a commercial database such as Dow Jones News/Retrieval Service or CompuServ, your system must include a modem. The modem can either be integrated into the micro circuitry or attached externally.

Multiplexer

When there is a need for multiple terminals to share the channel at the same time, multiplexers can be added to each end. A **multiplexer** is a device that permits the simultaneous sending and receiving of multiple messages. The effect of adding the multiplexers is like converting a one-lane road into a multi-lane highway.

The equipment up to this point—terminals, the cluster control unit, the modem, and the multiplexer—are the property of the using firm. The channel can also be included when it is a LAN. For WAN networks, however, the channel is the property of a firm that provides communications facilties for a fee. Such a firm is known as a common carrier, and we will provide more information on their role later in the chapter.

The Channel

Figure 10.7 shows how a WAN channel can be subdivided into sections that perform the transmission function in different ways.

The Local Loop   When the signals leave the sender's modem they travel along a **local loop,** which provides the connection between the firm's equipment and the central office of the telephone company in the sender's city. The local loop ordinarily consists of wires or coaxial cables. Four wires are necessary and they

FIGURE 10.7
The Channel of a Wide Area Network

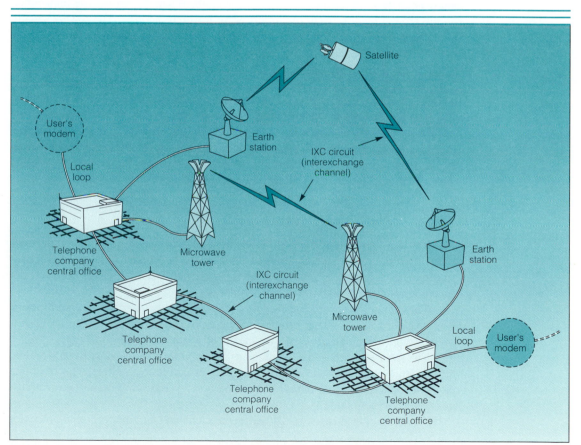

are twisted in pairs. The **twisted pair** is the most common type of circuit. A **coaxial cable (coax)** consists of a single wire covered with insulation, and contained within an outer cylindrical shell. The coaxial cable used by the common carrier usually consists of several individual cables bundled together. A bundle two inches in diameter can handle as many as 20,000 calls at one time.

The Interexchange Channel   When the message reaches the telephone company central office a decision is made determining which route the message will follow on its next leg. The portion of the channel that spans the greatest distance is the **interexchange channel circuit,** often shortened to **IXC circuit.**

Originally, the IXC circuit existed in the form of wires strung on telephone poles or metal cables buried underground, connecting the central offices in the various cities. The wires and metal cables still exist, but they are being replaced by newer technologies such as fiber optics and microwave.

Fiber-optical cables consist of hair-thin strands of glass through which pulses of light are passed. The pulses are coded to represent the data. **Microwave signals** are very short electromagnetic waves transmitted in a line-of-sight manner and cannot bend to conform to the curvature of the earth. When the signals are transmitted on the ground they go from one **microwave tower** to another. The towers usually are spaced from twenty to thirty miles apart. The microwave signals can also be bounced off of a satellite that is 23,300 miles above the earth, orbiting at a speed that permits it to remain stationary in relationship to the earth. The transmission stations that both send and receive the satellite signals are called **earth stations,** and have the same appearance as the dishes used to receive satellite TV signals.

The decision as to which IXC path to follow is made by a computer in the telephone company central office and is based on the volume of traffic at that particular time. For example, if you place three calls from Philadelphia to Baltimore, the first might go by earth-bound microwave transmission, the second by satellite microwave, and the third by underground cable.

The Front-end Processor

The **front-end processor** handles the incoming and outgoing data communications traffic for the host computer. Both computers can be of any type but a common configuration consists of a special type of minicomputer that serves as the front-end processor and a mainframe that is the host.

The channel we have described up to this point is but a single path to the host. It is possible to have many, perhaps hundreds, of such channels, and each is connected to the front-end processor by means of a **port** as shown in Figure 10.8.

The front-end processor functions as an *input unit* of the host by assembling the incoming messages and making that data available to the host. The front-end processor functions as an *output unit* of the host by receiving messages for transmission to the terminals.

While the transmission speed between the channel and the front-end processor

FIGURE 10.8

The Front-end
Processor

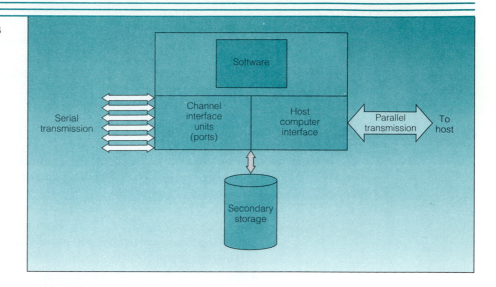

can be relatively slow (in most cases the bits are transmitted **serially,** one after the other), the transmission speed between the front-end processor and the host can be fast (several bits can be transmitted at the same time—in **parallel**).

Some front-end processors perform **message switching** by routing messages from one terminal to another without involving the host. If, for any reason, the receiving terminal cannot receive the message (perhaps it is in use or is out of service), the front-end processor can hold the message in its secondary storage and send it later—a capability called **store and forward.**

The Host

The **host** performs the data processing for the network. The incoming messages are handled in the same manner as data received from any other type of input unit. After the processing, messages can be transmitted back to the front-end processor for routing.

Putting Data Communications Equipment in Perspective

All datacom networks do not include the variety of hardware units we described. Our equipment mix is typical of larger organizations that use mainframes. Firms using minicomputers and microcomputers have more modest configurations. Even so, all network designs reflect the basic communication model.

The data communications equipment provides the circuitry to tie together the firm's operations that can be scattered over a wide area. But just like computing hardware the datacom equipment is useless without data communications software.

DATA COMMUNICATIONS SOFTWARE

Software enables all of the datacom hardware units to work as one system. Most of the software is located in the host and the front-end processor, but some can be located in the cluster control units and the terminals. Different names are used for the software, depending on its location.

Software in the Host

The datacom software in the host is called the **telecommunications monitor (TCM).** Although the functions performed by the TCM software vary from system to system, it typically enables the host to:

- Put messages in a particular order based on their priorities.
- Perform a security function by maintaining a log of activity for each terminal and verifying that a particular terminal is authorized to perform the requested task.
- Interface the datacom network with the DBMS. Most mainframe DBMSs have versions that permit networked users.
- Handle minor disruptions in processing (such as the temporary loss of power) by periodically saving the status of primary storage.

The TCM software supplements the portion of the operating system that handles the data transmission between the host and the front-end processor.

Software in the Front-end Processor

The name used for the datacom software in the front-end processor is **network control program (NCP).** A few of its more important functions include:

- Determine if terminals want to use the channel. One approach is to **poll** the terminals. Various techniques can be used, with the most straightforward being **roll call polling,** where each terminal is asked in sequence if it wants to use the channel.
- Maintain a record of channel activity by assigning a **date and time stamp** to each message, along with a unique serial number.
- Convert the codes used by one type of equipment (such as IBM) to another (such as DEC).
- Perform an editing function on incoming data by checking for errors and rearranging the format.
- Add and delete routing codes. Codes are added to outgoing messages to route them to the proper terminals, and codes are deleted from incoming messages before transmitting them to the host.

- Maintain a history file in secondary storage of messages handled during the past twenty minutes or so. The file can be used to recover from a disruption.
- Maintain statistics on network use.

It is easy to see why the NCP is called the workhorse of the network.

BASIC NETWORK APPROACHES TO PROCESSING

The first two generations of computing hardware featured stand-alone systems. When the third generation of computing hardware was introduced in 1964 that featured integrated chip circuitry, the idea of using the new systems in data communications networks was conceived. The first approach was timesharing. Next came distributed processing. Now, a new concept called client/server computing is attracting the most attention.

Timesharing

A **timesharing** network is one that consists of a *single* computer shared by multiple users who gain access by means of terminals. The first users were scientists and mathematicians who used the large computers at their firms' headquarters to perform computations. Figure 10.9 illustrates a timesharing system.

FIGURE 10.9
A Timesharing Network

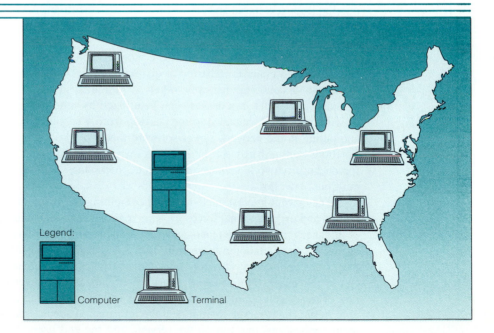

Legend:

Computer   Terminal

Distributed Processing

When small computers became popular, the firms changed their strategy and began *distributing* the minis and micros throughout the organization. When these systems are interconnected, the technique is known as **distributed processing** or **distributed data processing (DDP).**

It is important to understand that even though small computers stimulated the DDP approach, such networks can include computers of all sizes. Distributed processing replaced timesharing as the favorite network strategy during the late 1970s and 80s.

Client/Server Computing

Client/server computing is an approach to network use that is based on the notion that some functions are handled best on a local basis and some are handled best on a central basis. Therefore, client/server computing is a blend of the timesharing approach that features central use, and the distributed processing approach that emphasizes local use. Client/server computing can involve WANs, but the configuration typically consists of one or more interconnected LANs.

In a typical client/server computing network, application processing is shared between clients and one or more servers. A **client** is a user that accesses the network by means of a desktop computer. **Desktop computer** is the name given to a microcomputer that is used as a PC or a workstation. A **workstation** is a micro configuration that is tailored to a user's needs. Workstations are used by employees ranging from secretarial and clerical workers to executives. A **server** can be a computer of any size—a mainframe, a mini, a workstation, or even a micro—that provides a control function for the network.

Client/server computing is a much more complex hardware and software configuration than either timesharing or distributed processing. Any system in the network can access and use any other available systems. In this way, unused computing capacity in a desktop can be utilized by other desktops in the network, or work can be downloaded to the desktop from a server. The key to client/server computing is the network server software that provides control points for critical functions such as hardware sharing, data sharing, database management, storing and forwarding, network management, batch processing, and the interconnection of multiple networks.

The current interest in client/server computing is a result of technological, economic, and organizational forces working together. The technological forces consist of advances in microcomputers and data transmission technologies, database management systems tailored to network use, and graphical user interfaces. Economic forces are applied by an international marketplace that demands maximum efficiency in the use of information resources. Organizational forces include the migration of many computing activities from the central computing center to user areas.

In the client/server environment the information specialists focus on the firm's main applications that run on the servers, and the end users develop applications to run on their desktops. In order to take full advantage of client/server computing, applications must be developed specifically to run in such an environment. The concept is so new that there are only a handful of applications today that were developed with such a specific use in mind.

COMMON CARRIERS

A **common carrier** is a private company that provides communications services for a fee. The fee is called a **tariff.** Major common carriers include AT & T, the seven Bell Operating Companies, GTE, MCI, and US Sprint. Regulatory agencies such as the Federal Communications Commission (FCC) and the Public Utility Commission (PUC) control the tariffs.

Common Carrier Services

Common carriers typically provide public-measured services and private leased services. In **public-measured service** charges are based on the frequency and the distance of the communications service that is used. Most of your telephone calls are of this type. In a **private leased service** you enter into an agreement with the common carrier to receive an exclusive service such as a private line. A **private line,** or **dedicated line,** is one that is for your exclusive use—twenty-four hours a day, seven days a week.

Common Carrier Billing Methods

Common carriers use the same methods to charge you for data communications services that they use for voice charges. The simplest arrangement is a **dial-up circuit** that is established by dialing the receiver's number. A firm can make an unlimited number of local transmissions for a flat fee, and long-distance transmissions are billed separately. If there is much long-distance activity during the month, the firm can contract with the common carrier for **Wide Area Telecommunications Service,** a **WATS circuit,** which provides lower rates as the usage increases.

Both a dial-up circuit and a WATS circuit are **voice grade circuits**—they were designed to handle voice traffic. While the circuits are adequate for that purpose, they often do not offer the quality required to transmit the hundreds or thousands of data communications bits at a reasonable speed. The local loop equipment in some regions is very old and adds considerable noise to the circuit. Noise can also be added as the message is routed through the telephone company central offices where some of the circuits pass through mechanical relays. A firm can avoid the noise problem by leasing a private line that the common carrier specially conditions by adding such special devices as filters at the central offices. Such a specially conditioned circuit is called an **above-voice grade circuit.**

An example of a private leased service that holds much promise for business communications networks is ISDN.

ISDN

The **integrated services digital network (ISDN)** is a digital communications network architecture for simultaneous voice, data, text, and video communications. It is a worldwide effort to provide a single network technology. The basic building block of ISDN is a 64 kbps (thousand bits per second) channel, referred to as a **B-channel.** Each B-channel is used to transmit user information. Another channel, called the **D-channel,** carries signaling and control information that is used to initiate, redirect, or terminate calls.

The ISDN service operates in two standard structures, called basic access and primary access. **Basic access** consists of two B-channels and one 16 kbps D-channel, and is primarily intended for residential users. **Primary access** provides twenty-three B-channels and one 64 kbps D-channel, and is aimed at business users.

ISDN provides high-quality, digital, end-to-end transmission over multiple channels. The B-channel gives the user simultaneous access to office automation applications such as video conferencing, videotex, and FAX, as well as multimedia database systems, multiple microcomputers and multiple telephone lines. The D-channel provides special features such as calling number identification, automatic callback, and call forwarding.

As an example of how ISDN can be used in business, assume that a firm uses an ISDN network for purchasing replenishment stock from its suppliers. A buyer in the purchasing department dials the supplier's sales order department and explains what is needed. The supplier's salesperson retrieves pricing and delivery information from the database, and the information is simultaneously displayed on the screens of the salesperson and the buyer. Both persons can view the same image while they discuss the transaction.

NETWORK TOPOLOGIES

When multiple computers are included in a network, as is the case with distributed processing and client/server computing, the processors can be interconnected in several different topologies. A **topology** is simply a particular network pattern. The names star, ring, tree, and hybrid have been coined for the more popular topologies.

Star Network

A star network includes a central computer that is called the **central node,** as shown in Figure 10.10. A **node** is a point in the network where the circuits are interconnected by one or more units. The other nodes of the network can be computers of any size, and some nodes can be terminals. Although the star topology guarantees centralized control, any failure in the central node can be devastating.

Ring Network

A **ring network** is one that does not include a central node. Figure 10.11 shows the arrangement. Here, the control is distributed throughout the network, but a failure in any link poses a problem for the entire network.

FIGURE 10.10
A Star Network

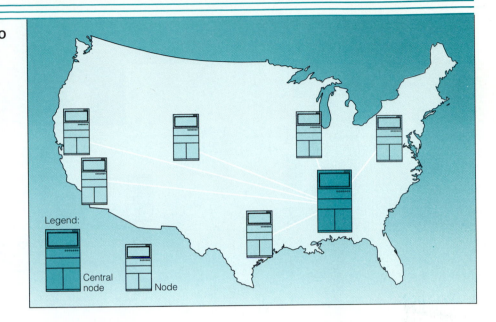

Tree Network

When more than two levels of computers exist in a hierarchy, as in Figure 10.12, the structure is called a **tree network.** The term **hierarchical network** is also used. The tree structure is ideal for firms with many organizational levels.

FIGURE 10.11
A Ring Network

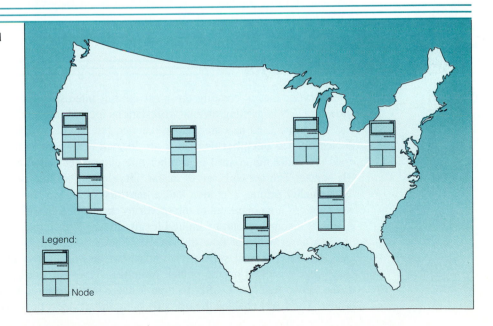

FIGURE 10.12
A Hierarchical, or
Tree, Network

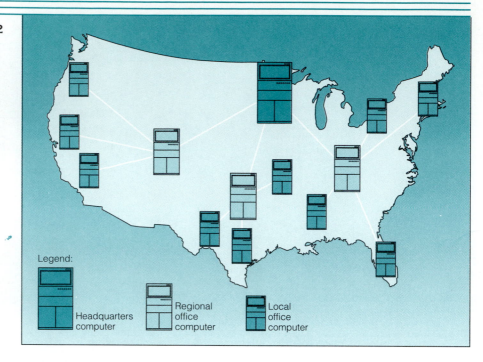

Legend:

Headquarters computer

Regional office computer

Local office computer

Hybrid Network

The star and ring topologies can be used alone, or they can be combined to form a hybrid topology.

LOCAL AREA NETWORKS

The network that is creating the most current interest is the LAN. Figure 10.13 shows a LAN consisting of four workstations located in users' offices. Each workstation can be used in a standalone manner, but can also access storage or output devices, called **peripherals,** which are located elsewhere in the network. Peripherals are under the control of another microcomputer called a **network server** or **file server.** The network server in the figure controls three peripheral devices—a letter quality printer, a plotter, and a hard disk drive. In this particular LAN, the workstations are connected to the server by means of a bus to form a star network. A **bus** is a single circuit of limited length and is an example of a tree topology.

As an example of how the LAN in Figure 10.13 might be used, Manager 1 can use expert system software stored in the network server DASD to prepare a graph that is plotted on the plotter. Manager 2 can use word processing software in the network server DASD to type a letter that is printed on the letter quality printer. The LAN enables the users to share the devices, thus saving money.

FIGURE 10.13

A Local Area Network

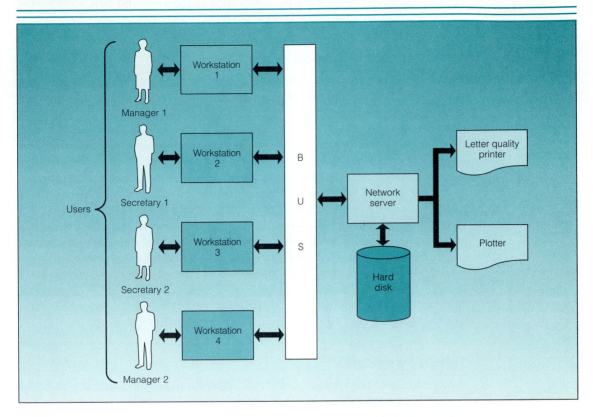

LAN Circuitry

All of the LAN equipment and circuitry is owned and operated by the firm. A common carrier is not involved unless the LAN interconnects with an IXC. The type of circuitry that is used depends on such factors as distance, susceptibility to interference on the circuit, and cost. Twisted pairs are the least expensive but have the most limited capability. Coaxial and fiber-optical cables can carry video signals that enable the firm to engage in videoconferencing. Fiber-optical cables provide a high-quality channel and the costs are decreasing as the technology becomes more widely adopted. One advantage of fiber optics is that it is extremely difficult for a computer criminal to tap into the circuit.

LAN Software

Special software enables workstations to share the peripherals. Most of the software is located in the network server, but some is located in each workstation. One of the most popular LAN software systems is NetWare, marketed by Novell, Inc. In a Novell network, the network server contains the NetWare operating system, and each workstation contains a NetWare shell. It is called a **shell** because it fits around the microcomputer's operating system.

LAN Control Methodologies

The way that messages transverse a LAN is determined by the type of LAN control that is used. Two popular control methodologies are the contention-based approach and the token-passing approach.

Contention-based Control
When **contention-based control** is applied, any microcomputer node that wants to transmit a message first listens to the network for a busy signal. When a signal is not detected, the node sends the message.

Since there is no centralized control, two or more nodes may attempt transmission at exactly the same time. This is called a **collision.** In order to avoide collisions, it is necessary to implement certain control schemes. With the contention-based approach, the network control is relatively simple, however network performance can quickly degrade when the transmission load becomes heavy.

Contention-based control is implemented in Ethernet, one of the earliest LAN designs that was developed jointly by Xerox, DEC, and Intel. Still very popular, Ethernet is based on a bus-oriented wiring scheme that enables data to be transmitted at speeds up to 10 mbps (million bits per second).

Token Passing

When **token-passing control** is employed, centralized network control is achieved by means of a token. A **token** is a set of data bits that are passed from node to node. A node can only send a message when it has the single token of the network. The method is similar to a track relay in which a runner can run only with the baton.

The network control is more complicated in token passing than in a contention-based scheme, but the token passing guarantees regulated access. Token-passing control is implemented in IBM's Token Ring Network and in General Motor's Manufacturing Automation Protocol.

PROTOCOLS AND NETWORK ARCHITECTURES

One of the characteristics of the datacom field since its inception has been the wide variety of hardware and software products on the market. The products are marketed by computer manufacturers, common carriers, and manufacturers who specialize in data communications hardware or software. This variety has been a blessing for datacom users, as it has stimulated competition among the suppliers and made available a wide selection of models. However, the variety has been a burden in that it has made it difficult to interconnect different suppliers' products.

In the datacom field the name **protocol** is used to describe a rule for interfacing, or interconnecting, the various units. The datacom devices follow the protocols in communicating with one another. This is called *shaking hands.*

Luckily, some of the suppliers saw the problems coming before the situation got out of hand. IBM was among the first. In 1970 IBM was marketing 200 different datacom products that could be interconnected fifteen different ways. IBM management decided that a set of standards should be defined to serve as a guide for future developments.

SNA

IBM named its system of protocols **Systems Network Architecture (SNA).** In designing SNA, IBM considered all of the activities necessary for transmitting data through a network with a user at one end (called the **user node**), the host computer at the other (called the **host node**), and several **intermediate nodes** that consist of such devices as the front-end processor and cluster control units.

IBM separated the *physical* activities that transmit the data from the *logical* activities that control the physical transmission. SNA was aimed at the logical activities.

SNA classified the logical activities into *layers.* The purpose of the layers was to insulate the user from changes in the datacom hardware and software. For example, the firm could convert from a network of dial-up lines to a LAN and the change would not affect the user or the user's software.

Other Manufacturers' Protocols

SNA was received so well that other computer manufacturers developed their own standards. For example, Burroughs announced its Burroughs Network Architecture (BNA), and Honeywell developed its Distributed System Environment (DSE). However, users did not regard the large number of manufacturers' "standards" as the solution to their problem. For example, IBM's SNA made it easy to interface IBM hardware and software, but it did not help the user who wanted to mix IBM products with those of other datacom suppliers.

The OSI Model

The problem of incompatibility between datacom products affected users on a worldwide basis, and in 1978 the International Standards Organization announced a system of network protocols and named it the **OSI model.** OSI stands for **Open Systems Interconnection.** Like SNA, the OSI model uses layers to define the logical and physical activities.

Figure 10.14 illustrates the OSI model. The host node is at the right, the user node is at the left, and the intermediate nodes that include the front-end processor and the cluster control unit, are in between.

FIGURE 10.14

The OSI Model

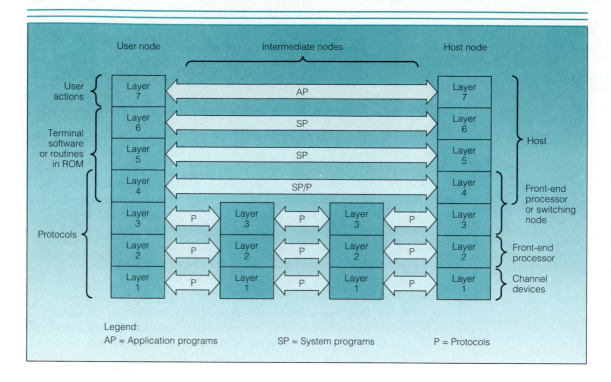

The brackets at the right of the figure indicate which hardware units are used in performing the functions of the various layers. The brackets at the left indicate whether the functions are performed by user actions, terminal software or routines in the terminal ROM, or by protocols.

The arrows linking the nodes at each layer are labeled to indicate the form of the linkage—application programs (AP), system programs (SP), and protocols (P). A layer in one node "talks" to the corresponding layer in another node. Each of the layers is described briefly. The numbers below match the layer numbers in the figure.

1. **Physical layer**—Transmits the data from one node to another.
2. **Data link layer**—Formats the data into a record called a **frame**—and performs error detection.
3. **Network layer**—Causes the physical layer to transfer the frames from node to node.
4. **Transport layer**—Enables the user and host nodes to communicate with each other. It also synchronizes fast- and slow-speed equipment as well as overburdened and idle units.
5. **Session layer**—Initiates, maintains, and terminates each session. A **session** consists of all the frames that comprise a particular activity, plus sig-

nals that identify the beginning and the end. A session is like a telephone call that begins with "hello" and ends with "good-bye." Standard log-on and user identification routines are used to initiate datacom sessions.

6. **Presentation layer**—Formats the data so that it can be presented to the user or the host. For example, information to be displayed on the user's screen is formatted into the proper number of lines and number of characters per line.

7. **Application layer**—Controls user input from the terminal and executes the user's application program in the host.

You will note that the bottom three layers appear in all nodes, but the upper four layers appear in only the host and user nodes.

How the Architecture Handles the User/Host Interface

Let us assume that the user wants to use a mathematical model located in the host to select the best pricing strategy. The user indicates that the pricing model is to be used by entering instructions in the terminal, under control of Layer 7 (the application layer). Layer 6 (the presentation layer) changes the input data into the format used for transmission, and Layer 5 (the session layer) initiates the session. Layer 4 (the transport layer) selects the route the message will follow in traveling from the user to the host node, and Layers 3 and 2 (the network layer and data link layer respectively) cause the data to be transmitted through Layer 1 (the physical layer).

When the message reaches the host node, control moves up the layers to the application program (the model) in the host. Communication from the host back to the user follows the same pattern—down the layers in the host node, across to the user node, and up the layers in the user node.

Some OSI Protocol Examples

An example of a protocol on the physical layer is the RS232c plug used to interconnect datacom hardware. The plug, pictured in Figure 10.15, is used by all manufacturers of datacom equipment.

An example of a Layer 2 (data link layer) protocol is the format for a message frame, pictured in Figure 10.16. The flags identify the beginning and the end of the frame, and the address causes the message to be routed to its destination. The control field specifies the type of frame, and the frame check character field is used to detect (and possibly correct) errors.

Putting Datacom Protocols in Perspective

Because of IBM's large customer base, SNA quickly became an unofficial standard among mainframe users. However, DEC's network architecture, called DECnet, also has achieved a large following—primarily among users of smaller-scale systems.

FIGURE 10.15

An Example of a
Physical
Protocol—the
RS232c Plug

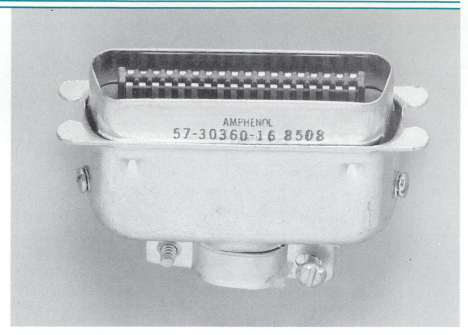

Courtesy of Amphenol.

The OSI model has picked up support rather slowly. One reason is that protocols for all of the layers have evolved gradually. Protocols for the first three layers were announced in 1978 but did not receive widespread use until the mid-1980s. Eventually, the OSI model will become the true datacom architecture standard. That process is being stimulated by the computer manufacturers who have modified their architectures so that they are compatible with the OSI model.

NETWORK MANAGEMENT

Networks are often the core of the firm's operations, and network failures can cost thousands of dollars every minute that the system is out of service. Network management is aimed at reducing the opportunity for network failures primarily through planning and control.

FIGURE 10.16

An Example of a
Logical Protocol—
a Message Frame

Beginning flag	Address	Control	Message	Frame check character	Ending flag

Network Planning

Network planning consists of all of the activity aimed at anticipating the firm's network needs. Network planning includes three main components—capacity planning, staff planning, and performance monitoring. **Capacity planning** analyzes and plans for traffic volumes that the network can handle. **Staff planning** helps determine the number of people necessary to manage a network, and their needed levels of expertise. **Performance monitoring** includes analyzing response times for a given level of traffic to anticipate the effects of potential changes on network performance.

Network Control

Network control involves the day-to-day monitoring of the network to ensure that it maintains the desired level of operation. Network control includes procedures such as fault detection, fault isolation, and network restoration. Ideal network control systems alert the operator to network failures or potential failures, identify the troubled components, and help correct the problem.

In order to achieve and maintain network control, firms need operation standards, design strategies, failure control procedures, and problem solving methodologies. These control elements should be updated as changes occur in computing technology, the network, or the organization.

The Network Manager

When we studied the database we saw that a specialist, called the DBA, is added to the information services organization to manage that part of the CBIS. The same approach has been taken with datacom. A **network manager** is responsible for planning, implementating, operating, and controlling the firm's datacom network, or networks. The network manager reports to the CIO.

Depending on the size of the firm and the complexity of the datacom activity, the network manager's staff can consist of several datacom specialists with different skills. The specialists can include **network analysts** who perform the same function as systems analysts, only restricted to communications-oriented systems, **software analysts** who program and maintain datacom software, and **datacom technicians** who are concerned with hardware and operations.

In some firms persons are designated as **LAN managers.** The LAN managers can be members of information services, but a more logical arrangement is for them to be members of the using organizations.

THE ROLE OF DATACOM IN PROBLEM SOLVING

Datacom has a positive influence on both individual problem solvers in the firm, and the firm itself.

Before datacom, the only problem solvers who could receive computer output in a reasonable length of time were those persons at the computer location. The printed reports, responses to database queries, and simulation results were delivered to the managers through the company mail—perhaps the same day, or, in the worst case, the next day. Managers at remote sites had to wait several days before receiving their information through the postal system. Today, information describing the firm's widespread operations is at *all* user's fingertips, assuming that the database and software library contain the necessary ingredients.

The combined benefits to individual problem solvers give the firm practically unlimited flexibility in terms of its enterprise strategies. With a sound datacom network, a firm can pursue a strategy of either centralized or decentralized decision making.

In a firm that stresses **centralized decision making,** all of the important decisions are made by top management at headquarters. Datacom contributes to this arrangement by providing for the flow of data from the firm's operations into the headquarter's computer, where information is made available to top management. Datacom also contributes by providing a means of communicating top management's decisions throughout the organization.

In a firm that practices **decentralized decision making,** top management delegates the authority for making certain decisions to lower-level managers. In this scenario lower-level managers can access the central computer and use the hardware, software, and data that typically reside at headquarters. Lower-level managers can solve their own problems by using the central computer in a timesharing manner or by using any of the computers in the network when distributed processing or client/server computing is practiced.

SUMMARY

The basic data communications schematic has the same general appearance as the basic communication model. All of the interconnected computer and communications devices are called a network. A fundamental network consists of a terminal and a computer that can both send and receive, modems that code and decode the messages, and a circuit that provides one or more channels.

The two basic network types are WAN, for wide area network, and LAN, for local area network.

A typical configuration of communications hardware consists of multiple terminals. There are six basic terminal types— keyboard, push-button telephone, POS, data collection, RJE, and special purpose. Cluster control units control multiple terminals in an area. Modems are always needed, even when the channel transmits the messages in a digital, rather than analog, fashion. Multiplexers are added to each end of the channel to enable the transmission of multiple messages at the same time. The channel consists of three major sections—a local loop, the IXC circuit, and another local loop. The IXC circuit can consist of twisted pairs, coaxial cables, fiber-optical cables, land-based microwave, or satellite microwave.

The front-end processor plays a key role in the network, coordinating the channel devices, selecting message routes, and converting the serial transmissions from the channel to a parallel form for the host and vice versa. It is possible for the front-end processor to perform some functions independent of the host, such as message switching.

Most of the datacom software resides in the front-end processor and the host. It is also possible to locate software nearer the user, such as in the cluster control unit and even the terminal.

Networks are used for timesharing, distributed processing, or client/server computing. A timesharing network includes only one computer, and a distributed processing network includes more than one. A client/server network enables work to be done both centrally and locally, using all of the resources in the network.

Common carriers provide data communications channels as either a public-measured service or a private leased service. You pay for the channel in the same manner as for voice transmission by using a dial-up circuit or a WATS circuit. Lease of a private circuit is one way to raise the quality to above-voice grade and ensure circuit availability around the clock. A common carrier service that is receiving much current attention is the integrated services digital network, or ISDN. ISDN permits simultaneous transmission of multiple communications media.

When multiple computers are included in a network, they can be arranged in four basic topologies—star, ring, tree, or hybrid.

The LAN is an in-house network that is completely owned and operated by the firm. Control can be achieved in a contention-based manner or by means of token passing.

In an effort to standardize the interfacing of datacom equipment, several network architectures have been devised. IBM introduced SNA and was followed by the other mainframe manufacturers with their own versions. ISO also announced its OSI model. These architectures typically view the logical tasks that control the physical movement of data as multiple layers. These layers use combinations of hardware, software, and protocols to accomplish the transmission.

When a firm has a sizable investment in datacom, it is a good strategy to manage the overall network planning and control by assigning that responsibility to a network manager. In a large firm the network manager oversees a staff of network analysts, software analysts, and datacom technicians, and coordinates the activities of LAN managers.

In a firm that uses datacom for data gathering and decision transmission, all problem solvers have access to the same computing resources. Datacom also makes it possible for a firm to follow a strategy of either centralized or decentralized decision making.

We have now completed the part of the text that explains information technology. Understanding this will enable us to next examine each of the subsystems of the CBIS in Part Four.

KEY TERMS

channel	circuit, line
data communications, teleprocessing, telecommunications, telecom, datacom	modem
	network

point of sale (POS) terminal
data collection terminal
cluster control unit
multiplexer
local loop
interexchange channel circuit, IXC circuit
front-end processor
host
telecommunications monitor (TCM)
network control program (NCP)
timesharing
distributed processing
common carrier
public-measured service

private leased service
dial-up circuit
Wide Area Telecommunications Service, WATS
   circuit
private line
integrated services digital network (ISDN)
node
contention-based control
token-passing control
protocol
SNA (Systems Network Architecture)
OSI (Open Systems Interconnection) model
network manager

KEY CONCEPTS

How the basic communication model provides
   the basis for the basic data
   communications schematic
The distinction between WAN and LAN
Distribution of datacom software throughout the
   network
The way that clients in a client/server
   computing environment can share the
   network resources

The network topologies—star, ring, tree, and
   hybrid
The separation of datacom activities into logical
   and physical components
How datacom facilitates problem solving in
   both an individual and organizational sense

QUESTIONS

1. What are the five components of the basic communication model?

2. What device performs the coding and decoding function in a datacom network? Is it always required?

3. Name one feature that distinguishes a LAN from a WAN.

4. List the six types of terminals. Identify with an asterisk the types a manager would use.

5. If a terminal is not used by the manager, what role does it play, if any, in problem solving? Answer in terms of each terminal type that you did not asterisk in Question 4.

6. In which functional area of the firm would you most likely find POS terminals? Data collection terminals?

7. What determines the transmission speed of a channel?

8. What technologies can be used in the local loop to transmit data? What technologies exist in the IXC circuit?

9. What role does the front-end processor play in a datacom network?

10. What is roll call polling? Which unit in the network performs it?

11. Distinguish between timesharing and distributed processing.

12. In a client/server network, who develops the central applications? The local applications?

13. Name two advantages to a firm that leases a private line.

14. What are the two types of channels included in an ISDN network? Which one transmits data? What does the other one do?

15. Which topologies can form the basis for a client/server network? Which would you most likely find in a firm with several organizational levels?

16. How can a LAN save a firm money?

17. Which circuitry will be used in a LAN when the firm wants to engage in video-conferencing? Which circuitry offers the greatest security?

18. What is a token and what is its significance?

19. What is a protocol?

20. How many layers of the OSI model connect all nodes? How many transmit data?

21. What are the three main components of network planning?

22. Where would you find a network manager? A LAN manager?

23. How does datacom provide flexibility in carrying out the firm's decision-making philosophy?

TOPICS FOR DISCUSSION

1. How do the front-end processor and host contribute to network security?

2. What accounts for the popularity of client/server computing?

3. What could a network analyst offer that a systems analyst could not? Do you think that the idea of having network analysts is a good one?

4. Someone has predicted that someday the CIO's responsibilities will consist only of network management. What is the basis of that prediction? Do you agree?

PROBLEM

Refer back to the general systems model of the firm illustrated in Figure 3.16. Redraw this figure, adding datacom hardware at those points where it would be used. Suggestion: First sketch the model on a large sheet of paper, leaving space between the boxes. You will have to redraw the information processor box so that it specifies the types of computers used. Then, overlay boxes on the arrows, and label them with the datacom hardware names. Use a legend if there is not enough space in the added boxes for the names. Try to incorporate as many of the appropriate hardware types as you can. When you are satisfied with your work, redraw the model. This would be a good application of a graphics package such as MacDraw.

Hudson Bay Builders Supply

You are the CIO of the Hudson Bay Builders Supply, one of the largest retail building materials firm in North America. The headquarters and the information systems division are located in Toronto.

Lumber and other construction supplies are bought from suppliers in both Canada and the U.S., and stored in warehouses in Vancouver, Edmonton, Regina, Winnipeg, Montreal, Ottawa, and Toronto. A total of 125 retail stores throughout the Western provinces sell the products to both contractors and do-it-yourself homeowners.

Your headquarters computer center consists of a large IBM mainframe computer with ample secondary storage and other peripherals. At each of the seven warehouses, IBM AS/400 minicomputers are used in a stand-alone manner. IBM personal computers are located in the headquarters, warehouses, and all of the retail stores. However, no personal computers at the same site are connected, and communication between the sites is accomplished by telephone and overnight mail.

Each store and warehouse maintains its own inventory record—reducing levels when sales are made and increasing them when replenishment stock is received. When reorder points are reached at the retail store level, purchase requisition forms are mailed to the warehouses. Company policy requires that a store order from the nearest warehouse in that province.

When a warehouse has to reorder, purchase orders are mailed to the Toronto headquarters where they are processed by the headquarters purchasing division.

This overall system has worked reasonably well in the past except when a warehouse runs out of stock for an item. Because of the centralized purchasing policy of the company, the warehouse cannot fill an order for that item from stock that often exists in other warehouses. This situation quite often generates backorders and customers have to wait for weeks to receive shipment. Further, some of the items that are badly needed in one warehouse are a surplus in another.

A week ago the president, Charles Stewart, attended an executive seminar on information technology. Stewart was so impressed with the notion of the decision support systems and business data communications that he asked the lecturer for advice on what Hudson Bay could do to apply the seminar concepts. The lecturer recommended that all of the computers be linked in a network. Thus, the retail stores and warehouses would be relieved of the responsibility for maintaining their own inventory records. Instead, those records would be maintained in the large headquarters computer.

This morning, Stewart asked you about the networked business environment. He said: "I think we ought to do something about our information systems. I would like the executive committee to consider it, but first we need some idea of its possible impacts on our business operations and what it's going to cost. Also, why don't we provide some terminals to our managers? I think we ought to start making better use of computers as well in our decision making processes. Let's start off with some terminals for our executive team—myself and the six vice presidents. What do you think?"

You respond: "If you use the computer, I think the others will follow suit. Let me take a cut at it. I'll get back to you next Monday. Is that OK?" Stewart nodded.

You see no problem in terms of the headquarters mainframe. It has adequate capacity to assume the increased workload. Furthermore, the warehouse and stores could continue to use their present hardware, and the relief from the inventory processing would make capacity and resources available for additional applications. Retail stores and warehouses will keep headquarters updated on sales and inventory status in a networked environment. You also know that the heaviest telephone and mailing activities are between Toronto and Montreal, and Toronto and Vancouver while traffic among other areas is relatively moderate.

Assignments

1. Prepare a geographic map and identify the warehouse locations. Connect warehouses by considering the volume of data transmission and the network topologies you learned. Are there any alternative networks you can design? If so, identify them, and briefly explain why they were not chosen.

2. What are the benefits of networking isolated computers to manage sales and inventory functions?

3. Make a list of communications hardware and software that will be necessary for each warehouse and each retail store. Consider communication circuit options between public-measured services and private leased services. Which option do you recommend? Why?

4. How would you justify the costs of building a networked environment?

5. What kind of information would be useful for executive decision makers such as the president and vice presidents? Would this be information about daily sales or inventory status or something else? What type of computing equipment would you provide to these executives? Explain your choice.

6. Describe key management tasks that the network manager will perform in the new networked environment.

SELECTED BIBLIOGRAPHY

Aversano, Nina. "The Telephone as Computer." *Review of Business* 11 (Fall 1989): 5–8.

Davis, Dwight. "Where Client/Server Fits." *Datamation* 37 (July 15, 1991): 36–8.

Francis, Bob. "Novell's Enterprising NetWare." *Datamation* 37 (January 1, 1991): 30*ff.*

Green, Paul, and Kanter, Jerry. "New Kid on the Block: Tracking the Evolution of the Modern Telecom Manager." *Computerworld* 23 (September 4, 1989): 73–80.

Green, Roedy. "Remote Connections." *Byte* 16 (July, 1991): 161–68.

Hindin, Eric. "Sharing the Load: Client/Server Computing." *Data Communications* 18 (March 21, 1989): 15–22.

Horwitt, Elisabeth. "ISDN to Reach the Masses." *Computerworld* 25 (January 28, 1991): 1*ff.*

Jackson, Brad M.; Butler, Charles W.; and Richardson, Gary L. "Information System Network Architecture." *Journal of Systems Management* 40 (February 1989): 28–34.

Joseph, Celia, and Muralidhar, Kurudi. "Integrated Network Management in an Enterprise Environment." *IEEE Network Magazine* 4 (July, 1990): 7–13.

Kerr, Susan. "The Politics of Network Management." *Datamation* 34 (September 15, 1988): 50–54.

Kerr, Susan. "The Applications Wave Behind ISDN." *Datamation* 36 (February 1, 1990): 64–66.

Kriz, Kenneth J. "ISDN: Communications of the Future for Banks." *Bank Administration* 64 (January 1988): 48*ff.*

McCusker, Tom. "The Latest In High-Speed Protocols." *Datamation* 37 (January 15, 1991): 48*ff.*

Markoff, John. "Soon: Faster and Wiser Networks." *New York Times Business Computing,* (April 3, 1991): 6.

Moskowitz, Robert. "Building Server-Based LANs." *Modern Office Technology* 37 (May 1992): 50*ff.*

Musgrave, Bill. "Network Management: Keeping the Connection." *Datamation* 33 (September 1, 1987): 98*ff.*

Panchak, Patricia. L. "Network Alternatives: Making the Right Choice." *Modern Office Technology* 37 (March 1992): 22*ff.*

Patterson, Raymond A., and Strouble, Dennis D. "Critical LAN Success Factors: An Implementation Model." In *Managing Information Technology in a Global Society,* edited by Mehdi Khosrowpour. Harrisburg, Pa: Idea Group Publishing, 1991. pp. 16–26.

Pinella, Paul. "Organizational Computing Arrives." *Datamation* 36 (November 15, 1990): 42*ff.*

Powell, Dave. "Signaling System 7: The Brain Behind ISDN." *Networking Management* 10 (March, 1992): 36–40.

Quarterman, John S., and Hoskins, Josiah C. "Notable Computer Networks." *Communications of the ACM* 29 (October 1986): 932–71.

Sinha, Alok. "Client-Server Computing." *Communications of the ACM* 35 (July 1992): 77-97.

Stamps, David. "Mapping OSI Migration Moves." *Datamation* 36 (July 1, 1990): 79–82.

Steinbart, Paul John, and Nath, Ravinder. "Problems and Issues in the Management of International Data Communications Networks: The Experiences of American Companies." *MIS Quarterly* 16 (March 1992): 55–76.

Tillman, Matthew A., and Yen, David (Chi-Chung). "SNA and OSI: Three Strategies for Interconnection." *Communications of the ACM* 33 (February 1990): 214–24.

Wexler, Joanie M. "Despite Progress, Doubt Still Remains with ISDN." *Computerworld* 25 (March 4, 1991): 85.

Wood, Lamont. "Local Area Network Management: What You Need to Know." *Modern Office Technology* 37 (April 1992): 56*ff.*

THE COMPUTER-BASED INFORMATION SYSTEM

The jobs that computers perform are called **applications.** Very often the term **systems** is used. In the beginning, the only computer application was *data processing.* The firm's data processing system consisted of subsystems such as payroll and inventory.

As the larger firms successfully implemented their data processing applications, new challenges were sought. The computer was recognized as a tool that could produce information for management decision making. First, there was the concept of the *management information system,* or *MIS.* Then, a refinement known as the *decision support system,* or *DSS,* appeared. MIS and DSS have received most of the attention of managers and information specialists during the past twenty years.

Today, two new areas of computer use are emerging, and they apply the computer in completely different ways. One, aimed at employing the computer and other electronic devices for the purpose of improving communications, is *office automation.* The other, aimed at using the computer to imitate certain aspects of human reasoning, is *artificial intelligence* and its subset *expert systems.*

In Part Four we explore each of these five major application areas in separate chapters. The descriptions illustrate how the fundamentals that you have learned in other parts of the text are applied by business organizations in using the computer as a problem-solving tool.

Part IV

THE COMPUTER-
BASED INFORMATION
SYSTEM

Chapter 11

The Data Processing System

LEARNING OBJECTIVES

After studying this chapter, you should:

- Understand what data processing is
- Know what types of technology can be used in data processing
- Understand the tasks that a data processing system performs
- Know the characteristics of a data processing system
- Be familiar with an integrated set of data processing subsystems that are found in many organizations
- Have a good appreciatrion for how data flow diagramming is used to document a business system
- Understand the role of data processing in problem solving

INTRODUCTION

The data processing system performs the firm's accounting applications. The first data processing systems were completely manual, but most were eventually augmented with keydriven machine, punched card, and computer technologies.

Data processing consists of four major tasks—data gathering, data manipulation, data storage, and document preparation. A firm does not have a choice of whether to have a data processing system; it is a requirement. Also, all firms perform the procedures basically the same way. The data processing system is data oriented rather than information oriented, and the data is largely historical. Consequently, the data processing system provides relatively little problem-solving information when compared to the other CBIS subsystems.

In this chapter we use data flow diagrams to document a data processing system that we call the distribution system. The system is used by firms such as manufacturers, wholesalers, and retailers that distribute products to their customers.

Although the data processing system is data oriented, it does produce some information. And, it provides the important database that other CBIS subsystems, such as decision support systems and expert systems, are built on.

WHAT IS DATA PROCESSING?

Data processing (DP) is the manipulation or transformation of symbols such as numbers and letters for the purpose of increasing their usefulness. The term **transaction processing (TP)** is gaining use to describe data processing as applied to business data. Although the terms data processing and transaction processing can be used interchangeably, we will use data processing since it is the most established.

THE DATA PROCESSING SYSTEM

A firm's data processing tasks are performed by a **data processing system** that gathers data describing the firm's activities, transforms the data into information, and makes the information available to users. In our view, the data processing system is the same as the accounting system. This view is based on the fact that early computers were applied only to accounting tasks, and the use was called **electronic data processing (EDP).** In taking this view, we recognize that data processing can involve nonaccounting activities such as use of mailing lists to prepare form letters, preparation of statistical tables, and so on.

Figure 11.1 is a model of a data processing system. It is a derivation of the general systems model of the firm that we described in Chapter 3. The input, transformation, and output elements of the physical system of the firm are at the bottom. Data is gathered from throughout the physical system and the environment, and

FIGURE 11.1

A Model of a Data Processing System

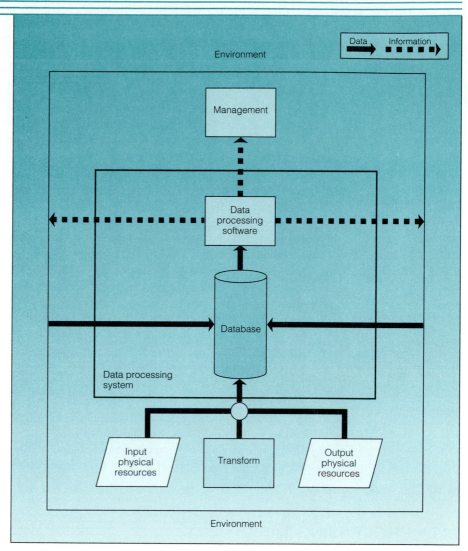

entered into the database. Data processing software transforms the data into information for the firm's management and for individuals and organizations in the firm's environment.

It is important to recognize the information flow to the environment. The data processing system is the *only* CBIS subsystem that has the responsibility of meeting information needs outside of the firm. The data processing system has a responsibility to furnish information to each environmental element except competitors.

DATA PROCESSING TECHNOLOGIES

Four different types of data processing systems have evolved over the years, distinguishable by their use of technology.

- **Manual** The first systems were manual. They included only people, pens or pencils, and ledger books for posting the entries. The ledger books represented the record of the firm's operations. Many small firms still use manual systems, and larger firms use manual procedures to supplement other technologies.
- **Keydriven machine** The invention of keydriven machines such as the cash register, typewriter, and desk calculator provided a degree of relief in handling large volumes of data. The machines enabled the firm's activity to be posted to the ledger books faster and more accurately than with manual systems. The only keydriven machine that is still used to any real degree is the pocket calculator.
- **Punched card machine** During the first half of this century, the larger organizations recorded their transactions in punched card form and used punched card machines to perform the necessary file maintenance and processing. The holes in the cards represented the status of the firm. Today, the only place you can find punched card machines is in the museum.
- **Computer** Today, all of the larger organizations and many of the smaller ones rely on computers for data processing.

All of the firm's data processing systems do not lend themselves computer processing. The volume of data that is processed by many systems is small, or the activities occur only infrequently. For those reasons, the modern business organization processes its data using a combination of computer, keydriven machine, and manual methods, with the computer playing the primary role.

DATA PROCESSING TASKS

Regardless of the data processing technology, four basic tasks are performed.

Data Gathering

As the firm provides products and services to its environment, each action is described by a data record. When the action involves an environmental element, it is called a **transaction,** hence the term transaction processing.

The data processing system gathers the data that describes each of the firm's *internal actions* and its *environmental transactions.*

Data Manipulation

It is necessary to manipulate the data to transform it into information. Data manipulation operations include:

Classifying   Certain data elements in the records are used as codes for identifying and grouping the records. In the computer field a **code** is one or more characters that are used for identification purposes. For example, a payroll record includes codes that identify the employee (employee number), the employee's department (department number), and the employee's payroll classification (payroll class).

Sorting   The records are arranged in certain sequences based on the codes or other data elements. For example, the file of payroll records is arranged so that all of the records for each employee are together.

Calculating   Arithmetic and logic operations are performed on the data elements to produce additional data elements. In a payroll system, for example, the hourly rate is multiplied times the hours worked to produce the gross earnings.

Summarizing   There is so much data that it is necessary to synthesize it, or boil it down, into the form of totals and subtotals.

Data Storage

In a small firm there are hundreds of transactions and actions each day; in a large firm there are thousands. Each transaction is described by several data elements. For example, a sales record identifies *who* makes the purchase (the customer number), *what* is purchased (the item number), *how much* is purchased (the quantity), *when* it is purchased (the sales date), and the customer's *authorization* (the customer purchase order number).

All of this data must be kept somewhere until it is needed, and that is the purpose of data storage. As explained in Chapter 9, the data is stored on secondary storage media, and the files can be logically integrated to form a database. *Most of the data in the database is produced by the data processing system.*

Document Preparation

The data processing system produces outputs for individuals and organizations both inside and outside the firm. The outputs are triggered in two ways:

- **By an action**   Outputs are produced when something happens. An example is the bill that is prepared each time a customer order is filled.
- **By a time schedule**   Outputs are produced at a particular time. An example is a payroll check that is prepared each Friday.

In most cases the outputs are in the form of documents. The documents are usually printed on paper, called **hard copy.** However, more and more users are making increased use of screen displays.

CHARACTERISTICS OF DATA PROCESSING

There are several characteristics of data processing that clearly distinguish it from the other CBIS subsystems. Data processing systems:

- **Perform necessary tasks**   Unlike the other major computer applications— MIS, DSS, OA, and expert systems—the firm does not decide whether it wants to perform data processing. The firm is required by law to maintain a record of its activity. Elements in the environment such as the government, stockholders and owners, and the financial community demand that the firm engage in data processing. But even if the environment did not demand it, the firm's management invariably would implement data processing systems as a means of achieving and maintaining control.
- **Adhere to relatively standardized procedures**   Regulations and accepted practices spell out how data processing is to be performed. Organizations of all types process their data basically the same way.
- **Handle detailed data**   Since the data processing records describe the firm's activities in a detailed way, they provide an audit trail. An **audit trail** is a chronology of activities that can be traced from the beginning to the end, and from the end to the beginning.
- **Have a primarily historical focus**   The data gathered by the data processing system generally describes what happened in the past. That is certainly the case when batch processing is used.
- **Provide minimal problem-solving information**   The data processing system produces *some* information output for the firm's managers. The standard accounting reports such as the income statement and the balance sheet are examples.

Whereas the line separating the other CBIS subsystems is often fuzzy, the data processing system can be distinguished by the above characteristics.

A SAMPLE DATA PROCESSING SYSTEM

A good example of a data processing system is the one that is used by distribution firms—firms that distribute products or services to their customers. We call the system the **distribution system.** As you study this system, it will help to think of a product-oriented firm such as a manufacturer, wholesaler, or retailer. But, the distribution system can also be found in service organizations such as the United Way and hospitals, and in government agencies such as the military and the IRS. *All* organizations are in the distribution business in one form or another.

Also keep in mind that you probably cannot find a firm that processes their data *exactly* the same way as described here. Our model is a general one—fitting most firms in a general way.

SYSTEM OVERVIEW

We will use data flow diagrams, or DFDs, to document the system.[1] DFDs document a system in a hierarchical manner, and the diagram in Figure 11.2 represents the highest level. The diagram is called a **context diagram** because it presents the system in the context of its environment.

[1] As we describe the system, we will also describe the basics of data flow diagramming. If you require a more detailed explanation, refer to Chapter 6.

FIGURE 11.2

A Context Diagram of the Distribution System

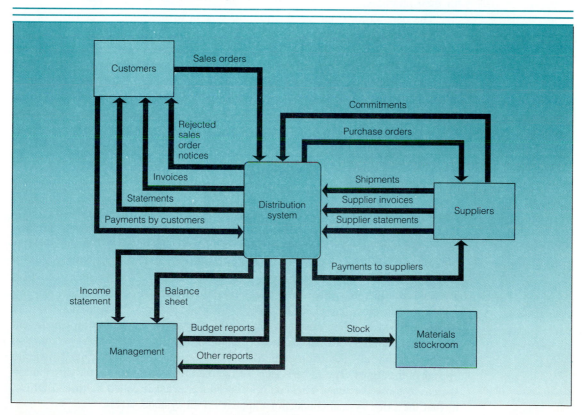

The entire system is represented by the upright rectangle in the center. A circle can also be used. The environmental elements are represented by rectangles, and are connected to the system by arrows called data flows.

The environmental elements of the distribution system include customers, suppliers, the materials stockroom, and management. In DFD terminology, the term *environment* applies to the *system* that is documented. For that reason, some environmental elements, such as management and the materials stockroom, exist within the firm.

The data flows that connect the firm with its customers are quite similar to the flows that connect the firm with its suppliers. That is because the firm is a customer of its supplier. The orders that the firm receives from its customers are usually named *Sales orders,* whereas the orders that the firm places to its suppliers are named *Purchase orders.* In some cases the firm will first obtain verbal *Commitments* from its suppliers before the purchase orders are prepared. Very often the firm will have to send *Rejected sales order notices* to its customers—perhaps their credit rating is bad. Although suppliers also send rejected purchase order notices to the firm, we have omitted that flow for simplicity. Both the firm and its suppliers use *Invoices* to advise customers how much money they owe, and use *Statements* to collect unpaid bills. Finally, both the firm and its customers must make *Payments* for their purchases.

The data flows from the distribution system to management consists of the standard accounting reports.

All of the data flows in the Figure 11.2 diagram consist of conceptual resources except the one from the suppliers to the system labeled *Shipments,* and the one from the system to the materials stockroom labeled *Stock.* Data flows can reflect both conceptual and physical resources, and the conceptual resources can include data or information.

THE MAJOR SUBSYSTEMS OF THE DISTRIBUTION SYSTEM

The context diagram is fine for defining the boundary of the system—the environmental elements and the interfaces. But we need to learn more about the processes that are performed. We accomplish that by identifying the three major subsystems in Figure 11.3. In DFD terminology, Figure 11.3 is called a *Figure 0 diagram.* Shortly, you will see how that name was derived. When a series of DFDs are used in a hierarchy, they are called **leveled DFDs.**

The subsystems are identified by the numbered rectangles. The first subsystem is concerned with filling customer orders, the second with ordering replenishment stock from suppliers, and the third with maintaining the firm's general ledger. You will notice that all four of the environmental elements from the context diagram appear in the figure. The same is true for the data flows connecting the distribution system to those elements. This condition produces what is called **balanced DFDs,** in that the same system connections appear on all systems levels.

FIGURE 11.3

A Figure 0 Diagram of the Distribution System

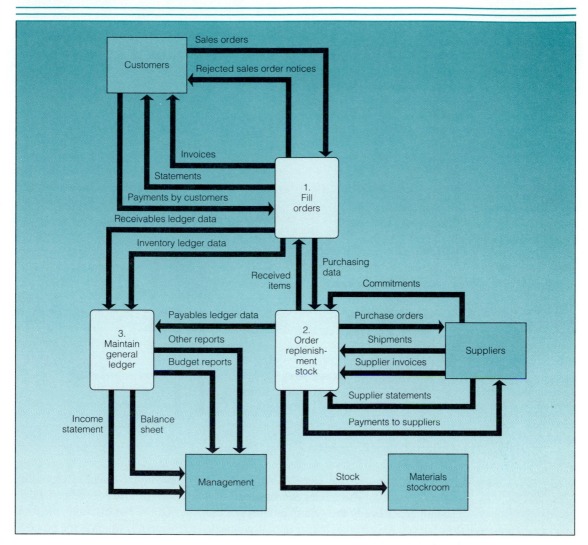

Systems that Fill Customer Orders

Figure 11.4 shows the four main systems that are involved in filling customer orders—order entry, inventory, billing, and accounts receivable. Figure 11.4 is an explosion of Process 1 in the Figure 0 diagram. For this reason, it is called a **Figure 1 diagram.** The figure number refers to the corresponding process number on the *next higher level* DFD. Since the context diagram used no figure numbers, the next lower level DFD is called the **Figure 0 diagram.**

FIGURE 11.4

A Figure 1 Diagram of the Systems That Fill Customer Orders

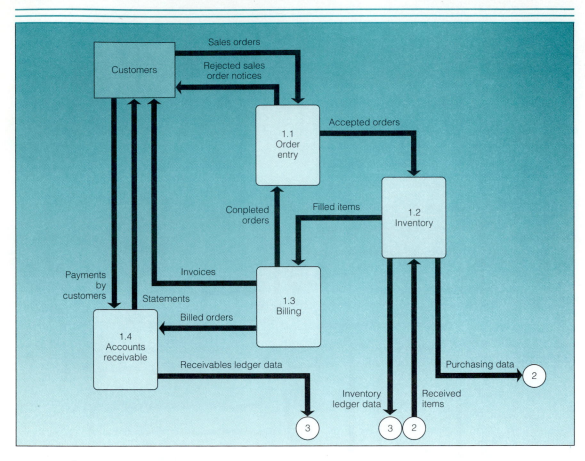

You will notice that some of the arrows are connected to small circles with numbers in them. The circles are **connectors** that establish flows to other DFDs. The numbers identify the system numbers of the other DFDs. For example, the data flow labeled *Receivables ledger data* is connected to Process 3, which is the process that maintains the general ledger.

We will learn more about the four order-filling systems later, but, for now, just understand that the **order entry system** enters customer orders into the system, the **inventory system** maintains the inventory records, the **billing system** prepares the customer invoices, and the **accounts receivable system** collects the money from the customers.

Systems That Order Replenishment Stock

In a similar manner, we identify the subsystems that are concerned with ordering replenishment stock from suppliers. This detail is shown in Figure 11.5, and it is

FIGURE 11.5

A Figure 2 Diagram of the Systems That Order Replenishment Stock

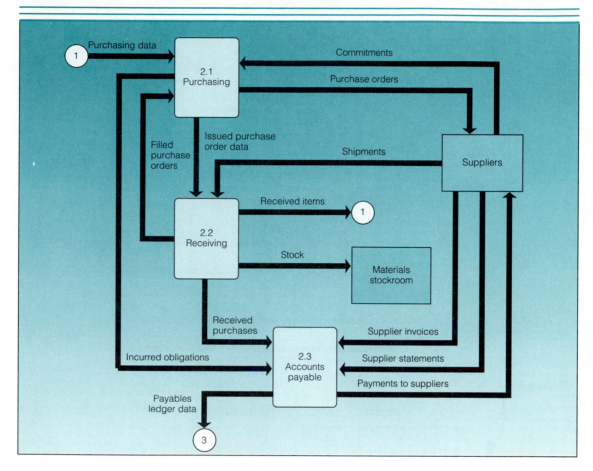

called a Figure 2 diagram since it explodes Process 2 of the Figure 0 diagram. The **purchasing system** issues purchase orders to suppliers for the needed stock, the **receiving system** receives the stock, and the **accounts payable system** makes payment.

Systems That Perform General Ledger Processes

Figure 11.6 shows the detail for the last of the three processes in the Figure 0 diagram—Maintain general ledger. The **general ledger system** is the accounting system that combines data from other accounting systems for the purpose of presenting a composite financial picture of the firm's operations. The file that contains the combined accounting data is the **general ledger.**

Two subsystems are involved. The **general ledger maintenance** subsystem posts the records that describe the various actions and transactions to the general

FIGURE 11.6

A Figure 3 Diagram of the Systems That Perform General Ledger
Processes

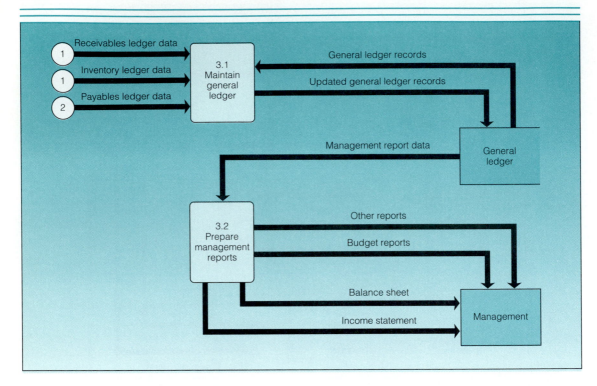

ledger. The **report preparation** subsystem uses the contents of the general ledger to prepare managers' reports.

We will not document the general ledger system in any greater detail than shown here. The Figure 3 diagram is adequate to understand the system.

A unique feature of Figure 11.6 is the inclusion of a **data store**—the DFD term for a file. The store is the General Ledger. We did not include stores in the higher-level DFDs because we wanted to keep those diagrams as uncluttered as possible. As we drop down to the next level of detail, we will encounter more data stores.

Now that we have a good overview of the distribution system, we will describe the subsystems that are used in filling customer orders and ordering replenishment stock.

FILL CUSTOMER ORDERS

In our description of each subsystem, we will use the numbers from the DFDs to make it easier for you to relate the narrative to the diagrams. We will also assume that the system is computer-based, although the type of technology has no influence on the way the DFDs are drawn. DFDs are *logical* representations of systems, not *physical* representations.

1.1 Order Entry

Figure 11.7 documents the order entry system. It is a *Figure 1.1* diagram—it documents in greater detail the processing in Step 1.1 of the higher-level diagram (Figure 11.4).

1.1.1 Edit order data   Firms use sales order forms to record the data that is necessary to process a customer order. A sample sales order is shown in Figure 11.8. When the sales order is received from the customer, it is checked for missing

FIGURE 11.7

A Figure 1.1 Diagram of the Order Entry System

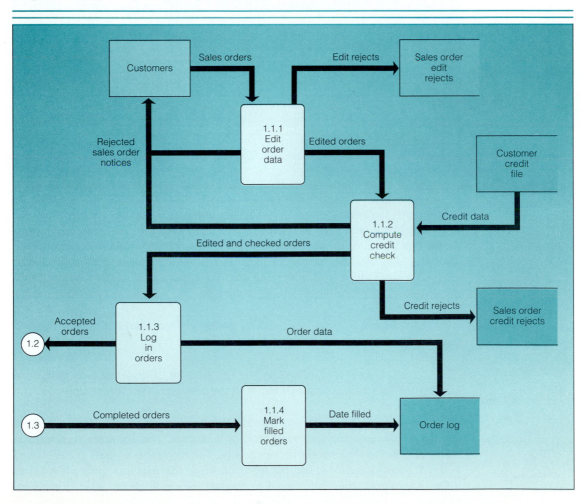

FIGURE 11.8

A Sales Order Form

ORDER FORM

SRA

Science Research Associates
P.O. Box 5380
Chicago, Illinois 60680-5380

Date 10-31-89

Please enter my order subject to the terms and conditions for Materials contained in the SRA Training Source Catalog (2-7310).
All orders are subject to acceptance by SRA in Chicago, Illinois. Orders from individuals require prepayment, plus all applicable taxes, plus 15% for transportation, but not less than $1.00.

Bill To:

Name: ONLINE PUBLISHING SERVICES
Address: 460 HAMPTON COURT
Address:
City: ROSELLE State: IL Zip: 60172
Attention To: MR. TIMOTHY TAYLOR
Purchase Order No. / Authorized Person: 55016
Person ordering: MR. TIMOTHY TAYLOR
IBM Customer Number:
Delivery (Check One):
☒ Regular (Generally UPS)
☐ $30 Expedite Processing Charge
Phone Number: (312) 351-0669

Ship To:

Name: ONLINE PUBLISHING SERVICES
Address: 460 HAMPTON COURT
Address:
City: ROSELLE State: IL Zip: 60172
Attention To: MR. TIMOTHY TAYLOR

Purchase

Quan.	Catalog Order No.	Course Code	Title	Purchase Price
8	212042	32193	USING TSO/E TEXT	30.00
8	208831	32343	COBOL COMPILER TEXT	30.00
8	208758	32322	COBOL OUT PROGRAM TEXT	30.00

License
NOT AVAILABLE TO INDIVIDUALS
NOT AVAILABLE ON VISA NOR MASTERCARD

Quan.	Catalog Order No.	Course Code	Title	License Price 60 Days	12 Months

Order written by _____ (Signature)   27103

or incorrect data. The order entry clerk corrects errors when possible, such as by looking up a customer number. But if that is impossible, such as reconciling a difference between item number and name, the clerk prepares a *Rejected sales order notice* that is sent to the customer asking that the corrected order be resubmitted. The clerk also files the sales order in a file named *Sales Order Edit Rejects*. The rejected orders will be held in that file until the customers resubmit new orders, or the orders are placed in some type of history file. We will not include that activity in our system.

The third output from Process 1.1.1 consists of the *Edited orders* that passed the edit. These orders are the input to the next step.

1.1.2 Compute credit check The purpose of this step is to determine whether the firm wants to do business with the customer. This is accomplished with a credit check.

One approach to conducting a credit check considers the impact of the order amount on the customer's accounts receivable amount. The **accounts receivable** is the money due to the firm for previous sales. The receivable amount is maintained in the Accounts Receivable file, but we also include that data in a special file, called a Customer Credit file, that is used to conduct the credit check. Also in the Customer Credit file are the customer credit limits. A **credit limit** is the total amount of receivables that the firm is willing to accept from a customer.

The data flow labeled *Credit data* includes both the receivable amount and the credit limit. The order amount is added to the receivable amount and the sum is compared to the credit limit. When the credit limit is exceeded, the order is rejected. Orders that do not pass the credit check are filed in the *Sales Order Credit Rejects* file, and *Rejected sales order notices* are sent to the customers.

The third output from the credit check is the *Edited and checked orders* that are input to the next step.

1.1.3 Log in orders   When an order is accepted, a brief identifying description is entered in an Order Log, and an *Accepted orders* record is written, which is input to the inventory system. The **Order Log** is used to follow up on orders to make certain that they are filled and contains such data elements as customer number, customer order number, customer order date, and order received date. Orders in the file are called **open orders.** That means that they are unfilled.

1.1.4 Mark filled orders   The first three order entry steps form a connected chain. They are linked by data flows, with no intervening data stores. Step 1.1.4 is separate because it is performed later—when the billing system signals that orders have been filled. The *Completed orders* data flow is created by the billing system to serve as the signal. In Step 1.1.4 the Order Log records for the filled orders are marked *by entering the date filled* as a way to indicate that they are no longer open.

By recording the date filled in the Order Log, the informational value of that file is increased. The computer can scan the date-filled fields to determine the open orders. It can also compare the dates that the orders were filled with the dates that they were received to determine how long it takes to fill orders. This information is valuable to managers.

1.2 Inventory

Once a decision has been made to accept the orders, a determination must be made as to whether they can be filled. Figure 11.9 shows the four main processes of the inventory system. Two processes (1.2.1 and 1.2.2) accomplish the order filling. The other processes (1.2.3 and 1.2.4) have other responsibilities.

1.2.1 Check the balance on hand   The first step is to check the balance on hand for each ordered item. The *Item record* for the ordered item is retrieved from the Inventory file. The balance on hand field from the record is compared with the order quantity from the accepted orders record to see if adequate stock exists to fill the order. For those orders that cannot be filled, *Backorder records* are entered in the Backorder file. A **backorder** means that "We cannot fill the order now, but we will later when we replenish our inventory."

This is the point in the system where all of the data elements relating to the inventory item are obtained. The inventory record includes elements such as item

FIGURE 11.9

A Figure 1.2 Diagram of the Inventory System

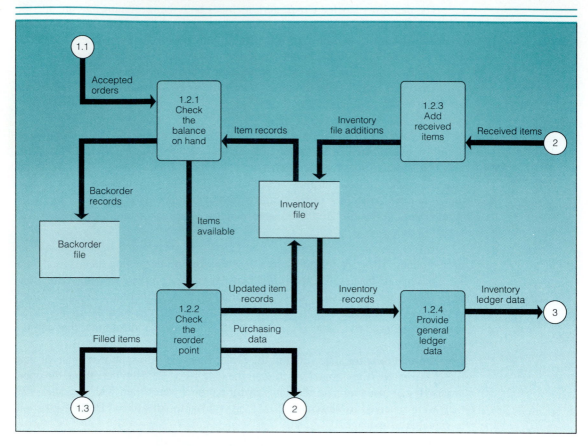

description and warehouse location that will be used later. By retrieving that data here and carrying it along with the transaction data, it will not be necessary to access the Inventory file again in the system. The time to access records is usually the most time-consuming part of any system and is to be minimized as much as possible.

When the order can be filled, an *Items available* data flow provides the linkage to the next process.

1.2.2 Check the reorder point   In the case of filled orders, the next step is to determine whether the new, lowered balance on hand caused the reorder point to be reached. Each item record contains a reorder point field. The **reorder point** is the inventory quantity that triggers a stock replenishment activity. When the balance on hand drops to the reorder point, it is time to reorder. The reorder point is set high enough so that the new supply will be received before all of the stock is completely exhausted—a **stockout.** When the reorder point has been reached, reorder data is recorded as *Purchasing data* to be used by the purchasing system.

The order-filling process is completed by writing the *Updated item records* back to the Inventory file. Each of these updated records contains the new balance on hand.

The *Filled items* data flow provides the linkage to the next order-filling system—billing.

1.2.3 Add received items

The above processes reduce inventory balances when orders are filled. Another process increases balances when replenishment stock is received from suppliers. Step 1.2.3 uses the *Received items* data flow from the receiving system and updates the balance on hand fields of the received items in the Inventory file.

1.2.4 Provide general ledger data

Inventory data is an important input to the general ledger system. The value of the inventory is included as an asset on the balance sheet. This step extracts data from the Inventory file that the general ledger system needs, and passes it along to that system in the form of the *Inventory ledger data* flow.

1.3 Billing

An **invoice,** or **bill,** is the official notice that the firm sends to its customers to advise them of the amount of money that is owed. Figure 11.10 pictures a typical

FIGURE 11.10

An Invoice

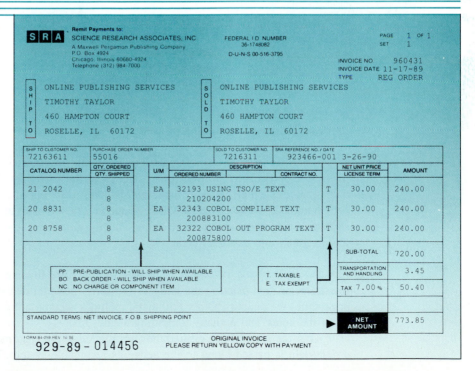

FIGURE 11.11

A Figure 1.3
Diagram of the
Billing System

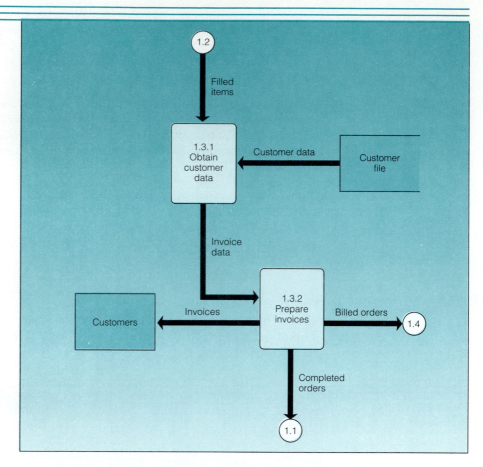

invoice. The system that prepares the invoices is the billing system. Figure 11.11 illustrates the two main billing processes.

1.3.1 Obtain customer data   First, the inventory data for the *Filled items* is supplemented with customer data from the Customer file. The customer data includes such elements as name and address, shipping instructions, and sales-person number. These elements will be printed on the invoices and other documents such as management reports. The output *Invoice data* from this step contains both the inventory and customer data.

1.3.2 Prepare invoices   The preparation of the invoices requires that each **line item,** or item listed in the body of the form, be **extended** by multiplying the price times the quantity. Other arithmetic includes accumulating a total amount for all of the items, and perhaps computing a sales tax.

After the *Invoices* are printed they are mailed to the customers, and the *Billed orders* data is passed along to the accounts receivable system. The *Billed orders* data does not include detail about each line item. Rather, it summarizes the billing transaction by identifying the invoice number, invoice date, customer number, customer name and address, customer order number, salesperson number, and invoice amount.

Now that the order has been filled, it is necessary to notify the order entry system so that the filled status can be reflected in the order log. This notification is accomplished with the *Completed orders* data flow.

1.4 Accounts Receivable

Figure 11.12 shows four processes performed by the accounts receivable system. This system has a unique structure in that each process is conducted separately from the others. This situation exists because each process has its own trigger.

FIGURE 11.12

A Figure 1.4 Diagram of the Accounts Receivable System

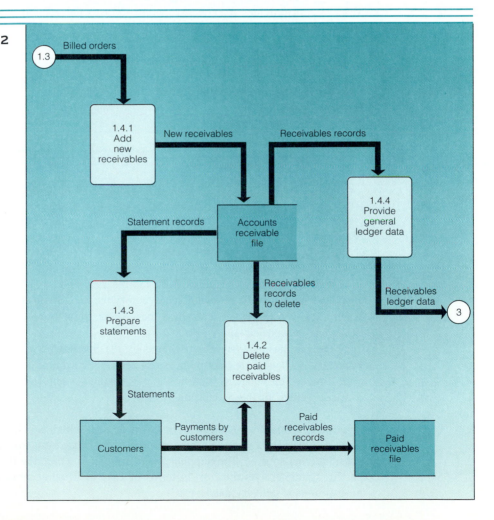

1.4.1 Add new receivables   Records are added to the Accounts Receivable file immediately following billing. The *Billed orders* trigger occurs daily.

1.4.2 Delete paid receivables   Likewise, records are removed from the Accounts Receivable file to reflect *Payments by customers.*

1.4.3 Prepare statements   On a monthly basis, the Accounts Receivable file is used to prepare *Statements.* A **statement** is a reminder that money is owed on one or more invoices. It is common practice to give the customer thirty days to pay an invoice. The receivable is considered **current** until thirty days have passed since the billing date. Then, the receivable becomes **past due.**

A statement contains a single line for each **outstanding invoice**—an invoice that has not been paid. A sample of a statement appears in Figure 11.13.

1.4.4 Provide general ledger data   Also on a monthly basis, the receivables system provides *Receivables ledger data* to the general ledger system that appears on the balance sheet as an asset.

At this point we have completed one major portion of the distribution system. We have handled all of the activity related to customer orders. Next it is necessary to respond to the reorder point signals of the inventory system, and procure replenishment stock.

ORDER REPLENISHMENT STOCK

The three systems that work together to order, receive, and pay for replenishment stock are purchasing, receiving, and accounts payable.

2.1 Purchasing

The purchasing department consists of a number of **buyers** who usually specialize in particular inventory categories. For example, one buyer might specialize in adhesives and another in electronics. The inventory record contains a field that identifies the inventory category so that when the reorder point is reached the responsible buyer can be notified.

The purchasing system is triggered by the inventory system in Step 1.2.2 of Figure 11.9 when the reorder point is reached. A record is added to the *Purchasing data* flow, which serves as input to the purchasing system. Figure 11.14 shows the four subsystems of the purchasing system.

2.1.1 Select suppliers   The buyer decides which suppliers should be considered to provide the replenishment stock, using data from the Supplier file and possibly other sources. The Supplier file maintains data that describes the suppliers' past transactions with the firm in terms of material quality, prices, and ability to meet promised delivery dates.

FIGURE 11.13

A Statement

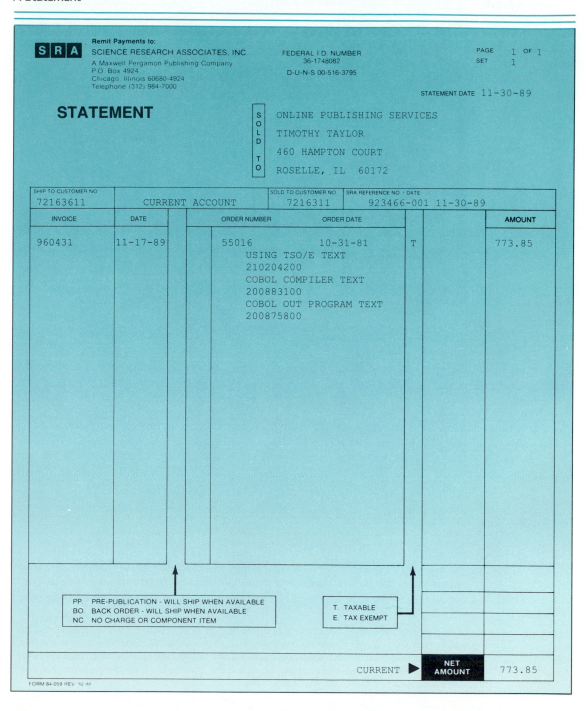

FIGURE 11.14

A Figure 2.1 Diagram of the Purchasing System

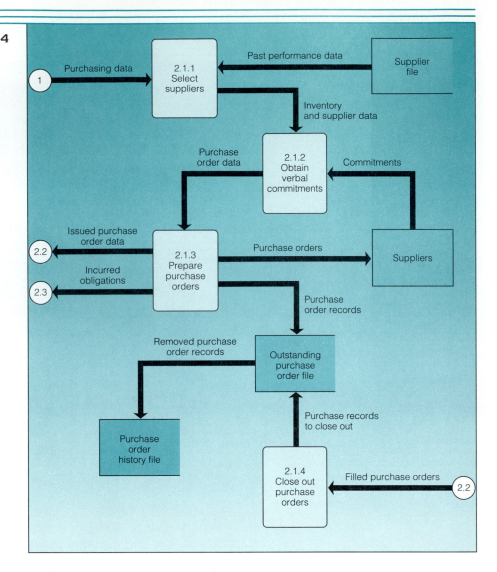

2.1.2 Obtain verbal commitments When the buyer determines which suppliers are the best prospects, they are contacted by means of telephone or perhaps an ISDN network for the purpose of reaching an agreement.[2] For each supplier

---

[2] We described ISDN in Chapter 8 as a modern type of data communications channel that can handle multiple media simultaneously. For example, a buyer can use ISDN to bring up a screen from the supplier's database, which displays information concerning an item to be ordered. Then, the buyer and a supplier sales representative can use the same channel to conduct a telephone conversation concerning the item.

the buyer attempts to negotiate the lowest possible price and obtain a commitment to meet a particular shipping date. These negotiations enable the buyer to select the supplier to be used for each order.

2.1.3 Prepare purchase orders   The buyer then fills out a purchase requisition form that is used to prepare the purchase order, either typed by a typist in the purchasing department or printed by the computer. Figure 11.15 is a computer-prepared purchase order.

Another output is the *Purchase order records* that are added to the Outstanding Purchase Order file. This file provides a degree of control over purchase orders becoming lost in the mail or shipments not being made as promised. When this file is stored on a magnetic medium, the computer can scan each record on a daily basis and advise the appropriate buyers of each **outstanding purchase order**— one that should have been filled but has not. The buyers can follow up with the suppliers to determine the reasons.

The other two outputs from Step 2.1.3 are notifications to other systems that a purchase has been made. The *Issued purchase order data* flow alerts the receiving system that a shipment is due. Also, the *Incurred obligations* data flow notifies the accounts payable system that an invoice is expected from the supplier. We will see shortly how these two notifications are used.

2.1.4 Close out purchase orders   It is necessary to remove records from the Outstanding Purchase Order file when the orders are filled. This signal comes from the receiving system in the form of the *Filled purchase orders* data flow. The *Removed purchase order records* are filed in the Purchase Order History file.

Of all the subsystems in the distribution system, purchasing is the one that has been the most difficult to computerize. The main reason is the fact that the human element is so important. All of the activities revolve around the negotiations of the buyer with the suppliers.

This situation seems to be changing. Innovative communications technologies such as ISDN, EDI, and videotex are being applied in the purchasing area to improve the flow of information between the firm and its suppliers. In addition, expert systems are being programmed to make some portion of the buyer's decisions.[3]

A purchasing system is not in sight that completely eliminates the buyer. However, the degree of computer support that is made available to the buyer should continue to increase.

---

[3] We presented EDI in Chapter 2 as a tool for achieving competitive advantage by establishing electronic linkages between separate firms. The buyer can use EDI to directly access the supplier's database, for example. Videotex is described in Chapter 13 as an office automation application capable of making textual material such as suppliers' catalogs available electronically. Expert systems are described in Chapter 14, and they are capable of capturing knowledge, such as that applied by the buyer, and applying that knowledge in a consistent manner.

The purpose of these inspections is to ensure that the supplier shipped the merchandise that was ordered, and that the merchandise that the supplier shipped was actually received. When everything checks out, the *Stock* is routed to the materials stockroom and *Receipt information* is assembled.

2.2.2 Notify other systems The *Receipt information* consists of all the data elements that will be used by other systems. A *Received items* data flow is directed to the Inventory system to advise the item numbers and quantities that will be used to update the Inventory file. A *Filled purchase orders* data flow is directed to the purchasing system for use in closing out the outstanding purchase orders. We will see how the *Received purchases* data flow is used by the accounts payable system in the next section.

Communications-oriented data processing systems, called **online transaction processing (OLTP)** systems, do a good job of transmitting the three receipt notices. Terminals in the receiving area can signal the other systems almost instantaneously. In manual systems, it can take days for the notifications to reach everyone.

2.3 Accounts Payable

The accounts payable system is responsible for paying the suppliers for the purchases. Before payment is made, the firm wants to make certain that the money is actually owed. This certainty is established when three conditions exist:

1. There is proof that the *stock was ordered.* This proof is provided by a file copy of the purchase order for the same dollar amount as on the supplier invoice.
2. There is proof that the *stock was received.* This proof is provided by the Received Purchases file that contains the notification of the receipt by the receiving system.
3. An *invoice has been received* from the supplier.

Figure 11.17 shows the processes of the accounts payable system.

2.3.1 Set up supplier payables records Records are added to the Accounts Payable file when the *Incurred obligations* data flow is received from the purchasing system. Considerable time then might elapse before the items are received.

2.3.2 Make supplier payments *Supplier invoices* and *Supplier statements* are filed in the Invoice and Statement file, where they are held until payment is made. Payments are made when all three above conditions have been met. *Payment data* from the Accounts Payable file and *Invoice data* from the Invoice and Statement file are used in making the *Payments to suppliers.*

2.3.3 Delete paid payables When a supplier payment is made, the corresponding record is removed from the Accounts Payable file.

FIGURE 11.17

A Figure 2.3 Diagram of the Accounts Payable System

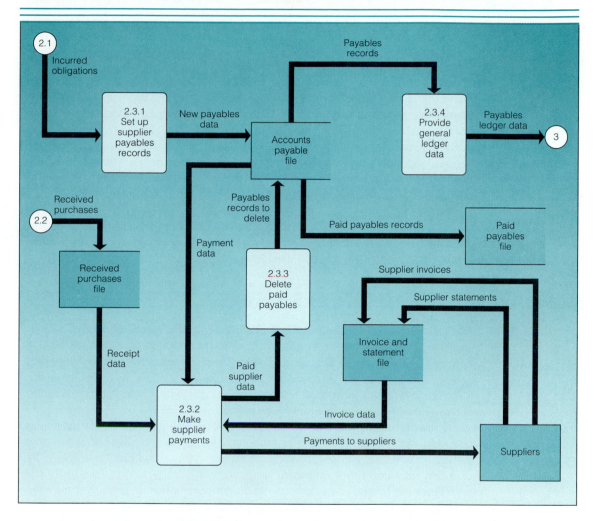

2.3.4 Provide general ledger data   The accounts payable system provides data to the general ledger system. Payables are shown as liabilities on the balance sheet.

This concludes our journey through the distribution system. Although it may have seemed complex, our system is very simple compared to those that most companies use. We omitted quite a few **exception routines**—activities that happen only infrequently but must be accounted for in the design of an operational system. For example, we did not include the processes of removing rejected sales orders from their suspense files or following up on backorders. But even though the system has been simplified, it provides a good taste of what constitutes data processing.

THE ROLE OF DATA PROCESSING IN PROBLEM SOLVING

Since data processing is characterized by large volumes of data rather than information, it is easy to get the idea that it contributes little to problem solving. This is misleading for two reasons. First, data processing systems produce *some* information output in the form of standard accounting reports. These reports are especially valuable in the financial area of the firm and at top-management levels. Second, and most important, the data processing system provides the rich database that can be used in problem solving. The database provides much of the input to other CBIS subsystems—especially MIS and DSS, and, to a lesser extent, expert systems.

Data processing is the foundation upon which other problem-solving systems are built. The first step in providing the manager with computer support for problem solving is to implement a sound data processing system.

SUMMARY

The data processing system maintains a detailed financial record of the firm's operations and produces information that describes those operations. The information exists in the form of printed and displayed documents that are used by managers and nonmanagers in the firm, and by all environmental elements except competitors. The systems of most modern organizations consist of a combination of computer, manual, and keydriven machine methods.

Data processing consists of four basic tasks—data gathering, data manipulation, data storage, and document preparation. Manipulation consists of classifying, sorting, calculating, and summarizing. Document preparation can be triggered by either an action or a time schedule.

There are several characteristics of data processing that distinguish it from the other application areas. Data processing performs necessary tasks, adheres to relatively standardized procedures, handles detailed data, has a primarily historical focus, and provides problem-solving information as a byproduct of its other activities.

A distribution firm uses an integration of nine data processing subsystems. The order entry, inventory, billing, and accounts receivable subsystems process customer orders. The purchasing, receiving, and accounts payable subsystems obtain replenishment stock. Two subsystems maintain the general ledger and produce standard management reports.

Data processing contributes to problem solving by producing standard reports that summarize the firm's financial condition, and providing the database that is used by other CBIS subsystems.

KEY TERMS

data processing (DP),
    transaction processing (TP)
data processing system
transaction
distribution system
order entry system
inventory system
billing system
accounts receivable system
purchasing system
receiving system
accounts payable system
general ledger system
accounts receivable
credit limit

order log
open order
backorder
reorder point
stockout
invoice, bill
statement
current receivable
past-due receivable
outstanding invoice
buyer
outstanding purchase order
packing slip
online transaction processing (OLTP) system

KEY CONCEPTS

How data processing captures the details of the firm's daily activity

How the basic data processing tasks remain the same regardless of the technology that is used—manual, keydriven machine, or computer

Why data manipulation is necessary to make the data meaningful to users

How the data flows from subsystem to subsystem in the distribution system

The data processing system as the major contributor to the database

QUESTIONS

1. Who uses the output of the data processing system?

2. What four technologies have been used to process data? Which one is obsolete? Which one(s) would you find in a firm such as American Airlines?

3. What are the four data manipulation operations?

4. Why must a firm have a data processing system?

5. What are the questions that are answered by the data elements of a sales transaction?

6. What can trigger an output from the data processing system?

7. What is the form of the problem-solving information that is provided to the firm's managers by the data processing system?

8. Why is the top-level DFD called a context diagram?

9. What are the four environmental elements of the distribution system? Which exist inside the firm? Which outside?

10. Does a DFD show physical or conceptual flows? Explain.

11. What two basic screening processes are conducted before a firm decides to accept a sales order?

12. How can a manager use the Order Log to improve the performance of the portion of the distribution system that fills customer orders?

13. In what subsystem would you find an open order? An outstanding invoice? An outstanding purchase order?

14. Distinguish between a backorder and a stockout.

15. Explain why you check the reorder point only when the order is filled.

16. Distinguish between an invoice, a bill, and a statement.

17. What numbers are multiplied together when a line item is extended?

18. As a general rule, when does a receivable become past-due?

19. Which systems does the receiving system notify when a shipment is received? For each, specify the data flow that is used.

20. What are the three conditions that must exist before a firm pays a supplier's invoice?

21. Name two ways that the data processing system contributes to problem solving.

TOPICS FOR DISCUSSION

1. What codes would you expect to find in your student record maintained by your college?

2. Which of the data flows in Figure 11.2 would be the easiest to accomplish by means of electronic transmission? Explain why. Are there any data flows of data or information that could not be handled electronically? If so, which ones?

3. The chapter says that each of the four accounts receivable processes has its own trigger. Are these triggers produced by actions or time schedules?

PROBLEMS

(Note: The tools used to work the following problems are described in Chapters 6 and 7.)

1. Draw a system flowchart of the order entry subsystem of the distribution system. Include all of the processing except the marking of the Order Log to reflect filled orders.

2. Use structured English to document the first two processes of the inventory system— check the balance on hand and check the reorder point.

3. Document the Order Log with a data store dictionary entry, a data structure dictionary entry, and the necessary number of data element dictionary entries.

4. Document the data flow in the billing system labeled *Billed orders*. Use a data flow dictionary entry, a data structure dictionary entry, and the necessary number of data element dictionary entries.

TeleWare, Inc.

TeleWare is a software marketing firm, headquartered in Memphis, that sells its products by telephone and mail order. Customers can call the TeleWare 800 number or mail or FAX their orders. All payments are made by credit card. Telemarketing clerks in the order department key the order data into the computer, which performs the inventory processing and produces a three-part output document. One part is used by the warehouse personnel as a picking ticket to pull the items from the shelves, one is enclosed with the shipping carton to serve as a packing list, and one is mailed to the customer as an invoice.

TeleWare president Gus Wallensak has learned that there are some rough spots in the order-filling procedure. In an effort to get to the bottom of the situation he sent the following electronic mail message to Patricia Vaughn, the manager of the order department; Buzz Barclay, the warehouse manager; Mary O'Neil, the manager of the accounts receivable section of the accounting department; and Clair Mandell, the MIS manager.

TO: Pat, Buzz, Mary, Clair
FROM: G.W.
SUBJECT: Problems in filling customer orders

During the past month, I have received an increasing number of complaints from our customers concerning the way we fill orders. Specifically, customers are complaining that:
1. Orders become lost.
2. We do not meet our promised delivery dates even though the shipments arrive by overnight mail service.
3. We send statements even though customers have made payment.

Please review these problems with your personnel and be prepared to discuss them at our managers' meeting next week.

PAT VAUGHN (Order department manager): I checked with our telemarketing clerks, and I'm told that the problem of lost orders is mainly those we receive by phone. The clerks key the data into the computer while they're talking on the phone, and there is no hard copy record. If the order gets lost later on, such as the computer output being misplaced, there is no record to refer back to.

GUS WALLENSAK (President): What about the mail and FAX orders? You have a record of them, don't you?

INTRODUCTION

The MIS is one of the five major CBIS subsystems and has the purpose of meeting the general information needs of all the managers in the firm, or in some organizational subunit of the firm. Subunits can be based on functional areas or management levels. All functional information systems can be viewed as a system of input subsystems, database, and output subsystems.

Behavioral influences are always important to the performance of information systems, but they are especially crucial to organizational information systems such as the MIS. Managers and information specialists can establish programs designed to transform the negative effects of the behavioral influences into positive results.

The MIS reflects an attitude by the executives that they want to make the computer available to all of the firm's problem solvers. When the MIS is in place, and functioning as intended, it can help managers and other users within the firm identify and understand problems.

WHAT IS AN MIS?

It was the mid-1960s, and most large firms had finally overcome the pains of implementing their first computers. It had been a difficult task since those organizations had accumulated huge volumes of data over the years, and much effort was required to put the data in a form that was acceptable to the computers. The computer literacy within the firms was limited to the handful of information specialists, and those specialists had no real experience in guiding the implementation through the steps of the system life cycle. Accomplishments came slowly—by trial and error.

The firms had one point in their favor during those hard times: the computer was applied in exactly the same way as the keydriven and punched card machines had been—in performing data processing. The tasks were well defined and affected primarily the firm's accounting departments. Computer implementation consisted essentially of transforming the older routines into a computer form.

Early MIS Efforts

With the data processing systems on the air, both the firms' information specialists and the computer manufacturers wanted to keep the computer activity moving, so they sought new application areas. It did not take long to realize that the informational output of the data processing systems left much to be desired. For many years the technology—the keydriven and punched card machines—had been incapable of providing management information. When it first became clear that the computer could fill that gap, it looked as if it would be an easy task.

The firms that attempted the first MISs learned otherwise. The big barrier turned out to be the managers. As a group they knew nothing about the computer. They knew their jobs and they had developed their own approaches to solving problems, but they had not given much formal thought to the role of information in their activities. As a result, it was difficult for the managers to articulate exactly what they needed from the MIS.

This situation was frustrating to the information specialists. Since they knew little about management, they did not know what questions to ask. The information specialists decided that the only solution was for them to design and implement systems to produce information that *they thought* the managers needed. This was done: in many cases the information specialists had guessed wrong, and the systems were not used.

Over time managers learned about the computer, they became aware of the underlying logic of the processes that they followed in solving problems, and they were able to describe their information needs. Information specialists, in turn, learned the basics of management and how to work with managers in designing information systems. The MISs were redesigned so that they more closely fit managers' needs, and the MIS eventually became established as a major computer application area.

The Different Views of MIS

There has never been complete agreement on what the term MIS means.[1] Although there have been a seemingly infinite number of views, we can boil them all down into three categories. One view of MIS is that it has been replaced. A second is that MIS includes all business applications of the computer. A third is that the MIS is an organizational resource.

The View that MIS Has Been Replaced   The MIS was a dramatic break from EDP, recognizing that the computer could be used for something other than processing data. During the period from the mid-1960s until the mid-1970s, there were only two computer applications in business—EDP and MIS. Of the two, MIS received most of the attention. However, when the DSS concept came along in the early 1970s, it lured many supporters from the MIS camp.

The people who gave up on MIS undoubtedly were influenced by the early MIS failures. The failures were seen as evidence of a faulty concept. In some cases, the MIS was viewed as an example of the **total systems approach**—an effort to achieve one single information system that could satisfy *all of the information needs of all managers*. Had that been the guiding principle of the MIS concept then it deserved failure, because no single system can achieve that goal. However, that was never the intent.

To this day, many people equate the term MIS with voluminous printouts. The system is seen as providing more information than managers can handle and doing

---

[1] For a good sample of the early controversy surrounding the MIS concept, *see* Russell L. Ackoff, "Management Misinformation Systems," *Management Science* 14 (December 1967), B147–B156 and Alfred Rappaport, "Management Misinformation Systems—Another Perspective," *Management Science* 15 (December 1968), B133–B136. *See also* Walter J. Kennevan, "MIS Universe," *Data Management* 8 (September 1970), 62–64 and John Dearden, "MIS Is a Mirage," *Harvard Business Review* 50 (January–February 1972), 90–99.

more harm than good. This situation is called **information overload**. In too many instances that also happened, but, again, it was not the intent.

The weakness of this view that DSS replaced MIS is the argument that the MIS did not support decision making. That is simply not the case. From the very beginning, the main objective of the MIS has been to help managers make decisions. Writing in 1966, Philip Kotler, a professor of marketing at Northwestern University, described a special information system for marketing called the MIAC (Marketing Information and Analysis Center). According to Kotler, the MIAC

> "... will function as the marketing nerve center for the company and will not only provide instantaneous information to meet a variety of executive needs but also will develop all kinds of analytical and decision aids for executives...."[2]

Another MIS pioneer, Joel D. Aron of IBM, defined MIS in 1969 as "an information system which provides the manager with that informtion he needs to make decisions."[3]

Early MIS failures were not due to a faulty concept but to a faulty implementation of a concept that remains inherently sound. The MIS concept was, and still is, the recognition that managers use information in making decisions, and the computer can provide some of that information.

The View that MIS Includes All Computer Applications   Another group did not attempt to completely eliminate MIS when DSS came along but, instead, gave it a new role. MIS became the umbrella for all business applications of the computer. This view is a popular one. On college campuses you find students majoring in MIS, there are MIS professors and MIS research centers, and in college libraries you find MIS journals. In many companies you find that the computer department is named the MIS department, that it is headed by a vice president of MIS, and that executive guidance is provided by an MIS committee.

The problem with this view, however, is that by making the MIS mean everything, it means nothing. There is no specific computer application that can be labeled MIS. What, then, do you do about concepts that are currently stimulating a great deal of interest—concepts such as the executive information system and the human resource information system?

The View that the MIS is an Organizational Resource   One way to overcome the limitations of the first two views—that the MIS still exists and that it must mean something specific—is to view MIS as it was originally conceived—as an organizational resource.

This is the view expressed in Chapter 1, when we identified the computer-

---

[2] Philip Kotler, "A Design for the Firm's Marketing Nerve Center," *Business Horizons* 9 (Fall 1966), 70.

[3] Joel D. Aron, "Information Systems in Perspective," *Computing Surveys* 1 (December 1969), 213–36.

based information system, or CBIS, as the umbrella for all business applications, and the MIS as a CBIS subsystem. In this structure, MIS represents organizational efforts to apply the computer as an information resource for decision making, and DSS represents efforts of individual managers, or small, well-defined groups of managers working as teams, to apply the computer in the same manner.

This means that the MIS and DSS can use the same hardware, software, and database, and that the information can be provided in the same forms. The *main* distinction is in terms of *who* uses the systems and *how* the information is applied.

If a system is designed to help a *large group of managers*, such as those in the entire firm or in a functional area or on an organizational level, solve a problem by providing information about the *problem*, then the system is an MIS or an MIS subsystem. The managers must decide whether the information is of value, and, if so, where in the problem-solving process it can be used. The managers must use their own judgment in applying the information.

If, on the other hand, a system is designed to help a *single manager or a small group of managers working as a team* solve a problem by providing information about *specific decisions*, then the system is a DSS. Less is required of the manager in determining how to apply the information because that capability has been built into the DSS. However, the manager, as with the MIS, must use his or her judgment in evaluating the output. We will return to the distinction between MIS and DSS in Chapter 13 when we describe the DSS.

A Definition of MIS

We define a **management information system (MIS)** as a computer-based system that makes information available to users with similar needs. The users usually comprise a formal organizational entity—the firm or a subsidiary subunit. The information describes the firm or one of its major systems in terms of what has happened in the past, what is happening now, and what is likely to happen in the future. The information is made available in the form of periodic reports, special reports, and outputs of mathematical simulations. The information output is used by both managers and nonmanagers in the firm as they make decisions to solve problems.

An MIS Model

Our definition can be illustrated with the MIS model in Figure 12.1. The database contains the data provided by the data processing system. In addition, both data and information are entered from the environment. The database contents are used by software that produces periodic and special reports, and mathematical models that simulate various aspects of the firm's operations. The software outputs are used by persons within the firm, who have the responsibility of solving the firm's problems. Unlike the data processing system, the MIS has no obligation to provide information to the environment.

FIGURE 12.1

An MIS Model

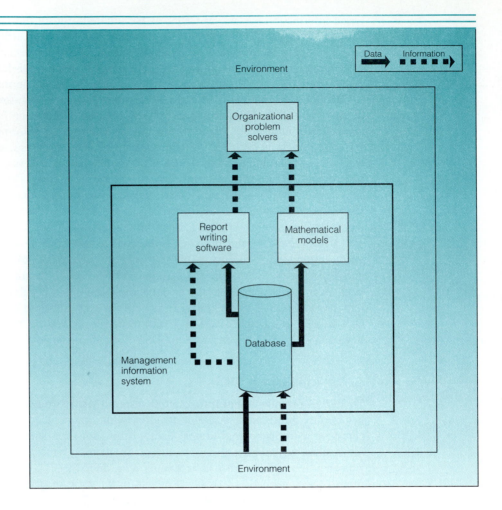

THE CONCEPT OF ORGANIZATIONAL
INFORMATION SUBSYSTEMS

As firms gained experience in implementing company-wide MIS designs, managers in certain areas began applying the concept to their own needs. These **functional information systems**, or subsets of the MIS that are tailored to meet users' needs for information concerning the functional areas, received much publicity in some areas and somewhat less in others. Marketing was the first area to conceive the notion of a functional information system, and considerable effort was spent in describing how the computer could be applied to the entire range of marketing operations. There was also considerable interest in accounting, where the concept of an accounting information system became established. An **accounting infor-**

mation system is essentially the data processing system that we described in the previous chapter.

In the following sections we introduce the MIS subsystems that are closely aligned with the major oganizational subunits. We first recognize information systems designed for use by executives. Then we describe information systems for functional areas—marketing, manufacturing, finance, and human resources.

As we discuss these organizational subsystems, it is important that you keep in mind that there is nothing *physically* separating them. They can be illustrated with a diagram, such as the one in Figure 12.2, which shows clear lines of separation, but this is not a physical separation. Much of the database that is used by one organizational subsystem can also used by others, and there may be much sharing of programs. Organizational information systems are a *logical*, rather than a *physical*, way of thinking about the MIS.

Another important point is that the functional systems are not an *alternative* to having a firm-wide MIS. It would be difficult for a firm to have a good MIS if one or more of the functional areas did not contribute. The recommended strategy is to first implement an MIS, and then follow up with organizational subsystems.

FIGURE 12.2
Organizational
Information
Systems

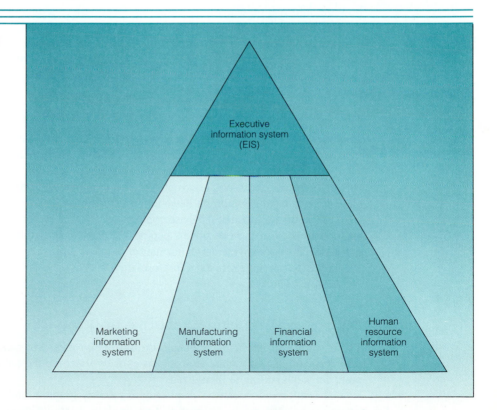

Executive
information system
(EIS)

Marketing
information
system

Manufacturing
information
system

Financial
information
system

Human
resource
information
system

EXECUTIVE INFORMATION SYSTEMS

The organizational information system that is intended for use by the firm's executives is just now getting off the ground. The main reason for its late start is because executive activity is not very well structured, and information specialists have less understanding of problem solving on the executive level than on lower management levels. As a result, computer use has gradually worked its way up through the organization and now is receiving attention in the executive suite. EIS is now one of the hottest areas in business computing. An **executive information system (EIS)** is a system that is designed specifically for managers on the strategic planning level.

Executive Support Systems (ESS)

Sometimes the term executive support system, or ESS, is used. Just as information scientists have had difficulty in distinguishing MIS and DSS, the distinction between EIS and ESS is also not well defined. Comshare, the leading marketer of mainframe EIS and ESS software, refers to its Executive Edge system as an ESS. According to Comshare, an EIS meets the *information* needs of executives, but an **executive support system (ESS)** supports their *information*, *communications*, and *analysis* needs. The ESS does this by providing **intelligence**—an understanding of how the information can affect operations. That understanding is gained primarily through the use of mathematical modeling.

Although there is a difference between the ESS and the EIS in terms of their definitions, the term EIS has been adopted as the general term that describes all executive computer use. For this reason, we will use EIS in our discussion.

An Executive Information System Model

A model of an EIS is pictured in Figure 12.3. The firm's database contains primarily data from the data processing system and is supplemented with electronic mailboxes that the executives use to send and receive electronic mail, and electronic calendars, which executives use to plan their appointments. Staff members have the capability of keying in current news and explanations.

EIS software uses the database contents to produce preformatted displays that are downloaded to the executive's personal computer and stored in the executive database. The executive enters information requests and receives the displays.

All EISs are not restricted to preformatted displays, but that approach has been the most popular.

Dialog between the Executive and the EIS

The executive enters instructions into the system by means of menus. Menu selection is accomplished by means of a mouse, or by touching the screen. The requirement for keyboarding is minimized.

The information can be displayed in tabular, graphic, and narrative forms. Some of the software is designed to first produce a tabular display that the exec-

FIGURE 12.3

An Executive Information System Model

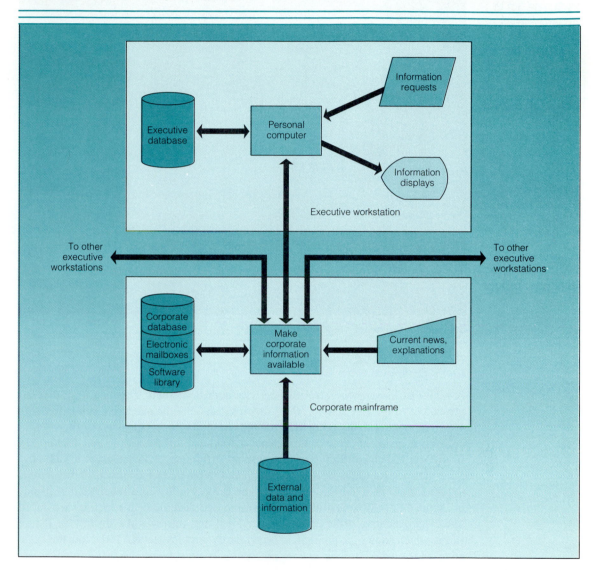

utive can quickly switch to a graphic display. A narrative explanation of the tabular or graphic data can be keyed in by a staff assistant, or it can be produced by artificial intelligence. Figure 12.4 shows a display produced by the EIS, marketed by Comshare. The explanation in the right hand half of the screen was produced by the system's artificial intelligence feature.

FIGURE 12.4

An Information Display That Includes a Computer-generated Narrative Explanation

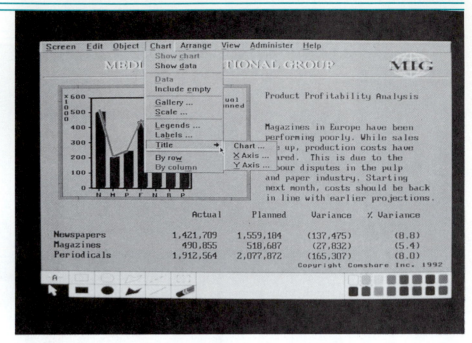

Courtesy of Canshare 1992 Commander 3.0

Drill Down

A term that has grown out of EIS activity is drilled down. This is a term that has grown out of the EIS activity. **Drill down** means that the executive can begin with an overview and then gradually retrieve information in greater detail. Figure 12.5 contains a series of three screen displays produced by the Command Center EIS from Pilot Executive Software. The display in Figure 12.5a indicates a high negative variance for radio profit when compared to the budget or quota. The executive requests more detailed information on the radio product and receives the display in Figure 12.5b. It is now clear that research and development expenses are out of line. The executive drills down another level and retrieves the display in Figure 12.5c, which shows the problem to be primarily with Project RA100. Now the executive knows where to concentrate problem-solving activity.

Routes to the EIS

There are three main routes to obtaining the software that produces the executive information.

1. The firm's information specialists can develop *custom software*.
2. The executives can use *application-development software* such as electronic spreadsheets, database management systems, and graphics packages.
3. The firm can purchase *special EIS software*.

FIGURE 12.5
The Drill-down
Technique

AMERICAN ELECTRONICS STANDARD FINANCIAL REPORTS
Consumer

Current Month	Actual	% Total	Budget	% Total	Variance	% Var.
Profit Before Tax						
Radio ◆	1,771	24.83%	2,084	28.71%	– 313	– 15.0%
Stereo	2,256	31.63%	2,193	30.21%	63	2.9%
Tape Recorder	569	7.98%	504	6.94%	65	12.9%
Television	2,537	35.57%	2,478	34.14%	59	2.4%
Total	7,133	100.00%	7,259	100.00%	– 126	– 1.7%

(a) Summary Display

**(b) Display One
Level Down**

AMERICAN ELECTRONICS STANDARD FINANCIAL REPORTS
Consumer Radio

Current Month	Actual	% Total	Budget	% Total	Variance	% Var.
Net Sales	12,986	100.00%	12,741	100.00%	245	1.9%
Cost of Sales	– 7,488	– 57.66%	– 7,213	– 56.61%	– 275	3.8%
Gross Margin	5,498	42.34%	5,528	43.39%	– 30	– .5%
Research & Devel. ◆	1,694	13.04%	1,412	11.08%	282	20.0%
Selling & Mktg.	1,505	11.59%	1,498	11.76%	7	.5%
General & Admin.	511	3.94%	522	4.10%	– 11	– 2.1%
Interest Income	60	.46%	62	.49%	– 2	– 3.2%
Interest Expense	– 77	– .59%	– 74	– .58%	– 3	4.1%
Before Tax Profit	1,771	13.64%	2,084	16.36%	– 313	– 15.0%

AMERICAN ELECTRONICS STANDARD FINANCIAL REPORTS
Consumer Radio Research & Devel.

Current Month	Actual	% Total	Budget	% Total	Variance	% Var.
Project RA100 ◆	517	30.52%	303	21.46%	214	70.6%
Project RA200	179	10.57%	176	12.46%	3	1.7%
Project RA300	115	6.79%	80	5.67%	35	43.8%
Project RA400	315	18.60%	288	20.40%	27	9.4%
Project RA500	231	13.64%	225	15.93%	6	2.7%
Project RA600	337	19.89%	340	24.08%	– 3	– .9%
Total R&D Expense	1,694	100.00%	1,412	100.00%	282	20.0%

**(c) Display Two
Levels Down**

Courtesy of Pilot Executive Software.

The third approach of using software designed especially for executives is creating the most interest. These off-the-shelf systems are available for computers of all sizes and feature user-friendly interfaces. The firm's information services staff can incorporate the same techniques into the custom EIS software.

It is too soon to tell whether the EIS and ESS concepts will stick at the executive level. Thus far, the reception has been good. It is likely that innovations pioneered at the executive level, such as the easy retrieval of preformatted displays, will trickle down to lower management levels in future MIS and DSS designs.

MARKETING INFORMATION SYSTEMS

A **marketing information system** is a subset of the management information system, which provides information to be used in solving the firm's marketing problems.

Figure 12.6 is a model that shows the basic structure of the marketing information system. We will use the same format for all of the other functional information systems as well. The **input subsystems** gather data and information that is entered in the database. The **output subsystems** consist of computer programs that transform the data into information for the users.

Marketing Input Subsystems[4]

Much of the marketing data and information is provided by the **data processing subsystem** that was described in Chapter 11. This data provides a detailed record of sales activity, which can provide the basis for periodic reports and mathematical models.

[4]The classification of the input subsystems is based on Philip Kotler, *Marketing Management: Analysis, Planning, and Control,* 2d ed. (Englewood Cliffs, NJ: Prentice-Hall, 1972), 292–361.

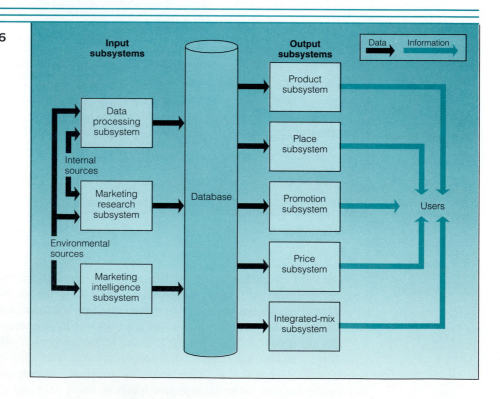

FIGURE 12.6
A Model of a Marketing Information System

The **marketing research subsystem** gathers data concerning any aspect of the firm's marketing operations but primarily those that involve customers and prospective customers. Data is gathered primarily by means of surveys.

The **marketing intelligence subsystem** gathers data and information concerning the firm's competitors. Historically, this system has operated in a very informal manner. For example, the firm's marketing representatives shop at competitors' stores and attend open houses of competitors' offices and plants. Recently, however, there has been a high level of activity in buying intelligence in the form of commercial databases.

The intelligence activity of the functional information systems is an ethical activity and is not to be confused with **industrial espionage**, which is a form of spying.

You will notice from the model in the figure that the input subsystems gather data and information from a combination of internal and environmental sources. This pattern is typical for all of the functional information systems.

Marketing Output Subsystems[5]

All of the products and services that are offered by the marketing function are referred to as the **marketing mix**. They include the *product*; the *place* where the product is sold; *promotion*, such as personal selling and advertising; and the product *price*.

The model uses the mix ingredients as a way to classify the output subsystems. All software that informs the manager about the product is included in the **product subsystem**. All software that describes how the product is distributed to the customers is included in the **place subsystem**. Likewise, the software that keeps the manager posted concerning personal selling and advertising is in the **promotion subsystem**, and all information about pricing is provided by the **pricing subsystem**. The manager can use these subsystems separately or in combination. The **integrated-mix subsystem** allows the manager to develop marketing strategies that use the mix ingredients in a combined manner.

Each output subsystem box in the model can represent multiple computer programs. There are programs that print or display periodic reports, programs that facilitate database queries, and programs that serve as mathematical models.

A Marketing Information System Example

A classic example of how problem-solving information can be produced from data provided by the data processing system is sales analysis. **Sales analysis** is the study of the firm's sales activity in terms of *which products* are being sold, *which cus-*

---

[5]The output subsystems are based on Richard H. Brien and James E. Stafford, "Marketing Information Systems: A New Dimension for Marketing Research," *Journal of Marketing* 32 (July 1968), 19–23.

FIGURE 12.7

A Sales by
Product Report

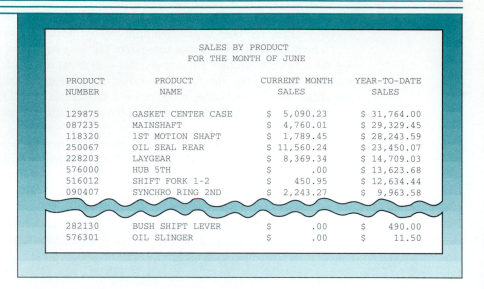

```
                        SALES BY PRODUCT
                      FOR THE MONTH OF JUNE

     PRODUCT        PRODUCT           CURRENT MONTH      YEAR-TO-DATE
     NUMBER         NAME                  SALES             SALES

     129875     GASKET CENTER CASE    $    5,090.23     $  31,764.00
     087235     MAINSHAFT             $    4,760.01     $  29,329.45
     118320     1ST MOTION SHAFT      $    1,789.45     $  28,243.59
     250067     OIL SEAL REAR         $   11,560.24     $  23,450.07
     228203     LAYGEAR               $    8,369.34     $  14,709.03
     576000     HUB 5TH               $         .00     $  13,623.68
     516012     SHIFT FORK 1-2        $      450.95     $  12,634.44
     090407     SYNCHRO RING 2ND      $    2,243.27     $   9,963.58


     282130     BUSH SHIFT LEVER      $         .00     $     490.00
     576301     OIL SLINGER           $         .00     $      11.50
```

tomers are buying the products, and *which sales representatives* are selling the products.

A **sales by product report** appears in Figure 12.7. The products are listed in a descending sequence based on year-to-date sales so that the highest-selling products are listed first. This technique illustrates how the sequence of the report information can be used to facilitate management by exception.

For each of the output systems, management decided that certain information could be helpful in solving marketing problems. Software was developed to provide the information on the marketing mix ingredients in a variety of ways.

MANUFACTURING INFORMATION SYSTEMS

Managers in the manufacturing area have used the computer as both a component of the physical system and as a conceptual information system. The computer is used in the physical production system for such applications as computer-aided design (CAD) and computer-aided manufacturing (CAM), which were introduced in Chapter 8. As a conceptual information system, use has also been made of computers in scheduling production, controlling inventory, controlling production quality, and reporting on production costs. All of these applications, physical and conceptual, have been given the name **computer integrated manufacturing (CIM)**.

Information system applications have been integrated into the model of a manufacturing information system in Figure 12.8. A **manufacturing information sys-**

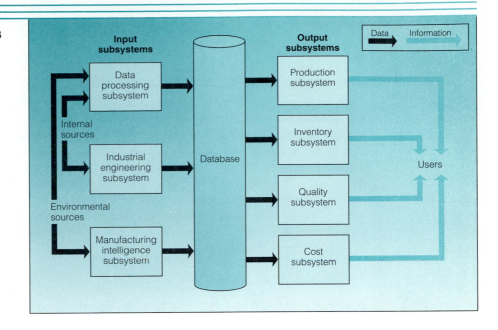

FIGURE 12.8

A Model of a
Manufacturing
Information
System

tem is a subset of the management information system, which provides information to be used in solving the firm's manufacturing problems. The model does not include the physical applications such as CAD/CAM.

Manufacturing Input Subsystems

The data collection terminals described in Chapter 9 are an example of how the **data processing subsystem** is used in manufacturing. The terminals are located throughout the plant to record each major activity—from receipt of raw materials to shipment of finished goods. The terminals enable the computer to be an up-to-the-minute conceptual representation of the physical manufacturing system.

Additional data describing the internal manufacturing operation is provided by the **industrial engineering subsystem**. This subsystem consists of the industrial engineers, or IEs, who study production processes for the purpose of making them more efficient. IEs spend much of their time designing *physical* production systems by deciding where to locate plants, how to arrange production lines, and the sequence in which processes should be performed. The IEs also are involved in *conceptual* systems such as scheduling and inventory. The data and information that are provided by the IEs represent the industrial engineering subsystem.

The **manufacturing intelligence subsystem** provides data and information about two elements in the firm's environment—the suppliers, and labor unions. Supplier data supplements that which is provided by the purchasing and receiving subsystems of the data processing system. Labor union data can be gathered by means of special studies, and labor union information can be gathered informally by personal contact with union leaders and members.

Manufacturing Output Subsystems

The four output subsystems measure separate dimensions of the production process. The **production subsystem** measures the process in terms of *time*—tracking the work flow from one step to the next. The **inventory subsystem** measures the *volume* of production activity as the inventory is transformed from raw materials into work-in-process and finally into finished goods. The **quality subsystem** measures the *quality* of the materials as they are transformed. Raw materials are checked for quality when they are received from suppliers, quality-control checks are made at different points in the production process, and a final check is made of finished goods before they leave the plant. The **cost subsystem** measures the *costs* that are incurred in the production process.

A Manufacturing Information System Example

As an example of how the production subsystem tracks the flow of a job, let us assume that a company manufactures bicycle flashlights—the type that you strap on your leg so that the light bobs up and down as you pedal. A clear lens mounted on the front provides some light ahead, and a red lens at the rear warns the motorists behind.

The lights are assembled from several parts. The list of parts is called the **bill of material**, and it is like a recipe. Both the flashlight and its bill of material are pictured in Figure 12.9.

The process of assembling the flashlights follows the production flows that are illustrated in Figure 12.10. The industrial engineer has determined that work can be done on two flows simultaneously to reduce production time. One flow is for assembling the cylinder, represented by the circles that are numbered 1 through 4. Each number represents a step in the production process. The other flow is for the top and is represented by the squares that are numbered 5 through 8. In Step 9 the top assembly is attached to the cylinder assembly and the result is a finished flashlight.

The **production schedule** determines when the steps of the production process will be performed. A program in the production subsystem creates the schedule that appears in Figure 12.11. On the left-hand side the date and time are printed for the release of each of the parts from raw materials inventory. When the parts are released, they are transported to the workstation where they will be used. The nine production steps are listed in the center, along with a start date and time for each. The *expected completion* dates and times on the right-hand side are computed from production standards that have been provided by the industrial engineering subsystem and the data processing subsystem.

FIGURE 12.9
Component Parts
and Bill of
Material of a
Finished Product

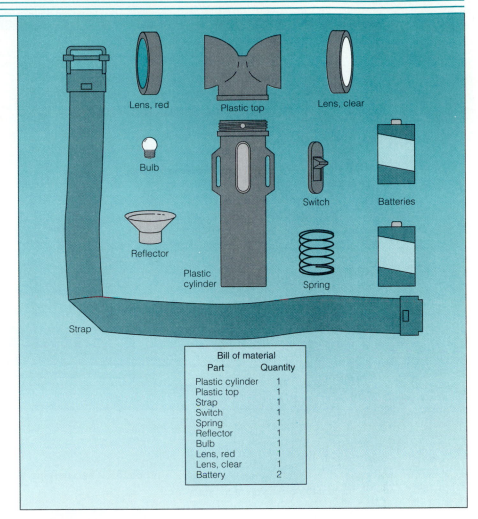

As the work is performed, employees use data collection terminals at their workstations to record the start and stop times for each step. The terminal data reflects *actual completion* dates and times, which can be compared to the planned figures. The comparison gauges the efficiency of the production operation, as well as the accuracy of the production standards.

The production subsystem provides management with a picture of not only production plans but also the current status. A manager, who is seeking to determine the status of a particular job, can query the database and obtain a display such as the one illustrated in Figure 12.12.

In this example, manufacturing management determined that an ability to query the database to learn the status of jobs in progress would be valuable in

FIGURE 12.10

Job Flow through
the Plant

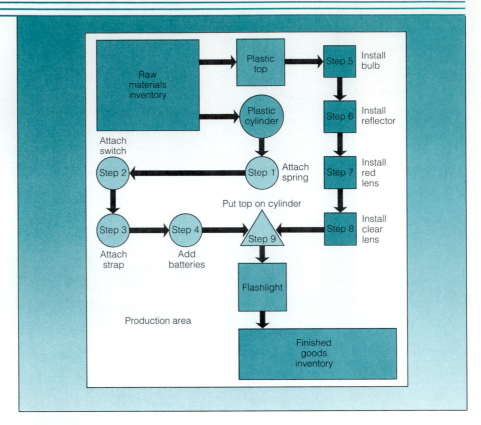

solving a wide range of production problems. The querying ability is provided by
the database management software.

FINANCIAL INFORMATION SYSTEMS

The **financial information system** pictured in Figure 12.13 is designed to provide
information concerning the money flow to users throughout the firm. The users are
primarily managers who use the information to manage their resources.

Financial Input Subsystems

An **internal audit subsystem** assists the **data processing subsystem** in providing
internal data and information. Larger firms usually have a staff of **internal auditors**

FIGURE 12.11

A Production
Schedule

```
                          PRODUCTION SCHEDULE

       JOB NAME        BICYCLE FLASHLIGHT
       JOB NO.         79-133

        RAW              RELEASE       PRODUCTION      START        COMPLETION
       MATLS          DATE   TIME        STEP        DATE   TIME    DATE   TIME

       CYLINDER       10-24  0800
       SPRING         10-24  0800     1-ATTCH SPRG   10-24  0838    10-24  1430
       SWITCH         10-24  1430     2-ATTCH SW     10-24  1500    10-26  0900
       STRAP          10-26  0930     3-ATTCH STRP   10-26  0950    10-26  1330
       BATTERY        10-26  1345     4-ADD BATTS    10-26  1404    10-26  1700
       TOP            10-23  0900
       BULB           10-23  0900     5-INST BULB    10-23  0930    10-23  1522
       REFLECTOR      10-23  1530     6-INST REF     10-23  1600    10-25  1000
       LENS RED       10-25  1030     7-INST LNSR    10-25  1100    10-26  0920
       LENS CLEAR     10-26  0930     8-INST LNSC    10-26  1000    10-26  1620
                                      9-ATTCH TOP    10-27  0800    10-27  1352
```

who periodically study the firm's conceptual systems to ensure that the integrity of the data is maintained.

The **financial intelligence subsystem** gathers information from the environmental elements that influence the money flow—the financial community, stockholders and owners, and the government. As with marketing intelligence, the approach to gathering data and information by informal means is changing to incorporate computer technology. It is possible to subscribe to computer-based financial databases and news services, and many firms are taking advantage of those opportunities.

Financial Output Subsystems

The **forecasting subsystem** conducts long-range forecasts five to ten years into the future to provide the basis for strategic planning. The **funds management subsystem** is concerned with the flow of money through the firm. Management wants to know in advance of cash surpluses and deficits so that they can plan how to handle them. The **control subsystem** prepares the annual operating budget and then provides feedback information to the managers so that they can monitor their actual expenses compared with the budget.

A Financial Information System Example

Our first two examples of functional information systems have emphasized the output subsystems. The input subsystem can create information value as well.

FIGURE 12.12

A Job Status
Report Displayed
on a Screen

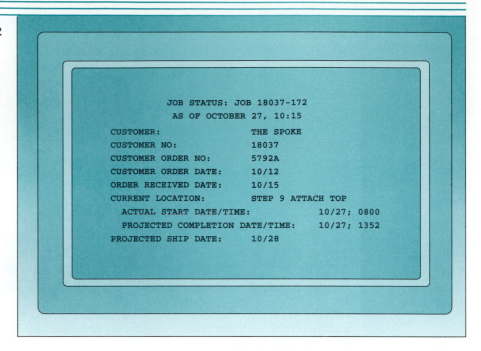

```
                    JOB STATUS: JOB 18037-172
                    AS OF OCTOBER 27, 10:15
         CUSTOMER:                    THE SPOKE
         CUSTOMER NO:                 18037
         CUSTOMER ORDER NO:           5792A
         CUSTOMER ORDER DATE:         10/12
         ORDER RECEIVED DATE:         10/15
         CURRENT LOCATION:            STEP 9 ATTACH TOP
           ACTUAL START DATE/TIME:              10/27; 0800
             PROJECTED COMPLETION DATE/TIME:    10/27; 1352
         PROJECTED SHIP DATE:    10/28
```

FIGURE 12.13

A Model of a
Financial
Information
System

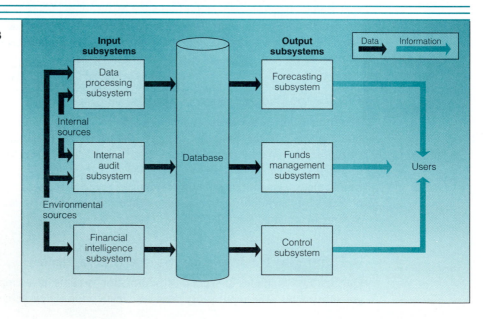

Many firms make financial intelligence available to their managers in the form of financial databases such as the Dow Jones News/Retrieval Service. The DJNRS provides the ability to obtain current information from *The Wall Street Journal* in the form of screen displays. Firms subscribe to the service, and users query the DJNRS database to remain current on the financial environment. Figure 12.14 provides an example of the output that is possible.

HUMAN RESOURCE INFORMATION SYSTEMS

Personnel is one of the physical resources that flow through the firm, and the human resources department plays a key role in that flow. The human resources department, called HR, is a functional area of the firm, performing a staff function. In a large firm, HR might be headed by a vice president of human resources.

HR is responsible for bringing personnel from the environment into the firm. This involves recruiting, interviewing, and testing. Once personnel have been hired, HR maintains employee records and can offer various types of educational and training programs. For example, HR instructors may assist systems analysts in educating users and participants during the implementation phase of the SLC. When

FIGURE 12.14
A Display of Dow Jones Information

FIGURE 12.15

A Model of a
Human Resource
Information
System

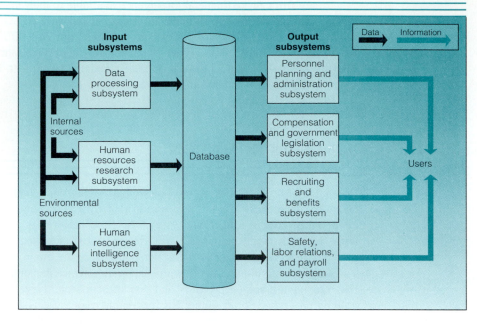

personnel terminate their employment, HR conducts exit interviews to gain insight concerning the firm's human relations policies and administers benefit programs to retired employees.

The system that provides information on the firm's human resources is the **human resource information system (HRIS)**. The name **human resource management system (HRMS)** is also being used to an increasing degree. The model of the HRIS is shown in Figure 12.15.

HRIS Input Subsystems

The **data processing subsystem** provides primarily financial data that relates to the firm's personnel. The responsibility for all or part of the firm's payroll application is usually included in the HRIS. This financial data is combined with nonfinancial data to present a complete picture of the firm's personnel resources.

Special studies of the firm's jobs are performed by the **human resources research subsystem**. These studies reveal the tasks that are performed, the knowledge and skills that are required, and the appropriate levels of compensation. Some of these studies require an expertise that is not found within the HR units, and the talents of HR consultants are used.

HR must remain current on the environmental influences that affect the personnel flow, and this is the responsibility of the **human resources intelligence subsystem**. Information is gathered from:

- The *financial community*, which provides economic forecasts that influence long-range personnel planning.
- *Labor unions*, the *local community*, and even *competitors*, who serve as the sources of new hires.
- *Suppliers*, such as employment agencies, colleges, and executive search firms, which channel personnel to the firm.
- The *government*, which passes legislation supporting and administering equal employment opportunity (EEO), the affirmative action program (AAP), and the occupational safety and health administration (OSHA). Such legislation exerts a strong influence on the firm's personnel policies and practices.

No other functional area has a responsibility for staying current on so many environmental elements as does HR.

HRIS Output Subsystems [6]

The **personnel planning and administration subsystem** includes applications such as performance appraisal, organization charting, training, and attendance. The common practice is for the managers to formally appraise the performance of each of their employees on an annual basis. The computer ensures that the appraisals are performed, and stores the results. An example of an organization chart, drawn with special charting software, appears in Figure 12.16.

The **compensation and government legislation subsystem** has been computerized to a greater degree than any of the other output subsystems because it deals with employee pay and government influence.[7] Pay applications include merit increases, executive compensation, salary forecasts, and bonus incentives. Legislation applications include EEO records and EEO analysis.

The **recruiting and benefits subsystem** includes applications such as applicant tracking that assists in bringing new employees into the firm, relocation studies that assist management in assigning current employees, and benefits applications that support retired employees. Many firms have instituted *cafeteria-style benefits plans*. Such plans enable employees to select the benefits that they want but make administration extremely complex.

The output subsystem that has been achieved to the least degree is the **safety, labor relations, and payroll subsystem**.[8] The most popular application in this category is payroll. Many less firms have implemented applications that deal with accidents, health records, toxic substance, grievances, and disciplinary action.

---

[6]These output subsystems are based on the categories of HRIS applications that are used by the Association of Human Resource Systems Professionals.

[7] *1990–1991 Systems Survey* (Dallas, TX: The Association of Human Resource Systems Professionals, 1991), 19.

[8] *Ibid*, 21.

FIGURE 12.16

Special Charting Software Enables Management to Keep Documentation Current on the Dynamic Organizational Structure

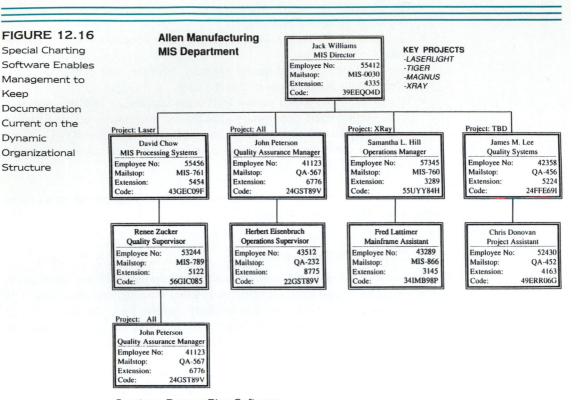

Courtesy Banner Blue Software

An HRIS Example

Job profile matching is an example of an application in the personnel planning and administration subsystem. It helps management plan career paths within the firm that can be made available to the employees.[9] Each job in the company is studied to determine the tasks that are performed and the amount of time spent on each. Jobs often consist of a hundred or more tasks. The list of tasks and times represent the **job profile**.

All of the job profiles are then matched by the computer to determine the degree of similarity. Similarity is measured in terms of **overlap**—the percentage of time spent on the same tasks.

Figure 12.17 shows the overlap between jobs in the computer operator job family. The arrows connecting the job titles are labeled with the overlap percent-

[9]Material for this section was contributed by Dwain R. Boelter of Personnel Decisions, Inc. of Minneapolis, and P. R. Jeanneret of Jeanneret & Associates, Inc. of Houston. The author also acknowledges the assistance provided by Richard D. Arvey and Gerardine DeSanctis of the University of Minnesota.

FIGURE 12.17

Job Overlap Helps to Identify Career Paths

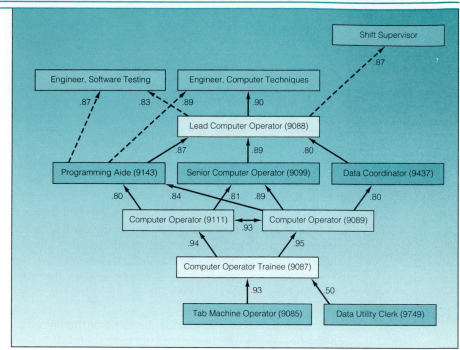

ages. The solid arrows indicate that an individual should be able to progress from one position to the next given the training and experience gathered in the lower-level position. The dotted arrows indicate that the progression to the higher-level position would require education or training not typically received in the lower-level position.

This application identifies a series of higher positions that involve many of the tasks employees now perform. When employees are promoted, only the new tasks must be learned. The result is better job performance, more frequent promotions, and higher morale than if career planning is not accomplished.

THE MIS AND HUMAN FACTORS CONSIDERATIONS

Computer applications and projects that develop those applications have always been subjected to certain behavioral influences. The first computer projects stimulated fear in employees, that they would lose their jobs. As it turned out, the computer did not produce mass layoffs, but fear still persists. Today's employees fear the impact that the computer will have on their interpersonal relationships and even their health and safety. All of these influences that can affect the performance of employees as they perform their computer-related tasks are termed **human factors considerations**.

Fear as the Underlying Human Factors Consideration

The employees of the firms that installed the first data processing systems experienced fear. They feared that the computers would put them out of work, and in some firms that actually happened. However, even in those firms where management had no intention of replacing people with the computer, the employees were still distrustful and expected the worst. These fears often increased the difficulty of implementing the data processing systems.

Many employees reacted in the same way when firms embarked on their second stage of computer use by implementing management information systems. The employees feared that "Big Brother" would use the systems to spy on them and invade their privacy. Some office automation applications, such as electronic mail, have had this same influence. In at least one firm, the employees accused management of using electronic mail for eavesdropping on their internal communications.[10]

What must be kept in mind is the fact that the DP system, the MIS, and OA applications such as electronic mail are *organizational* systems. As such, they are implemented to meet the general needs of large groups rather than individuals. Individual employees who perceive no real benefit from the systems cannot only fail to lend their support but can actively work toward their destruction.

DSSs and expert systems, on the other hand, offer much less of a behavioral threat. The reason is that these systems are usually implemented at the request of the users who stand to benefit from their use.

How Employees Express Their Fears When employees are afraid of the computer they can react in various ways. The healthiest response is to openly express their fears to management. Management then has the opportunity to respond and put the fears to rest. Many times, however, the employees will keep their fears to themselves and secretly take action to sabotage the system.

How Managers Express Their Fears Rank and file employees are not the only ones who can throw up roadblocks to computer use. Managers can have fears of their own. At times the managers in one functional area do not want to share their information with others. Their reasoning is that they have gone to the expense of gathering the information and should be able to control its use. While

---

[10] Glenn Rifkin, "Do Employees Have a Right to Electronic Privacy," *New York Times,* December 8, 1991, Section 3, Page 8.

such attitudes are clearly not in the best interests of the firm as a whole, they are a reality of human nature.

A Program to Minimize Fear and Its Effects

The designers of information systems must be aware of how fear on the part of both employees and managers can affect the success or failure of development projects and operational systems. The firm's management, assisted by the information specialists, can minimize fear and its detrimental effects by taking the four following steps:

1. Use the computer as a means of achieving **job enhancement** by giving the computer the task of doing the redundant, boring work, and giving the employees the tasks that challenge their abilities.
2. Use **formal communications** to keep the employees aware of the firm's intentions. The announcements by top management at the beginning of the analysis and implementation phases of the system life cycle are examples of this strategy.
3. Build a relationship of **trust** between the employees, the information specialists, and management. Such a relationship is achieved by being honest about the projected impacts of computer systems, and in living up to promises. Such formal communications and the inclusion of users on the project teams go a long way to achieve trust.
4. Align the **employees' needs** with the objectives of the firm. First, identify the employees' needs. Then, motivate the employees by showing them that work toward the firm's objectives also helps them to meet their own needs.

Information specialists can contribute to each of these four steps. These specialists often observe the resistance that employees keep hidden from management and can also detect managers who are not putting their full weight behind projects. Information specialists should be trained to recognize and respond to resistance. These behavioral skills are just as important as technical skills.

PUTTING THE MIS IN PERSPECTIVE

Although the topic of the chapter is the organization-wide MIS, we have devoted the majority of the discussion to functional information systems. We took this approach because most of the current MIS developmental effort is being mounted by organizational subunits. The manufacturing area has been the most aggressive over the long term in implementing CAD/CAM, materials requirements planning (MRP) systems, and computer integrated manufacturing (CIM). But two other subunits are currently exhibiting the highest level of activity. The HR area is implementing HRISs, and the strategic planning level is implementing EIS and ESSs. All of this activity is expected to continue.

The MIS and Problem Solving

The MIS and its organizational subsystems contribute to problem solving in two basic ways. First, they provide organization-wide information resources to large numbers of managers. Second, they lend especially strong support in problem identification and understanding.

Organization-Wide Information Resources　The MIS is an organization-wide effort to provide problem-solving information. The system is a formal commitment by executives to make the computer available to all managers. The MIS sets the stage for accomplishments in the other areas—DSS, OA, and expert systems.

Problem Identification and Understanding　The main idea behind the MIS is to keep a continuous supply of information flowing to the manager. The manager uses the MIS primarily to signal problems or impending problems, and then to understand them by pinpointing their locations and causes.

The main weakness of MIS is that it is not aimed at the specific needs of the individual problem solvers. Very often the MIS does not provide exactly the information that is needed to solve problems once they have been identified and understood. The decision support system concept was created in response to that need, and we will turn our attention to this CBIS subsystem in the next chapter.

SUMMARY

Early MIS efforts were largely unsuccessful because managers had difficulty articulating their information needs. Over time the communication barrier between managers and information specialists dissolved and firms implemented successful systems.

There has always been disagreement concerning what an MIS is. Some people feel that the MIS is a thing of the past, whereas others regard it as meaning all business computing. We take the position that it is an organizational resource. An MIS provides information to groups of managers with similar needs. The information spans the past, the present, and the future, and is provided in the form of periodic reports, special reports, and simulation results. The information is used by managers in decision making.

The MIS concept was so well received that managers in the functional areas began incorporating software and data into the systems to meet their own needs. Marketing led the way and was followed by manufacturing and finance. The most current attention is being focused on the executive level and the human resources function.

Executive information systems and executive support systems feature user-friendly interfaces and emphasize database retrieval. Executives can drill down to the level of detail that they need.

The functional information systems that have been developed in marketing, manufacturing, finance, and human resource all fit a uniform architecture that consists of input subsystems, a database, and output subsystems. Three input subsystems are standard. The data processing subsystem appears in all functional information systems. A second input subsystem conducts special research projects, and a third gathers data and information from the environment. The output subsystems transform the contents of the database into formats that meet the particular needs of the users.

The behavioral influences that can affect a computer project or an operational system are called human factors considerations. The underlying factor is fear by the employees and managers that the computer will affect them in an adverse way. Management and information specialists can minimize the fear factor by using the computer to enhance jobs, keeping lines of communication open, creating an atmosphere of trust, and building systems that are compatible with employees' needs.

The MIS is an organization-wide commitment to a quality information resource. The MIS is especially valuable in identifying problems and helping managers to understand them so that they can be solved.

KEY TERMS

information overload
management information system (MIS)
functional information system
executive information system (EIS), executive
    support system (ESS)
drill down
marketing information system
computer integrated manufacturing (CIM)

manufacturing information system
bill of material
financial information system
human resource information system (HRIS),
    human resource management system
    (HRMS)
human factors considerations

KEY CONCEPTS

The MIS as an organization-wide commitment to providing problem-solving information to users on all levels within the firm

How the MIS uses the database that is provided by the data processing system

How an information system can be tailored to the special needs of managers within certain organizational subunits such as management levels or functional areas

The use of preformatted displays to keep executives current on the firm's activities

A functional information system structure that consists of input subsystems, a database, and output subsystems

The data processing subsystem as an input subsystem to all functional information systems

The need of each functional information system

for an input subsystem that is devoted to special research projects

How the input intelligence subsystems specialize in gathering data from certain environmental elements

The use of the marketing mix ingredients as a framework for providing information on marketing activity

The use of the four dimensions of production

as a framework for providing information on manufacturing activity

How the financial information system reflects the flow of money through the firm

How the human resource information system reflects the flow of personnel through the firm

Fear as the underlying human factors consideration

QUESTIONS

1. What factor minimized the task that was faced by the designers of early computer systems?

2. Why did many early MIS efforts fail?

3. What are the three different views of the MIS?

4. Is the MIS an example of the total systems approach? Explain.

5. Can a manager receive too much information? Explain.

6. Why is one functional information system not physically separate from other such systems?

7. Is there a real difference between the EIS and ESS? If so, what is it?

8. What are the three routes to the EIS? Which one is stimulating the most interest?

9. Is the drill down technique of interest to only the top management level? Support your answer.

10. Is marketing intelligence a form of industrial espionage? Explain.

11. Which functional area has done the best job of using the computer in both a physical and a conceptual way?

12. Which input subsystem includes data collection terminals?

13. Does an industrial engineer (IE) solve physical or conceptual problems?

14. What are the four dimensions of production? Specify the output subsystem that measures each dimension.

15. Why would a person who works in the raw materials stockroom need to know the production schedule?

16. Which functional information system has the responsibility for monitoring the most environmental elements? Can you explain why?

17. What is a prime underlying cause of resistance to computer projects?

18. What are four things that managers and information specialists can do to overcome fear of the computer by other managers and employees?

19. What are the two ways that the MIS supports problem solving?

20. What is the main weakness of the MIS?

TOPICS FOR DISCUSSION

1. Do you think that an individual manager can implement an MIS? What about a functional information system? A DSS?

2. Using the diagram of the eight environment elements in Figure 2.1 as a guide, which functional area has the main responsibility for each element?

3. The chapter lists four things that can be done to overcome computer fear on the part of both employees and managers. What, if anything, can be done before a person goes to work for a company to accomplish the same results?

PROBLEMS

1. Using the models of the four functional information systems as a guide, draw a general model that could be used as a guide for any type of organizational information system.

2. Using your general model from Problem 1, draw a model of an executive information system. Hint: Try to apply management the-ory in identifying the output subsystems. For example, have any of the management theorists such as Henri Fayol, Henry Mintzberg, or Robert Anthony given us any frameworks that can be used? What about management scientists such as Herbert Simon?

Hilo Wheels

Your career is progressing nicely—six successful years with one of the Big Six accounting firms in its management services division. Your performance as a computer consultant was so outstanding that you got a job offer from one of your clients, a new company that became an overnight success selling inline skates in competition with the industry leader, Rollerblades. You managed the conversion from a batch to an online transaction processing system for Hilo so well that the company offered you the job of CIO. Sue Rankin, the Hilo president, told you that the next step was to develop a firm-wide MIS, with supporting functional information systems, and she needed someone to achieve the implementation. The system you installed earlier does all the essential data processing tasks, and does them well.

During your first day on the job, you meet with Rankin to learn more about her expectations. She tells you that she has formed an MIS steering committee consisting of Rick Guenther (vice president of manufacturing), Don Lehnert (vice president of marketing), Cheryl Mitchell (vice president of finance), and you. Rankin wants you to call on each member, introduce yourself, and set a date and time for the first planning meeting.

On your way out the door of Rankin's office, you ask: "Aren't you going to be on the committee?" "No," Rankin replies. "I'm too busy planning our entry into the Taiwan market area next year. My time is completely booked up. That's why I hired you."

You already know Mitchell, having worked with her on the installation of the DP system. You know that she is extremely computer literate and anxious to expand the scope of computer applications. You have heard of Guenther and Lehnert but haven't met them.

Your first stop is Guenther's office. You find him extremely likeable—a warm handshake, boundless energy, and a great sense of humor. You spend two hours in his office, getting to know him and talking about the computer. Guenther wants to get started immediately.

"I've just been waiting for someone like you," he says. I've known about MIS and how it can help us in manufacturing from my previous job, but we haven't had anyone here at Hilo to pick up the ball and run with it. I want data collection terminals in every work area. I would like to be reporting all production activities within three months because I need good data to establish production standards. I want all manufacturing managers to have terminals in their offices, and I want to conduct in-house training courses that show the managers how to use the computer in problem solving. I can't want to get started."

Neither can you. You are so excited after talking with Guenther that you almost run down the hall to Lehnert's office. When his secretary ushers you into his office and his greeting is: "Well, what do *you* want?" you suspect tough skating. You introduce yourself and explain your purpose. You feel uncomfortable when Lehnert continues to shuffle papers on his desk as you talk. When you pause to catch your breath, he says: "Listen, I don't have time to get involved with Sue's MIS. We're planning to expand our market area and I have to find three new distributors by the end of the month. I can't do that sitting around talking about computer programs. Now, I have to get back to work. I want you to talk with my manager of marketing administration, Willie Campbell. The MIS is really in Willie's area. He'll get you fixed up. Listen, I've enjoyed meeting you, and I know that you will give us a good MIS. I wish you all the luck in the world on your project."

Assignments

1. Is there a problem here? If so, state it in one sentence that begins: "The problem is. . . ."

2. What are your chances of achieving a good, organization-wide MIS in this setting? Explain your reasoning.

3. What are your chances of achieving the functional information systems that Sue wants? Support your answers.

4. How can you get Lehnert actively involved in implementing a marketing information system? Think of two different approaches, and explain why one is better than the other.

5. Who should be the chair of the MIS steering committee? Explain your reasoning. What would be a good strategy to follow in getting that person to take the job.

SELECTED BIBLIOGRAPHY

Barthel, Ronald C., and Lindeman, Robert G. "Modeling Helps It Happen." *EDGE* 3 (January/February 1990): 31*ff.*

Cholak, Paul M., and Simon, Sidney H. "HRIS Asks, 'Who's the Boss?'" *Personnel Journal* 70 (August 1991): 74–76.

Davis, Leila. "On the Fast Track To HR Integration." *Datamation* 37 (September 15, 1991): 61*ff.*

Cox, James F., and Steven J. Clark, "Problems in Implementing and Operating a Manufacturing Resource Planning Information System," *Journal of Management Information Systems* 1 (Summer 1984): 81–101.

Duchessi, Peter; Schaninger, Charles M.; and Hobbs, Don R. "Implementing a Manufacturing Planning and Control Information System." *California Management Review* 31 (Spring 1989): 75–90.

Ferranti, Marc. "Wingz-Based EIS Tool Released for Windows." *PC Week Software* 9 (April 6, 1992): 38.

Hanold, Terrance. "An Executive View of MIS." *Datamation* 18 (November 1972): 65–71.

"HRIS Buyers' Guide." *Personnel Journal* 70 (May 1992): 126–37.

Jones, Jack William, and McLeod, Raymond, Jr. "The Structure of Executive Information Systems: An Exploratory Analysis." *Decision Sciences* 17 (Spring 1986): 220–49.

Kotler, Philip. "A Design for the Firm's Marketing Nerve Center." *Business Horizons* 9 (Fall 1966): 63–74.

Lapalme, Guy; Rousseau, Jean-Marc; Chapleau, Suzanne; Cormier, Michel; Cossette, Pierre; and Roy, Serge. "GeoRoute: A Geographic Information System for Transportation Applications." *Communications of the ACM* 35 (January 1992): 80–88.

Leonard, Bill. "The Myth of the Integrated HRIS." *Personnel Journal* 70 (September 1991): 113–15.

McElroy, John. "The HRIS As An Agent of Change." *Personnel Journal* 70 (May 1991): 105*ff*.

McLeod, Raymond, Jr., and Rogers, John C. "Marketing Information Systems: Their Current Status in Fortune 1000 Companies." *Journal of Management Information Systems* 1 (Spring 1985): 57–75.

Meal, Harlan C. "Putting Production Decisions Where They Belong." *Harvard Business Review*. 62 (March-April 1984): 102–10.

Nardoni, Ren. "Planning Promotes HRIS Success." *Personnel Journal* 70 (January 1992): 61*ff*.

Snyder, Christy. "Slashing Your Information Overload." *EDGE* 3 (May/June 1990): 28*ff*.

Stamps, David. "Human Resources: A Strategic Partner or IS Burden?" *Datamation* 36 (June 1, 1990): 47*ff*.

Teicholz, Eric. "Computer Integrated Manufacturing." *Datamation* 30 (March 1984): 169*ff*.

Viahos, George E., and Ferratt, Thomas W. "Use of Information Technology by Managers of Corporations in Greece to Support Decision Making." In *Proceedings of the 1992 ACM SIGCPR Conference*, ed. Albert L. Lederer, 1992, 136–51. New York, NY: ACM Press.

Wetherbe, James C. "Executive Information Requirements: Getting It Right." *MIS Quarterly* 15 (March 1991): 51–65.

Chapter 13

Decision Support Systems

LEARNING OBJECTIVES

After studying this chapter, you should:

- Have an expanded theoretical base for understanding decision making and the decision support system (DSS) concept
- Understand the objectives of DSS
- Understand one definition of the DSS and its accompanying model
- Understand the role of each type of DSS output in problem solving
- Know the basic characteristics of reports and how to improve their information content
- Know the different types of mathematical models, and understand the basic modeling terms
- Know the main advantages and disadvantages of modeling
- Appreciate that graphs are not always better than tables for conveying information, and know the situations where graphs tend to do the best job
- Know how to apply the DSS concept to group problem solving

INTRODUCTION

We have discussed two of the CBIS subsystems—data processing and MIS. We have seen that managers can obtain some information from the data processing system and considerably more from the MIS. These systems, however, are tailored to the information needs of large numbers of managers—those comprising the entire firm or an organizational unit. In many cases this information is not adequate for making specific decisions to solve specific problems. The DSS concept was conceived as a way to meet this need.

Much of the theoretical base for the decision support system (DSS) concept is from Herbert Simon. His distinction between programmed and nonprogrammed decisions, and his decision-making phases are reflected in current DSS thinking. However, it was not Simon who coined the term DSS. Rather, it was G. Anthony Gorry and Michael S. Scott Morton who incorporated the term in their grid, which contrasted problem structure and management levels. Steven Alter provided empirical support with his study of operational DSSs, which formed the basis of his DSS topology.

Unlike the MIS, which is aimed at problems of all types, the DSS is intended to support managers in solving semistructured problems. In addition, the DSS has an objective of effectiveness rather than efficiency.

The DSS provides both problem-solving information and a communications capability. The information is produced in the form of periodic and special reports, and outputs from mathematical models and expert systems. The communications are used when groups of managers engage in problem-solving.

From the beginning of the DSS era, mathematical modeling has been recognized as an integral component. Modeling provides the manager with some real advantages, but there are disadvantages as well.

Another component of the DSS that continually receives much publicity is computer graphics. Research has shown, however, that graphs are good only in certain situations, and in those situations some graph types are more effective than others.

The most recent embellishment of the DSS concept is the GDSS—group decision support system. The GDSS endeavors to improve communications among group members by providing stimulating environments. Advanced versions of GDSS feature mathematical models and expert systems.

DECISION MAKING

In earlier chapters, we laid a good foundation for the study of decision making. In Chapter 1 we included the **decision support system** in the CBIS, and defined the **DSS** as an information-producing system aimed at a particular problem that a manager must solve and decisions that a manager must make. In Chapter 4 we recognized that decisions are made to solve problems and described the steps of the systems approach. In Chapters 6 and 7 we explained some of the more popular problem-solving tools, such as data flow diagrams and entity relationship diagrams. In this chapter we expand on this foundation and add some theoretical constructs.

Simon's Types of Decisions

According to Herbert A. Simon, Nobel-prize winning management scientist at Carnegie-Mellon University, decisions exist on a continuum with programmed decisions at one end and nonprogrammed decisions at the other. **Programmed decisions** are "repetitive and routine, to the extent that a definite procedure has been worked out for handling them so that they don't have to be treated *de novo* (as new) each time they occur."[1] **Nonprogrammed decisions** are "novel, unstructured, and unusually consequential. There is no cut-and-dried method for handling the problem because it hasn't arisen before, or because its precise nature and structure are elusive or complex, or because it is so important that it deserves a custom-tailored treatment."[2]

Simon explained that the two decision types are only the black and white ends of the continuum, and that the world is mostly gray. However, the concept of programmed and nonprogramed decisions is important because each calls for a different technique.

Simon's Phases of Decision Making

Another of Simon's contributions is his description of the four phases that a manager goes through when solving a problem. Simon's phases are:

- **Intelligence activity**—searching the environment for conditions calling for solution.
- **Design activity**—inventing, developing, and analyzing possible courses of action.
- **Choice activity**—selecting a particular course of action from those available.
- **Review activity**—assessing past choices.

The left-hand side of Figure 13.1 shows how Simon's four phases relate directly to the steps of the systems approach that we described in Chapter 4. His intelligence activity relates to our steps of proceeding from a system to a subsystem level and analyzing system parts in sequence. His design activity corresponds to our steps of identifying and evaluating alternatives, and his choice activity relates to our step of selecting the best solution. Finally, his review activity relates to our steps of implementing the solution and following up. Simon's phases, therefore, are

---

[1] Herbert A. Simon, *The New Science of Management Decision*, rev. ed. (Englewood Cliffs, NJ: Prentice-Hall, 1977), 46.

[2] *Ibid.*

FIGURE 13.1

The Relationship
Between the
Systems
Approach,
Simon's Problem
Solving Phases,
and Interative
DSS
Implementation

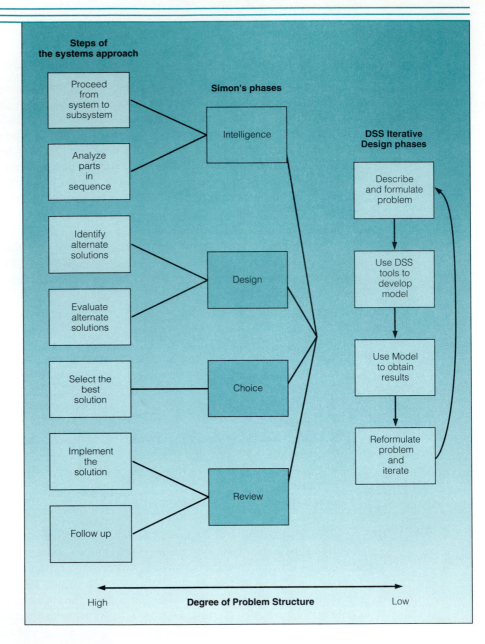

another interpretation of the systems approach. Managers follow these patterns in either a specific or a general way when they solve problems that face their units. Information specialists also follow these patterns when they engage in systems development.

The Prototyping Approach to DSS Development

The right-hand side of Figure 13.1 shows how the systems approach and Simon's phases relate to the prototyping approach to systems development.[3] We discussed prototyping in Chapter 5 and recognized it as a part of rapid application development (RAD).

As noted by the scale at the bottom of Figure 13.1 the less the degree of problem structure, the greater the need for prototyping. Therefore, prototyping is especially applicable to the development of complex DSSs and expert systems.

The iterative prototyping process begins with a description and formulation of the problem. Flexible DSS software generators and tools are then used to develop a small but usable DSS. The DSS is actually a working model. Its output provides a partial solution to the problem but, more importantly, provides the user with a better understanding of the problem. The problem is then reformulated, and the process is repeated until a stable system to be used in solving the problem is developed.

THE DSS CONCEPT

The DSS concept got its start in the late sixties with computer timesharing. For the first time a person could interact directly with the computer without having to go through information specialists.

The Term DSS Is Coined

It was not until 1971, however, that the term DSS was coined by G. Anthony Gorry and Michael S. Scott Morton, both MIT professors.[4] They felt a need for a framework to channel computer applications toward management decision making and developed what has become known as the *Gorry and Scott Morton Grid*. The grid, illustrated in Figure 13.2, is based on Simon's concept of programmed and nonprogrammed decisions and Robert N. Anthony's management levels.

Gorry and Scott Morton described decision types in terms of problem structure, ranging from structured to semistructured, to unstructured. You recall from Chapter 1 that Anthony used the names *strategic planning*, *management control*, and *operational control* to describe the top, middle, and lower management levels, respectively.

Simon's phases of decision making are used to determine problem structure. A fully **structured problem** is one in which the first three of Simon's phases—intelligence, design, and choice—are structured. That is, it is possible to specify algorithms, or decision rules, that allow the problem to be identified and under-

---

[3] Based on Efraim Turban, *Decision Support and Expert Systems* 2d ed. New York: Macmillan, 1990, 168–83.

[4] G. Anthony Gorry and Michael S. Scott Morton, "A Framework for Management Information Systems," *Sloan Management Review* 13 (Fall 1971), 55–70.

FIGURE 13.2

The Gorry and Scott Morton Grid

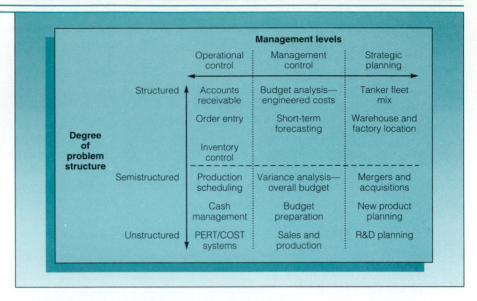

stood, alternate solutions to be identified and evaluated, and a solution to be selected. An **unstructured problem**, on the other hand, is one in which none of the three phases is structured. A **semistructured problem** is one in which one or two of the phases is structured.

Gorry and Scott Morton entered types of business problems into their grid. As an example, accounts receivable is solved by managers on the operational-control level making structured decisions. R&D planning is accomplished by strategic-planning managers making unstructured decisions.

The dotted line across the middle of the grid is significant. It separates the problems that had, at that time, been successfully solved with computer assistance (above) from those problems that had not been subjected to computer processing. The upper area was named *structured decision systems* (*SDS*), and the lower area was named *decision support systems* (*DSS*).

Gorry and Scott Morton initially regarded DSS as describing only future computer applications. Subsequently, the term has been applied to *all* computer applications dedicated to decision support—both current and future.

Alter's DSS Types

Steven L. Alter, a doctoral student at MIT, built upon the Gorry and Scott Morton framework by conducting a study of fifty-six decision support systems.[5] The study enabled him to develop a taxonomy of six DSS types based on the degree of problem-solving support. The six types are illustrated in Figure 13.3.

---

[5] Steven L. Alter, "How Effective Managers Use Information Systems," *Harvard Business Review* 54 (November–December 1976), 97–104.

FIGURE 13.3

Alter's DSS Types

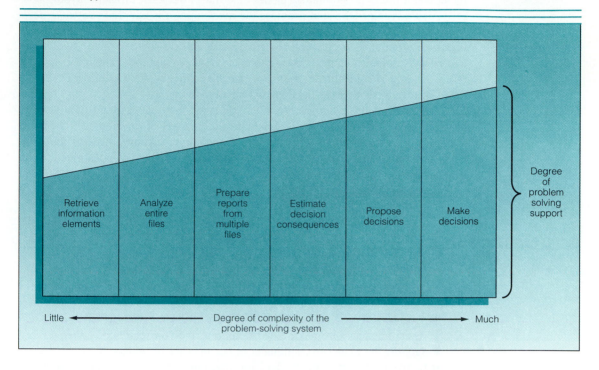

The type that offers the least support is one that enables the manager to *retrieve information elements*. The manager might query the database to obtain a sales figure for one of the marketing regions. Slightly more support is provided by a DSS that permits the manager to *analyze entire files*. The manager might query the database for a special report that uses data from the Inventory file. Another example is a monthly payroll report that is prepared from the Payroll file. Still more support is provided by systems that *prepare reports from multiple files*. Examples of such reports are an income statement and an analysis of product sales by customer.

These first three DSS types provide support in the form of special reports in response to database queries, and periodic reports. The final three DSS types involve the use of mathematical models.

A DSS that lets the manager see the possible effects of various decisions is a model that can *estimate decision consequences*. Perhaps the manager enters a price into a pricing model to see the effect on net profit. The model response, in effect, says that, "If you lower the price to $25, the net profit will increase by $5,000." The model is unable to determine that $25 is the *best* price, only what *might* happen if such a decision is made. These models also allow the user to assign subjective probabilities. An example is a risk analysis model that uses estimated probability distributions for each of the key factors.

More decision support is provided by a model that can *propose decisions*. For example, a manufacturing manager enters data that describes a plant and its equipment, and a linear programming model determines the most efficient layout.

Alter's type of DSS that provides the most support is one that can *make decisions* for the manager. Alter used the example of a computer model that determines insurance premiums. A data entry operator keys in data such as "male, under age 25, Trans Am, Houston, $100 deductable," and so on, and the computer computes the premium. The insurance company management has such confidence in the model that they let it make those particular decisions.

The Alter study is important for two reasons. First, it was the initial attempt to study DSSs actually in use. It supported the concept of developing systems to address particular decisions. Second, the classification includes systems that produce a variety of information outputs, emphasizing that a DSS is not limited to the more exotic approaches of database querying and decision modeling. The DSS also includes periodic reporting.

DSS OBJECTIVES

Another DSS pioneer at MIT, Peter G. W. Keen, teamed with Scott Morton to define the three objectives that a DSS should achieve.[6] They believed that the DSS should:

- Assist managers in making decisions to solve *semistructured problems*.
- *Support* the manager's judgment rather than try to replace it.
- Improve the manager's decision-making *effectiveness* rather than its efficiency.

These objectives correlate with three fundamental principles of the DSS concept—problem structure, decision support, and decision effectiveness.

Problem Structure

It is difficult to find problems that are completely structured or unstructured. The vast majority are semistructured—Simon's gray area. This means that the DSS is aimed at the area where most problems are found.

Decision Support

The DSS is not intended to replace the manager. Figure 13.4 illustrates this relationship between problem structure and the degree of support that the computer can provide. The computer can be applied to the structured portion of the problem, but the manager is responsible for the unstructured portion—applying judgment or intuition, and conducting analyses. The manager and the computer work together

[6] Peter G. W. Keen and Michael S. Scott Morton, *Decision Support Systems: An Organizational Perspective,* Reading, MA: Addison-Wesley Publishing Company, 1978, 1.

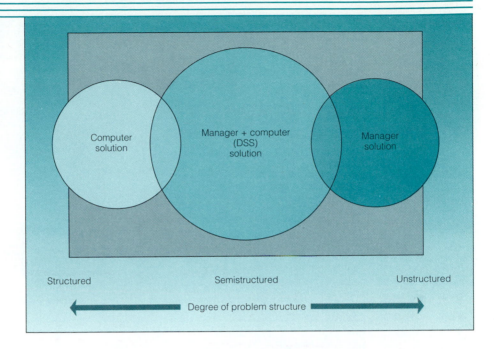

FIGURE 13.4
The DSS
Focuses on
Semistructured
Problems

Computer
solution

Manager + computer
(DSS)
solution

Manager
solution

Structured

Semistructured

Unstructured

Degree of problem structure

as a problem-solving team in solving problems that fall in the large semistructured area.

Decision Effectiveness

The objective of the DSS is not to make the decision-making process as efficient as possible. The manager's time is valuable and should not be wasted, but the main benefit from using a DSS is better decisions.

When making a decision, the manager does not always try to achieve the *best* one. Some mathematical models will do that for the manager. However, in most cases, it is the manager who must decide which alternative is best. Quite possibly the manager could spend extra time to fine-tune the solution so that it approaches the optimum, but the increased precision would not be worth the time and effort. The manager uses judgment in determining when a decision will contribute to a problem solution.

A DSS MODEL

We have presented models of the data processing system and the management information system in the two previous chapters, and can use a similar structure for a DSS model. As shown in Figure 13.5, data and information are entered into the

FIGURE 13.5

A DSS Model

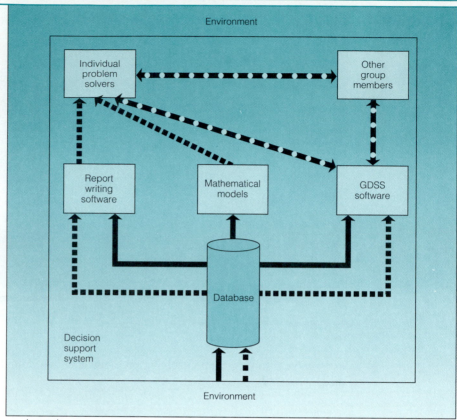

Environment

Individual
problem
solvers

Other
group
members

Report
writing
software

Mathematical
models

GDSS
software

Database

Decision
support
system

Environment

Legend:

Data   Communication   Information

database from the firm's environment. The database also contains data that is provided by the data processing system. The contents of the database are used by three software subsystems.

■ **Report-writing software** produces both periodic and special reports. Periodic reports are typically produced by software that is coded in a procedural language such as COBOL or PL/I. The special reports are produced in response to database queries by users who use the query language of the database management system. As a general rule, periodic reports reflect what happened in the past, and special reports have the capability of describing what is happening now.

■ **Mathematical models** produce information as a result of simulations that involve one or more components of the physical system of the firm, or facets of its operations. As we recognized in Chapter 3, mathematical models have the unique capability of enabling the user to project decision consequences into the future.

■ **GDSS software** enables multiple problem solvers, working together as a group, to use the DSS. In this case the term **GDSS**, **group decision support system**, is used. Perhaps the problem solvers represent a committee, or a project team.

The three software systems support decision making in three basic ways. Report-writing software produces information in the form of *reports*; mathematical models produce information in the form of *simulation results*; and GDSS software facilitates *communications* between the group members as the problem-solving process unfolds. You can see that the group members communicate with one another both directly and by means of the GDSS software.

HOW INFORMATION FROM THE DSS IS USED

Managers make two basic uses of the information from the DSS—to define problems and to solve them. Problem definition is the *definition effort* of the systems approach. It corresponds to Simon's *intelligence* phase. Next, managers use information to solve the problems that have been identified. This is the *solution effort* of the systems approach, and Simon's *design* and *choice* phases.

As a general rule, periodic and special reports are used primarily in definition effort, and simulations are used in solution effort. These two uses are shown in the conceptual diagrams that appear in Figure 13.6.[7]

Periodic reports can be designed to *identify problems* or potential problems. Managers can also query the database to find problems or to learn more about problems that have already been identified. Simulations can also uncover hidden problems, because weaknesses tend to stand out when part of the firm's operation is manipulated mathematically.

Periodic and special reports can also help the manager *solve problems* by identifying alternatives, evaluating and selecting alternatives, and providing follow-up information. However, this is the area where simulation shines. Mathematical models can project the expected results of alternate decisions.

You will note that the manager uses other means to define and solve problems in addition to computer information.

With this understanding of the role played by these output methods in problem solving, we will learn more about reports and modeling. In discussing these topics,

---

[7]This situation is believed to exist and probably holds true most of the time; however, exceptions would be expected. The diagram is a theory of information use, yet to be supported by empirical evidence. Such a situation is typical of many of the MIS concepts.

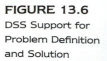

FIGURE 13.6
DSS Support for
Problem Definition
and Solution

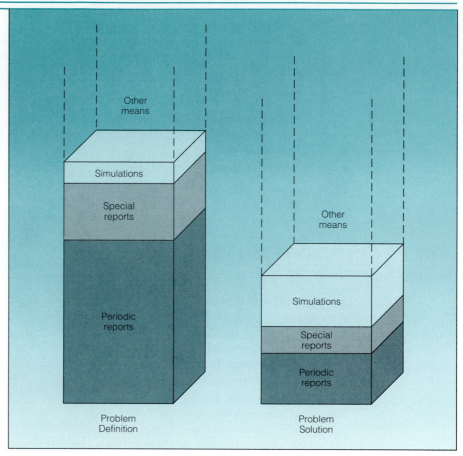

we will recognize the increasing popularity of graphic output, as compared with the more traditional tabular format. In addition, we will recognize the unique communications capabilities of GDSSs.

PERIODIC AND SPECIAL REPORTS

If you were to pick up a report from a manager's desk, you could not tell whether it was a periodic report or a special report. Both can look exactly alike. What distinguishes them is the manner in which they are triggered. A **periodic report** is prepared according to a certain schedule. An example is a monthly analysis of sales by customer. A **special report** is prepared when something out of the ordinary happens. One example is an accident report; another is a response to a database query.

Incorporating Management by Exception into Reports

The information content of both periodic and special reports can be improved by incorporating the concept of management by exception. We introduced the concept in Chapter 3 when we described the general systems model of the firm. In this model the information processor compares actual performance against standards and advises the manager when performance falls outside the acceptable range.

Management by exception can be incorporated into reports in four basic ways.

Prepare the Report Only when Exceptions Occur   This is the technique incorporated in the general systems model, and the overtime earnings report in Figure 13.7 is an example of the output produced by the information processor. The report is printed only when employees work overtime; each entry on the report is an exception.

Use the Report Sequence to Highlight the Exceptions   It is possible to sort report records into either an ascending or descending sequence based on one or more key fields, so as to call the user's attention to particular records.

For example, a report of customer sales records can be sorted into descending sequence based on the current month's sales amounts. This sequence results in the customers with the largest sales amounts being listed first, calling the manager's attention to them. Such a report might be titled the **monthly high sales amount report**. We illustrated this technique in Chapter 3. See Figure 3.9

An example of the use of an ascending sequence is a **slow moving items report**. The inventory items are listed in ascending sequence based on their year-

FIGURE 13.7
An Overtime
Earnings Report

```
                        OVERTIME EARNINGS REPORT

                     FOR WEEK ENDING AUGUST 19


    --------------------------------------------------------------------
                                             OVERTIME EARNINGS
    DEPARTMENT NO.    DEPARTMENT NAME     CURRENT MONTH    YEAR-TO-DATE
    --------------------------------------------------------------------


       16-10          RECEIVING           $ 2,305.00       $ 5,319.20
       16-11          INSPECTION          $ 1,025.60       $ 4,386.12
       16-12          MATERIALS HANDLING  $ 3,392.50       $12,629.00
       16-13          TOOLING             $    78.00       $ 1,049.00
       16-14          ASSEMBLY            $     0.00       $   792.80
       16-15          PLATING             $ 3,504.90       $12,635.20
       16-16          SHIPPING            $ 5,219.16       $18,294.16

                      TOTALS              $15,525.16*      $55,105.48*
```

FIGURE 13.8

An Aged
Accounts
Receivable Report

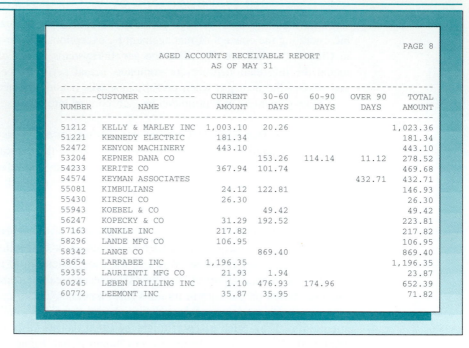

```
                                                                    PAGE 8
                    AGED ACCOUNTS RECEIVABLE REPORT
                            AS OF MAY 31

    -------------------------------------------------------------------
    -------CUSTOMER ----------   CURRENT    30-60    60-90   OVER 90    TOTAL
    NUMBER       NAME             AMOUNT     DAYS     DAYS     DAYS     AMOUNT
    -------------------------------------------------------------------
    51212    KELLY & MARLEY INC  1,003.10   20.26                    1,023.36
    51221    KENNEDY ELECTRIC      181.34                              181.34
    52472    KENYON MACHINERY      443.10                              443.10
    53204    KEPNER DANA CO                 153.26   114.14    11.12    278.52
    54233    KERITE CO             367.94   101.74                     469.68
    54574    KEYMAN ASSOCIATES                                432.71   432.71
    55081    KIMBULIANS             24.12   122.81                     146.93
    55430    KIRSCH CO              26.30                               26.30
    55943    KOEBEL & CO                     49.42                      49.42
    56247    KOPECKY & CO           31.29   192.52                     223.81
    57163    KUNKLE INC            217.82                              217.82
    58296    LANDE MFG CO          106.95                              106.95
    58342    LANGE CO                       869.40                     869.40
    58654    LARRABEE INC        1,196.35                            1,196.35
    59355    LAURIENTI MFG CO       21.93    1.94                      23.87
    60245    LEBEN DRILLING INC      1.10   476.93   174.96           652.39
    60772    LEEMONT INC            35.87    35.95                      71.82
```

to-date sales volume. Those items that have not sold well this year have low volumes and are listed first, calling the manager's attention to them.

Group the Exceptions Together   The report can be designed so that the manager can look in certain areas for the exceptions. The aged accounts receivables

FIGURE 13.9

A Sales by
Salesperson
Report

```
                        SALES BY SALESPERSON REPORT
                        FOR MONTH ENDING MARCH 31

    ----SALESPERSON-----   -----CURRENT-MONTH----   -----YEAR-TO-DATE-----
      NO.      NAME        QUOTA  ACTUAL VARIANCE   QUOTA  ACTUAL VARIANCE

     0120   JOHN NELSON    1200    1083    -117     3600    3505    -95
    10469   LYNN SHERRY    1000    1162    +162     3000    3320    +320
    19261   DARVIN UPSHAW   800    1090    +290     2400    2510    +110
    20234   JANIE EVANS    1500    1305    -195     4500    4110    -390
    61604   TRAVIS BURKE   2000    2333    +333     6000    6712    +712
    62083   CATHY HAGER    1000     990     -10     3000    2319    -681
    63049   STEVE JENNER   1100    1250    +150     3300    2416    -884
    64040   SAM MOSELEY    1050     985     -65     3150    3020    -130

            TOTALS         9650   10198     548    28950   27912   -1038
```

report in Figure 13.8 lists receivables in separate columns. If the manager is interested in receivables over ninety days old, this column is scanned to pick them out.

Show the Variance from the Norm   Actual activity is compared to planned activity and the difference is shown as a variance. In the Figure 13.9 example, the manager scans the two variance columns to pick out the very large and very small amounts—the exceptions.

An important point to keep in mind is that these report format suggestions should be considered not only by the information specialists but by the manager as well. The manager can incorporate management by exception into reports that are to be used in end-user computing.

MATHEMATICAL MODELING

A **model** is an abstraction of something; it represents some phenomenon—an object or an activity. The phenomenon is called the **entity**. If a model represents a firm, the firm is the entity. If a model represents the fluctuation in the firm's sales volume, the sales volume is the entity.

In Chapter 3 we identified four types of models—physical, narrative, graphic, and mathematical. The mathematical model is the type that plays such an important role in the DSS.

There are several different ways to classify mathematical models.

Static or Dynamic Models

A **static model** does not include time as a variable. It deals with a situation at a particular point in time. It is like a snapshot. A model that includes time as a variable is a **dynamic model**. The model represents the behavior of the entity over time, like a motion picture.

Probabilistic or Deterministic Models

Another way to classify models is based on whether the formulas include probabilities. A **probability** is the chance that something will happen. Probabilities range from 0.00 (for something with no chance) to 1.00 (for something that is a sure thing). A model that includes probabilities is called a **probabilistic model**. Otherwise, it is a **deterministic model**.

Optimizing or Suboptimizing Models

An **optimzing model** is one that selects the best solution among the alternatives. For a model to be able to do this, the problem must be very well structured. A **suboptimizing model**, often called a **satisficing model**, permits a manager to enter a set of decisions, and the model will project *an outcome*. The model does not identify the decisions that will produce the best outcome but leaves that task to the manager.

SIMULATION

When a model represents its entity, the process is called **simulation**, or **modeling**.

The Modeling Scenario

The term **scenario** is used to describe the setting in which a simulation occurs. For example, if you are simulating an inventory system, as shown in Figure 13.10, the scenario specifies the beginning balance and the daily sales units. The data elements that establish the scenario are called **scenario data elements**. Models can be designed so that the scenario data elements are variables, thus enabling different values to be assigned.

Decision Variables

The input values that the manager enters to gauge their impact on the entity are known as **decision variables**. In the Figure 13.10 example the decision variables include the order quantity, reorder point, and lead time (the time required for the supplier to furnish replenishment stock).

Simulation Technique

The manager usually executes an optimizing model only a single time; it produces the best solution using the particular scenario and the decision variables. However, it is necessary to execute a suboptimizing model over and over, searching for the combination of decision variables that produces a satisfying outcome. This iterative process of "trying out" decision alternatives is called playing the **what-if game**.

Each time the model is executed, only one of the decision variables should be changed so that its influence can be seen. In using the Figure 13.10 model, for example, the manager manipulates the order quantity until its proper level is identified. Then the reorder point is manipulated, and then lead time.

Format of Simulation Output

It is a good practice to include the scenario elements and decision variables on the same screen or page as the output, as shown in Figure 13.10. Then it is always clear which inputs produced the output.

A MODELING EXAMPLE

A firm's executives might use a mathematical model to make several key decisions. Perhaps the executives want to simulate the effect of: (1) the *price*, (2) the amount of *plant investment* that will be necessary to provide the capacity for producing the

FIGURE 13.10

The Output from
an Inventory
Model

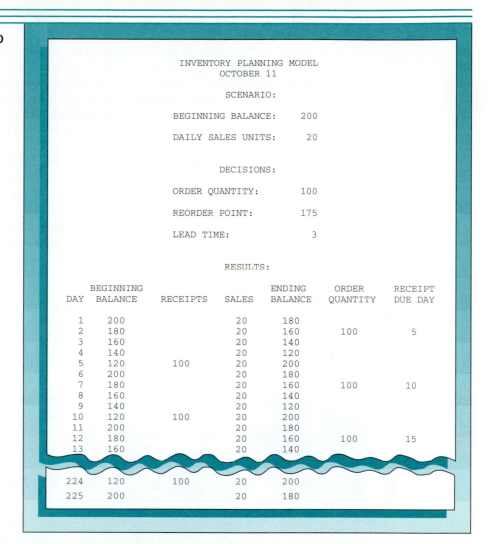

INVENTORY PLANNING MODEL
OCTOBER 11

SCENARIO:

BEGINNING BALANCE: 200

DAILY SALES UNITS: 20

DECISIONS:

ORDER QUANTITY: 100

REORDER POINT: 175

LEAD TIME: 3

RESULTS:

DAY	BEGINNING BALANCE	RECEIPTS	SALES	ENDING BALANCE	ORDER QUANTITY	RECEIPT DUE DAY
1	200		20	180		
2	180		20	160	100	5
3	160		20	140		
4	140		20	120		
5	120	100	20	200		
6	200		20	180		
7	180		20	160	100	10
8	160		20	140		
9	140		20	120		
10	120	100	20	200		
11	200		20	180		
12	180		20	160	100	15
13	160		20	140		
224	120	100	20	200		
225	200		20	180		

product, (3) the amount to be invested in *marketing* activity such as advertising and personal selling, and (4) the amount to be invested in *R & D* (research and development).

Further, the executives want to be able to simulate four quarters of activity and produce two reports—an operating statement that includes key nonmonetary values such as market potential (demand) and plant capacity, and an income statement that reflects the results in monetary terms. They want a dynamic, deterministic, and suboptimizing model. A model of such complexity would most likely be created by information specialists.

Model Input

Figure 13.11 shows the input screen that is used to enter the scenario elements and decision variables. The values for the first quarter have already been entered in the portion of the screen above the white area. The top three data lines contain the scenario for the *last quarter*. You can identify the data lines by the brackets. Some of the values relate to the firm—its plant capacity, the number of units that were produced, the dollar value of raw materials, and so forth. The others relate to the influence of the firm's environment—economic index, seasonal index, competitor price, and competitor marketing.

The fourth data line contains scenario elements for the *next quarter*. The executives indicate that they want to simulate four quarters. Then they enter estimates for the economic and seasonal indexes, and for the competitor's price and marketing.

The fifth data line (immediately above the white area) includes the four decisions, with space at the right where the results will be displayed.

Model Output

The next quarter's activity (Quarter 1) is simulated, and after-tax profit is displayed on the screen. The executives study the figure and decide on the set of decisions to be used in Quarter 2. These decisions are entered and the simulation is repeated.

FIGURE 13.11

A Model Input Screen

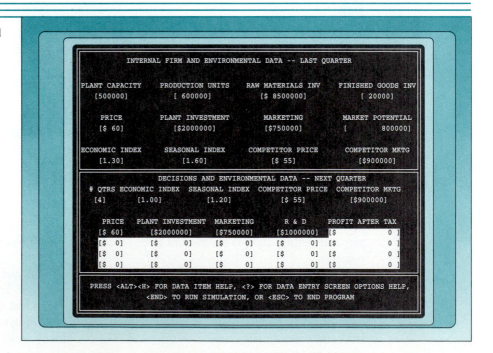

```
          INTERNAL FIRM AND ENVIRONMENTAL DATA -- LAST QUARTER

PLANT CAPACITY    PRODUCTION UNITS   RAW MATERIALS INV    FINISHED GOODS INV
   [500000]          [ 600000]          [$ 8500000]           [ 20000]


    PRICE         PLANT INVESTMENT       MARKETING          MARKET POTENTIAL
   [$ 60]            [$2000000]          [$750000]        [           800000]

ECONOMIC INDEX     SEASONAL INDEX      COMPETITOR PRICE     COMPETITOR MKTG
   [1.30]             [1.60]              [$ 55]             [$900000]

         DECISIONS AND ENVIRONMENTAL DATA -- NEXT QUARTER
 # QTRS ECONOMIC INDEX  SEASONAL INDEX  COMPETITOR PRICE  COMPETITOR MKTG
   [4]      [1.00]          [1.20]          [$ 55]          [$900000]

    PRICE    PLANT INVESTMENT  MARKETING       R & D      PROFIT AFTER TAX
   [$ 60]      [$2000000]      [$750000]    [$1000000]   [$          0 ]
   [$  0]      [$       0]     [$     0]    [$       0]   [$          0 ]
   [$  0]      [$       0]     [$     0]    [$       0]   [$          0 ]
   [$  0]      [$       0]     [$     0]    [$       0]   [$          0 ]

 PRESS <ALT><H> FOR DATA ITEM HELP, <?> FOR DATA ENTRY SCREEN OPTIONS HELP,
        <END> TO RUN SIMULATION, OR <ESC> TO END PROGRAM
```

FIGURE 13.12
Summary Output
Is Displayed on
the Screen

```
         INTERNAL FIRM AND ENVIRONMENTAL DATA -- LAST QUARTER

PLANT CAPACITY    PRODUCTION UNITS    RAW MATERIALS INV    FINISHED GOODS INV
   [561914]         [ 786680]          [$ 8500000]          [       0]

    PRICE          PLANT INVESTMENT        MARKETING        MARKET POTENTIAL
   [$ 56]            [$2000000]           [$750000]         [     2101650]

ECONOMIC INDEX     SEASONAL INDEX      COMPETITOR PRICE     COMPETITOR MKTG
   [1.00]             [1.20]              [$ 55]              [$900000]

         DECISIONS AND ENVIRONMENTAL DATA -- NEXT QUARTER
 # QTRS ECONOMIC INDEX  SEASONAL INDEX  COMPETITOR PRICE  COMPETITOR MKTG
  [4]      [1.00]          [1.20]           [$ 55]          [$900000]

    PRICE    PLANT INVESTMENT   MARKETING      R & D     PROFIT AFTER TAX
   [$ 56]      [$2000000]       [$750000]   [$1000000]  [$    14,897,832 ]
   [$ 58]      [$2000000]       [$750000]   [$1000000]  [$    12,241,367 ]
   [$ 60]      [$2000000]       [$750000]   [$1000000]  [$     6,953,955 ]
   [$ 60]      [$2000000]       [$750000]   [$1000000]  [$     6,154,826 ]

  PRESS <ALT><H> FOR DATA ITEM HELP, <?> FOR DATA ENTRY SCREEN OPTIONS HELP,
         <END>  TO RUN SIMULATION, OR <ESC> TO END PROGRAM
```

This process continues until all four quarters have been simulated. At this point the screen has the appearance shown in Figure 13.12. The decisions and resulting after-tax profit are listed in reverse sequence at the bottom of the screen, with the figures for the fourth quarter on top.

The executives can obtain more detailed output in displayed or printed form, as in Figure 13.13. The operating statement and income statement are displayed on separate screens.

MODELING ADVANTAGES AND DISADVANTAGES

A manager who uses mathematical models can expect to benefit in the following ways:

- The modeling process can be a *learning experience*. Invariably, something new is learned about the physical system with each modeling project.
- The *speed* of the simulation process provides the ability to evaluate the impact of decisions in a short period of time. In a matter of minutes, it is possible to simulate several months, quarters, or years of company operations.

FIGURE 13.13
Detailed Output
Can Be Displayed
or Printed

```
DATE: 10/26/89                 PRICING MODEL OUTPUT                PAGE 1 OF 2


          ---------------[C U R R E N T  P E R I O D  D E C I S I O N S]---------------

                          QUARTER 1    QUARTER 2    QUARTER 3    QUARTER 4

PRICE                   $       60 $        60 $        58 $        56
PLANT INVESTMENT        $ 2,000,000 $ 2,000,000 $ 2,000,000 $ 2,000,000
MARKETING               $   750,000 $   750,000 $   750,000 $   750,000
RESEARCH & DEVELOPMENT  $ 1,000,000 $ 1,000,000 $ 1,000,000 $ 1,000,000

          ------------------[O P E R A T I N G  S T A T E M E N T]------------------

                          QUARTER 1    QUARTER 2    QUARTER 3    QUARTER 4

MARKET POTENTIAL          341539       375692       626778      2101650
SALES VOLUME              341538       375692       626778       786680
PRODUCTION UNITS          341538       375692       626778       786680
FINISHED GOODS INV.            0            0            0            0
PLANT CAPACITY            516071       531741       547019       561915


   PRESS: <PG UP>, <PG DN>, PAGE NUMBER, <ALT><0> TO SAVE, <ALT><P> TO PRINT
               <RETURN> FOR DATA ENTRY SCREEN, OR <ESC> TO END PROGRAM
```

```
DATE: 10/26/89                 INCOME STATEMENT                   PAGE 2 OF 2

RECEIPTS, SALES REVENUE                                  $    123,441,004
EXPENSES, MARKETING                  $  3,000,000
   RESEARCH AND DEVELOPMENT          $  4,000,000
   ADMINISTRATION                    $  1,200,000
   MAINTENANCE                       $  1,583,016
   LABOR                             $ 13,985,031
   MATERIALS                         $ 13,191,000
   REDUCTION, FINISHED GOODS         $    240,000
   DEPRECIATION                      $  3,774,305
   FINISHED GOODS CARRYING COSTS $            0
   RAW MATERIALS CARRYING COSTS      $  1,700,000
   ORDERING COSTS                    $    200,000
   PLANT INVESTMENT EXPENSE          $  1,600,000
   SUNDRIES                          $  1,592,855
TOTAL EXPENSES                                           $     46,067,007
PROFIT BEFORE INCOME TAX                                 $     77,373,997
INCOME TAX                                               $     37,126,018

NET PROFIT AFTER INCOME TAX                              $     40,247,979


   PRESS: <PG UP>, <PG DN>, PAGE NUMBER, <ALT><0> TO SAVE, <ALT><P> TO PRINT
               <RETURN> FOR DATA ENTRY SCREEN, OR <ESC> TO END PROGRAM
```

- Models provide a *predictive power*—a look into the future—that no other information-producing method offers.
- Models are *less expensive* than the trial-and-error method. The modeling process most certainly is costly in terms of development time and the soft-

ware and hardware required for the simulations, but the cost is not nearly as high as that of bad decisions.

These modeling advantages can be offset to some degree by two basic disadvantages of models:

- The *difficulty of modeling a business system* will produce a model that does not capture all of the influences on the entity. For example, in the model just described, someone in the firm must estimate the values for the scenario data elements. This means that considerable judgment must be applied in implementing the decisions that are based on the simulation results.
- A *high degree of mathematical skill* is required to personally develop more complex models. Also, such skill is necessary to properly interpret the output.

For a long time most managers perceived the disadvantages of modeling to outweigh the advantages. That situation is changing due to a combination more user-friendly modeling tools and more computer and information literate managers.

COMPUTER GRAPHICS

Until the early 1980s computer graphics were not seriously considered as an output option for MISs and DSSs. Then, along came the micro and Lotus. The Lotus PrintGraph system enabled managers to display and print the five types of graphs illustrated in Figure 13.14. The ease and economy of micro-based graphics software generated a high level of interest in using information in a graphic form rather than tabular.

The success of Lotus also stimulated other suppliers to develop graphics software and hardware. These products have been promoted as contributing to improved decision making. In many cases they do, but success is not always assured. Rather, graphs seem to work best in some situations, and tabular formats work best in others.

When to Use Graphs

Sirkka L. Jarvenpaa, an MIS professor at the University of Texas at Austin, and Gary W. Dickson, an MIS professor the University of Minnesota recommend the use of graphs when:[8]

- Seeking a quick summary of data
- Detecting trends over time
- Comparing points and patterns of different variables

[8] Sirkka L. Jarvenpaa and Gary W. Dickson, "Graphics and Managerial Decision Making: Research Based Guidelines," *Communications of the ACM* 31 (June 1988), 772.

FIGURE 13.14

The Five Basic Types of Lotus Graphs

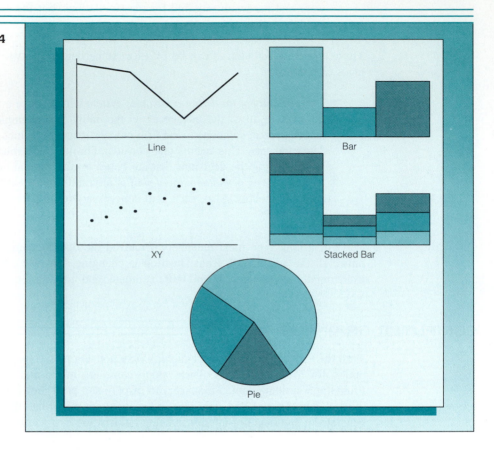

- Forecasting activities
- Seeking relatively simple impressions from a vast amount of information

The researchers recommend that a tabular presentation be used when it is necessary to read individual data values.

Which Graphs to Use

Jarvenpaa and Dickson also offer the following tips when choosing between the various types of graphs:

- Line or bar charts are preferred for summarizing data.
- Grouped line or bar charts are good for showing trends over time. Examples of these graph types are shown in Figure 13.15.
- Grouped bar charts are better than pie charts for presenting parts of a whole.

FIGURE 13.15

Grouped, Multiple Line and Bar Charts

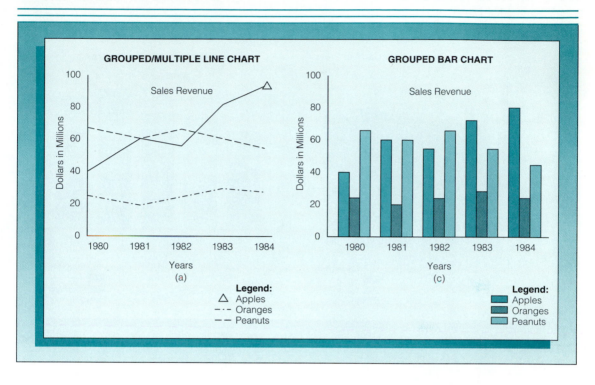

This is surprising since the pie chart has long been considered an effective way to display information.[9]

■ Grouped line or bar charts are good for comparing patterns of variables; do not use stacked line or bar charts. Figure 13.16 shows examples of the stacked graphs.

■ Use horizontal rather than vertical bars when comparing variables. This is a revealing insight in light of the fact that vertical bars are so frequently used. Lotus, for example, features vertical, not horizontal, bars.

■ Use single line or bar charts to compare individual data points between variables.

■ Put data values on the top of the bars in a bar chart for easier reading.

It is important for the manager and the information specialist to study the task to be performed and tailor the output accordingly. The most success will be achieved by designing outputs for use in solving specific types of problems.

[9] *See,* for example, Blake Ives, "Graphical User Interfaces for Business Information Systems," *MIS Quarterly* (Special Issue 1982), 17.

FIGURE 13.16

Stacked, Divided Bar and Line Charts

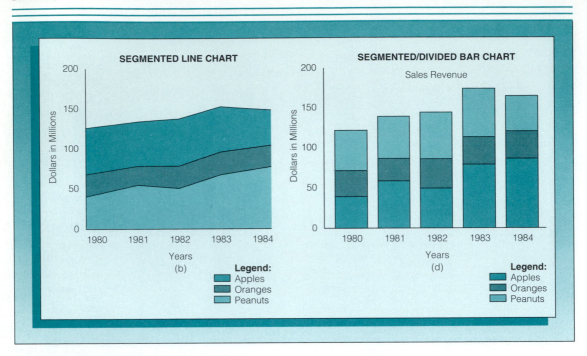

GROUP DECISION SUPPORT SYSTEMS

It has always been an accepted fact that managers seldom solve problems alone. Very often a manager will enlist the help of peers, superiors, and subordinates in defining a problem or perhaps in identifying and evaluating alternate solutions. The committees and project teams that exist in most companies are also examples of group approaches to problem solving.

The GDSS Concept

A **group decision support system (GDSS)** is "a computer-based system that supports groups of people engaged in a common task (or goal) and that provides an interface to a shared environment."[10] Other terms have also been coined to describe the application of information technology to group settings. These terms include **group support system (GSS)**, **computer-supported cooperative work (CSCW)**, **computerized collaborative work support**, and **electronic meeting system**

---

[10]Clarence Ellis, Simon Gibbs, and Gail Rein, "Groupware: Some Issues and Experiences," *Communications of the ACM* 34 (January 1991), 40.

TABLE 13.1
The GDSS
Addresses
Needs and Diffi-
culties of Group
Interaction

Group Problem or Need	GDSS Feature
Sending and receiving information efficiently among all parties or specific group members	Electronic messaging, broadcast or point-to-point
Access to personal data files or corporate data during the course of a meeting	Computer terminal for each group member; gateway to a local area network or central computer
Display of ideas, votes, data, graphs, or tables to all members simultaneously	Large common viewing screen or "public" screen at each group member's terminal
Reluctance of some members to speak due to their shyness, low status or controversial ideas	Anonymous input of ideas and votes
Failure of some members to participate due to laziness or "tuning out"	Active solicitation of ideas or votes from each group member
Failure to efficiently organize and analyze ideas and votes	Summary and display of ideas; statistical summary and display of votes
Failure to quantify preferences	Provide rating scales and/or ranking schemes; solicit and display ratings and rankings.
Failure to develop a meeting strategy or plan	Provide a mock agenda which the group can complete
Failure to stick with the meeting plan	Continuously display the agenda; provide a time clock; automatically display agenda items at the appropriate time

Reprinted by permission of Gerardine DeSanctis and R. Brent Gallupe, "A Foundation for the Study of Group Decision Support Systems," *Management Science,* 33, May 1987. Copyright, 1989, The Institute of Management Sciences.

(**EMS**).[11] The software that is used in these settings has been given the name **groupware**.

Most GDSSs are designed to help groups become more productive by supporting the exchange of ideas, opinions, and preferences within the group.[12] You know from experience that people who communicate in groups have special needs, and that difficulties often arise. Table 13.1 lists the more common needs and difficulties and identifies corresponding GDSS features.

[11] For more information on EMS *see* Alan R. Dennis, Joey F. George, Len M. Jessup, Jay F. Nunamaker, Jr., and Douglas R. Vogel, "Information Technology to Support Electronic Meetings," *MIS Quarterly* 12 (December 1988), 591–624.

[12] R. Brent Gallupe and Gerardine DeSanctis, "Computer-Based Support for Group Problem-Finding: An Experimental Investigation," *MIS Quarterly* 12 (June 1988), 278.

How the GDSS Contributes to Problem Solving

The underlying assumption of the GDSS is that improved communications make possible improved decisions. Improved communications are achieved by keeping the discussion focused on the problem, resulting in less wasted time. The time gained can be devoted to a more thorough discussion of the problem, contributing to a better problem definition. Or, the time gained can be used in identifying more alternatives than otherwise would be possible. The evaluation of more alternatives increases the likelihood of arriving at a good solution.

GDSS Environmental Settings

The GDSS contributes to problem solving by providing a setting that is conducive to communications. Figure 13.17 shows four possible GDSS settings based on the size of the group and where the members are located.

In each setting group members may meet at the same time or at different times. When the members meet at the same time it is called a **synchronous exchange**, and an example is a committee meeting. When the members meet at different times, it is called an **asynchronous exchange**, and an example is communication by means of electronic mail or computer conferencing. We discuss the electronic applications in Chapter 14 when we address office automation.

Decision Rooms   A **decision room** is the setting for small groups, which meet face-to-face. The room contributes to communication through a combination of furnishings, equipment, and layout.

FIGURE 13.17
GDSS Environmental Settings

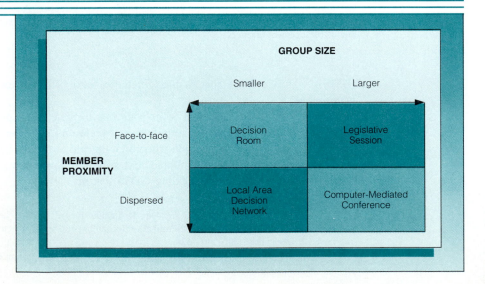

FIGURE 13.18

The Layout of a
Decision Room

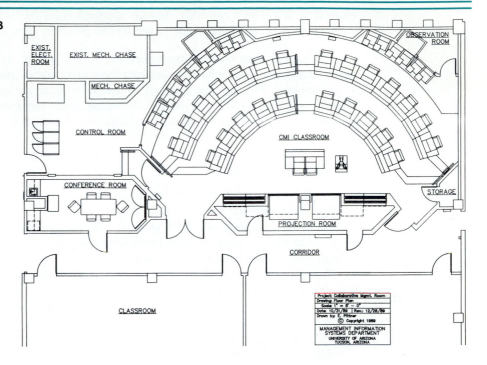

Figure 13.18 is a layout of the decision room at the Center for the Management of Information at the University of Arizona. This room includes twenty-four IBM Personal System 2 workstations, thirty-eight audio pick-up microphones, and six video cameras.

In the center of the room is a facilitator's console. A **facilitator** is a person whose chief task is to keep the discussion on track.

Based on the arrangements that are established for each session, one group member's keyed-in messages to another member may be displayed on a large screen for the entire group to see. Other material pertinent to the discussion can also be displayed from such media as videotapes, color slides, and transparencies.

Equipment in the control room performs a variety of tasks—keeping a record of the computer inputs from all members as well as audio and video recordings of the discussion.

Local Area Decision Network   When it is impossible for small groups to meet face-to-face, the members can interact by means of a local area network, or LAN. A member enters comments in a keyboard terminal and views the comments of the other members on the screen.

Legislative Session   When the group is too large for a decision room, a legislative session is required. The large size imposes certain constraints on the communications. Either the opportunity for equal participation by each member is removed, or less time is available. Another approach is for the facilitator to decide which material is displayed on the screen for the group to view.

Computer-mediated Conference   Several office automation (OA) applications permit communication between large groups with geographically-dispersed members. These are the applications that are collectively known as teleconferencing, and they include computer conferencing, audio conferencing, and video conferencing. We discuss teleconferencing in the OA chapter. You can see that there is a strong tie between the GDSS and OA.

A GDSS Example

In a typical GDSS session using the University of Arizona's GroupSystems, a group will meet in the decision room shown in Figure 13.18. Participants will write comments about a topic such as "What goals should our company have for the next year?" using the *Electronic Brainstorming* (*EBS*) program. This program provides for both parallel communication and anonymity.

Parallel communication is when all participants write comments at the same time, and **anonymity** is when nobody is able to tell who wrote a particular comment. Anonymity allows each participant to write what she or he really thinks without fear of ridicule from other group members. Also, it allows each idea to be evaluated on its merits rather than on who offered it.

After approximately a half hour of writing comments about the central topic, group members consolidate the comments into categories using another program called *Idea Organizer*. For example, all comments relating to one particular goal may be grouped together, while comments regarding other goals are put into other categories.

Finally, group members use the *Vote* program to rank the list of categories outlined by Idea Organizer, in terms of some criterion such as the overall importance to the firm. Each member generates his or her own list and is not influenced by someone else's ranking. A summary of the ranked lists is then shown on the public screen to give the group an idea about their consensus concerning the meeting topic.

GDSS Levels

The GDSS concept is still a relatively new approach to decision making. The next several years should see substantial improvement in the level of decision support that is offered. MIS professors Gerardine DeSanctis of the University of Minnesota, and R. Brent Gallupe of Queen's University, Ontario have identified three GDSS levels:[13]

■ A **Level 1 GDSS** is designed to facilitate communication. The features listed in Table 13.1 are examples of a Level 1 GDSS.

[13] Gerardine DeSanctis and R. Brent Gallupe, "A Foundation for the Study of Group Decision Support Systems," *Management Science* 33 (May 1987), 593–95.

TABLE 13.2 The Level 2 GDSS Facilitates Decision Making	Group Problem or Need	GDSS Feature
	Need for problem structuring, planning, and scheduling	Planning models, e.g., PERT, CPM, Gantt
	Decision-analytic aids for uncertain future events	Utility and probability assessment models, e.g., decision trees, risk assessment
	Decision-analytic aids for resource allocation problems	Budget allocation models
	Decision-analytic aids for data-oriented tasks	Statistical methods, multi-criteria decision models
	Decision-analytic aids for preference tasks	Social judgment models
	Desire to use a structured decision technique but insufficient knowledge or time to use the technique	Automate the Delphi, Nominal, or other idea-gathering and compilation technique(s); provide an online tutorial for the group or a human facilitator

Reprinted by permission of Gerardine DeSanctis and R. Brent Gallupe, "A Foundation for the Study of Group Decision Support Systems," *Management Science,* 33, May 1987. Copyright 1989, The Institute of Management Sciences.

- A **Level 2 GDSS** extends the abilities of Level 1 to include modeling software and other aids to be used in decision making. These features are listed in Table 13.2.
- A **Level 3 GDSS** features machine-induced group communication patterns, and can include the use of expert systems. See Table 13.3.

Most of the DSS developmental activity thus far has been aimed at establishing Level 1 settings, although some accomplishments have been made toward Levels 2 and 3. Milam Aiken, Olivia Liu Sheng, and Doug Vogel, for example, have shown how the integration of expert systems with GDSSs can improve data retrieval, group communication, facilitator control, network utilization, and GDSS tool selection.[14]

Putting Group Problem Solving in Perspective

Pioneer work on the GDSS concept during the early 1980s involved both academia and industry. One of the first decision rooms was constructed at EXECUCOM, under the leadership of its founder, Gerald Wagner. Another was built at Southern Methodist University by Professor Paul Gray, now at Claremont Graduate School. That tradition of both industrial and academic research has continued with decision

[14]Milam Aiken, Olivia Liu Sheng, and Doug Vogel, "Integrating Expert Systems with Group Decision Support Systems," *ACM Transactions on Information Systems* 9 (January 1991), 75–95.

TABLE 13.3 The Level 3 GDSS Incorporates Expert Systems	Group Problem or Need	GDSS Feature
	Desire to enforce formalized decision procedures	Automated Parliamentary Procedured or Robert's Rules of Order
	Desire to select and arrange an array of rules for discussion	Rule base; facility for rule selection and application
	Uncertainty about options for meeting procedures	Automated counselor, giving advice on available rules and appropriate use
	Desire to develop rules for the meeting	Rule-writing facility

Reprinted by permission of Gerardine DeSanctis and R. Brent Gallupe, "A Foundation for the Study of Group Decision Support Systems," *Management Science,* 33, May 1987. Copyright 1989. The Institute of Management Sciences.

rooms being used daily at business organizations such as the XEROX Palo Alto Research Center and universities, such as the University of Minnesota, the University of Georgia, and the University of Arizona. University facilities are typically made available to industry for a fee.

Industry recognizes the GDSS as a concept that has real practical value, and the concept is attracting the interest of academic researchers as well. The GDSS should continue to be one of the most intense areas of DSS development.

THE ROLE OF THE DSS IN PROBLEM SOLVING

We saw in the previous chapter that the MIS is best suited to identifying problems and helping managers understand them. The DSS can extend this support through the remaining steps of the problem-solving process. This added capability is not because of the tools that are used, since MIS and DSS both employ the same ones. The reason for the more complete support is the fact that the DSSs are tailored to the specific needs of specific managers.

SUMMARY

Herbert Simon made two key contributions to the DSS concept—the distinction between programmed and nonprogrammed decisions, and the four phases of problem solving. Gorry and Scott Morton used his concept of decision structure as the basis for one of the dimensions of their grid. The other dimension came from Robert Anthony in the form of his management levels.

The Alter DSS taxonomy is important, as it recognizes that DSS support can range from single information elements to decisions that are made for the manager by mathematical models.

DSSs support managers as they solve semistructured problems. The emphasis is on the effectiveness of the decisions rather than the efficiency of the decision-making process.

A DSS consists of three types of information-producing subsystems. Report-writing software provides information in the form of periodic and special reports. Mathematical models provide information in the form of simulation results. GDSS software provides for communications links among group members.

Management by exception can be incorporated into reports by preparing them only when exceptions occur, using an ascending or descending sequence to highlight exceptions, grouping exceptions together, and using variance columns.

A mathematical model simulates an entity and can be static or dynamic, probabilistic or deterministic, and optimizing or suboptimizing. Models are designed so that the manager can specify the scenario and then assign values to decision variables. A manager who engages in modeling can expect to learn from the modeling experience, be able to consider a larger number of alternatives because of the simulation speed, gain a certain predictive power, and possibly avoid the costs of bad decisions. However, the manager must recognize that the model is only an approximation of reality, and the requirement for mathematical skills increases as the models become more complex.

Although computer graphics are intuitively appealing, research has not supported their superiority over tabular displays in all instances. In general, graphs are best for making rather simple analyses, and certain types of graphs are better than others, depending on the task.

Initial DSS research was directed at supporting the individual, but recently the needs of decision-making groups have received attention. Most GDSS activity thus far has been aimed at improving communications by providing stimulating environmental settings. Future designs will make greater use of mathematical models and expert systems.

During the 1970s and 1980s the DSS stimulated more interest than any other CBIS subsystem. Its popularity will continue, for the soundness of the DSS concept is beyond question. During the 1990s, however, the CBIS subsystem that will probably generate the most hardware and software sales is office automation. OA is the subject of the next chapter.

KEY TERMS

programmed decision
nonprogrammed decision
periodic report
special report
model

entity
static model
dynamic model
probabilistic model
deterministic model

optimizing model

suboptimizing model, satisficing model

simulation, modeling

scenario

scenario data element

decision variable

what-if game

group decision support system (GDSS)

groupware

synchronous exchange

asynchronous exchange

decision room

facilitator

parallel communication

KEY CONCEPTS

The continuum of decisions that ranges from programmed to nonprogrammed

How Simon's problem-solving phases parallel the steps of the systems approach

Problem structure

Alter's DSS taxonomy

How the manager and the computer work together in solving semistructured problems

The way that periodic and special reports

contribute primarily to problem definition, and how mathematical modeling contributes primarily to problem solution

The incorporation of management by exception into reports

How the manager uses a suboptimizing model in a what-if manner

How the environmental setting of the GDSS facilitates communication, which in turn facilitates decision making

QUESTIONS

1. What are Simon's two major contributions to DSS theory?

2. How did Gorry and Scott Morton initially view the DSS?

3. Which of Alter's DSS types refers to database queries?

4. At the time that Alter developed his taxonomy, expert systems were not popular. Where would they fit in his six categories, or would they? Support your answer.

5. Does Alter's *Make decisions* type of DSS replace the manager? Explain.

6. Why would a manager settle for anything less than the optimum decision?

7. Why has the GDSS become so popular?

8. Which of the three methods for obtaining information from the DSS are best suited to problem definition? To problem solution?

9. When is a special report prepared?

10. What types of computer devices would a firm need if it wanted to print periodic reports one day after the end of the period?

11. What are four ways to incorporate management by exception into reports?

12. Which type of model is like a motion picture? Like a snapshot?

13. Why design a model so that the scenario elements are variables rather than constants?

14. Why is it a good practice to manipulate only a single decision variable at a time?

15. Why include the scenario elements and decision variables on the model output?

16. What feature does modeling offer that is not found in periodic or special reports?

17. What effect have electronic spreadsheets had on modeling disadvantages?

18. If you were designing a weekly report for a department head, showing the hours that each employee worked each day, would you use a graph or a tabular display? Support your answer.

19. How can bar graphs be designed so that the user can read individual data values?

20. Give an example of a synchronous exchange in a legislative session.

TOPICS FOR DISCUSSION

1. According to the Gorry and Scott Morton grid, what factor has the greatest influence on the difficulty of implementing an application on the computer?

2. What is the connection, if any, between Simon's programmed and nonprogrammed decisions and problem structure ranging from structured to semistructured to unstructured?

3. Why has the DSS been more successful in providing problem solving support than has MIS, or has it?

PROBLEMS

1. The president of a retail chain has a favorite report that she calls her *stars report*. It lists the items that are selling the best. She reviews the report before touring a store so that she can ask the store personnel why the items are selling so well. Then, she trys to think of ways to achieve the same results for the items that are not selling. How could the report be designed to facilitate management by exception? Write a one-page explanation, titled "Incorporation of Management by Exception into a Fast-Moving Items Report." Your instructor will give you the details on the paper format.

2. Design the data record that would be used to print the stars report. Include all necessary data elements. Unless your instructor tells you otherwise, use the data dictionary forms in Chapter 6 to document the record.

International Business Machines[15]

A plant manager was having trouble identifying problem areas that were hindering shop floor control. His subordinates seemed unable to isolate causes of the problem and possible solutions that could result in improved productivity. A two-hour meeting of six key plant personnel had resulted in quite a few arguments but no solutions.

The manager decided to use the company's GDSS in an attempt to resolve the problem and develop a plan of action including information system requirements. The manager met with the company's GDSS facilitator to set the agenda of the meeting and to understand how the GDSS could be used to resolve the problem. The manager and facilitator decided to use the Electronic Brainstorming, Idea Organizer, and Vote programs and to invite ten of the plant employees, in addition to the manager and two junior analysts assigned to investigate the problem. The manager and facilitator decided that the topic of the meeting should be "What are the key issues in improving shop floor control?"

During the GDSS session the meeting participants used the Brainstorming program for thirty-five minutes and generated 645 lines of comments about the topic. At the end of the brainstorming session, the manager saw that for the first time he was able to get concrete, meaningful answers to questions associated with shop floor control issues. The two analysts saw that they were beginning to better understand the complex nature of the overall shop floor control process.

After using Electronic Brainstorming, the group participants used Idea Organizer for thirty minutes to identify key issues or focus on items related to shop floor control. They then spent forty-five minutes organizing the 645 lines of comments into these key issues, and forming a consolidated list of requirements for effective shop floor control improvement.

Finally the Vote program was used. Each group member prioritized the list of requirements developed using Idea Organizer in terms of importance to improved shop floor control. The accumulated results were displayed to the group. After ten minutes of discussion, the meeting was concluded with the manager thanking the participants. The manager was given a printout of all of the group's comments, the consolidated list of requirements, and the results of the group vote.

Assignments

1. What was the problem faced by the manager?
2. What were the basic alternatives open to the manager for pursuing a problem solution?

[15] Adapted from Jay Nunamaker, Doug Vogel, Alan Heminger, Ben Martz, Ron Grohowski, and Chris McGoff, "Experiences at IBM with Group Support Systems: A Field Study," *Decision Support Systems* 5 (June 1989), 183–96.

3. Do you think that the GDSS was a good way to come to grips with the problem? Explain your answer.

4. Do you think that the group included too many plant employees? Why or why not?

5. Was it wise to include the information specialists? Why or why not?

6. Was this an example of following the systems approach to problem solution? Explain your reasoning.

Racine Paper Products

"Ms. Vance? I'm Blanca San Miguel. I'm from information services, and we're conducting a survey of all the people who receive reports to see if there is any way they can be improved. According to our records you get the monthly product sales report. Is that true?"

Susan Vance, sales manager for Racine Paper Products, began to shuffle the papers on her desk and said, "I think I have it here somewhere. I usually don't keep it, but I think I received one yesterday. I really don't use it. The manager who was here before me ordered it and it just keeps coming. I've been meaning to call you people and tell you to stop, but I just never got around to it. Too busy I guess. Oh, here it is." Ms. Vance pulled the thick report out of a stack of papers.

"Do you mind if I sit down?" Blanca asked. "It looks like the report could use some improvement. Why don't you take a look at it and tell me what's wrong?"

Susan said, "Well, to begin with, this report is for the month of October and my secretary's date stamp says that we received it on November 12. Why does it take so long to get it to me? By the time I get it, it's past history."

"It's probably because its so lengthy," Blanca replied. "We have a lot of reports like that, and it takes a long time to print all of the pages. Add to that the time required to route it through the company mail, and you've got a long delay. I grant you that we should be able to get it out sooner. All of the data is in the computer at the end of the month. Let me see what I can do to speed things up. Anything else?"

"As a matter of fact, yes. Isn't there some way to boil all of this down? That would certainly make the report easier to read. I imagine that we have a lot of products that are just dead weight—we haven't sold any in ages and aren't likely to sell any more in the future. It would be best to just get rid of them. I know that if I spent several days going through this printout I could spot the nonprofitable items, but that seems to be a tremendous price to pay. I just don't have that kind of time."

"Oh, I am sure that we can give you a report that would help you make that decision without taking up all of your time," Blanca replied. "What constitutes a product that isn't selling? Could you give us some guidelines?"

"Well, if it hasn't sold in six months I'd like to know about it. Could you tell me that?"

Blanca pulled a sheet of paper out of a folder and said, "Here is the data dictionary description of the record that we use to print the report. It doesn't have the date of the last sale in it, but I'm sure we could add it. Then it would be a simple matter to select out those records that have been dormant for six months—or for any period."

Just then Susan's secretary walked into the room and said "Ms. Vance. They're ready for you in the conference room. Shall I tell them that you will be a little late?"

"No. I'm on my way. Ms. San Miguel, I appreciate you taking the time to go over this report with me. If you could do some of the things we talked about, I'm sure I would use it more often."

"One last question," Blanca asked as Susan headed toward the door. "Have you ever used the computer?"

"Oh no," Susan replied. "I'm no programmer."

Assignments

1. Does it sound as though Susan needs a special report or a periodic one? Explain your answer.

2. What could be done to cut down on the delay in getting the report to Susan?

3. Would you recommend an ascending or descending sequence? What would be the control field?

4. Was Blanca on safe ground in assuring Susan that the date field could be added? Explain why or why not.

5. Assume that the company decides to offer an inhouse course for managers in the use of a query language. What reasons could Blanca give Susan that she attend?

SELECTED BIBLIOGRAPHY

Alter, Steven L. *Decision Support Systems: Current Practice and Continuing Challenges*. Reading, MA: Addison-Wesley, 1980.

Benbasat, Izak; Dexter, Albert S.; and Todd, Peter. "An Experimental Program Investigating Color-Enhanced and Graphics Information Presentation: An Integration of the Findings." *Communications of the ACM* 29 (November 1986): 1094–105.

Chen, Edward T., and Hwang, Hsin-Ginn. "Group Decision Support Systems (GDSS): Supporting Management Teamwork in the 21st Century." In *Managing Information Technology in a Global Society*, edited by Mehdi Khosrowpour, Memphis, TN; n.p. 1991. Pp. 194–200.

Dyson, Esther. "Why Groupware Is Gaining Ground." *Datamation* 36 (March 1, 1990): 52*ff.*

Fuerst, William L., and Martin, Merle P. "Effective Design and Use of Computer Decision Models." *MIS Quarterly* 8 (March 1984): 17–26.

George, Joey F. "The Conceptualization and Development of Organizational Decision Support Systems." *Journal of Management Information Systems* 8 (Winter 1991–92): 109–125.

Guimaraes, Tor; Igbaria, Magid; and Lu, Ming-te. "The Determinants of DSS Success: An Integrated Model." *Decision Sciences* 23 (March/April 1992): 409–30.

Huber, George P. "Issues in the Design of Group Decision Support Systems." *MIS Quarterly* 8 (September 1984): 195–204.

Keen, Peter G. W. "Decision Support Systems: Translating Analytic Techniques into Useful Tools." *Sloan Management Review* 21 (Spring 1980): 33–44.

Kirkpatrick, David. "Here Comes the Payoff from PCs." *Fortune* 125 (March 23, 1992), 93*ff.*

Liberatore, Matthew J.; Titus, George J.; and Dixon, Paul W. "The Effects of Display Formats on Information Systems Design." *Journal of Management Information Systems* 5 (Winter 1988/89): 85–99.

Martin, Merle P. "Management Reports." *Journal of Systems Management* 33 (June 1982): 32–38.

Nunamaker, Jay F., Jr.; Applegate, Lynda M.; and Konsynski, Benn R. "Facilitating Group Creativity: Experience with a Group Decision Support System." *Journal of Management Information Systems* 3 (Spring 1987): 5–19.

Philippakis, Andrew S., Green, Gary I. 1988. "An Architecture for Organization-Wide Decision Support Systems." In *Proceedings of the Ninth International Conference on Information Systems*, ed. Janice I. DeGross, and Margrethe H. Olson., 257–63. Minneapolis, MN.

Silver, Mark S. "Decisional Guidance for Computer-Based Decision Support." *MIS Quarterly* 15 (March 1991), 105–22.

Straub, Detmar W., Jr., and Beauclair, Renee A. "Current and Future Uses of Group Decision Support System Technology: Report on a Recent Empirical Study." *Journal of Management Information Systems* 5 (Summer 1988): 101–16.

Umanath, Narayan S., and Scamell, Richard W. "An Experimental Evaluation of the Impact of Data Display Format on Recall Performance." *Communications of the ACM* 31 (May 1988): 562–70.

Weber, E. Sue, and Konsynski, Benn R. "Problem Management: Neglected Elements in Decision Support Systems." *Journal of Management Information Systems* 4 (Winter 1987/88): 64–81.

Chapter 14

Office Automation

LEARNING OBJECTIVES

After studying this chapter, you should:

- Know the different application areas within office automation
- Understand the role that office automation plays in problem solving

INTRODUCTION

Automation began in the factory and spread to the office in the form of office automation, or OA. Originally, OA was targeted at secretarial and clerical workers, but its ability to facilitate both formal and informal communications with persons both inside and outside the firm added managers and professionals as users. All of these users use OA to increase their productivity.

There are at least eleven OA applications. Some require the use of the computer, and some do not. All, however, can provide problem-solving information.

OA can be tailored to the communications needs of each manager. A particular manager's OA mix is influenced by the type of organization, the manager's personal preference, and the OA resources that are available.

Although information scientists have not lavished as much attention on OA as they have on other CBIS subsystems, such as DSS and expert systems, OA has been widely embraced by practitioners. OA appeals to managers on all levels because it not only supplements their traditional interpersonal communications media but offers some new communications capabilities as well.

AUTOMATION IN THE FACTORY

Automation is the use of machinery to perform physical tasks that normally are performed by human beings. The first applications of automation were in the factory. In the late 1950s production machines were designed so that they could be controlled by holes punched in paper tape. The application was called **numerical control**, and the machines could do the work faster and more accurately than when human operators were used. Then the machines were designed so that they could be controlled directly by a minicomputer—**direct numerical control**. More recently **robotics** (the use of robots), **CAD (computer-aided design)** and **CAM (computer-aided manufacturing)** have contributed to automation in the production area.

Firms quickly recognized factory automation as a means of achieving greater productivity and thus competing better in world markets. During the 1970s firms spent an average of $25,000 for the purpose of increasing each factory worker's productivity. The investment paid off as productivity rose an average of 85 to 90 percent.[1]

OFFICE AUTOMATION

The picture in the office, however, has been different. During the 1970s the capital investment per office worker was in the $2,000 to $4,000 range, and productivity rose only 4 percent. When these figures were compared to those in the factory, managers realized that office productivity had been neglected.

[1]The figures from this and the next section are from Nancy B. Finn, *The Electronic Office* (Englewood Cliffs, NJ: Prentice-Hall, 1983), 8–9.

Unplanned Growth

Although factory automation has been impressive, it has not followed any grand plan. As the innovations in technology came along, manufacturing managers simply took advantage of them. The same thing has happened in the office.

The origin of office automation can be traced back to the early 1960s when IBM coined the term *word processing* to describe the activity of its electric typewriter division. The term expressed the concept that office activity is centered around the processing of *words*. The intent was to draw the same attention to office products that had been lavished on computers and *data processing*.

The first tangible evidence of this new concept came in 1964 when IBM placed on the market a machine called the MT/ST. The letters stood for Magnetic Tape/Selectric Typewriter. The Selectric had been the name given to IBM's typewriter that featured the rotating-ball typing element. The MT/ST was a Selectric typewriter with a magnetic tape unit attached. As a form letter was typed, it was stored on tape. The letter could be typed over and over from the tape. The typist only had to type in the name and address of the recipient. The letter looked as if it had been typed especially for the recipient.

What Is Office Automation?

Since the debut of word processing, other technologies have been applied to office work, and together they are known as office automation. **Office automation (OA)** includes all of the formal and informal electronic systems primarily concerned with the communication of information to and from persons both in and outside the firm.

Formal and Informal Electronic Systems   Some OA systems are formal in that they are planned and documented in the form of a written procedure. These formal systems are implemented on a firm-wide basis to meet organizational needs—in much the same manner as an MIS.

Most OA systems, however, are neither planned nor described in writing. These informal OA systems are implemented by individuals to meet their own unique needs—in much the same manner as a DSS.

Communication of Information   The key word that distinguishes OA from the other CBIS subsystems is *communication*. OA is intended to facilitate all types of communication, both oral and written.

Persons Both in and outside the Firm   When we hear the term office automation, it is easy to think of persons communicating within a single office. This restricted view no longer applies. Today's OA systems provide communications not only among persons in a firm but also between those persons and others in the firm's environment.

Who Uses Office Automation?

OA is used by all of the people who work in offices. Essentially there are four categories of users—managers, professionals, secretaries, and clerical employees.

FIGURE 14.1
Office Workers

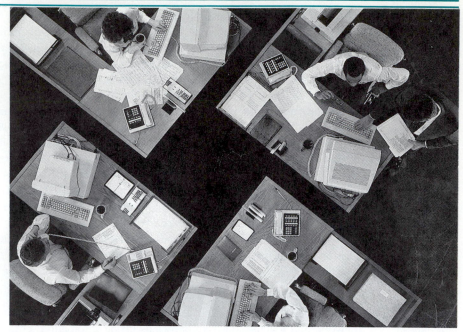

PhotoEdit

We know who the **managers** are. They are the persons who have responsibility for managing the firm's resources, primarily personnel. **Professionals** are persons who do not manage others but contribute some special skill that distinguishes them from secretarial and clerical employees. Examples of professionals are buyers, salespersons, and such special staff assistants as marketing researchers, statisticians, and administrative assistants. The managers and professionals are collectively known as **knowledge workers** since their main contribution to their activities is their knowledge.

Secretaries and clerical workers support the knowledge workers. **Secretaries** usually are assigned to particular knowledge workers to perform a variety of duties such as handling correspondence, answering the telephone, and maintaining appointments calendars. **Clerical employees** perform tasks for the secretaries, relieving them of such activities as operating copying machines, assembling documents, filing, and mailing.

An OA Model

A model of an OA system is illustrated in Figure 14.2. Since OA has no data processing capability, its use of the database is restricted to the information contents. This information is gathered from the physical system of the firm at the bottom of the model in the same manner that the data processing system gathers its data. In fact, some of the information that is used by OA is provided by data processing.

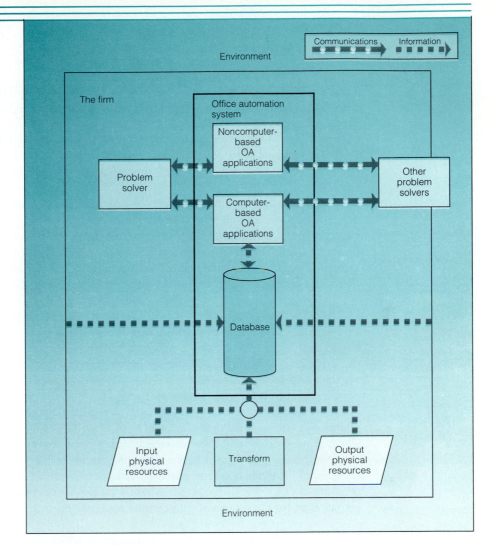

FIGURE 14.2

An OA Model

An example is an income statement produced by DP, which a manager incorporates into a memo prepared with word processing. Information is also provided by the environment.

The information serves as input to such *computer-based OA applications* as word processing, electronic mail, and computer conferencing. The computer-based applications enable one problem solver to communicate information to other problem solvers, both inside and outside the firm. Notice how the box labeled "Other problem solvers" straddles the line that separates the firm and the environment.

The model also reflects the use of such *noncomputer-based OA applications* as FAX to facilitate communications between problem solvers.

The Objective of Office Automation

Until about 1980 OA was seen as a way of increasing the productivity of only secretaries and clerical employees. OA products enabled these office workers to process more documents faster and better. Then it became apparent that the knowledge workers could benefit as well. OA could make it easier for the knowledge workers to prepare *outgoing correspondence*. For example, the knowledge workers or their secretaries could use word processing to prepare letters, memos, and reports.

But the outgoing correspondence of one person is the incoming correspondence of another. Viewed as a means of stimulating *incoming correspondence*, OA becomes a tool to be used in problem solving. Compared with media transmitted by manual office communications systems, the OA information arrives sooner, in a better form, and with a more attractive appearance. In sum, OA information communicates better and thereby provides better information for decision making.

Higher Revenues versus Cost Avoidance
Many firms use computers as a means of achieving **cost avoidance**. The computers do not replace current employees, but they do delay the hiring of additional employees needed to handle the expanding workload. This strategy applies especially to OA where firms see the increased secretarial and clerical productivity made possible by OA as a means of delaying the addition of more personnel.

Although these avoided clerical costs are good objectives, they are modest when compared with the potential benefits of using OA as a problem-solving tool. The improved decisions of the managers, which come as a result of the improved communications, have the potential of producing higher revenues for the firm in the form of increased sales and improved return on investments. The potential contribution of OA to the firm's profits is much greater for the problem-solving applications than for the secretarial and clerical applications.

Group Problem Solving
The manner in which OA contributes to communications both to and from managers makes it especially applicable to group problem solving. In Chapter 13 we recognized that managers seldom solve problems alone. They communicate with other members of the problem-solving team at each step of the process, and OA can be used for some of the communication.

A Supplement—Not a Replacement
OA is not without its limitations as a means of business communication. It will not replace *all* traditional interpersonal communications—face-to-face conversations, telephone conversations, notes jotted on memo pads, and the like. Those informal communications will continue, since they are both convenient and effective. OA should have the objective of *supplementing* the traditional communications. Used in combination, OA and the tra-

ditional media provide the manager with the most powerful communications capability.

OA APPLICATIONS

The OA applications have grown one-by-one until there are now at least eleven:[2]

- Word processing
- Electronic mail
- Voice mail
- Electronic calendaring
- Audio conferencing
- Video conferencing
- Computer conferencing
- Facsimile transmission
- Videotex
- Imaging
- Desktop publishing.

We will discuss each of the applications below.

Word Processing

Word processing is the use of an electronic device that automatically performs many of the tasks necessary to prepare typed or printed documents.

During 1970s, special electronic devices, called dedicated word processors, were built especially for that application. A **dedicated word processor** is a key-driven device designed to perform only word processing, and its specialized hardware and software work together as a unit. Practically all of the dedicated word processors have given way to the use of general-purpose computers. A general-purpose computer achieves its word processing capabilities through software. The computer can be a mainframe, a minicomputer, or a microcomputer. A major advantage of using a general-purpose computer is its ability to incorporate contents of the database into documents.

Figure 14.3 shows the primary units of a word processing system. The operator uses a keyboard to type the material, which is displayed on the screen. The operator uses the display to add and delete words, move sentences around, adjust the format, and so on. Then the material is stored in secondary storage and printed.

Word processing is the most well-established of the OA applications. It has been around the longest, and its outputs touch almost everyone in business. The

---

[2]Some application lists include **telecommuting,** the use of electronic communications facilities to link employees who work at home with their firms. We do not include telecommuting since it does not offer a unique communications technology. In fact, telecommuting can use *any* of the eleven OA applications in our list.

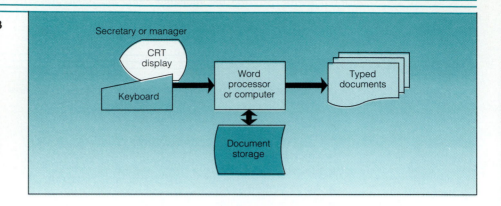

FIGURE 14.3
A Word
Processing
System

suppliers of the leading packages such as WordStar, WordPerfect, and Microsoft Word, continue to make improvements, but new innovations also emerge. One such innovation is the **graphic word processor** that displays characters in exactly the same size and shape as they will appear on paper. The term WYSIWYG (What you see is what you get) describes the effect. The operator does not have to wait to see the hard copy to view the output.[3]

Word processing contributes to problem solving by enabling the manager to prepare more effective written communications. The manager realizes a return on her or his investment when the persons with whom the manager communicates use word processing in preparing memos, letters, and reports for the manager.

Electronic Mail

Electronic mail, popularly known as **E-mail**, is the use of a networked computer that allows users to send, store, and receive messages using the computer's terminals and storage devices. Figure 14.4 shows the system configuration. A user types a message using his or her terminal keyboard, and the message is placed in the recipient's **electronic mailbox** in computer storage. The message is retrieved at the convenience of the recipient, using his or her terminal and providing the proper password. Electronic mail software controls the process.

Electronic mail is intended to solve a multitude of problems that plague conventional telephone use. According to a study by AT & T, in 75 percent of the calls, the caller does not obtain the desired information.[4] Too frequently, the two parties play **telephone tag**, the game of alternately returning calls only to find that the other person is out or is unavailable.

---

[3] For more information on graphic word processors, *see* Rick Cook, "A Bold New Look For Word Processing," *Datamation* 36 (September 1, 1990), 35*ff*.

[4] Jules DeVigne, "Automated Telephones And Office Efficiency," *The Office* 113 (February 1991), 28.

FIGURE 14.4

An Electronic Mail System

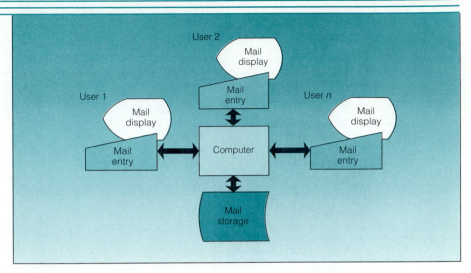

Electronic mail handles only one-way communications, but that limitation is not as serious as it first appears. The AT & T study found that 50 percent of all business calls are only requests for information.[5] However, if you desire two-way conversation, you must either send multiple E-mail messages back and forth or use another medium.

Several optional E-mail features are available, depending on the prewritten software package that is used. If you want everyone in the firm with a terminal to read the message, it is placed on an **electronic bulletin board**, which everyone can access. If you want to receive a confirmation when the recipient retrieves your message, it can be sent as **registered mail**. The confirmation is called a **receipt notice**. If you do not want the recipient to route the message to others in the network you can send it as **private mail**.

Electronic Mail Services   When a firm decides to implement electronic mail, it has two basic choices. It can acquire its own hardware and software, and install an inhouse system. Or, it can subscribe to an **electronic mail service** that provides the necessary computing and communications facilities for a fee. A subscriber need only furnish the terminals to tie into the network. Table 14.1 lists the seven largest publicly available electronic mail networks in the U.S.

The first services were implemented as **closed systems**, in that they were designed to use only the suppliers' communications standards, or protocols. Suppliers now are seeking to implement **interconnected systems**, which allow a user of one service to communicate with a user of another service. The interconnected systems will greatly facilitate the use of E-mail for interfirm communications.

[5] *Ibid.*

TABLE 14.1

The Most Popular Electronic Mail Services

Network/Carrier		1989 Revenues ($ millions)	Market Share (percent)
Easy Link	Western Union	$100	.28
SprintMail	U.S. Sprint	50	.14
Dialcom	British Telecom	40	.11
AT & T Mail	AT & T	30	.09
CompuServe	CompuServe	30	.09
MCI Mail	MCI	30	.09
Quik-Comm	General Electric	30	.09

Voice Mail

Voice mail is just like electronic mail only you send messages by speaking them into your telephone rather than typing them, and you use your telephone to retrieve messages that have been sent to you. Voice mail requires a computer with an ability to store the audio messages in a digital form and then convert them back to an audio form upon retrieval, as illustrated in Figure 14.5. Each user has a **voice mailbox** in secondary storage, and special equipment converts the audio messages to and from the digital form.

Voice Mail for Group Communications   A voice mail feature that has application to group problem solving is the **message distribution list**, which identifies all of the persons who are to receive the same message. The caller provides the distribution list, and the voice mail system periodically calls each person on the

FIGURE 14.5

A Voice Mail System

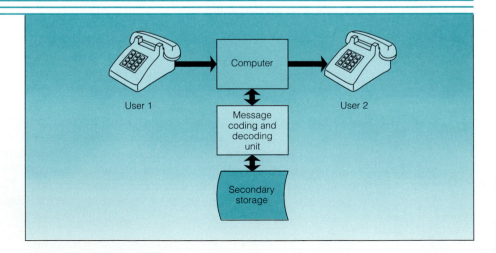

list until their receipt notice has been received. The system can also provide a list of those persons who have not acknowledged receipt.

The main advantage of voice mail over electronic mail is that the manager does not have to type. Voice mail also makes it easy to include persons in the firm's environment in communications networks. If the manager wants to use voice mail to communicate with persons outside the firm, it is only necessary to reserve a voice mailbox for that person. The external contact can both send and receive voice mail messages using the manager's system. The downside of this arrangement is that it opens the door for someone outside the firm to breach the firm's computer security.

Electronic Calendaring

Electronic calendaring is the use of a networked computer to store and retrieve a manager's appointments calendar. This process is shown in Figure 14.6. The manager or manager's secretary can enter appointments, make changes, and review the calendar using a keyboard terminal. You will notice that this equipment configuration is exactly the same as for E-mail. In fact, it is common for E-mail software to include an electronic calendaring capability.

Figure 14.7 illustrates how a manager's calendar might appear in electronic form.

It is possible to access other managers' calendars in addition to your own. If you want to schedule a meeting, the electronic calendar software can cause the computer to check the other calendars to pick a mutually convenient time. If you want to walk down the hall to talk with someone, you can check their calendar

FIGURE 14.6

An Electronic Calendaring System

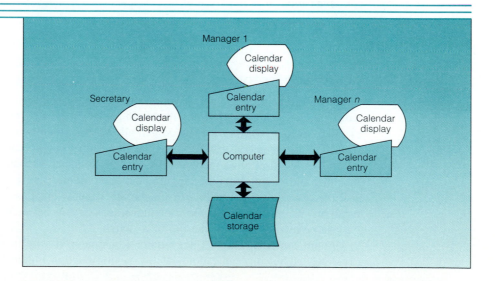

FIGURE 14.7
An Electronic
Calendar

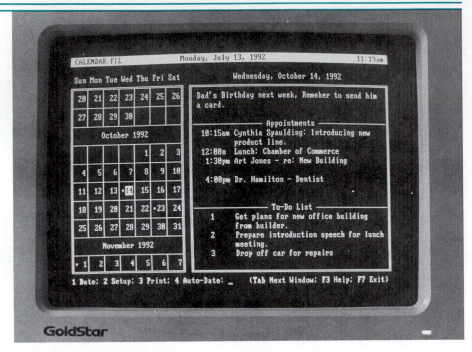

© Ogust/The Image Works

first to determine if they are available. If you prefer, you can prevent others from accessing all or part of your own calendar.

Electronic calendaring is unique among the OA applications in that it does not actually communicate *problem-solving* information. Rather, it sets the stage for the communication. It is most useful to managers on upper levels who have complicated appointments schedules.

Audio Conferencing

Audio conferencing is the use of voice communications equipment to establish an audio link between geographically dispersed persons for the purpose of conducting a conference. The **conference call**, which allows more than two persons to participate in a telephone conversation, was the first form of audio conferencing and is still in use. If a firm has a modern PBX, or private branch exchange, that switches incoming and outgoing telephone calls, the audio conferencing capability can be easily added. However, much more elaborate systems are possible. Some firms install private, high-quality audio communications circuits between conference sites that can be established with the flip of a switch.

Audio conferencing does not require a computer. It only involves the use of a two-way audio communications facility as illustrated in Figure 14.8.

FIGURE 14.8
An Audio
Conferencing
System

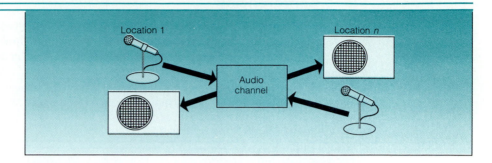

Advantages of Audio Conferencing
Audio conferencing offers three advantages over video conferencing, which we will discuss in the next section:[6]

- The cost of the equipment that is needed for an audio conference is within reach of practically all firms.
- People feel at ease speaking on the telephone.
- An audio conference can be arranged in minutes. Either an operator notifies the participants, or the participants are given a telephone number to call.

How to Make Audio Conferences More Efficient
Audio conferences can be made more efficient if a few simple rules are followed:

- The person who organizes the conference should serve as a **moderator**, making certain that all persons have an opportunity to participate, and the objectives of the conference are achieved.
- The number of participants should be kept to a manageable size. When the number exceeds a half dozen or so, it is difficult to keep the discussion on track.
- A copy of the conference agenda should be sent to the particpants in advance. Another OA application, FAX, which will be discussed later, is an excellent way to accomplish this transmission.
- When persons speak, they should identify themselves.
- A taped record of the conference should be kept.
- A hard copy record should be prepared from the taped record, and distributed to all participants.

Audio conferencing appeals only to firms that are spread over a wide area. When all of the problem solvers reside in the same location, a face-to-face meeting provides a better communications setting.

---

[6]Material in this section is based on Belden Menkus, "Why Not Try 'Audio Teleconferencing?," *Modern Office Technology* 32 (October 1987), 124*ff.*

Video Conferencing

Video conferencing is the use of television equipment to link geographically disbursed conference participants. The equipment provides for audio as well as video linkage. Like audio conferencing, video conferencing does not involve the use of a computer.

Figure 14.9 shows a video conference room where the images of participants in other locations can be viewed as the conference takes place. The firm can con-

FIGURE 14.9

A Video Conference

© 1991 Matthew Borkoski/Stock, Boston

FIGURE 14.10

Video
Conferencing

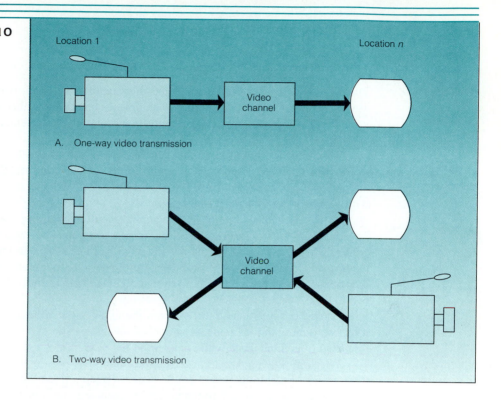

Location 1

Location *n*

Video
channel

A.   One-way video transmission

Video
channel

B.   Two-way video transmission

struct its own rooms, or rent them from such organizations as telephone companies and larger hotel chains.

Three basic video conferencing configurations are possible, based on the signal capabilities.

- **One-Way Video and One-Way Audio**   Video and audio signals are sent from a single transmitting site to one or more receiving sites. A good application is use by a project leader to disseminate information to team members at remote sites.
- **One-Way Video and Two-Way Audio**   The two-way audio capability enables persons at the receiving sites to engage in conversation with persons at the transmitting site while everyone views the same video images. Figure 14.10A illustrates one-way video.
- **Two-Way Video and Audio**   The video and audio communications between all sites are two-way. This setup is the most expensive of the electronic-aided conferencing approaches. Figure 14.10B illustrates two-way video.

Firms have found that video conferencing *reduces* travel expenses involved with bringing people together for face-to-face meetings, but it does not *eliminate* such travel. When a meeting is necessary to discuss an especially complex problem it is best for the members to assemble in person.

Computer Conferencing

There is a fine line between computer conferencing and E-mail. Both applications use the same software and the same equipment configuration that was illustrated in Figure 14.3. The distinguishing features are *who* uses the system, and the *subject matter*.

We can define **computer conferencing** as the use of a networked computer to allow members of a *problem-solving team* to exchange information concerning the *problem* that is being solved. E-mail, on the other hand, can be used by *anyone* with access to the system, for *any purpose*.

Unlike an audio conference, a computer conference group can consist of a large number of participants. One of the largest computer conferences was formed within IBM to include all of the persons who had an interest in the IBM PC. Its membership exceeded 40,000, and there were over 4,000 separate topic areas. The conference caused such a flood of internal communications that IBM management had to enact special policies governing its use.[7]

Computer conferencing differs from the other two conferencing types in that it can be used within a single geographical site. A person can use computer conferencing to communicate with someone in the next office.

Teleconferencing The term **teleconferencing** has been coined to describe all three forms of electronic aided conferencing—audio, video, and computer. Teleconferencing can be used throughout the problem-solving process for exchanging information among the problem-solvers who are not at the same location. This capability enables persons who otherwise would be left out for reasons of geography to contribute to problem solution.

Facsimile Transmission

If there is anyone on this planet who does not know what a FAX is, they have probably been marooned on a Pacific island for the past several years. No other OA application has pervaded our daily lives to the extent of FAX. **FAX**, for **facsimile transmission**, is the use of special equipment that can read a document image at one end of a communication channel and make a copy at the other end, as diagrammed in Figure 14.11.

A FAX machine is the easiest piece of OA equipment to implement and operate. It uses an ordinary voice-grade telephone line, and operation requires no more skill than a copying machine.

The first FAX machines were dedicated to that application; they could do nothing but send and receive FAXs. However, in 1985, an innovation called a **FAX**

---

[7] H. Jeff Smith, "IBM Computer Conferencing," *Harvard Business School Case N9–188–039,* copyright 1988 by the President and Fellows of Harvard College, Boston, MA.

FIGURE 14.11

Facsimile

Transmission

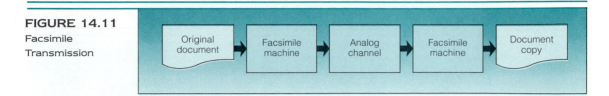

board was introduced that enables a microcomputer to function like a FAX machine. By adding the board, you can receive FAX messages and store them for later display or printing. You can also send FAX messages by keying them into the keyboard. The market for computer-based FAX equipment is expected to increase dramatically during the 1990s, as illustrated in Figure 14.12. As shown in the figure the FAX capability can be made available both to standalone PCs and to LANs.

FAX contributes to problem solving by disseminating documents to members of the problem-solving team quickly and easily, regardless of their geographic location. Of special value to problem solvers is the ability to transmit graphic as well as narrative and tabular material. Anything that can be copied on an office copier can be transmitted.

Like voice mail, a manager can establish a FAX linkage with environmental contacts. The factor making this linkage possible is the set of FAX protocols that have been established on an international basis.

FIGURE 14.12

The Expanding
Market for
Computer-based
FAX Equipment

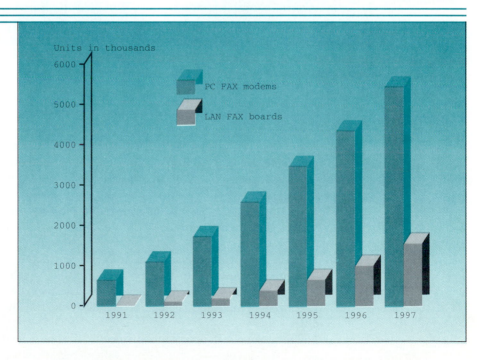

FIGURE 14.13

A Videotex Display

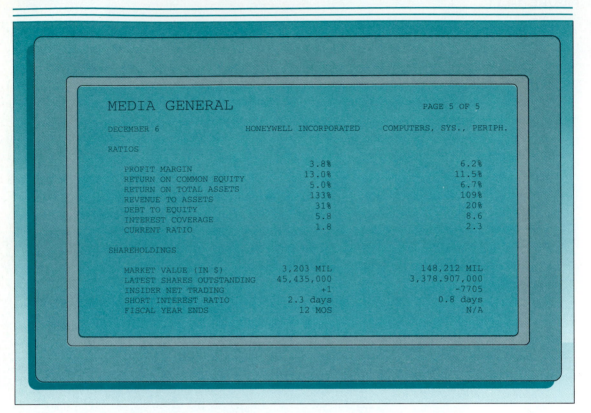

Dow Jones News/Retrieval

Videotex

Of all the OA applications, the one that has received the least amount of publicity is videotex. **Videotex** is the use of a computer for the purpose of providing the display of stored narrative and graphic material on a CRT screen. Figure 14.13 shows a typical display.

When a firm wants to provide information to problem solvers in a videotex form, there are three basic sources of the material.

- The firm can create videotex files in its *own computer.*
- The firm can subscribe to a *videotex service*, which enables users to access the videotex files provided by the service. The files are stored in the service's online secondary storage or are distributed in the form of optical disks.
- The firm can obtain access to the videotex files of *other firms.*

Thus far firms have shown the least amount of interest in the first and third approaches. Firms have been unwilling to go to the expense of creating their own videotex files, and they have been slow to realize the potential for sharing their information storage with other firms. A good example of the potential for shared storage is in the purchasing area. Suppliers could make their catalogs and price lists available to their customers' buyers in videotex form. Buyers would not have to maintain bulky catalogs as is now the practice and would simply query the supplier's videotex storage as prices or specifications are needed.

Most of the videotex interest has centered around the second approach. A **videotex subscription service** provides access to their files of videotex material for a fee. You can subscribe in much the same manner as you subscribe to a newspaper or magazine. In fact, it is possible to receive the *New York Times* in videotex form. There is an ever-increasing number of such videotex services, but two provide good examples of what is available.

- **Dow Jones News/Retrieval Service**   Subscribers to DJNRS can use their terminals to access current or recent business information stored in the Dow Jones central computer. Two types of information are made available—business news items and stock prices. Business news items are valuable in signaling problems or potential problems to managers in all functional areas. The stock prices are especially valuable to financial managers. Many executive information systems include DJNRS as a standard feature.
- **Lotus One Source**   This videotex service comes in the form of optical disks that the firm can use with its own computer. One of the disks is a videotex file named *CD/Corporate* that contains financial information on topics such as SEC filings, U.S. mergers and acquisitions, and U.K. public companies. Figure 14.14 is a sample display of CD/Corporate data. Financial analysts can bring contents such as these up on their screens, and can transport the data into their 1-2-3 spreadsheets for additional processing.

After initial acceptance in Europe, videotex began to make an impact in the United States. At first, home use was considered to offer the greatest potential. Now, the suppliers are turning their interest to business. The popularity of videotex should continue to increase as additional subscription services are offered and firms create information storage files for their own use and for use by their suppliers and customers.

Imaging

Some firms have large volumes of documents, which they must maintain in files so that the information can be retrieved when needed. Insurance companies and banks fit into this category. Initially, these firms maintained the files in paper form, but the space requirements became intolerable. The solution was to store an *image* of the document rather than the document itself. This OA application has recently been given the name imaging and is the OA application that is currently stimulating

FIGURE 14.14

The CD/Corporate Videotex Disk from Lotus One Source Permits the
Retrieval of Financial Information On U.S. and European Firms

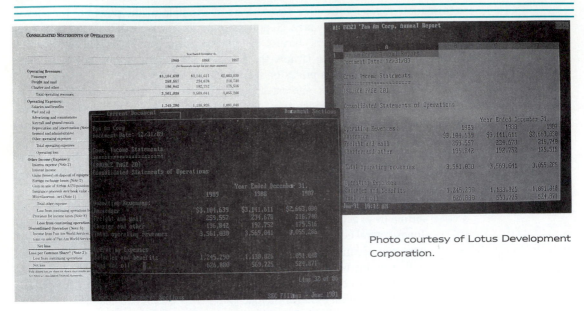

Photo courtesy of Lotus Development
Corporation.

the most interest. **Imaging**, as it is now practiced, is the use of optical character recognition to convert paper or microfilm records to a digital format for storage in a secondary storage device. Once stored, the images can be retrieved for display or printing.

Imaging processes are performed by a **document management (DM)** system such as that illustrated in Figure 14.15. The system consists of one or more optical character recognition (OCR) units for converting the document images to a digited form. Document management software is used to store the digitized data in optical disk storage, and make the images available to users who access the system from their workstations. The workstations are equipped with high-resolution screens.

The technology that has made DM practical is the optical disk. Previously, the best storage medium was microform, which consists of either roll-type microfilm, or microfiche. Many firms still use that technology.[8] The main advantage of the optical disk is its capacity. One 5 1/4 inch optical disk can store about 200,000 pages that fill about twenty file cabinets.[9]

Imaging is just getting off the ground, and the legal aspects are still being worked out. A few states have passed legislation that makes the digitized images admissable as evidence in court.

[8] "Document Storage and Retrieval Takes a Step Forward," *Modern Office Technology* 37 (March 1991), 28–29.

[9] Janet Mann, "An Image of Document Management," *Datamation* 37 (November 15, 1991), 81–82.

FIGURE 14.15

A Document
Management
System

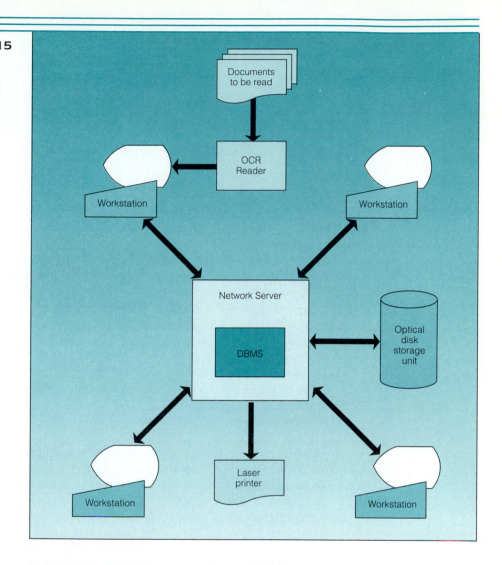

Imaging is used in problem solving when it is necessary to review historical documents for the purpose of understanding a problem. An operator accesses the DM system from a workstation, and produces a hard copy output for the manager.

Desktop Publishing

The newest member of the OA application family is desktop publishing. **Desktop publishing (DTP)** is the preparation of printed output that is very close in quality to that produced by a typesetter.

FIGURE 14.16

A Desk-Top
Publishing
System

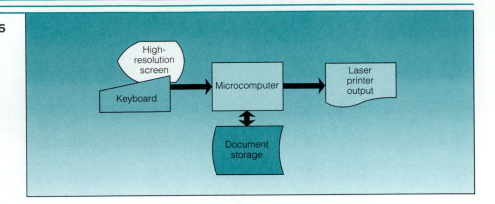

A DTP system consists of a microcomputer configuration shown in Figure 14.16. The configuration includes a high-resolution CRT screen and a laser printer, and is driven by DTP software. The high-resolution screen enables the operator to display the image in a WYSIWYG form. The laser printer produces the high-quality output. The DTP software permits the selection of the type fonts and sizes, hyphenation and right-margin justification, addition of horizontal and vertical lines, and layout of pages (including graphics).

Many of the magazines that you read and appear to have been typeset, have actually been produced using DTP. Macintosh has pioneered this application, using DTP software such as PageMaker.

DTP applications fall into three areas.[10]

- **Administrative applications** include documents intended for such internal use as correspondence, reports, and newsletters.
- **Technical applications** include such training materials as slides, overhead transparencies, and manuals.
- **Corporate graphics** include advertisements, brochures, and other documents intended for use outside the firm.

The use of DTP as a problem-solving tool includes both administrative and technical applications. Members of the problem-solving team can use DTP to prepare proposals and reports to communicate among themselves and with others in the organization. The attractive, professional appearance of the documents adds to their communicating effectiveness. In addition, slides and transparencies produced from DTP documents can be used in group problem-solving sessions—perhaps in a GDSS decision room.

[10]This classification was taken from Pamela Jarvis, "Desktop Publishing: Is It for Every Office?", *The Office* 105 (June 1987), 65*ff.*

THE ROLE OF OFFICE AUTOMATION IN PROBLEM SOLVING

Information comes to the manager in the form of both computer and noncomputer media. Although we have emphasized the role of computer media, a much greater volume comes from noncomputer sources—primarily interpersonal communications. The persons with whom the manager communicates are located on higher levels in the organizational hierarchy (**superiors**), on lower levels (**subordinates**), on the same level (**peers**), and in the environment.

A Manager's OA Mix Model

We introduced Henry Mintzberg in Chapter 1 by identifying his theory that managers play various roles while discharging their duties. Mintzberg identified ten roles, and we offered brief definitions in Table 1.1. These roles offer an excellent framework for viewing how a manager can apply OA. We refer to this framework, shown in Figure 14.17, as the **manager's OA mix model**.

This model uses circles to identify sources and receivers of the manager's communications, uses rectangles to identify the managerial roles, and uses parallelograms to identify places where OA can be applied.

Managerial Roles

Five interperesonal and information roles are instrumental in sending and receiving information.

- The *Monitor* role in the center serves as a traffic cop, receiving information, and passing it along to others or keeping it for use in decision making.
- The *Spokesperson* role transmits information to superiors, the environement, other operating units in the firm, and internal support units such as information services and accounting.
- The *Liaison* role receives information from the environment, other units, and support units.
- The *Leader* role receives information from superiors and subordinates.
- The *Disseminator* role sends information to subordinates.

The information that the manager does not pass along to others is used in the four decisional roles in the lower-left-hand corner of the model.

Selecting the Manager's OA Mix

The task of the manager (and of the information specialist working with the manager) is to select the OA applications to be used on each of the paths of the model.

FIGURE 14.17

A Manager's OA Mix Model

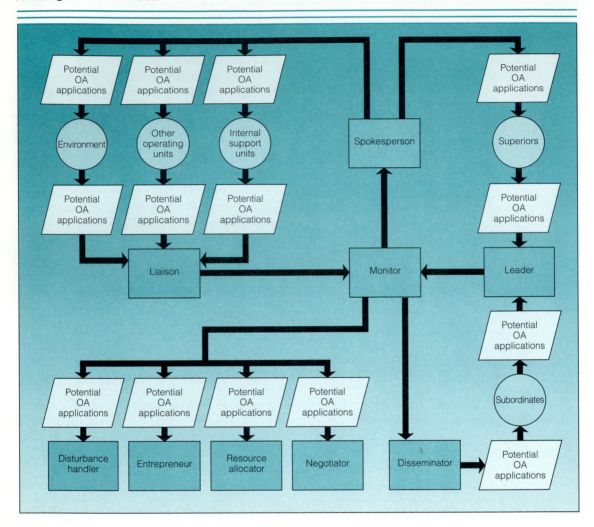

Three main factors influence the choice.

- **Type of Organization**   As reflected in Table 14.2, a manager in a firm with only one location will not consider audio and video conferencing. The exception to this rule is when the single-site firm is involved with another firm on a project such as the use of EDI. In that case, all eleven OA applications can be used.
- **Personal Preference**   Managers who prefer face-to-face communication are attracted to video conferencing and make good use of electronic cal-

TABLE 14.2		Firm with a Single Location	Firm with Geographically Disbursed Operations
The Influence of the Organiza-tion on the Manager's OA Mix	OA application		
	Electronic calendaring	X	X
	Word processing	X	X
	Electronic mail	X	X
	Voice mail	X	X
	Image storage/retrieval	X	X
	Facsimile transmission	X	X
	Videotex	X	X
	Audio conference		X
	Video conference		X
	Computer conference	X	X
	Desktop publishing	X	X

endaring. Those who like a written record use word processing, and those who spend much time on the telephone are the best prospects for electronic or voice mail. When considering OA applications to replace or improve traditional media, the grid in Figure 14.18 can be used. For example, a manager who makes frequent use of memos can consider word processing, electronic and voice mail, imaging, FAX, and DTP as ways to replace memos or to improve their content.

■ **Available OA Resources**   The manager's mix is limited to the OA resources that are available in the firm.

When these factors are considered, the manager's mix can appear as in Figure 14.19. In this example, all eleven applications are utilized.[11]

Keeping OA in Perspective

In terms of its potential for supporting problem solving, OA is a sleeping giant. Too often it has been regarded as a secretarial tool, since the manager does not always personally use the applications. This same criticism can be directed at the other problem-solving tools as well. The manager will not always code programs, or personally query the database and use mathematical models. It does not matter who operates the equipment as long as the manager benefits.

Of all the information used in solving a problem, that provided by interpersonal communications accounts for a major portion. The manager and information

---

[11] The mix in this example is a composite of five executives' communications preferences as reported in Raymond McLeod, Jr. and Jack W. Jones, "A Framework for Office Automation," *MIS Quarterly* 11 (March 1987), 87–104.

FIGURE 14.18

OA Applications Can Replace or Improve Conventional Communications Media

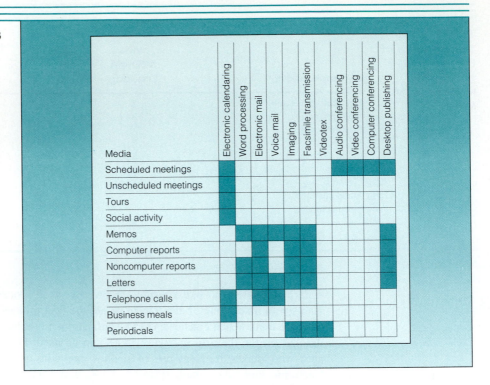

specialist should view OA as a means of supplementing these interpersonal communications. In many instances OA offers the opportunity for better communications than are possible using traditional media.

SUMMARY

Factory automation led the way, and now office automation is stimulating interest. What began as a single effort called word processing has blossomed into a booming industry.

Most early OA attention was directed at secretarial and clerical activities. More recently the communication needs of managers and other knowledge workers have been recognized. The main objective of OA, regardless of who uses it, is increased productivity. For problem solvers, OA offers the opportunity for faster and better decisions that benefit the firm in the form of higher revenues.

Word processing can be performed on a dedicated word processor or a general-purpose computer. Regardless of the type of hardware, the main advantage of word processing is the ease with which changes to copy can be made. The writer is able to refine a document until it communicates exactly the desired message.

FIGURE 14.19

A Sample Manager's OA Mix

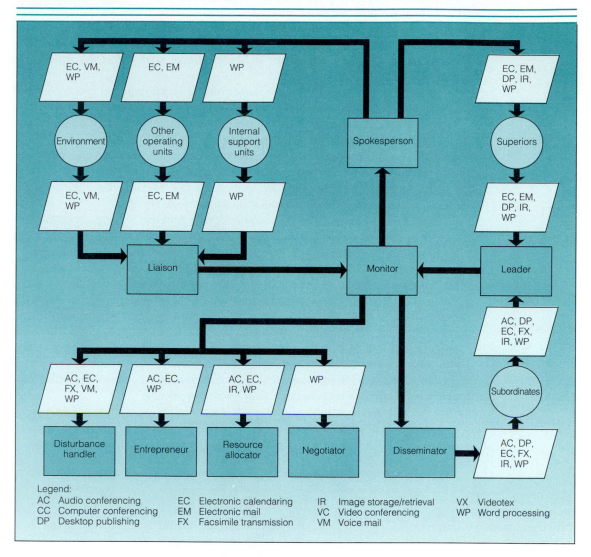

Legend:
AC	Audio conferencing	EC	Electronic calendaring	IR	Image storage/retrieval	VX	Videotex
CC	Computer conferencing	EM	Electronic mail	VC	Video conferencing	WP	Word processing
DP	Desktop publishing	FX	Facsimile transmission	VM	Voice mail		

Electronic and voice mail were conceived as ways to combat telephone tag. In both cases the users have their own mailboxes in the computer's storage that they can check at their convenience. Electronic mail will become a means for gathering environmental information with the increased availability of interconnected systems. Voice mail can also have an environmental capability when the manager provides external contacts with their own voice mailboxes.

Electronic calendaring enables a person in the firm to access the appointments calendars of others for scheduling meetings and visits.

There are three forms of teleconferencing—audio, video, and computer. The appeal of audio conferencing is its availability to anyone with a telephone. Video conferencing can combine both sound and picture in one-way and two-way configurations. Computer conferencing is like electronic mail except the participants and their topics are more restricted.

FAX is long-distance copying that permits the transmission of graphic as well as textual material. Videotex makes both graphic and textual material available from computer storage. The storage can be that of the firm, a videotex subscription service, or another organization such as a supplier.

Modern imaging systems overcome the limitations of paper and microfilm storage by applying OCR and optical disk technologies.

Desktop publishing is the OA application that provides the "icing on the cake" by producing printed communications that look typeset.

One word describes the OA contribution to problem solving—communication. A systematic way to evaluate the communication potential of OA applications is to consider how they can provide pathways to connect the managerial roles.

A manager will select the mix of OA applications based on characteristics of the organization, personal preferences, and the resources available. Some OA applications are alternatives to traditional communication methods. For example, word processing provides a means of preparing letters and memos, and electronic and voice mail can substitute for certain telephone calls. Other applications offer new opportunities. Video conferencing can link persons in different cities in a setting that approximates face-to-face communication, electronic calendaring provides a way to coordinate information exchanges, and computer conferencing offers participants a way to communicate at their own convenience.

OA is a problem-solving tool even when the manager does not personally operate the equipment.

KEY TERMS

office automation (OA)	electronic calendaring
professional	audio conferencing
knowledge worker	video conferencing
word processing	computer conferencing
electronic mail, E-mail	teleconferencing
electronic mailbox	facsimile transmission (FAX)
telephone tag	videotex
electronic bulletin board	imaging
voice mail	document management (DM) system
voice mailbox	desktop publishing (DTP)

KEY CONCEPTS

How office processes, just as manufacturing processes, lend themselves to automation

How OA evolved from separate applications—with no grand plan

How OA facilitates receiving information as well as sending it

How OA can make a greater contribution to profit by increasing revenues through improved decisions than by avoiding secretarial and clerical costs

The fact that OA will not replace the traditional communications methods

The ability to include persons outside the company in electronic mail and voice mail systems

How a manager tailors an OA mix to fit personal needs within the constraints imposed by the organization

QUESTIONS

1. What was the first OA application?

2. What four categories of employees use OA?

3. What effect does increased productivity of secretaries and clerical employees have on the firm's profit? What about increased productivity of knowledge workers? Which approach offers the greatest profit potential? Why?

4. Why did dedicated word processors lose out to general-purpose computers in terms of popularity?

5. Which type of E-mail system holds promise for stimulating environmental communications?

6. In what ways are electronic mail and voice mail alike? In what ways are they different?

7. Which OA application is not used to directly communicate information?

8. Which of the suggestions for conducting an audio conference would also apply to a video conference?

9. What distinguishes computer conferencing from E-mail?

10. What is teleconferencing?

11. What are the three sources of videotex material?

12. How does the Dow Jones News/Retrieval Service differ from Lotus One Source in the way information is made available?

13. What is a big advantage of optical disks?

14. Which of the four types of OA users would be least likely to personally use a DM system? Explain why.

15. What are the three DTP application areas? Which are involved in problem solving?

16. List the OA applications to which the firm can subscribe, rather than install its own system?

17. What factors influence the choice of OA applications for a particular manager?

18. Why would a firm with a single location consider audio or video conferencing?

TOPICS FOR DISCUSSION

1. Which of the OA applications would be most likely implemented on an firm-wide basis, rather than on an individual basis?

2. Some OA applications do not require that the the sender and user be online to the communications channel at the same time.

For example, a person can use computer conferencing to send a message to someone who is in a meeting, on a plane, or even playing golf. These communications are called **asynchronous communications**.

Communications where the sender and receivers must be on line at the same time are called **synchronous communications**. What are the asychronous OA applications?

PROBLEM

Draw a grid similar to Figure 13.17. Enter the OA applications in the boxes where they would contribute to group problem solving. In a separate narrative, explain why each of the entered OA applications is appropriate for that particular GDSS environmental setting. Also, explain why the applications that were not entered do not fit the GDSS.

CASE PROBLEM

North American Plywood and Gypsum

Edwin Kirby is chief information officer for North American Plywood and Gypsum. P and G, as it is called in the construction industry, has its headquarters in Arlington, Virginia, and seven plants are located across the South, Southwest, and Far West. Each plant manufactures and ships a full line of building materials to retailers in its area. Kirby's major responsibility at present is the implementation of a new inventory system that will link the mainframe computer at headquarters with minis at the plant locations. The network will enable each plant to fill orders from stock at other plants when its own stock has been depleted. This is an additional application for P and G's computer network. All managers have terminals in their offices, and a WATS line makes telecommunications both fast and economical.

The inventory project has been underway for about three months and is approaching the design phase. The plan is to implement the new system one plant at a time. A headquarters implementation team will travel from plant to plant, providing assistance to the local information services personnel as needed. Implementation at the first plant is scheduled one year from now.

Each Monday morning at 8 A.M. Kirby and the top information services personnel at headquarters have a telephone conference with the managers of information services at the plants. The purpose of the conference is to review the previous week's progress and plan this week's activity.

"Is everybody here?" Kirby asks in a voice loud enough to be heard without the telephone hookup. The four others seated around the conference table in Kirby's office are silent as the plant participants identify themselves, their voices coming from the speaker behind Kirby's desk.

When the final voice says "Sacramento's here," Kirby responds, "You sound like you're half asleep, Brenda." The voice replies, "No. Actually I'm *all* asleep. You forget that it's five o'clock in the morning out here. After this meeting I'm going to eat a good breakfast."

Kirby does not reply, but walks over to an easel that displays a large bar chart. "This might take some time today, people. I want to review the chart that Andy (Andrew Salem, the corporate manager of systems analysis) prepared. It shows the remainder of our implementation activity. I'd like to use it as the basis of our project planning. It shows each type of activity, such as local educational programs and database conversion, by plant and also by time period. I'm sure you know what it looks like. You've seen millions of bar charts and it's no different."

Kirby proceeds to explain the chart, but is continually interrupted by voices from the speaker "Could you run over that again?" "I didn't get that, Ed." "Oh, I thought you meant *after* the team arrives." This went on for about twenty minutes and finally, in desperation, Kirby announces in an even louder voice: "O.K. everybody. I've had enough. This is impossible. Listen, I'll have Andy make a copy of the chart and mail it to you. We can discuss it in next Monday's meeting. We'll handle it that way from now on. Andy can send you an updated chart each week. It'll throw our planning about a week behind, but I don't want to go through this every time. Now, let's discuss what we did last week."

The telephone conference lasts for another forty-five minutes without any more incidents. After Kirby gives his usual "Let's hit it hard this week" farewell and presses the off button on the speaker, the others file out of the office. Kirby breathes a heavy sigh and sits down at his desk. His eyes focus on a magazine on top of his in basket. The title reads "OA As a Way to Make Meetings More Effective."

Assignments

1. Assume that Kirby reads the article and becomes interested in OA. Which applications *that could be implemented on existing computing hardware* could Kirby use in communicating with the members of his project team? Make a list and, for each, include a brief explanation of how it would be used. The applications do not necessarily have to *solve* his communications problem; they only need to *contribute* to his communications ability.

2. Assume now that cost is not a limiting factor and Kirby decides to consider *all* OA applications, regardless of whether they require additional equipment. Make a list of the mix of OA applications you feel would provide the best support, and briefly explain how each one would be used. You do not have to explain the applications identified in Assignment 1.

SELECTED BIBLIOGRAPHY

Brown, Carolyn M. "Next Best Thing to Being There." *Black Enterprise* 22 (February 1992): 53–54

Ferguson, Cortney S.; Watson, Hugh J.; and Gatewood, Robert. "Strategic Planning for Office Automation." *Information & Management* 21 (November 1991): 201–15.

Fernberg, Patricia M. "Tailoring the Workstation to the Worker." *Modern Office Technology* 37 (June 1992): 26*ff.*

Fisher, Marsha J., "Digging Out With Image Technology," *Datamation* 35 (April 15, 1989): 18*ff.*

Giuliano, Vincent E. "The Mechanization of Office Work." *Scientific American* 247 (September 1982): 148–64.

Hamilton, Dennis. "Is Mainframe Word Processing Extinct?" *EDGE* 3 (April 1990): 16–22.

Jones, Jack William; Saunders, Carol; and McLeod, Raymond, Jr. "Information Media and Source Patterns Across Management Levels: A Pilot Study." *Journal of Management Information Systems* 5 (Winter 1988–89): 71–84.

Kydd, Christine T., and Ferry, Diane L. "A Behavioral View of Computer Supported Cooperative Work Tools." *Journal of Management Systems* 3 (Number 1, 1991): 55–67.

Lasher, Donald R.; Ives, Blake; and Jaravenpaa, Sirkka L. "USAA-IBM Partnerships in Information Technology: Managing the Image Project." *MIS Quarterly* 15 (December 1991): 551–65.

Lee, Soonchul. "The Impact of Office Information Systems on Potential Power and Influence." *Journal of Management Information Systems* 8 (Fall 1991): 135–51.

Leinfuss, Emily. "USAA's Image of Success." *Datamation* 36 (May 15, 1990): 77*ff.*

McLeod, Raymond, Jr., and Bender, Donald H. "The Integration of Word Processing into a Management Information System." *MIS Quarterly* 6 (December 1982): 11–29.

Olson, Margrethe H., and Lucas, Henry C., Jr. "The Impact of Office Automation on the Organization: Some Implications for Research and Practice." *Communications of the ACM* 25 (November 1982): 838–47.

Paddock, Charles E. "An Assessment of Productivity and Operations Control as Motives for Office Automation." *Journal of Management Information Systems* 1 (Spring 1985): 76–86.

Rice, Ronald E. "Computer-Mediated Communication and Organizational Innovation." *Journal of Communication* 37 (Autumn 1987): 65–94.

Romei, Lura K. "Desktop Publishing: What's the Outlook?" *Modern Office Technology* 34 (March 1989): 100*ff.*

Romei, Lura K. "Fax Integration: More Uses, Less Equipment." *Modern Office Technology* 37 (February 1992): 38–39.

Romei, Lura K. "Telecommuting: A Workstyle Revolution?" *Modern Office Technology* 37 (May 1992): 38–40.

Ryan, Donald J. "Emerging Opportunities for Integrating Fax and Voice Messaging." *Business Communications Review* 21 (February 1991): 68*ff.*

Sproull, Lee, and Kiesler, Sara. "Reducing Social Context Cues: Electronic Mail in Organizational Communication." *Management Science* 32 (November 1986): 1492–1512.

Wolk, Sue. "Your Imaging Connection." *Modern Office Technology* 37 (June 1992): A3*ff.*

Chapter 15

Expert Systems

LEARNING OBJECTIVES

After studying this chapter, you should:

- Know what is meant by the term artificial intelligence, and what areas in addition to expert systems are included
- Understand the appeal of expert systems and how they compare with DSS
- Know the component parts of an expert system and how they work together
- Understand how an expert system is developed
- Appreciate the potential role of the expert system in solving business problems, and know its advantages and limitations
- Be able to decide when to use an expert system
- Have an awareness of the biologically inspired models referred to as neural networks, and how they might affect expert systems designs of the future

INTRODUCTION

The CBIS subsystem that is stimulating the greatest amount of attention among computer scientists and information specialists is expert systems—a subset of artificial intelligence, or AI. Unlike DSSs, expert systems have the potential to extend a manager's problem solving ability beyond his or her normal capabilities.

An expert system consists of four main parts: a user interface, a knowledge base, an inference engine, and a development engine. The knowledge base uses rules to express the logic of the problem that the expert system is designed to help solve. The inference engine uses reasoning, in much the same manner as a human, in processing the contents of the knowledge base. The development engine consists of either programming languages or prewritten inference engines called expert systems shells. Prototyping is especially applicable to the development of an expert system.

Expert systems offer advantages both to the using firms and managers, but they have significant limitations. Continued research such as that involving neural networks is expected to expand the capabilities of future expert systems.

ARTIFICIAL INTELLIGENCE

For the past fifteen or so years there has been an increasing interest in using the computer for artificial intelligence. **Artificial intelligence (AI)** is the activity of providing such machines as computers with the ability to display behavior that would be regarded as intelligent if it were observed in humans.[1] AI represents the most sophisticated computer application to date, seeking to duplicate some types of human reasoning.

History of AI

From all of the attention one would think that AI is a recent innovation. The fact is that the seeds of AI were sown only two years after General Electric installed the first computer for business use. The year was 1956, and the term artificial intelligence was coined by John McCarthy as the theme of a conference held at Dartmouth College. That same year the first AI computer program, called Logic Theorist, was announced. Logic Theorist's ability for limited reasoning (proving calculus theorems) encouraged researchers to develop another program called the General Problem Solver (GPS) intended for use in solving problems of all kinds. The task turned out to be too much of a challenge.

AI research continued, but it took a backseat to the less ambitious computer applications such as MIS and DSS. Over time, however, persistent research continued to push back the frontiers of using the computer for tasks that normally require human intelligence.

---

[1] This definition paraphrases one found in Clyde W. Holsapple and Andrew B. Whinston, *Business Expert Systems* (Homewood, IL: Irwing, 1987), 4.

Areas of AI

If you ask a businessperson how AI has been applied in business, you are likely to get "expert systems" in response. An **expert system**, also known as a **knowledge-based system**, is a computer program that attempts to code the knowledge of human experts in the form of heuristics. The term **heuristic** is derived from the same Greek root as eureka (to discover), and it refers to a rule of thumb or a rule of good guessing. Heuristics do not guarantee results as absolutely as do conventional algorithms such as those incorporated in a DSS, but the rules offer results that are specific enough most of the time to be useful. The rules allow the system to function in a manner consistent with a human expert, advising the user how to solve a problem. Since the expert system functions as a consultant, the act of using it is called a **consultation**—the user consults the expert system for advice.

In addition to expert systems, AI includes work in the following areas: neural networks, perceptive systems, learning, robotics, AI hardware, and natural language processing. These areas are illustrated in Figure 15.1, and there is a certain amount

FIGURE 15.1

Areas of Artificial Intelligence

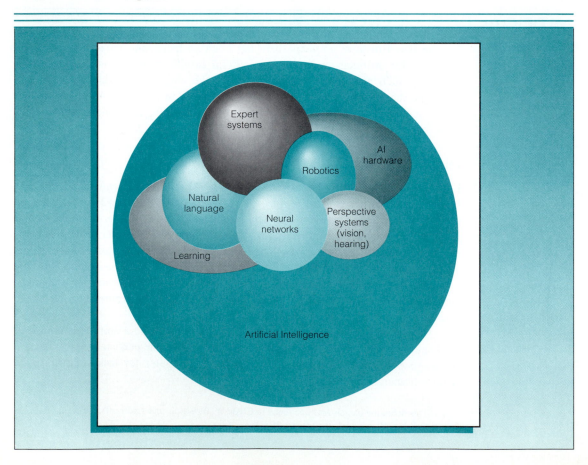

of overlap among the areas. The overlap illustrates the way that one area can benefit the others.

- **Neural Networks** are highly simplified models of the human nervous system that exhibit abilities such as learning, generalization, and abstraction. These abilities enable the models to learn human-like behavior.
- **Perceptive Systems** use visual images and auditory signals to instruct computers or other devices, such as robots.
- **Learning** encompasses all of the activity that enables the computer or other device to acquire knowledge in addition to what has been entered into its memory by its manufacturer or by programmers.
- **Robotics** consists of computer-controlled devices that mimic the motor activities of humans.
- **AI Hardware** includes the physical devices that aid in AI application. Examples are hardware that is dedicated to knowledge-based systems, neural computers used to speed up calculations, and electronic retina and cochlea.
- **Natural Language Processing** enables users to communicate with the computer in languages such as Spanish, German, Japanese, Chinese, English, or French.

Each of these areas has the potential for use in solving business problems, but thus far the main benefits have come in the form expert systems.

THE APPEAL OF EXPERT SYSTEMS

Certain tasks require such specialized knowledge that experts are required. Unfortunately, not every manager can afford a staff of full-time specialists or can call in outside consultants each time a special problem is faced. The concept of expert systems is based on the assumption that an expert's knowledge can be captured in computer storage and then applied by others when the need arises.

How an Expert System Differs from a DSS

An expert system is very similar to a DSS in that both are intended to provide a high level of problem-solving support to their users. However, the two CBIS subsystems differ in two major ways.

First, a DSS consists of routines that reflect how the manager believes a problem should be solved. The decisions produced by the DSS reflect the manager's style and capabilities. An expert system, on the other hand, offers the opportunity to make decisions that exceed the manager's capabilities. For example, a new investments officer for a bank can use an expert system designed by a leading financial expert and incorporate the expert's knowledge into his or her investments decisions.

The second distinction between an expert system and a DSS is the ability of the expert system to explain the line of reasoning that is followed in reaching a particular solution. Very often, the explanation of how a solution was reached is more valuable than the solution itself. For example, medical students using an expert system for diagnosis of cardio-pulmonary trauma can learn through a review of the system's reasoning what factors are important for consideration in different circumstances.

AN EXPERT SYSTEM MODEL

The model of an expert system in Figure 15.2 consists of four main parts. The **user interface** enables the user to interact with the expert system, and the **knowledge base** houses the accumulated knowledge of the particular problem to be solved.

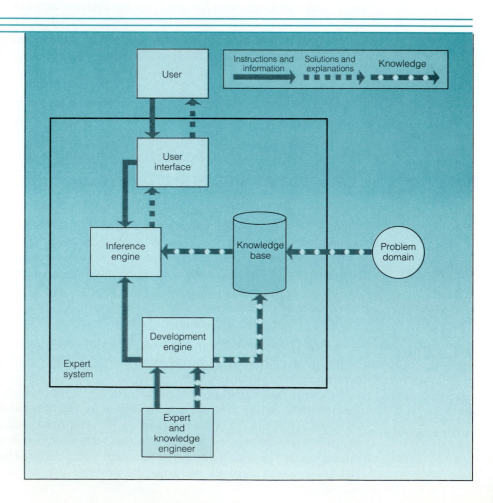

FIGURE 15.2
An Expert
System Model

The **inference engine** provides the reasoning ability that interprets the contents of the knowledge base. The expert and the systems analyst use the **development engine** to create the expert system.

THE USER INTERFACE

The user interface enables the manager to enter *instructions* and *information* into the expert system and to receive information from it. The instructions specify the parameters that guide the expert system through its reasoning process, and the information is in the form of values assigned to certain variables.

Expert System Inputs

The manager can use four methods for input: menus, commands, natural language, and customized interfaces. *Menus* are like those of Lotus, *commands* are like the dot commands used with dBASE III Plus (LIST FILES ON A: LIKE PAY-ROLL.*), and *natural language* is like that used with a 4GL query language (WHO ARE THE EMPLOYEES IN OUR NEW YORK OFFICE WITH A COLLEGE EDUCATION). *Customized interfaces* vividly reflect particular aspects of the problem being solved. Figure 15.3 contains an example of a graphic developed by Ford Motor Company for use with the Texas Instruments Personal Consultant expert system in diagnosing robot problems.

Expert System Outputs

Expert systems are designed to recommend solutions. These solutions are supplemented by explanations. There are two types of explanations:

1. **Explanation of questions**   The manager may desire explanations while the expert system performs its reasoning. Perhaps the expert system will prompt the manager to enter some information. The manager asks why the information is needed, and the expert system provides an explanation.
2. **Explanation of the problem solution**   After the expert system provides a problem solution, the manager can ask for an explanation of how it was reached. The expert system will display each of the reasoning steps leading to the solution.

Although the inner workings of the expert system can be complex, the user interface is user-friendly. A manager, accustomed to interacting with a computer, should have no difficulty in using an expert system. In fact, some executive information systems incorporate an expert systems capability. The Executive Edge EIS marketed by Comshare is an example.

FIGURE 15.3
A Customized
Interface

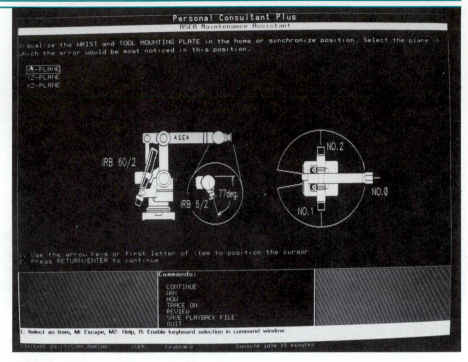

Courtesy of Texas Instruments, Inc.

THE KNOWLEDGE BASE

The knowledge base contains facts that describe the problem area, or **problem domain**, and also knowledge representation techniques that describe how the facts fit together in a logical manner.

Rules

The most popular knowledge representation technique is the use of rules. A **rule** specifies what to do in a given situation and consists of two parts: a *condition* that may or may not be true and an *action* to be taken when the condition is true. An example of a rule is:

```
IF ECONOMIC.INDEX > 1.20 AND SEASONAL.INDEX > 1.30
THEN SALES.OUTLOOK = ''EXCELLENT''
```

All of the rules contained in an expert system are called the **rule set**. The rule set can vary from a dozen or so rules for a simple expert system to 500, 1000, or 10000 rules for a complex one.

FIGURE 15.4
A Rule Set That Produces One Final Conclusion

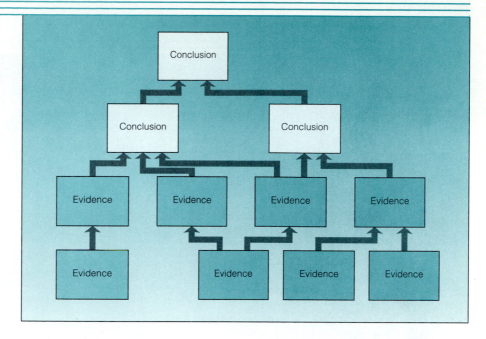

Networks of Rules

The rules of a rule set are not physically linked, but their logical relationships can be illustrated with a hierarchical diagram as in Figure 15.4. The rules at the bottom of the hierarchy provide *evidence* for the rules on the upper levels. The evidence enables the rules on the upper levels to produce *conclusions*.

The top level might consist of a single conclusion as shown in the figure, indicating that the problem has only a single solution. The term **goal variable** is used to describe the solution that can be a computed value, an identified object, an action to be taken, or some other recommendation. For example, if an expert system is to advise top-level management whether to enter a new market area, a value of *Yes* or *No* would be assigned to the single goal variable `MARKET.DECISION`.

It is also possible for the top level of the hierarchy to include multiple conclusions, indicating the possibility of more than one solution. An example is an expert system that makes recommendations concerning the best strategy to follow in reacting to increased competitive activity. The system might select among possible strategies of improving the quality of the firm's products, investing more in advertising, or lowering prices.

The Problem of Rule Selection

The main difficulty in using rules to represent knowledge is efficiently selecting them from the knowledge base. Very often, only a subset of the total rule set is necessary to solve the problem. Take, for example, the expert system diagrammed

FIGURE 15.5
A Rule Set That Can Produce More than One Final Conclusion

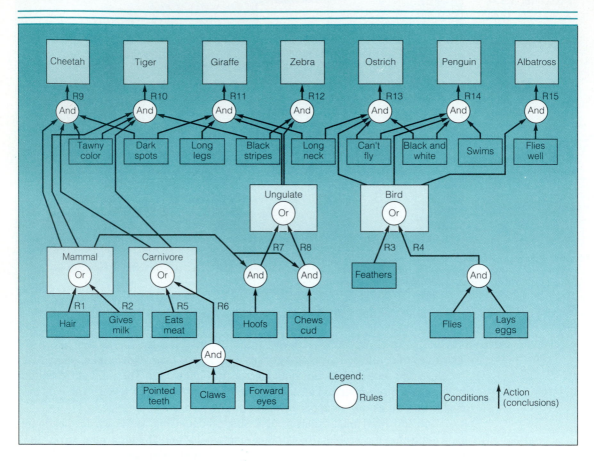

in Figure 15.5. The seven animals listed across the top can be identified, based on the fifteen rules below. The rules are represented by circles, the rectangles below the circles are the conditions, and the arrows leading upward from the circles represent the actions or conclusions. Using this expert system, it is possible to identify an animal as a bird by using only rule R3 (it has feathers) or R4 (it flies and lays eggs).

The task is to condition the expert system so that it considers only the proper subset of rules. Several techniques can be used, but the most straightforward is for the user to enter parameters that narrow the rule selection. For example, if the user specifies that the animal is a bird, only Rules 13, 14, and 15 are necessary to identify the specific type of bird.

THE INFERENCE ENGINE

The inference engine is the portion of the expert system that performs reasoning by using the contents of the knowledge base in a particular sequence.

During the consultation, the inference engine examines the rules of the knowledge base one at a time, and when a rule's condition is true the specified action is taken. In expert systems terminology, the rule is *fired* when the action is taken.

Two main methods have been devised for the inference engine to use in examining the rules: forward reasoning and reverse reasoning.

Forward Reasoning

In **forward reasoning**, also called **forward chaining**, the rules are examined one after the other in a certain order. The order might be the sequence in which the rules were entered into the rule set or some other sequence as specified by the user. As each rule is examined, the expert system attempts to *evaluate* whether the condition is true or false.

Rule Evaluation   When the condition is *true*, the rule is fired and the next rule is examined. When the condition is *false*, the rule is not fired and the next rule is examined.

It is possible that a rule cannot be evaluated as true or false. Perhaps the condition includes one or more variables with unknown values. In that case the rule condition is *unknown*. When a rule condition is unknown, the rule is not fired, and the next rule is examined.

The Iterative Reasoning Process   The process of examining one rule after the other continues until a complete pass has been made through the entire rule set. More than one pass usually is necessary in order to assign a value to the goal variable. Perhaps the information needed to evaluate one rule is produced by another rule that is examined subsequently. For example, after the eleventh rule is fired, the fifth rule can be evaluated on the next pass.

The passes continue as long as it is possible to fire rules. When no more rules can be fired, the reasoning process ceases.

An Example of Forward Reasoning   Figure 15.6 shows the forward reasoning process. The rectangles represent rules. The lines connecting the rules represent logical dependencies. For example, Rule 4 cannot be fired until Rule 7 has been fired.

Letters are used for the conditions and actions to keep the illustration simple. In Rule 1, for example, if Condition A exists, then Action B is taken. Condition A might be `THIS.YEAR.SALES > LAST.YEAR.SALES.` and Action B might be `MARKET = ''Growing''`. Likewise in Rule 2, if Condition C exists, Action D is taken.

FIGURE 15.6

The Forward
Reasoning
Process

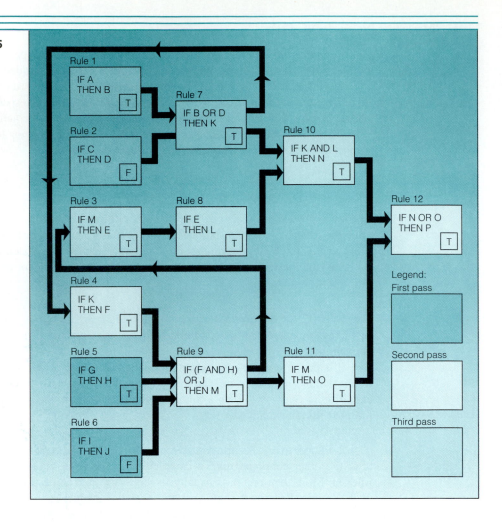

You will note that some of the conditions include only one variable and others include two. When multiple condition variables are involved, they can be connected with the words AND or OR. In Rule 7 if *either* Condition *B or D* is true, the rule is fired. In Rule 10 *both* Condition *K and L* must be true for the rule to be fired.

The objective of the sample expert system is to compute a sales forecast. Rule 12 produces the forecast Variable *P*, which is the goal variable. We will assume that the manager provides the values for condition Variables *A, C, G,* and *I* in Rules 1, 2, 5, and 6 prior to the evaluation of the rules by the inference engine. These values are shown in the squares inside the rectangles. The manager assigns a value of true to Variable *A* in Rule 1, a value of false to Variable *C* in Rule 2, a value of true to Variable *G* in Rule 5, and a value of false to Variable *I* in Rule 6.

The legend indicates the pass during which the rules can first be evaluated as true or false. In this example rules are fired during three passes. The letters T and F identify the outcome of the evaluation.

On the fourth pass no rules are fired and reasoning stops. If Rule 12 has been fired, the value assigned to the goal Variable P becomes the sales forecast. If the expert system was unable to fire Rule 12, then insufficient information exists for a solution to the problem. In our example, Rule 12 was fired on both the second and third passes. Condition O was determined to be true on the second pass and Condition N was determined to be true on the third pass.

You might ask why reasoning does not stop with the assignment of the initial value to the goal variable. The answer is that subsequent firings might improve the solution.

Reverse Reasoning

In **reverse reasoning**, also called **backward chaining**, the inference engine selects a rule and regards it as a problem to be solved. Using the same rule set as the previous figure, Rule 12 is the problem since it assigns a value to the Goal Variable P. The inference engine attempts to evaluate Rule 12 but recognizes that Rule 10 or Rule 11 must be evaluated first. Rules 10 and 11 become *subproblems* of Rule 12 as shown in Figure 15.7. The inference engine then selects one of the subproblems to evaluate, and the selected subproblem becomes the new problem.

The First Logical Path is Pursued   We will assume that Rule 10 becomes the problem as shown in Figure 15.8. The inference engine then determines that Rules 7 and 8 must be evaluated before Rule 10 can be evaluated. Rules 7 and 8 become the subproblems. The inference engine continues to subdivide a problem into its subproblems in this manner, searching for a rule that can be evaluated.

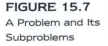

FIGURE 15.7

A Problem and Its Subproblems

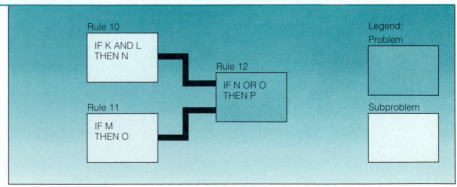

FIGURE 15.8

A Subproblem
Becomes the
New Problem

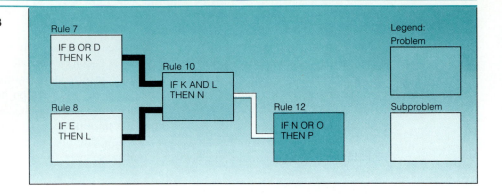

The first five problems that are identified are shown in Figure 15.9. The circled step numbers and the heavy arrows indicate the sequence in which the rules are examined. Since Rule 1 is evaluated as true, it is possible to evaluate Rule 7 as true without examining Rule 2. With a value of true assigned to Variable *K*, Rule 10 can be reexamined. However, since Rule 10 requires that both Condition *K* and *L* be true, it is necessary to next evaluate Rule 8. In order to evaluate Rule 8, it is

FIGURE 15.9

The First Five
Problems Are
Identified

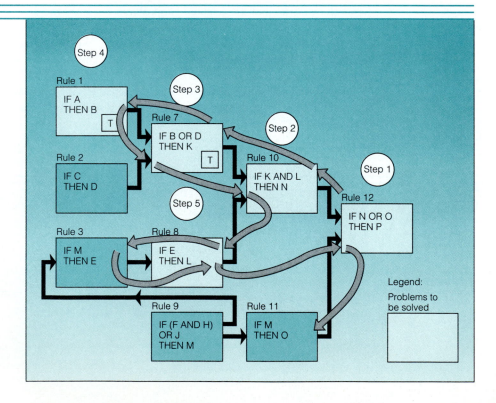

necessary to evaluate Rule 3. This is a dead end since the Rule 3 condition (Variable *M*) depends on the outcome of Rule 9. In this situation, the inference engine addresses the other subproblem of Rule 12—Rule 11.

The Next Logical Path is Pursued   Figure 15.10 shows how the reasoning proceeds as the expert system attempts to evaluate Rule 11. Rule 9 becomes the problem, and it can be evaluated using the outcomes of Rules 4 and 5. Since both Rules 4 and 5 are true, Rule 9 can be evaluated as true without the need to examine Rule 6.

Once Rule 9 is fired, Rule 11 can be fired as well. This makes it possible to assign a value to Goal Variable *P* since Rule 12 is fired if either Rule 10 or 11 is true.

Comparing Forward and Reverse Reasoning

Reverse reasoning proceeds faster than forward reasoning since it does not have to consider all of the rules and does not make multiple passes through the rule set. However, forward reasoning is appropriate when:

- There is no single goal variable
- All or most all of the rules must be examined in the process of reaching a solution
- There are only a few rules

FIGURE 15.10
The Next Four Problems Are Identified

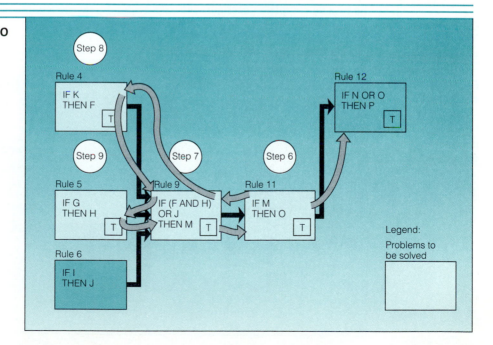

Some inference engines are designed to perform both forward and reverse reasoning. In that case the user specifies which one to use.

Providing Needed Information

As the reasoning process proceeds, it may become necessary for the inference engine to obtain additional information. The inference engine can obtain the information from databases, electronic spreadsheets, mathematical models, or other expert systems. Or, it can prompt the user for the needed information. This is a good place to incorporate GUI (graphical user interfaces). Figure 15.11 illustrates these various information sources.

How the Inference Engine Handles Uncertainty

You are seldom 100 percent certain about the information provided to an expert system. The uncertainty can apply to entire rules or to rule conditions. As an example of an *uncertain rule*, a system developer might not know for certain that a rule dealing with a raw material supplier's financial status has an influence on the material quality but might be 80 percent certain that it does. As an example of an *uncertain condition*, a marketing manager using an expert system to project a sales forecast might be only 80 percent certain that the economic index for next year will be strong.

Expert systems use **certainty factors (CFs)**, to handle varying degrees of uncertainty. The CFs are analogous to probabilities and can range from 0, which represents complete uncertainty, to 100, which represents complete certainty.

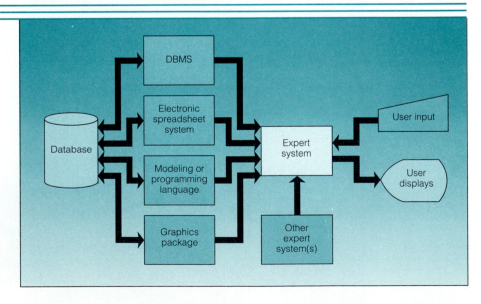

FIGURE 15.11
The Expert System Obtains Needed Information from Other Sources

In keeping with the notion that "a chain is no stronger than its weakest link" the expert system advises the user when the conclusion is less than 100 percent certain. For example, assume that four rules lead to a conclusion, and three of them can be evaluated with 100 percent certainty. However, the fourth rule has a CF of 80, meaning that the certainty of its action is 80 percent. The expert system keeps track of the various rule CFs throughout the reasoning process and indicates the degree of certainty for the goal variable at the end of the consultation, such as:

```
SALES FORECAST = $12,450,500              CF = .80
```

The weak link approach is only one way to handle uncertainty. The user can select the method that best fits the particular situation.

THE DEVELOPMENT ENGINE

The fourth major component of the expert system is the development engine, which is used to create the expert system. Essentially this process involves building the rule set. There are two basic approaches: programming languages and expert system shells.

Programming Languages

You can create an expert system using any programming language, however two are especially well suited to the symbolic representation of the knowledge base: Lisp and Prolog. Lisp was developed by John McCarthy (one of the members of that first AI meeting in 1959), and work on Prolog was begun by Alain Colmerauer at the University of Marseilles in 1972.

For several years, Lisp enjoyed its greatest popularity in the United States, and Prolog was preferred by European and Japanese users. Such geographic preferences no longer prevail. Prolog has gained supporters in the United States, and there is considerable Lisp activity in Europe. The Japanese have cast their lot with Prolog, selecting it as the basis for their new generation of computers.

Expert System Shells

One of the first expert systems was Mycin, developed by Edward Shortliffe and Stanley Cohen of Stanford University, with the help of Stanton Axline, a physician. Mycin was created to diagnose certain infectious diseases.

When the success of Mycin had been established, the developers looked for other ways to apply their accomplishments. They discovered that the Mycin inference engine could be tailored to another type of problem by replacing the Mycin knowledge base with one reflecting the other problem domain. This finding signaled the start of a new approach to building expert systems: the expert system shell. An **expert system shell** is a ready-made processor that can be tailored to a specific problem domain through the addition of the appropriate knowledge base. In most cases the shell can produce an expert system quicker and easier than by programming.

Today, most of the interest in applying expert systems to business problems involves the use of shells. The first commercial shell was KEE—for Knowledge Engineering Environment. KEE was designed for use on a computer designed especially for the Lisp language—a **Lisp machine**. However, the introduction of faster devices such as RISC (for reduced instruction set computing) has caused most development to move away from dedicated Lisp machines and onto the new platforms. Developmental work is also beginning to branch out to multiprocessing machines that combine multiple CPUs.

The Role of the Systems Analyst

The term **knowledge engineer** has been used to describe the person who works with the expert in designing an expert system. In the case of the previously described Mycin, professors Shortcliffe and Cohen were the knowledge engineers, and physician Axline was the expert. In a business organization, the knowledge engineer is likely to be the systems analyst.

In addition to the skills used in developing conventional computer applications, the analyst must:

1. Understand how experts apply their own knowledge in solving problems.
2. Be able to extract a description of that knowledge from the expert. The process of extracting the knowledge has been termed **knowledge acquisition**, and several different approaches have been devised.

Actually, these two skills are appropriate for the design of *any* type of CBIS subsystem.

The System Development Process

We discussed the system development process in general in Chapter 5 when we addressed the system life cycle. We explained how the information specialists work with the manager in developing the system. The process of developing an expert system varies from that pattern in that it involves a third player—the expert.

Figure 15.12 illustrates how the systems analyst works with the expert to initiate the development process and develop the expert system prototype, and then gain user participation. We described the fundamentals of prototyping as a systems design tool in Chapter 7 and explained its relationship to the systems approach in Chapter 13 when we described the DSS.

Initiate the Development Process The task of the systems analyst in Step 1 is to study the problem domain and decide whether development work should continue. If so, the analyst becomes sufficiently knowledgeable about the problem domain to continue the project.

FIGURE 15.12

Prototyping Is
Incorporated in
the Development
of an Expert
System

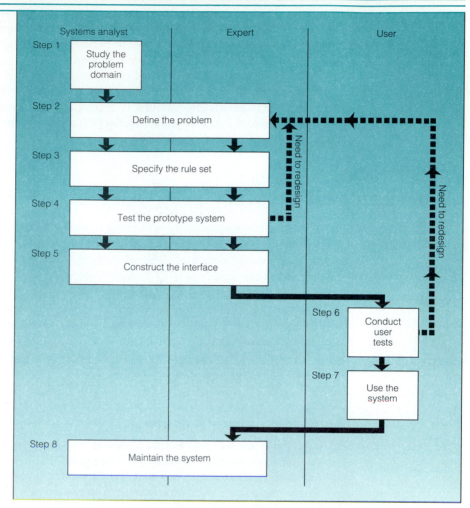

Develop the Expert System Prototype   In Steps 2 through 5 the analyst works with the expert. In some cases the manager who identified the need for the system serves as the expert. Or, the expert could be another manager in the firm or someone from the outside such as a consultant or one or more managers in other firms. It might even be necessary to enlist the help of several experts to acquire the necessary knowledge.

The analyst and expert follow the systems approach by first defining the problem in Step 2. They then specify the rule set in Step 3. The rules are incorporated in the prototype.

The analyst and expert test the prototype in Step 4, and if the tests do not go well the prototype is revised beginning with Step 2. If everything goes as it should, the analyst and expert add the user interface in Step 5.

User Participation   It is next necessary for the user to subject the prototype to tests. The systems analyst and expert provide the necessary user training, and in Step 6 the user tests the prototype. If the user is not pleased with the results, the analyst and expert take a fresh approach beginning with Step 2. If the tests go well, the user puts the expert system to use in Step 7.

Expert System Maintenance   An expert system must be maintained just as any other CBIS subsystem, and this is accomplished in Step 8. Changes are made, which enable the expert system to reflect the changing nature of the problem domain and to achieve greater efficiency.

A SAMPLE EXPERT SYSTEM

Most of the expert systems activity in business began in the late 1980s. The systems that have been achieved are aimed mainly at the responsibilities of lower-level managers or staff specialists such as financial analysts. A sample of such a financial expert system is the credit approval system developed by Professors Venkat Srinivasan of Northeastern University and Yong H. Kim of the University of Cincinnati, working with a Fortune 500 company, which we will identify as SRR.[2]

SRR's credit policy consists of two activities: (1) setting credit limits for new customers and reviewing them once a year, and (2) handling exceptions on a daily basis. Srinivasan and Kim interviewed credit managers and observed credit analysts making the credit decisions. A senior credit manager served as the expert.

The Credit Approval Decision

Table 15.1 shows the five information categories that form the basis for the credit approval decision—financial strength, payment record, customer background, geographical location, and business potential. The categories have different weightings, depending on the amount of credit requested. You can see that the financial strength category has the most influence.

The Knowledge Base

The knowledge base of the expert system consists of two components: (1) rules that reflect the credit approval logic, and (2) a mathematical model that determines the credit limit. Figure 15.13 includes a sample set of rules that are used to determine the customer's financial strength. When one of these rules is fired, the customer is given a rating of *Excellent* in the corresponding category.

---

[2] Venkat Srinivasan and Yong H. Kim, "Designing Expert Financial Systems: A Case Study of Corporate Credit Management," *Financial Management* 17 (Autumn 1988), 32–44.

TABLE 15.1
**Weightings of
the Information
Categories**

Category	$5,000–$20,000	$20,000–$50,000
Financial strength	0.65	0.70
Payment record	0.18	0.20
Customer background	0.10	0.05
Location	0.05	0.03
Business potential	0.02	0.02
Total	1.00	1.00

Source: Venkat Srinivasan and Yong H. Kim, "Designing Expert Financial Systems: A Case Study of Corporate Credit Management," *Financial Management* 17 (Autumn 1988): 41. Reprinted by permission.

The User Interface

As the inference engine proceeds through the rule set in a forward-chaining manner, the credit analyst is asked to make pairwise comparisons. For example, the inference engine might display the prompt:

```
What is the relative importance of Customer Background
over Payment Record if the objective is to improve over-
all credit performance?
```

The credit analyst enters a code that reflects the comparison, and the forward chaining proceeds. When the chaining is completed, the output appears as a series of screens. The three lines in the upper screen in Figure 15.14 summarize the analysis process. The customer has a `Credit Need of $30,000` but currently is allowed no credit (`Existing Line = 0`). Based on the consultation the expert system recommends that no credit be granted (`Suggested Line = 0`).

The remainder of the first screen summarizes the customer's rating on four dimensions. The expert system determined that the customer has a *Good* record in terms of pay experience, background, and bank, but financial strength is *Poor*.

The expert system then explains how it arrived at its conclusion. The second screen in Figure 15.14 shows how the Good rating on pay experience was derived. The AHP Intensity Value is a score computed by the mathematical model.

The credit analyst is able to display screens such as these, which explain the logic followed by the expert system in making the credit decision.

Expert systems have been well received in the financial area, being applied to decisions that are difficult to make and require the knowledge of experts. In the case of the Fortune 500 company all of the credit analysts had seven to eight years

FIGURE 15.13

Sample Rules

Profitability		
If	sales trend is	*Improving*
And	customer's net profit margin is	*Greater than 5%*
And	customer's net profit margin trend is	*Improving*
And	customer's gross margin is	*Greater than 12%*
And	customer's gross profit margin trend is	*Improving*
Then	customer's profitability is	*Excellent*
Liquidity		
If	sales trend is	*Improving*
And	customer's current ratio is	*Greater than 1.50*
And	customer's current ratio trend is	*Increasing*
And	customer's quick ratio is	*Greater than 0.80*
And	customer's quick ratio trend is	*Increasing*
Then	customer's liquidity is	*Excellent*
Debt Management		
If	sales trend is	*Improving*
And	customer's debt to net worth ratio is	*Less than 0.30*
And	customer's debt to net worth ratio trend is	*Decreasing*
And	customer's short-term debt to total debt is	*Less than 0.40*
And	customer's short-term debt to total debt trend is	*Decreasing*
And	customer's interest coverage is	*Greater than 4.0*
Then	customer's debt exposure is	*Excellent*
Overall Financial Health		
If	customer's profitability is	*Excellent*
And	customer's liquidity is	*Excellent*
And	customer's debt exposure is	*Excellent*
Then	customer's financial health is	*Excellent*

experience. It is not easy to capture the logic that these experts use when making decisions, but it can be done.

ADVANTAGES AND DISADVANTAGES OF EXPERT SYSTEMS

As with all computer applications, expert systems offer some real advantages, but there are also disadvantages. The advantages can accrue to both managers and the firm.

The Advantages of Expert Systems to Managers

Managers who use expert systems can expect to make better decisions by considering more alternatives, applying a higher level of logic in evaluating the alterna-

FIGURE 15.14
The First Output Screen

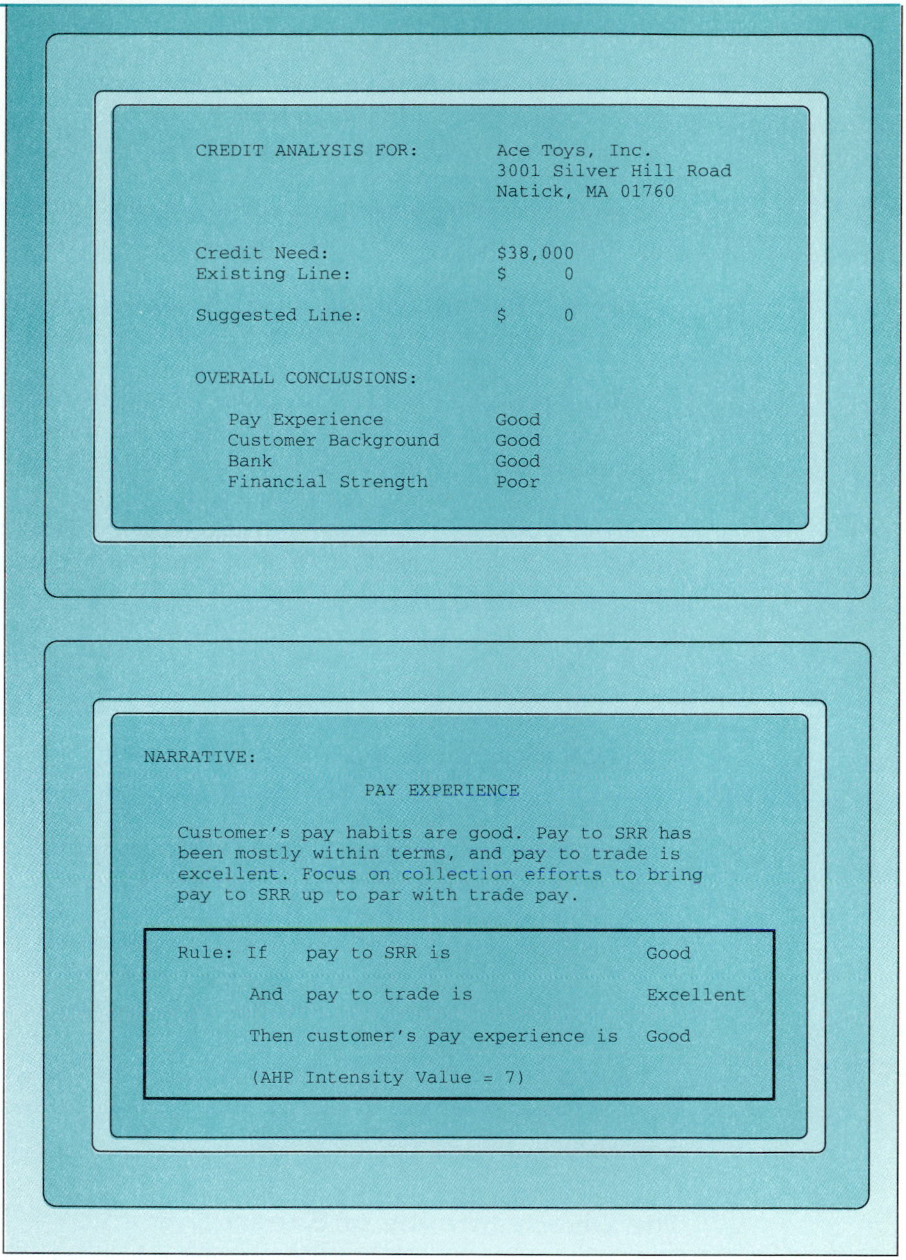

```
CREDIT ANALYSIS FOR:        Ace Toys, Inc.
                            3001 Silver Hill Road
                            Natick, MA 01760


Credit Need:                $38,000
Existing Line:              $      0

Suggested Line:             $      0


OVERALL CONCLUSIONS:

    Pay Experience          Good
    Customer Background     Good
    Bank                    Good
    Financial Strength      Poor
```

```
NARRATIVE:

                    PAY EXPERIENCE

    Customer's pay habits are good. Pay to SRR has
    been mostly within terms, and pay to trade is
    excellent. Focus on collection efforts to bring
    pay to SRR up to par with trade pay.

    Rule: If    pay to SRR is              Good

          And   pay to trade is            Excellent

          Then customer's pay experience is  Good

          (AHP Intensity Value = 7)
```

tives, having more time for the evaluation, and achieving a consistency in the decisions that are reached.

Consider More Alternatives An expert system can enable a manager to consider more alternatives in the process of solving a problem. For example, a financial manager who has been able to track the performance of only thirty stocks because of the volume of data that must be considered can track 300 with the help of an expert system. By being able to consider a greater number of possible investment opportunities, the likelihood of selecting the best ones is increased.

Apply a Higher Level of Logic A manager using an expert system can apply the same logic as that of a leading expert in the field.

More Time to Evaluate Decision Results The manager can obtain advice from the expert system quickly, leaving more time to weigh the possible results before action has to be taken.

More Consistent Solutions The computer does not have good days and bad days like the human manager. Once the reasoning is programmed into the computer, the manager knows that the same solution process will be followed for each problem.

The Advantages of Expert Systems to the Firm

A firm that implements an expert system can expect:

- **Better Performance for the Firm** As the firm's managers extend their problem-solving abilities through the use of expert systems, the firm's control mechanism is improved. The firm is better able to meet its objectives.
- **Maintain Control over the Firm's Knowledge** Expert systems afford the opportunity of making the experienced employees' knowledge more available to newer, less experienced employees and of keeping that knowledge in the firm longer—even after the employees have left.

In today's world economy firms are seeking ways to compete, and they see expert systems as one way to cultivate their management resource and keep that resource in the firm for a longer period.

The Disadvantages of Expert Systems

Two characteristics of expert systems limit their potential as a business problem-solving tool. First, they cannot handle inconsistent knowledge. In business, few things hold true all of the time because of the variability in human performance. Second, expert systems cannot apply the judgment and intuition that we recognized as important ingredients of problem solving when we discussed the systems approach in Chapter 4.

The Bottom Line

The big constraint in applying expert systems to business problems is the problem structure. For an expert system to be feasible, the problem must be highly structured, and we have seen that most business problems do not fit this mold.

There is no doubt that during the next few years effective expert systems will continue to be successfully applied. However, the accomplishments will not come easy. Among possible application domains, the ones that are selected will be the ones that best meet the firm's overall objectives in terms of maximizing payoff and minimizing risk of failure.

Deciding When to Use an Expert System

While all CBIS development projects are expensive, expert systems usually represent the highest potential cost. The reason is the extended amount of time required to develop the knowledge base. It is not uncommon for efforts to last several years. Digital Equipment Corporation, for example, began work on its XCON expert system in 1979, had a usable prototype in 1980, and used the evolving production system from 1981 until 1987 when the code was rewritten.[3] So, the realization of an expert system is not a "get rich quick" affair.

As the firm's executives make the important decision whether to develop an expert system, it is helpful to address each of the factors that can influence the success of the project and the system. These factors are illustrated in Figure 15.15.[4] A particular *task* exists within the *problem domain*, and a *development project* produces an expert system to perform that task. The project is influenced by the *expert*, working with *domain personnel* and the *systems analyst*. In addition, there are *general considerations*.

The factors and the conditions that influence the factors are listed below:

- General Considerations
    1. Conventional programming (algorithmic) approaches to the task are unsatisfactory.
    2. There are recognized experts who can solve the problem.
    3. Expertise is not or will not be available on a reliable or continuing basis.
    4. No alternative solutions are currently available.
    5. The completed system is expected to have a significant payoff for the firm.
    6. The selected problem domain represents the best combination of payoff versus risk.

- The Problem Domain
    1. The problem domain is characterized by the use of expert knowledge, judgement, and experience.

---

[3] Virginia E. Barker and Dennis E. O'Connor, "Expert Systems for Configuration at Digital: XCON and Beyond," *Communications of the ACM* 32 (March 1989), 298–318.

[4] Based on John Sviokla, "Business Implications of Knowledge-based Systems," *Database* 17 (Summer 1986), 5–19.

FIGURE 15.15
Factors That
Influence the
Success of an
Expert System

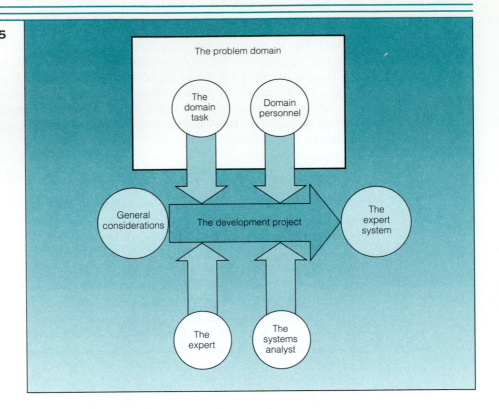

2. Formal knowledge exists about the domain, perhaps in the form of books.
3. The domain is fairly stable, and the expert system will serve a long-term need.

■ The Domain Task
   1. The task is neither too easy nor too difficult.
   2. The task requires primarily symbolic reasoning.
   3. The task requires the use of heuristics.
   4. The task does not require knowledge from a very large number of areas.
   5. The task is clearly defined.
   6. The amount of knowledge required by the task is large enough to necessitate use of a knowledge base.
   7. The important task concepts number no more than several hundred.
   8. The task skills can be taught to novices.

■ Domain Personnel
   1. There is strong management support.
   2. Potential users have realistic expectations.
   3. Results will not be politically sensitive.
   4. The system will exert a minimal change on standard procedure.

- The Expert
    1. There exists a qualified expert who can commit time to the project.
    2. The expert is credible.
    3. The expert is cooperative, easy to work with, and communicates well.

    4. The expert can supply most of the necessary expertise.
    5. If many experts are needed, they agree on the "right" answer.
    6. If many experts are needed, one serves as chief expert.

- The Systems Analyst
    1. There exists an analyst who already understands the problem domain or can learn it.
    2. The analyst is able to extract the expert's knowledge.

- The Development Project
    1. The system developers agree on task goals.
    2. The system can be phased in, with useful results accruing from the series of prototypes.
    3. Test cases are available.

These factors contribute to the ideal environment for the development of an expert system. The more factors that exist, the greater the chance of success.

NEURAL NETWORKS

Although expert systems have been successfully applied to many business problems, there are some difficulties that have severely hampered their development.[5] These are:

- **The knowledge engineering bottleneck**—the enormous time and effort required to extract the expert's knowledge and translate it into the IF/THEN rules upon which an expert system is based.
- **The programming bottleneck**—the difficulty of programming the system and maintaining the code.
- **The learning problem**—the inability of an expert system to use inductive learning and inference to adapt to changing relationships in the decision environment.

Although these problems have received considerable attention from information specialists, the difficulties still exist. It is possible that the real solutions lie in unconventional techniques that are still in early research stages. One such technique is neural net design.

---

[5]Delvin D. Hawley, John D. Johnson, and Dijjotam Raina, "Artificial Neural Systems: A New Tool for Financial Decision-Making," *Financial Analysts Journal* 46 (November/December 1990), 63–72.

Neural net design consists of efforts of scientists to model human intuition by simulating the physical process upon which intuition is based. The objective of neural net design is to simulate the process of adaptive biological learning, although on a much less complex scale.[6]

Neural net design is actually a bottom-up approach since it looks at the physical brain for inspiration in the creation of intelligent behavior. In contrast are the top-down approaches that have been developed by proponents of the more traditional AI areas mentioned earlier.

Biological Comparisons

The design of neural networks has been inspired by the physical design of the human brain.[7] The component of the brain that provides an information-processing capability is the **neuron**, illustrated in Figure 15.16.

The Neuron   The neuron is actually a very simple structure consisting of three basic regions—dendrites, soma, and axon. The **dendrites** specialize in the input of electrochemical signals, the **soma** performs processing on the signals, and the **axon** provide output paths for the processed signals.

Dendrites   Dendrites form a dendritic tree, which looks like a very fine branch-like region of thin fibers around the cell body. Dendrites are the input components of the cell and receive the electrochemical impulses that are carried from the axons of neighboring neurons.

Axons   Axons are long fibers, which carry signals from the soma. The end part of the axon splits into a tree-like structure and each branch terminates in a small endbulb that almost touches the dendrites of other neurons.

The Synapse   The **synapse** is the endbulb that serves as a contact point to connect dendrites and axons. Each neuron may be connected to a thousand or more neighbors via this network of dendrites and axons.

The Soma   The **soma** is the processor component of the neuron and is essentially a summation device that can respond to the total of its inputs within a short time period. The aggregation of signals is compared to an **output threshold**, which is the level of stimulation that is necessary for the neuron to fire or send an impulse along its axon to other connected neurons. The strength of the synaptic

---

[6] *Ibid.*, 63.

[7] *See* Delvin D. Hawley and John D. Johnson, "Artificial Neural Networks: Past, Present and Future. An Overview of the Structure and Training of Artificial Learning Systems," forthcoming in Andrew Whinston and John D. Johnson eds., *Advances in Artificial Intelligence in Economics, Finance and Management,* (Greenwick, CN: JAI Press), 1992. *See also* Jacek M. Zurada, *Introduction to Artificial Neural Systems,* Saint Paul, MN: West Publishing, 1992.

FIGURE 15.16

A Simple Biological Neuron

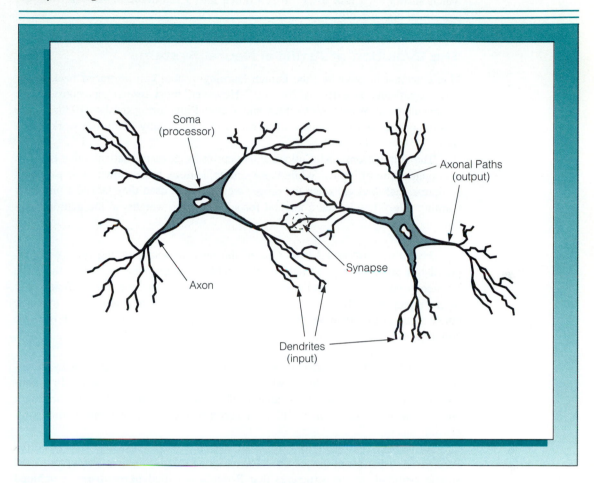

connection between the axon of the firing cell and the dendrite of the receiving cell determine the effect of the impulse.

Through this very simple mechanism, input signals from neighboring neurons can be assigned priorities or weights in the soma's accumulation process. These weights most likely serve as storage or memory to the network.

Even though the response time for a single neuron is approximately a thousand times slower than the digital switches in a computer the brain is capable of solving complex problems such as vision and language. This is accomplished by linking together a tremendous number of inherently slow neurons (processors) into an immensely complex network. The number of neurons in the human brain has been estimated to be around 10^{11}, and each neuron forms approximately 104 synapses with other neurons. This is an example of **parallel distributed processing (PDP)**, which allows each task to be broken down into a multitude of subtasks that are performed concurrently.

The Evolution of Artificial Neural Systems

Man's interest in modeling the human learning system can be traced back to the Chinese artisans as early as 200 B.C.[8] However, most researchers consider the achievements of Warren McCulloch and Walter Pitts during the late 1930s on the development of a simple neuron function as the beginning of formal work in the area.

The output from a McCulloch-Pitts neuron has a mathematical value equal to a weighted sum of inputs. While these simple neurons were shown to be excellent computational devices, when the proper weights were used they lacked a universal learning rule. They lacked a method for adjusting the weights in the neuron function.

Hebb's Learning Law   One of the most famous learning rules was proposed five years later by Donald Hebb.[9] Hebb's learning law states that the more frequently one neuron contributes to the firing of a second, the more efficient will be the effect of the first upon the second. Thus, memory is stored in the synaptic connections of the brain and learning occurs with changes in the strength of these connections.

The First Neurocomputers   In the early 1950s Marvin Minsky developed a device called the Snark, which is considered by many to be the first **neurocomputer**, or computer-based analog of the human brain. Although the Snark was technically successful, it failed to perform any significant information processing function.[10]

In the mid 1950's, Frank Rosenblatt, a Cornell neurophysicist, developed the Perceptron, a hardware device used for pattern recognition. The Perceptron used simple artificial neuron structures that Rosenblatt called **perceptrons**, combined with a simple learning rule.[11] The Perceptron was able to generalize and respond to unfamiliar input stimuli.

The success of Rosenblatt's work fueled speculations that artificial brains were just around the corner. The interest in neural nets reached an all-time high. It seemed as if this "technological tidal wave would carry on its back the surfers of

---

[8] *See* Raymond Kurzweil, *The Age of Intelligent Machines,* Cambridge, MA: MIT Press, 1990, for an excellent history of the development of AI.

[9] D. O. Hebb, *The Organization of Behavior,* New York: John Wiley & Sons, 1949.

[10] *See* Robert Hecht-Nielsen, *Neurocomputing,* Reading, MA: Addison-Wesley, 1990.

[11] Frank Rosenblatt, "The Perceptron: a Probabilistic Model for Information Storage and Organization in the Brain," *Psychological Review,* 65, (November 1958), 386–408.

tommorrow's technology and sweep out to sea all those unfortunates who didn't catch the wave in time."[12]

Rather than be swept out to sea along with their traditional top-down technologies, Marvin Minsky and his colleague Seymour Papert carefully demonstrated that the perceptrons of Rosenblatt could not solve simple logic problems such as the *exclusive OR*. Their demonstration put a temporary damper on neural net research.

The Artificial Neural System (ANS)

The **artificial neural system (ANS)** that is the subject of today's research is not an exact duplicate of the biological system of the human brain, but it does exhibit abilities such as generalization, learning, abstraction, and even intuition. An ANS is made up of a series of very simple artificial neuron structures or neurodes. The structures are often referred to as perceptrons due to the influence of Rosenblatt, however they are a direct extension to the mathematical model developed by McCulloch and Pitts. An example of an artificial neuron structure is illustrated in Figure 15.17.

These artificial neurons are the processing elements of the ANS architecture. The neuron sums the weighted inputs from its neighbors, compares this sum to its threshold value and passes the result through a transfer function. The **transfer function** is a relationship between the output of the weighted sum and the threshold value of the cell. When the weighted sum exceeds the threshold value, the neuron "fires."

The Multi-layer Perceptron

These simple neurons are combined to form a multi-layer ANS referred to as a **multi-layer perceptron**. Within each, the input nodes are linked to the output nodes through one or more hidden layers as illustrated in Figure 15.18.

The multi-layer perceptron is a **feedforward network** meaning that the flow of data moves in only a single direction from the input layer to the output layer. However, the hidden layers permit an interaction between individual input nodes. This interaction allows for a flexible mapping between inputs and outputs that facilitates their training.

Network Training

A neural net is not *programmed* in the traditional sense. Rather, it is *trained* by example. The training consists of many repetitions of inputs that express a variety of relationships. By progressively refining the weights of the system nodes (the

---

[12] *See* Gene Woolsey, "On Inexpert Systems and Natural Intelligence in Military Operations Research," *Interfaces* 21 (July–August 1991), 2.

FIGURE 15.17

A Single Artificial
Neuron

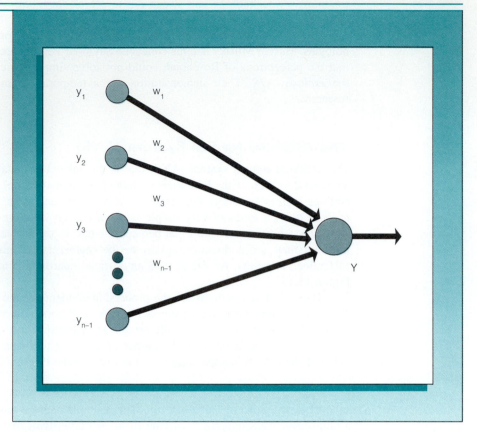

FIGURE 15.17

A Single Artificial Neuron

simulated neurons), the ANS "discovers" the relationships among the inputs. This discovery process constitutes learning.[13]

This ability to learn based on adaptation is the major factor that distinguishes ANS from expert system applications. Expert systems are programmed to make inferences based on data that describes the problem environment. The ANS, on the other hand, is able to adjust the nodal weights in response to the inputs and, possibly, to the desired outputs.[14]

PUTTING ARTIFICIAL INTELLIGENCE AND EXPERT SYSTEMS IN PERSPECTIVE

Expert systems represent the most advanced application of the computer to solve business problems. Although the dividing line that separates expert systems from DSS is often fuzzy, the expert systems provide managers with the potential to

[13] Hawley, Johnson, and Raina, Artificial Neural Systems, 65.

[14] Ibid.

FIGURE 15.18

The Multi-layered Perceptron

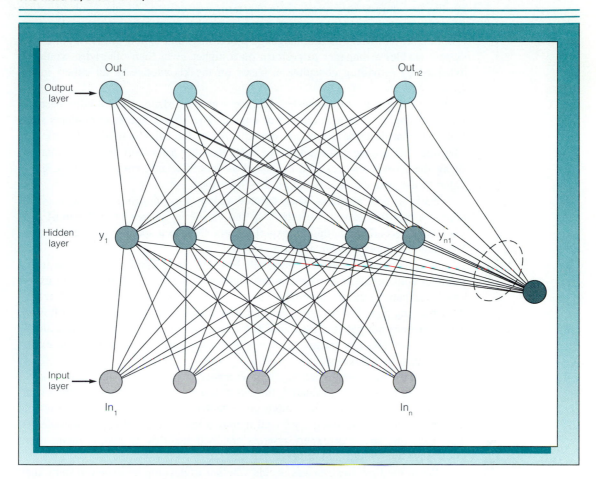

exceed their own capabilities. The firm is able to perform at a higher level because of the improved problem-solving capabilities of its management team. Expert systems enable this superior performance to persist over a long period by insulating the firm from knowledge loss due to turnover.

A major limitation of expert systems is their inability to apply judgment and intuition. Neural net development is intended to overcome this limitation, at least in part by providing the expert system with a learning ability. The artificial neural system (ANS) can exhibit not only learning but abilities, such as generalization, abstraction, and intuition.

During the coming years, expert systems will be developed that incorporate neural nets, giving the systems the combined ability to provide expert consultation and to improve their own expertise over time based on learning.

SUMMARY

During the almost forty years since the term was coined, AI has evolved into a field that includes such areas as neural networks, perceptive systems, learning, robotics, AI hardware, natural language processing, and expert systems. An expert system enables a manager to perform on a higher level than otherwise would be expected by providing consultation based on the knowledge of an expert in the field.

The parts of an expert system include a user interface, a knowledge base, an inference engine, and a development engine. The knowledge base contains rules and facts that describe a problem domain. All of the rules comprise the rule set. The inference engine can examine the rules in either a forward or reverse manner, firing them when they can be evaluated as true. The inference engine assigns a value to the goal variable based on the fired rules.

Early expert systems were created using programming languages. That approach is still followed, with the Lisp and Prolog languages being the most popular. More recently, adapting an expert system shell to a specific problem domain has gained support—especially in business.

A systems analyst who understands how an expert applies knowledge in the problem domain, and can extract a description of that knowledge from the expert can participate in the development of an expert system. The difficulty of getting the reasoning right the first time dictates that a prototyping approach be followed. The user does not get involved until the analyst and expert are satisfied with the system. User tests can trigger further prototyping. Once implemented, the expert system must be maintained.

Expert systems enable managers to consider more decision alternatives, use a higher level of logic in evaluating the alternatives, have more time for the evaluation, and make decisions in a more consistent fashion. The systems also enable the firm to do a better overall job and maintain its resource of expert knowledge. The main limitations of expert systems are their inability to handle inconsistent knowledge and employ intuitive skills.

When the firm's executives decide whether to develop an expert system, they consider the influence of the problem domain, the domain task, domain personnel, the expert, the systems analyst, and the development project, as well as general considerations.

More accomplishments will be necessary before expert systems are solidly established as an effective management problem-solving tool. Those accomplishments may come in the form of artificial neural systems that hold the promise of providing expert systems with a learning ability. Unlike expert systems, artificial neural systems are not programmed but are taught. The teaching involves the repetitive input of varying signals that allow the system to adjust the weights of the simulated neurons. The advantage of the artificial neural system over the expert system as we know it today is the ability of the ANS to improve its consultation over time.

KEY TERMS

artificial intelligence (AI)
expert system, knowledge-based system
heuristic
consultation
neural network
knowledge base
inference engine
development engine
problem domain

rule set
goal variable
certainty factor (CF)
expert system shell
knowledge engineer
knowledge acquisition
parallel distributed processing (PDP)
artificial neural system (ANS)

KEY CONCEPTS

How expert systems enable managers to
    perform on the level of experts
How a problem domain can be described by
    facts and rules in the knowledge base
Forward and reverse reasoning
The expert system shell as a general-purpose

expert system waiting to receive a
    knowledge base
An artificial neural system (ANS) as a
    computer-based mathematical model of the
    human brain

QUESTIONS

1. Which concept is older, artificial intelligence or DSS?

2. Why is use of an expert system called a consultation?

3. What are the two main ways that an expert system differs from a DSS?

4. What are the two types of inputs that a manager enters into an expert system?

5. What are the four methods for entering inputs into an expert system?

6. What are the two types of explanations produced by an expert system?

7. What term is used to describe the solution that the expert system seeks? Can there be more than one solution?

8. What is the main difficulty in using rules as a knowledge representation technique?

9. When is a rule fired? When is it not fired?

10. How does the expert system know to conclude the forward reasoning process?

11. Why is reverse reasoning faster than forward reasoning?

12. List the situations where you would favor forward reasoning over reverse reasoning.

13. Where can the expert system obtain the information that it needs?

14. What types of uncertainty can the expert system handle? What term is used to describe the degree of uncertainty?

15. What are two primary approaches to developing expert system software?

16. What special skills does the systems analyst need in order to work with the expert in developing an expert system?

17. In what basic way does the development of an expert system differ from that of another CBIS subsystem such as a DSS?

18. Name two major limitations of expert systems.

19. Would you characterize the domain task as a structured, semistructured, or unstructured problem?

20. What are the three problems that hinder the development of expert systems?

21. Is the neuron an open or closed system? Is it an open-loop or closed-loop system?

22. Which component of the neuron functions as the processor?

23. How was Hebb's learning law applied to the McCulloch-Pitts concept of neuron weights?

24. What was the big limitation of Rosenblatt's perceptron?

25. Is the ANS a good example of feedback?

26. What advantage does an ANS have over a conventional expert system?

TOPICS FOR DISCUSSION

1. Explain how each of the AI areas, with the exception of expert systems, can help business.

2. Why is prototyping recommended for expert system development?

3. Would an expert use an expert system that she or he had developed? If so, why? If not, why not?

4. Is the expert system intended to replace the manager?

PROBLEMS

1. Refer to the explanation of forward and reverse reasoning. Using the sample rule set in Figure 15.6, make two lists with the following headings:

Sequence   Rule   Evaluation   Explanation

For the first list, enter the rules in the order in which they are evaluated in the process of performing forward reasoning. For each rule, specify its evaluation (true, false, unknown), and then a brief explanation. For example, the first three entries in your table should appear as:

Sequence	Rule	Evaluation	Explanation
1	1	True	Entered by manager
2	2	False	Entered by manager
3	3	Unknown	Cannot be fired until Rule 9 is fired

The second list should illustrate the rule evaluation sequence for reverse reasoning.

2. Assume that you are a systems analyst who has been assigned to work with an expert in developing an expert system. Design a questionnaire that you and the expert can use to obtain information from domain managers. You want to know whether the factors that exist within the domain are conducive to a successful project. The managers will fill out the questionnaires in your presence.

The chapter includes a list of factors and conditions that influence the decision to implement an expert system. Use that list as a basis. Include only questions that a domain manager would be expected to answer, such as: "Does formal knowledge exist concerning the domain in the form of books?" Limit the questionnaire to only two pages.

Newcastle Homes

More and more young married couples are remodeling older houses as a way of avoiding the high costs of new ones. The smart couple will purchase a house with remodeling potential and then request bids from contractors to do the work they cannot do themselves. In the Wilmington, Delaware, area there are about a half-dozen construction firms specializing in remodeling. One is Newcastle Homes owned by Alvin and James Moreland.

When contractors are asked by home owners to bid on a construction project, the two parties meet to inspect the house and discuss the work to be done. Then the contractors estimate the cost. Since the contractors know that they invariably will encounter some unanticipated difficulties once work begins, they add a cushion to their bids. The Morelands know their business so well that they do not have to add much of a cushion. That is one reason for their success.

One rainy morning when the Morelands could not work outdoors, they were in the office talking about their computer. They use it in preparing their proposals. Alvin has written some programs in BASIC, which compute certain materials costs, and James has developed a word processing file used in preparing the written document. Alvin suggested that they should develop an expert system for bidding to keep their competitive edge. Their main objective was to reduce the amount of time necessary to make a written bid. The reduced time per bid would enable them to make more bids and perhaps obtain more jobs. The supply of remodeling jobs in Wilmington seemed virtually unlimited and Alvin and James intended to eventually branch out into other cities. Because they had been pleased with the support provided by their computer, they decided to proceed with the project.

The first task was to develop the knowledge base of the expert system. Because they did not know exactly what went through their heads when developing a bid, they kept notes as they worked up bids over a two-month period. They also carried clipboards as they checked out each house and took greater pains in making complete notes than they had in the past. After they accumulated a good set of notes, they developed a form that they could fill out for each job. This form included data such as the number of rooms, room size, condition of the wiring, plumbing, and so on. Then it was a simple matter of entering the data from the form into the expert system.

Next, Alvin purchased an inexpensive microcomputer-based expert system shell that was advertised in one of the computer magazines he read from cover to cover each month. After a few days of getting familiar with the program, he began entering the rules that he and James had developed. The resulting expert system contained 120 rules.

Alvin and James continued to construct bids manually for a couple of months while comparing their results with those of the expert system. They found that using the expert system not only saved time, but they were also surprised to learn that the system was more accurate than they were. For example, they found out that they had not been consistent in writing bids and occasionally forgot some of the variables that had been encoded in the knowledge base.

Assignments

1. Do you think that Alvin should have developed the expert system using Lisp or Prolog instead of using an expert system shell?

2. What do you think about Alvin and James marketing their expert system to other contractors around the country? Would they need to change the knowledge base?

3. What other expert systems do you think Alvin and James could develop to help with their home remodeling business?

4. Besides a reduced time and a higher accuracy with each bid, what other benefits could arise from the expert system?

5. Do you think a neural net would have been better than an expert system in this case? Explain.

SELECTED BIBLIOGRAPHY

Bobrow, Daniel G.; Mittal, Sanjay; and Stefik, Mark J. "Expert Systems: Perils and Promise." *Communications of the ACM* 29 (September 1986): 880–94.

Braden, Barbara; Kanter, Jerome; and Kopcso, David. "Developing an Expert Systems Strategy." *MIS Quarterly* 13 (December 1989): 459–67.

Carlson, David A., and Ram Sudha. "An Architecture for Distributed Knowledge-Based Systems." *DATA BASE* 22 (Winter/Spring 1991): 11–21.

Cronan, Timothy P.; Glorfeld, Louis W.; and Perry, Larry G. "Production System Development for Expert Systems Using a Recursive Partitioning Induction Approach: An Application to Mortgage, Commercial, and Consumer Lending." *Decision Sciences* 22 (September/October 1991): 812–45.

Cupello, James M., and Mishelevich, David J. "Managing Prototype Knowledge/Expert System Projects." *Communications of the ACM* 31 (May 1988): 534–41.

Danford, Thomas S. "VP-Expert." *Decision Line* 23 (March 1992): 7–9.

Dhar, Vasant. "On the Plausibility and Scope of Expert Systems in Management." *Journal of Management Information Systems* 4 (Summer 1987): 25–41.

Holsapple, Clyde W., and Whinston, Andrew B. *Business Expert Systems.* Homewood, IL: Irwin, 1987.

Kinnucan, Paul. "Computers that Think Like Experts." *High Technology* 4 (January 1984): 30*ff.*

Liou, Yihwa Irene. "Knowledge Acquisition: Issues, Techniques and Methodology." *DATA BASE* 23 (Winter 1992): 59–64.

Luconi, Fred L.; Malone, Thomas W.; and Scott Morton, Michael S. "Expert Systems: The Next Challenge for Managers." *Sloan Management Review* 27 (Summer 1986): 3–13.

Meador, C. Lawrence, and Mahler, Ed G. "Choosing an Expert Systems Game Plan." *Datamation* 36 (August 1, 1990): 64–69.

Murray, Thomas J., and Tanniru, Mohan R. "A Framework for Selecting between Knowledge-based and Traditional Systems Design." *Journal of Management Information Systems* 4 (Summer 1987): 42–58.

Meyer, Marc H., and Curley, Kathleen Foley. "Putting Expert Systems Technology to Work." *Sloan Management Review* 32 (Winter 1991): 21–31.

Myers, Ware. "Introduction to Expert Systems." *IEEE Expert* 1 (Spring 1986): 100–109.

Nelson, Carl W., and Balachandra R. "Choosing the Right Expert System Building Approach." *Decision Sciences* 22 (Spring 1991): 354–68.

Newquist, Harvey P. III. "Experts at Retail." *Datamation* 36 (April 1, 1990): 53*ff.*

Prietula, Michael J., and Simon, Herbert A. "The Experts in Your Midst." *Harvard Business Review* 67 (January–February 1989): 120–24.

Remus, William E., and Kottemann, Jeffrey E. "Toward Intelligent Decision Support Systems: An Artificially Intelligent Statistician." *MIS Quarterly* 10 (December 1986): 403–18.

Sipior, Janice C., and Garrity, Edward J. "Merging Expert Systems with Multimedia Technology." *DATA BASE* (Winter 1992): 45–49.

Sviokla, John J. "An Examination of the Impact of Expert Systems on the Firm: The Case of XCON." *MIS Quarterly* 14 (June 1990): 127–40.

Turban, Efraim. *Decision Support and Expert Systems.* 2d ed. New York: Macmillan, 1990.

Turban, Efraim, and Watkins, Paul R. "Integrating Expert Systems and Decision Support Systems." *MIS Quarterly* 10 (June 1986): 121–36.

Weitzel, John R., and Kerschberg, Larry. "Developing Knowledge-Based Systems: Reorganizing the System Development Life Cycle." *Communications of the ACM* 32 (April 1989): 482–88.

Yoon, Youngohc, and Guimaraes, Tor. "Developing Knowledge-Based Systems: An Object-Oriented Organizational Approach." *Information Resources Management Journal* 5 (Summer 1992): 15–32.

PART V

ORGANIZATIONAL INFORMATION SYSTEMS

In this part of the text you will see examples of how certain companies are using their computers. We will divide the CBIS into subsystems based on how their *users* are grouped in the organization. This structure is illustrated in Figure Five.1.

We briefly introduced this structure in Chapter 12. There is an *executive information system*, or *EIS*, for use by the firm's executives. There are also *functional information systems*—one for each of the major functional areas of the firm. In this text we describe marketing, manufacturing, finance, and human resource information systems. The functional subsystems are information systems that are tailored to the activities in those areas. The executive information system and the functional information systems are examples of *organizational information systems*.

Each of the five organizational information systems makes use of the five CBIS subsystems discussed in Part Four—data processing, MIS, DSS, OA, and expert systems. This relationship is illustrated in Figure Five.2.

Functional Information Systems

The key point concerning the *functional* information systems is that a firm should not implement one by itself without regard to the others. All of the systems should be present. Let us use marketing as an example. Much of the marketing data comes from

FIGURE Five.1

The Composition of Organizational Information Systems

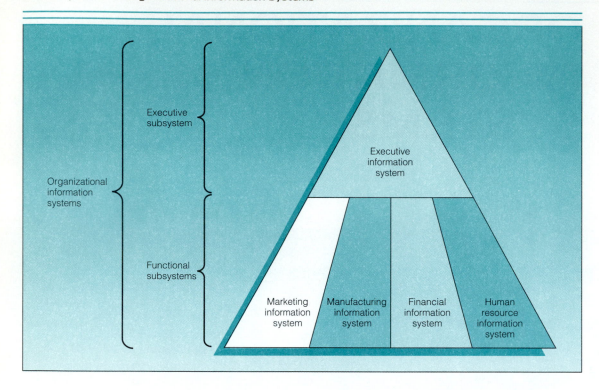

the finance and manufacturing areas. If finance and manufacturing do not attempt to achieve the same high quality in their databases and software libraries as marketing, then those two areas cannot provide the type of support that marketing needs. The situation is analogous to property values in a neighborhood. Everyone's values are higher when all of the homeowners maintain their property. There is a **synergism** among the parts—the whole is greater than the sum of the parts. The utility of the overall CBIS is maximized when *all* of the functional subsystems are present and functioning in an integrated manner.

The Executive Information System

The situation is different for the executive information system. The concept of a *computer-based* executive information system is brand new, and only the more progressive firms have implemented

FIGURE Five.2

Each Organizational Information System Includes the Five CBIS
Subsystems

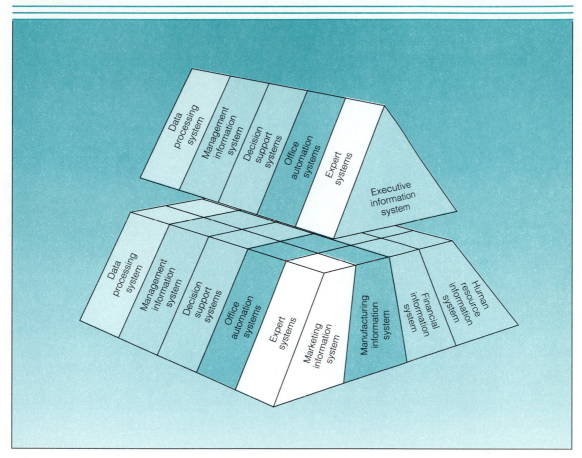

them. Many organizations have the four functional information systems, but no executive information system. This situation is changing, however, and someday the executive information system will become as popular as the functional information systems.

We devote Chapter 16 to the executive information system, and Chapters 17 through 20 to the marketing, manufacturing, financial, and human resource information systems. In studying these chapters, keep in mind that the descriptions are normative, or ideal. The examples represent what leading-edge firms are doing. However, firm size is not always a determining factor; many small firms have impressive systems.

The reason that we take a normative approach is because it provides you with an understanding of how firms *ought* to use their computers. This understanding will be useful to you as you pursue your career.

Chapter 16

Executive Information Systems

LEARNING OBJECTIVES

After studying this chapter, you should:

- Have a better understanding of what executives do, and how they think
- Understand the general characteristics of executives' information systems in terms of where the information comes from and the form that it takes
- Recognize the need for a computer-based executive information system, or EIS, to satisfy some of the information needs of executives
- Know five steps that executives can take to improve their information systems
- See how management concepts can be incorporated into an EIS
- Be aware of the options that exist for acquiring EIS software
- Know the factors that influence the success of an EIS
- Be alert to possible future EIS trends

INTRODUCTION

"A rich man is not just a poor man with more money."

Pierre Martineau[1]

Pierre Martineau, in his study of social class in America, recognized inherent differences between the rich and the poor, differences that could not be measured by the amount of money that each did or did not have. As we address the special information needs of executives, we recognize that there is something that distinguishes them from managers on lower levels. Executives *are* different—not in terms of personal characteristics but in terms of the job and how it is performed. We can paraphrase Martineau and say:

"An executive is not just a lower-level manager on a higher level."

The job changes drastically when the manager reaches the top, and the manager must be capable of meeting the challenge. In this chapter we describe how the CBIS can lend support when the manager becomes an executive.

If we did not include an executive information system and only included functional information systems, the CBIS would have the appearance of the model in Figure 16.1. Top-level managers would receive all of their information from the functional subsystems, and these executives would have to distill and synthesize the data into a form that would be meaningful to them. The executive information sytem relieves the executives of that work.

The executive information system sits atop the functional systems as shown in Figure 16.2 and makes information available to the executives. The information originates both within the firm and its environment. It is generally accepted that environmental information is especially important at the top level.

WHAT DO EXECUTIVES DO?

The term **executive** is rather loosely applied. There is no clear dividing line that separates the executives from the remaining managers. The term is used to identify managers on the upper level of the organizational hierarchy, who exercise a strong influence on the firm. The influence is gained by engaging in strategic planning and setting the policies of the firm.

In addition to their long-term planning horizon, executives can often be distinguished from managers on lower levels by their attitude. Executives assign a higher value to the welfare of the firm than to the welfare of individual units within the firm. In this respect, executives are company oriented. Some but by no means all managers on lower levels tend to put the welfare of their own units first.

---

[1] Pierre Martineau, director of research and marketing for *The Chicago Tribune,* quoted in Stuart U. Rich and Subhash C. Jain, "Social Class and Life Cycle as Predictors of Shopping Behavior," *Journal of Marketing Research* 5 (February 1968), 41.

FIGURE 16.1

A Firm without an
Executive
Information
System

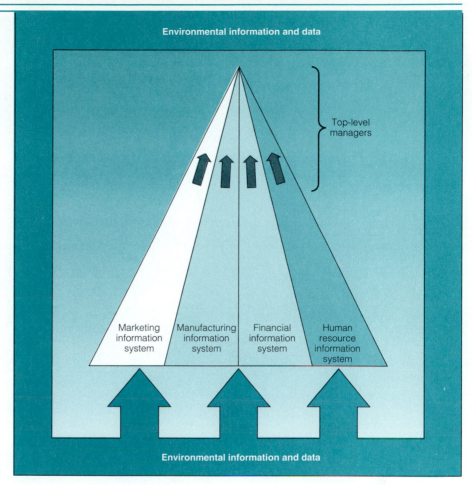

We can gain an additional insight to what the executive does by examining the contributions made by three management theorists—Henri Fayol, Henry Mintzberg, and John Kotter.

Fayol's Management Functions

Henri Fayol believed that all managers perform the same management functions—plan, organize, staff, direct, and control. The widespread belief is that planning is emphasized most on the executive level, while other functions are more critical to performance at lower levels. That is the reason why Robert Anthony used the term strategic planning level for managers at the top.

FIGURE 16.2

A Firm with an Executive Information System

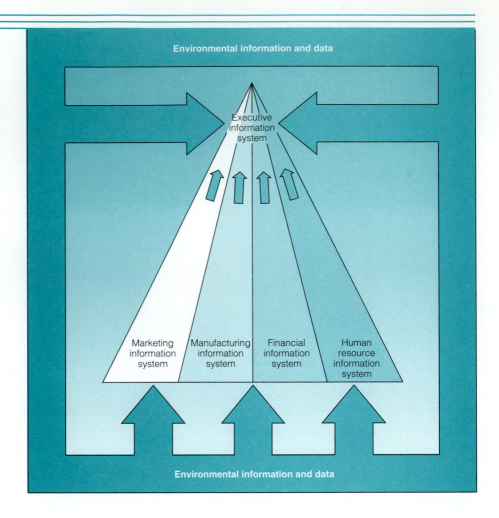

Mintzberg's Managerial Roles

We can also define the executive's duties in terms of Henry Mintzberg's managerial roles. He believes that all managers perform all roles, but the orientation is different on each level. One of the decisional roles is that of negotiator, and Mintzberg gives the example of a top-level manager negotiating a merger, and a lower-level manager negotiating a delivery date with a supplier. Both negotiate but with different orientations.

Mintzberg found in his study of CEOs that they did not spend equal amounts of time discharging the decisional roles. They concentrated on making long-range, entrepreneurial improvements to the firm and responding to unanticipated disturbances, while leaving much of the resource allocating and negotiating to managers at lower levels.

Kotter's Agendas and Networks

Harvard professor John P. Kotter believes that executives cope with the challenges of their jobs by following a three-step strategy.[2] First, they establish **agendas**—the objectives that the firm is to achieve. Long-term agendas tend to be estimates, such as a general idea of what kinds of products that the firm should be selling five, ten, or even twenty years from now. Short-term agendas are more specific, such as the market share that each of the firm's current products should achieve.

Second, executives build **networks.** These are not computer networks but are cooperative relationships among those people who are to accomplish the agendas. Hundreds or thousands of network members can be found both inside and outside the firm.

Third, executives work to establish the right **environment** of norms and values so that the network members can work to achieve the agendas. Executives establish face-to-face contact with as many of the network members as possible but concentrate on subordinates.

HOW DO EXECUTIVES THINK?

Most of the research dealing with managers focuses on observable behavior. Very little attention has been given to what goes on inside a manager's head while this behavior occurs. The manager's mind is often regarded as a black box, not to be opened.

Harvard professor Daniel J. Isenberg studied the thought processes of more than a dozen executives over a two-year period to gain insight into what executives think about and how they apply their thinking.[3]

What Executives Think About

Isenberg found that executives think about two general classes of problems—how to get things done and how to deal with a few overriding concerns or general goals. In thinking about how to get things done, executives are more concerned with the organizational and personal issues in getting subordinates to solve a problem than with what the specific solution will be.

Although executives may be facing a large number of issues or concerns at any one time, they tend to be preoccupied by only a few. As an example, a particular executive might see the need for greater discipline in the organization. That passion weaves its way in and out of everything the executive does.

[2] John P. Kotter, "What Effective General Managers Really Do," *Harvard Business Review* 60 (November–December 1982), 156–67.

[3] Daniel J. Isenberg, "How Senior Managers Think," *Harvard Business Review* 62 (November–December 1984), 81–90.

Thought Processes while Solving Problems

Isenberg observed that an executive will often skip from problem definition forward to solution implementation and then back to alternative evaluation. Executives *do* make rational decisions, but the decisions might not always come as the result of following a series of well-defined steps in the same order.

Isenberg believes that executives use intuition at each step of the problem-solving process. Intuition probably plays a more important role at the executive level than any other because of the unstructured nature of the problems and also the vast reservoir of experience that executives can apply.

UNIQUE INFORMATION NEEDS OF EXECUTIVES

Just as executives have unique responsibilities and engage in unique thought processes, they also have unique information needs. There have been a number of studies of executives' use of information, and we will discuss three. The first two deal with the executive's overall information system. The third one focuses on computer use.

The Mintzberg Study

Mintzberg was the first to conduct a formal study of the information needs of executives. He identified five basic activities that accounted for his five CEOs' time—desk work, telephone calls, unscheduled meetings, scheduled meetings, and tours. His findings appear in Figure 16.3.

Mintzberg did not specifically include computer output in his study, lumping all written media into a documents category. He emphasized the role of the informal systems that communicate oral information, and concluded: "It would appear that it is more important for the manager to get his information quickly and efficiently than to get it formally."[4]

Much has changed in terms of computer use since Mintzberg gathered his data in the early 1970s. However, his research has value as we consider modern CBIS designs. In Chapter 14 we presented a framework for determining a manager's mix of office automation applications, which is based on Mintzberg's role concept.

The Jones and McLeod Study[5]

This author, working with professor Jack W. Jones of Texas Christian University, saw a need to learn more about the executive's information sources and media than had been reported by Mintzberg. We conducted a study of the incoming information flows of five executives. The executives included a CEO of a retail chain, a bank

---

[4] Henry Mintzberg, *The Nature of Managerial Work* (New York: Harper & Row, 1973), 47.

[5] For more detail on the study, refer to the Jones and McLeod entries in the bibliography at the end of the chapter.

FIGURE 16.3

How Mintzberg's CEOs Spent Their Time

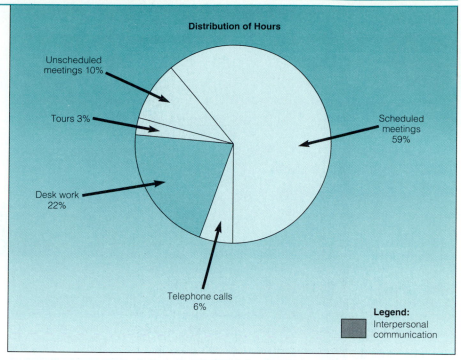

Source: *The Nature of Managerial Work* by Henry Mintzberg. Copyright © 1973 by the author. Reprinted by permission of Harper & Row, Publishers, Inc.

CEO, a president of an insurance company, a vice president of finance, and a vice president of tax. The study was designed to answer the questions:

1. *How much* information reaches the executive?
2. What is the *value* of the information?
3. What are the *sources* of the information?
4. What *media* are used to communicate the information?
5. What *use* is made of the information?

Answers to these questions, even though they apply to only five executives, provide an insight into information needs at the executive level.

How Much Information Reaches the Executive?   During a two-week period, the executives and their secretaries logged 1,454 information transactions that flowed to the executives. A **transaction** is a communication involving any medium—computer report, memo, observational tour, telephone call, letter, meeting, and so on.

The executives received an average of twenty-nine information transactions per day. As Figure 16.4 shows, there was considerable variation in volume from

FIGURE 16.4

The Volume of Information Reaching the Executives

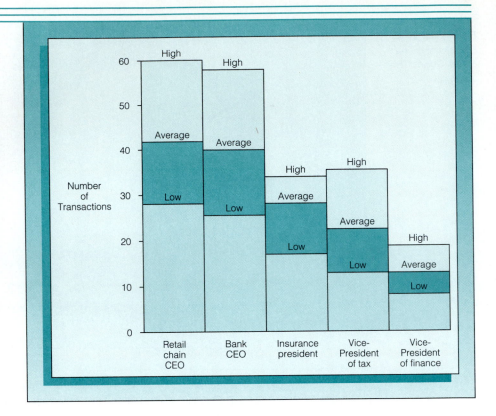

one executive to another, and considerable fluctuation from one day to the next for the same executive. The two CEOs had the highest volume, and the two vice presidents had the lowest, with the president in between.

What Is the Value of the Information?   The executives assigned a value ranging from zero (no value) to ten (maximum value) to each transaction. Figure 16.5 contains a bar graph that shows the distribution of the values for all of the executives. The executives gave 26 percent of the transactions very low values— zero (the most frequently assigned value), one, or two. At the other extreme the executives gave only 6 percent of the transactions a nine or a ten.

There was also a variation in the level of values assigned by each executive, ranging from an average of 2.9 for the vice president of tax to 5.5 for the bank CEO. The distribution of values for these two executives is shown as lines in the figure. The two vice presidents had the lowest averages. Perhaps because of the narrower scope of their roles, it was easier for them to see that incoming information had little value.

What Are the Sources of the Information?   Figure 16.6 shows the information sources. Each source is represented by a rectangle. The upper number

FIGURE 16.5

The Value of
Information
Reaching the
Executives

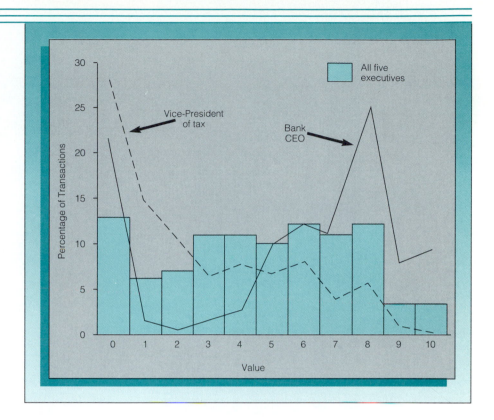

in a rectangle represents the volume of transactions supplied by that source, stated as a percentage of the total transactions. The lower number is the average transaction value.

The firm's environment is represented by the rectangle to the left of the dashed line. The internal sources are to the right. The environment provided the largest volume, but it also provided the information with the lowest average value. Conversely, the source providing the lowest volume was committees, but they provided the information with the highest value. In terms of both volume and value, the two levels immediately below the executives represented the best mix.

What Media Are Used to Communicate Executive Information?

Written media accounted for 61 percent of the number of transactions as shown in Figure 16.7. Telephone calls were the only oral communication that accounted for a large volume. Unfortunately for the executives, the three media that they control the least (letters, memos, and telephone calls) accounted for 60 percent of the transactions.

If executives do prefer oral media, as Mintzberg stated, then those media should have received higher values than written media. Table 16.1 lists the media and their average values. As predicted, oral media occupy the top four positions.

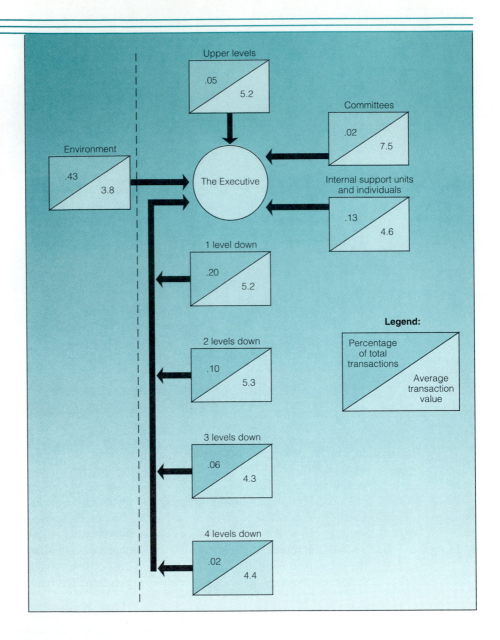

FIGURE 16.6

The Sources of Information Reaching the Executives

Telephone calls and business meals are the only oral media outranked by written media.

The term computer reports was used for all computer output. At the time of the study none of the executives were querying the firm's databases or engaging in mathematical modeling. They were receiving only computer reports and did not regard them as a major medium. The executives relied more heavily on noncom-

FIGURE 16.7
The Media Pie (in
Percentages of
Total
Transactions)

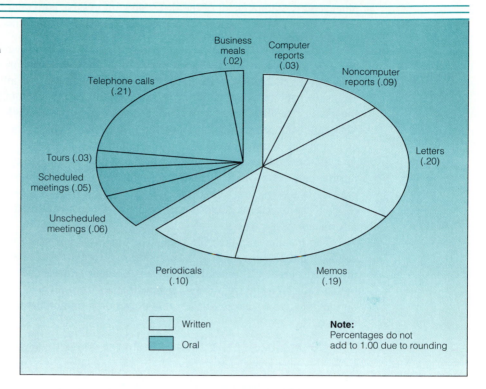

Business
meals
(.02)

Computer
reports
(.03)

Noncomputer
reports (.09)

Telephone calls
(.21)

Tours (.03)

Scheduled
meetings (.05)

Unscheduled
meetings (.06)

Letters
(.20)

Periodicals
(.10)

Memos
(.19)

☐ Written
▨ Oral

Note:
Percentages do not
add to 1.00 due to rounding

TABLE 16.1
Ranking of
Media by Value

Medium	Mode	Average Value
Scheduled meetings	Oral	7.4
Unscheduled meetings	Oral	6.2
Tours	Oral	5.3
Social activity	Oral	5.0
Memos	Written	4.8
Computer reports	Written	4.7
Noncomputer reports	Written	4.7
Letters	Written	4.2
Telephone calls	Oral	3.7
Business meals	Oral	3.6
Periodicals	Written	3.1

puter reports. Although all of the firms have impressive computer resources, almost three-fourths of the executives' reports were prepared some other way.

What Use Is Made of the Information? The researchers, assisted by the executives, assigned a decisional role to each information transaction. The assignment reflected how the executive would likely use the information. Figure 16.8 shows the distribution. You can see that most of the information was intended for use in handling disturbances, being an entrepreneur, and allocating resources. Very little was earmarked for negotiation, supporting Mintzberg's observation that executives seldom negotiate.

Six percent of the transactions could not be identified with any role. Their information value was 1.1, compared with much higher average values for entrepreneur (4.8), resource allocator (4.7), disturbance handler (4.6), and negotiator (3.8). If the executive could not associate a piece of information with a role, the information was given a low value.

The manner in which the executive obtains information to play the roles is anything but simple. As Figure 16.9 shows, information comes from a number of different sources as each role is played. Both the disturbance handler and entrepreneur roles on the right draw on information from all five of the sources listed on the left. The resource allocator role draws on four, and the negotiator role draws on two.

Significance of the Study Findings Three findings of the study appear to be the most significant:

■ Most of the executives' information came from environmental sources, but the internal information was valued higher.

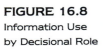

FIGURE 16.8
Information Use
by Decisional Role

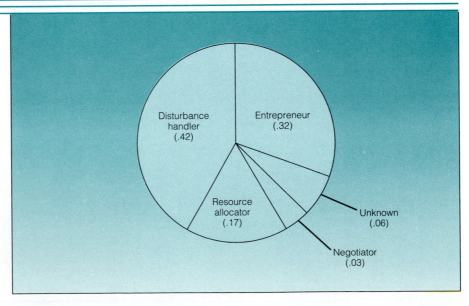

FIGURE 16.9
Sources of Decisional Information

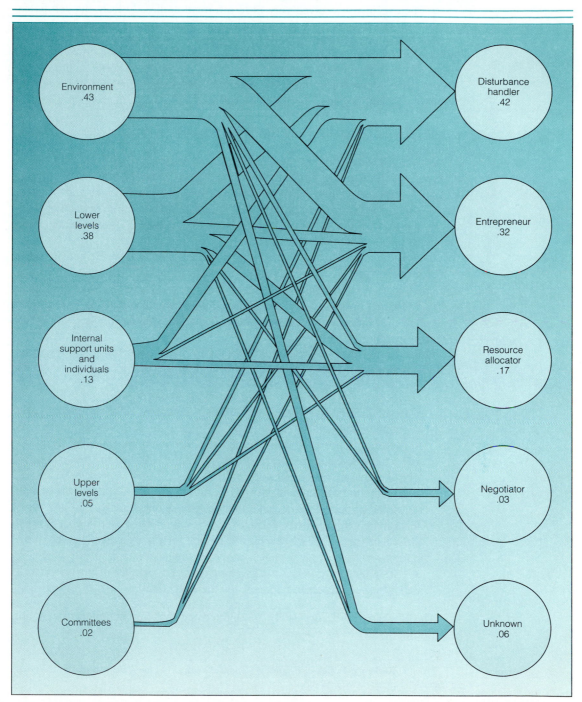

- Most of the executives' information came in a written form, but the oral information was valued higher.
- The executives received very little information directly from the computer.

No executive information system is going to be completely computer based. Rather, the computer will be superimposed on top of noncomputer flows. For that reason, the information systems of the five study executives serve an important purpose. They show the intricate nature of the information flows that executives establish to obtain problem-solving information.

The Rockart and Treacy Study

If one were asked to pinpoint the single research effort that triggered the interest in executive information systems, it would be difficult to decide between the Mintzberg study and one conducted in the early 1980s by John Rockart and Michael Treacy, both of MIT.[6] In their study of executive computer use in sixteen companies, at least one of the top three officers—most often the CEO—personally used computers.

One of the most dedicated computer supporters was Ben W. Heineman, CEO of Northwest Industries. Heineman had a terminal in his office, one at home, and took one with him on vacations. Heineman stated that: "There is a huge advantage to the CEO to get his hands dirty in the data." Another executive commented that: "You learn the nature of the real question you should have asked when you muck around in the data."[7]

The term *executive information system,* or *EIS,* first appeared in the report of the Rockart and Treacy study. Although no definition was provided, the researchers recognized that such systems feature:

- **A Central Purpose**—Executives employ computer information primarily in planning and controlling.
- **A Common Core of Data**—The database contains information on industries, customers, competitors, and business units in three time periods—history, present, and future.
- **Two Principal Methods of Use**—Executives use the EIS to access current status and projected trends, and conduct personalized analyses of the data.
- **A Support Organization**—The executives are helped by EIS coaches and EIS chauffeurs. An **EIS coach** is a member of the executive's staff, information services, or an outside consulting organization, who provides help in setting up the system. An **EIS chauffeur** is a member of the executive's staff who operates the equipment for the executive.

The Rockart and Treacy study spotlighted the fact that computer use is not beneath the dignity of executives.

[6] John F. Rockart and Michael E. Treacy, "The CEO Goes On-Line," *Harvard Business Review* 60 (January–February 1982), 82–88.

[7] Ibid, 86.

Putting the Computer in Perspective

Although some executives rely heavily on the computer, the fact of the matter is that there is a smaller proportion of computer users on the executive level than any other. Two possible reasons stand out. First, the problems at the executive level are less structured and therefore more difficult to support with computer processing. Second, executives tend to be older and less likely to have had the benefit of formal computer training. Age in itself is not an issue, as proven by the many executives approaching retirement who have embraced computer processing. Also, the lack of training is something that can easily be overcome if the executive is willing.

Perhaps computer use is influenced mainly by the problem-solving nature of the executive. If the executive emphasizes rational problem solving and recognizes the potential contribution of the computer to the process, then he or she likely will make use of computer information.

The important points in this discussion are that (1) computer use is a personal thing, and (2) computer information is only a portion of all of the information reaching an executive. All executives want to receive good information from any source. Heineman, as strong a computer advocate as one could ever expect to find on the executive level, expressed this feeling when he said that he believed in "not being the captive of any particular source of information."[8]

SUGGESTIONS FOR IMPROVING EXECUTIVE INFORMATION SYSTEMS

One cannot help but feel that the computer represents an untapped information resource for executives. Executives should take steps to elevate the role of the computer in their information systems. But, in doing so, executives should strive to improve the noncomputer components as well. A five-step program to this end is outlined below:

1. **Take an inventory of incoming information transactions.** The Jones and McLeod study has revealed that executives do not always have a clear perception of their information systems.[9] Executives may view certain sources and media as contributing more than they really do. By the same token, other sources and media may be underrated. Executives, assisted by their secretaries, can maintain logs similar to those of the Jones and McLeod study. The data can be entered into a database, and reports can be prepared that enable the executives to answer the Jones and McLeod questions as they relate to their own systems.

2. **Stimulate high-value sources.** With the high value sources identified, executives can then take steps to make it easier for those sources to com-

---

[8] Ibid, 85.

[9] Raymond McLeod, Jr., Jack W. Jones, and Joe L. Poitevent, "Executives' Perceptions of Their Information Sources," in *Fourth International Conference on Decision Support Systems,* ed. Robert W. Zmud (Dallas: IADSS, April 1984), 2–14.

municate. The bank CEO provides a good example of how this can be done. Perhaps his most valuable information came from his management committee. In order for each member to feel equally free to participate, the CEO specified that a round conference table be used.

3. **Take advantage of opportunities.** When a good piece of information comes along, the executive should grab it. The vice president of finance followed this strategy when he positioned his desk against the wall so that his back was to the door. This might seem like a maneuver to discourage communication, but the intent was just the opposite. As he explained, when someone enters his office he does not want to carry on a conversation looking across a sea of unfinished paperwork. With his desk against the wall, he can swivel around and give his caller his complete attention.

4. **Tailor the system to the individual.** As the Jones and McLeod study data shows, each executive has a unique information gathering style. What is good for one executive may not work for another. The retail CEO serves as a case in point. The previous CEO built a private outside entrance to his office so that he could come and go without confronting anyone. The study CEO had exactly the opposite philosophy, preferring instead to use the main entrance to the building so that he could have personal contact with as many employees as possible along the way.

5. **Take advantage of technology.** Executives are generally open-minded concerning their information systems and will consider any means of improving them. Younger executives who studied computers in high school and college know the potential of computer use, but their computer literacy must be kept current. Older executives require a more fundamental consulting service in terms of what the computer can and cannot do. Keeping all executives informed of developments in information technology is an important responsibility of the information services organization.

Interest in EIS took off like a rocket during the late 1980s. The interest was a combination of a greater computer awareness on the part of the executives and the availability of improved hardware and software.

COMPUTER-BASED EXECUTIVE INFORMATION SYSTEMS

An **executive information system (EIS)** is a system that provides information to the executive on the overall performance of the firm. The information can be easily retrieved and can provide varying levels of detail. The term **executive support system (ESS)** is also used. We will use EIS and assume that the system incorporates the computer.

An EIS Model

The configuration of a computer-based EIS usually includes a personal computer. In large firms the PC is networked to a mainframe as shown in the EIS model in

FIGURE 16.10

An EIS Model

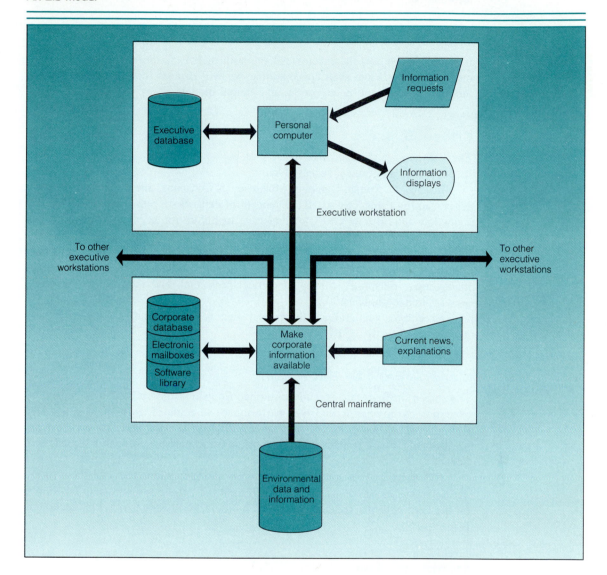

Figure 16.10. The executive's personal computer serves as the **executive workstation.** The hardware configuration includes secondary storage, most likely in the
form of hard disk, which houses the executive database. The **executive database**
contains data and information that has been preprocessed by the firm's mainframe.
The executive selects from menus to produce preformatted screen displays, or perform a minimum amount of processing. The system also permits use of the firm's
electronic mail system and access to environmental data and information. In some

cases, EIS support personnel enter current news items and explanations of the information.

The Incorporation of Management Concepts

It is easy to see how the executives have built their EISs on fundamental management concepts. Three such concepts that we will discuss include critical success factors, management by exception, and mental models.

Critical Success Factors

The EIS enables the executive to monitor how well the firm is doing in terms of its objectives and critical success factors.

In 1961 D. Ronald Daniel of McKinsey & Company, one of the nation's largest consulting firms, originated the concept of **critical success factors.** He felt that a few key activities, or **CSFs,** spell success or failure for any type of organization, and they vary from one organization to the next. For example, in the automobile industry the CSFs are believed to be styling, an efficient dealer network, and tight control of manufacturing cost. In life insurance they are the development of agency management personnel, control of clerical personnel, and innovation in creating new insurance products.[10]

Executives who embrace the critical success factors concept use their EISs to monitor each of the CSFs.

Management by Exception

The screen displays that executives retrieve frequently incorporate management by exception by comparing budgeted performance to actual. Figure 16.11 is a screen that superimposes a pie chart on a tabular display. The pie chart shows the composition of actual performance, and the tabular portion compares actual with budget.

EIS software can automatically identify the exceptions and call them to the executive's attention. For example, a highlight bar can be automatically positioned on the item with the greatest variance. Figure 16.11 illustrates how this technique is used.

Mental Models

The primary role of the EIS is to synthesize, or distill, a large volume of data and information to increase its utility. This distillation has been called **information compression,** and it produces a view, or a **mental model,** of the firm's operations.

John Rockart and David DeLong of MIT, in their book on executive support

---

[10]The CSFs quoted here are from John F. Rockart, "Chief Executives Define Their Own Data Needs," *Harvard Business Review* 57 (March–April 1979), 85.

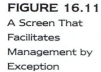

FIGURE 16.11
A Screen That Facilitates Management by Exception

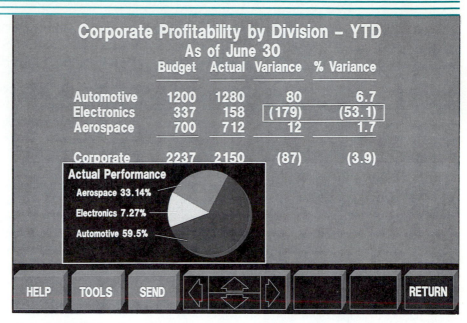

Copyright 1988 by Comshare.

systems, give P. N. Johnson-Laird credit for coining the term mental model. They quote his explanation that mental models "enable individuals to make inferences and predictions, to understand phenomena, to decide what action to take and to control its execution, and above all to experience events by proxy."[11]

The CBIS is a mental model, as are each of its subsystems. The EIS is the mental model that is of most interest and value to the executive.

EIS IMPLEMENTATION DECISIONS

When a company considers whether to implement a computer-based EIS, three key implementation decisions must be made. First, there is the question: "Should we develop an EIS?" When the answer is *No,* the executives continue to rely on their present systems.

When the answer is *Yes,* the next question is: "Is there prewritten application-development software available to meet the executives' needs?" If so, it is purchased.

If not, the next question is: "Should we purchase prewritten EIS software?" If so, it is purchased. If not, the firm's information services staff creates custom EIS software.

[11] John F. Rockart and David W. DeLong, *Executive Support Systems* (Homewood, IL.: Dow Jones-Irwin, 1988), 54.

Prewritten Application-development Software

Application-development software is general purpose software that any type of organization can use to develop its own applications. Examples are DBMSs, electronic spreadsheet packages, graphics packages, and project management systems. If this type of software is acceptable, then it is the best option, as it is the least expensive. The main limitation is that the executives may perceive it as not being user friendly enough or not keyed to their special needs.

Prewritten EIS Software

When the firm decides not to go the application-development software route, the next option is **prewritten EIS software,** which is specially designed to meet the information needs of executives. Such systems usually provide information compression and the drill-down capability that we discussed in Chapter 12.

The first examples of EIS software were designed for mainframe systems, and the leading suppliers were Pilot Executive Software, Inc. of Boston, and Comshare, Inc. of Ann Arbor, Michigan. Execucom Systems Corporation of Austin, Texas belonged to this pioneering group, but was recently acquired by Comshare. Today, prewritten EIS software is available for all sizes of computers, with most of the packages aimed at owners of PCs.

This class of software offers three major advantages over the other categories. First, it enables the firm to get a system up and running in a hurry. Second, the EIS implementation project does not put as much of a burden on the firm's information services staff as when they must develop the EIS from scratch. Third, EIS software is specifically intended for the executive and offers a good chance of being used. A disadvantage could be the inability to tailor the system to the executive's particular needs.

Custom EIS Software

When the firm elects not to purchase prewritten software of either type, the remaining option is for the information services staff to create custom EIS software.

One of the most highly publicized examples of custom EIS software is the MIDS (for Management Information and Decision Support) system implemented by Lockheed-Georgia.[12] Figure 16.12 shows a sample output from MIDS. An interesting feature of this display is the identification in the upper-right-hand corner of the persons who are expert in the data that is displayed. These persons are called **data managers.** If the executive has a question about the display, she or he contacts one or the other of the data managers for an explanation.

Another interesting feature of MIDS is the fact that it required a support staff of six information analysts and two computer analysts to keep the system running.

---

[12] George Houdeshel and Hugh J. Watson, "The Management Information and Decision Support (MIDS) System at Lockheed-Georgia," *MIS Quarterly* 11 (March 1987), 127–40.

FIGURE 16.12

The Screen Identifies Who Is Responsible for the Data

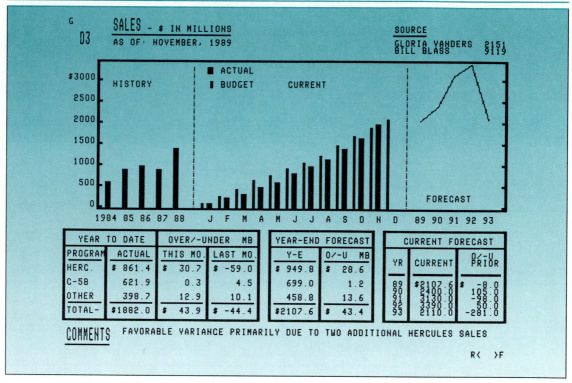

Courtesy of Lockheed Aircraft, Incorporated.

That is a characteristic of EISs that is often overlooked; there are many people behind the scenes who make the system work.

AN EIS CASE STUDY

Linda Volovino of Canisius College and Stephen Robinson of Execucom Systems Corporation studied the EIS experiences of a large bank.[13] Marine Midland Bank developed and implemented an EIS called Compass in 1987. The EIS was created with the Pilot Command Center EIS software and was designed to support 100 users, from the CEO to divisional vice presidents. The system was designed to work in conjunction with the bank's decision support system. Both systems were to run

---

[13] For more information on this example, *see* Linda Volovino and Stephen Robinson, "EIS Experiences at Marine Midland Bank, N.A.," *Journal of Information Technology Management* 2 (Number 2, 1991), 33–38.

on the same mainframe computer, and the DSS was to provide Compass with a central repository of compressed data. Compass was intended to become the foundation of the bank's executive office of the future.

During the development process, information specialists tried to meet with the bank's executives in order to determine their information needs. This proved difficult for two reasons: (1) the executives had little time to devote to such interviews, and (2) many of the executives had no experience with EIS and had little understanding of what was possible. As a result, several design decisions were made by the specialists rather than by the executives.

Compass was designed to identify the sources of displayed information by name, address, and telephone number. The date that the information was entered was also included. The design called for Compass to generate no new data, but to display data gathered from other systems. The data was to be updated weekly.

System use was high from the very beginning. In fact, people who were not executives, including controllers and administrative assistants, began to use it. As a result, response time began to degrade, and by mid-1988 system usage dropped off significantly.

Why the decrease in popularity? First, the executive who had been the strongest supporter of Compass left the company, depriving the system of any central direction. Second, the system was not designed to be integrated into the bank's management process. It could not function as a communication tool. In fact, the bank's electronic mail system ran in a completely separate environment. Third, the lack of hardware that was dedicated to the EIS aggravated the problem of poor response time. Fourth, the weekly update schedule became inadequate as users' expectations increased. Fifth, the system had been designed to be flexible, but this feature rendered some applications too complicated for executive use. Rather than learn to use an application, the executives declined to use the system at all.

After a careful examination, systems developers estimated that it would cost hundreds of thousands of dollars to address the problems. At the time that Volovino and Robinson wrote their article, Compass was on the list of systems to be eliminated as part of a general budget reduction plan.

EIS CRITICAL SUCCESS FACTORS

Although EIS experiences such as those at Marine Midland are to be avoided, they serve a useful purpose in alerting firms to the possibility that the systems do not always work as intended. Firms benefit from these experiences and incorporate features into their EIS development programs that offer the best assurance of success.

Rockart and DeLong identify eight critical success factors for achieving a successful EIS.[14] We have supplemented the list by adding experiences of firms in applying the CSFs.

---

[14] Rockart and DeLong, *Executive Support Systems,* 153–54.

1. **A Committed and Informed Executive Sponsor**—A top level executive, preferably the CEO, should serve as the **executive sponsor** of the EIS by encouraging its implementation. The most successful EIS efforts have been those where the first user was a top executive. At Gillette, the president of the company's North American unit inaugurated the EIS. At Lockheed-Georgia, the system came at the urging of the president. Unfortunately, at Marine Midland, the executive sponsor left. Since such an eventuality cannot be prevented, the best strategy is to have a substitute waiting in the wings.

2. **An Operating Sponsor**—The executive sponsor will most likely be too busy to devote much time to implementation. That task should be given to another top-level executive, such as the executive vice president. The **operating sponsor** works with both the using executives and the information specialists to ensure that the work gets done.

3. **An Appropriate Information Services Staff**—Information specialists should be available who not only understand the information technology but also how the executive will use the system. The areas of information technology that are especially applicable include data communications, database, and graphical user interfaces. There will be situations, however, where information services does not develop the system. The operating sponsor may elect to assign the task to other managers in the executives' units or to consultants.

4. **Appropriate Information Technology**—EIS implementers should not get carried away and incorporate unnecessary hardware or software. The system must be kept as simple as possible and should give the executive exactly what he or she wants—nothing more and nothing less.

5. **Data Management**—It is not sufficient to simply display the data or information. The executive should have some idea of how current the data is. This can be accomplished by identifying the day and, ideally, the time of day that the data was entered into the system. The executive should also be able to pursue a data analysis. The analysis can be accomplished by drill down, by following up with data managers, or both.

6. **A Clear Link to Business Objectives**—Most successful EISs are designed to solve specific problems or meet needs that can be addressed with information technology. Many firms will be constrained from jumping on the EIS bandwagon because they have not developed these well defined statements of where they are headed and how they should get there.

7. **Management of Organizational Resistance**—When an executive resists the EIS, efforts should be taken to gain support. A good strategy is to identify a single problem that the executive faces and then quickly implement an EIS, using prototyping, to address that problem. Care must be taken to select a problem that will enable the EIS to make a good showing. Then, additional applications can be added.

8. **Management of the Spread and Evolution of the System**—Experience has shown that when upper-level management begins receiving information from the EIS, lower-level managers want to receive the same output. The lower-level managers want to be able to anticipate problems and solve them before the upper-level managers view the situation as being out of hand. EIS use therefore trickles down the management levels. However, care must be taken to add users only when they can be given the attention that they need to get their systems up and running. One reason for the success of the EIS concept has been the high level of user education and training.

These CSFs essentially boil down to good planning—anticipating needs and then putting the required resources and procedures in place. If the firm has embraced information resources management and does a good job of strategic planning for information resources, the achievement of a good EIS and other organizational informational sytems as well is a realistic goal.

PUTTING THE PIECES TOGETHER

Earlier in the chapter we presented a five-step program for improving an EIS. We then identified the three alternate software choices. These steps are combined with the EIS critical success factors to achieve the overall EIS development plan in Figure 16.13.

FUTURE EIS TRENDS

Incorporation of the computer into executives' information systems has been slow, but the situation is rapidly changing. Whereas the Ben Heinemans of the early 1980s were rare, it is not unusual for today's executive to be a computer user. As support for the EIS continues to increase, we can expect to see its influence in several forms.

EIS Use in Large Firms Will Become Commonplace

More and more middle-level managers with computer backgrounds are moving up into the executive ranks. Some of these new executives will be attracted to the prewritten EIS software. Others will allocate information services resources to the development of custom systems. All of this activity will result in EISs in practically all of the larger firms.

There Is a Need for Lower-priced Special EIS Software

The future adoption rate for smaller firms is not so clear. Application-development software may not be a suitable alternative. The most appealing alternative for

FIGURE 16.13

An Overall EIS
Development Plan

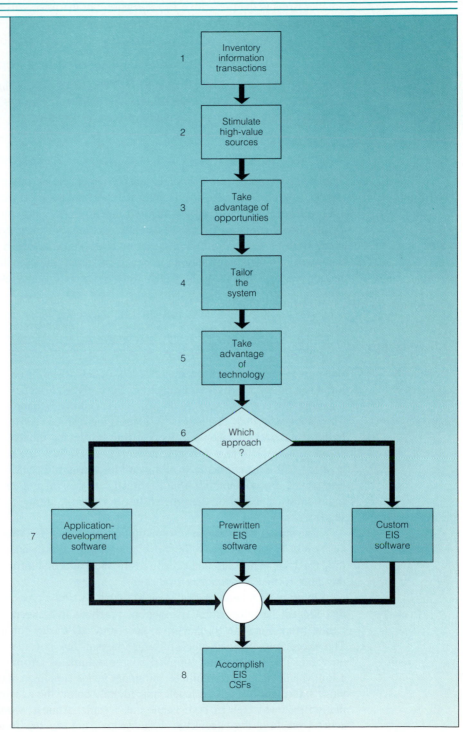

smaller firms is the prewritten EIS software, but the price will have to be reduced. This will happen as more suppliers enter the market.

Tomorrow's MIS and DSS Will Look Like Today's EIS

More effort has gone into achieving user acceptance of EIS than any other application. We will see new classes of MIS and DSS software designed for managers on lower levels, which contain many of the EIS features.

Executives Will Keep the Computer in Perspective

The trend is clearly toward increased computer use at the executive level, but nobody is predicting that the computer will become the most important information source. Executives have always favored face-to-face communication, and that situation should continue. Executives are recognizing, however, that the computer can meet some of their information needs in a superior manner. By incorporating the computer into their information systems, new opportunities will open up for information retrieval and analysis, which were never before available at the executive level.

SUMMARY

Executives are managers on upper levels of an organization who exert a strong influence on its activities and direction. Executives are believed to emphasize the planning function, as well as the roles of disturbance handler and entrepreneur. They cope with their challenges by identifying agendas for their firms to achieve, building networks of people to work toward achieving the agendas, and creating a stimulating environment for their networks. Executives are concerned more with how to get their networks to work toward the agendas than with specific decisions. Executives use both intuition and rational analysis in problem solving, applying intuition at each step of the process but not always taking the steps in the same sequence.

Executives have unique information needs. Mintzberg studied the information systems of five CEOs, recording how they spent their time and the main media that they used. He concluded that executives favored informal information systems over the more formal computer-based designs.

Jones and McLeod expanded on Mintzberg's media types and designed a study that logged the information transactions reaching five executives. Daily volumes varied from executive to executive, and from day-to-day for the same executive. The executives obtained much information that they considered to be of little or no value. The environment supplied a large volume of information usually having a low value, whereas committees and upper levels supplied small volumes of high-value information. The two levels immediately below the executive supplied information that was high in both value and volume. Almost two-thirds of the transactions reaching the executives were written, but the top four media, based on average transaction value, were oral. The major findings of the study are that the executives' information systems did not always provide information from the preferred sources, using the preferred media, and that the computer played a relatively minor role.

Rockart and Treacy reported on sixteen firms where the executives were eager to use the computer themselves. The researchers coined the term executive information system, or EIS, and identified four main features—central purpose, a common core of data, two principal uses to assess and analyze data, and a support organization.

If the modern executive wishes to make greater use of the computer, a five step program can be followed. This program will improve the entire EIS and begins with an inventory of information inputs. The executive then stimulates high-value sources, takes advantage of opportunities, and tailors the system to her or his unique style. Finally, the executive takes advantage of EIS technology.

An EIS usually consists of a PC networked to a mainframe. The PC serves as the executive workstation, providing access to the executive database. Applied management concepts include critical success factors, management by exception, and mental models.

A firm can base its EIS on application-development software, prewritten EIS software, or custom software developed in-house. Application-development software is least expensive but not specifically intended for executive use. Prewritten EIS software can be inflexible and expensive but offers the advantages of quick implementation and a high probability of executive acceptance.

When the firm's executives decide to take advantage of computer technology, they should pay attention to the eight EIS critical success factors. These factors include having executive and operating sponsors; making use of information services resources; using appropriate technology; linking the EIS to business objectives; and managing data problems, organizational resistance, and system evolution.

We will see continued acceptance of the EIS by executives. Lower-level managers will make use of the same systems and will stimulate development of systems that are similar to those for executives but geared to lower-level needs. In addition, more prewritten EIS software will be developed for use on stand-alone micros by small firms.

Although the computer is achieving greater acceptance by executives, it will continue to be only one of several sources of information. Executives will continue to solicit good information from many sources, using both oral and written media.

With this look at the information needs of executives, we turn our attention in the next four chapters to the MIS subsystems that support functional areas.

KEY TERMS

executive
agendas (of objectives)
networks (of cooperative relationships)
environment (of norms and values)

EIS coach
EIS chauffeur
executive information system (EIS), executive
    support system (ESS)

executive workstation
executive database
critical success factor (CSF)
information compression

mental model
data manager
executive sponsor
operating sponsor

KEY CONCEPTS

The uniqueness of each executive's information system—molded to fit her or his particular interests, plus the demands of the organization and its environment

The fact that executives gather information from many sources both inside and outside the firm, using both written and oral media

The reality that an executive can manage some but not all of his or her information sources and media

The importance of an executive gaining an understanding of his or her information system before attempting to make improvements in that system

The influence of today's EIS on tomorrow's MIS and DSS designs

QUESTIONS

1. Name a basic distinction between an executive and a lower-level manager.

2. Which of Fayol's management functions is supposed to be the most critical at the executive level?

3. Which of Mintzberg's managerial roles is supposed to be the most critical at the executive level?

4. How does Kotter's use of the term environment differ from how we have been using it?

5. Do executives follow the systems approach? Explain.

6. How did Mintzberg's executives spend most of their time?

7. List the eight major sources of executive information identified in the Jones and McLeod study. Place an asterisk next to the ones that offer the best combination of high volume and high value.

8. Does the potential use of information have any influence on its value, according to the Jones and McLeod study? If so, explain.

9. Did the Rockart and Treacy study support the belief that executives prefer summary information? Support your answer.

10. Distinguish between an EIS coach and an EIS chauffeur.

11. What are the five steps that an executive can take to improve his or her information system?

12. Is it necessary for the EIS to include computer-produced information?

13. Why are the three alternatives for achieving an EIS examined in the sequence described?

14. List three reasons why a firm should consider purchase of prewritten EIS software.

15. Is a data manager the same as a DBA? Explain.

16. List the EIS critical success factors that Marine Midland did not incorporate into their Compass development program.

17. If the executive sponsor wants to engage in the day-to-day development activity, will there be a need for an operating sponsor?

18. What is the best way to combat organizational resistance to the EIS?

19. Why does EIS use trickle down through the organization?

20. Ten years from now, which of the three alternate EIS software avenues do you think small firms will be selecting the most?

TOPICS FOR DISCUSSION

1. Is the owner and operator of a newstand in a hotel an executive?

2. Why do you think that executives prefer oral information over written information?

3. Why do executives receive so many information inputs with little or no value?

4. Do you think the day will ever come when executives will obtain all of their information from the computer?

PROBLEMS

In Chapter 12 we described the drill-down technique and illustrated it with Figure 12.5. Assume the executive wants you to modify the system so that each tabular screen in the figure is supplemented by two other screens—a graph and a narrative. The graph will present the tabular data in a graphic form, and the narrative will explain the reason for any exceptions.

1. Sketch out the graph for each tabular screen. You can select the type of graph. Your instructor will tell you whether to use a graphics package for the final product.

2. Write a short narrative for each tabular screen that could enable the executive to quickly grasp the reason for the exceptional performance. This narrative would be generated by an artificial intelligence capability incorporated in the EIS. Hint: The cause of each exception is revealed by the tabular screen on the next lower level. This means that you will have to fabricate the cause for the lowest-level screen. Let your imagination run wild.

SERVCO

Kevin Flanagan is president and CEO of SERVCO, the nation's largest manufacturer of janitorial supplies. SERVCO has been using a computer since the mid-1970s, but there have been more failures than successes. A continual turnover of computer personnel, including managers, has prevented SERVCO from achieving the level of computer use that Flanagan had envisioned.

Six months ago Melissa Grover was hired as the new computer manager. She is currently putting together a long-range computing plan. She is also devising new personnel policies intended to attract and retain professional information specialists. Several members of the present staff are expert in database management systems and computer graphics, but the remaining staff and their skills are nothing to write home about.

As Flanagan looks over his appointments calendar for the day, he sees that his consultant, Guy Winstead, is scheduled for 9:30 and Melissa for 10:00.

"Guy, it's good to see you. Please sit down and tell me what's on your mind."

"I'm surprised you can't guess, Kevin. Every time we talk, I try to convince you to put together a good set of business objectives."

"You know, Guy, I wish I had the time to take you up on that, but I'm too busy putting out fires. I've got a real inferno going now." Kevin pulls a computer printout from a drawer and drops it on his desk with a thud. "Look at this. I've been after good information from my computer people for years, and this is all I've got to show for it."

Guy leans over and thumbs through the report. "I can't help you much on this. Computing is something I've never gotten into. Your new manager, Grover— maybe she can help you."

"I certainly hope so. She's due in here at ten, and I'm going to try to get something rolling."

Guy looks at his watch and decides to take advantage of his remaining time. "I would expect you to make some real progress. I recall that you and your secretary kept all of those records of where your information comes from, and you always try to stay in contact with your good sources of information. You certainly pick my brains every chance you get. I think you've got the makings of an information system that suits you to a T—the noncomputer part of it anyway. It's a shame that your computer people have always let you down. Well, I can see my time's up. Let me know when we can work on those objectives. You know the saying: "When you don't know where you're going, any road will take you there."

"It's not that bad, Guy. We're making some real progress in some areas. Come back any time. You're always welcome."

As Guy leaves, he passes Melissa and the two exchange greetings. She then enters Kevin's office and takes a seat in front of his desk. "Kevin, I wanted to bring you up to date on the long-range plan I've been working on."

"Go ahead, Melissa. You know that I'm all ears when it comes to that topic. Take all the time you need."

"Well, the hard facts are that we just don't have any computer applications that are well established. We not only haven't made any real progress toward an MIS or DSS, we don't even have a good data processing system. We are still struggling with data entry, trying to cut down on errors and get the data into the system sooner. And, our DP programs have been patched so many times that maintenance is next to impossible. After I get my staff established, my top priority is to recode all of the DP programs using structured programming and create some good documentation. But, that's probably going to take a year."

"Melissa, I think that's the place to start. If it takes a year, fine. I was going to talk with you about something else, but it can wait. Let's get a good data processing system established, and we can go from there. Keep me posted, and you know that you can count on me for help."

Melissa leaves the office and Kevin picks up his phone, dials a number, and says: "Rick, how are things in marketing research? Listen, I've been thinking about what you said the other day about setting me up with my own executive information system. Go ahead and order the PC and the dBASE IV and Lotus packages. As soon as you have them, give me a call and let's get started."

Assignments

1. Using Figure 16.13 as a guide, list the reasons why Kevin should be optimistic about achieving a good EIS.

2. Now, list the reasons why he might be in for some disappointment.

3. Assume that Kevin has asked you for advice. What would you recommend? List the steps in order.

SELECTED BIBLIOGRAPHY

Armstrong, David A. "How Rockwell Launched its EIS." *Datamation* 36 (March 1, 1990): 69–72.

Carlisle, Judith P., and Alameddine, Kimberly D. 1990. "A Study Evaluating Existing Executive Information Systems Products." In *Proceedings of the Twenty-Third Annual Hawaii International Conference on Systems Sciences,* ed. Jay F. Nunamaker, Jr. Vol. III, "Decision Suport and Knowledge Based Systems," 160–169. Los Alamitos, CA: IEEE Computer Society Press.

Chung, Kae H., and Friesen, Michael E. "The Critical-Success-Factor Approach To Management at Boeing." *Journal of Management Systems* 3 (No. 2, 1991): 53–63.

Dearden, John. "Will the Computer Change the Job of Top Management?" *Sloan Management Review* 25 (Fall 1983): 57–60.

Ferranti, Marc. "Wingz-Based EIS Tool Released for Windows." *PC Week* 9 (April 6, 1992): 38.

Friend, David. "EIS: Straight to the Point." *Information Strategy* 4 (Summer 1988): 25–30.

Houdeshel, George. 1990. "Selecting Information for an EIS: Experiences at Lockheed Georgia." In *Proceedings of the Twenty-Third Annual Hawaii International Conference on Systems Sciences,* ed. Jay F. Nunamaker, Jr. Vol. III, "Decision Suport and Knowledge Based Systems," 178–85. Los Alamitos, CA: IEEE Computer Society Press.

Hough, Paul, and Duffy, Neil. "Top Management Perspectives on Decision Support Systems." *Information & Management* 12 (1987): 21–31.

Jenster, Per V. "Firm Performance and Monitoring of Critical Success Factors in Different Strategic Contexts." *Journal of Management Information Systems* 3 (Winter 1986/87): 17–33.

Jones, Jack William, and McLeod, Raymond, Jr. "The Structure of Executive Information Systems: An Exploratory Analysis." *Decision Sciences* 17 (Spring 1986): 220–49.

Jones, Jack William; Saunders, Carol; and McLeod, Raymond, Jr. "Information Media and Source Patterns Across Management Levels: A Pilot Study." *Journal of Management Information Systems* 5 (Winter 1988/89): 71–84.

Kador, John. "The Current State of Executive Support Systems." *Planner* 11 (Winter 1989): 9–14.

Kador, John. "Executive Support Systems Keep Executives in Control." *Planner* 11 (Spring 1989): 1–5.

Leifer, Richard. "Matching Computer-Based Information Systems with Organizational Structures." *MIS Quarterly* 12 (March 1988): 63–73.

McLeod, Raymond, Jr., and Jones, Jack William. "Making Executive Information Systems More Effective." *Business Horizons* 29 (September/October 1986): 29–37.

Mohan, Lakshmi; Holstein, William K.; and Adams, Robert B. "EIS: It Can Work in the Public Sector." *MIS Quarterly,* 14 (December 1990): 435–48.

Pinella, Paul. "An EIS for the Desktop." *Datamation,* 37 (May 1, 1991): 26–30.

Stamps, David. "EIS Prices Finally Get Real." *Datamation.* 37 (January 15, 1991): 65–66.

Turban, Efraim. *Decision Support and Expert Systems.* New York: Macmillan, 1988. Pp. 289–310.

Viahos, George E., and Ferratt, Thomas W. 1992. "The Use of Information Technology by Managers of Corporations in Greece to Support Decision Making." In *Proceedings of the 1992 ACM SIGCPR Conference,* ed. Albert L. Lederer, 136–51. New York: ACM Press.

Watson, Hugh J.; Rainer, R. Kelly, Jr.; and Koh, Chang E. "Executive Information Systems: A Framework for Development and a Survey of Current Practices." *MIS Quarterly* 15 (March 1991): 13–30.

Wetherbe, James C. "Executive Information Requirements: Getting It Right." *MIS Quarterly* 15 (March 1991): 51–65).

Zaleznik, Abraham. "Managers and Leaders: Are They Different?" *Harvard Business Review* 70 (March–April 1992): 126–35.

Chapter 17

Marketing Information Systems

After studying this chapter, you should:

- Recognize the high level of interest that marketing has shown in functional information systems and appreciate how their theoretical models benefit other functional areas as well
- Visualize a functional information system as a group of input and output subsystems connected by a database
- Understand how the input subsystems gather data and information both internally and from the environment
- Recognize that the output subsystems include various types of software that transform data into information describing the functional area
- Have an awareness of how information technology has been incorporated into marketing research and the gathering of marketing intelligence
- Be familiar with some of the programs in the software library, which support decisions relating to product, place, promotion, price, and the integrated mix
- Know how *Fortune 500* firms use their marketing information systems

603

INTRODUCTION

The trend is definitely toward functional information systems, but they pose a threat of undermining the efficiency and effectiveness of an integrated CBIS. Marketing was the first functional area to exhibit an interest in MIS. Shortly after the MIS concept originated, marketers tailored it to their area and called it the MKIS. Early graphic models of MKISs provide a basis for organizing all functional information systems.

The model structure that we will use in this and the next three chapters consists of input subsystems that gather data and information from inside the firm and from its environment, a database where the data is kept, and output subsystems that transform the data into information.

The MKIS consists of three input subsystems: data processing, marketing research, and marketing intelligence. The output subsystems address the information needs of the four ingredients of the marketing mix (product, place, promotion, and price), plus an integration of the four.

Managers in large firms changed their preferences for marketing information during the 1980s. MKISs today are providing more balanced decision support than did earlier versions.

FUNCTIONAL ORGANIZATION STRUCTURE

Business firms traditionally have been organized in terms of the tasks, or functions, that are performed. All types of organizations have marketing, finance, human resources, and information services functions, although these names do not always appear on doors and organization charts. The only firms with a manufacturing function are those that produce the products that they sell. Other functions include engineering, and research and development.

In this and the next three chapters we will focus on the marketing, manufacturing, finance, and human resources functions. Throughout the text we have directed our attention at the information services function.

FUNCTIONAL INFORMATION SYSTEMS

The functional organization influence is so prevalent that information systems can be organized functionally as well, as is illustrated in Figure 17.1. The conceptual systems are mirror images of the physical systems that they represent.

The Risk of Emphasizing Functional Information Systems

It is important to understand that functional information systems are not a substitute for a single integrated system for the firm—the CBIS. Functional subsystems must work together. They must derive at least some of their data from a common data-

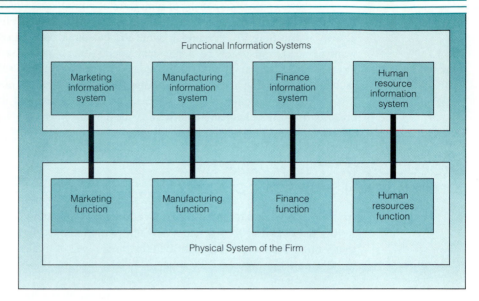

FIGURE 17.1
Functional
Information
Systems
Represent
Functional
Physical Systems

base, and decisions made in one area must be compatible with those made in others and with the overall objectives of the firm.

The remainder of the chapter will be devoted to the first functional information system to emerge—the marketing information system. In their enthusiasm for applying the computer, the marketers built a solid theoretical base upon which information systems for all functional areas can be built.

MARKETING PRINCIPLES

Many people think of marketing in narrow terms—as including only selling and advertising. Marketers, however, define it very broadly. One definition states that **marketing** "consists of individual and organizational activities that facilitate and expedite satisfying exchange relationships in a dynamic environment through the creation, distribution, promotion, and pricing of goods, services, and ideas."[1]

Such a view suggests the broad range of problems that marketing managers must solve as well as the broad range of information that is needed to solve the problems.

The Marketing Mix

Marketing managers have a variety of resources with which to work. The objective is to develop strategies that apply these resources to marketing the firm's goods, services, and ideas.

[1] William M. Pride and O. C. Ferrell, *Marketing Concepts and Strategies,* 7th ed. (Boston: Houghton Mifflin Company, 1991), 4.

Marketing strategies consist of a mixture of ingredients, which has been named the **marketing mix**: product, promotion, place, and price. Collectively they are known as **the four Ps. Product** is what the customer buys to satisfy a perceived want or need, and it can be a physical good, some type of service, or an idea. **Promotion** is concerned with all the means of encouraging the sale of the product, including advertising and personal selling. **Place** deals with the means of physically distributing the product to the customer through a channel of distribution. **Price** consists of all the elements relating to what the customer pays for the product.

EVOLUTION OF THE MARKETING INFORMATION SYSTEM CONCEPT

In 1966 Professor Philip Kotler of Northwestern University used the term **marketing nerve center** to describe a new unit within marketing to gather and process marketing information.[2] He identified the three types of marketing information that are illustrated in Figure 17.2.

- **Marketing intelligence**—information that flows into the firm from the environment
- **Internal marketing information**—information that is gathered within the firm
- **Marketing communications**—information that flows from the firm outward to the environment

Kotler recognized the decision support intent of the nerve center: "... complex marketing decisions such as dropping a price, revising sales territories, or increasing the advertising expenditure level can be preevaluated and postevaluated through the scientific analysis of available data."[3] Although he did not use the name marketing information system, it is what Kotler had in mind.

We can define a **marketing information system (MKIS)** as a computer-based system that works in conjunction with other functional information systems to support the firm's management in solving problems that relate to marketing the firm's products. Two elements in the definition make key points. First, all of the functional information systems must work together, and second, the problem-solving support is not limited to marketing managers.

The Kotler Model

During the period 1967–74, no fewer than five models of MKISs were described in the literature. One was prepared by Kotler and is illustrated in Figure 17.3. The core consists of four subsystems: internal accounting, marketing intelligence, mar-

---

[2] Philip Kotler, "A Design for the Firm's Marketing Nerve Center," *Business Horizons* 9 (Fall 1966), 63–74.

[3] Ibid, 73.

FIGURE 17.2
Kotler's
Information Flows

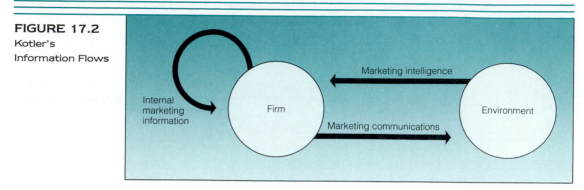

Source: Reprinted from *Business Horizons* (9, Fall 1966). Copyright 1966 by the Foundation for the School of Business at Indiana University. Used by permission.

FIGURE 17.3
The Kotler Model of a Marketing Information System

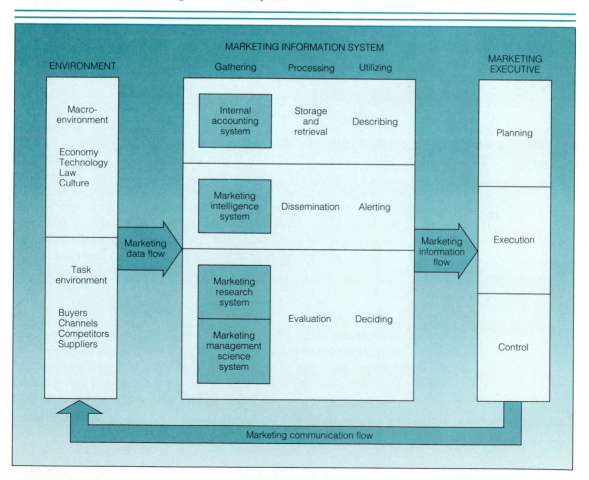

keting research, and marketing management science. These subsystems take data from the environment and transform it into information for the marketing executive.

By including the *internal accounting system,* Kotler recognized the symbiotic, or dependent, relationship among the functions of the firm. The internal accounting system provides a common bond throughout the firm.

The *marketing intelligence system* is concerned primarily with disseminating information to alert managers to new developments in the marketplace. It differs from the accounting system in that the intelligence output is oriented toward the future, rather than the present or the past.

The *marketing research system* has a twofold purpose of: (1) gathering current data that describes marketing operations, and (2) presenting the findings to management in a form that facilitates decision making. The emphasis is on the timeliness of the information. The typical approach is to conduct special projects that gather data describing a particular problem. On the other hand, the *marketing management science system* emphasizes the use of sophisticated quantitative techniques, such as mathematical modeling. Kotler saw the marketing executive using the information output for planning, execution, and control.

Professor Kotler produced a good structure for identifying the primary methods of generating marketing information. However, his model assigned most of the problem-solving techniques to the marketing research and marketing management science systems. For our purposes, we need a finer breakdown so as to accomodate the wealth of information technology that has been made available during the past thirty years.

A MARKETING INFORMATION SYSTEM MODEL

All of the decisions that a marketing manager makes relate to one or more of the mix ingredients. For that reason the ingredients are a good way to categorize the activities of the MKIS. The MKIS can be designed so that it supports decisions relating to each of the ingredients.[4] Our model of such a system is illustrated in Figure 17.4. It consists of a combination of input and output subsystems connected by a database.

Output Subsystems

Each output subsystem provides information about its part of the mix. The **product subsystem** provides information about the firm's products. The **place subsystem** provides information about the firm's distribution network. The **promotion subsystem** provides information about the firm's advertising and personal selling activ-

---

[4]The idea of using the mix ingredients as the basic model structure came from Richard H. Brien and James E. Stafford, "Marketing Information Systems: A New Dimension for Marketing Research," *Journal of Marketing* 32 (July 1968), 19–23.

FIGURE 17.4

A Model of a
Marketing
Information
System

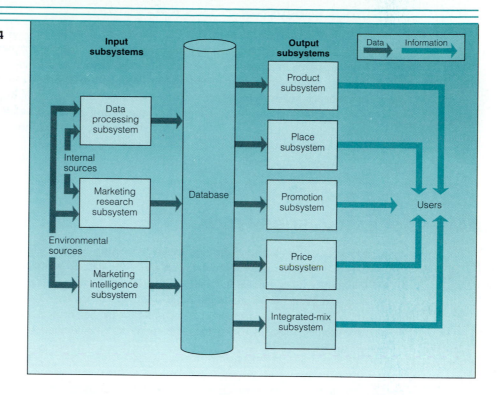

ities. The **price subsystem** helps the manager make pricing decisions. In addition, there is a fifth subsystem labeled the **integrated-mix subsystem,** which enables the manager to develop strategies that consider the combined effects of the ingredients. An example of the information provided by the integrated-mix subsystem is the sales forecast, which considers the interaction of all of the mix ingredients.

Each of the output subsystems consists of programs in the software library. These programs enable the manager to obtain information in the form of periodic and special reports, the results of mathematical simulations, communications, and expert systems advice.

It is important that you realize that the output subsystems draw on each of the CBIS subsystems that we described in Part Four—data processing, MIS, DSS, OA, and expert systems. This relationship was illustrated in Figure Five.2. The output subsystems of *all* functional information systems contain *all* types of CBIS software.

Database

The data that is used by the output subsystems comes from the database. Some of the data in the database is unique to the marketing function, but much is shared with other functional areas.

Input Subsystems

The input subsystems that provide the data for the database all come from Kotler's model. We rename the internal accounting subsystem the **data processing system.** It gathers data that describes the firm's marketing transactions and enters that data into the firm's accounting system as we described in Chapter 11. The **marketing intelligence subsystem** gathers information from the firm's environment that has a bearing on marketing operations. The **marketing research subsystem** conducts special studies of marketing operations for the purpose of learning customer needs, and improving marketing efficiency.

We will now describe each of the subsystems in greater detail, beginning with the input subsystems.

DATA PROCESSING SUBSYSTEM

Marketing plays a role in the firm's data processing system by providing sales order data. Perhaps the sales representatives enter the data from customer offices, using telephones for terminals. Or, sales order personnel at headquarters take order data over the phone or by mail, and enter it into keyboard terminals.

The data is used to prepare information in the form of periodic and special reports. The data also provides the input for mathematical models and expert systems.

Data for Preparation of Periodic Reports

Examples of periodic marketing reports include the *sales by product report* that we illustrated in Chapter 12. *See* Figure 12.7. Managers can use the report to identify which products are selling well, and which are not. In a similar fashion, periodic reports can be prepared for customers and salespersons. We illustrated a *sales by salesperson report* in Chapter 13 when we explained how to incorporate management by exception into a report. *See* Figure 13.9.

Data for Preparation of Special Reports

The vast majority of data that is used to respond to managers' database queries likely comes from data provided by the data processing system. An example is the sales analysis report that we illustrated in Chapter 8 when we described the FOCUS 4GL. The *product unit sales analysis* in Figure 8.15 summarizes product sales by sales region.

Data for Mathematical Models and Expert Systems

When we discussed the DSS in Chapter 13 we described how the firm's executives could use a pricing model to gauge the effects of price changes on profit. All of the output information from the pricing model was produced from data provided by the data processing system.

The key point is that if a firm does not have a good data processing system, it cannot expect to provide its problem solvers with good information.

MARKETING RESEARCH SUBSYSTEM

Marketing managers can use **marketing research** to gather any type of information, but most activity is aimed at customers and prospects. Marketers use the term **consumers** to describe both groups.

Primary and Secondary Data

Two types of data are gathered—primary and secondary. **Primary data** is data that the firm collects. Data gathered by the firm's salespersons is an example. Data that has been collected by someone else is called **secondary data.**

Using Marketing Research to Gather Secondary Data   Some secondary data must be purchased and is often made available in the form of magnetic tapes or diskettes for easy entry into the CBIS. Other secondary data, such as that found in libraries, is free for the asking. Computer-based information retrieval systems, available in many libraries, minimize the collection time. Mailing lists are another example of secondary data. These lists are available in many forms, including magnetic tape, diskettes, gummed labels, and index cards. The lists enable the firm to establish contact with very select markets, usually by direct mail. For example, the Alvin B. Zeller company of New York City offers lists on t-shirt retailers, women by height, high school cheerleading directors, and hypnotists.

Using Marketing Research to Gather Primary Data   Almost everyone has been approached by someone conducting a survey. A **survey** involves asking the same questions of a number of persons, by personal interview, telephone, or mail. The number of persons may be relatively small, say thirty, or quite large, say several thousand. Figure 17.5 shows a personal interview being conducted in a shopping mall—a convenient place to ask shoppers about their shopping habits.

When questions are asked of a small number of people, such as three or four, the technique is known as an **in-depth interview.** The time devoted to the interview is much longer than that spent with someone participating in a survey. Also, the emphasis of the in-depth interview is on obtaining explanations of *why* consumers behave as they do. This contrasts with the emphasis of surveys on *what* they do.

A third marketing research technique is **observation,** either watching a certain behavior or looking for evidence that it occurred. Marketing researchers often note license plate numbers in a shopping mall parking lot to determine how far people have driven. Instances have also been recorded of researchers going through people's garbage to learn what products they buy.

Marketers have also applied the technique of the **controlled experiment** from the physical and behavioral sciences, and both the real marketplace and the classroom are used as laboratories. College students often serve as subjects in experi-

FIGURE 17.5
A Personal
Interview

© Rhoda Sidney/Stock, Boston

ments designed to measure the effect of a particular treatment (such as a certain type of ad) on behavior (such as the ability to recall the ad).

Electronic Consumer Recording

Marketing research firms often enlist the participation of consumers in recording data. Recently, research programs have been designed to obtain all of the data from a consumer that bears on a purchase. This is called **single-source data.**

The Arbitron Company gathers single-source data by providing consumers with an electronic recording unit that sits on top of the TV set and keeps a record of the programs and ads that are tuned in. Every fifteen minutes a prompt appears on the TV screen and the viewers use a remote-control device to identify themselves. The device contains buttons that are labeled with the family members' names. As the appropriate buttons are pressed the information is stored in the TV recording unit.

The system is also used to record items that the family purchases. When a shopper arrives home, a cordless data wand is removed from its holder in the TV recording unit and is used to scan the UPC (universal product code) bar codes on the purchased items. Figure 17.6 shows the consumer using the wand. Each 24-hour period, usually during the wee morning hours, the Arbitron central computer in Maryland polls the TV recorders and retrieves the stored data. This data, combined with demographic data that the family members have provided, enables Arbi-

FIGURE 17.6
Consumers Use
Data Wands to
Record Purchases

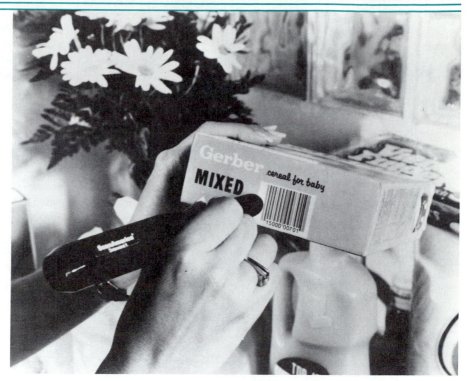

Arbitron Ratings Company. A Control Data Company. Used by permission.

tron to identify (1) the ads that are being watched, (2) who is doing the watching, and (3) the items that are being purchased. The data can be correlated to link purchases with ads as a way of measuring the effectiveness of the ads.

Marketing Research Software

Until a few years ago only the largest firms could conduct their own marketing research. Smaller organizations had to rely on marketing research organizations or do without. Now, there are a large number and variety of marketing research software packages available. The packages, most of which are for micros, perform a variety of applications that range from assisting telephone interviewers to conducting sophisticated statistical analyses. There are also packages that produce graphics of the research findings. Color maps are popular ways to display research data that relates to trade areas.

Although the software makes marketing research a reality to firms of all sizes, it is not the key to effective research. The key is the expertise that is used to design research projects and interpret the findings. If the expertise does not exist within the firm, it can come from consultants, or the firm can enroll employees in marketing research courses.

MARKETING INTELLIGENCE SUBSYSTEM

Each functional area has a responsibility to interface the firm with particular elements in the environment. Figure 17.7 shows that marketing has responsibility for the customers and competititors; manufacturing for suppliers and labor; finance for stockholders or owners, and financial community; and human resources for the government and local community. All of the functional areas have responsibilities in terms of the government and local community.

Marketing Responsibilities for Environmental Data and Information

Our third input subsystem, marketing intelligence, gathers data and information concerning one of marketing's two environmental responsibilities—the competitors. Marketing has no responsibility to establish an outgoing flow to the competitors but must establish an incoming flow.

Data and information concerning the firm's second environmental responsibility, customers, are gathered by both the data processing system and marketing research.

What Is Marketing Intelligence?

The term marketing intelligence may bring to mind visions of one firm spying on another—an activity called **industrial espionage.** A certain amount of such under-

FIGURE 17.7
Each Functional Area Has Responsibility for Gathering Environmental Data and Information

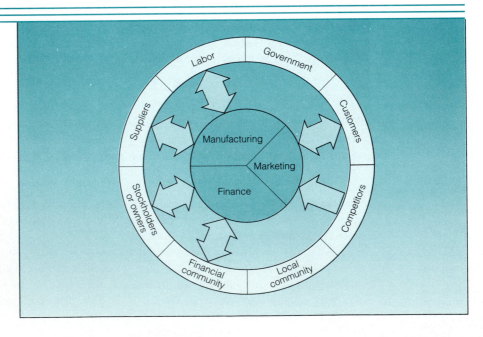

cover work surely must go on in the competitive world of business. However, few instances have been publicized since firms are hesitant to report thefts of proprietary information for fear of damaging their corporate image. Also, such violations are difficult for authorities to prosecute.

Some accusations of unethical data gathering involve computerized databases. Frontier Airlines accused United of monitoring competitors' activity as recorded in the APOLLO reservation system and then using the information to either lower prices or broadcast special messages to travel agents.[5] When Braniff filed for bankruptcy, it made similar charges against American.

There is really no reason to break the law to obtain information because it is so easy to obtain legally. **Marketing intelligence** refers to the wide range of ethical activities that may be used to gather information about competitors. It does not refer to unethical or clandestine activities.

The Booming Interest in Business Intelligence

During the 1960s and 1970s U.S. firms did not pay too much attention to gathering information about their competitors. However, the increased competition from foreign firms, especially those in Japan, during the 1980s has changed things dramatically. Today, the gathering, storage, and dissemination of competitive information represents an important computer application in many companies. Sometimes the terms **competitive intelligence (CI)** and **business intelligence** are used. The information that is gathered is called **intelligence.**

Basic Intelligence Tasks[6]

Competitive intelligence involves five basic intelligence tasks, which are illustrated in Figure 17.8. Some firms establish a special intelligence unit to perform the tasks. Other firms assign the tasks to existing units as an added responsibility.

Collect Data   The firm may acquire either primary data or secondary data. Much secondary data is available, such as data describing supermarket and drug store sales, and is collected by organizations such as Nielsen Marketing Research.

Evaluate Data   Whether the data is primary or secondary, it should be checked to ensure its accuracy.

Analyze Data   Seldom does the data tell the entire story. It is necessary to fill in the gaps. The term **lateral thinking** describes how you examine the data from a variety of angles, looking for patterns. In the words of one CI consultant,

[5]James I. Cash and Benn R. Konsynski, "IS Redraws Competitive Boundaries," *Harvard Business Review* 63 (March–April 1985), 135.

[6]Tamar Gilad and Benjamin Gilad, "Business Intelligence—The Quiet Revolution," *Sloan Management Review* 27 (Summer 1986), 53.

FIGURE 17.8

The Five Basic Intelligence Tasks

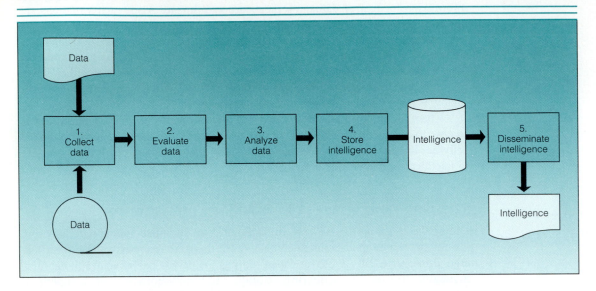

"If you can't find a foot, ... look for a footprint."[7] The purpose of the analysis step is to transform data into intelligence.

Store Intelligence If the intelligence is purchased in a machine-readable form such as optical disk, or is available online, entry into the computer is no problem. However, if the intelligence exists in a printed form, it must be entered either by optical character recognition (OCR) or by keying. When keying is necessary, some firms outsource the work to a company in a foreign country, usually in the Caribbean or Asia, where the labor costs are low.[8]

Once in the computer, the intelligence must be stored in such a manner that easy retrieval will be possible. The difficulty of this task is the fact that most of the intelligence is in a narrative form. Most DBMSs are intended for digital data, but some are marketed for use in storing narrative data. An example is INQUIRE/Text from Infodata Systems, Inc. In the INQUIRE/Text DBMS you can have alphanumeric fields of any length and can have as many fields as you need. An abstract, or an entire document, can be stored in a single field.

Disseminate Intelligence Once in secondary storage, the text of the document or abstract is retrieved in the same manner as any data record. Figure 17.9 contains a sample display, using INQUIRE/Text.

[7] Tim Miller, "Staying Alive in the Jungle," *Online Access* 12 (March/April 1987), 47.

[8] Uday Apte and MaryAnne Winniford, "Global Outsourcing of Information Systems: Opportunities and Challenges," in *Managing Information Technology in a Global Society,* ed. Mehdi Khosrowpour. (Harrisburg, PA: Idea Group Publishing, 1991), 58–67.

FIGURE 17.9
An INQUIRE/Text
Display

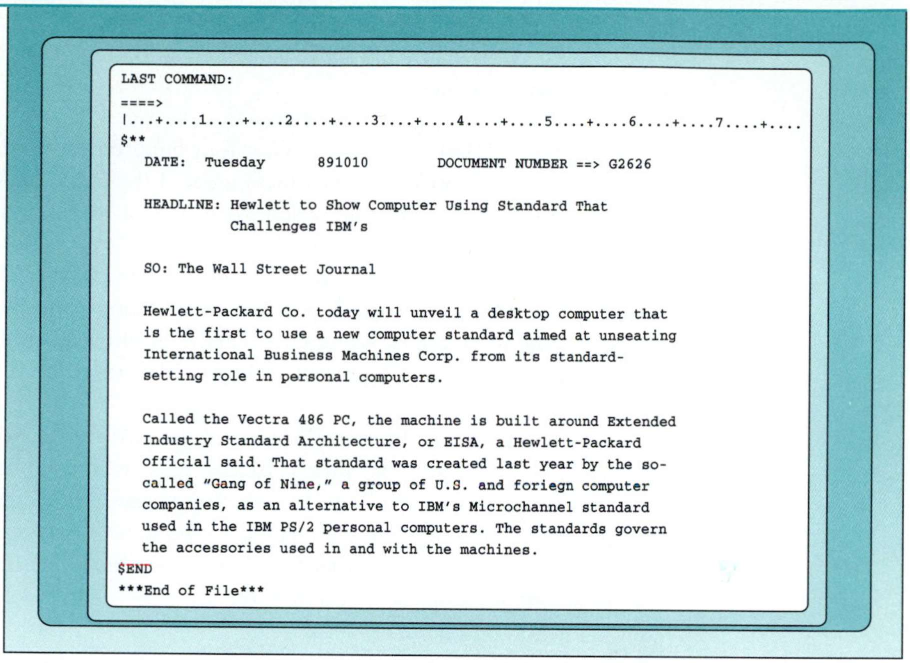

```
LAST COMMAND:
====>
|...+....1....+....2....+....3....+....4....+....5....+....6....+....7....+....
$**
    DATE:  Tuesday      891010        DOCUMENT NUMBER ==> G2626

    HEADLINE: Hewlett to Show Computer Using Standard That
             Challenges IBM's

    SO: The Wall Street Journal

    Hewlett-Packard Co. today will unveil a desktop computer that
    is the first to use a new computer standard aimed at unseating
    International Business Machines Corp. from its standard-
    setting role in personal computers.

    Called the Vectra 486 PC, the machine is built around Extended
    Industry Standard Architecture, or EISA, a Hewlett-Packard
    official said. That standard was created last year by the so-
    called "Gang of Nine," a group of U.S. and foriegn computer
    companies, as an alternative to IBM's Microchannel standard
    used in the IBM PS/2 personal computers. The standards govern
    the accessories used in and with the machines.
$END
***End of File***
```

A sophisticated approach to dissemination is to prepare an **intelligence profile** for each user, describing in a coded form the intelligence topics that the user wants to monitor. This profile is entered in the computer, and when a piece of intelligence arrives that matches the profile, the intelligence is made available to the user. This technique is called **selective dissemination of information (SDI).** The information is made available to only those who have an interest in it.

Online Data Services

Previously in the text we have mentioned online data services such as the Dow Jones News/Retrieval Service. In Chapter 14 we recognized that DJNRS is an example of videotex and is included in many executive information systems.

DJNRS is only one of thousands of online databases that are available worldwide. Some are aimed at consumers to facilitate activities such as electronic shopping, and some are aimed at professionals such as doctors and lawyers. The major business database services include BRS and DIALOG.

Bibliographic Retrieval Service (BRS)

BRS is a product of BRS Information Technologies and offers three business related services. One is BRS/Search, a 24-hour-a-day, 7-day-a-week service that enables users to use command language to access bibliographic citations and abstracts from over a hundred and fifty databases. The second service is After Dark, a user-friendly, menu-driven access to over a hundred and ten databases (some are the same as BRS/Search) at reduced rates for evening and weekend use only. The third service is BRS/Colleague, a menu-driven access to basically the same databases as BRS/Search, but targeted to executives and professionals.

DIALOG   DIALOG includes over four hundred separate databases, primarily in the business, scientific, and technical areas. Like BRS, DIALOG makes its services available on a worldwide basis and has over 140,000 customers in approximately one hundred countries.

These online data service suppliers make their databases available for a fee. There may be a relatively small onetime setup charge, and then you pay a certain amount per hour of use or per query. This is an area of computer service that is growing very rapidly and represents a huge CBIS resource.

The area of competitive intelligence is the part of the MKIS that is currently receiving the most attention. Firms usually have well-established data processing capabilities, and those firms with a marketing research need have created their own departments or are aligned with research agencies. Now, firms are seeking to improve the input subsystem that was long neglected—intelligence.

This concludes our description of the three input subsystems. We now turn our attention to the output subsystems.

PRODUCT SUBSYSTEM

The product is usually the first ingredient in the marketing mix to be specified. The firm decides to provide a product to satisfy a particular market need. Subsequently, the remaining ingredients (place, promotion, and price) are identified and described.

The Product Life Cycle

The task of the marketing manager is to develop strategies and tactics for each ingredient in the marketing mix and then to integrate these into an overall marketing plan. A framework called the product life cycle guides the manager in making these decisions. As its name implies, the **product life cycle** traces the sales of a product from its introduction to its withdrawal from the market. The four stages in the life cycle are introduction, growth, maturity, and decline.

Figure 17.10 shows these stages along with the three time periods during which the product subsystem helps the marketing manager make product-oriented decisions. The first period precedes the introduction of the product, when a decision is made whether to develop and market the product. The second period includes the time when various strategies must be considered to keep sales healthy. The final period is during the decline, when product deletion is an alternative.

A number of techniques have been developed to provide the manager with the information needed for making product oriented decisions. The technique discussed

FIGURE 17.10
The Product Life Cycle and Related Decisions

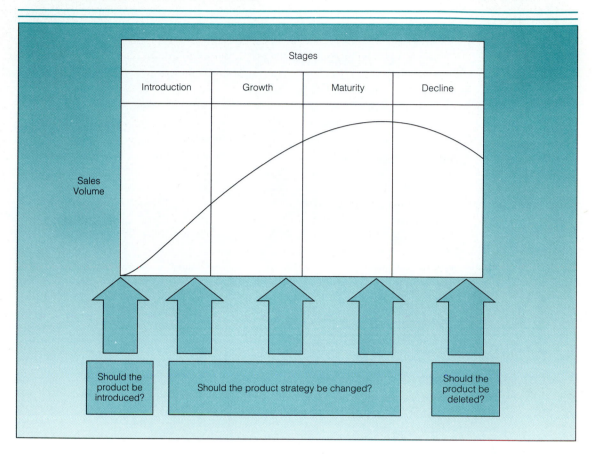

below helps the manager decide whether to introduce a product. The product subsystem consists of techniques such as these.

A New Product Evaluation Model

The decision to develop a new product should be carefully considered, have a sound financial basis, and be made by executives. Firms that introduce many new products develop a formal procedure that considers factors such as potential profitability and the efficient utilization of resources. The firm may have a **new product committee,** which performs a screening function by using a **new product evaluation model** to compute scores for new product candidates. The firm's executives use the scores in making new product decisions.

FIGURE 17.11

Quantitative Evaluation of a New Product Candidate

A--UTILIZATION OF PRODUCTION RESOURCES (PROPOSED NEW PRODUCT JXL5005)

DECISION CRITERIA	CRITERIA WEIGHT	VERY GOOD (10)		GOOD (8)		AVERAGE (6)		POOR (4)		VERY POOR (2)		TOTAL	CRITERION EVALUATION (TOT. EV X WEIGHT)
		P	EV	P	EV	P	EV	P	EV	P	EV		
PLANT CAPACITY	.20	.2	2.0	.6	4.8	.2	1.2	0	0	0	0	8.0	1.60
LABOR SKILLS	.30	.2	2.0	.7	5.6	.1	.6	0	0	0	0	8.2	2.46
ENGINEERING KNOW-HOW	.30	0	0	.2	1.6	.2	1.2	.6	2.4	0	0	5.2	1.56
EQUIPMENT AVAILABILITY	.10	0	0	0	0	.7	4.2	.3	1.2	0	0	5.4	.54
MATERIAL AVAILABILITY	.10	0	0	0	0	.1	.6	.6	2.4	.3	.6	3.6	.36

TOTAL PRODUCTION RESOURCES VALUE 6.52

(a) Utilization of production resources

B--UTILIZATION OF MARKETING RESOURCES

DECISION CRITERIA	CRITERIA WEIGHT	VERY GOOD (10)		GOOD (8)		AVERAGE (6)		POOR (4)		VERY POOR (2)		TOTAL	CRITERION EVALUATION (TOT. EV X WEIGHT)
		P	EV	P	EV	P	EV	P	EV	P	EV		
PRODUCT COMPATABILITY	.20	0	0	.2	1.6	.5	3.0	.2	.8	.1	.2	5.6	1.12
SALES KNOWLEDGE	.20	.1	1.0	.5	4.0	.3	1.8	.1	.4	0	0	7.2	1.44
DISTRIBUTION FACILITIES	.30	.3	3.0	.5	4.0	.2	1.2	0	0	0	0	8.2	2.46
LONG-TERM DEMAND	.30	0	0	.2	1.6	.6	3.6	.2	.8	0	0	6.0	1.80

TOTAL MARKETING RESOURCES VALUE 6.82

(b) Utilization of marketing resources

C--UTILIZATION OF FIRM RESOURCES

RESOURCE	VALUE	WEIGHT	WEIGHTED VALUE
PRODUCTION	6.52	.40	2.61
MARKETING	6.82	.60	4.09

TOTAL 6.70

(c) Utilization of firm's resources

Figure 17.11 illustrates output from a new product evaluation model.[9] In this example, a new product candidate is evaluated in terms of both its production and marketing features. An acceptable new product is one that fits both the production and marketing capabilities of the firm.

The decision criteria for considering the production aspects of the product candidate appear in the upper band. The criteria for the marketing aspects appear in the middle band. For each of the production and marketing criteria, a weighting factor (*criteria weight*) is included that reflects the relative importance. The center portion of the tables consists of ratings that each criterion receives, from very good to very poor. The ratings each have values from a high of 10 for very good to a

[9] Based on Stewart H. Rewoldt, James D. Scott, and Martin R. Warshaw, *Introduction to Marketing Management*, 3d ed. (Homewood, IL: Richard D. Irwin, 1977), 253–62. The technique is not new; an early description appeared in John T. O'Meara, "Selecting Profitable Products," *Harvard Business Review* 39 (January–February 1961), 83–89.

low of 2 for very poor. In the column beneath each rating is listed the probability (*P*) of the new product scoring the indicated rating on each specific criterion.

For example, the new product committee decides that the probability of the new product performing *very good* in terms of its effect on plant capacity is .2. This probability is multiplied by the value of 10 for a very good rating to produce an *expected value* (*EV*) of 2.0. The second column from the right contains a summation of the expected values for each criterion, and these are multiplied by the appropriate criteria weights to obtain the figures in the right-hand column. The total of the right-hand figures represents a *total production resources value* of 6.52 for the new product.

The marketing considerations are evaluated the same way. Then, both the production and marketing resource utilization scores are multiplied by their respective weights in the bottom band, and the weighted values are added. The total score of 6.70 represents the company production and marketing resource utilization for the new product. Similar scores are computed for the other products under consideration to aid the executives in making the new product decision.

PLACE SUBSYSTEM

The channels of distribution that a firm uses to get its products to the consumer comprise the place ingredient in the marketing mix. For some firms the channels are short—Mary Kay Cosmetics, for example, sells directly to the consumer. For other operations, the channels are long. Farmers' products, for example, reach the supermarket through a network of intermediaries, which includes wholesalers, brokers, and distributors.

The product, or material, is not the only resource to flow through the channel. Figure 17.12 shows the resources flowing through a channel that includes a supplier, manufacturer, wholesaler, retailer, and consumer. The material flow originates with the supplier and ends with the consumer. The money flow is just the reverse, and an information conduit provides a *two-way* flow that connects *all* participants.

Each channel member must know the details of the product flow as it relates to their role in the distribution process. For example, the manufacturer must know the rate at which wholesalers are buying the product, the rate at which retailers are buying from wholesalers, and the rate at which consumers are buying from retailers. It would be a mistake for the manufacturer to continue production of a product that is gathering dust on the retailers' shelves.

If the manufacturer expects feedback from the channel members, then something must be offered in return. Quite possibly this need only be information. The term **feedforward information** describes the flow of information toward the consumer. Feedforward information from the manufacturer to the wholesaler and retailer can include announcements of new products, sales and promotion aids, and forecasts of demand. Feedforward information to the consumer can include instructions for use, safety tips, and warranties.

FIGURE 17.12

Material, Money, and Information Flow through the Distribution
Channel

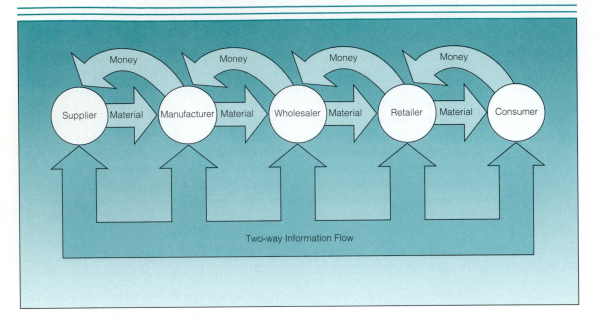

Information that flows in the opposite direction to the material flow is called
feedback information. We are expert in feedback, having introduced the feedback
loop in Chapter 3 when we described the general systems model of the firm.

Computer-based Information Flow

A channel system that permits information to flow freely among many firms provides an edge over competitive systems without that capability. In Chapter 2 we
described the concept of competitive advantage, and explained how firms such as
American Airlines, American Hospital Supply, and McKesson Drug had achieved
it. Each of these firms established electronic links with other organizations, a capability called **electronic data interchange (EDI).** EDI is excellent for achieving
competitive advantage, and the conceptual system that causes it to happen is the
place subsystem.

PROMOTION SUBSYSTEM

It has been extremely difficult to apply the computer to the promotion area. Companies have been using data from the data processing system to conduct sales analyses since punched card days, but the reports provide only a look at the past. Even
less has been accomplished in advertising because of its creative nature. There have
been a number of efforts, primarily by advertising agencies and academicians, to

FIGURE 17.13

A Salesperson
Can Use a
Portable
Microcomputer to
Communicate

Courtesy of PowerTek Industries, Inc.

develop mathematical models for use in making advertising media decisions, but none has met with much success—at least not publicized success.

One promotional area were the computer can be applied is salesperson communications. If the firm wants to provide its sales force with a flexible means of communication, this can be accomplished with portable microcomputers. The laptop in Figure 17.13 incorporates a modem and a telephone handset to facilitate its use as a terminal.

Salespersons carry the portables with them as they cover their territories and use them to:

■ Query the database to answer questions that the consumer asks about products being considered for purchase—availability, price, shipping costs, and the like.

- Enter sales order data into the order entry system.
- Submit **call reports** that summarize each sales call, specifying who was contacted, what was discussed, what the next sales objective will be, and so on. It is a simple matter to design the call report so that it contains space for recording competitive intelligence. In fact, the report can be designed so that different types of intelligence can be gathered from one month to the next, varying with competitive activity.

When marketing management decides to implement such electronic communications systems, it is important that salespersons see how their sales will increase. For example, the systems can provide salespersons with: (1) information about new prospects, (2) information about existing consumers such as historical patterns of previous purchases, and (3) information about the most profitable products to sell, taking into account factors such as varying commission rates, bonuses, and contests.

All of this information enables salespersons to do their job better. Everybody benefits—salespersons increase their commissions, the company increases its sales, and the consumers receive improved service.

PRICING SUBSYSTEM

The price area can run a close second to promotion in terms of decision support difficulty, depending on the firm's pricing policies.

Cost-based Pricing

Some firms engage in **cost-based pricing** by determining their costs and then adding a desired markup. This approach is a rather cautious one. You make your desired profit when you sell the items, but there is a chance that the consumer would have paid more.

When the firm has a good data processing system, it is an easy task for the pricing subsystem to support cost-based pricing by providing accurate cost data.

Demand-based Pricing

A less cautious pricing policy is **demand-based pricing,** which establishes a price compatible with the value that the consumer places on the product. The key to this approach is correctly estimating demand. This requires a good understanding of the consumer and also of the market, including the state of the economy and competition.

When the firm follows a demand-oriented pricing approach, computer support can come in the form of a mathematical model. The model enables the manager to play the What-If game in locating the price level that maximizes profit yet does not intensify competitive activity. We described a pricing model in Chapter 13 when we discussed DSS, and included samples of the input and output screens in Figures

13.11 through 13.13. Such a model is typical of the software that comprises the pricing subsystem.

INTEGRATED-MIX SUBSYSTEM

The integrated-mix subsystem supports the manager as the ingredients of the marketing mix are combined to form a particular strategy. This is accomplished by projecting the possible outcomes of various mixes.

Descriptions of integrated-mix subsystems in the literature are rare, a fact that is probably due more to the difficulty of the task than to firms' desire for secrecy. The integrated-mix model receiving the most publicity is BRANDAID, developed by MIT professor John D. C. Little.[10]

BRANDAID includes submodels for advertising, promotion, price, personal selling, and retail distribution. It simulates the activities of a manufacturer that sells to consumers through retailers in a competitive environment. This environment, including the main elements and the influences that interconnect them, is shown in Figure 17.14. The solid arrows represent the influences flowing from the manufacturer, retailer, competitor, and business environment. The dashed arrows represent responses to those influences.

The basic approach of the model is to estimate the effect of the various influences on the manufacturer's sales. The influences are listed next to each solid arrow. Figures 17.15 and 17.16 illustrate how the influences interact to produce a combined effect. Figure 17.15 shows the behavior of four of the variables, and if only one were present, sales would fluctuate as shown. Figure 17.16 shows the combined influence as projected by the model along with actual sales. You can see that BRANDAID did a good job.

A mathematical model, however, cannot handle unexpected events. This happened when the company using BRANDAID was hit by a strike, followed by an unexpectedly good sales response to a new package. The effect of these influences is pictured in Figure 17.17.

An integrated-mix model such as BRANDAID can be a powerful tool, not only for marketing managers but for other managers in the firm as well.

A STUDY OF MARKETING INFORMATION SYSTEMS IN *FORTUNE 500* FIRMS

This author, working with Professor John Rogers of California Polytechnic State University at San Luis Obispo, conducted a mail survey of *Fortune 500* firms in 1980. The study revealed how the firms used the computer as an MKIS.[11]

---

[10] John D. C. Little, "Decision Support Systems for Marketing Managers," *Journal of Marketing* 43 (Summer 1979), 9–26. For a detailed description of BRANDAID, *see* John D. C. Little, "BRANDAID: A Marketing-Mix Model, Parts 1 and 2," *Operations Research* 23 (July–August 1975), 628–73.

[11] Raymond McLeod, Jr. and John C. Rogers, "Marketing Information Systems: Uses in the Fortune 500," *California Management Review* 25 (Fall 1982), 106–18.

FIGURE 17.14

The BRANDAID Integrated-mix Model

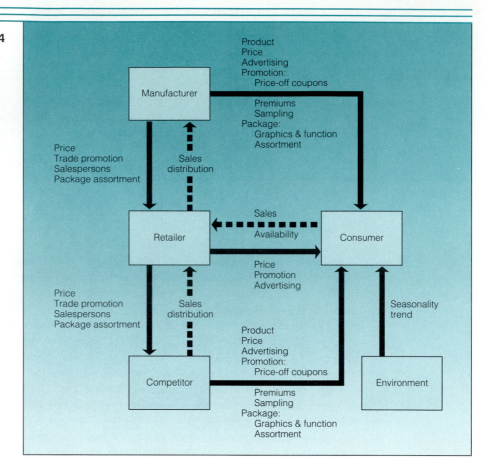

In 1990, the authors were joined by Professor Eldon Li, also of Cal Poly, and a second study of the *Fortune* firms was conducted. Usable questionnaires were returned by 131 marketing executives, for a 26 percent response rate.

The two studies reveal some interesting trends in the use of the computer as a strategic marketing tool.

Terminal Use

The 1980 and 1990 studies were not the first efforts to learn about the MKISs of the *Fortune 500* firms. In 1972, Professors Louis Boone and David Kurtz surveyed the same population and learned that 10 percent of the marketing managers had terminals.[12] In the 1980 study by McLeod and Rogers, this figure had risen to 51

[12]Louis E. Boone and David L. Kurtz, "Marketing Information Systems: Current Status in American Industry," in *Relevance in Marketing: Problems, Research Action,* ed. Fred C. Allwine, (Chicago: AMA Proceedings, 1972), 163–67.

FIGURE 17.15

Influence of Four Variables, Considered Separately

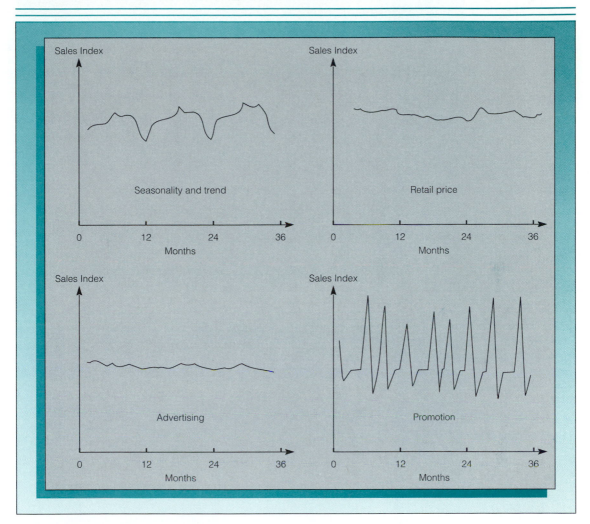

percent, and in 1990 it was 93 percent. Since some managers are close-minded to terminal use, the 1990 figure could very well represent a saturation point. Clearly, the situation today in *Fortune* 500 companies is one where a terminal is available to every marketing manager who wants one.

Not only are more managers using terminals, they are using them more frequently. Seventy percent of the 1990 managers use their terminals daily, up from 44 percent ten years ago. Monthly use is down from 7 percent to 2 percent, and only 7 percent of the 1990 terminal owners never use them on a regular basis, compared to 12 percent in 1980.

In 1980 managers used their terminals most often for retrieving information

FIGURE 17.16
Influence of Four
Variables, Taken
Together

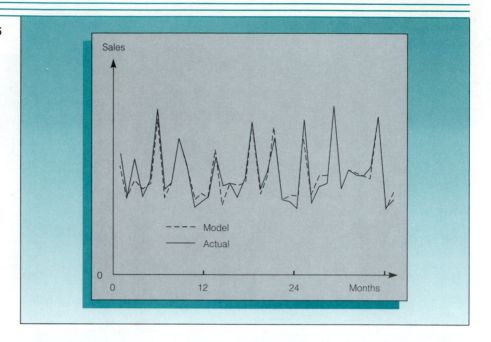

FIGURE 17.17
A Model Cannot
Cope with
Unexpected
Events

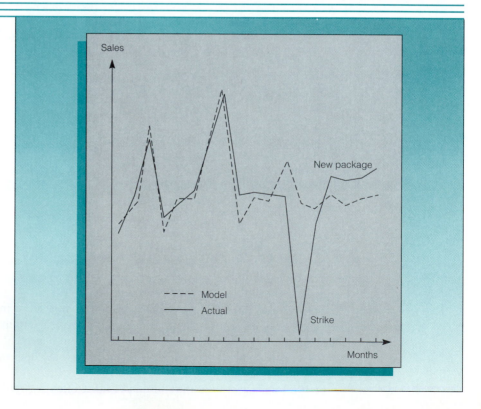

from the database (75 percent), followed by producing reports (61 percent), storing data (56 percent), mathematical modeling (51 percent), and coding programs (40 percent). In 1990 database retrieving had increased to 92 percent, report producing to 77 percent, and data storing to 64 percent. However, the 1990 managers had a new use in fourth place—processing data. Fifty-eight percent of the managers use their terminals to process data, strong evidence of end-user computing. The 1990 managers also use their terminals to send and receive reports (48 percent) and display graphs (42 percent), but have cooled down in their program coding activities to a level of 14 percent.

Preprocessed Information

One reason for the increased use of terminals to retrieve data and information from the database is the availability of preprocessed information. Seventy-one percent of the 1990 firms follow this practice of anticipating managers' database queries and doing the processing ahead of time. This technique, popularized with executive information systems, reduces the delay in providing the information to the managers, and is up substantially from the 50 percent level in 1980.

Mathematical Modeling

In 1972 the Boone and Kurtz study revealed that 20 percent of firms engaged in mathematical modeling. This situation changed dramatically by 1980 with 60 percent using modeling to develop the operating budget, 48 percent to determine prices, 38 percent to select new products, 37 percent to compute reorder points, 36 percent to compute economic order quantities, and 30 percent to locate facilties and to delete products.

However, these high levels of modeling were not reported by managers in 1990, as is shown in Table 17.1 The only applications showing an increase are product deletion and advertising media selection. Otherwise, modeling use is down across the board. This situation ties in with the infrequent use of terminals for modeling. Only 30 percent of managers use their terminals for decision simulation.

TABLE 17.1
Uses of
Mathematical
Modeling

1980	1990
1. Operating budget (.60)	1. Operating budget (.50)
2. Pricing (.48)	2. Pricing (.45)
3. New product evaluation (.38)	3. New product evaluation (.34)
4. Reorder point (.37)	4. Product deletion (.33)
5. Economic order quantity (.36)	5. Economic order quantity (.20)
6. Facility location (.30)	6. Salesperson assignment (.18)
7. Product deletion (.30)	7. Facility location (.16)
8. Salesperson assignment (.23)	8. Reorder point (.13)
9. Salesperson routing (.13)	9. Ad media selection (.13)
10. Ad media selection (.11)	10. Salesperson routing (.09)

Note: The percentages are based on the number of firms reporting the particular model uses.

The decrease in modeling activity was unanticipated. If anything, an increase should have been in order due to the availability of user-friendly modeling software in the form of electronic spreadsheets. However, the respondents may not have regarded the spreadsheets as models, or perhaps the managers have replaced much modeling activity with database querying. Whatever the reason, marketing managers perceive that they rely less on modeling than they did in the early 80s.

Support for Management Levels

In addition to the overall decrease in modeling, some significant shifts in model use in terms of management levels were reported, as shown in Figure 17.18.

In 1980, 70 percent of the respondents believed that management-control-level (middle-level) managers were receiving the most support from models. Only 17 percent felt that the strategic-planning level (top level) was the main user, and 13 percent chose the operational-control level (lower level). That situation was recognized as a healthy sign since early criticisms of the MIS labeled it as a support system for only the lower-level managers. Figure 17.18 shows the increased popularity of models at the top and lower management levels.

FIGURE 17.18
Model Use Is More Balanced Today than in 1980 in Terms of Management Levels

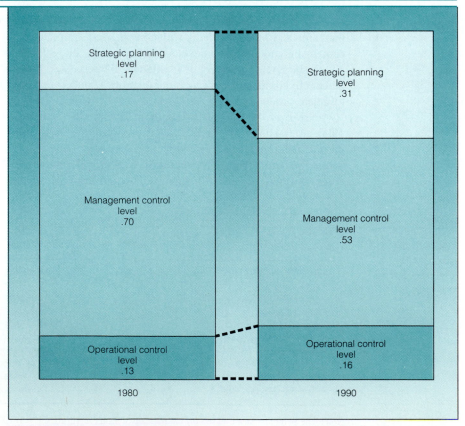

Note: The percentages are based on the number of respondents ranking the particular management levels first.

In 1990 model support at the management-control level slipped substantially to 53 percent, but support at the strategic-planning level increased to 31 percent. In a similar fashion, the support for the operational-control level was up to 16 percent.

The same trend toward a more balanced computer use among the management levels can be seen in the overall support provided by the MKIS. When asked to rank the levels of marketing management based on the degree of support received from the MKIS, 57 percent of the 1980 managers first listed the management-control level, followed by the strategic-planning level (25 percent), and finally the operational-control level (17 percent).[13] In 1980 the MKIS designs were clearly aimed at supporting middle-level managers.

In 1990 support for the management-control-level managers was down 11 percent to 46 percent, support for the strategic-planning level was up to 32 percent, and for the operational-control level it was up to 34 percent. Figure 17.19 illustrates these substantial shifts.

[13] Percentages do not always add to 100 due to rounding.

FIGURE 17.19

Overall Support from the Marketing Information System Is More Balanced Today than in 1980

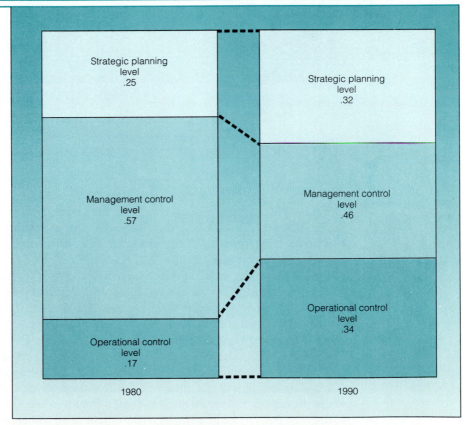

Strategic planning level .25

Strategic planning level .32

Management control level .57

Management control level .46

Operational control level .17

Operational control level .34

1980

1990

Note: The percentages are based on the number of respondents ranking the particular management levels first.

FIGURE 17.20

The 1990 Managers Placed More Emphasis on Planning and Less on Directing than Did Their 1980 Counterparts

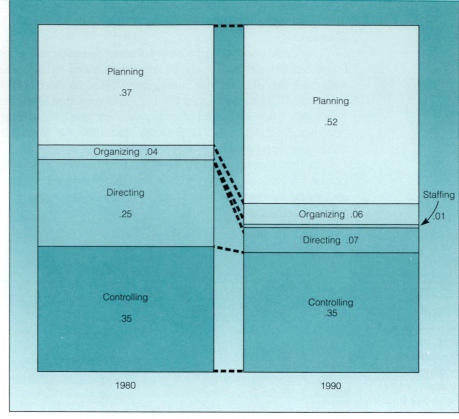

Note: The percentages are based on the number of respondents ranking the particular management functions first.

Support for Management Functions

Other shifts in support can be seen in Fayol's management functions. The left-hand bar in Figure 17.20 shows the distribution of support provided by the MKIS in 1980. The managers viewed the system as primarily being aimed at planning, directing, and controlling.

A corresponding distribution can be seen for 1990 in the right-hand bar. Fifty-two percent of managers believed planning to hold the top position, and support for controlling remained stable at 35 percent. The big shift is in directing; its support has slipped dramatically, with 33 percent of managers relegating it to last place. Organizing gained some support, as did staffing. However, the portion of managers who believed that staffing was supported the least ballooned to 73 percent.

Some of these shifts are easier to explain than others. The increased popularity of planning ties in with the increased CBIS support at upper-management levels where planning is so important. The slightly improved support for organizing and staffing can possibly be linked with recent emphasis on human resource information systems (HRIS). Perhaps marketing managers are taking advantage of the HRIS as they go about their organizing and staffing.

The loss of support for directing is difficult to explain. This is an area of office automation strength. Managers could use word processing, electronic mail, voice mail, and computer conferencing to communicate their directives to their subordinates. Perhaps managers are using these applications but do not regard them as part of the MKIS.

Support for Ingredients of the Marketing Mix

When asked to rank the mix ingredients in terms of support from the MKIS, 49 percent of the 1980 managers gave first-place honors to product, followed by price (27 percent), place (16 percent), and promotion (8 percent). Figure 17.21 shows this allocation.

The 1990s have seen no real change in support for place decisions, with only 15 percent associating that ingredient with the highest level of support. The previously strong support for product decisions has fallen to 32 percent, and the slack

FIGURE 17.21
Marketing Managers Are Using the Computer More Today for Making the Difficult Price and Promotion Decisions than in 1980

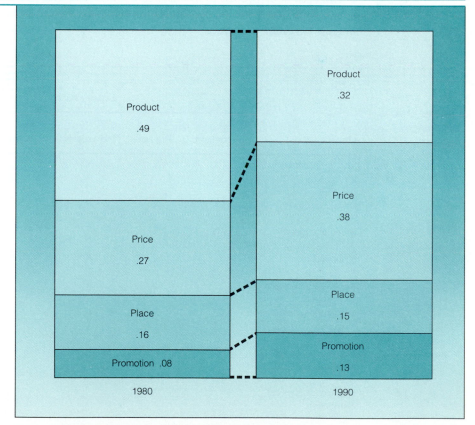

Note: The percentages are based on the number of respondents ranking the particular mix functions first.

has been taken up by price (38 percent) and promotion (13 percent). The emergence of price as the ingredient supported the most is a dramatic one. It indicates that marketing managers are focusing the computer on one of their most important, and difficult, decision areas.

As with the shift in support for the management levels, the 1990 MKIS is providing more balanced support for marketing mix decisions.

HOW MANAGERS USE THE MARKETING
INFORMATION SYSTEM

The *Fortune 500* studies provide a good view of how the industry giants are using the computer as a marketing tool. In applying all of the material in the chapter, we see marketing managers using the MKIS to learn about consumer needs and wants, to formulate the marketing mix, and to follow up on how well the mix is received by the consumers.

Other managers in the firm also use the MKIS. We have seen that competitive intelligence is of interest to the firm as a whole and that executives get involved in setting prices. Table 17.2 identifies the subsystems that would likely be of most interest to certain managers.

TABLE 17.2
Users of the Marketing Information System

| User | Subsystem | | | | |
	Product	Place	Promotion	Price	Integrated Mix
Vice president of marketing	X	X	X	X	X
Other executives	X	X	X	X	X
Brand managers	X	X	X	X	X
Sales manager			X	X	
Advertising manager			X	X	
Manager of marketing research	X	X	X	X	X
Manager of product planning	X				
Manager of physical distribution		X			
Other managers	X	X	X	X	X

Although the name of a functional information system implies that it is only for managers in that area, the information output can be of value to other managers and executives as well.

SUMMARY

The emergence of functional information systems shortly after the MIS concept originated was the first real evidence of a movement toward end-user computing. This movement benefits the firm except when it undermines efforts to achieve coordinated computer use.

Our model of the marketing information system, or MKIS, is based on the pioneering work of several marketing theorists. The input subsystems include data processing, marketing research, and marketing intelligence.

The data processing subsystem provides the input for software that produces information in the form of periodic and special reports, and outputs from mathematical models and expert systems.

Marketing research utilizes a variety of data gathering techniques—surveys, in-depth interviews, observations, and controlled experiments. New technology enables data to be recorded in consumers' homes.

Most of the current MKIS activity is aimed at establishing an intelligence-gathering capability. The basic tasks include collecting, evaluating, analyzing, storing, and disseminating. SDI directs intelligence to the persons who have a need. Online data services such as BRS and DIALOG bring intelligence as close as the nearest keyboard.

The product life cycle provides a framework for all marketing decisions. The product subsystem provides product-related information prior to introduction, during the period of healthy sales, and when deletion is considered. For example, a new product evaluation model can provide executives with some degree of structure in deciding whether to introduce a product.

The framework that holds the place subsystem together is the distribution channel. Data communications facilitates both feedforward and feedback information. This is the most popular way that firms have achieved competitive advantage, using information technologies such as EDI.

Both pricing and promotion have represented tough challenges to decision makers, but the MKIS seems to be making inroads. The promotion subsystem provides an opportunity to use portable computers to improve salesperson communications, and mathematical models in the pricing subsystem provide support for demand-based strategies.

A good integrated-mix subsystem is hard to find, in the literature anyway, but BRANDAID gives an idea of what can be achieved. Such models can be extremely accurate in handling expected events.

Although they hardley serve as a barometer for all computer users, the *Fortune 500* firms shed light on how operational MKISs match the model as well as management and marketing concepts. Terminals are available to everyone, and they are used to bring up a variety of information, some in a preprocessed form. During the

1980s managers on the strategic-planning and operational-control levels increased the amount of support that they received from the MKIS.

Another change occurred in terms of management functions. Support shifted in a big way to planning and in a modest way to organizing and staffing—all at the expense of directing. Although more functions are supported today, the distribution of support is far from even.

Such was not the case for the 4 Ps. The mix ingredients that had posed the stiffest challenges in 1980, price and promotion, increased their support levels. In fact, price is now supported the best.

With this understanding of how marketers use the computer, we can treat the other functional areas the same in the next three chapters.

KEY TERMS

primary data

secondary data

survey

in-depth interview

observation

controlled experiment

single-source data

industrial espionage

marketing intelligence, competitive intelligence (CI), business intelligence

intelligence

intelligence profile

selective dissemination of information (SDI)

feedforward information

cost-based pricing

demand-based pricing

KEY CONCEPTS

How functional information systems correspond to the functionally organized physical resources of the firm

The marketing information system (MKIS)

How a functional information system can be viewed as a combination of input and output subsystems, connected by a database

How the firm's data processing system provides data for all types of information output

The responsibilities of each of the functional areas for gathering intelligence from particular environmental elements

The product life cycle

The distribution channel as a pathway for material, money, and information flows

QUESTIONS

1. Why does a functional information system not stand alone but depend on the rest of the CBIS?

2. What three information flows did Kotler identify?

3. Does Kotler's model of an MKIS reflect the systems concept? Explain.

4. Are Kotler's four subsystems dedicated to input, output, or both? Explain.

5. What role does the integrated-mix subsystem play?

6. What types of computer output are generated from data provided by the data processing system?

7. What are the two basic types of data?

8. What are the four basic means of gathering primary data? Which one can be conducted without the knowledge and approval of the persons providing the information?

9. Explain what single-source data is.

10. What is the difference between industrial espionage and marketing intelligence?

11. What are the three time periods in the product life cycle where information support is provided?

12. Who uses the output from the new product evaluation model?

13. In the new product evaluation model explained in the chapter, would a good product receive a high or a low score? Support your answer.

14. Why is feedforward information important?

15. Why can a firm that uses EDI compete better than a firm that does not?

16. What are the three ways that salespersons can use portable computers?

17. What are the two basic approaches to pricing? Which receives support from the pricing subsystem? How?

18. What are the four sources of influence on consumer behavior in the BRANDAID model?

19. What was the most popular terminal application for the 1980 *Fortune 500* managers? The 1990 managers?

20. Which management level in the *Fortune 500* firms was the most heavily involved in mathematical modeling in 1990? Was that usage up or down from 1980?

21. Which management function was supported the best by the *Fortune 500* MKISs in 1990?

22. Does it appear that the *Fortune 500* managers are attempting to achieve a level support for all four Ps?

23. Are all managers in a firm interested in the outputs of all of the output subsystems?

TOPICS FOR DISCUSSION

1. How could selective dissemination of information work in a firm that does not have a computer?

2. Is the new product decision structured, unstructured, or semistructured?

3. The sample new product in the chapter received an overall score of 6.70. Is that good or bad? Should the firm introduce it?

PROBLEMS

1. Design a telephone interview form in order to obtain the following information. Approach the task in much the same way you would plan the logic of a computer program. The questions should flow, one after the other, in a logical manner. Prepare the layout so that it can be easily administered by some-

one else. Note that the following items are listed in a random sequence.
   a. age?
   b. education?
   c. if college, which degree?
   d. if no college, how many years?

e. if computer major, which programming languages studied?

f. current job?

g. worked way through college?

h. name?

i. if business degree, which major?

2. Go to the library and find three recent articles that contain examples of intelligence relating to the Apple computer organization. List the references, using the same style as the end-of-chapter bibliographies. For each reference write a single paragraph summarizing the intelligence that is contained. Assume that you are doing the research for your boss, who regards Apple as a competitor. Attach a cover memo. Your boss is Bradley Murph, Sales Manager.

CASE PROBLEM

Universal Foods

Universal Foods operates six frozen food processing plants in Florida. The products are sold to wholesalers who, in turn, sell to retailers. Approximately 80 percent of the retail outlets are small "Mom and Pop" grocery stores, but they account for only about 15 percent of the sales. The remaining 20 percent of the outlets are giant supermarket chains. They account for about 85 percent of the sales. Universal sells in all fifty states, and their chief competitors are the other frozen foods firms such as Birds Eye, Stouffer's, and Swanson.

Universal's main computing center is located in Bradenton, Florida. It houses a mainframe that is linked to minis at the food processing plants by means of a front-end processor and WATS lines.

Like all food companies of its size, Universal invests heavily in advertising. Most of the ads run on TV and are aimed at consumers. Some advertising, however, is aimed at Universal's customers—the wholesalers. Universal's thirty sales reps call on approximately 850 food wholesalers and also the headquarters of the larger supermarket chains. The reps try to make at least one call per month on each contact.

You are Roger Potuzak, the manager of marketing research. Your group consists of five researchers who design questionnaires and use statistical techniques to analyze the results and write reports. Everybody has enough work to do, and there is about a six-month backlog of research projects.

One morning you are on your way to coffee when you meet your boss in the hallway. He is Lyle Branstetter, the vice president of marketing.

"Oh, good morning Roger. I'm glad I ran into you. I just got out of the executive committee meeting and we decided to beef up our intelligence activity. The market is getting so competitive these days that we have to know more about what the competition is doing. We haven't decided yet how to go about it. The other executives suggested that we set up a special intelligence unit reporting directly to the CEO. I recommended that we let your shop handle it.

Could you put together something for me to use in our next meeting? First, let me know if you think marketing research should have the responsibility and give me your reasons. Then, describe how competitive intelligence could be gathered without using the computer—you know, a manual system. Last, describe how it could be tied into our computer operation. If we would need any new equipment, specify what it is and how it would be used.

Now, if you could have that ready by Friday, I would really appreciate it. Check my electronic calendar and make an appointment. See you Friday."

Assignments

1. Prepare a memo to Lyle, advising him whether you would like for marketing research to also gather marketing intelligence. Give your reasons.

2. Prepare a list that can be attached to the memo (Attachment A), explaining what types of competitive intelligence could be gathered without involving the computer.

3. Prepare a second list (Attachment B) that explains how Universal could engage in a computer-based intelligence activity. Assume there are no budget constraints and list any hardware needs that are not met by the current configuration.

SELECTED BIBLIOGRAPHY

Beath, Cynthia Mathis, and Ives, Blake. "Competitive Information Systems in Support of Pricing." *MIS Quarterly* 10 (March 1986): 85–96.

Collins, Robert H. "Salesforce Support Systems: Potential Applications to Increase Productivity." *Journal of the Academy of Marketing Science* 15 (Summer 1987): 49–54.

Cox, Donald F., and Good, Robert E. "How to Build a Marketing Information System." *Harvard Business Review* 45 (May/June 1967): 145–54.

Crissy, W. J. E., and Mossman, Frank. "Matrix Models for Marketing Planning: An Update and Expansion." *MSU Business Topics* 25 (Autumn 1977): 17–26.

Davis, Leila. "Retailers Go Shopping for EDI." *Datamation* 35 (March 1, 1989): 53*ff.*

Deshpande, Rohit, and Zaltman, Gerald. "A Comparison of Factors Affecting Use of Marketing Information in Consumer and Industrial Firms." *Journal of Marketing Research* 24, no. 1 (February 1987): 114–18.

Ferreira, Joe, and Treacy, Michael E. "It's More Than Just Laptops." *Datamation* 34 (November 1, 1988): 127–31.

Gilad, Tamar, and Gilad, Benjamin. "Business Intelligence—The Quiet Revolution." *Sloan Management Review* 27 (Summer 1986): 53–61.

Goslar, Martin D. "Marketing and The Adoption of Microcomputers: An Application of Diffusion Theory." *Journal of the Academy of Marketing Science* 15 (Summer 1987): 42–48.

Ives, Blake, and Learmonth, Gerard P. "The Information System as a Competitive Weapon." *Communications of the ACM* 27 (December 1984): 1193–1201.

King, William R., and Cleland, David I. "Environmental Information Systems for Strategic Marketing Planning." *Journal of Marketing* 38 (October 1974): 35–40.

Leong, Siew Meng; Busch, Paul S.; and John, Deborah Roedder. "Knowledge Bases and Salesperson Effectiveness: A Script-Theoretic Analysis." *Journal of Marketing Research* 26 (May 1989): 164–78.

Malhotra, Naresh K.; Tashchian, Armen; and Mahmoud, Essam. "The Integration of Microcomputers in Marketing Research and Decision Making." *Journal of the Academy of Marketing Science* 15 (Summer 1987): 69–82.

McLeod, Raymond, Jr., and Rogers, John C. "Marketing Information Systems: Their Current Status in Fortune 1000 Companies." *Journal of Management Information Systems* 1 (Spring 1985): 57–75.

Mentzer, John T.; Schuster, Camille P.; and Roberts, David J. "Microcomputer Versus Mainframe Usage by Marketing Professionals." *Journal of the Academy of Marketing Science* 15 (Summer 1987): 1–9.

Montgomery, David B., and Urban, Glen L. "Marketing Decision-Information Systems: An Emerging View." *Journal of Marketing Research* 7 (May 1970): 226–34.

Rangaswamy, Arvind; Eliashberg, Jehoshua; Burke, Raymond; and Wind, Jerry. "Developing Marketing Expert Systems: An Application to International Negotiations." *Journal of Marketing* 53 (October 1989): 24–39.

Rao, Vithala R., and McLaughlin, Edward W. "Modeling the Decision to Add New Products by Channel Intermediaries." *Journal of Marketing* 53 (January 1989): 80–88.

Steinberg, Margery, and Plank, Richard E. "Expert Systems: The Integrative Sales Management Tool of the Future." *Journal of the Academy of Marketing Science* 15 (Summer 1987): 55–62.

Whitten, Patrick. "Using IT to Enhance the Role of Market Research." *Journal of the Market Research Society* 33, No. 2 (1991): 113–25.

Chapter 18

Manufacturing Information Systems

After studying this chapter, you should:

- Be familiar with the major efforts to automate the factory, including CAD/CAM and robotics
- Understand the concepts of reorder point systems, material requirements planning (MRP), and manufacturing resource planning (MRP II)
- Understand the basic features of the just-in-time (JIT) approach to manufacturing
- Appreciate the contribution that a data collection network can make to gathering attendance and job data in real time
- Recognize the industrial engineer (IE) as a source of input data for the manufacturing information system
- Be familiar with ways that the firm can obtain information on labor unions and suppliers
- Understand how the manufacturing information system can be used in making plant location decisions
- Understand the fundamentals of inventory management
- Understand how the manufacturing information system can enable the firm to achieve the dual objectives of high quality and low cost
- Be aware of the trend in computer-based manufacturing systems that is expected to characterize the 1990s

INTRODUCTION

In the previous chapter we saw that marketing has the responsibility for determining what consumers want and need. Once this determination has been made, and the firm's executives decide to meet those wants and needs, it is the responsibility of the manufacturing function to produce the products.

Manufacturing management uses the computer both as a conceptual system and as an element in the physical production system. Computer-aided design (CAD), computer-aided manufacturing (CAM), and robotics all represent ways to use computer technology in the physical system.

The evolution of the computer as a conceptual manufacturing system is easiest to see in the inventory area. Initially there were systems that keyed on reorder points. Then came the MRP concept—first applied as material requirements planning and then as manufacturing resource planning. The MRP systems offer one way to accomplish inventory management. Another way is just-in-time, or JIT. JIT is unique among modern production concepts in that it does not rely heavily on computer technology.

The manufacturing information system consists of three input subsystems and four output subsystems. The data processing subsystem captures data in real time describing the utilization of the physical resources. The industrial engineering subsystem provides production standards that facilitate management by exception. The manufacturing intelligence subsystem enables management to stay current on activities of its labor unions and suppliers.

This input data is transformed into information by the output subsystems. The production subsystem enables management to both build and operate manufacturing facilities. The inventory subsystem uses mathematical formulas for determining when to reorder and how much. The quality subsystem enables the firm to achieve product quality by monitoring the flow of material beginning with receipt from suppliers, through the production process, and ending with consumption or use by the firm's customers. The cost subsystem permits management to control the cost of these production activities by means of information feedback.

Our main interest is how the computer is used as a conceptual system. However, that use is being blended with applications in the physical system by a concept called computer-integrated manufacturing, or CIM.

THE COMPUTER AS A PART OF THE PHYSICAL SYSTEM

Much has been accomplished in the use of computer-controlled machines in the production area. These machines can do jobs that were formerly done by workers. The machines cost less than the workers and are capable of performing better in some cases. Attempts to automate the factory initially met with resistance from organized labor. Over time, however, resistance has diminished as it becomes clear that a firm must take advantage of computer technology if it is to survive in a world market.

Computer-Aided Design (CAD)

Computer-aided design (CAD), increasingly being referred to as **computer-aided engineering (CAE),** involves the use of a computer to assist in the design of a product that is to be manufactured. CAD first appeared in the aerospace industry around 1960, and it was later adopted by automobile manufacturers. It has subsequently been used to design everything from complex structures such as buildings and bridges to small parts.

In Chapter 8 we showed a design engineer in Figure 8.8 using a CRT terminal equipped with a special **light pen** that is used for input. The engineer uses the pen to sketch the design on the screen, and the CAD software refines the drawing by smoothing and straightening the lines. Once the design is entered into the computer, the engineer can subject the design to various tests to detect weak points. The CAD software can even make parts move as they would when in use. When the design becomes finalized, the CAD software can prepare the detailed specifications that are necessary to produce the product. Those specifications are stored in a **design database**.

Computer-Aided Manufacturing (CAM)

Computer-aided manufacturing (CAM) is the application of the computer in the production process. Special, computer-controlled production machines such as drills and lathes produce the products using the specifications obtained from the design database. Some of the production machines have built-in microprocessors, and some are controlled by minicomputers. A single minicomputer can control several production machines at one time.

Much factory automation today consists of CAM technologies. Production can proceed faster and with greater precision than when human workers provide the control. The greater precision achieved makes possible fewer rejected parts and less scrap.

Robotics

Another application of the computer in the factory is **robotics.** Robotics involves the use of **industrial robots (IR),** devices that automatically perform certain tasks in the manufacturing process. Industrial robots, such as the one pictured in Figure 18.1, were introduced in the automobile industry about 1974 and, like CAD and CAM, have spread to many other industries. A popular robotics application is the feeding of raw materials to a machine tool that is automated by CAM.

Robots enable firms to cut costs and achieve high levels of quality, but they also perform hazardous jobs such as working in areas where the temperature is very high.

FIGURE 18.1

An Industrial
Robot

© Pickerell/The Image Works

THE COMPUTER AS AN INFORMATION SYSTEM

We use the name **manufacturing information system** to describe the CBIS subsystem that provides information concerning the production operations. The information is used not only by manufacturing managers, but by managers throughout the firm who have an interest in the production operation. The output from the manufacturing information system is used to both create and operate the physical production system.

You will not find many references to manufacturing information systems in the literature. The reason is that other names have been used—ROP, MRP, MRP II, JIT, and CIM. These are all approaches to managing the manufacturing process, and all use information. With the exception of CIM, we will explain each of these terms in the next sections. CIM, or computer-integrated manufacturing, is a new concept that is just now evolving, and we will discuss it at the end of the chapter.

Reorder Point (ROP) Systems

After the first computers were successfully applied in the accounting area, they were given the task of controlling inventory. The most simple approach is a *reactive* one of waiting for an item balance to reach a particular level and then triggering a purchase order or a production process. The item level that serves as the trigger

FIGURE 18.2
The Reorder Point with No Safety Stock and with a Safety Stock

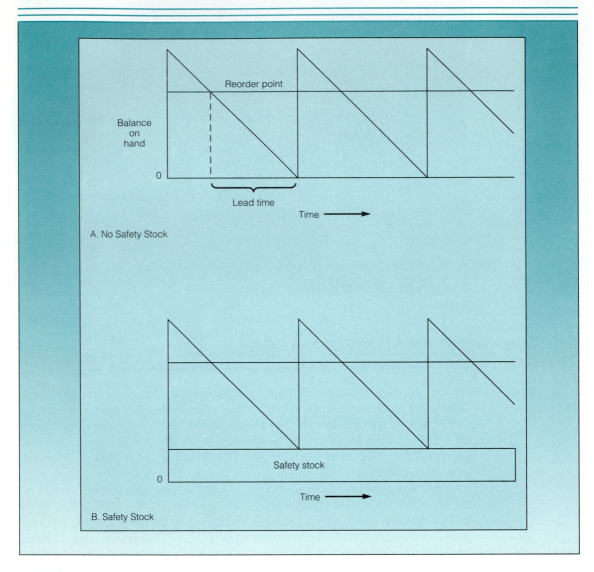

is called the **reorder point,** and a system that bases the purchasing decision on the reorder point is called a **reorder point system.**

Figure 18.2A is a diagram of the activity of an inventory item over time. The sawtooth shape illustrates how stock is gradually depleted, either through use in the manufacturing process, if it is a raw material, or by sales activity, if it is a finished good. According to the diagram, just as soon as the balance on hand drops to zero, replenishment stock arrives from the supplier, and the balance on hand returns to its peak level. This cycle is repeated over and over.

Figure 18.2A illustrates an ideal situation—replenishment stock arrives just as a stockout condition is reached. A **stockout** means that there is no inventory available. The company anticipates the stockout and places an order with the supplier when the balance on hand reached the reorder point. The amount of time that the supplier needs to fill the order is called the **lead time.**

Managers do not like to cut things so close. There is always the chance that the supplier shipment will be late or that usage will accelerate during the lead time period for some reason. As a precautionary measure an extra amount of inventory, called **safety stock,** is held in reserve. Safety stock is illustrated in Figure 18.2B. The firm hopes that it never has to use its safety stock, but it is there just in case— like a spare tire.

The Reorder Point Formula   The manufacturing manager does not have to guess where to position the ROP. It can be computed, using the following formula:

$$R = LU + S$$

Where: R = reorder point
L = supplier lead time (in days)
U = usage rate (number of units used or sold per day)
S = safety stock level (in units)

For example, if it takes the supplier fourteen days to provide the ordered materials, and you use ten units per day, you will use 140 units while waiting for the supplier to fill the order. Add to this a safety stock of sixteen, and the reorder point is 156.

Reorder point systems worked well during the late 1950s and early 1960s. In fact, many firms still use them as the basis for managing their materials.

Material Requirements Planning (MRP)

In the early 1960s Joseph Orlicky of the J. I. Case Company devised a new approach to materials management called **material requirements planning (MRP).** MRP is a *proactive* materials strategy. Rather than wait until it is time to order, MRP looks into the future and identifies the materials that will be needed, their quantities, and the dates that they will be needed.

Figure 18.3 illustrates the major components of an MRP system. The numbered systems below correspond to the numbers in the figure.

1. The **production scheduling system** uses four data files in preparing the master production schedule. The input data includes The Customer Order file, the Sales Forecast file, the Finished-Goods Inventory file, and the Production Capacity file. The **master production schedule** projects the pro-

FIGURE 18.3

An MRP System

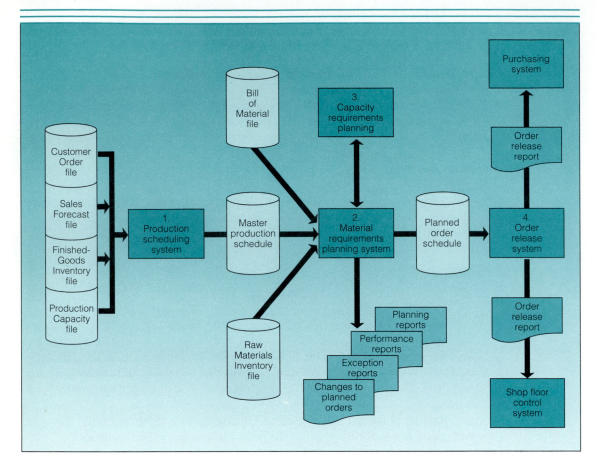

duction far enough into the future to accommodate the production process that accounts for the longest combination of supplier lead time and production time. It is not uncommon for production schedules to look more than a year into the future.

2. The **material requirements planning system** determines how much material will be needed to produce the desired number of units. The Bill of Material file is used to **explode the bill of material** for each item scheduled for production by multiplying the quantities on the bill of material times the number of units to be produced. The purpose of the explosion is to determine the total material requirements, called the **gross requirements,** that will be needed to produce the scheduled products. Next, the Raw Materials Inventory file is used to determine which of the materials are already on hand. The materials on hand are subtracted from the gross

requirements to identify the **net requirements**—the items that must be purchased in order to meet the production schedule.[1]

3. The material requirements planning system works in conjunction with the **capacity requirements planning system** to ensure that the scheduled production will fit within the plant capacity. After that determination has been made, the material requirements planning system produces several outputs. The main output is the **planned order schedule,** which lists the needed quantities of each material by time period. Other outputs include:

   - **Changes to planned orders** that reflect canceled orders, expedited orders, and modified order quantities.
   - **Exception reports** that flag items requiring management attention.
   - **Performance reports** that indicate how well the system is performing in terms of stockouts and other measures.
   - **Planning reports** that can be used by manufacturing management for future inventory planning.

4. The **order release system** uses the planned order schedule for input and prints an **order release report.** One copy is sent to buyers in the purchasing department for use in negotiating with suppliers, and the other copy is sent to shop floor managers for use in controlling the production process.

MRP enables the firm to do a better job of managing its materials. It can avoid stockouts caused by waiting until the last minute and learning that replenishment stock is unavailable. Also, knowing their future materials needs, buyers can negotiate purchase agreements with suppliers and receive quantity discounts.

Although a large number of firms implemented MRP, they did not always realize the anticipated benefits.[2] Experience showed that MRP fit certain production environments better than others. Many firms still use MRP to manage their materials, but others have either abandoned their systems or expanded on the concept in hopes of achieving even greater benefits.

Manufacturing Resource Planning (MRP II)

Oliver Wight and George Plossl, consulting partners, are given credit for expanding the MRP concept beyond the manufacturing area so that it could encompass the entire firm. The result was given the name **MRP II,** and the meaning of the letters was changed to **manufacturing resource planning.**

---

[1] We illustrated a bill of material with Figure 12.10 in Chapter 12, when we described the bicycle manufacturing process. Assume that the firm wants to produce 2200 flashlights, and that each one uses two batteries. The gross requirements for the batteries are 4400. Also, assume that there are 500 batteries on hand. The net requirements are 3900.

[2] James F. Cox and Steven J. Clark, "Problems in Implementing and Operating a Manufacturing Resource Planning Information System," *Journal of Management Information Systems* 1 (Summer 1984), 82.

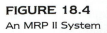

FIGURE 18.4

An MRP II System

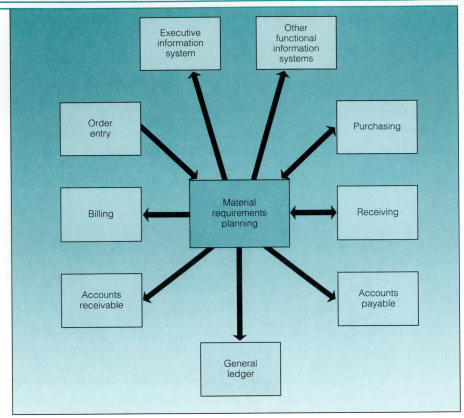

An MRP II system integrates all of the processes within manufacturing that deal with materials management. It also interfaces with other CBIS subsystems as shown in Figure 18.4. It can provide information to the executive information system and to the other functional information systems. It also exchanges data with the subsystems of the data processing system, which are involved in the material flow—order entry, billing, accounts receivable, purchasing, receiving, accounts payable, and general ledger.[3]

Guidelines for Implementing MRP II

As with MRP, not all of the MRP II firms have achieved their high expectations. Studies indicate that the degree of success realized with MRP II depends on per-

---

[3] Based on Peter Duchessi, Charles M. Schaninger, and Don R. Hobbs, "Implementing a Manufacturing Planning and Control Information System," *California Management Review* 31 (Spring 1989), 76.

formance in three areas—top management commitment, the implementation process, and hardware and software selection.[4]

1. *Top management commitment* is demonstrated when the executives actively participate in a steering committee, establish MRP II as a top-priority project in the company, set clear goals for the implementation, and use the system to run the business.
2. *The implementation process* proceeds most smoothly when project teams are appointed with representation from throughout the firm, a detailed requirements analysis is conducted to identify user needs, a detailed project plan is established with responsibilities assigned to particular individuals, necessary controls are built into the physical production system, and emphasis is placed on user education and training.
3. *Hardware and software selection* is best accomplished when a formal RFP (request for proposal) is provided to suppliers, and the ones with the best bids are required to demonstrate their products using the firm's own data.

You can see that the prescribed approach to implementing MRP II is very similar to our description of the system development life cycle in Chapter 5. Many of the MRP II recommendations have come about by means of trial and error in applying the SDLC.

Benefits of MRP II

When a firm creates the prescribed MRP II climate, it can expect benefits in one or more of the following areas:[5]

- **More efficient use of resources**   Reductions can be anticipated in both work-in-process and finished-goods inventories, plant equipment can be better utilized, bottlenecks in work centers can be spotted, and equipment maintenance can be better scheduled.
- **Better priority planning**   The amount of time required to get jobs into production can be reduced, and the production schedule can be more easily modified to reflect changing customer needs.
- **Improved customer service**   The ability of the firm to meet promised delivery dates is enhanced, and the opportunity exists for improved quality and reduced prices.
- **Improved employee morale**   Employees have confidence in the system, and coordination and communication between departments are improved.
- **Better management information**   The information from the system can provide management with an improved insight into the physical production system, as well as a means for measuring the performance of that system.

[4] *Ibid,* 79–89.

[5] Based on Cox and Clark, *Manufacturing Resource Planning Information System,* 86.

In addition, the firm's executives and managers from all functional areas can do a better job of long-range planning.

The MRP family of systems represent the mainstream activity of North American and European manufacturers in applying the computer as an information system. However, during recent years, the Japanese have popularized a new approach that is given credit for much of their manufacturing success.

Just-In-Time (JIT)

Just-in-time (JIT) keeps the flow of materials through the plant to a minimum by scheduling them to arrive at the workstations "just in time."

JIT goes counter to the traditional philosophy of mass production that is based on large lot sizes. A **lot size** is the number of items to be produced at one time. The objective of a large lot size is to minimize setup and production costs and to obtain quantity discounts from suppliers. Our description of the bicycle manufacturing process in Chapter 12 is an example of mass production using large lot sizes.

Mass production also carries with it high inventory costs. In the bicycle flashlight example the firm would have large raw-materials, work-in-process, and finished-goods inventories. Large inventories represent a sizable investment and carry with them various maintenance costs such as insurance and security.

JIT attempts to minimize inventory costs by producing in smaller quantities. The ideal lot size would be "1" in a JIT system. The single unit moves from workstation to workstation until its production is completed.

Timing is the key to a JIT system. A supply of raw materials arrives from the supplier just before a production run is scheduled to begin; there is no raw-materials inventory to speak of. Small quantities of raw materials are received at a time; perhaps a supplier makes several deliveries a day.

The raw materials start down the assembly line. The first worker finishes the first production step and sets the item aside. The next worker picks up the item and performs the second step. This process continues from one production step to the next. When a worker is ready for the next item, he or she signals the previous worker. A **kanban**—Japanese for "card" or "visible record"—is used to make the signal. The kanban can be a displayed card, flashing lights, or even a golf ball rolling down a pipe. An example of a kanban appears in Figure 18.5. In this example the kanban is a card that accompanies a material container between two work centers.

Kanban signals enable the work to flow rapidly. The kanban *pulls* the material through the assembly process, as opposed to the manner in which a large lot size *pushes* its way from station to station. Since there is less material in the work flow, the amount of work space is reduced, and the work area is neater.

In contrast to MRP, which emphasizes long-term planning and requires the use of a computer, JIT emphasizes timing and the use of noncomputer signals.

Growing interest in JIT has caused firms that invested heavily in MRP to second guess their wisdom. Some firms have scrapped MRP for JIT, while others remained dedicated to MRP or integrated JIT into MRP. During the past few years

FIGURE 18.5

A Kanban

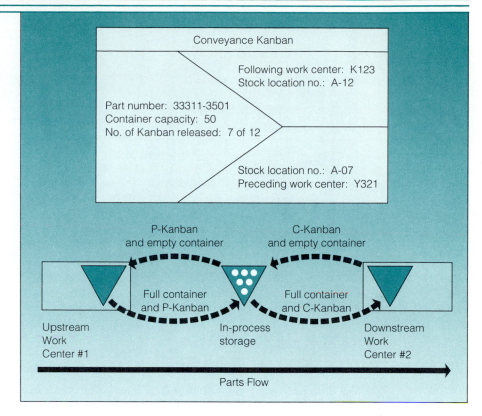

Conveyance Kanban

Following work center: K123
Stock location no.: A-12

Part number: 33311-3501
Container capacity: 50
No. of Kanban released: 7 of 12

Stock location no.: A-07
Preceding work center: Y321

P-Kanban
and empty container

C-Kanban
and empty container

Full container
and P-Kanban

Full container
and C-Kanban

Upstream
Work
Center #1

In-process
storage

Downstream
Work
Center #2

Parts Flow

it has become clear that MRP will withstand the JIT threat. This is not to say that JIT is a thing of the past. Rather, like all other production management concepts, JIT is better suited to certain environments than others. One type of environment that has proven especially difficult for JIT is one of frequent variations in production volume caused by changes in customer demand. But then, that situation causes difficulties for MRP as well.

Both JIT and MRP stand the best chance of success when management establishes firm control over the production process and enforces the discipline of a formal system.

A MODEL OF A MANUFACTURING INFORMATION SYSTEM

The manufacturing information system encompasses all of the applications of the computer in the manufacturing area as a *conceptual* system. A model of such a system is illustrated in Figure 18.6. The basic structure consists of input subsystems, a database, and output subsystems.

FIGURE 18.6

A Model of a
Manufacturing
Information
System

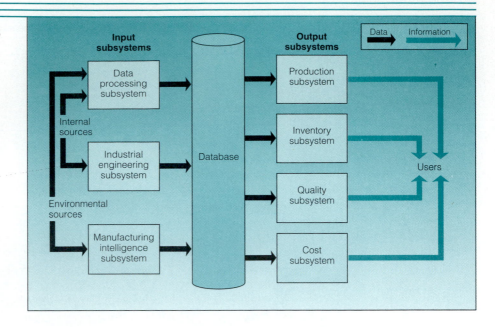

Input Subsystems

The **data processing subsystem** gathers internal data describing the manufacturing operation and environmental data describing the firm's transactions with its suppliers.

The **industrial engineering subsystem** is like the marketing research subsystem in that it consists primarily of special data gathering projects. The two subsystems are dissimilar in that the industrial engineering subsystem gathers data from inside the firm rather than from the environment.

The **manufacturing intelligence subsystem** gathers data from the environment. Suppliers and labor unions are the special responsibility of manufacturing. Suppliers provide much data in the form of catalogs and price lists. Much of the data describing labor unions never finds its way into the computer but is communicated by word of mouth and in a hard copy form.

Output Subsystems

The **production subsystem** describes each step of the transformation process—from the ordering of raw materials from suppliers to the release of the finished goods to marketing.

The **inventory subsystem** maintains the conceptual record of materials as they flow from one production step to the next—from raw materials to work in process and finally to finished goods.

The **quality subsystem** is used to assure that the quality level of raw materials received from suppliers meets the required standards. This subsystem then reports on the quality level at each critical step of the transformation process and finally ensures that the quality of the finished product is at the intended level.

The **cost subsystem** keeps the firm's executives and manufacturing management informed concerning the cost of the transformation process. The cost data can be compared with predetermined standards. Excessive costs call for decisions that make the material flow and transformation process more efficient.

We will now discuss each of the subsystems in greater detail.

DATA PROCESSING SUBSYSTEM

The task of gathering data describing the production operations is best performed with the use of data collection terminals. Production employees enter data into the terminals using a combination of machine-readable media and the keyboard. The media most often take the form of documents with bar codes that can be read optically. Other media include documents with pencil marks that can be read optically and plastic badges with recording strips that can be read magnetically. After the data is read, it is transmitted to the central computer where it is used to update the database to reflect the current status of the physical system.

Figure 18.7 shows twelve data collection terminals located throughout a factory. Terminal 1 is in the receiving area. When raw materials are received from suppliers, receipt data is entered into the terminal. All material receipts then undergo a quality control inspection, and the results are recorded on Terminal 2. As the accepted receipts enter the raw-materials storeroom, the action is logged on Terminal 3. The same terminal is also used to record the release of materials to the production process. Terminals 4 through 10 are used by production employees to signal the start and completion of each step of the production process. When the final product is finished, Terminal 11 is used to show the entry of the goods into the finished-goods storeroom. Terminal 11 also signals the release of finished goods to the shipping department. When the goods are shipped to customers, the action is recorded on Terminal 12.

The terminal use that is illustrated in the figure is called **job reporting,** as it provides data that describes the production jobs. In addition to reporting on the material flow, job reporting also reports on machine utilization. Management knows which machines are used and for how long.

Terminals also record the use of personnel resources. **Attendance reporting** is accomplished when workers insert their plastic badges into the terminals as they report for work in the morning and repeat the operation as they leave in the afternoon.

Through job and attendance reporting, the data collection system records every important production action. Manufacturing management uses this rich database to monitor the activities of the entire production system.

FIGURE 18.7
Location of Data Collection Terminals

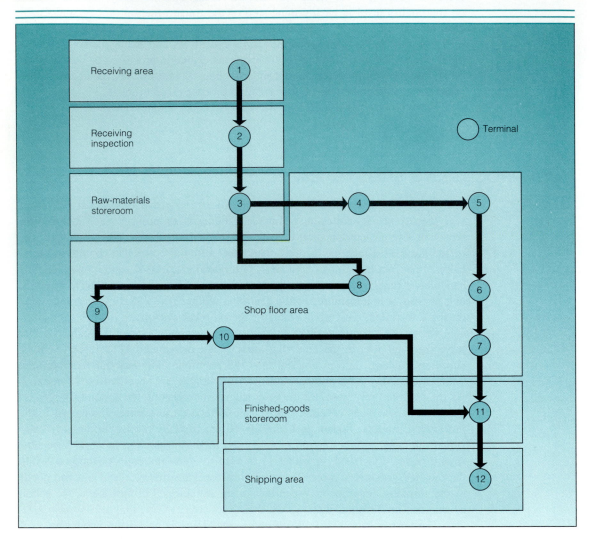

INDUSTRIAL ENGINEERING SUBSYSTEM

An **industrial engineer (IE)** is a specially trained systems analyst who studies the manufacturing operation and makes recommendations for improvement. The IE specializes in the design and operation of physical systems but is knowledgeable in conceptual systems as well. The IE can be a member of the project teams that develop the data processing system and each of the output subsystems.

An important part of the IE's work involves the setting of production standards—a critical ingredient in applying management by exception in the manufacturing area. The IEs set the standards by studying production processes to determine how long they should take. The standards are stored in the database and are compared to actual performance data provided by the data processing system. Any exceptional variance is reported to management.

MANUFACTURING INTELLIGENCE SUBSYSTEM

Manufacturing management must remain current on the sources of labor, material, and machines, and that is the objective of the manufacturing intelligence subsystem.

Labor Information

Manufacturing managers pay particular attention to the labor unions that organize, or attempt to organize, the firm's workers. When workers vote for unionization, a contract describes the expectations and obligations of both the firm and the union. Information describing the actual performance of both parties must be gathered so that management can ensure that the terms of the contract are met.

Figure 18.8 shows that both formal and informal systems are used to generate the flow of labor information.

Formal Systems
Manufacturing management initiates the flow of personnel information by preparing personnel requests that are sent to the human resources department. Human resources then gathers information from various environmental elements and establishes contact with the applicants. After the applicants are screened, applicant data is sent to manufacturing management. When an applicant is hired, personnel information is entered into the database of the human resource information system (HRIS) and also into the Payroll file. A formal flow also exists when employees are terminated. A formal information flow, detailing the degree to which the terms of the union contract are being followed, can also link manufacturing management and upper-level management.

Informal Systems
The flow of information between employees and manufacturing management is largely informal. It consists of the day-to-day contact between the employees and their supervisors. There is also an informal communication link between union officials, the firm's industrial relations department, and upper-level management. These groups work together in resolving labor related problems.

Supplier Information

Most purchasing departments have several buyers who specialize in procuring certain classes of materials. Selection of the best suppliers is a key element in achieving production efficiency and quality. Ordered materials must arrive on schedule and at the expected quality level.

FIGURE 18.8

Flow of Labor Information

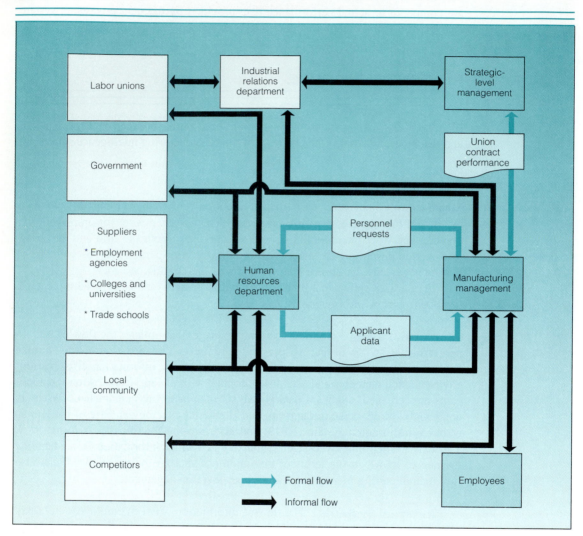

Supplier Selection   Suppliers are selected by means of a screening process. A thorough screening consists of the following steps:

1. Each potential supplier completes a questionnaire that asks for information describing production resources and the importance placed on quality control. Data from these forms is stored in the database and kept current.
2. The firm conducts a financial analysis of each supplier. The supplier's balance sheet and income statement items indicate the long-term ability of the supplier to perform as a reliable source of materials or machines.

3. Buyers visit supplier plants to observe the quality control procedures.
4. Supplier representatives are invited to visit the firm's plant to become familiar with how their materials are used in the firm's products.

Once a supplier has been selected, buyers remain current on the supplier's capabilities.

Supplier Data   Data is maintained in the database that describes each supplier. Figure 18.9 illustrates three sources.

Supplier input is provided when the supplier's sales representatives make personal calls on the buyers and furnish manuals and catalogs. The firm's buyers also contact the supplier by telephone to ask specific questions. This is a good point to apply ISDN or videotex. And, each time a firm obtains materials from a supplier, the data processing system creates a record of the transaction.

Quality control input consists of data that is provided by quality control inspectors as the materials flow through the production process.

Customer service input is a responsibility of the marketing function. The customer service unit provides supplier information as a result of repairs and replacements, and also surveys of customer satisfaction.

A complete supplier record provides an analysis of the organization as well as the performance of its materials from receipt to end-product use.

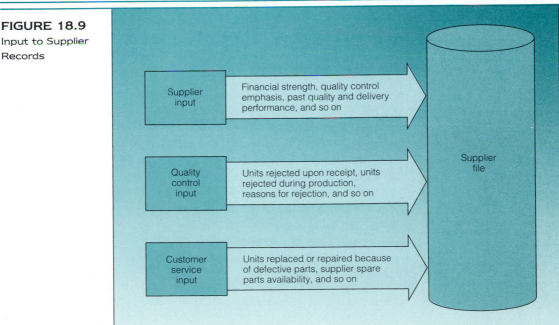

FIGURE 18.9

Input to Supplier Records

Supplier input — Financial strength, quality control emphasis, past quality and delivery performance, and so on

Quality control input — Units rejected upon receipt, units rejected during production, reasons for rejection, and so on

Customer service input — Units replaced or repaired because of defective parts, supplier spare parts availability, and so on

Supplier file

This concludes the discussion of how data is entered into the manufacturing information system by the three input subsystems. The remaining discussion will deal with the output subsystems.

PRODUCTION SUBSYSTEM

Manufacturing management uses the production subsystem primarily to manage the daily production processes as illustrated by the bicycle flashlight example in Chapter 12.

Another use of the production subsystem is to support the manager in creating new production facilities. Such decisions are normally made at the top-management level because of the long-term effects and the large investment amounts. If the firm has an executive committee or a management committee comprised of the executives from the functional areas, it is likely that such a committee would make the decisions.

The Decision to Build a New Plant

There can be any number of reasons why a new plant would be needed. Perhaps the existing plant is worn out or obsolete. Perhaps the market for the firm's products has shifted and the plant is no longer in a good location. Or, perhaps the existing plant cannot handle the increased volume.

The Decision Where to Locate the Plant

Once the decision has been made to build a new plant, it is next necessary to determine where it should be located. This is a step-by-step process that gradually narrows down the site. Middle-level managers from the manufacturing function may contribute expertise to the decision making process.

1. **Select the Region** The managers must select a particular region of the U.S. or another country. Some of the factors influencing this decision include the concentration of customers, availability of a labor supply, availability of raw materials, climate, and strength of unionization.
2. **Select the City** The selection of a particular city in a region considers such factors as taxes, transportation, community services (police, fire, and so on), community attitudes, cultural resources, and management preferences.
3. **Select the Area of the City** Management must choose a particular area of the selected city. Influencing factors include land costs, public transportation, utilities, and zoning restrictions.

The region, city, and area decisions are semistructured. Some factors, such as land costs, taxes, and transportation facilities, can be measured quantitatively. Other factors, such as community attitudes and cultural resources, are difficult to measure.

The production subsystem can help management make any of the location decisions. A mathematical model can be used to address the structured portion of the problem. A technique called linear programming, or LP, has been used since the beginning of the computer era for making decisions of this type.

A more recent application of information technology is the use of graphic output. The results of the modeling process can be displayed in the form of graphs such as maps, which facilitate the location decisions. Figure 18.10 is an example of graphic output as applied to the plant location decision.

FIGURE 18.10
Graphic Outputs Assist Management in Making the Plant Location Decision

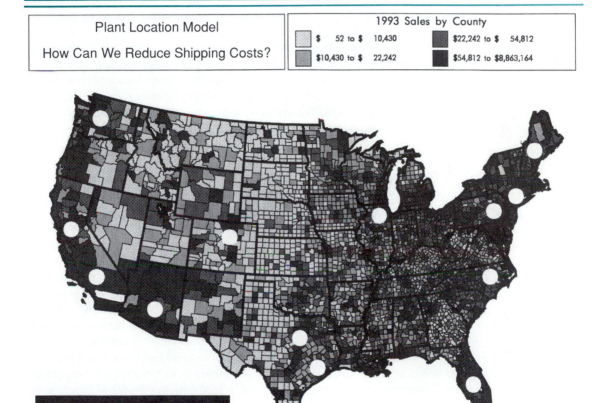

Plant Location Model

How Can We Reduce Shipping Costs?

1993 Sales by County

$ 52 to $ 10,430
$10,430 to $ 22,242
$22,242 to $ 54,812
$54,812 to $8,863,164

Locations of existing plants

INVENTORY SUBSYSTEM

Manufacturing management has always been responsible for the raw-materials and the work-in-process inventories. In many cases, marketing is responsible for the finished-goods inventory.

Maintenance Costs

The annual cost of keeping an inventory varies, depending on the type of material stored. For example, a pharmaceutical company that stores drug products in environmentally controlled rooms with tight security incurs very high costs. An oil field supply company, on the other hand, incurs very low costs in storing iron pipe outdoors.

The **maintenance cost,** or **carrying cost,** is usually expressed as an annual percentage of the cost of the item, and the cost includes factors such as spoilage, pilferage, obsolescence, taxes, and insurance. An important characteristic of maintenance cost is the fact that it varies directly with the inventory level—the higher the level, the higher the cost. Therefore, if a firm wants to minimize its maintenance costs, it keeps its inventory level low.

Inventory Level

The level of a firm's inventory is very important because it represents a substantial investment. Money that is tied up in inventory cannot be used elsewhere.

The level of a particular item is influenced primarily by the number of units that are ordered from a supplier at one time. The average inventory level can be estimated at half of the order quantity plus the safety stock. The diagram in Figure 18.11 shows this effect. In the upper example, a quantity of twenty is ordered from the supplier. Sometimes (just after receipt) there are twenty-five units in inventory, counting the safety stock of five units. Sometimes (just before receipt) there are only five—the safety stock. On the average there are fifteen. In the lower example a quantity of sixteen is ordered and the average level drops to thirteen.

If a firm wants to keep its inventory level low to minimize its investment, one approach is to order in smaller quantities. Another is to establish a lower reorder point. Manufacturing management can use a mathematical model to simulate the effects of these alternate decision strategies.

Backorders

Earlier in the chapter we identified safety stock as a means of preventing or minimizing stockouts. Safety stock can also reduce the number of backorders. A **backorder** is an order from a customer, which cannot be filled because of a stockout. The firm says, in effect, "We cannot fill your order now . . . but will fill it when we receive replenishment stock."

FIGURE 18.11

The Effect of Order Quantity on Average Inventory Level

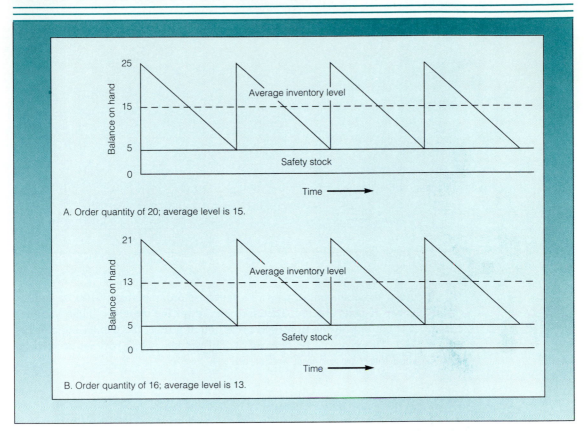

A. Order quantity of 20; average level is 15.

B. Order quantity of 16; average level is 13.

A backorder can be viewed as a negative balance on hand, as shown in Figure 18.12. When replenishment stock arrives, the backorders are filled, but the balance on hand does not reach its normal height—Level 1. Instead, it reaches a lower level—Level 2. The fact that the new usage sequence begins with a lower level increases the likelihood of more stockouts and backorders.

Purchasing Costs

We have seen that there are good reasons for a firm to keep its inventory level low, and one way to do it is to order in small quantities. This would always be a good objective if it were not for another cost that increases as the order quantity decreases. This is the **purchasing cost,** which includes costs that are incurred when materials are ordered—buyer time, telephone expense, secretary time, purchase order forms, and so on.

FIGURE 18.12

A Backorder Is a
Negative Balance
on Hand

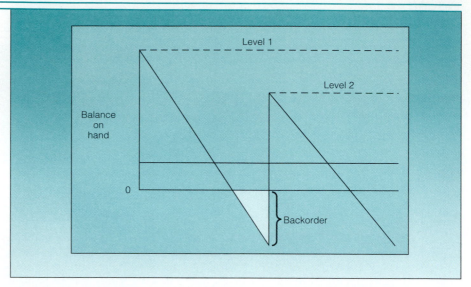

It costs a fixed amount to prepare a purchase order, perhaps $100, regardless of the number of units ordered. Therefore, the fewer the units, the higher the purchasing cost per unit. If the firm orders one unit at a time, the purchasing cost per unit is $100. This cost can be reduced to $50 per unit when two are ordered, to $33.33 when three are ordered, and so on.

Economic Order Quantity

The **EOQ (economic order quantity)** balances the maintenance and purchasing costs and identifies the lowest combined cost. Figure 18.13 includes a diagram that captures the concept and includes the EOQ formula. An EOQ is established for each item in raw-materials inventory and is included as a data element in the inventory record. The EOQ is used for ordering replenishment stock from *suppliers.*

Economic Manufacturing Quantity

Another economic quantity can be used for the finished-goods inventory. This is the **economic manufacturing quantity (EMQ),** also called the **economic lot size.** The EMQ balances the costs of carrying the inventory with the costs of production inefficiencies. The EMQ is used for ordering replenishment stock from the firm's own *manufacturing function.*

The EOQ and EMQ are optimum; they cannot be improved upon without changing the values of the variables. Once the quantities have been computed, the inventory subsystem can make the order quantity decisions. The manager only becomes involved when exceptional situations arise.

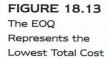

FIGURE 18.13
The EOQ
Represents the
Lowest Total Cost

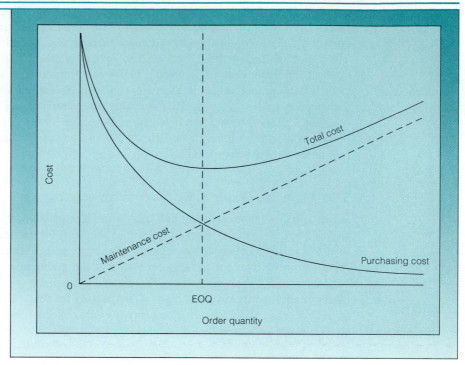

A   Graphic model

$$EOQ \sqrt{\frac{2 \times PC \times S}{M}}$$

Where: EOQ = economic order quantity

PC = purchasing cost (in dollars)

S = annual sales (in units)

M = maintenance cost (in dollars)

B   Mathematical model

QUALITY SUBSYSTEM

In the past all firms have not had superior product quality as an objective. Many firms have aimed their products at the low end of the market where sales success depends on a low price. These firms equated low price with low quality, and the strategy seemed sound. Things worked out fine until the market expanded to international scope. Because of several factors such as a large supply of inexpensive labor, Third World countries were able to offer products at low prices *and* high quality. This new competition forced many firms to rethink their quality strategies. The period of the late 1980s was marked by a new awakening of firms that recognized the importance of producing high-quality products at a profit. You only have to look at the current products of U.S. automakers and compare them with their models ten years ago to see the results of an emphasis on quality.

The CBIS subsystem that is largely responsibile for the firm's product quality is the manufacturing information system, and its component that plays the leading role is the quality subsystem.

The Role of Quality Control Inspectors

When a firm wants to achieve high quality in its production, it is not sufficient to simply check the quality of the products as they roll off the end of the assembly line. It's really too late at that point to do much good. Instead, quality control checks must be incorporated into each step of the production process, beginning with the receipt of raw materials. The persons who make the quality checks are called **quality control inspectors—QC inspectors** for short. They enter the results of their checks into the database by using the data collection terminals or keyboard terminals in their offices.

Practices that Contribute to Product Quality

Studies of firms that have been successful in achieving production quality reveal the following practices:[6]

- **Top management is actively interested in the question of quality.** In some firms the subject of quality appears on the weekly agenda of the executive committee meeting.
- **Annual targets are set for quality levels.** These targets can be established for each inspection point on the assembly line. Information describing assembly line rejects and field failures is quickly made available to management.
- **Production machinery is well maintained, the work areas are kept clean and orderly, and the workers are well trained.** This is one area where JIT has an advantage over MRP. Because work-in-process inventory levels in a JIT shop are lower, the production area can be kept neater.
- **The importance of raw material quality is emphasized, and the quality control inspectors play a role in supplier selection.** The four-part program

[6]Based on David A. Garvin, "Quality on the Line," *Harvard Business Review* 61 (September–October 1983), 64–75.

that we described earlier for selecting suppliers is typical of firms that emphasize raw material quality.

If a firm is to compete in world markets, it must be able to produce high-quality products at low costs. The quality subsystem is the main vehicle for achieving the quality objective, and the cost subsystem has the responsibility in terms of costs.

COST SUBSYSTEM

The cost subsystem can contain programs that prepare both periodic and special reports. The periodic reports can be printed and distributed, or they can be stored in a preformatted form in the database for later retrieval.

An Example of a Cost Report

The report in Figure 18.14 shows how the cost subsystem can be used to keep the costs of maintaining production machines in line. Some machines require little or no maintenance. A personal computer is a good example. You use it until something breaks and then have it fixed. Other machines, however, must be maintained on a periodic basis. A good example is a large mainframe computer. Accepted practice is to set aside one or two hours each day for **preventive maintenance (PM),** which

FIGURE 18.14

A Maintenance Report

EQUIPMENT MAINTENANCE SUMMARY

EQUIPMENT NUMBER	DESCRIPTION	SCHEDULED HOURS	RUNNING HOURS	BREAKDOWN HOURS	PARTS COST	LABOR COST	MAINTENANCE COST PER RUNNING HR.	COST GRTR 0.15?	TOTAL MAINTENANCE COST
1103	BURGMASTER DRILL	330.0	315.0	15.0	130.0	75.0	0.6508	*	205.0
1161	WARNER SWAZEY LATHE	495.0	400.0	95.0	60.0	1350.0	3.5250	*	1410.0
1178	CINCINNATI MILL	495.0	490.0	5.0	3.0	60.0	0.1286		63.0
1183	MAZAK N/C LATHE	330.0	328.0	2.0	5.0	10.0	0.0457		15.0
1195	FISCHER N/C LATHE	495.0	450.0	45.0	70.0	50.0	0.2667	*	120.0
2015	EXCELLO WORK CTR	495.0	420.0	75.0	700.0	100.0	1.9048	*	800.0
2113	EXCELLO BORING MILL	165.0	160.0	5.0	10.0	45.0	0.3438	*	55.0
2205	LINCOLN WELDER	330.0	330.0	0.0	0.0	0.0	0.0000		0.0
2213	FROREIP VERT LATHE	495.0	470.0	25.0	40.0	30.0	0.1489		70.0

is intended to prevent breakdowns. PM includes such activities as cleaning and oiling the mechanical parts, and checking and replacing electronic components.

Manufacturing management uses PM as a way to minimize **breakdown hours**—the time that production machines are out of service awaiting repair. When the breakdown hours listed in the center column of the Figure 18.14 report are believed to be too high for a given machine, its maintenance can be performed more often. When the breakdown hours are minimal, maintenance can be performed less often, freeing mechanics for other work.

Manufacturing management can also use the report in deciding when it is time to purchase replacement equipment. You will notice that the report reflects management by exception. When the maintenance cost per running hour for a machine exceeds $0.15, an identifying asterisk is printed. The manager can scan the asterisk column looking for exceptions that call for a replacement decision.

Basic Ingredients of Cost Control

An effective cost control program is built on two key ingredients: (1) good performance standards and (2) a system for reporting the details of the activity as it occurs. The data collection network can contribute in both areas. When manufacturing employees (machine operators, inspectors, maintenance mechanics, and so on) perform their tasks, they can use the data collection terminals to record the activity so that manufacturing management knows what is happening in the plant. This actual data can also be accumulated over time and combined with other inputs, such as that from the IEs, to set the standards and keep them current.

HOW MANAGERS USE THE MANUFACTURING INFORMATION SYSTEM

The manufacturing information system is used both in the creation and operation of the physical production system. The information is used by the firm's executives, managers in the manufacturing area, and managers in other areas as well. This usage is shown in Table 18.1.

The executives, including the vice president of manufacturing, receive information from all output subsystems. The plant superintendent also uses summarized output describing the entire operation.

Managers in marketing and finance also use the output. Marketers are interested in aspects of production such as cost, quality, and availability since those factors influence product sales. Financial managers have a special interest in the inventory subsystem, as it is used in determining the level of inventory investment, and in the production subsystem, as it is used to make important decisions concerning plant construction or expansion.

The important point to keep in mind is the fact that the manufacturing information system provides information to managers throughout the firm. Regardless of the users' information needs, the manufacturing information system can meet

TABLE 18.1
Users of the Manufacturing Information System

User	Subsystem			
	Inventory	Quality	Production	Cost
Vice-President of manufacturing	X	X	X	X
Other executives	X	X	X	X
Plant superintendent	X	X	X	X
Manager of planning and control	X		X	
Manager of engineering		X	X	X
Manager of quality control		X		
Director of purchasing	X	X		X
Manager of inventory control	X			
Other managers	X	X	X	X

those needs. The key is the availability of a database that describes the production operation in detail. Modern information technology, such as data collection terminals, makes this database a reality.

A SYSTEMS VIEW OF MANUFACTURING— COMPUTER-INTEGRATED MANUFACTURING

Computer applications in the manufacturing area have experienced a relatively unplanned growth pattern. The applications have proceeded on several fronts at the same time, and manufacturing managers have taken advantage of the opportunities. The problem is that now there are so many computer applications that it is difficult to manage them all.

CIM (computer integrated manufacturing) is the management philosophy that all production and information technologies must work together. CIM is a way of looking at the firm's production resource as a single system and defining, funding, managing, and coordinating all improvement projects in terms of how they effect the entire system. CIM is a systems view of production rather than the past molecular view of only dealing with the parts separately.

Some firms have already achieved CIM or are well on their way. One, Allen-Bradley, built a new plant in Milwaukee based on the CIM philosophy. The venture

FIGURE 18.15

CIM Includes Both Physical and Conceptual Systems

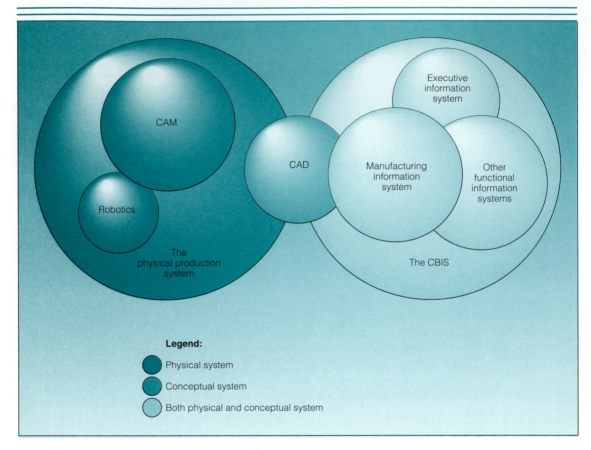

has been a success, with raw-materials inventory being completely eliminated and a quality level of only fifteen parts rejected per million produced.[7]

When implemented to its fullest extent in a manufacturing firm, CIM integrates both the physical production system and the CBIS as shown in Figure 18.15. CAD provides the interface between the two main system types, producing the design specifications that are used to guide CAM and robotics in the physical system. The CBIS subsystems that represent the strongest linkages with CAD are the manufacturing information system, the executive information system, and the other organizational subsystems.

[7] For more information about this installation and the management philosophy behind it, *see* Bernard Avishai, "A CEO's Common Sense of CIM: An Interview with J. Tracy O'Rourke," *Harvard Business Review* 67 (January–February 1989), 110–17.

SUMMARY

Manufacturing managers have applied computers in two basic ways: as physical systems, and as information systems. CAD, CAM, and robotics are used in the physical production system to perform tasks better and reduce costs.

The application of the computer as a conceptual system in the manufacturing area began with inventory. The first system design was the reorder point approach, but it was superseded by the more proactive MRP concept. The letters MRP initially meant material requirements planning. Later the concept was expanded to integrate with other systems throughout the firm, and the name was changed to manufacturing resource planning, or MRP II.

During the 1980s, firms were provided with another production strategy—JIT. JIT is a revolutionary concept in two respects. First, it goes against the time-honored philosophy of mass production. Second, it ignores the communications capability of computer technology in favor of physical signals.

Now that the newness has worn off JIT, firms realize that they do not all have to abandon their MRP systems. Some firms can benefit more from JIT, and some from MRP. Some integrate JIT into MRP.

A manufacturing information system consists of input subsystems, a database, and output subsystems.

The data processing subsystem gathers internal data, often using data collection terminals, and gathers environmental data as a result of transactions with suppliers. The industrial engineering subsystem gathers internal information that relates to the physical production system. The manufacturing intelligence subsystem gathers environmental data describing labor unions and suppliers.

Management uses the production subsystem to build new production facilities and operate existing facilities. The inventory subsystem uses formulas to program the two important decisions of when to place an order and how much. The quality subsystem uses a combination of quality standards, feedback information, and quality control inspectors to achieve the high quality that is necessary to meet international competition. The cost subsystem also assists in achieving competitive advantage by providing information that enables management to keep production costs low.

The manufacturing information system is a robust application of information technology in production, but it is only one dimension of computer use. CIM is a management philosophy aimed at integrating all of the separate computer-based information systems plus factory automation. Achieving CIM will provide a difficult challenge for managers, industrial engineers, and information specialists as we approach year 2000.

KEY TERMS

reorder point system
stockout
lead time

safety stock
gross requirements
net requirements

lot size
kanban
industrial engineer (IE)
maintenance cost, carrying cost
backorder

purchasing cost
EOQ (economic order quantity)
EMQ (economic manufacturing quantity),
economic lot size

KEY CONCEPTS

CAD/CAM and robotics as the application of computer technology to the physical production system

The proactive nature of material requirements planning (MRP), and manufacturing resource planning (MRP-II)

The relative simplicity of just-in-time (JIT)

The manufacturing information system as a combination of input and output subsystems, integrated by a database

How data collection terminals provide data describing the physical production system in real time

Components of inventory costs, and the means of keeping the costs down

How both supplier selection and quality control inspections play key roles in achieving high quality in production output

Computer-integrated manufacturing (CIM)

QUESTIONS

1. How does CAD communicate information to CAM?

2. Name two ways that computer technology can be used in CAM.

3. Why is a reorder point system a reactive strategy?

4. When a firm decides to use safety stock, does that decision have any effect on the reorder point? What about the average inventory level? If yes to either question, explain.

5. What are the four subsystems of a material requirements planning (MRP) system? Which one explodes the bill of material?

6. What data files are used in computing the gross requirements? The net requirements?

7. Who receives order release reports? What do they do with them?

8. In what way does MRP II reflect an organizational influence on computing?

9. List the actions that a manager can take to influence the success of MRP II.

10. Does JIT have a pull or a push influence on job flow through the plant? Explain.

11. Explain how data collection terminals are used to manage materials, machines, and personnel.

12. How does the work of the IE contribute to management by exception?

13. What two environmental elements are the focus of the manufacturing intelligence subsystem?

14. What are four steps of gathering supplier data?

15. What is structured about a plant location decision? What is unstructured?

16. What two costs are incorporated in the EOQ formula?

17. When would an EMQ be used instead of an EOQ?

18. Why would a marketing manager be interested in manufacturing cost?

19. Explain why CAD is part of the conceptual system. Explain why it is part of the physical system.

TOPICS FOR DISCUSSION

1. How could a firm that has embraced JIT use the computer in manufacturing?

2. How can the four output subsystems of the manufacturing information system contribute to high product quality? Address each subsystem separately.

PROBLEMS

1. Use the computer to determine the reorder points for the following items. Your instructor will advise you what material to turn in.

Item number	Lead time (in days)	Usage rate (in units)	Safety stock (in units)	Reorder point (in units)
10	23	104	45	————
12	17	49	10	————
14	3	65	100	————
16	11	94	250	————
18	120	8	30	————
20	25	3	12	————

2. Use the computer to determine the economic order quantities for the following items.

Item number	Purchasing cost (in $)	Annual sales (in units)	Maintenance cost (in $)	EOQ (in units)
10	$100	26,000	$ 12.50	————
12	$100	12,250	$ 25.00	————
14	$100	16,250	$ 0.25	————
16	$100	23,500	$ 2.50	————
18	$100	2,000	$ 37.50	————
20	$100	750	$250.00	————

CASE PROBLEM

Newtone Plastics, Inc.

June 12

MEMO TO: Members of the Executive Committee:
    Dorothy Murray, Vice President of Finance
    Fred Sheinberg, Vice President of Manufacturing
    Andrea Willis, Vice President of Marketing
    Charles Hinkle, Vice President of Information Services
FROM: James Whitworth, President
SUBJECT: Agenda for Next Executive Committee Meeting

Fred has asked that our first topic at next week's meeting be MRP II. He will bring us up to date on it, and we can decide whether to pursue the subject.

June 16

FRED: As most of you know, we are presently using what is called a reorder point system to trigger purchase orders for raw materials. Most of the industry has replaced their reorder point systems with something called MRP II. MRP II uses the production schedule as a basis for the ordering. You look at the schedule and identify when certain materials will be needed, and you place orders ahead of time. It's less risky because if you wait until the reorder point is reached the supplier might not be able to fill your order.

CHARLES: I've heard about MRP. Most everyone purchases prewritten software. That would probably be the only way Information Services could support such an effort since we've committed our programmers to the HRIS and EIS for the next three years. But, those MRP packages are really expensive. You can spend up to $1 million, can't you?

FRED: That's right. That's about what a mainframe package costs, including installation. I know it sounds like a lot, but if it does what it is supposed to do, it could easily pay for itself.

ANDREA: We just got through automating the factory. I don't think we've recovered our investment on that; have we, Dorothy?

DOROTHY: Not yet. We still have about a year to go on the robotics and another eighteen months on CAD/CAM.

ANDREA: See what I mean? We haven't even paid for your last project, Fred, and now you ask for more. What about the other areas of the company? What about marketing? We've been trying to automate our distribution centers for years and we keep getting pushed aside by manufacturing. Our customers are suffering from the lack of attention that we give to marketing systems.

FRED: Well, I'm sure that if we implemented MRP your customers would benefit. I can't give you any specifics because I didn't bring that material with me.

ANDREA: Well, if we can't talk specifics, I suggest we move on.

JAMES: That's a good idea. We have too many other things to cover today. Fred, why don't you put together a list of benefits for marketing, and we can discuss them next week. If nobody objects—next topic. Andrea, tell us how the sales reps are liking their new laptops.

Assignment

Prepare a list of benefits that would accrue to marketing if MRP II is implemented. For each benefit, include a brief explanation (one or two sentences) of how it is achieved with MRP II. **Hint:** You might structure your benefits along the lines of the ingredients of the marketing mix. This is a language that Andrea will understand.

SELECTED BIBLIOGRAPHY

Attaran, Mohsen. "The Automated Factory: Justification and Implementation." *Business Horizons* 32 (May–June 1989): 80–86.

Beischel, Mark E., and Smith, K. Richard. "Linking the Shop Floor to the Top Floor." *Management Accounting* 73 (October 1991): 25–29.

Berkley, Blair J., and Kiran, Ali S. "A Simulation Study of Sequencing Rules in a Kanban-Controlled Flow Shop." *Decision Sciences* 22 (July/August 1991): 559–82.

Berlant, Debbie; Browning, Reese; and Foster, George. "How Hewlett-Packard Gets Numbers It Can Trust." *Harvard Business Review* 68 (January–February 1990): 178ff.

Ebrahimpour, Maling. 1990. "A Comparison of American and Japanese Quality Management Practices in the United States." In *Proceedings 1990 Annual Meeting Decision Sciences Institute,* ed. Betty Whitten and James Gilbert, 1520–22, San Diego, CA.

Francis, Bob. "MRP II Rides the PC Bandwagon." *Datamation* 36 (August 15, 1990): 45ff.

Gold, Bela. "Computerization in Domestic and International Manufacturing." *California Management Review* 31 (Winter 1989): 129–43.

Hall, Robert W., and Vollmann, Thomas E. "Planning Your Material Requirements." *Harvard Business Review* 56 (September–October 1978): 105–12.

Hebditch, David. "Opening Up CIM Opportunities." *Datamation* 36 (June 1, 1990): 111–13.

Howery, C. Kenneth; Bennett, Earl D.; and Reed, Sarah. "How Lockheed Implemented CIM." *Management Accounting* 73 (December 1991): 22–28.

Kendall, Walter R., and Scott, C. Richard. "Information As a Factor of Production." *Journal of Information Technology Management* 1 (Number 2, 1990): 39–43.

Krajewski, Lee J.; King, Barry E.; Ritzman, Larry P.; and Wong, Danny S. "Kanban, MRP, and Shaping the Manufacturing Environment." *Management Science* 33 (January 1987): 39–57.

Liker, Jeffrey K.; Fleischer, Mitchell; Nagamachi, Mitsuo; and Zonnevylle, Michael S. "Designers and their Machines: CAD Use and Support in the US and Japan." *Communications of the ACM* 35 (February 1992): 77–95.

McGrath, Michael E., and Hoole, Richard W. "Manufacturing's New Economies of Scale." *Harvard Business Review* 70 (May–June 1992): 94–102.

Mehra, Satish, and Inman, R. Anthony. "Determining the Critical Elements of Just-In-Time Implementation." *Decision Sciences* 23 (January/February 1992): 160–74.

Misterek, Susan D. A.; Anderson, John C.; and Dooley, Kevin J. "The Strategic Nature of Process Quality." 1990. In *Proceedings 1990 Annual Meeting Decision Sciences Institute,* ed. Betty Whitten and James Gilbert, 1517–19, San Diego, CA.

Moad, Jeff. "Tools to Automate Quality Production." *Datamation* 37 (April 15, 1991): 63–64.

Morecroft, John D. W. "A Systems Perspective on Material Requirements Planning." *Decision Sciences* 14 (January 1983): 1–18.

Raymond, Louis, and Pare', Guy. "Measurement of Information Technology Sophistication in Small Manufacturing Businesses." *Information Resources Management Journal* 5 (Spring 1992): 4–16.

Ricciuti, Mike. "Connect Manufacturing to the Enterprise." *Datamation* 38 (January 15, 1992): 42*ff.*

Schartner, Andreas, and Pruett, James M. "Interactive Job Shop Scheduling: An Experiment." *Decision Sciences* 22 (November/December 1991): 1024–46.

Schonberger, Richard J. "Some Observations on the Advantages and Implementation Issues of JIT Production Systems." *Journal of Operations Management* 2 (November 1982): 1–12.

Schroeder, Roger G.; Anderson, John C.; Tupy, Sharon E.; and White, Edna M. "A Study of MRP Benefits and Costs." *Journal of Operations Management* 2 (October 1981): 1–9.

Weston, Frederick C., Jr. "Why IS Must Be a Partner in CIM." *Datamation* 36 (September 15, 1990): 111–12.

Chapter 19

Financial Information Systems

After studying this chapter, you should:

- Appreciate the interest that members of the firm's environment have in the financial information system
- Have an improved understanding of the role played by the data processing system in the CBIS
- Appreciate the necessity for including internal auditors in CBIS design and evaluation
- Understand how a corporation gathers information from its stockholders
- Be aware of the growing availability of financial intelligence in the form of online data services and CD-ROM disks
- Know the basic facts of forecasting, and be alert to nonquantitative as well as quantitative methods
- Have an introductory understanding of how forecasting can be accomplished with a statistics package
- Be familiar with a popular financial analysis tool—the cash flow model
- Understand a procedure that many firms follow in preparing their annual operating budgets

INTRODUCTION

Mechanized financial information systems have been used in business for one hundred years or more. Punched card machines, which were the only real alternative for large firms before the computer came along, were used primarily in the financial function. The same situation held true for keydriven bookkeeping machines.

The application of these machines was restricted to the processing of accounting data, and little attention was paid to the information needs of managers—even the financial managers. When computers came onto the scene, they were applied the same way. It was not until the mid-1960s that financial information systems were developed beyond the basic accounting tasks.

We have recognized that the financial function is concerned with the money flow through the firm. First it is necessary to acquire enough money to support the manufacturing, marketing, and other activities. Then it is necessary to control those funds to make certain they are used in the most effective way.

All managers in the firm have financial responsibilities. As a minimum they are given an operating budget and are expected to keep expenditures within those limits. Information describing the money flow—both budgeted and actual—permits managers to meet their financial responsibilities. This information is provided by the financial information system.

The financial information system has two input subsystems that are also found in the other functional information systems—data processing and intelligence. The third input subsystem consists of the firm's internal auditors. These auditors analyze the firm's conceptual systems to ensure that they process financial data the proper way.

The three output subsystems exert an influence on the firm's money flow in a sequential nature. First the forecasting subsystem projects the firm's long-range activity in an economic environment. Next the funds management subsystem manages the money flow as it occurs—seeking to keep it balanced and positive. Finally the control subsystem provides managers of the firm's operating units with financial information that they use in managing all of their resources.

INTERNAL AND EXTERNAL INTEREST IN FINANCIAL INFORMATION

We use the term **financial information system** to describe the CBIS subsystem that provides information concerning the firm's financial matters. Information is provided in the form of periodic reports, special reports, results of mathematical simulations, office automation communications, and the advice of expert systems. Managers throughout the firm use this information in managing their resources. All of the resources can be expressed in financial terms, and managers are evaluated based on how well they use the financial resources that are available to them.

Many elements in the firm's environment also have an interest in the firm's financial matters. The firm's stockholders, members of the financial community, the government, and suppliers require different kinds of information describing the firm's financial condition. Also, much financial information is directed to groups and organizations that are never directly associated with the firm—securities analysts, educators, and potential investors.

From the standpoint of its environmental interface, the financial information system has a greater exposure to outsiders than do any of the other functional information systems. The public's view of the firm's operations is influenced to a great extent by the capabilities of the financial information system.

MODEL OF THE FINANCIAL INFORMATION SYSTEM

The financial information system has three basic tasks: (1) to identify future money needs, (2) to assist in the acquisition of those funds, and (3) to control their use. These tasks are represented as output subsystems in the financial information system, illustrated in Figure 19.1. This system has the same structural arrangement that we used for the marketing and manufacturing information systems.

Input Subsystems

There are three input subsystems: the data processing subsystem, the internal audit subsystem, and the financial intelligence subsystem.

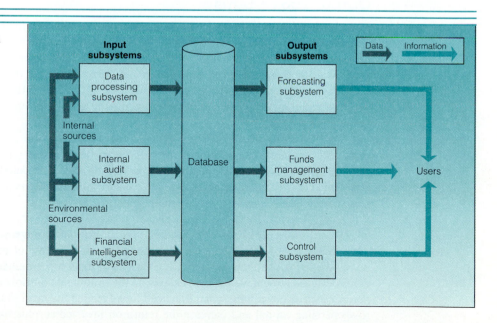

FIGURE 19.1
A Model of a Financial Information System

Data Processing Subsystem   The data processing subsystem gathers both internal and environmental data. In Chapter 18 we saw how data collection terminals in the manufacturing area gather internal data. Those terminals are a part of the data processing subsystem. Other internal data is captured from source documents and entered into the database using terminals or networked micros located throughout the firm.

The data processing subsystem also gathers environmental data as a result of business transactions with other firms. In Chapter 11 we saw how the order entry and accounts receivable systems gather customer data and how the purchasing, receiving, and accounts payable systems gather supplier data.

Internal Audit Subsystem   The internal audit subsystem is similar to the marketing research and the industrial engineering subsystems in that it is designed to conduct special studies of the firm's own operations. The **internal audit subsystem** consists of the firm's staff of internal auditors, who assure top management that the conceptual financial system represents the physical system in an accurate way.

Financial Intelligence Subsystem   The **financial intelligence subsystem** gathers data from the financial community—banks, government agencies, securities markets, and the like. This subsystem monitors the pulse of the nation's economy and informs the firm's executives and financial analysts of trends that can affect the firm. Within the past few years, the environment that this subsystem monitors has broadened from national to international in scope.

Output Subsystems

The output subsystems include the forecasting subsystem, the funds management subsystem, and the control subsystem. The early versions of these subsystems produced their outputs in the form of periodic reports. Then database management systems made it easy to query the database and prepare special reports, and mathematical models enabled the managers to simulate the effects of financial decisions. More recently, expert systems have been applied to all of the output subsystems.

Forecasting Subsystem   The **forecasting subsystem** prepares intermediate and long-term projections of the activity of the firm for ten or more years into the future. The changing needs of customers must be anticipated, as should the economic climate. Forecasting models are used to solve problems that become less structured as the planning horizon lengthens.

Funds Management Subsystem   The **funds management subsystem** uses projections of the firm's operations to determine the flow of money into and out of the firm. The manager can use a cash flow model to simulate several strategies designed to achieve the best balance in the inflow and outflow during a future period, such as the coming year. Balanced flows reduce the need to needlessly borrow operating capital and increase the return on invested surplus funds.

Control Subsystem   The **control subsystem** consists primarily of programs that use data gathered by the data processing subsystem to produce reports that show how monies are being spent. The reports typically compare actual financial performance to a budget. The control subsystem enables managers to track their cost control activity.

PREWRITTEN FINANCIAL SOFTWARE

More prewritten application software has been developed for the financial area than for any other. These are mostly data processing packages such as payroll, inventory, and accounts receivable. Financial managers and analysts also make good use of electronic spreadsheets. The spreadsheet rows are excellent for representing financial data such as sales and cost of goods sold, and the columns can represent the time periods such as months, quarters, or years.

These prewritten software systems enable small firms to achieve good financial control without investing in large information services staffs. The systems also enjoy widespread use in large firms, where their user friendliness is the main stimulus to end-user computing.

We will now describe each of the subsystems of the financial information system in more detail.

DATA PROCESSING SUBSYSTEM

We devoted Chapter 11 to the data processing system. Subsequently, we have recognized the ability of the data processing system to provide input to the executive, marketing, and manufacturing information systems. In this chapter, we recognize that it plays the same role in the financial information system.

The data processing subsystem is the only subsystem that appears in all of the functional information systems. Even more fundamentally: *The data processing system is the foundation upon which all information-oriented CBIS subsystems are built.* If the firm does not have a good data processing system, it cannot expect to have a good MIS, DSSs, and expert systems.

The Importance of Accounting Data

Accounting data provides a record of everything of monetary importance that happens in the firm. A record is made of each transaction, describing what happened, when it happened, who was involved, and (in many cases) how much money was represented. This data can be analyzed in various ways to meet management's information needs.

We have seen how a marketing manager can receive a **sales analysis report** (Figure 12.7) that shows how well products are selling. We have also seen how a manufacturing manager can receive a **maintenance report** (Figure 18.14) that shows the costs of running the various production machines. Also, a financial manager, such as a credit manager, can receive a report such as an **aged accounts receivable report,** which classifies the receivables amounts based on how long they have been owed. We illustrated this report in Figure 13.8 when we described management by exception in Chapter 13. All of these reports are prepared from accounting data.

INTERNAL AUDIT SUBSYSTEM

Firms of all sizes rely on **external auditors** to audit the accounting records to verify their accuracy. External auditors work for such accounting firms as Arthur Andersen and Price Waterhouse. Annual stockholder reports contain a *Statement to the Stockholders* that such an audit has been conducted.

Larger firms have their own staffs of **internal auditors,** who perform the same analyses as external auditors but have a broader range of responsibilities. We include internal auditing as an input subsystem of the financial information system because of its ability to independently appraise and influence the firm's operations from a financial standpoint.

Figure 19.2 shows a popular way to position internal auditing in the organization. The board of directors includes an **audit committee,** which defines the responsibilities of the internal auditing department and receives many of the audit reports. The **director of internal auditing** manages the internal auditing department and usually reports to the CEO or the CFO. The **CFO, chief financial officer,** is the person who manages the financial function and typically holds the title of vice president of finance. This top-level positioning of internal auditing within the organization ensures that it is recognized as an important activity and receives the cooperation of managers on lower levels.

The Importance of Objectivity

A unique ingredient that internal auditors offer is objectivity. They operate independently of the firm's functional units and have no ties with any individuals or groups within the firm. Their only allegiance is to the board, the CEO, and the CFO.

In order for the auditors to retain their objectivity, they make it clear that they do not want operational responsibility for systems that they help develop. They work strictly in an advisory capacity. They make recommendations to management, and management decides whether to implement those recommendations. In this respect, internal auditors perform in exactly the same manner as systems analysts.

Types of Auditing Activity

There are four basic types of internal auditing activity: financial, operational, concurrent, and control system design. One internal auditor can engage in all four types.

FIGURE 19.2

The Position of
Internal Auditing
in the
Organization

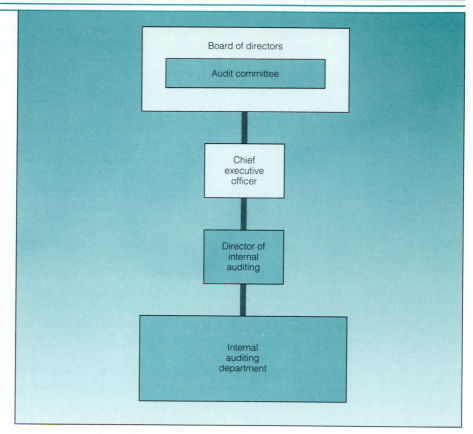

Financial Auditing   A **financial audit** verifies the accuracy of the firm's records and is the type of activity performed by external auditors. Internal auditors also conduct special financial audits separately from those of external auditors or can work jointly with external auditors.

Operational Auditing   An **operational audit** is not conducted to verify the accuracy of records but rather to validate the effectiveness of procedures. The systems studied are almost invariably conceptual rather than physical, but do not necessarily involve the computer. An auditor who works with computer-based systems has traditionally been called an **EDP auditor.** However, this title is being used less frequently as more auditors become expert in computing.

When internal auditors conduct operational audits, they look for three basic system features:

- **Adequacy of controls**   Is the system designed to prevent, detect, or correct errors?

- ■ **Efficiency** Are the operations of the system carried out so as to achieve the greatest productivity from the available resources?
- ■ **Compliance with company policy** Does the system enable the firm to meet its objectives or solve its problems in the prescribed way?

When information specialists develop systems, they should also look for these same features.

Concurrent Auditing A **concurrent audit** is the same as an operational audit except that the concurrent audit is ongoing. For example, internal auditors may randomly select employees and personally hand them their pay checks rather than use the company mails. This activity ensures that the names on the payroll represent real employees and are not simply fictitious entries made by an unscrupulous supervisor who wants to receive some extra pay checks.

Internal Control Systems Design In operational and concurrent auditing the internal auditors study existing systems. However, an auditor should not wait until a system is implemented to exert an influence. Internal auditors should actively participate in systems development. There are two basic reasons why this is a good idea. First, the cost of correcting a system flaw increases as the system life cycle progresses. According to Figure 19.3, it costs 4,000 times as much to correct a design error during operation and maintenance of a system than when the design is being conceptualized.

The second reason for involving the internal auditors in system development is that they offer expertise that can improve the quality of the system.

The Internal Auditor as a Member of the CBIS Team

The contributions that internal auditors can make to the CBIS depend on a combination of their knowledge and skills, and the attitude of top management.

The Auditors' Required Knowledge and Skills Contrary to what you might think, internal auditors do not always major in accounting in college; they come into auditing with a variety of backgrounds. This situation, combined with the fact that business systems are complex, makes it necessary for a new internal auditor to undergo a training period of several years. All of this means that internal auditors, like information specialists, can contribute in varying degrees to system projects based on their particular backgrounds and experiences.

Top Managements' Attitude Toward Auditing Perhaps an even greater influence on the auditor's contribution is the attitude of top management. If management sees the auditors as simply watchdogs whose main mission is to detect weaknesses in already installed systems, the auditors' contributions will be minimal. On the other hand, if management sees the auditors as active contributors throughout the SLC, then the level of the auditors' contributions can be high.

FIGURE 19.3

The Escalating Cost of Correcting Design Errors as the System Life
Cycle Progresses

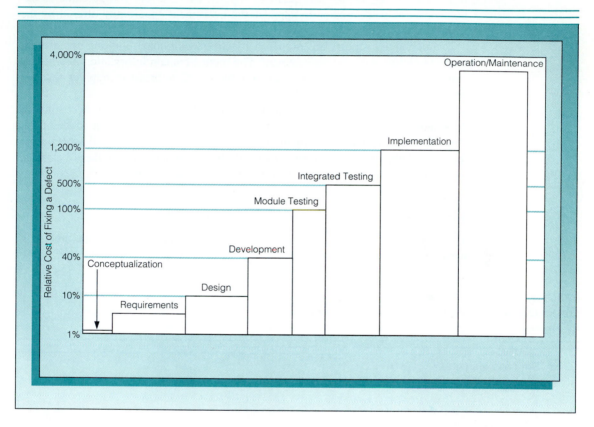

FINANCIAL INTELLIGENCE SUBSYSTEM

Since the financial function controls the money flow through the firm, information is needed to expedite the flow. The financial intelligence subsystem seeks to identify the best sources of additional capital and the best investments of surplus funds. In order to accomplish this task, the financial intelligence subsystem gathers data and information from stockholders and the financial community. Like the other functional intelligence subsystems, it also gathers data and information from the government. Much information that affects the money flow comes from the federal government and, to a lesser extent, state and local government.

Stockholder Information

All corporations have one or more people who are responsible for stockholder relations. The stockholder relations department is usually located within the financial function. This department maintains the communication link between the firm and its stockholders. Most of the information flows from the firm to the stockholders in the form of the annual and quarterly reports. Both current and potential stockholders use this information to appraise the investment opportunity offered by the firm.

Stockholder reports are prepared by the stockholder relations department working closely with top management. The reports contain information in a highly summarized form. Figure 19.4 is an example of the impressive graphics that are characteristic of stockholder annual reports.

Stockholders also use the stockholder relations department as a conduit to communicate complaints, suggestions, ideas, and other information to the firm. Once a year stockholders have the opportunity to attend the annual stockholder meeting. Although the firm does most of the communicating at these sessions, stockholders often express their views to the corporate executives.

Financial Community Information

The best developed intelligence activity of the firm is most likely the one involving the financial community. Long before the computer era, managers and staff in the

FIGURE 19.4

Stockholder Annual Reports Use Graphics to Communicate
Information

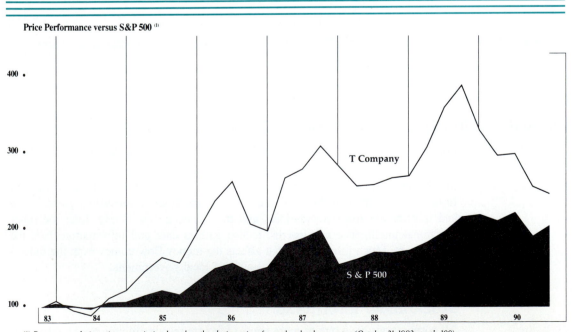

(1) *Represents relative price appreciation based on the closing prices for each calendar quarter. (October 31, 1983 equals 100)*

FIGURE 19.5
Stockholders Are Often Given a Chance to ''Have Their Say'' at Annual Stockholder Meetings

The Picture Cube

financial function had systems in place that gathered information describing the financial environment.

There are two reasons why firms have established this information flow. First, the information is readily available, existing in the form of printed material and databases that contain economic and environmental information. Second, top management recognizes the influence of the economic environment on the firm and wants to remain alert to changes that must be acted upon.

Environmental Influence on the Money Flow

The environment exerts both an indirect and a direct influence on the flow of money through the firm.

A good example of indirect influence is how the Federal Reserve System speeds up or slows down the money flow. When the Fed wants to speed up the flow, it releases its various controls, such as by lowering the prime interest rate. When the Fed wants to slow down the flow, it tightens the controls, such as by raising the rate.

The manner in which the financial community—banks, savings and loan associations, mortgage loan firms, and insurance companies—responds to the actions of the Fed is a direct influence. The members of the financial community respond by raising or lowering the interest rates that they charge their customers. The firm feels this direct influence when it borrows money or invests surplus funds.

Methods for Obtaining Financial Intelligence

Firms gather financial intelligence in three basic ways: informal communications, written publications, and computer databases.

Informal Communications Much financial intelligence is gathered by means of informal communications between the firm's managers and staff, and members of the financial community. This information is communicated by telephone and in face-to-face conversation, such as that which takes place over a business lunch.

This is an area where office automation can contribute. The firm's environmental sources of financial intelligence can be given voice mailboxes to make it easier for them to communicate. And, the firm's managers and analysts can use electronic calendaring to schedule meetings with the environmental contacts.

Written Publications Much financial intelligence can be gleaned from newspapers, newsletters, and magazines. Examples of such publications include *The Wall Street Journal,* the *Federal Reserve Bulletin,* and *Business Week.* Office automation can contribute here as well. Some of these publications are available in a videotex form in addition to the traditional hard copy.

Computer Databases When we described videotex as an office automation application in Chapter 14, we identified the Lotus One Source as a provider of financial informtion in the form of its CD/Corporate database. We illustrated the CD/Corporate output in Figure 14.14. When we described executive information systems in Chapter 12, we recognized that the Dow Jones/News Retrieval Service (DJNRS) is often included. We illustrated a DJNRS display in Figure 12.15.

Another example of a computer database of financial information is *CANADIAN BUSINESS AND CURRENT AFFAIRS* that is available as a part of the DIALOG OnDisc package offered by DIALOG Information Services, Inc. *CANADIAN BUSINESS AND CURRENT AFFAIRS* is compiled by Micromedia Limited of Toronto and indexes more than 200,000 articles a year from 200 business periodicals, 300 magazines, and ten newspapers. Figure 19.6 is a sample of the type of financial intelligence that can be provided.

The time period covered by *CANADIAN BUSINESS AND CURRENT AFFAIRS* includes 1981 to present, and the database comes in the form of a single optical disk that is updated quarterly. The hardware requirements include an IBM PC or PS/2 or compatible with a CDROM drive and a modem. *DIALOG OnDisc CANADIAN BUSINESS AND CURRENT AFFAIRS* illustrates how financial intelligence is available on an international basis.

This concludes our discussion of the input subsystems of the financial information system. We now turn our attention to the output subsystems.

FIGURE 19.6
An Example of Financial Intelligence Available from a Computer
Database

DIALOG OnDisk® CANADIAN BUSINESS AND CURRENT AFFAIRS   March, 1992

71 of 99 Complete Record
02681644
Painfully slow: Canada's economy should be stronger by year end
(Gazette interview with 3 economists)
This Week In Business January 6, 1992 pg 8-9+
Special Features: Photograph; Graphic Abstraction available
Descriptors: Forecasts (Economics)

Clement Gignac, Senior Economic Advisor at the National Bank of Canada,
George Saba, Chief Economist at Montreal Trust, and Earl Sweet, Assistant Chief
Economist at the Royal Bank of Canada agree that 1992 will show very slow
economic recovery because of very poor consumer confidence and high consumer
debt loads. On the positive side, interest rates are down to 8%, home
construction is growing again, and both inflation and interest rates fell
faster than expected. This will lead to growth in the economy by the end of
1992, if nothing drastic happens in the constitutional arena. The higher
Canadian dollar and the Goods & Services Tax have made shopping in the United
States very attractive, hurting the retail sector even more. While interest
rates are much lower than their peak, they are still high in real terms,
leaving manufacturers unable to raise prices or to invest in their businesses.
93% of the job losses were in Ontario and Quebec, and the effect of the Free
Trade Agreement deepen the sense of the recession. The high dollar may force
manufacturers to restructure and reorganize the economy. The US will be in
the same position in 1992 as Canada, although Canada is likely to outperform
the US in the last six months. Canadian business is not in bad shape and is
ready to succeed internationally.

FORECASTING SUBSYSTEM

When you pursue your business career and prepare to engage in forecasting, you
will have to select the forecasting method, or methods, to use. In making the selection, you should keep three basic facts in mind:

- **All forecasts are projections of the past.** The best basis for predicting what
  will happen in the future is to look at what has happened in the past. All

types of forecasting follow this approach. This is the reason why accounting data is so important in forecasting; it provides the historical base.

▪ **All forecasts consist of semistructured decisions.** Forecasting decisions are a good example of the semistructured type that are supported by the DSS. The decisions are based on some variables that can be easily measured and some that cannot.

▪ **No forecasting technique is perfect.** Not even the most sophisticated mainframe forecasting package can be expected to predict the future with 100 percent accuracy.

Since managers are aware of these facts, they apply much judgment in using the forecast as a basis for future planning.

Short-term and Longer-term Forecasting

Short-term forecasting is performed by the functional areas. The marketing function projects sales for the near future, say the next one to three years. All of the functional areas use the sales forecast as the basis for determining the resources that they will need to support the projected level of activity. For example, the sales forecast is a basis for the MRP projections made by manufacturing.

Longer-term forecasting is usually done by an area other than marketing—by the financial function or by a special group that has planning as its only responsibility. Some large corporations have a strategic planning group that reports to the executive level.

Forecasting Methods

Although it is natural to think of forecasting as involving only quantitative methods, an increasing amount of attention is being directed at nonquantative methods.

Nonquantitative Methods   A **nonquantitative forecasting method** does not involve computations of data but is based on subjective estimates. The manager follows reasoning such as: "We sold two thousand units last year, and we should be able to improve on that. So I think we will sell twenty-five hundred next year."

Forecasts such as this may seem like the manager is flying by the seat of the pants, but they can result from an insight into the business that comes from years of experience. Many managers are very good at the nonquantitative approach.

Some firms have established formal systems that encompass nonquantitative methods. Two such formal systems are panel consensus and the Delphi method.

▪ The **panel consensus** technique consists of a group of experts who openly discuss the factors bearing on the future and arrive at a single projection based on the combined inputs. The experts can meet on a regularly scheduled basis, follow a prescribed agenda, and have the discussion recorded in a written form.

■ The **Delphi method** involves a group of experts who do not meet in person but instead submit responses to a series of questionnaires that are prepared by a coordinator. Each round of questionnaires incorporates inputs from previous rounds, thus gradually refining the content.

Nonquantitative methods can be used in conjunction with output from quantitative systems. For example, executives can discuss output from a computer-based forecast in a panel consensus setting.

Quantitative Methods Forecasting was one of the very first applications of quantitative techniques to business, and many forecasting techniques have been developed over the years.[1]

One forecasting technique that has remained popular over the years is regression analysis. **Regression analysis** involves establishing a relationship between the activity to be forecast called the **dependent variable** and another activity called the **independent variable.** The activity to be forecast depends on the other activity.

Figure 19.7 illustrates the relationship between the dependent and independent variables. In this example, the firm's sales are the dependent variable, and the number of salespersons are the independent variable. The sales depend on the number of sales reps.

When there is only a single independent variable, the technique is called **simple regression,** or **bivariate regression.** When there are more than one independent variable, the names are **multiple regression,** or **multivariate regression.**

A line has been plotted through the data points in the figure so that the total distance from each of the points to the line is at a minimum. This line is called the **regression line,** and it is the best fit to the points. Management can use the regression line to forecast sales based on a particular number of salespersons. For example, if the firm employs twenty salespersons, it can assume that sales will approximate two thousand units.

When there is only a single independent variable, such as in the figure, forecasting can be accomplished graphically by using the regression line. However, it is more common to use a mathematical formula. Prewritten programs are used to perform regression analysis on the computer. These programs are mathematical models that usually are part of a set that performs different types of statistical analyses. Some of the more popular **statistics packages,** or **stat packages,** are BMD, SAS, and SPSS. Some of the packages are available for micros.

Regression analysis permits the mathematical model to specify the relationship between the dependent and independent variables very exactly. The models can produce graphic outputs such as the one in the figure, and they can also produce outputs in the form of tabular reports or displays.

---

[1] For an analysis of eighteen different forecasting techniques, *see* John C. Chambers, Satinder K. Mullick, and Donald D. Smith, "How to Choose the Right Forecasting Technique," *Harvard Business Review* 49 (July–August 1971), 45–74.

FIGURE 19.7

Using the Number of Salespersons to Project Sales

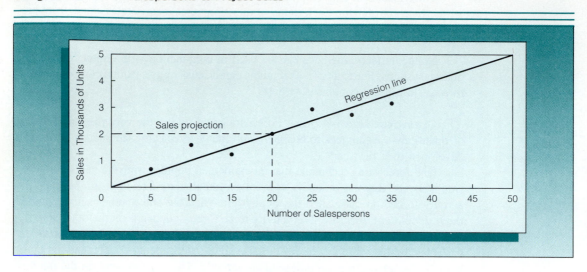

TABLE 19.1

Sales Forecast Data

Year	Sales (Y)	Advertising (X_2)	Price ratio (X_3)
		Historical Data	
1	24	4	80
2	27	4	80
3	31	5	90
4	29	5	100
5	33	6	100
6	38	7	110
7	37	8	120
8	40	8	100
9	45	9	90
10	49	10	100

A Forecasting Example

Assume that you own a creamery that sells ice cream to supermarkets. You have been in operation for ten years and have accumulated some statistics on your operation. The statistics presented in Table 19.1 represent your annual sales (Y) in thousands of dollars, your advertising budget (X_2), also in thousands of dollars, and a ratio (X_3) of your price compared with your competitors' average price. To compute the ratio, your price is divided by the competitors' average price, and the result is multiplied by 100.

You want to use the SAS statistical package, and both the data and the SAS instructions can be entered through the keyboard of a terminal or a micro. It is possible to use data already stored in the database, in which case you only enter the SAS instructions. We will assume that the historical data in the table is not in your database, so you enter:

```
DATA;
INPUT SALES ADVER PRICE 7-9;
CARDS;
24      4       080
27      4       080
31      5       090
29      5       100
33      6       100
38      7       110
37      8       120
40      8       100
45      9       090
49     10       100
PROC GLM;
MODEL SALES = ADVER PRICE;
```

The word DATA tells SAS to create a file. The word INPUT is used to define the format of the input record. The first field is SALES, the next is ADVER, and the third is PRICE. The word CARDS indicates that the data records follow.

The instruction PROC (pronounced *prock*) is a request for SAS to process the data. GLM stands for general linear model, the part of SAS that performs the regression. The MODEL expression first identifies the dependent variable (SALES) and then the independent variables (ADVER and PRICE).

The SAS output appears in Figure 19.8. The equation data is in the lower left-hand corner:

```
INTERCEPT       16.50961065 (16.51 rounded)
ADVER            3.92557910 (3.93 rounded)
PRICE           -07338590 (0.07 rounded)
```

FIGURE 19.8

Sales Forecast Produced by SAS

S T A T I S T I C A L   A N A L Y S I S   S Y S T E M

GENERAL LINEAR MODELS PROCEDURE

DEPENDENT VARIABLE: SALES

SOURCE	DF	SUM OF SQUARES	MEAN SQUARE	F VALUE	PR > F	R-SQUARE	C.V.
MODEL	2	556.41542632	278.20771316	110.12	0.0001	0.969196	4.5027
ERROR	7	17.68457368	2.52636767		STD DEV		SALES MEAN
CORRECTED TOTAL	9	574.10000000			1.58945515		35.30000000

SOURCE	DF	TYPE I SS	F VALUE	PR > F	DF	TYPE IV SS	F VALUE	PR > F
ADVER	1	551.00594059	218.10	0.0001	1	443.50691568	175.55	0.0001
PRICE	1	5.40948572	2.14	0.1868	1	5.40948572	2.14	0.1868

PARAMETER	ESTIMATE	T FOR H0: PARAMETER=0	PR > |T|	STD ERROR OF ESTIMATE
INTERCEPT	16.50961065	3.94	0.0056	4.18787189
ADVER	3.92557910	13.25	0.0001	0.29627964
PRICE	-0.07338590	-1.46	0.1868	0.05015139

When these values are incorporated in the regression equation, it becomes:

$$Y = 16.51 + 3.93X_2 - 0.07X_3$$

Sales for a given year can be expected to be the sum of $16,510 plus 3.93 times each thousand dollars invested in advertising minus 0.07 times the price ratio. Management can use this regression equation in deciding on the appropriate mix of advertising and pricing strategies.

Putting Forecasting in Perspective

Managers on all levels and in all areas engage in forecasting. Both nonquantitative and quantitative methods can be used, very often in concert. Very seldom will a quantitative method be used without the injection of judgment by the manager.

The higher the management level, the longer the planning horizon of the forecast. Intermediate and long-term forecasting must consider the influences of the national and possibly international economies. The preparation of the intermediate and long-term forecasts is the responsibility of the forecasting subsystem of the financial information system.

FUNDS MANAGEMENT SUBSYSTEM

The flow of money from the environment, through the firm, and back to the environment is important because money is used to obtain the other physical resources. The flow can be managed to achieve two goals: (1) to assure that the revenue inflow is greater than the expense outflow, and (2) to assure that this condition remains as stable as possible throughout the year.

A firm could show a good profit on the year's activities, yet have periods during the year when expenses exceed revenues. This situation can be seen in Figures 19.9 and 19.10 where a manufacturer of garden equipment produces at a constant level throughout the year, but enjoys high sales to wholesalers in the fall and low sales in the spring. From March through May the monthly sales of $300,000 are not high enough to cover the monthly manufacturing expenses of $360,000. Money outflow during March through May exceeds inflow, even though profit for the year is substantial.

The figures are examples of a **cash flow analysis** that tracks the inflow and outflow by month. The software that performs this task is called a **cash flow model.** It can be a custom-programmed model or application-development software such as an electronic spreadsheet. Output can be displayed in both a tabular and a graphic form.

FIGURE 19.9

A Graphic Display Shows That During Some Months Sales Are Less Than Manufacturing Expenses

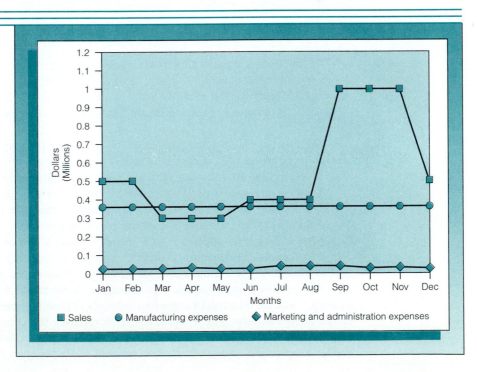

FIGURE 19.10

A Tabular Display Provides More Detail Concerning the Months with
Negative Sales Revenue

	JAN	FEB	MAR	APR	MAY	JUN	JUL	AUG	SEP	OCT	NOV	DEC	TOTAL
MONEY INPUT													
SALES	500	500	300	300	300	400	400	400	1000	1000	00	500	6600
MONEY OUTPUT													
MANUFACTURING													
EXPENSES													
WAGES	82	82	82	82	82	82	82	82	82	82	82	82	984
MATERIALS	220	220	220	220	220	220	220	220	220	220	220	220	2640
OTHER MFG.													
EXPENSES	58	58	58	58	58	58	58	58	58	58	58	58	696
TOTAL MANU-													
FACTURING													
EXPENSES	360	360	360	360	360	360	360	360	360	360	360	360	4320
MARKETING AND													
ADMIN. EXP.	26	26	26	28	28	28	40	40	40	30	30	30	372
NET CHANGE IN													
MONEY	114	114	-86	-88	-88	12	0	0	600	610	610	110	1908

Although the annual results of the garden equipment manufacturer are good, the money flow throughout the year is anything but stable. What can be done with the surplus during the fall months? What about the deficit during the spring? The managers can simulate several different strategies in an effort to find the best solution.

One approach is to match production to sales rather than produce at a constant level. The managers use the cash flow model to consider the effect of this strategy, but the results are unsatisfactory. There are still too many peaks and valleys.

Another strategy is tried. If arrangements can be worked out with the suppliers, payments for raw materials can be delayed for four months. The managers simulate this solution, which is illustrated in Figure 19.11. A four-month interest charge of four percent has been added to each month's material expenses to reflect the delayed payments. The months of significant negative flows are eliminated. If this flow is satisfactory to the managers, no further simulations are performed.

The cash flow model enables the managers to select and implement the best strategy. The cash flow model is the best example of how the computer can be used in managing the money flow because it encompasses the entire pipeline—from cash receipts to cash disbursements. Many subsidiary decisions must be made within this pipeline, and the funds management subsystem can provide support.

FIGURE 19.11

A Strategy of Delaying Supplier Payments Eliminates the Months of Negative Sales Revenue

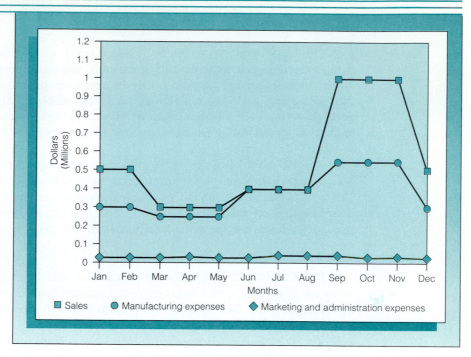

Putting Funds Management in Perspective

The firm is not at the complete mercy of its environment. In terms of the money resource, the firm can influence the flow to and from the environment. The programs in the funds management subsystem enable management to make the decisions that influence the flow in the desired manner.

CONTROL SUBSYSTEM

Managers have operational objectives to achieve, such as producing or selling a certain number or value of items. The managers are given an **operating budget,** an amount of money that is available for use in meeting the operational objectives. The budget usually covers operations for one **fiscal year,** or financial year.

The Budgeting Process

The budgeting process consists of a number of semistructured decisions. Considerable supporting data is available in the form of historical accounting records but much judgment must be applied.

There are three general approaches that a firm can take in setting its budget—top-down, bottom-up, and participative.

The Top-Down Approach   When a top-down approach is taken, the firm's executives determine the budget amounts, and then impose those amounts on the lower levels. The rationale is that the executives have the best grasp of the firm's long-term goals and can allocate funds that enable the firm to meet those goals. However, such a budget might be viewed by managers on lower levels as an unrealistic objective, imposed by persons who do not know the real situation.

The Bottom-Up Approach   When a bottom-up approach is taken, the budgeting process begins at the lowest organizational level and works its way up. The logic is that persons on the lower levels are closer to the action and can best determine their resource needs. However, this logic frequently escapes the executives, who reason that the lower-level managers will ask for unrealistically high amounts.

The Participative Approach   Because of the shortcomings of the top-down and bottom-up approaches, the general practice is to follow a **participative budgeting** process.[2] That is to say, the persons who will receive the funds participate in setting the levels of those funds. It is a *give and take* approach with managers on the various levels negotiating to achieve a budget that is satisfactory to all. Middle-level managers play a key role in this process, bringing into focus the long-range views of the executives and the immediate needs of the managers on the lower level.

Figure 19.12 illustrates the participative budgeting process. The numbered paragraphs below correspond to the numbers in the figure. This example assumes that the firm makes maximum use of mathematical modeling.

1. The starting point is the sales forecast, prepared by marketing. A **forecasting model** bases its projections on inputs from lower-level marketing managers, combined with adjustments by marketing executives.
2. Top management examines the forecast and makes adjustments based on their subjective evaluations plus other inputs.
3. The approved forecast data is then entered into a **resource planning model** that converts the sales objectives into resource requirements for each functional area. For example, if the firm is to sell 230,000 units next year, eight new salespersons must be hired, a new drill press must be purchased, two new accounting clerks must be added, and an additional disk drive must be installed. The MRP model that we discussed in Chapter 18 can be a part of the resource planning model—projecting the material needs.

---

[2]Research on the relative merits of participative budgeting has identified instances where it works well and instances where it does not. For more details, *see* Peter Chalos and Susan Haka, "Participative Budgeting and Managerial Performance," *Decision Sciences* 20 (Spring 1989), 334–47.

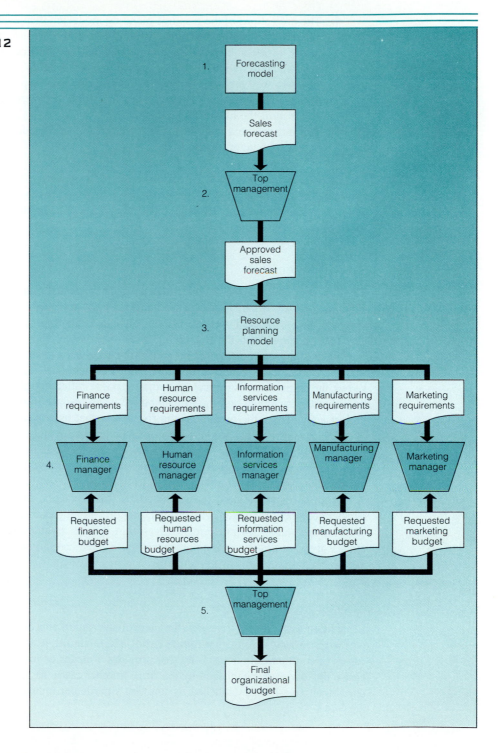

FIGURE 19.12
The Budgeting
Process

4. The projections of the resource planning model are then evaluated by managers in each of the functional areas. These managers use their knowledge of the business to adjust the amounts as they see fit. Each manager works in conjunction with his or her superior to arrive at an acceptable budget. The two-way arrows connecting this and the next step illustrate the way that recommendations bounce back and forth between the management levels until the budget is finalized.

5. Top management combines the approved functional budgets to obtain the operating budget for the firm.

This budgeting process is performed once each calendar year, just prior to the beginning of the fiscal year. As an example, a firm might schedule its budgeting activity for September and October, so that the plan will be in place when the fiscal year begins on November 1.

Budget Reports

The operating budget for a unit, such as a department or division, consists of amounts for each of the basic expense items (salaries, telephone, rent, supplies, and so on). These expense items are usually allocated monthly throughout the fiscal year to correspond with the fluctuating level of activity.

Each manager with budget responsibility receives a monthly report showing actual expenditures for her or his unit compared with the budget. Figure 19.13 shows the format that is typical of budget reports, reflecting performance against both the current month and the to-date budget. The **to-date budget** consists of the budget amounts for the months of the fiscal year that have passed.

The manager's goal is to meet the total budgeted amount for the year, and the reports enable the manager to stay on track during the year by responding to significant variances. The drill-down technique that has been popularized by executive information systems is an effective way to obtain more details on the variances.

Budget reports seldom go unnoticed by the managers. In some firms, management compensation plans are based in part on budget performance. For example, bonuses are paid when performance is within budget. Even when budget performance does not directly affect compensation, it most certainly can affect the manager's evaluation by his or her superior.

Performance Ratios

In addition to the budget reports, the control subsystem can produce a number of performance ratios. A **performance ratio** is a relationship of two or more indicators of an organization's activity that provides a means of measurement. In some cases, the ratios are established by the firm. In other cases the ratios represent standards that have been established by the firm's particular industry or perhaps business as a whole.

FIGURE 19.13

A Budget Report

```
                        BUDGET REPORT
                      AS OF JANUARY 31
                        MIDWEST REGION

                 CURRENT MONTH                    YEAR-TO-DATE
   ITEM        BUDGET    ACTUAL    DOLLARS     BUDGET    ACTUAL    DOLLARS

SALARIES       $23,500   $22,000   $1,500-     $59,000   $54,250   $4,750-
TRAVEL          8,250     9,000      750+       23,500    28,100    4,600+
ENTERTAINMENT   1,400     1,635      235+        4,200     5,100      900+
TELEPHONE        200        85       115-         600       225       375-
RENT             535       535         0         1,605     1,605        0
FURNITURE         0         0          0           420       505       85+
SUPPLIES         625       410       215-        1,875     1,320      555-
MISC.            400       620       220+        1,200     1,963      765+

TOTAL          $34,910   $34,285    625-       $92,400   $93,070     670+
```

Among the most popular of the ratios is the current ratio. The **current ratio** measures the extent to which a firm or an organizational unit can cover its short-term debts with assets that are easily converted into cash.

$$\text{Current ratio} = \frac{\text{current assets}}{\text{current liabilities}}$$

A ratio of 1.0 or greater is desirable since it means that the debts can be covered without having to sell some of the assets.

Another popular ratio is **inventory turnover,** which measures the firm's sales in terms of the inventory investment. For example, assume that a firm has an inventory that is worth $1 million, and the cost of the inventory that is sold during a particular time period, such as a year, is $3 million. You can think of the inventory as turning over, or being sold, three times.

$$\text{Inventory turnover ratio} = \frac{\text{cost of goods sold}}{\text{average inventory value}}$$

Generally, the higher the inventory turnover ratio, the better. The ratio is an indication of the manager's ability to achieve high sales levels without heavy investments in inventory.

Ratios such as these are used by managers and by outsiders such as financial analysts, potential investors, and stockholders to monitor the performance of the firm. The ratios are highly distilled representations of accounting data and provide a handy way to come to grips with the data.

Putting the Control Subsystem in Perspective

The computer has probably done a better job in the control area than in any other. When an accurate and current database exists, it is a simple process to compare actual and budgeted expenses, produce reports, and compute ratios. The reports and ratios have been provided for so long that managers take them for granted, and would feel lost without them.

HOW MANAGERS USE THE FINANCIAL INFORMATION SYSTEM

Table 19.2 identifies the users of the financial information system. Executives in the financial function such as the vice president of finance and the controller use the information produced by all three output subsystems. Other executives, including members of the board of directors, also use all of the outputs. Lower-level managers and members of the professional staff favor those subsystems that relate directly to their areas of responsibility. For example, an investments analyst uses the funds management subsystem, and a store manager relies on the control subsystem.

Every day, managers throughout the firm use financial information.

TABLE 19.2
Users of the Financial Information System

User	Subsystem		
	Forecasting	Funds management	Control
Vice president of finance	X	X	X
Other executives	X	X	X
Controller	X	X	X
Manager of accounting			X
Manager of financial planning	X		X
Director of budgets			X
Other functional managers	X	X	X

SUMMARY

Members of the firm's environment join the firm's managers in using the output of the financial information system. The heart of the system is the data processing subsystem, which provides detailed data concerning everything of a monetary nature that happens to the firm. Unless a firm has a good data processing subsystem, it cannot hope to have a good CBIS.

The firm's internal auditors form the internal audit subsystem and engage in four types of audits—financial, operational, concurrent, and internal control systems design. The internal auditing staff can exert a strong influence on systems design when the staff members have the required knowledge and skills, and top management recognizes their potential contribution.

The financial intelligence subsystem monitors the economic environment of the financial community and also interfaces with the firm's stockholders. Financial intelligence can be gathered by means of informal communications, written publications, and computer databases such as the *CANADIAN BUSINESS AND CURRENT AFFAIRS* service from DIALOG.

All forecasts are projections of the past, consist of semistructured decisions, and lack complete perfection. Marketing engages in short-term forecasting of sales, and this forecast provides the basis for all functional planning. The responsibility for longer-term forecasting is performed by the forecasting subsystem, using both quantitative and nonquantitative techniques. Two examples of nonquantitative techniques are panel consensus and the Delphi method. A popular quantitative technique is regression analysis. A firm rarely creates its own forecasting programs but uses prewritten packages such as SAS.

The funds management subsystem assists management not only in tracking the flow of money through the firm but in influencing that flow. A cash flow model can be used to simulate the effect of alternate decisions on the flow.

A firm's outgoing money flow is influenced by the firm's operating budget. Managers throughout the firm use the budget as a control mechanism. Monthly budget reports during the fiscal year advise managers how well they are performing compared to their budgets. Managers also use ratios to compare their units' performance with standards established by the firm, the firm's industry, and business in general.

We have now concluded our study of the functional areas that have historically been the biggest users of the computer. In the next chapter, we will consider the new member of the group—human resources.

KEY TERMS

external auditor
internal auditor
audit committee
chief financial officer (CFO)

EDP auditor
panel consensus
Delphi method
regression analysis

statistics package
cash flow analysis
cash flow model
operating budget
fiscal year

to-date budget
performance ratio
current ratio
inventory turnover

KEY CONCEPTS

The financial information system as a combination of input and output subsystems, integrated by a database

The way that accounting data forms the foundation for all systems that provide information

Different types of audits

The three basic features that internal auditors and information specialists seek to incorporate into systems designs.

The importance of good historical data to forecasting

The need to supplement quantitative forecasts with nonquantitative methods and judgment

The relevance of cash flow analysis to all financial management

The way that participative budgeting integrates the top-down and bottom-up approaches

How output from mathematical models is blended with management judgment to produce the operating budget

QUESTIONS

1. Why would environmental elements with no direct involvement in the firm's operations be interested in the financial information system?

2. What are the three basic tasks of the financial information system in terms of the money flow?

3. Give an example of internal data gathered by the data processing subsystem. Of environmental data.

4. In what way do internal auditors resemble marketing researchers and industrial engineers?

5. How does the aged accounts receivable report reflect management by exception?

6. What role do external auditors play in the annual report to stockholders?

7. Why not position internal auditing within the finance function?

8. What distinguishes an operational audit from a concurrent audit?

9. Both internal auditors and systems analysts look for three basic system features. What are they?

10. Which department in the corporation serves as the interface with the stockholders?

11. How could voice mail be used to gather financial intelligence?

12. How does DIALOG keep its *CANADIAN BUSINESS AND CURRENT AFFAIRS* database current?

13. Why are manufacturing, finance, human resources, and information services interested in the sales forecast?

14. What is a similarity between the panel consensus and the Delphi method? What is a dissimilarity?

15. How many variables are involved in simple regression? What are their names?

16. How many dependent variables are included in multiple regression? How many independent variables?

17. What are the two goals of managing the money flow?

18. Explain why an electronic spreadsheet is a good vehicle for achieving a cash flow model.

19. Although the text does not say, which managers would use the cash flow model? Consider management levels and functional areas. Justify your answer.

20. In what way were the users of the cash flow model for the garden equipment manufacturer aware of the influence of the environment on their cash flow policies?

21. What keeps executives from simply turning the forecasting responsibility over to the managers on the operational control level?

22. Which management level is the key to making participative budgeting work?

23. What is the relationship between sales forecasting and the budgeting process?

24. Who sets the desired values for financial performance ratios?

TOPICS FOR DISCUSSION

1. Why has so much prewritten software been aimed at the financial function?

2. What is the role of data processing in the MIS? In a DSS? In an expert system?

3. How could a corporation stimulate an inflow of information from its stockholders?

4. The chapter explains how the Fed can exercise an indirect influence on the firm's money flow. Explain how the firm's competitors could accomplish the same effect.

5. Can you think of an instance when a forecast would not be a projection of the past?

PROBLEMS

1. Go to the library and obtain the most recent annual reports for three firms in the same industry. Compute the current ratio and the inventory turnover ratio for each firm using data contained in the reports. Based on this data, which firm do you believe to be in the best financial condition? Prepare a one-page, double-spaced summary of your findings.

2. Use a statistics package such as SAS to develop a regression equation using the following historical data:

Year	Sales revenue (in thousands)	Number of sales persons	Advertising budget (in thousands)	Sales promotion budget (in thousands)
1	12.1	25	0.5	0.2
2	12.4	25	0.9	0.2
3	12.9	26	1.1	0.2
4	12.7	26	1.0	0.3
5	13.2	26	1.2	0.3
6	13.6	27	1.2	0.3
7	14.1	27	1.5	0.0
8	13.8	28	1.5	0.3
9	14.1	28	2.0	0.3
10	14.0	30	2.0	0.4
11	14.5	29	1.5	0.4
12	14.6	30	2.0	0.5
13	15.3	31	2.5	0.5
14	15.5	31	2.2	0.5

What sales revenue would be expected if the firm has 33 salespersons, invests $2,500 in advertising, and $750 in sales promotion?

Sound Business

Sound Business is an electronics manufacturer with a plant in Eugene, Oregon, and stores throughout the Pacific Northwest. The company has a new president, Tony Albert. Tony was appointed by the board of directors to replace Catherine Figer, who retired. Tony has called a meeting of the executive committee. In addition to Tony, the members include Barbara Scott-White (Vice President of Information Services), Alice Wingate (Vice President of Finance), Wayne Babers (Vice President of Manufacturing), and Don Frame (Vice President of Marketing).

TONY ALBERT (President): The first thing I want to accomplish is to establish better control. In my opinion, the main reason why sales have been so poor is the lack of control. I've seen it everywhere—in the plant, in the stores, even here at headquarters. I want each manager on each level to have absolute control over his or her own area. What I would like from you today is your suggestions on where we should start. Alice, what are the main control mechanisms we have in finance, and how well are they working?

ALICE WINGATE (Vice President of Finance): As I see it, the budget is the main control mechanism for the entire company. Each spring the board of directors meets to plan the strategy for the next fiscal year. In the fall we have a weekend meeting at an area resort to get away from the interruptions. All managers, except those on the lowest level, attend. Each manager presents her or his case, and we thrash out any differences. When we leave, we have a budget.

DON FRAME (Vice President of Marketing): I'd like to interrupt. That sounds all well and good, but I've always pointed out that marketing really doesn't have much say in the budgeting process. The board of directors sets the objectives so that the price of the stock will increase as much as possible. That's their only concern; they couldn't care less about our capabilities. They specify what they want to achieve and then the company has to come up with a plan. I've seen some annual plans that are a real joke.

WAYNE BABERS (Vice President of Manufacturing): Well, I'm sure the board is not about to let marketing tell them what Sound Business is going to accomplish. Your store managers know that if they submit an optimistic forecast they will end up with a high quota that will be hard to make. Since their compensation is based on their quota performance, it's to their benefit to come in with low estimates. Then, when they exceed their quotas they look good. That's why the board always increases your forecasts.

TONY: Let's not get into an argument now. I'd like to hear everybody's views. Don, what controls does marketing have?

DON: Regardless of what Wayne says, we have a good control mechanism in our sales quotas. We let the store managers set their own because they know the local situation better than anyone. We tried setting the quotas for them and they rebelled. By the way, Barbara gives us really good support in the form of the monthly sales reports. All of the store managers know exactly where they stand in terms of quota, month by month.

TONY: Sounds good. Wayne, what's the situation in manufacturing?

WAYNE: As you know from your tour last week, we're really excited about our new MRP system. Once we get it up and running, it ought to give us all the control we need.

TONY: What do you see as the key to getting it "up and running," as you say?

WAYNE: Well, there's no question but what we need some performance standards. We have only one industrial engineer, and she's overworked. We let her set the standards, but the workers on the shop floor complain because they say the standards aren't realistic. We really can't come back with any good arguments because we don't have any historical records to back us up.

BARBARA SCOTT-WHITE (Vice President of Information Services): You don't have the records because you didn't install the data collection system we recommended.

WAYNE: Well, that's true, but we had no choice. Again, it was the people on the shop floor. They just don't want the terminals—"Big Brother" they say. And, I think the union had a big influence. Since we had to lay off some people because of poor sales the union has become more of a factor.

TONY: Well, I'm not so sure that you are going to get your MRP system "up and running" any time soon under those conditions. Barbara, what about controls in information services?

BARBARA: We have the usual ones. We keep backup files of all the databases and programs. The computer room is off limits to everyone except our operators; the analysts and programmers can't even get in. I think everything is working pretty well. We don't hear many complaints, except from the internal auditors. If it were left up to them, we would spend so much time building in controls that we would never get a system on the air. On the few projects where they were involved, we had a lot of friction. Our analysts just don't want somebody else telling them how to design systems—at least somebody who isn't a computer professional.

ALICE: I would like to say something on behalf of the auditors even though they are not in my area. Tony, they report directly to the board. I admit that our auditors are short on computer skills, but I don't think that is necessarily a hindrance. The controls that they have recommended should be built into any system—manual or computer. I think that the analysts just don't want anybody else criticizing their work. They are probably gun-shy after having to redo the payroll system because it was computing the income tax wrong.

TONY: Well, all of this is very interesting. I'm sure we could go on like this all day, but I think I've heard enough. I appreciate the input. Give me some time to think it over and then we can decide what our strategy will be. It sounds like we have some work to do. Let's try to put together a preliminary control plan at our meeting next week. See you then.

Assignments

1. Assuming that everyone's perceptions represent the true facts, what is the root cause of the control problem at Sound Business? Explain it in one sentence, beginning with: "The main reason for lack of control is . . ."

2. Is there anything that Tony can do to improve the system of controls from a company standpoint? Explain what they are and how he should go about it.

3. Does finance have a control problem? If so, what is it? Who will be involved in solving it, and how will they go about it?

4. Repeat Question 3 in terms of marketing.

5. Repeat Question 3 in terms of manufacturing.

6. Repeat Question 3 in terms of information services.

SELECTED BIBLIOGRAPHY

Barthel, Ronald C., and Lindeman, Robert G. "Modeling Helps It Happen." *EDGE* 3 (January/February 1990): 31*ff.*

Cloud, Avery C. "An EDP Control Audit With Teeth." *Journal of Systems Management* 41 (January 1990): 13*ff.*

Cornell, David W., and Coates, J. Dennis. "Harnessing the New Cash Flow Statement." *Business Credit* 94 (March 1992): 20–23.

Czyzewski, Alan B., and Hicks, Donald W. "Hold Onto Your Cash." *Management Accounting* 73 (March 1992): 27–30.

Dunmore, David B. "Farewell to the Information Systems Audit Profession." *Internal Auditor* 46 (February 1989): 42–48.

Eom, Hyun B.; Lee, Sang M.; Snyder, Charles A.; and Ford, F. Nelson. "A Multiple Criteria Decision Support System for Global Financial Planning." *Journal of Management Information Systems* 4 (Winter 1987–88): 94–113.

Fair, Ray C., and Shiller, Robert J. "Comparing Information in Forecasts from Econometric Models." *The American Economic Review* 80 (June 1990): 375–89.

Figliozzi, John P. "Capture Major Risk Trends with a Financial Analysis Model." *Business Credit* 94 (June 1992): 18–19.

Gallegos, Frederick. "Audit Contributions to Systems Development." In *EDP Auditing.* Boston, MA: Auerbach Publishers, 1991. Section 72–01–40, 1–14.

Gentry, James A. "State of the Art of Short-Run Financial Management." *Financial Management* 17 (Summer 1988): 41–57.

Gershefski, George W. "Building a Corporate Financial Model." *Harvard Business Review* 47 (July–August 1969): 61–72.

Greenberg, Robert R., and Murphy, David Smith. "Systems Development and the Internal Auditor: Where Are We Now?" *Internal Auditor* 46 (August 1989): 52–57.

Holsapple, Clyde W.; Tam, Kar Yan; and Whinston, Andrew B. "Adapting Expert System Technology to Financial Management." *Financial Management* 17 (Autumn 1988): 12–22.

Lovejoy, Jeff. "Companies Grow with Proper Cash Flow." *Business Credit* 92 (April 1990): 10–12.

Lynch, John J. "Eliminate the Auditors?" *Internal Auditor* 49 (April 1992): 26–32.

McIntosh, Willard. "Forecasting Cash Flows: Evidence from the Financial Literature." *The Appraisal Journal* 58 (April 1990): 221–29.

Sawyer, Lawrence B. "The Political Side of Internal Auditing." *Internal Auditor* 49 (February 1992): 26–33.

Schiff, Johathan B., and May, Claire B. "How Useful Are Management Reports on Financial Statements?" *Business Credit* 94 (February 1992): 14–17.

Seed, Allen H., III. "Improving Cost Management." *Management Accounting* 71 (February 1990): 27–30.

Srinivasan, Venkat, and Kim, Yong H. "Designing Expert Financial Systems: A Case Study of Corporate Credit Management." *Financial Management* 17 (Autumn 1988): 32–44.

Stocks, Kevin D.; Albrecht, W. Steve; Howe, Keith R.; and Schueler, Dennis R. "What Makes an Effective Internal Audit Department?" *Internal Auditor* 45 (April 1988): 45–49.

Taylor, Norman. "Spreadsheet Models Work for Forecasting." *Business Credit* 92 (April 1990): 8–9.

Weaver, Samuel C.; Peters, Donald; Cason, Roger; and Daleiden, Joe. "Capital Budgeting." *Financial Management* 18 (Spring 1989): 10–17.

Williams, Joseph D. "The Board of Directors' Reliance on the Internal Auditor." *Internal Auditor* 45 (August 1988): 31–35.

Zeune, Gary D. "Flawed Analysis: How Seasonality Inaccurately Alters Traditional Ratios." *Business Credit* 93 (September 1991): 15–18.

Chapter 20

Human Resource Information Systems

LEARNING OBJECTIVES

After studying this chapter, you should:

- Know the primary activities that are performed by the human resources (HR) function and how the human resource information system (HRIS) supports those activities
- Know where the HRIS can be positioned within the firm's organizational structure
- Be familiar with how the HRIS has evolved to its current status
- Understand the role played by the data processing system in the HRIS
- Recognize the need for special research projects to gather special HR data for the database
- Appreciate how the environment influences the flow of personnel resources through the firm, and be aware of how environmental databases can facilitate that flow
- Have a good understanding of the HRIS database—what it contains, where it is located, how it is managed, and how data entry is accomplished
- Be able to classify HRIS applications into four categories, and understand the degree of success that firms have had in developing applications for each category
- Know what value the firm's executives place on the HRIS in relation to other functional systems
- Appreciate the potential that exists for the HRIS

INTRODUCTION

All larger firms have a human resources function that handles much of the specialized processing concerning the firm's personnel. The conceptual system that is used in managing the personnel is called the human resource information system, or HRIS. The HRIS is usually located in the HR function.

For many years, the firm's top management placed little emphasis on the HRIS, as it evolved from a manual system housed in HR to a computer-based system with most of the hardware, software, and data located in information services. Government legislation, aimed at ensuring equality in firms' personnel practices, prompted top management to give the HRIS more attention than it had previously enjoyed. Along with this new status, the HRIS began to migrate from IS to HR, taking advantage of microcomputer technology.

The HRIS can conform to the same basic format as the other functional information systems, making use of input subsystems to enter data into the database and output subsystems to transform the data into information. The data processing subsystem provides personnel data of a financial nature, the human resources research subsystem conducts special research projects to gather new data, and the human resources intelligence subsystem gathers personnel-related data and information from the environment.

The HRIS database complements the personnel data with data describing both organizations and individuals in the firm's environment that influence the personnel flow. Although much of the HRIS processing in large firms has been downloaded from the mainframes to micros in HR, the HRIS database is still largely contained within the central computers. Data entry is performed by both managers and non-managers who reside both within and outside HR. Most of the output goes to users inside HR, but other users exist elsewhere in the firm and its environment.

The four output subsystems include personnel planning and administration; compensation and government legislation; recruiting and benefits; and safety, labor relations, and payroll. Many of the applications contained within each of these subsystems have been implemented by a large number of firms, but some are still in the process of development. Also, many of the applications are a part of the core HRIS, but some function in a stand-alone manner.

The HRIS has come a long way in the past decade, and many executives now regard it as being just as valuable as other functional information systems. However, there is still room for growth as the HRIS tackles some of the most difficult management problems.

THE HUMAN RESOURCES FUNCTION

The organizational structure of most firms includes a unit that has responsibility for many of the activities related to the personnel resource. The term **personnel** was originally given to these units, but the practice today is to use the name **human resources (HR),** recognizing that personnel are a valuable resource. HR can be a department or division within a functional area, or it can have functional status equal to marketing, manufacturing, finance, and IS. The manager of HR is the **HR director,** who can be a member of the executive committee.

Primary HR Activities

HR supports the other functional areas by assisting in obtaining new personnel, preparing personnel to do their jobs, and handling much of the recordkeeping that is related to personnel. In meeting its responsibilities, HR performs four primary activities, as illustrated in Figure 20.1.

- **Recruiting and Hiring**   HR helps bring new employees into the firm by running help wanted ads in newspapers, providing position requests to both government and private employment agencies, performing screening interviews on college campuses and at the firm's facilities, and administering employment tests. HR stays current on government legislation affecting employment practices and counsels management in the proper policies to establish.
- **Educating and Training**   During the period of employment, HR can administer educational and training programs that are required to cultivate the employees' job-related knowledge and skills. For example, members of

FIGURE 20.1

The Human Resources Function Facilitates the Flow of the Personnel Resources

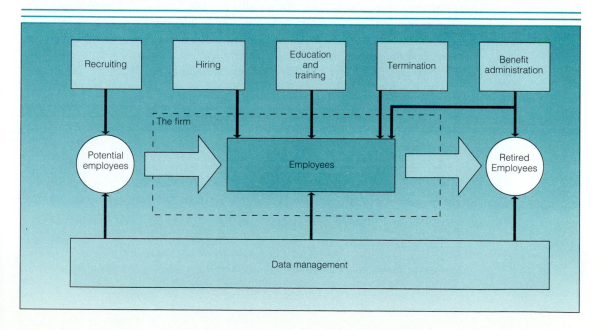

the HR staff can assist systems analysts in training users and participants during the implementation phase of the SLC.

- **Managing Employee Related Data** HR maintains a database of employee related data, and processes that data to meet users' information needs.
- **Termination and Benefit Administration** During the time that persons are employed by the firm they receive a package of benefits such as hospitalization, dental insurance, and profit sharing that is becoming increasingly difficult to administer. When employees terminate their employment, HR processes the necessary paperwork and often conducts exit interviews. One purpose of the interviews is to learn how the firm can better serve its employees in the future. After termination, HR administers the firm's retirement program to former employees who are eligible.

As the employees work for the firm they are not managed by HR but by the managers of the areas where they work. HR therefore performs a support function, facilitating the flow of the personnel resource through the firm.

THE HUMAN RESOURCE INFORMATION SYSTEM

Each firm must have a system for gathering and maintaining the data that describes the human resources, transforming the data into information, and reporting the information to users. This system has been named the **human resource information system (HRIS).** The name **human resource management system (HRMS)** is also being increasingly used, but we will use HRIS since it is more popular.

Although it is easy to think of the HRIS as a computer-based system, this view can be misleading for two reasons. First, a relatively large number of HRISs are noncomputer-based, and second, the term also applies to the *people* who work with the computer. The HR organization typically includes an HRIS section that has the responsibility for managing the conceptual system of human resource data and information.

The 1990-91 HRSP Survey

In 1990 and 1991, a study was conducted by the Association of Human Resource Systems Professionals (HRSP), and the findings from that study shed considerable light on the current status of the HRIS.[1] HRSP is an international organization of

[1] The study was conducted by the author and Gerardine DeSanctis of the University of Minnesota, working with James Stroop, the executive director of HRSP, and several HRSP members including Naomi Bloom, Betsy Evers, and John Hinojos. Also contributing was Kim Zitzmann of the University of Minnesota. The researchers greatfully acknowledge the assistance provided by HRSP in conducting the study. A complete report of the findings can be obtained from the Association of Human Resource Systems Professionals, P.O. Box 801646, Dallas, TX 75380–1646.

over 3,000 members who represent over 2,000 organizations in all fifty states, Canada, and many other countries. Most of the HRSP members are assigned to their firms' HRIS units, but some work in other areas.

The study consisted of a questionnaire that was mailed to 1861 HRSP members who had previously identified themselves as practitioners. Responses were received from 513 separate organizations—a response rate of 27.6 percent.

A wide variety of industries were represented, with manufacturing (20.5 percent of the respondents) being the most popular. Following closely behind were banking/financial services (14 percent), health care (6.8 percent), and insurance (5.7 percent). The firms also represented a wide range in terms of the span of their operations. More than one-third (35.5 percent) are multinational. At the other extreme 11.3 percent operate in only single metropolitan areas, and 6.6 percent are limited to single cities or towns. The annual revenues averaged over $400 million.

The Location of the HRIS within the Firm

Approximately 10 percent of the HRSP firms report that they have no formal HRIS unit, but, for those that do, it can be located in various places. Most of the units (73.5 percent) reside in HR, but some (8.4 percent) are a part of information services, some (1.8 percent) can be found in the payroll section of the accounting department, and some (4.9 percent) are located elsewhere such as outside service organizations. Our description will assume that the HRIS is a part of HR.

The Location of the HRIS within HR

The most popular arrangement is for the HRIS to report directly to the HR director (48.3 percent), but other possibilities exist. In some firms, HRIS is a subunit of another HR group such as compensation and benefits (20.1 percent), or HR planning (2.5 percent).

The number of full-time HRIS employees ranges from 0 to 260, but the HRIS unit is typically not divided into smaller subunits. That is the situation found in 65.9 percent of the HRSP firms.

Most of the HRIS employees are information specialists, augmented by managers and staff members. Table 20.1 shows the average number of employees in each group.

THE EVOLUTION OF THE HRIS

Early personnel systems stored employee data in paper files located in the personnel department. When firms obtained punched card machines, the files were moved to the data processing department (later to be named IS), and converted to punched card form. When computers replaced the punched card machines, the personnel data was converted to magnetic tape and disk.

	Category	Average Number
TABLE 20.1 Categories of HRIS Employees	Programmer/Analysts	5.87
	Data entry/terminal operator	4.28
	Systems analysts	4.20
	Specialists/technicians	3.49
	Supervisors/administrators	3.08
	Managers	1.87
	Directors	1.45
	Others	5.53

Source: *1990–1991 Systems Survey* (Dallas, TX: The Association of Human Resource Systems Professionals, 1991), p. 11. Reprinted with permission.

The Influence of Government Legislation

Until the 1980s, management did not give personnel data the attention that it deserved. The maintenance of the data was considered to be nothing more than a necessary task. Management did not view the data as a conceptual system for use in managing the personnel.

The stimulus for elevating the status of personnel data was provided by federal government legislation such as EEO (Equal Employment Opportunity), OSHA (Occupational Safety and Health Administration), and AAP (Affirmative Action Program), enacted during the 1960s and 70s. Firms were required to provide the federal government with statistics that showed the extent to which the firms' personnel practices conformed to the laws. The firms quickly learned that they could not keep up with the increasing reporting requirements without the aid of computer-based systems.

The firm's top management began allocating additional resources to the development of information-oriented personnel systems. The new systems were developed by information specialists from information services, working with users in HR. The processing was done on the large-scale computers located in IS. This situation persisted until the late 1970s, when an innovation in computing technology gave birth to the HRIS as it is known today.

The Influence of the Microcomputer

When microcomputers came onto the scene, HR began installing them in their area. Some were used in a stand-alone manner, and some were networked together to form LANs, or to tie in to the firm's central computing facility. Some HR organizations even installed their own minicomputers and even mainframes.

The HRSP firms report an average of 37.9 micros dedicated to the HRIS, with slightly more than 40 percent being networked. There are also keyboard terminals (34.1 per firm), as well as workstations (an average of 13.8). The average of 3.7 minicomputers and 2.4 mainframes emphasize the huge hardware accumulations in the larger units.

A MODEL OF A HUMAN RESOURCE INFORMATION SYSTEM

One feature of the HRIS that distinguishes it from other functional information systems is the wide variety of applications that are performed. Figure 20.2 gives you an idea of the variety of applications that are possible. This figure is typical of the many HRIS models that have been developed in an effort to come to grips with the diversity of the applications.

In devising our model of an HRIS, we use the same general format of input subsystems, database, and output subsystems that we have used for the other functional areas. The input subsystems are the standard combination of data processing, research, and intelligence. In most firms the database is housed in computer storage. Only 5.7 percent of the HRSP firms reported using a noncomputer database. The output subsystems use the classification of applications, which has been adopted by HRSP. These input, storage, and output components form the HRIS model, which appears in Figure 20.3.

DATA PROCESSING SUBSYSTEM

The database of human resources data and information exists in two basic forms—personnel records and accounting records.

Personnel records contain relatively permanent, nonfinancial data concerning each employee, such as name, sex, date of birth, education, and employment history. These personnel records are created by HR at the time of employment and are kept current as long as the employees work for the firm. Similar records are also kept for retired employees.

Accounting records contain primarily financial data, which tends to be more dynamic than that of the personnel records. Accounting records contain data such as hourly rate, monthly salary, current gross earnings, and year-to-date income tax.

The data processing subsystem makes the accounting data available to the HRIS so that the database contains a complete picture of the personnel resource—financial as well as nonfinancial.

Although the flow of accounting data is important, it is not as important to

FIGURE 20.2

The HRIS Applications Network

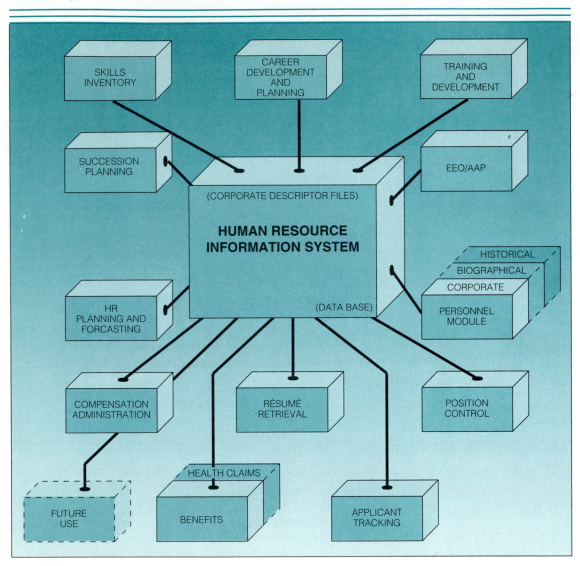

the HRIS as it once was. At one time, payroll was a major HR application, and the data processing subsystem provided the input. However, the responsibility for payroll has gradually been assumed by the accounting department, and now management of the payroll data is no longer an HRIS responsibility in many firms. Figure 20.4 shows payroll data management to be ranked seventeenth in a list of eighteen HRIS responsibilities as reported in the 1990-91 HRSP survey. However,

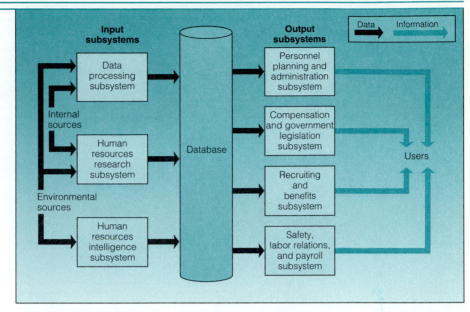

FIGURE 20.3

A Model of a Human Resource Information System

regardless of its low ranking, the graph shows payroll to be important for a large number of firms.

HUMAN RESOURCES RESEARCH SUBSYSTEM

The human resources research subsystem gathers data by means of special research projects. Examples of such research are succession studies, job analyses and evaluations, and grievance studies.

- **Succession studies** are conducted for the purpose of identifying persons in the firm who are candidates for positions becoming available. Perhaps a department head is retiring, and top management wants to know who can be considered for promotion to that position.
- **Job analyses and evaluations** study each job in an area for the purpose of defining its scope and identifying the knowledge and skills that are required.
- **Grievance studies** follow up on complaints filed by employees for a variety of reasons.

In each of these examples, a need exists for certain information that cannot be produced from the HRIS database, and a special study is conducted to gather the data.

FIGURE 20.4

HRIS Responsibilities

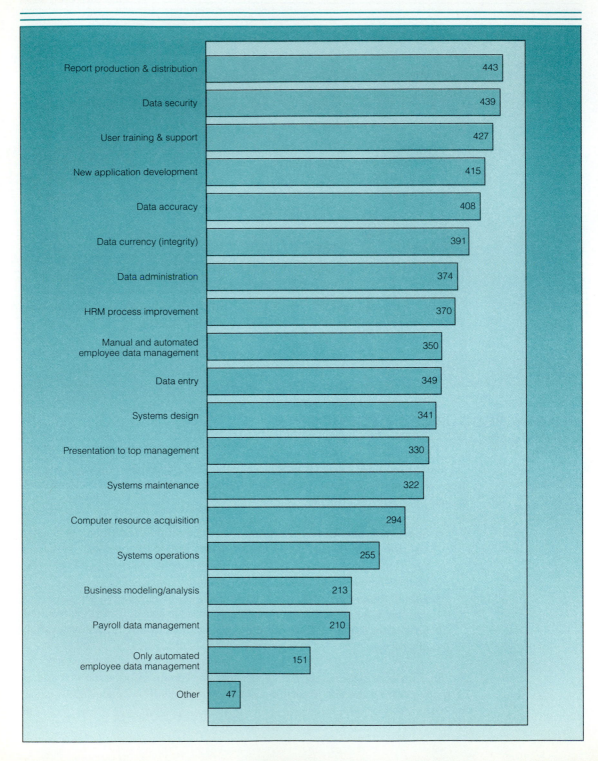

Category	Value
Report production & distribution	443
Data security	439
User training & support	427
New application development	415
Data accuracy	408
Data currency (integrity)	391
Data administration	374
HRM process improvement	370
Manual and automated employee data management	350
Data entry	349
Systems design	341
Presentation to top management	330
Systems maintenance	322
Computer resource acquisition	294
Systems operations	255
Business modeling/analysis	213
Payroll data management	210
Only automated employee data management	151
Other	47

HUMAN RESOURCES INTELLIGENCE SUBSYSTEM

The human resources intelligence subsystem gathers data, relating to human resources, from the firm's environment. Environmental elements that provide this data include the government, suppliers, labor unions, the local community, the financial community, and competitors.

- **Government Intelligence**   The government provides data and information that assist the firm in complying with the various employment laws.
- **Supplier Intelligence**   The suppliers include other firms such as insurance companies, which provide employee benefits, and university placement centers and employment agencies, which serve as sources of new employees. These suppliers provide data and information that enable the firm to manage its human resources.
- **Labor Union Intelligence**   Labor unions provide data and information that are used in administering the labor contracts between the unions and the firm.
- **Local Community Intelligence**   The local community provides information that describes local resources such as housing, education, and recreation. This information is used in recruiting prospective employees and in integrating current employees into the community.
- **Financial Community Intelligence**   The financial community provides economic data and information that are used in personnel planning.
- **Competitive Intelligence**   In certain industries where highly specialized knowledge and skills are required, such as the computer industry, there is a frequent flow of personnel from one competitive firm to another. Some firms regard their competitors as excellent sources of personnel, and gather information concerning their competitors' personnel practices, and perhaps even information on individuals who are potential recruits.

Much of this environmental intelligence is gathered by means of informal systems, such as word of mouth, but an increasing volume is being provided by formal, computer-based systems.

Environmental Human Resources Databases[2]

There are over 150 U.S. suppliers of computer-based resume databases that firms can use in their recruiting programs. These databases exist in five categories:

- **Executive Search Firm Databases**   Executive search firms specialize in finding applicants for executive positions. Access to a search firm's database is restricted to the firm's own recruiters, or to recruiters of other similar firms that form a tightly knit network.

---

[2] This section is based on Rod Wilis, "Recruitment: Playing the Database Game," *Personnel* 67 (May 1990), 25–29.

- **University Databases**   Approximately 200 colleges and universities make resume databases available to recruiters as a service to their graduating students and alumni who are seeking employment.
- **Employment Agency Databases**   Some of the larger employment agencies such as Snelling & Snelling maintain their own databases. Other databases are for the use of specified agencies that form a network. Access to this category of databases is not as restrictive as the first two types.
- **Public Access Databases**   These databases are available to any user for a fee. One of the largest is the Career Placement Registry that is accessed through the DIALOG Information Services network. Approximately 60 percent of the resumes are for students, and access fees range from $12 for a student to $45 for a candidate in the $45,000 salary range.
- **Corporate Job Banks**   Several large firms such as IBM, Hewlett-Packard, Travelers, and Wells Fargo maintain their own databases of persons who can work as temporary employees. The firms use the job banks when finding temporary replacements for regular employees who are sick, taking maternity leave, going on vacation, and so on.

These recruiting databases represent formal systems for gathering intelligence from the firm's suppliers. Similar formal systems can be used with the government and financial community.

THE HRIS DATABASE

The increasing complexity of personnel-related issues, caused by mounting government legislation and an expanding selection of benefits, has made it almost a necessity to maintain the data in the computer. For the computer-based HR database, several alternatives exist in terms of database contents, location, management, and data entry.

Database Contents

The HRIS database can contain data describing not only employees, but also organizations and individuals in the firm's environment, which influence the human resource in some way.

Employee Data   Most of the HRIS database contains data concerning the firm's current employees. In 82.5 percent of the HRSP firms, employee data is the only type that is maintained, but hundreds of data elements can be stored for each employee. Table 20.2 provides a sample of the wide variety of data that is possible.

Nonemployee Data   When asked to describe nonemployee data in their databases, 8 percent of the HRSP respondents identified data that describes *organizations* in the firm's environment such as employment agencies, colleges and uni-

TABLE 20.2
Sample HRIS
Database
Contents

Address (work)
Address (home)
Birthdate
Child support deductions
Citizenship
Claim pending (description)
Claim pending (outcome)
Claim pending (court)
Claim pending (date)
Date on current job
Department
Dependent (sex)
Dependent (number of)
Dependent (relationship)
Dependent (birthdate)
Dependent (name)
Discipline (appeal date)
Discipline (appeal outcome)
Discipline (date of charge)
Discipline (hearing date)
Discipline (outcome)
Discipline (type of charge)
Division
Driver's license (number)
Driver's license (state)
Driver's license (expir. date)
Education in progress (date)
Education in progress (type)
Educational degree (date)
Educational degree (type)
Educational major
Educational minor
Educational level attained
EEO-1 code
Emergency contact (phone)
Emergency contact (name)
Emergency contact (relation)
Emergency contact (address)
Employee weight
Employee number
Employee height
Employee date of birth
Federal job code
Full-time/part-time

Grievance (type)
Grievance (outcome)
Grievance (filing date)
Handicap status
Health plan coverage
Health plan (# dependents)
Injury (date)
Injury (type)
Job location
Job preference
Job position number
Job title
Leave of absence (start date)
Leave of absence (end date)
Leave of absence (type)
Life insurance coverage
Marital status
Marriage date
Medical exam (date)
Medical exam (restrictions)
Medical exam (blood type)
Medical exam (outcome)
Miscellaneous deductions
Name
Pay status
Pension plan
Performance rating
Performance increase ($)
Performance increase (%)
Phone number (work)
Phone number (home)
Prior service (hire date)
Prior service (termination date)
Professional license (type)
Professional license (date)
Race
Religious preference
Salary
Salary (previous)
Salary (change date)
Salary (change reason)
Salary (change type)
Schools attended
Service date

Service branch
Service discharge type
Service ending rank
Service discharge date
Sex
Sick leave (used)
Sick leave (available)
Skill function (type)
Skill subfunction (type)
Skill (number of years)
Skill (proficiency level)
Skill (date last used)
Skill (location)
Skill (supervisory)
Social security number
Spouse's employment
Spouse's date of death
Spouse's name
Spouse's birthdate
Spouse's sex
Spouse's social security
number
Start date
Stock plan membership
Supervisor's name
Supervisor's work address
Supervisor's work phone
Supervisor's title
Termination (date)
Termination (reason)
Training schools (attended)
Training schools (date)
Training schools (held)
Training schools (completed)
Transfer date
Transfer reason
Union code
Union deductions
United Way deductions
Vacation leave (available)
Vacation leave (used)
Veteran status

Based on: Cynthia D. Fisher, Lyle Schoenfeldt, and James B. Shaw, *Human Resources Management* (Boston, Mass.: Houghton Mifflin 1990), p. 299.

versities, labor unions, and governments. Also identified was data describing *individuals* such as applicants, dependents, beneficiaries, and survivors.

Location of the HRIS Database

In the HRSP firms, most of the HRIS databases are housed in the firms' central computers, but other databases reside in HR, in other functional areas, and in outside service centers. Figure 20.5 illustrates the relative popularity of these locations. As the trend to organizational end-user computing continues, it is expected that more databases will be shifted from their central location to HR.

Database Management Software

HRIS units have implemented database management systems (DBMSs) to manage their HRIS databases. Figure 20.6 lists the more popular DBMSs, as reported by the HRSP study. IMS, FOCUS, and DB2 are all mainframe DBMSs, and their top rankings emphasize the key role that mainframes play in the HRIS. dBASE is the most popular microcompter-based system. The 194 systems listed in the "Other" category indicate the wide variety of software that is in use.

Data Entry

The data is entered into the database from several sources, according to the HRSP study. Nonmanagers within HR are the most popular source (86.9 percent of the

FIGURE 20.5

Possible HRIS Database Locations

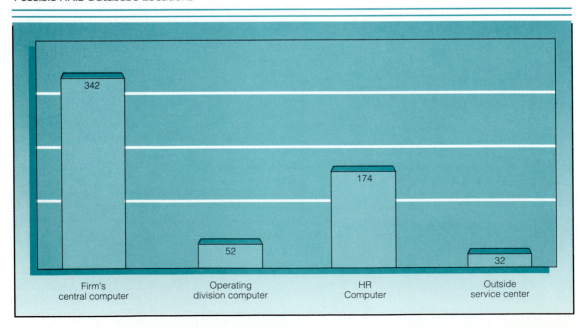

Firm's central computer	Operating division computer	HR Computer	Outside service center
342	52	174	32

firms), followed by nonmanagers outside of HR (36.1 percent), managers outside of HR (7.8 percent), and managers within HR (30.8 percent). Data entry from the environment is still relatively rare, being reported by only 24.2 percent of the firms.

HRIS OUTPUT

In the HRSP firms, 65.3 percent of the users are located within HR, 29.1 percent are elsewhere in the firm, and 10.2 percent are in the firm's environment. Figure 20.7 shows that HR managers, including the HR director, use the HRIS more fre-

FIGURE 20.6
HRIS Database Management Systems

Number	DBMS
112	IMS
108	FOCUS
87	DB2
86	dBASE
69	Revelation
51	IDMS
27	Mark IV, V
27	Rbase
22	NOMAD
18	ADABAS
14	RAMIS
11	IDEAL/DataCOM
5	INQUIRE
194	Other

FIGURE 20.7

Users of HRIS
Output

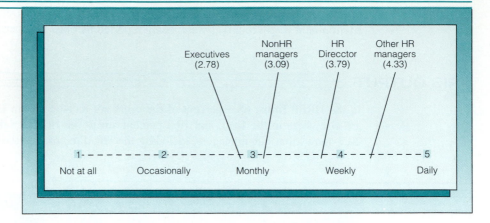

quently than do the firm's executives and managers outside of HR. The HR managers tend to use the HRIS on a weekly basis, whereas the firm's other managers are more likely to follow a monthly routine.

Basic Forms of Output

The HRIS users usually receive their output in the form of periodic reports and responses to database queries. Mathematical models are used to some extent, and there is some use of expert systems. Figure 20.8 shows the percentage of firms reporting each of the output types.

HRIS Software

The output subsystem software can be in a prewritten form that is purchased from software suppliers, or it can be developed within the firm. More custom software is developed jointly by HR and IS than by HR or IS alone, and it is least likely to be produced by outside firms.

Varieties of Software

We have seen that HRIS users demand information on a wide variety of applications. These applications are packaged in the four HRIS output subsystems.

Each of the subsystems contains multiple applications. Some of the applications are well established, and others are in the process of development. Also, some of the applications are part of the core HRIS, and others are stand alone. The **core HRIS** is an integration of software subsystems that function as a unit. The subsystems share a common database, and the outputs of one system serve as inputs to another. A **stand-alone system,** on the other hand, operates apart from other systems. A stand-alone system is not dependent on other systems for a database, inputs, or outputs.

FIGURE 20.8

Basic Forms of
HRIS Output

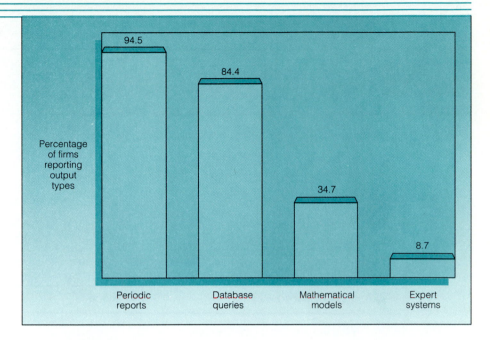

Percentage of firms reporting output types

94.5 — Periodic reports

84.4 — Database queries

34.7 — Mathematical models

8.7 — Expert systems

The descriptions of the four output subsystems are illustrated with tables. The upper portion of each table reveals the extent to which the applications have been achieved, and the lower portion reports on the separation between core HRIS and stand-alone versions.

PERSONNEL PLANNING AND ADMINISTRATION SUBSYSTEM

Table 20.3 lists the applications that are involved with the planning for future personnel needs, and the administration of the firm's current workforce.

We see that the most popular applications are performance appraisal, organization charting, and training. Most of the development effort is aimed at training, position control, skills/competency, and succession, with more than one hundred firms currently involved in developing those applications.

The three applications that have been achieved to the least degree—succession, planning, and workforce models—all take a future orientation. From this ranking, it is easy to see that computer systems are used more for managing the current workforce than in planning future personnel needs.

The lower portion of the table reveals that most of the applications are part

TABLE 20.3
Applications of the Personnel Planning and Administration Subsystem

In Use	Being Developed	Application
244	60	Performance appraisal
238	58	Organization charting
216	102	Training
191	69	Attendance
177	108	Position control
115	107	Skills/competency
110	102	Succession
68	61	Planning
66	29	Workforce models

Part of core HRIS	Stand Alone	Application
242	48	Performance appraisal
230	40	Position control
187	113	Training
173	74	Attendance
172	37	Skills/competency
72	45	Planning
63	121	Succession
59	237	Organization charting
55	33	Workforce models

Source: *1990–1991 Systems Survey* (Dallas, TX: The Association of Human Resource Systems Professionals, 1991) p. 18. Reprinted with permission.

of the core HRIS, with only training, succession, and organization charting seeing heavy use as stand-alone systems. Organization charting is a good example of stand-alone software. There are many microcomputer-based packages on the market that draw organization charts, and do nothing else.

In summary, the applications that enable management to plan and administer the firm's personnel are still in the process of development in many firms, and most fit within the core HRIS.

COMPENSATION AND GOVERNMENT
LEGISLATION SUBSYSTEM

The compensation and government legislation subsystem reflects the strength of government influence on the HRIS, being the output subsystem with the largest number of installed applications. As shown in the upper portion of Table 20.4, most of the applications are up and running with more than three out of every four HRSP firms currently handling merit increases and maintaining EEO records. Those are the highest percentages of any HRIS applications. EEO analysis, executive compensation, salary forecasting, and bonus incentives also represent well-established applications. Job analysis/evaluation is the only area where any real developmental

TABLE 20.4
Applications of the Compensation and Government Legislation Subsystem

In Use	Being Developed	Application
404	36	Merit increases
402	43	EEO records
352	47	EEO analysis
273	39	Executive compensation
237	47	Salary forecast
230	31	Bonus incentives
176	66	Job analysis/evaluation
165	13	Union increases

Part of core HRIS	Stand Alone	Application
373	58	EEO records
338	79	Merit increases
277	103	EEO analysis
172	104	Salary forecast
166	134	Executive compensation
157	21	Union increases
144	101	Bonus incentives
105	124	Job analysis/evaluation

Source: *1990–1991 Systems Survey* (Dallas, TX: The Association of Human Resource Systems Professionals, 1991), p. 19. Reprinted with permission.

work is being applied. In the lower listing, all of the applications are included in core systems to a great extent, but many also function in a stand-alone manner.

RECRUITING AND BENEFITS SUBSYSTEM

The recruiting and benefits subsystem, shown in Table 20.5, handles the increasingly complex benefit plans. The current trend is to offer **flexible benefits,** which

TABLE 20.5
Applications of the Recruiting and Benefits Subsystem

In Use	Being Developed	Application
275	38	Defined contribution
270	47	Defined benefits
235	98	Application tracking
234	57	Benefit statements
195	55	Flexible benefits
149	16	Stock purchase
121	33	Relocation
111	56	Internal search
88	11	Claims processing

Part of core HRIS	Stand Alone	Application
204	80	Defined benefits
192	87	Defined contribution
171	94	Benefit statements
162	65	Flexible benefits
143	164	Applicant tracking
115	44	Internal search
80	68	Stock purchase
46	101	Relocation
34	56	Claims processing

Source: *1990–1991 Systems Survey* (Dallas, TX: The Association of Human Resource Systems Professionals, 1991), p. 20. Reprinted with permission.

include a menu of benefits from which the employees can choose. The employees tailor their benefits to meet their own particular needs.

In addition to the variety of the benefit plans, the complexity of some makes them extremely difficult to administer. Defined contribution, defined benefits, and stock purchase plans represent real challenges, even for computer-based systems.

As a rule, firms are generally satisfied with these applications, and they are usually a part of the core HRIS. Applicant tracking and relocation are more likely to function in a stand-alone manner than be a part of the core.

SAFETY, LABOR RELATIONS, AND PAYROLL SUBSYSTEM

The fourth output subsystem has the least amount of activity. Table 20.6 shows that the only application to have been implemented to any extent is payroll. Although the accounting department has assumed the responsibility for the overall payroll system in most firms, HR is still involved to some degree.

TABLE 20.6 Applications of the Safety, Labor Relations, and Payroll Subsystem

In Use	Being Developed	Application
389	21	Payroll
109	44	Accidents
102	41	Health records
80	32	Toxic substance
66	31	Grievances
63	39	Disciplinary

Part of core HRIS	Stand Alone	Application
289	97	Payroll
66	28	Disciplinary
65	67	Health records
62	86	Accidents
49	44	Grievances
30	76	Toxic substance

Source: *1990–1991 Systems Survey* (Dallas, TX: The Association of Human Resources Systems Professionals, 1991), p. 21. Reprinted with permission.

The nonpayroll applications have not only failed to achieve a high level of implementation, but they are not stimulating much developmental activity. This situation indicates a relatively low level of interest by management in adding them to the HRIS portfolio.

Some of the nonpayroll applications are those that are identifiable with a concern for the health and safety of the workers. Although not all firms have problems with accidents and toxic substance, only 30 percent of the HRSP reporting firms have made efforts to implement systems that maintain health records.

APPLICATIONS INTEGRATION

Surprisingly, the HRSP respondents reported that only 70.9 percent of their applications are computer-based. This leaves a large number that are still being performed manually or with noncomputer technology. In most of the firms, the applications that are on the computer are integrated. Fifty-three firms (10.3 percent) reported *all* applications to be integrated, and 227 firms (44.2 percent) claim that *most* are. Firm size has no affect on the integration, but age of the HRIS does. The newer HRISs are more likely to be integrated.

CURRENT STATUS OF THE HRIS

When asked how top management views the HRIS, the HRSP respondents gave the answers shown in Figure 20.9. In 242 (47.2 percent) of the firms the executives value the HRIS on a par with other functional systems. This is a healthy situation, and the twenty-nine firms where the HRIS enjoys a preferred position is encouraging. But, the 225 firms where the HRIS is viewed as having less value than the other systems is distressing to those who regard the firm's personnel as its most valuable physical resource.

Since HRIS was relatively late in jumping on the computer bandwagon it could well be the functional area with the greatest potential for applying the computer to problem solving. The HRIS is aimed at the management functions of organizing, staffing, and directing, which have been largely ignored by other information systems.

SUMMARY

The HR function has four primary activities—recruiting and hiring, educating and training, managing employee related data, and termination and benefit administration. The conceptual system that helps the firm's managers manage the personnel resource is called the human resource information system, or HRIS. A few firms have no computer-based HRIS, but those that do usually locate it in HR. In some firms, HRIS is a part of another unit such as IS or accounting. Within HR, HRIS

FIGURE 20.9

Executive Perception of HRIS Value

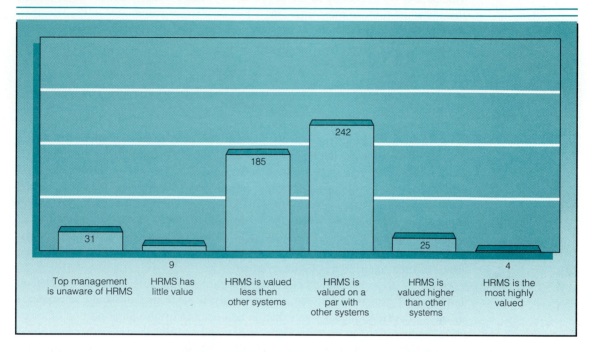

31	9	185	242	25	4
Top management is unaware of HRMS	HRMS has little value	HRMS is valued less then other systems	HRMS is valued on a par with other systems	HRMS is valued higher than other systems	HRMS is the most highly valued

usually reports to the HR director and is not subdivided into smaller units. The personnel within HRIS include managers and all types of information specialists.

Early personnel systems consisted of paper files maintained in HR, but the introduction of punched card machines caused the files to be moved to the data processing department. When the computer came along, the punched card files were converted to magnetic tape and disk, and remained in information services.

During recent years, two influences have had a big effect on the HRIS. First, government legislation called top managements' attention to the need for a good conceptual human resource system. Second, the microcomputer made it possible for HR units to have their own hardware and software—an expression of end-user computing. These two influences have served to heighten the visibility of HRIS at the strategic management level, and have triggered a migration of human resource applications from IS to HR.

The HRIS model includes three input subsystems: data processing, human resources research, and human resources intelligence. The data processing subsystem provides personnel data that is expressed in financial terms. Human resources research augments the database with data and information acquired through special research projects. Human resources intelligence gathers data and information from all of the environmental elements except the stockholders and owners, and the customers.

The HRIS database contains data not only on the employees but also on individuals and organizations in the firm's environment, which exert an influence on the personnel flow. In most firms, the HRIS database is maintained in IS. The most popular DBMSs are those of mainframe systems. The data can be entered by both managers and nonmangers in the firm, and, to a lesser extent, by elements in the environment.

HRIS output is most often in the form of periodic reports and database queries, but use is also made of mathematical models and expert systems. The outputs are produced by both custom and prewritten software, with the custom software most often coming as a joint effort by IS and HR.

Of the four output subsystems, the compensation and government legislation subsystem has enjoyed the widest implementation. The safety, labor relations, and payroll subsystem has seen the least operational use. The personnel planning and administration subsystem is attracting considerable developmental work, and the software is usually part of the core HRIS. The recruiting and benefits subsystem emphasizes the benefits, which have become extremely complex to administer. Many of the recruiting and benefits applications are stand alone. In spite of the large numbers of stand-alone systems, over half the HRSP firms report that most or all of their applications are integrated.

The 1980s saw the HRIS emerge as a legitimate functional information system, but it is still struggling for recognition. In the HRSP firms that would be expected to accord the HRIS higher status than in nonmember firms a large portion of executives are perceived to view the HRIS as having less value than the other functional systems. Much potential exists for the HRIS, but in order for that potential to be achieved, top management must increase its level of support.

KEY TERMS

human resources

human resource information system (HRIS),
    human resource management system
    (HRMS)

core HRIS

stand-alone system

KEY CONCEPTS

Human resources as a functional area that facilitates the flow of personnel through the firm

The HRIS as an organizational unit consisting of personnel who process human resource data using both computer and noncomputer technologies

The flow of human resource intelligence to the firm from most of the environmental elements

HR software consisting of both a core HRIS and stand-alone systems

How the mix of HR applications reflects both environmental influence and executive values

The opportunity for the HRIS to succeed in providing support for organizing, staffing, and directing, where the other information systems have failed

QUESTIONS

1. What are the four main activities that are performed by HR?

2. During which phase of the SLC can HR assist IS by performing one of its four main activities? What is the activity?

3. Why would a firm want to conduct a termination interview? Why would it be better for HR, rather than the employee's unit, to do it?

4. Give two reasons why you should not think of the HRIS as strictly a computer-based system.

5. Explain why punched card machines and early computers did little to enhance the status of HR within the firm.

6. Explain what someone might be talking about when they say: "Management did not decide to have an HRIS. It was forced on them."

7. What sort of hardware can you expect to find in the HRIS?

8. What are the two basic types of data that describe a firm's personnel? What are the characteristics of each?

9. Why does the HRIS rely less on accounting data than it once did?

10. What triggers an HR research project?

11. Assume that you are a recruiter who is looking for sales trainees with college degrees in marketing. Identify the environmental HR databases that you could use.

12. On the average, how often do the firm's executives ask for information from the HRIS?

13. Which form of output is the most popular with HRIS users? Which is the least popular?

14. Have most firms implemented personnel planning and administration subsystems, or are they in the process of developing them?

15. Which of the output subsystems has been implemented by most of the HRSP firms? Explain why.

16. What innovation in benefit plans has contributed to the complexity of the applications in the recruiting and benefits subsystem?

17. Which output subsystem has been implemented by the fewest HRSP firms? Can you explain why?

18. Why are the newer HRISs more likely to be integrated than the older ones?

19. Explain why the HRIS holds so much potential. Base your answer on Fayol's management functions.

TOPICS FOR DISCUSSION

1. Why would the HRSP members tend to rate the HRIS higher than nonmembers? Or, would they?

2. The text does not identify the firm's customers and the stockholders and owners as sources of HR intelligence. Can you think of any situations where that would not be the case?

3. Pick a large employer in your area, and identify the types of data that it would want to maintain in its database about your college.

4. Explain why a core HRIS would be better than using stand-alone systems. Explain why stand-alone systems would be best.

5. Explain why a firm's executives might value the HRIS lower than other systems such as the marketing information system.

PROBLEMS

1. Assume that your boss has asked you for suggestions concerning organizational charting software. Go to the library and research the subject. Write a memo identifying your source, or sources, and list three possible packages. for each package, give the name, the name and address of the supplier, the basic features, and the cost.

2. Assume that you are the HRIS manager, and that your company maintains a database of personnel data that is illustrated in Table 20.2. The HR director has requested a printed listing that shows the data elements for each employee that are relatively stable. That is, the elements are unlikely to change. Employee name is an example. Do not include data on nonemployees such as dependents. Prepare the layout of such a report, with report and column headings. Enter sample data for two employees.

Bill's Home Center

Bill's is a nationwide chain of building materials stores, geared to the do-it-yourself market. The headquarters is in Milwaukee, and you are applying for the position of Manager of Personnel Systems. Bill's uses the name Personnel Systems, or PS, rather than HRIS. PS reports to the Manager of Compensation and Benefits, who, in turn, reports to the Director of Personnel, Alma Bradley. Your interview is with Alma. Including Alma, there are eight managers and supervisors in Personnel, with the remaining eighteen employees divided almost equally between staff, secretarial, and clerical duties.

ALMA: Please call me Alma. We're on a first-name basis around here. Let me start by telling you about PS. PS consists of two full-time programmers, plus the manager position that we are hoping you can fill. The main function of PS is to serve as the interface between members of the Personnel Department who want computer support and our MIS Department. When the job request is fairly simple, such as the preparation of a special report, PS can provide what is needed. When the request is more complex, such as the design of a new system, PS forwards the request to the MIS Department. We have a policy that Personnel employees never contact MIS. They always go through PS. In fact, the Personnel employees regard PS as their own MIS department.

YOU: Does PS ever do any work for users outside of Personnel?

ALMA: Never. Any other requests within Bill's for personnel information is provided by MIS.

YOU: Does MIS always respond to your requests for help?

ALMA: No, the work is not automatically done. Before MIS can dedicate resources to a project, the project must be approved by the MIS committee. The MIS committee consists of the MIS Director, plus the managers of systems analysis, programming, and operations. There are no outside members. As far as our job requests go, MIS gives top priority to personnel systems that are required to comply with federal legislation, or to provide personnel information to Bill's parent company—Lombard Industries.

YOU: What about the two PS programmers? What languages do they use?

ALMA: They are not programmers in the true sense. They can't code in languages such as COBOL, for example. Rather, they are trained in the use of database query languages. The language that we use the most is FOCUS.

YOU: Do the programmers use FOCUS to access the Bill's central database from terminals?

ALMA: They do use terminals. We have two in PS—one for each of the programmers. But, the programmers don't access the central database. Instead, each week, MIS downloads selected personnel data to a personnel database that we use for report preparation.

YOU: So, the data that is used for report preparation might be a week old.

ALMA: That is correct. But, we haven't had too many complaints. The data really doesn't change that much from one week to the next.

YOU: Other than the two terminals, what computing equipment is located in Personnel?

ALMA: We have eight PCs. They belong to those people who have expressed an interest in using them. The machines are not networked. There is no sharing of software and data.

YOU: How does MIS feel about you doing your own computing? Are they supportive?

ALMA: Oh, they're all for it. They have more work than they can handle. They would be happy if we did it all.

YOU: What about the Bill's executives? What is their attitude about computer support?

ALMA: They've been the motivating force all along. Our executive committee, of which I am a member, consistently approves the requests by MIS for more hardware, software, and people. I would characterize the environment here at Bill's as very conducive to computing.

YOU: Is there a long-range, strategic plan for MIS?

ALMA: There is one for MIS, but it doesn't include any other areas. Our corporate strategy is to provide computer support on a centralized basis, and we really do not encourage user areas to expand their computing operations.

YOU: What about you, Alma? Would you like for PS to handle all of the requests for personnel information, not only within Personnel, but throughout Bill's?

ALMA: Certainly, I would prefer that we function in a full-service capacity but we simply do not have the resources. At least, not at the present time. If you decide to take the job, one of the first things I want you to do is help me draft a memo to the executive committee, recommending changes in our PS operation. Now, the key question? Do you accept the job?

YOU: I'm going to have to sleep on it. It's a big decision.

Assignments

1. Write a letter to Alma, advising her whether you will accept the job. Base your decision on the opportunity that exists in Bill's for a successful career beginning as HRIS manager. Give your reasons for acceptance or rejection.

2. Assume that you do accept the job. (Don't let this assignment influence your decision on the first one.) Write a memo that Alma can present to the executive committee, requesting changes in the PS operation.

SELECTED BIBLIOGRAPHY

Cholak, Paul M., and Simon, Sidney H. "HRIS Asks, 'Who's the Boss?'" *Personnel Journal* 70 (August 1991): 74–76.

Davis, Leila. "On the Fast Track to HR Integration." *Datamation* 37 (September 15, 1991): 61*ff.*

DeSanctis, Gerardine. "Human Resource Information Systems: A Current Assessment." *MIS Quarterly* 10 (March 1986): 15–26.

Duff, Kenneth. "HR-Link: An HRIS from Apple Canada." *Personnel* 67 (May 1990): 6*ff.*

Harris, Donald. "Beyond the Basics: New HRIS Developments." *Personnel* 63 (January 1986): 49–56.

"HRIS Buyers' Guide." *Personnel Journal* 70 (May 1992): 126–37.

Leonard, Bill. "The Myth of the Integrated HRIS." *Personnel Journal* 70 (September 1991): 113–15.

Manzini, Andrew O., and Gridley, John D. *Integrating Human Resources and Strategic Business Planning.* New York: American Management Association, 1986. Pp. 31–63.

McElroy, John. "The HRIS As An Agent of Change." *Personnel Journal* 70 (May 1991): 105*ff.*

Nardoni, Ren. "Planning Promotes HRIS Success." *Personnel Journal* 70 (January 1992): 61*ff.*

Perry, Steve. "An HRIS for the '90s." *Personnel Journal* 69 (August 1990): 75–78.

Simon, Sidney H. "The HRIS: What Capabilities Must It Have?" *Personnel* 60 (September–October 1983): 36–49.

Sirageldin, Camelia. "Training Drives the HRIS." *Personnel* 67 (May 1990): 15*ff.*

Stamps, David. "Human Resources: A Strategic Partner or IS Burden? *Datamation* 36 (June 1, 1990): 47*ff.*

Stright, Jr., Jay F. "Creating Chevron's HRMS: An Epic Tale." *Personnel Journal* 69 (June 1990): 72–81.

Taylor, G. Stephen, and Davis, J. Stephen. "Individual Privacy and Computer-Based Human Resource Information Systems." *Journal of Business Ethics* 8 (1989): 569–76.

Travis, William I. "How to Justify a Human Resources Information System." *Personnel Journal* 67 (February 1988): 83–86.

Part VI

FORCES THAT ARE INFLUENCING THE FUTURE

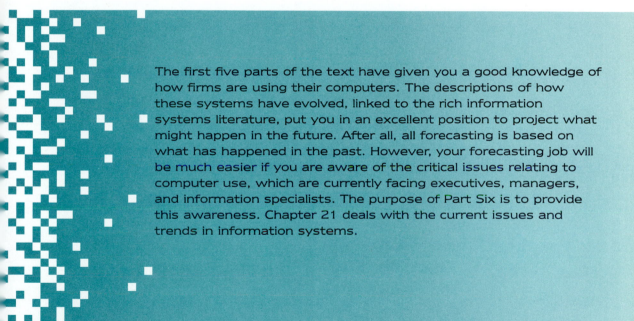

The first five parts of the text have given you a good knowledge of how firms are using their computers. The descriptions of how these systems have evolved, linked to the rich information systems literature, put you in an excellent position to project what might happen in the future. After all, all forecasting is based on what has happened in the past. However, your forecasting job will be much easier if you are aware of the critical issues relating to computer use, which are currently facing executives, managers, and information specialists. The purpose of Part Six is to provide this awareness. Chapter 21 deals with the current issues and trends in information systems.

Chapter 21

Current Issues and Trends in Information Systems

LEARNING OBJECTIVES

After studying this chapter, you should:

- Be familiar with some techniques that firms use in justifying expenditures on computing
- Know some strategies that firms can use to increase the contribution of information systems to profitability
- Know three strategies for handling outdated systems
- Understand how firms are dealing with new threats to systems security, such as computer viruses
- Recognize the responsibility of both government and industry to use their information resources in an ethical way

INTRODUCTION

Managers initially sought to justify computing expenditures on a strictly economic basis, using such techniques as break-even analysis, payback analysis, and net present value. The difficulty of placing a value on information forced the managers to also use noneconomic techniques such as the portfolio approach, information economics, and surrogate measures.

In today's hard economic times, executives are looking for ways to control the costs of information services. There are four main strategies that can be followed—consolidation, downsizing, outsourcing, and insourcing. All have a long-term impact on the firm's information resources.

One reason for the high cost of information resources is the need to respond to outdated systems. Firms are responding with three new strategies. Reverse engineering solves the problem of poor system documentation, and restructuring converts antiquated systems into a structured form. Reengineering builds on reverse engineereing and restructuring to repeat the entire SDLC.

All of these strategies that are being applied by the firm are taking place within environmental constraints. One constraint exists in the form of threats to the firm's computer security. The other represents expectations of ethical computer use.

These are some of the more critical issues facing computing today. As you pursue your career as a manager or information specialist, you will be expected to find solutions. This will be a big challenge, but the opportunity for rewards will be great.

ECONOMIC JUSTIFICATION

When management seeks justification of information resources, it looks for data to support its decisions. **Economic justification** is the comparison of monetary costs and benefits as a means of justifying an action. The term **cost-benefit analysis** is also used. When economic justification is applied to computing expenditures, there are three popular approaches—break-even analysis, payback analysis, and net present value.

Break-even Analysis

Break-even analysis compares the cost of the new system to that of the current one and identifies the **break-even point.** That is the point in time at which the two costs are the same. Table 21.1 provides an illustration. The costs of the current system gradually increase, indicating an inability to efficiently handle the firm's growing operations. The costs of the new system are high in the beginning, reflecting the developmental effort. The time prior to the break-even point is the **investment period,** and the time after is the **return period.**

TABLE 21.1
The Break-even
Point Identifies
where the
Costs of the
New and Cur-
rent Systems
are Equal

Year	Month	Current system Costs*	New system Costs*	Difference
1	1	7	22	+15
1	2	7	24	+17
1	3	7	25	+18
1	4	7	25	+18
1	5	7	27	+20
1	6	8	29	+21
1	7	7	28	+21
1	8	8	26	+18
1	9	8	28	+20
1	10	8	22	+14
1	11	8	19	+11
1	12	8	15	+ 7
2	1	8	13	+ 5
2	2	8	13	+ 5
2	3	8	13	+ 5
2	4	9	13	+ 4
2	5	9	12	+ 3
2	6	10	12	+ 2
2	**7**	**10**	**10**	**0**
2	8	11	10	− 1
2	9	11	9	− 2
2	10	12	9	− 3
2	11	12	8	− 4
2	12	12	8	− 4

*Monthly costs and benefits in hundreds of dollars

Payback Analysis

Payback analysis compares the cumulative costs of the new system with its cumulative benefits. The point at which the two are the same is called the **payback point,** and the time that is required to reach the payback point is the **payback period.** Table 21.2 includes the formula that subtracts new system costs from new system benefits to obtain cumulative benefits. Initially, the cumulative benefits are negative because of the high developmental costs. The point at which the cumulative benefits turn positive is the payback point.

Net Present Value

Net present value (NPV) is the discounted current value of money that will be received in the future, taking into account a particular interest rate. For example,

TABLE 21.2

The Payback Point Identifies where the Cumulative Benefits of the New System Equal the Cumulative Costs

	Year*				
	1	2	3	4	5
Current system costs	9	12	15	22	29
New system costs	29	13	8	11	13
New system benefits	−21	− 1	+7	+11	+16
Cumulative benefits	−21	−22	−15	−4	+12

$$PBP = Y + \frac{C}{V}$$

Where: Y = The last year that the cumulative benefits of the new system were negative
C = The cumulative benefits of the new system for the last year that they were negative
V = The absolute value of the cumulative benefits of the new system for (1) the last year that they were negative, and (2) the first year that they are positive.

Using the data in the table, the payback period is computed as:

$$PBP = 4 + \frac{4}{4 + 12} = 4 + \frac{4}{16} = 4.25 \text{ years,}$$

or 4 years and 3 months

*Annual costs and benefits in thousands of dollars

if you want to receive $100 five years from now, and the interest rate is 12 percent, you need only invest $56.74 today. Said another way, when the interest rate is 12 percent, $100 five years from now is worth only $56.74 today. Since the returns from a computer project can come well into the future, NPV can be used to express those returns in current values. Table 21.3 uses the same data as Table 21.2, and shows how the use of NPV reduces the cumulative benefits and prolongs the payback period.

Putting Economic Feasibility in Perspective

Management prefers an economic justification for its actions, but this is not always possible when it comes to computing because of the difficulty in obtaining the data. The costs can usually be estimated fairly accurately, but the same does not hold true for the benefits. Data processing systems are the easiest to justify because their benefits usually come in such forms as reduced or avoided clerical costs, reduced inventory investment, and increased production efficiency. MISs, DSSs, and expert systems are another story because their benefits require that a value be placed on information, a task that is not easy to do.

TABLE 21.3
The Net Pres-
ent Value of the
New System

	Year*				
	1	2	3	4	5
Current system costs	9	12	15	22	29
New system costs	29	13	8	11	13
New system benefits	−21	− 1	+ 7	+11	+16
Discount percent	0.893	0.797	0.712	0.636	0.567
Discounted benefits	−18.8	− .8	+ 5.0	+ 7.0	+ 9.1
Cumulative discounted benefits	−18.8	−19.6	−14.6	− 7.6	+ 1.5

$$\text{Discounted PBP} = 4 + \frac{7.6}{9.1} = 4.83 \text{ years,}$$

or 4 years and 10 months

*Annual costs in thousands of dollars; annual interest = 0.12

NONECONOMIC JUSTIFICATION

The difficulty of measuring information value caused management to consider noneconomic factors when deciding whether to implement such systems as MISs, DSSs, and expert systems. **Noneconomic justification** is the use of data other than that expressed in monetary terms as a basis for an action. Many approaches have been devised for justifying a computing expenditure in noneconomic terms, but the three that we will describe are the portfolio approach, information economics, and surrogate measures.

The Portfolio Approach

The **portfolio approach** is based on the idea that evaluation should not be limited to a single application but, rather, should consider the firm's entire portfolio of applications.[1] The reasoning is the same that underlies portfolios of financial invest-ments—that certain components perform better or worse than others. The com-bined performance of all the components, however, is what counts.

In applying portfolio analysis, management employs a three-pronged strategy:[2]

1. Minimize the number of high risk projects.
2. Include some sure winners, even if their expected payoffs are not large.

[1] A description of the portfolio approach first appeared in F. Warren McFarlan, "Portfolio Approach to Information Systems," *Harvard Business Review* 59 (September–October 1981), 142–50.

[2] Lee L. Gremillion and Philip J. Pyburn, "Justifying Decision Support and Office Automation Systems," *Journal of Management Information Systems* 2 (Summer 1985), 15.

3. Scrap a project just as soon as the risk appears to be greater than the expected reward.

Portfolio analysis relieves management of the impossible task of justifying each and every computer project that comes along by focusing attention on overall performance.

Information Economics

Information economics recognizes that a system has the potential to achieve a wide range of values, and incur a wide range of risks.[3]

Potential System Values   A proposed computer-based system can provide value to the firm in ways that are not always obvious. For example, a system can:

- Provide information to the elements in the firm's environment.
- Support the firm's long-term strategy.
- Provide the firm with a competitive advantage.
- Enable management to track its critical activities.
- Enable management to respond quickly to competitive actions.
- Support the firm's strategic plan for information resources.

The more of these types of values that a potential system can deliver, the better its chances of being approved for development.

Potential System Risks   Attention should also be paid to the risks that might prevent a potential system from contributing to a strong portfolio. A proposed system should not:

- Support a risky business strategy.
- Depend on unproven capabilities within the firm.
- Depend on cooperation from multiple functional areas of the firm when that cooperation might be difficult to acheive.
- Be based on poorly defined user needs.
- Depend on new and untried technology.

The fewer of these risks that characterize a potential system, the better the chances of its development project being approved.

[3] Marilyn M. Parker and Robert J. Benson, "Information Economics: An Introduction," *Datamation* 33 (December 1, 1987), 86*ff*.

Surrogate Measures

Peter G. W. Keen, one of the founders of the DSS concept, identifies four levels of nonmonetary benefits that can be observed *after* implementation of a new application.[4] In the following order, the use of the computer as an information system can lead to:

1. **Management action**   There is evidence that managers take certain actions as a result of receiving information from the computer.
2. **Management change**   The managers change the ways that they perform their functions and play their roles.
3. **Increased use of decision-support tools**   Managers acquire terminals or micros for thier offices, learn how to use software such as electronic spreadsheets and graphics packages, and use the tools to solve problems.
4. **Organization change**   The computer provides information that is used to change the organization's structure or the makeup of its personnel.

Putting Noneconomic Feasibility in Perspective

Today's computer-based applications are so complex and are so intertwined with all of the firm's operations, that it is almost impossible to measure their contribution in dollars and cents. Therefore, indirect measures must be used. The situation is similar to that of advertising, where the firm's executives spend huge sums of money, not knowing exactly what benefits the ads bring. Many decisions to make computing expenditures are based on the executives' faith that the systems are essential to the firm's operations. The noneconomic measures are the basis for much of that faith.

THE INCREASING IMPORTANCE OF JUSTIFYING INFORMATION RESOURCES

For the first thirty years or so of the computer era, the firm's executives used the economic and noneconomic methods for justifying *single* computer projects, or applications. That effort continues, but the executives are also giving thought to justifying their *entire* information services operations. Two situations have spurred this critical analysis. First, the depressed economic conditions that began in the 1970s have caused firms to experience severe belt-tightening in terms of their costs. Second, a new class of computer service companies have come onto the scene, anxious to take over the firm's computing operations.

[4]Peter G. W. Keen, "Computer-Based Decision Aids: The Evaluation Problem," *Sloan Management Review* 16 (Spring 1975), 17–29.

STRATEGIES FOR REDUCING THE COSTS
OF INFORMATION SERVICES

As the firm's executives look for ways to cut corners in their computer operations, yet maintain the effectiveness, they consider four main strategies: consolidation, downsizing, outsourcing, and insourcing.[5]

Consolidation

A **consolidation** strategy can be followed by reducing the number of separate locations where information resources are located. The reasoning is that a few large concentrations of resources can operate more efficiently than can many smaller ones.

This strategy is easiest to achieve in terms of the firm's information services organization. This is where most of the resources are located, and they may be scattered over a wide area in the form of regional data centers and the like. Consolidation is more difficult to apply to information resources located in user areas, where any strategy that is perceived to constrain end-user computing is resisted.

The best example of successfully applying a strategy of consolidation in user areas is the information center. An **information center** is a special area, apart from the firm's data center, that is reserved for end users. The area contains hardware and software that end users prefer, such as terminals, micros, letter-quality printers, electronic spreadsheet packages, graphics packages, and desktop publishing packages. The information center is conveniently located for end users, and they are encouraged to use it.

Downsizing

Downsizing is the transfer of the firm's computer-based applications from large equipment configurations, such as mainframes, to smaller ones, such as microcomputers. The ingredient that makes this strategy possible is the tremendous processing power that is now available in micros. We saw this trend in our discussion of human resource information systems in the previous chapter.

Outsourcing

If downsizing has caused the hearts of CIOs to skip a beat for fear of losing their grip on the firm's computer operation, outsourcing has caused coronary arrest. **Outsourcing** is the contracting out of all or a portion of a firm's computer operation to an outside service organization.

---

[5] These strategies come from Mario M. Morino, "IS Cost Reduction: A Matter of Survival," *Datacenter Manager* 3 (July/August 1991), 31*ff*.

The Growth of Outsourcing   Although outsourcing is receiving much current attention, it is not a new concept. During the late 1960s, firms such as banks sold excess time on their computers in the form of timesharing services. Other organizations, which were given the name **computer utilities,** were formed to offer the timesharing service in the same manner as a utility company provides electricity, water, and gas.

It was during this period that Ross Perot formed Electronic Data Systems, or EDS. Perot convinced organizations such as life insurance companies and the federal government that his firm could process their data at a lower cost than they could, and many organizations took his offer.

Who Are the Outsourcers?   During the 1970s and 80s, attention shifted from timesharing to distributed processing, but firms such as EDS continued to provide computer services and became known as outsourcers. We can define an **outsourcer** as a computer services firm that performs part or all of a customer firm's computing for a long period of time, such as five or ten years, as specified by a written contract.

Outsourcing contracts can involve huge sums of money. The agreement between General Dynamics and Computer Sciences Corporation (CSC) was for $3 billion, and the EDS contract with Continental Airlines was for $2.1 billion.[6] However, the contract that shocked the computer industry was Kodak. In 1989, Kodak outsourced its computer operations to IBM, its applications development to Andersen Consulting, and its telecommunications and network management to Digital Equipment Corporation. At the time, Kodak was recognized as a model computing operation, and when they decided to go outsourcing, executives throughout North America took notice.

Outsourcing Services   The services offered by outsourcers include the following:[7]

- Data entry and simple processing
- Contract programming
- Facilities management
- Systems integration
- Support operations for maintenance, service, or disaster recovery

Facilities management (FM) is the complete operation of a computing center. **Systems integration (SI)** is the performance of all the tasks of the system devel-

---

[6]Clinton Wilder, "Giant Firms Join Outsourcing Parade," *ComputerWorld* 25 (September 30, 1991), 91.

[7]Uday Apte and MaryAnne Winniford, "Global Outsourcing of Information Systems Functions: Opportunities and Challenges," in *Managing Information Technology in a Global Society*, ed. Mehdi Khosrowpour (Idea Group Publishing: Harrisburg, PA, 1991), 58–59.

opment life cycle. Once the system is implemented, the SI outsourcer turns it over to the customer.

Objectives of Outsourcing Firms have three main objectives in outsourcing:[8]

- To do a better job of controlling costs—reducing them, containing them, and predicting them
- To relieve management from the problems of systems maintenance so that attention can be given to systems that provide strategic value
- To acquire access to leading edge technology and knowhow.

The experts agree that outsourcing will continue to grow during the early and mid-1990s, but a survey of twenty-one large U.S. financial firms revealed that three-fourths were opposed to the idea.[9]

Insourcing

Not only are many firms cool toward the outsourcing strategy, some are moving in the opposite direction. **Insourcing** is the action of a firm to regain the processing that previously was farmed out to an outsourcer.

In 1987, NHP, Incorporated of Washington, D.C. reacquired the computing operation that they had previously outsourced, and were able to cut their annual information services budget by 52 percent. NHP personnel pointed out that outsourcers have no interest in controlling costs since "they make money when costs go up."[10] Other factors cited were the turning over of the processing "to people who don't really know your business," and a loss of control. The control issue was important with National Liberty Insurance, who decided to insource in 1981 because they felt "hostage" to their supplier's pricing policies."[11]

Putting Cost Reduction Strategies in Perspective

If things go well, outsourcing can prove to be a wise decision, but if they do not, the firm could find itself with a totally inadequate CBIS. The alternatives of consolidation, downsizing, and insourcing are less risky. Firms are likely to follow all four strategies to varying degrees in the future. All reflect the fact that top management is keenly aware of the CBIS as an organizational resource and is not hesitant to make strategic decisions concerning this resource. Even though some of the

---

[8] Ibid, 59–60.

[9] Sid L. Huff, "Outsourcing of Information Services," *Business Quarterly* 55 (Spring 1991), 64.

[10] Clinton Wilder, "Outsourcing: From Fad to Respectability," *Computerworld* 24 (June 11, 1990), 122.

[11] Morino, "IS Cost Reduction," 34.

decisions go counter to what would be preferred by information services, such a situation of executive awareness and involvement cannot be all bad.

BUSINESS PROCESS REDESIGN

A firm consists of many physical and conceptual systems. Some work as they should, and some do not. Many firms are beginning to critically analyze their systems for the purpose of redesigning them so that they function better. This strategy is called **business process redesign (BPR).** BPR requires that the firm take a critical look at its processes, and make whatever changes are necessary.

When a firm applies BPR to its overall operation or to its major systems the effort invariably results in the redesign of computer-based systems. Three techniques for applying BPR to the CBIS have been devised, and they are known as the *Three Rs*— reverse engineering, restructuring, and reengineeering. These components are applied either separately or in combination.

Reverse Engineering

Reverse engineering had its origin in business intelligence. A common way for a firm to keep current on its competitors' products is to purchase samples and take them apart to see how they are designed. The design specifications are derived from the products themselves, reversing the normal pattern where the design comes first.

As used in computing, **reverse engineering** is the process of analyzing a system to identify the elements and their interrelationships, and to create documentation in a higher level of abstraction than currently exists.[12]

Reverse engineering consists of two subareas—redocumentation and design recovery:

- **Redocumentation** is the preparation of system documentation, using the system as the basis. The starting point is the program code, which is analyzed for the purpose of preparing detailed documentation such as structured English and program flowcharts. This documentation can then be analyzed for the purpose of preparing more abstract descriptions such as data flow diagrams and system flowcharts.
- **Design recovery** is the application of human knowledge and reasoning to the documentation of the system in order to completely understand it. The information specialists and users "fill in the gaps" left by the documentation.

Reverse engineering does not seek to change systems. Rather, it seeks only to understand them. The objective of the understanding is to provide a basis for making changes by other means, such as restructuring or reengineering.

---

[12]The definitions used in this section are based on Elliot J. Chikofsky and James H. Cross II, "Reverse Engineering and Design Recovery: A Taxonomy," *IEEE Software* 7 (January 1990), 13–17.

Restructuring

Restructuring is the transformation of a system into another form without changing its functionality. By **functionality** we mean what the system is designed to do—the tasks that it performs.

A good example of restructuring is the transformation of a program written in "spaghetti code" into one in a structured format. The program still performs its original functions, but does so in a different form. Restructuring can involve data as well as processes. For example, the normalization of a database is an example of restructuring.

Firms engage in restructuring as a means of updating systems that were developed prior to the advent of structured techniques.

Reengineering

Reengineering is the complete redesign of a system with the objective of changing its functionality. It is a "clean slate" approach that can affect the entire firm. Reengineering usually begins with reverse engineering, followed by restructuring, and, finally, forward engineering. **Forward engineering** is the name given to the process of following the system development life cycle in the normal manner.

A Model of Business Process Redesign of Computer-based Systems

Figure 21.1 is a model that shows the interrelationships of the BPR components as they are applied to computer-based systems.

Forward engineering and reverse engineering take opposite paths through the SDLC as shown in the upper portion of the model. Although most descriptions of reverse engineeering focus on the activity of progressing from the implementation phase to the design phase, movement to earlier phases can be accomplished as well.

Reengineering begins with the implementation phase and backtracks, phase by phase, to the planning phase where a new SDLC begins. In its reverse movement through the phases, reengineering can use reverse engineering and restructuring as a means of providing improved documentation.

You can see at the bottom of the model that restructuring can be focused on any of the developmental phases.

The model illustrates two key points in relation to BPR activity. First, it shows how BPR of computer-based systems is not limited to implementation-phase activity, but can span the entire SDLC. Second, it shows how the BPR components can be applied in combination, depending on the degree of change that is sought.

Selection of the BPR Components

The selection of the component, or components, to use in a BPR project depends on the current state of the system in terms of its functional and technical quality. Figure 21.2 is a diagram that shows how these two situations influence the choice.

FIGURE 21.1
Business Process Redesign Can Span All Four Phases of the System
Development Life Cycle

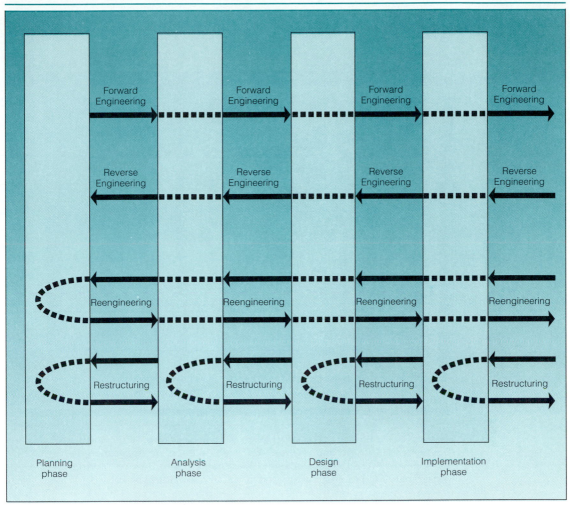

This model is based on one in Elliot J. Chikofsky and James H. Cross II, "Reverse Engineering and Design Recovery: A Taxonomy," *IEEE Software* 7 (January 1990), 14.

Functional quality is a measure of *what* the system does—the tasks that it performs. **Technical quality,** on the other hand, is a measure of *how* the tasks are performed. Essentially, technical quality is concerned with the degree to which the system reflects modern structured techniques.

According to the lower-left-hand quadrant of the figure, when both the functional and technical quality are poor, a forward engineering project is in order. Things are so bad that it is best to start over.

FIGURE 21.2
The Selection of BPR Components Is Based on Functional and
Technical Quality

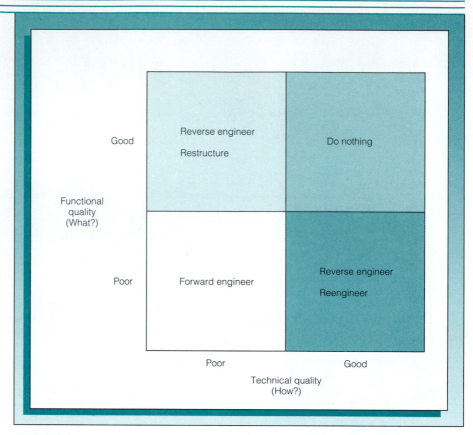

Sources: David Sharon, "The Psychology of Reengineering," *IEEE Software* 8
(November 1991): 74; and " Three 'R's: A White Paper on Application Re-
Development," The Re-Development Investigation Team, Texaco Information
Systems Enabling Center, Texaco, Inc., (January 30, 1992), p. 10.

When the functionality is good, but the technical quality is poor, reverse engineering followed by restructuring should be pursued. It is not necessary to refocus
the system; it is necessary only to modernize how the system performs its tasks.

When functionality is poor, but technical quality is good, reverse engineering
followed by reengineering is the proper route. Here, the system reflects modern
techniques, but is simply not doing the right job.

Finally, in the upper-right-hand quadrant, when both functionality and technical quality are good, it is best to leave things alone.

FACTORS CONTRIBUTING TO THE INTEREST IN BUSINESS PROCESS REDESIGN

Why is BPR creating so much attention in the computer field today? It is because of two influences—the increasing volume of legacy systems and the availability of special software.

Legacy Systems   A legacy is something that is left to you by an ancestor or someone else from a previous time period. For information services, a **legacy system** is one that was developed prior to the use of structured techniques.

Legacy systems are diminishing the effectiveness of information services in three ways:[13]

- They are becoming increasingly complex and costly to maintain.
- They are creating high turnover and morale problems within the ranks of the information specialists who perform the maintenance.
- They consume so many information resources that it is difficult for information services to respond to changing business needs.

Firms have long been aware of the problems of legacy systems, but only recently has it been feasible to do anything about them. The element that makes solution possible is BPR software.

BPR Software   The software industry has responded to the problems of poor functionality and technical quality with a large number of products that facilitate BPR. Table 21.4 lists some of these systems, and identifies where they may be used in the BPR process.

The *program analyzing* tools enable the firm to identify those programs that are the best candidates for BPR. For example, COBOL/Metrics, from Computer Data Systems, Inc., ranks programs in terms of the difficulty of maintenance, and prioritizes reengineering efforts.

COBOL/SF from IBM facilitates *restructuring* by converting unstructured programs to functionally equivalent, structured programs. It produces a top-down hierarchy of structured modules that feature single entry and exit points, and no GOTOs.

InterCASE from Interport Software Corporation performs *reverse engineering* by generating output that can be input to CASE tools and maintains that output in a repository.

[13] "The Three 'R's: A White Paper on Application Re-Development," (Houston, TX: The Re-Development Investigation Team, Texaco Information Systems Enabling Center, Texaco, Inc., January 30, 1992), 5–7.

TABLE 21.4
Examples of BPR Software

System name	Supplier	System type			
		Program analyzing	Restructuring	Reverse engineering	Reengineering
Application Development Workbench	KnowledgeWare				X
BACHMAN/Analyst Capture for COBOL	BACHMAN Information Systems			X	
BACHMAN/DBA Catalog Extract for DB2	BACHMAN Information Systems		X		
COBOL/Metrics	Computer Data Systems	X			
COBOL/SF	IBM	X	X		
Configure	Computer Data Systems		X		
Documentation System III	Marble Computer		X		
Inspector	KnowledgeWare	X			
InterCASE	InterPort Software		X	X	
Oracle*CASE	Oracle				X
Pacbase/PacReverse	CGI		X	X	
Pinpoint	KnowledgeWare	X	X		
SCAN/Analyzer	Computer Data Systems	X			
SCAN/COBOL	Computer Data Systems	X	X		
SuperStructure	Computer Data Systems	X	X		
XL/Dictionary	Intersolv			X	

Source: "The Three 'R's: A White Paper on Application Re-Development," (Houston, TX: The Re-Development Investigation Team, Texaco Information Systems Enabling Center, Texaco, Inc., January 30, 1992), 21–22.

The Bachman Reengineering Product set, which includes several systems such as Bachman Data Analyst and Bachman Database Administrator, provides several capabilities for *reengineering*. For example, it performs functions such as reverse engineering of IMS, DB2, and COBOL data structures, and produces entity-relationship diagrams.

Putting Business Process Redesign in Perspective

Systems maintenance has long been regarded as the ugly duckling of information services, with most of the attention aimed at the development of new, strategic systems. All the while, the maintenance albatross became increasingly impossible to bear. Today, BPR software provides a ray of hope that the problems of maintenance can be solved.

Thus far, BPR has focused on legacy systems, for they are the ones that require immediate attention. Once those problems are solved, however, firms can turn to systems that are performing in a more adequate manner, and seek to improve them.

Walter Viali, manager of Texaco's Information Systems Enabling Center, comments on the saying: "If it ain't broke, don't fix it." He maintains that: "If it ain't broke, break it and fix it so that it runs better."

When the computer industry is able to take Mr. Viali's advice, all four quadrants in Figure 21.2 will read: "Reengineer." Firms will use reengineering to make complete changes in how they do business.

SAFEGUARDING INFORMATION RESOURCES

It was not until the period of social unrest during the late 1960s and early 1970s that firms began protecting their computing centers from threats of intentional damage and destruction. More recently it has become clear that protection should also be offered from the damaging effects of natural disasters. The San Francisco and Oakland area earthquake of 1990 confirmed that firms must safeguard their information systems from threats of all kinds. Firms attempt to thwart computer criminals by means of systems security, and minimize the damage caused by threats of all kinds by means of contingency planning.

SYSTEMS SECURITY

Systems security refers to the protection of all of the firm's information resources from threats by unauthorized parties. The firm implements a program of effective systems security by identifying vulnerabilities of its information resources to certain threats, and by implementing the required countermeasures and safeguards.

Reasons for the Increasing Interest in Systems Security

Interest in systems security is higher now than ever before. The reasons are:[14]

- Firms are heavily dependent on information systems for their critical operations.
- Applications that feature electronic data interchange (EDI) allow other organizations to have access to the firm's valuable information resources.

---

[14] From *Systems Auditability and Control: Module 1 Executive Summary* (Altamonte Springs, FL: The Institute of Internal Auditors Research Foundation, 1991), 2.

- Most systems today feature online access from users located throughout the firm.
- Many end users tend to be lax in their security and recovery precautions.

These conditions are expected to continue through the 1990s, guaranteeing that systems security will remain a crucial ingredient in computer use.

Security Objectives

Systems security is intended to achieve three main objectives: confidentiality, availability, and integrity. Figure 21.3 shows how security threats impact the ability of the firm to achieve these objectives.

- **Confidentiality**   The firm seeks to protect its data and information from disclosure to unauthorized persons. Human resource information systems have the responsibility in terms of information describing the firm's employees. Other such systems as accounts receivable, purchasing, and accounts payable have the responsibility in terms of safeguarding the personal privacy of elements in the firm's environment.
- **Availability**   The purpose of the CBIS is to make its data and information available to those who are authorized to use it. This objective is especially important to the information-oriented CBIS subsystems.
- **Integrity**   All of the subsystems of the CBIS should provide an accurate reflection of the physical systems that they represent.

Historically, firms have spent the most money on maintaining confidentiality and the least on achieving integrity. However, availability is receiving increased management attention.[15]

Security Threats

The four main threats to the firm's information resources include unauthorized disclosure and theft, unauthorized use, unauthorized destruction and denial of service, and unauthorized modification.

- **Unauthorized disclosure and theft**   When the database and software library are made available to persons not entitled to have access, the result can be the loss of information or money. For example, industrial spies can gain valuable competitive information, and computer criminals can embezzle the firm's funds.
- **Unauthorized use**   Persons who are not ordinarily entitled to use the firm's resources are able to do so. Typical of this type of computer criminal is the

---

[15] Daniel E. White, Ernst & Young, address at the ACM Computer Security Seminar, Phoenix, Arizona, October 8, 1991.

FIGURE 21.3
Unauthorized Acts Threaten System Security Objectives

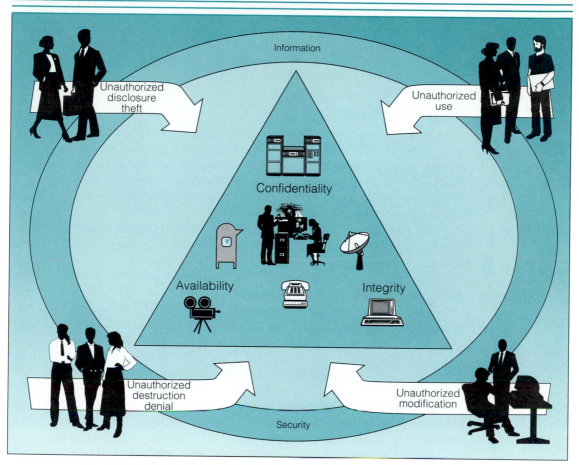

Source: Ken Cutler, "Hackers, Viruses, Thieves, and . . . Other Threats to Your Information Assets," in *Computer Security Seminar Course Material* (New York: The Association of Computing Machinery, 1991). Reprinted with permission.

hacker, a person who likes to play with the computer and enjoys mastering the details of its operation. A hacker, for example, can break into a firm's computer network, gain access to the telephone system, and make unauthorized long-distance calls.

■ **Unauthorized destruction and denial of service**   Persons can damage or destroy the hardware or software, causing a shutdown in the firm's computer operations. It is not even necessary that the computer criminals gain access to the computer room. The criminals can log onto the firm's computer network from remote terminals and cause physical destruction such as damaged monitors, crashed disks, jammed printers, and disabled keyboards.

■ **Unauthorized modification** Changes can be made to the firm's data, information, and software. One serious result of such modification is the wrong decisions made by managers when using the system's output.

Attacks by computer criminals intent on stealing a firm's funds are only one dimension of the harm that can be done. Of potentially greater loss is the damage that can accrue to information. Recently, much information damage has been caused by computer viruses unleashed by hackers.

Computer Viruses

A **computer virus,** known simply as a **virus,** is a piece of code that is attached to a host program. When the host is run, the virus code is executed and can play tricks or cause damage. In addition, the code can reproduce itself in another program, causing the virus to spread. Thus far, the primary targets of viruses have been microcomputers, and the most popular means of dissemination have been diskettes and electronic bulletin boards.

The first recorded instance of a computer virus occurred in the mid-1970s when a program attacked the idle workstations in a Silicon Valley research center's computer network. The program displayed random patterns on the screens, disabled the keyboards, and clogged the network. It was only years later, in 1984, when Fred Cohen of the University of Cincinnati first applied the term virus to software.

In December of 1987 a virus attacked the IBM internal communications network by drawing Christmas trees on the screens. It replicated itself many times and clogged the network, but was detected and quickly removed before any damage was done. The significance of the IBM Christmas tree virus is the fact that it is believed to have been attached to a data file, whereas viruses are usually attached to programs.

In August of 1989 there were less than one hundred viruses.[16] By 1991 the number had reached over one thousand.[17] Each is identified by one or more unique names.

When you suspect that your system has been attacked by a virus, it is not recommended that you attempt to repair the infected program. The repair process is not simple and may produce additional damage. Recovery is best accomplished by using **anti-viral software,** which deactivates a virus in a program, and restores the program to its original condition.

Access Control

The basis for security from viruses and other threats is access control. The reasoning is simple: if unauthorized persons are denied access to the information resources, then harm cannot be done.

[16] Eugene H. Spafford, Kathleen A. Heaphy, and David J. Ferbrache, "A Computer Virus Primer," in *Computers Under Attack: Intruders, Worms, and Viruses,* ed. Peter J. Denning (New York: ACM Press, 1990), 340–42.

[17] Ken Cutler, American Express, address at the ACM Computer Security Seminar, Phoenix, Arizona, October 8, 1991.

Access control is achieved by means of a three-step process that includes user identification, user authentication, and user authorization. The incorporation of these steps into a security system is illustrated in Figure 21.4.

1. **User identification**   Users first identify themselves by providing something that they *know*, such as a password. The identification can also include the user's *location*, such as a telephone number or network entry point.
2. **User authentication**   Once initial identification has been accomplished, users verify their right to access by providing something that they *have*, such as a smart card or token, or an identification chip. User authentication

FIGURE 21.4

Access Control Functions

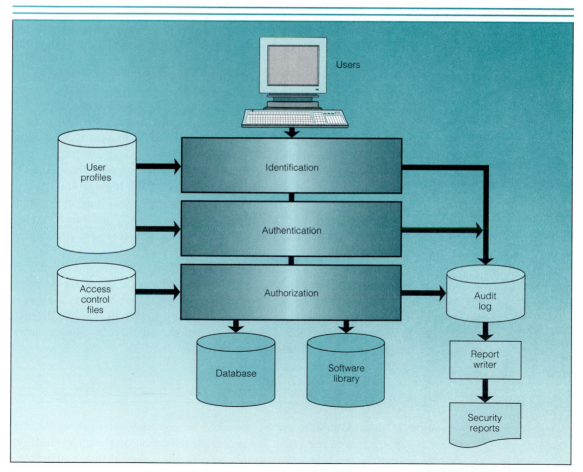

Source: Ken Cutler, "Hackers, Viruses, Thieves, and … Other Threats to Your Information Assets," in *Computer Security Seminar Course Material* (New York: The Association of Computing Machinery, 1991). Reprinted with permission.

can also be accomplished by providing something that they *are*, such as a signature or a voice or speech pattern.

3. **User authorization** With the identification and authentication checks passed, a person can then be authorized certain levels or degrees of use. For example, one user might be authorized to only read from a file, whereas another might be authorized to make changes.

Identification and authentication make use of **user profiles,** or descriptions of authorized users, that are maintained in DASD. Authorization makes use of **access control files** that specify the levels of access available to each user.

Once a user has satisfied the three access control functions, he or she can use the contents of the database and software library. A log is maintained in DASD of all access control activity and is used to prepare security reports.

Putting Systems Security in Perspective

Systems security becomes more serious each year because of the increasing complexity of the systems and the high level of computer literacy on the part of computer criminals.

The first computer criminals who could be identified with a particular group were the Vietnam war protesters who inflicted their anti-government and anti-business feelings on computer centers. Those protesters were replaced in the late 1970s and 1980s by embezzlers who sought to use the computer for illegal financial gain. More recently the criminals who have drawn the most attention have been persons intent on causing havoc in the form of viruses and other malicious software.

The most serious forms of computer criminals have not yet gone into action— at least, not on a grand scale. These criminals are called **high-grade threats** because (1) they have extensive resources in money, personnel, and clandestine technology, (2) they are more interested in long-term gain than immediate results, and (3) they are especially adept at circumventing physical and procedural safeguards.[18]

As far as business is concerned, the high-grade threat is the computer criminal who has the mission of stealing the firm's information for use by its competitors. As far as the federal government is concerned, the high-grade threat is the international terrorist who would engage in computer crime to disable national defense systems. Both firms and the federal government are currently implementing security systems for the purpose of thwarting high-grade threats.

CONTINGENCY PLANNING

A computer operation that cannot be disrupted by computer criminals or natural disasters is not achieved overnight. It requires the execution of a planned strategy. During the early years of computing, this activity was called **disaster planning,** but a more positive term, **contingency planning,** is currently enjoying popular use.

[18] Based on *Computers At Risk* (Washington, DC: National Academy of Science, 1991), 283–84.

Firms have found that, rather than relying on a single, large plan, the best technique is to develop several subplans that address specific contingencies.[19] Typical subplans include the emergency plan, the backup plan, and the vital records plan.

The Emergency Plan   The **emergency plan** specifies those measures that ensure the safety of the employees when disaster strikes. The measures include alarm systems, evacuation procedures, and fire suppression systems.

The Backup Plan   The firm should make arrangements for backup computing facilities in the event that the regular facilities are destroyed or damaged beyond use. Backup can be achieved by means of some combination of redundancy, diversity, and mobility.[20]

- **Redundancy**   Hardware, software, and data are duplicated so that when the original unit is down, the backup unit can continue the processing.
- **Diversity**   The information resources are not all installed at the same location. Large firms typically establish separate computing centers for different areas of their operations.
- **Mobility**   Small firms enter into a **reciprocal agreement** with other users of the same type of equipment so that each firm can provide backup to the other in the event of a catastrophe. Large firms can achieve mobility by contracting for backup service at hot or cold sites. A **hot site** is a complete computing facility that is made available by a supplier to its customers for use in the event of emergencies. A **cold site,** often called an **empty shell,** is constructed by the firm at a site separate from the main computing facility, and includes only the building facilities but not the computer. The computer is obtained from the supplier and installed in the empty shell when disaster strikes.

Because computers are subject to failure, and are essential to continued operations, all firms need some type of backup plan.

The Vital Records Plan   A firm's **vital records** are those paper documents, microforms, and magnetic storage media that are necessary for carrying on the firm's business. In addition to safeguarding the records at the computer site, backup copies should be stored at a remote location. All types of records can be physically transported to the remote location, but computer records can be transmitted electronically. Three electronic transmission services are currently available:

- **Electronic vaulting,** which came into use about 1988, involves the electronic transmission of backup files in a batch manner.

---

[19] The idea of separate subplans was first described in *Data Security Controls and Procedures— A Philosophy for DP Installations*, G320-5649 (White Plains, N.Y.: IBM Corporation, 1977), 17–22.

[20] Daniel E. White, Ernst & Young, address at the ACM Computer Security Seminar, Phoenix, Arizona, October 8, 1991.

- **Remote journaling** is similar to electronic vaulting, but accomplishes transmission as transactions occur.
- **Database shadowing,** the most sophisticated form of electronic vital-records backup, allows for entire duplicate databases to be maintained up-to-date at remote sites.

Putting Contingency Planning in Perspective

Contingency planning is one area of computer use where it is easy to see great improvement in just the past few years. During the late 1980s only a handful of firms had such plans, and those firms seldom put them to test. Today, such plans are commonplace, and the firms periodically engage in drills that include activating cold sites and travel to hot sites or to the computing centers of other firms.

In addition, contingency planning is no longer viewed as having secondary importance. Larger information services organizations include a **manager of contingency planning,** who has contingency planning as a main responsibility.

THE IMPORTANCE OF ETHICS

It is appropriate that the final topic in this text be ethics. It is a topic that is currently receiving much attention in business in general, and in computing in particular. There is a much greater opportunity to use the computer unethically today than there was just a few years ago.

Ethics as a Parameter of Behavior

All of us are guided in our behavior by laws, morals, and ethics.[21] The laws are the most obvious because they exist in a written form. **Morals** are generally accepted standards of what is right and what is wrong in terms of our conduct or character. **Ethics** are expressions of morals in the form of sets or codes that are intended to serve as guidelines. Some of our ethical codes are informal, shaped by our experience as we grow. Other codes are formal, documented in a written form by organizations.

At least five codes of ethics have been defined by professional computing organizations. The codes include the *Professional Conduct and Procedures for the Enforcement of the ACM Code of Professional Conduct* by the Association for Computing Machinery, the *Code of Ethics, Standards of Conduct and Enforcement Procedures* by the Data Processing Management Association (DPMA), the *Code of Conduct* by the British Computer Society (BCS), the *Code of Ethics* by the Institute

---

[21]Karen A. Forcht, "Assessing the Ethical Standards and Policies in Computer-Based Environments," in *Ethical Issues in Information Systems*, eds. Roy Dejoie, George Fowler, and David Paradice (Boston, MA: Boyd & Fraser Publishing Company, 1991), 57–59.

of Electrical and Electronics Engineers (IEEE), and the *Codes of Ethics and Good Practices* by the Institute for Certification of Computer Professionals (ICCP).[22]

Four Ethical Issues

Richard O. Mason, a professor at Southern Methodist University, has identified four ethical issues that face the information age. He uses the acronym **PAPA** to represent privacy, accuracy, property, and accessibility. Professor Mason explains each as follows:[23]

- **Privacy**   What information about ones's self or one's associations must a person reveal to others, under what conditions and with what safeguards? What things can people keep to themselves and not be forced to reveal to others?
- **Accuracy**   Who is responsible for the authenticity, fidelity and accuracy of information? Similarly, who is to be held accountable for errors in information and how is the injured party to be made whole?
- **Property**   Who owns information? What are the just and fair prices for its exchange? Who owns the channels, especially the airways, through which information is transmitted? How should access to this scarce resource be allocated?
- **Accessibility**   What information does a person or an organization have a right or a privilege to obtain, under what conditions and with what safeguards?

A Social Contract for Computer Use

Professor Mason concludes his discussion of the PAPA ingredients by stating five principles that ensure information technology and the information it handles are used to enhance the dignity of mankind.[24] Firms should enter into a social contract for computer use by ensuring that their information systems:

- Do not unduly invade a person's privacy.
- Are accurate.
- Protect the viability of the fixed conduit resource through which information is transmitted to avoid noise and jamming pollution.
- Protect the sanctity of intellectual property.
- Are accessible to avoid the indignities of information illiteracy and deprivation.

[22] *Ibid,* 61–62.

[23] Richard O. Mason, "Four Ethical Issues of the Information Age," *MIS Quarterly* 10 (March 1986), 5.

[24] *Ibid,* 11.

When these principles are followed, information will flow to create the kind of world in which we wish to live.[25]

A FINAL NOTE

We have addressed several issues in this chapter, which are exerting an especially strong influence on computer use. When you begin your career you will be expected to contribute to the solution of problems such as these. The computer field is approximately forty years old, but the fact is that there are more problems today than in 1954 when GE plugged in its first UNIVAC I. Although you will have far more sophisticated hardware and software resources at your disposal, the challenges are much greater than those faced by the early computer pioneers.

You should look at this situation in a positive way. That was the view taken by the manager who had a sign on his office wall that read: "Problems are opportunities in work clothes." There are a lot of opportunities that remain in applying the computer as a problem-solving system.

SUMMARY

Managers initially sought an economic justification for their decisions to install computers. In taking this approach, analyses were conducted to determine the break-even point, the payback point, and the net present value. The introduction of information-oriented systems necessitated the use of noneconomic measures, such as the portfolio approach, information economics, and surrogate measures. These methods for justifying computing expenditures take on an even greater meaning today as executives make decisions that can affect the entire information services unit.

The current economic climate forces firms to improve profitability by reducing their costs. The firm's executives are seeking cost reduction in information services by following strategies of consolidation, downsizing, outsourcing, and insourcing. Although outsourcing is receiving the most attention, it is the riskiest. Downsizing is the strategy that naturally complements the trend to end-user computing.

Another avenue that can lead to profitability is business process redesign, or BPR. The three main components of BPR that are applied to computer-based systems are reverse engineering, restructuring, and reengineering. The functionality and technical quality of systems determine the mix of components that is appropriate. When wholesale change is in order, the entire SLC can be repeated—a process called forward engineering. The high level of current interest in BPR is stimulated by both legacy systems and BPR software. When the burden of legacy systems has been lightened, firms will use reengineereing to make good systems perform even better.

[25] *Ibid,* 11–12.

Today's firms are especially vulnerable both computer criminals and natural disasters. Systems security seeks to achieve the objectives of confidentiality, availability, and integrity. Standing in the way of these objectives are the threats of unauthorized use, disclosure and theft, destruction and denial of service, and modification.

The basis of systems security is access control, which is achieved in a three-step fashion consisting of user identification, user authentication, and user authorization. Access control is aimed at computer criminals, such as protestors, embezzlers, and hackers, but is yet to be tested by high-grade threats such as industrial spies and international terrorists.

Since it is impossible to prevent disasters, contingency plans spell out what to do when one occurs. Subplans devoted to subjects such as emergencies, backup, and vital records are periodically tested.

The computer profession has recognized its ethical responsibilities and drafted several codes that address issues such as privacy, accuracy, property, and accessibility. By engaging in a social contract for computer use, firms ensure that information systems will contribute to the good of mankind.

KEY TERMS

break-even analysis
payback analysis
net present value
portfolio approach
information economics
surrogate measures
downsizing
outsourcing
insourcing
business process redesign (BPR)
reverse engineering
restructuring
functionality

reengineering
forward engineering
legacy system
systems security
computer virus, virus
high-grade threat
disaster planning, contingency planning
hot site
cold site, empty shell
electronic vaulting
remote journaling
database shadowing

KEY CONCEPTS

The consideration of both economic and noneconomic factors in justifying money spent on computing, and the broadening focus of the justification to include the firm's entire computing operation

How reverse engineering, restructuring, and reengineering work together to achieve business process redesign

Achieving systems security by controlling access

The use of subplans that address specific contingencies

Enhancing mankind by using the computer to ensure privacy and accuracy, protect property, and control accessibility

QUESTIONS

1. Distinguish between break-even analysis and payback analysis.

2. What are the two effects of using net present value in payback analysis calculations?

3. What are the three guidelines that management follows in pursuing a portfolio analysis strategy?

4. What are the two potential features of a system that are considered by information economics?

5. When can Keen's surrogate measures be observed?

6. Why is justification of computer systems by the firm's executives taking on added importance today?

7. How could a firm with a single data center and a high level of end-user computing use consolidation as a cost-reduction strategy?

8. What is it called when an outsourcer conducts the SDLC, and then turns the system over to the customer?

9. What is it called when a firm decides to cancel its outsourcing contract?

10. Of the four cost-reduction strategies, which is the most risky from the standpoint of ensuring a long-term computing capability? Which is most compatible with end-user computing?

11. Is reverse engineering accomplished completely by software? Explain.

12. If you wanted to transform a spaghetti-code program into a structured format, which BPR strategy would you use?

13. What question does functional quality address? What about technical quality?

14. In what ways do legacy systems strain information services?

15. What are the four categories of BPR software?

16. What currently popular application is making the CBIS more susceptible to computer crime by other organizations?

17. What are the three objectives of systems security?

18. What could someone have in their possession that would authenticate their right to access the computer system?

19. What is a high-grade threat?

20. What does an emergency plan seek to accomplish?

21. Distinguish between a hot site and a cold site.

22. What is the difference between electronic vaulting and remote journaling?

23. What do the letters in PAPA represent?

24. Which of Professor Mason's ethical principles is represented by a software licensing agreement? By the refusal of a firm to sell its customer name and address file to a mailing list company? By a university placement center that lets students read the reference letters in their files?

TOPICS FOR DISCUSSION

1. Assume that your boss, the CIO, has asked you to conduct a study in the firm to determine the extent to which Keen's surrogate measures have been acheved by a recently implemented system. What technique, or techniques, would you use for each one?

2. If many decisions to spend money on computing are based on faith, what factors can contribute to that faith being sound? For example, is there anything that you learn in this course that will help?

3. Rank the four security threats in order of seriousness to the firm. Defend your ranking.

4. Which type of threat is represented by the computer virus?

PROBLEMS

1. Go to the library and read a magazine or journal article on reengineering. Summarize it on two double-spaced pages. At the top of the first page, identify the source on six lines: (1) author or authors, (2) title, (3) publication name, (4) volume number and issue number, (5) date, and (6) page numbers.

2. The virus is only one example of malicious software, or software that causes the user some kind of harm. Conduct library research to identify other types. Select a type, and write a one-page, double-spaced description. Hint 1: You may find the other types described in articles on viruses. Hint 2: Back issues of the *Communications of the ACM* are a good source.

National Foods

National Foods is a leading manufacturer of food products, competing with firms such as General Mills and General Foods. A mainframe computer is installed at the Minneapolis headquarters, networked to minicomputers at plants and distribution centers across the country. Each of the firm's 625 sales representatives is equipped with a laptop computer with a modem. At the end of the day, the reps transmit sales call data to headquarters. The data identifies the number of units of each product, which were sold, plus status reports on special promotions, such as cooperative ads, coupons, and contests.

It's the Friday afternoon before Memorial Day, and Dan Kennerly, the CIO, is on his way out of his office when the telephone rings. It's Fred Ennen, the vice president of marketing, on the line. Dan cradles the phone between his shoulder and ear while listening to Fred and tossing papers into his briefcase with both hands.

Fred congratulates Dan on the new sales tracking system that has just been installed. The system uses the laptop data transmitted by the sales reps. Fred raves on and on about the system for at least five minutes, takes a deep breath, and then asks: "Why don't we install a sales tracking system that will track competitors' sales? We could limit it to only selected items at first, such as dog food where the number of competing brands is not large. I'd like to know about a competitor's plans to put a new brand on the market before it actually hits. Then I'd like to track the sales during the life cycle. When the sales start to decline we can predict a new product announcement. Doesn't that sound like a good idea?"

Dan replies: "It sure does, but I have a question. Just exactly where will we get the information? It seems to me like it would be hard to come by."

"Not really," Fred responds. "We get it from the store managers. We pay them a certain amount each month. The money is no problem. I've got enough in my budget. The managers ask the competitors' sales reps questions, and then pass the information along to our reps. Our reps can transmit it to headquarters with their laptops. Anything wrong with that?"

"I don't know, Fred. This is all hitting me at a bad time. I'm taking Alice and the kids to the lake this weekend, and I'm supposed to be home ten minutes ago. Let me think this over and get back with you on Tuesday." With that, Dan hangs up the phone, shuts his briefcase, puts it in the closet, and leaves the office.

Assignments

1. Assuming that the competitor sales tracking system is implemented as described by Fred, what are some problems that might be encountered in maintaining a continuous flow of information?

2. Comment on Fred's system from an ethical standpoint. Would you label it as ethical or unethical? Support your conclusion.

3. Are there any other ways that such a competitor tracking system could be implemented without involving store personnel? If so, list them and briefly describe each.

SELECTED BIBLIOGRAPHY

"A Sampling of Justification Methods." *Computerworld* 25 (November 11, 1991): 85.

Andrews, William C. "Contingency Planning for Physical Disasters." *Journal of Systems Management* 41 (July 1990): 28–32.

Caldwell, Bruce, and Perry, Linda. "Down and Out In Chicago." *InformationWeek* (April 20, 1992): 12–13.

Cohen, Eli, and Cornwell, Larry. "A Question of Ethics: Developing Information System Ethics." *Journal of Business Ethics* 8 (1989): 431–37.

Collier, Paul Arnold; Dixon, Robert; and Marston, Claire Lesley. "Computer Fraud: Research Findings from the UK." *Internal Auditor* 48 (August 1991): 49–52.

Haight, Nicholas, and Byers, C. Randall. "Disaster Recovery Planning: Don't Wait Until It's Too Late." *Journal of Systems Management* 42 (April 1991): 13–16.

Hammer, Michael, and Champy, James A. "What is Reengineering?" *InformationWeek* (May 5, 1992): 10*ff.*

Henry, Bill. "Measuring IS for Business Value." *Datamation* 36 (April 1, 1990): 89–91.

Horwitt, Elisabeth. "Downsizing Quandry for IS Pros." *Computerworld* 24 (March 5, 1990): 1*ff.*

Jakes, J. Michael, and Yoches, E. Robert. "Basic Principles of Patent Protection for Computer Software." *Communications of the ACM* 32 (August 1989): 922–24.

Keen, Peter G. W. "Value Analysis: Justifying Decision Support Systems." *MIS Quarterly* 5 (March 1981): 1–15.

Kerr, Susan. "Using AI to Improve Security." *Datamation* 36 (February 1, 1990): 57*ff.*

Krass, Peter. "A Delicate Balance." *InformationWeek* (May 5, 1992): 26*ff.*

Ladner, Richard E. "Computer Accessibility For Federal Workers With Disabilities: It's the Law." *Communications of the ACM* 32 (August 1989): 952–56.

Lederer, Albert L.; Mirani, Rajesh; Neo, Boon Siong; Pollard, Carol; Prasad, Jayesh; and Ramamurthy, K. "Information System Cost Estimating: A Management Perspective." *MIS Quarterly* 14 (June 1990): 159–76.

Leibs, Scott. "Get Radical." *InformationWeek* (May 5, 1992): 6–7.

Leibs, Scott, and Krass, Peter. "1992: The Squeeze Is On." *InformationWeek* (March 9, 1992): 34*ff.*

Moad, Jeff. "Disaster-Proof Your Data." *Datamation* 36 (November 1, 1990): 87*ff.*

O'Heney, Sheila. "Outsourcing Solutions to the DP Puzzle." *Bankers Monthly* 108 (July 1991): 26–28.

Schlack, Mark. "How To Keep Viruses Off Your LAN." *Datamation* 37 (October 15, 1991): 87*ff.*

Sharon, David. "The Psychology of Reengineering." *IEEE Software* 8 (November 1991): 73–75.

Shneiderman, Ben. "Socially Responsible Computing I: A Call to Action Following the L.A. Riots." *SIGCHI Bulletin* 24 (July 1992): 14–15.

Shneiderman, Ben. "Socially Responsible Computing II: First Steps On the Path to Positive Contributions." *SIGCHI Bulletin* 24 (July 1992): 16–17.

Skupsky, Donald S. "Establishing an Effective Records Retention Policy." *Modern Office Technology* 36 (November 1991): 58*ff.*

Straub, Detmar W. "Organizational Structuring of the Computer Security Function." *Computers & Security* 7 (1988): 185–95.

Summers, R. C. "An Overview of Computer Security." *IBM Systems Journal* 23 (1984): 309–25.

Taylor, G. Stephen, and Davis, J. Stephen. "Individual Privacy and Computer-Based Human Resource Information Systems." *Journal of Business Ethics* 8 (1989): 569–76.

Violino, Bob. "Kodak's Next Step." *InformationWeek* (February 3, 1992): 10–11.

GLOSSARY

Above-voice grade circuit. A specially conditioned communications circuit that permits the transmission of data at high speeds with a low error rate.

Accounting information system. A functional information system designed to support the needs of persons in the firm for accounting information.

Accounting system. *See* **Data processing system.**

Accounts payable system. A subsystem of the data processing system, which pays the firm's suppliers.

Accounts receivable system. A subsystem of the data processing system, which collects money from the firm's customers.

Activity. An arrow on a network diagram.

Ad hoc request. A request for information from the database, which has not previously been specified.

Agenda. Kotter's term for an objective that the firm seeks to achieve.

Analysis. *See* **Definition effort.**

Analysis phase. *See* **Definition effort.**

Anonymity. A characteristic of a GDSS, which enables participants to make comments and suggestions without being identified to the group as the source of those inputs.

Application generator. A CASE tool that permits the generation of computer code to perform an application.

Application software. The programs that process a firm's data. Examples are payroll, inventory, mathematical models, and statistical packages. Contrast with **Application-development software** and **System software.**

Application-development software. The name used in this text to describe software that does not clearly fit into the system or application categories, such as Lotus 1-2-3 and dBASE IV. These are not prewritten packages in the true sense, in that the user must tailor them to fit particular applications.

Artificial intelligence (AI). The use of electronics to provide machines with the ability to perform processes that normally raquire human intelligence. AI includes several areas, such as robotics and expert systems.

Artificial neural system (ANS). A mathematical model of a neural network, which can provide an expert system with a learning ability.

Asynchronous exchange. Dialog between one or more senders and receivers, which does not require messages to be received at the same time they are sent. Office automation applications such as computer conferencing, electronic mail, and voice mail have this characteristic, as do certain GDSS settings. Contrast with **Synchronous exchange.**

Attendance reporting. The recording of data that describes the number of hours worked by employees.

Attribute. A characteristic of a data entity. For example, employee number is an attribute of the employee entity. Some attributes describe entities (*See also* **Descriptor**), and some provide identification (*See also* **Identifier**).

Attribute value. A value that is assigned to an attribute, such as an employee number of 12382.

Audio conferencing. An office automation application that provides for only audio communication between geographically dispersed sites. It is a form of teleconferencing.

Audit committee. A committee composed of members of the board of directors, which oversees the firm's internal auditing operation.

Audit trail. A history of some aspect of a firm's activity, which enables a transaction to be traced from its source to its conclusion and from its conclusion to its source. The audit trail might be a detail report or a magnetic tape file containing a record for each transaction.

Availability. A basic security objective of making the information resources available when they are needed.

Backorder. A sales transaction consisting of an order for merchandise that is not available. The order is not rejected or canceled but is held until the merchandise becomes available.

Backward chaining. *See* **Reverse reasoning.**

Balanced DFD. A data flow diagram that uses the same names for the same data flows that are found in other DFDs of the set.

Batch processing. One of the two basic ways to process data, which is characterized by grouping transactions so that all are handled at one time. It is the most efficient way to use the computer, but it does not keep files current as transactions occur. Contrast with **Online processing.**

Bill. *See* **Invoice.**

Bill of material. The list of parts and subassembles, along with their quantities, that go into the production of a finished good. It is analogous to a recipe.

Billing system. A subsystem of the data processing system, which prepares invoices for customers, advising them of the amount of money owed to the firm for their purchases.

Black hole. A process in a data flow diagram with only data flows leading to it, and none leading from it. Also called an **infinite sink.**

Brainstorming. An approach to systems analysis and design where the participants discuss the application in an informal group setting.

Break-even analysis. A method for justifying a computer expenditure, which compares the costs of the new and old systems.

Budget. *See* **Operating budget.**

Business intelligence. *See* **Marketing intelligence.**

Business process redesign (BPR). An effort by the firm to rethink its procedures without being constrained by the way things are currently being done.

Buyer. The person in the purchasing department, who negotiates with suppliers to obtain replenishment merchandise.

Cache memory. A high-speed primary storage that resides between the processor and secondary storage. It is used to speed up the retrieval of the contents of secondary storage.

Carpal tunnel syndrome. An injury to the wrists, which is caused by holding the hands in an awkward position while using a keyboard.

Carrying cost. *See* **Maintenance cost.**

Cash flow analysis. A process that produces a report reflecting the money entering and leaving the firm during a coming time period such as a year.

Cash flow model. A mathematical model that is used to conduct a cash flow analysis. *See also* **Cash flow analysis.**

Cathode-ray tube (CRT). The electronic device that is most frequently used to display input and output on a keyboard terminal or microcomputer. The tube has the appearance of a TV screen, and a terminal using such a screen is called a **CRT terminal,** or simply a **CRT.**

CD-ROM. *See* **Optical disk.**

Certainty factor (CF). A measure of the degree of certainty that is used in an expert system. The certainty can apply to a rule or to a variable in a rule condition. The certainty factor is analogous to a probability in a mathematical model.

Channel. Used in data communications, this term applies to the pathway that connects the sender and the receiver. The channel can exist in various forms such as air space through which face-to-face communications travel, a telephone line, or a microwave circuit. Multiple channels can be provided by a single circuit. *See also* **Circuit.**

Chief information officer (CIO). The person in charge of the firm's information resources, who participates equally with the other executives in mapping out corporate strategy.

Child. *See* **Hierarchical structure.**

Choice activity. The term used by Simon for the selection of the best alternative.

Circuit. The transmission facility that provides one or more channels in a data communications network. Commonly used circuits are telephone lines, coaxial cables, fiber-optic cables, and microwave signals. Also called a **line.**

Client/server computing. The approach to network design, which recognizes the need to perform some processes centrally (by a server) and some processes locally (by a client using a desktop computer).

Closed system. A system that does not interface with its environment.

Closed-loop system. A system with a feedback loop. *See also* **Feedback loop.**

Cluster control unit. A piece of data communications equipment, which controls multiple terminals in a given area, such as a department.

Coaxial cable. Commonly called coax, a type of data communications circuit, which permits all types of office automation applications, including video conferencing.

Code. A character or group of characters used to represent something. For example, a particular employee number is a code.

Cold site. A backup computing facility that contains everything except the computer. Also called an **Empty shell.**

Common carrier. A company such as AT&T or GTE, which furnishes communications facilities for a fee.

Compact disk. *See* **Optical disk.**

Competitive advantage. An edge that a firm enjoys over its competitors in meeting the needs of its customers.

Competitive intelligence (CI). *See* **Marketing intelligence.**

Composite key. Multiple keys that are required to identify a data entity.

Computer conferencing. An office automation application that enables conference members to communicate with each other using their computer terminals. Members do not have to be online at the same time—a situation referred to as an asychronous exchange. Computer conferencing is a form of teleconferencing.

Computer integrated manufacturing (CIM). An organized, unified approach to all computer use in manufacturing—CAD, CAM, robotics, the manufacturing information system, and other systems.

Computer literacy. Knowledge of the computer—generally how it works, its terminology, its capabilities and limitations, and so on.

Computer virus. *See* **Virus.**

Computer-aided design (CAD). The use of a computer to design something, such as a bridge or an automobile. Also called **Computer-aided engineering.**

Computer-aided engineering. *See* **Computer-aided design.**

Computer-aided manufacturing (CAM). The use of a computer in the manufacturing process. Computer-controlled lathes, drill presses, and conveyor belts are examples.

Computer-aided software engineering (CASE). The complete set of computer-based tools facilitate system development and maintenance.

Computer-based information system (CBIS). The term used in this text to describe all of the computer applications in a firm—data processing, MIS, DSS, OA, and expert systems.

Conceptual resource. A resource that represents a physical resource. Examples are data and information.

Conceptual system. A system that represents a physical system. A good example is the MIS, which can represent the physical status of the organization. The representation is accomplished by the storage of data reflecting conditions (such as the level of inventory) and activities (such as the work flow).

Concurrent audit. An ongoing operational audit. *See also* **Operational audit.**

Confidentiality. A basic objective of computer security, which ensures the personal privacy of persons working in and with the firm.

Connectivity. The ability of a system to exchange data and programs with other systems using a data communications network. Also, the relationship between entities in an entity-relationship diagram (one-to-one, one-to-many, and many-to-many).

Connector. A symbol on a flowchart or data flow diagram, which serves to link processes or data.

Consolidation. An information resources management strategy that the firm follows for combining separate computing sites as a cost-cutting measure.

Consultation. The act of using an expert system.

Contention-based control. A "first come, first served" approach to controlling the use of a data communications network such as a LAN.

Context diagram. The highest-level data flow diagram. It presents the system in context with its environmental interfaces.

Contingency planning. The activity of formally outlining actions to be taken when any of the firm's computing resources are subjected to hazards.

Control mechanism. The portion of a closed-loop system, which adjusts the system so that the standards may be achieved.

Controlled experiment. A way of gathering information whereby the research setting is stabilized so as to isolate the effect of a treatment on behavior. It is used primarily by marketing researchers but can be used by systems analysts.

Cost avoidance. A strategy for computer justification whereby existing expenses are not reduced, but future expenses are not incurred.

Cost reduction. A strategy for computer justification whereby existing expenses are reduced.

Cost-benefit analysis. The activity of comparing the anticipated costs of a computer application or system with the anticipated benefits.

Critical path. The sequence of activities through a network diagram, which requires the least amount of time. *See also* **Network diagram.**

Critical path method (CPM). A type of network diagram that includes only a single estimate of the time required for each activity.

Critical success factor (CSF). A particular activity that is recognized as having a strong influence on the firm's success. Managers can use a few CSFs to monitor firm performance, rather than a larger volume of information relating to overall operations.

CRT. *See* **Cathode-ray tube.**

CRT terminal. *See* **Cathode-ray tube.**

Current ratio. A performance ratio used to evaluate a firm's financial position by comparing its current assets and liabilities.

Current state. The condition of an entity at the present time. The entity, such as a firm or one of its operations, is monitored by comparing the current state with the desired state. *See also* **Desired state.**

Data. Facts and figures that are relatively meaningless to the user. Data is transformed into information by an information processor. Data is the raw material of information.

Data collection terminal. A terminal that permits input of data in various ways, such as by means of the keyboard, OCR, or magnetically-encoded cards. It is often used by factory workers for attendance and job reporting but can be found in other settings, such as libraries.

Datacom. *See* **Data communications.**

Data communications. The transmission of data from one geographic location to another. Also called **Teleprocessing, Telecommunications, Telecom, and Datacom.**

Data description language (DDL). The syntax that is used to specify a database schema or subschema.

Data description language processor. The part of the database management system, which transforms the data dictionary into the schema. *See also* **Data dictionary,** and **Schema.**

Data dictionary. A description of all of the data elements that are used by all of the firm's computer programs. The description includes the data element name, the type of data (numeric, alphabetic, alphanumeric), the number of positions, how the element is used, and so on. Some data dictionaries are maintained in computer storage.

Data dictionary system. The software that is used to create the data dictionary, maintain it in computer storage, and make it available for use. *See also* **Data dictionary.**

Data element. The smallest unit of data in a record. Examples are name, age, and sex.

Data flow diagram (DFD). A top-down, structured analysis and design tool that consists of symbols representing environmental elements, processes, data flows, and data repositories.

Data management. All of the activities concerned with keeping the firm's data resource accurate and up-to-date.

Data manager. Used in its broadest sense, the data manager is the person responsible for all of the data in the firm. Used in conjunction with the executive information system (EIS), the data manager is the person who is responsible for one or more data elements. This person's name and telephone number are frequently included in EIS displays.

Data manipulation language (DML). The syntax that is incorporated into a program to process data retrieved from a database.

Data processing (DP). Operations on data, which transform it into a more usable form, such as sorted data, summarized data, or stored data. The term often is used to describe accounting applications as opposed to those of a decision-support nature. Also called **transaction processing.**

Data processing system. The group of procedures that are concerned primarily with processing the firm's accounting data. The term **accounting system** is also used.

Data store. The symbol in a data flow diagram, which represents a repository of data, such as a file or database.

Database. In the broadest sense, all of the data existing within an organization. In a narrower sense, only the data stored in the computer's storage in such a manner that retrieval is facilitated. The narrower view is the more prevalent.

Database administrator (DBA). The person in a firm, who has overall responsibility for the computer-based data resource. There may be several DBAs in a large firm.

Database management system (DBMS). The software that handles the storage, maintenance, and retrieval of data in a database. The DBMS establishes the logical integration between files and records that facilitates retrieval.

Database manager. The portion of the DBMS, which is main-memory resident and makes database contents available to users. *See also* **Database management system.**

Database shadowing. A security precaution that calls for a duplicate database at a remote site to be updated as transactions occur.

Datacom. The term used in this text to mean data communications.

Datacom network. *See* **Network.**

Decision. The selection of a course of action.

Decision making. The process of making a decision. A problem solver makes multiple decisions while solving a single problem.

Decision room. A room that is especially designed to facilitate group decision making.

Decision support system (DSS). A concept originating in the early 1970s, which focuses on the decisions necessary to solve single problems, usually of a semistructured nature.

Decision variable. A value that is entered by a user into a mathematical model to gauge its effect on the entity being simulated.

Dedicated line. *See* **Private line.**

Dedicated word processor. A microcomputer designed specifically to perform word processing.

Definition effort. The portion of the systems approach to problem solving, which consists of a definition of the problem—where it is located and what is causing it. Also called **Analysis,** the **Analysis phase,** and **Diagnosis.**

Delphi method. An approach to gathering nonquantitative data, which involves successive responses from a panel. For each round the panel leader provides feedback from the previous round, which serves to bring the divergent views together. This iterative process continues until the responses reflect a single position.

Descriptor. An attribute that describes a data entity but does not identify it. Contrast with **Identifier.**

Design. *See* **Solution effort.**

Design activity. The term used by Simon for the identification and evaluation of alternatives.

Desired state. The state or condition of the entity when it is meeting its objectives. A problem exists when the desired state is not the same as the current state. *See also* **Current state.**

Desktop publishing (DTP). An office automation application that produces high-quality printing, such as that found in a book or magazine.

Deterministic model. A model that does not include probabilities. Contrast with **Probabilistic model.**

Development engine. The portion of an expert system, which is used by the expert and the systems analyst in developing the system.

Diagnosis. *See* **Definition effort.**

Dial-up circuit. The ordinary type of transmission facility, which is obtained by dialing the telephone number of the receiver.

Dialog. *See also* **Guided dialog.**

Direct access storage device (DASD). A secondary storage unit that has the capability of sending the access mechanism directly to a certain location where data can be written or read.

Disaster planning. *See* **Contingency planning.**

Disk drive. The direct access storage device (DASD) that stores data on metal disks in the form of magnetic bits. Also called a **disk unit.**

Disk stack. A vertical arrangement of magnetic disks that are housed in a disk drive.

Disk unit. *See* **Disk drive.**

Distributed data processing (DDP). *See* **Distributed processing.**

Distributed processing. A data communications network consisting of multiple computers. Also called **Distributed data processing.**

Distribution system. The set of data processing subsystems commonly found in distribution firms—manufacturers, wholesalers, and retailers.

Document management (DM) system. The software that manages a documenting imaging system. *See also* **Imaging.**

Downsizing. The information resources management strategy that calls for the downloading, or transfer, of applications from the firm's mainframe computer to microcomputers.

Drill down. A term usually associated with executive information systems, whereby the user is able to retrieve successively more detailed displays.

DSS. *See* **Decision support system.**

Dynamic model. A mathematical model that includes time as a variable; it simulates activity over time. It is analogous to a motion picture.

Economic justification. Evidence that the monetary benefits of using a system outweigh the costs.

Economic lot size. *See* **Economic manufacturing quantity.**

Economic manufacturing quantity (EMQ). An optimum quantity to be manufactured, which minimizes the total costs of producing too little or too much. Also called an **Economic lot size.**

Economic order quantity (EOQ). An optimum quantity of replenishment stock to be ordered from a supplier, which minimizes the total costs of ordering too little or too much.

Edit routine. A program module that subjects one or more data elements to tests that are intended to detect errors.

EDP auditor. A internal auditor who has a computer literacy.

EIS chauffeur. The person who operates the computer for the executive.

EIS coach. The person who helps an executive develop an executive information system, or EIS.

Electronic bulletin board. A use of electronic mail whereby the same message is sent to all users of the system. It is a way of broadcasting information on a wide scale.

Electronic calendaring. An office automation application that maintains an appointments calendar for the user. Some systems enable one person to view another person's calendar for the purpose of scheduling appointments.

Electronic data interchange (EDI). The design of computer-based systems to facilitate the flow of data from one firm to another. Examples of EDI include electronic transmission of purchase orders, invoices, and even payments.

Electronic data processing (EDP). The term that was used initially to mean computer processing. It is sometimes used as a synonym for **data processing.**

Electronic funds transfer (EFT). The technique of transferring funds between individuals and organizations, using electronic media rather than paper documents.

Electronic mail. An office automation application that enables users in a computer network to use their terminals or micros to send messages to one another.

Electronic mailbox. The area in the computer's storage where electronic mail is stored for a specific user.

Electronic meeting system (EMS). An expansion of the Group DSS concept to include activity in addition to decision making.

Electronic vaulting. The batch transmission of data to a remote storage facility where it is held in the form of backup files.

Empty shell. *See* **Cold site.**

End user. The person who uses the output of the CBIS.

End-user computing. The development and use of a computer application by a user, or end user, independent of assistance from information specialists.

Enterprise. The firm.

Enterprise data model. A description of the firm's total data resource, which serves as a basis for long-range data planning. The entity-relationship diagram and the data dictionary provide a good means of documentation. *See also* **Entity-relationship diagram,** and **Data dictionary.**

Entity. The phenomenon being modeled—a condition or a process.

Entity-relationship diagram. The documentation tool that illustrates the data entities and the relationships that exist among them.

Environment. Used in this text to mean everything outside the firm. Used by Kotter, it means a firm's norms and values.

Environmental management. The ability of a firm to control its environment to a certain degree.

Ergonomics. The study of the physical and behavioral effect of computing equipment on its users. Also called **Human engineering.**

Error message. A printed or displayed notice that an error has been made while processing data, possibly accompanied by an explanation of how to correct the error.

Evaluation criteria. The factors used in measuring each alternate solution to a problem for the purpose of identifying the best one.

Executive. A manager on the top level who exercises a strong influence on the firm's mission, strategy, and policies.

Executive committee. The formal group of executives, which regularly make the key decisions in an organization.

Executive database. The personal database of an executive.

Executive information system (EIS). A computer-based system designed specifically to meet the needs of one or more executives. Information is typically made available in the form of preformatted displays.

Executive routine. *See* **Supervisor.**

Executive sponsor. The individual, usually the president, who is the driving force behind the firm's efforts to implement an executive information system.

Executive support system (ESS). A computer-based system that has the capability of supporting the information needs of executives through the use of mathematical modeling.

Executive workstation. The terminal used by an executive.

Expert system. A computer program that can function as a consultant to a problem solver by not only suggesting a solution, but also by explaining the line of reasoning that leads to the solution. Such a program is an example of artificial intelligence. Also known as a **Knowledge-based system.**

Expert system shell. An expert system that includes all of the components except the knowledge base. The shell is tailored to a particular problem domain by providing the applicable knowledge base. *See also* **Knowledge base.**

Explicit relationship. A logical relationship between records and files of a database, which is accomplished explicitly—by incorporating link fields into the records. Contrast with **Implicit relationship.**

Facilitator. The leader of a group DSS effort, who focuses the discussion on the problem. Also used to describe the organization that stimulates cooperation in an interorganizational system, or IOS.

Facilities management (FM). A service offered by an outsourcer, which involves operating the firm's computing facility or facilities.

Facsimile transmission (FAX). An office automation application that transmits a copy of a document over a data communications channel.

Feasibility study. The activity of determining whether a system or a project is practical from the standpoint of technology, economic factors, legal considerations, user acceptance, and time schedule.

Feedback loop. The portion of a system, which enables the system to regulate itself. Feedback is obtained from the system and transmitted to the control mechanism. The control mechanism makes adjustments to the system when necessary. *See also* **Closed-loop system, Open-loop system.**

Feedforward information. Information that flows through a distribution channel in the same direction as the products and services. Examples include announcements of new products and product safety instructions.

Figure 0 diagram. The data flow diagram that exists just below the context diagram in the top-down hierarchy.

Figure n diagram. A data flow diagram that exists on a level below the Figure 0 diagram. The n identifies the process on the next higher level.

File. A group of records relating to a particular subject.

File maintenance. The process of keeping a file up-to-date by adding, deleting, and modifying records.

File server. *See* **Network server.**

Financial audit. An audit that is conducted by an external or internal auditor for the purpose of verifying the accuracy of the firm's accounting figures.

Financial information system. The functional information system that meets the needs of the firm's managers for financial information.

Flat file. A two-dimensional file of data in rows and columns, which is used in a relational database. *See also* **Relational structure.**

Flowchart. A schematic diagram of a process, using standardized symbols. When the diagram is that of an entire system, it is called a **system flowchart**. When it is of only a single program within the system, it is a **program flowchart.**

Form-filling technique. One of three ways to enter data and instructions into a computer from an online keydriven device. The screen is designed to resemble a printed form so that you can move the cursor from field to field as the data elements are entered. Contrast with **Menu-display technique** and **Questions-and-answers technique.**

Forward chaining. *See* **Forward reasoning.**

Forward reasoning. One of the two basic approaches to rule-based reasoning, which an expert system uses, whereby each rule in the rule set is examined in sequence. When a rule condition is true, the rule is fired. Multiple passes are made until no more rules can be fired. Also called **Forward chaining.** Contrast with **Reverse reasoning.**

Fourth-generation language (4GL). The most recent breed of software that is intended to facilitate end-user computing. The name **natural language** is also used because of the user-friendly syntax, and the name **nonprocedural language** is used since it is not as necessary that the processes be specified in a particular order as with a programming language.

Front-end processor. The component of a data communications network, which performs most of the control functions. The front-end processor is often a minicomputer that relieves the larger host computer of much of the network-related responsibility so that the host can concentrate on data processing.

Functional area. *See* **Functional organization.**

Functional decomposition. A top-down systems analysis approach that involves subdividing each system into its subsystems.

Functional information system. A subset of the MIS, which is tailored to meet the needs of a particular functional area. Examples are manufacturing information systems and marketing information systems.

Functional organization. A segregation of the firm's resources based on the major functions that are performed. The four main functional areas are marketing, manufacturing, finance, and human resources.

Functionality. What a system does—the tasks that it performs.

Gantt chart. A chart that uses horizontal bars to represent tasks to be performed over time.

General ledger system. The accounting system that assembles data from other systems to maintain a composite record of the firm's operations. The data is maintained in a general ledger file that is used to print standard accounting reports such as the balance sheet and income statement.

Go/no-go decision. A decision whether to continue with a project or to terminate it.

Goal variable. The overall solution that is sought by an expert system. For example, the goal variable for an expert system designed to produce a sales forecast would be the forecast figure.

Graph generator. A software package that produces information in a graphic form. Also called a **Graphics package.**

Graphic model. A model that uses symbols and lines to represent its entity.

Graphic user interface (GUI). The feature of a computer-based system, which uses graphic symbols to communicate with the user.

Graphic word processor. A new breed of word processors, which displays information on the screen just as it will be printed on paper. It is an example of WYSIWYG. *See* **WYSIWYG.**

Graphics package. *See* **Graph generator.**

Gross requirements. The total quantity of materials needed for a production run, determined by multiplying the number of units in the job lot times the quantities of each item on the bill of materials.

Group decision support system (GDSS). A DSS that is used by several people who jointly make a decision.

Groupware. Software that supports a GDSS environment. *See* **Group decision support system.**

Guided dialog. The exchange of data and information between the computer and the user, which is controlled by the software.

Hard copy. A paper document.

Hard copy terminal. A keyboard terminal that produces output information in a printed form. Also called a **Teleprinter terminal.**

Hardware. The equipment that comprises a computer configuration.

Hashing scheme. *See* **Randomizing formula.**

Help message. A screen display that is intended to assist the user in overcoming a particular difficulty in using the computer.

Help screen. *See* **Help message.**

Heuristic. A rule of thumb or an "educated guess" that is incorporated into an expert system.

Hierarchical network. *See* **Tree network.**

Hierarchical structure. One of the basic database structures, which arranges data in a top-down hierarchy of one-to-one or one-to-many relationships. A data element on one level, called a **child,** is related to only a single data element immediately above, called the **parent.**

High-grade threat. A person or organization with the technological expertise and resources to inflict damage on a computer installation even though the installation may be well secured.

Host computer. The computer in a data communications network, which performs most of the processing. In a large network the host is usually a mainframe. Control of the network is shared by the host and the front-end processor. *See also* **Front-end processor.**

Hot site. A backup computer facility that contains everything needed, including the computer.

Human engineering. *See* **Ergonomics.**

Human factors considerations. Behavioral influences that determine the relationship between the computer and the people whom it affects.

Human resource information system (HRIS). The functional information system that meets the needs of the firm's managers for personnel information. Also called the **human resource management system (HRMS).**

Human resource management system (HRMS). *See* **Human resource information system.**

Hybrid network. A data communications network that consists of a combination of topologies, such as star and ring.

Identifier. An attribute that identifies an entity. For example, employee number identifies the employee entity.

Imaging. An office automation application featuring the storage and retrieval of document images using optical disks.

Immediate cutover. The stopping of the old system and the starting of the new system without any overlap.

Impact printer. A printing device that prints characters on paper by striking a hammer-like object with an embossed character against an ink ribbon, which, in turn, strikes the paper. It is the same technology as used by a typewriter.

Implementation. The actions required to transform a description of a system that exists on paper into one that consists of functioning physical components.

Implicit relationship. The linking of records and files in a database without addition of special fields. The relationships are implied using the contents of fields already in the records. This is accomplished through the use of a relational calculus, and is characteristic of the relational database structure.

In-depth interview. A lengthy, personal interview of a small number of people, conducted by marketing researchers or systems analysts.

Industrial engineer (IE). The person who studies a physical system for purpose of making it more efficient. The work also involves the establishment of conceptual systems to control the physical system.

Industrial espionage. Unethical techniques that a firm employs to gather information on its competitors.

Industrial robot (IR). A robot used to perform tasks in a manufacturing facility.

Inference engine. The portion of an expert system, which performs the logical reasoning.

Infinite sink. *See* **Black hole.**

Information. Processed data that is meaningful to the user.

Information center. An area in a firm, which provides hardware, software, and expertise to the firm's employees who want to engage in end-user computing.

Information compression. A term used in conjunction with an executive information system, which describes the manner in which information is boiled down to its essential elements.

Information economics. The approach to justifying computing expenditures, which recognizes all possible values and all possible risks.

Information engineering. A term coined by James Martin to describe the top-down implementation of computer-based systems, beginning with strategic planning, followed by a critical look at the firm's activities, and finally encompassing rapid application development. *See also* **Rapid application development.**

Information literacy. An understanding of how to use information in problem solving.

Information management. All of the activities involved with managing the firm's information resources.

Information overload. The situation when a problem solver is presented with more information than is needed.

Information processor. The unit that transforms data into information. It can be a human, a computer, or some other device.

Information resources management (IRM). A firm's formal program for utilizing its computing resources so that they enable the firm to meet its strategic objectives.

Information specialist. Any person whose primary occupation is concerned with providing computer-based systems. Examples are systems analysts, programmers, operators, network managers, and database administrators.

Information systems (IS). A term that is often used as a synomym for MIS when describing the entire field of business computing.

Information technology (IT). Resources of all types—hardware, software, personnel, and so on—that produce information.

Information-gathering style. The unique manner in which a manager obtains information. *See also* **Preceptive style** and **Receptive style.**

Information-using style. The unique manner in which a manager applies information in decision making. *See also* **Intuitive style** and **Systematic style.**

Input bottleneck. The situation that exists when a system cannot handle its volume of input data.

Input subsystem. A subsystem of a functional information system, which enters data and information into the database.

Insourcing. An information resources management strategy of a firm, which decides to recapture outsourced computing activity.

Integrated application generator. A prototyping tool that produces all of the components of an operational system—database, input screens, outputs, and so on.

Integrated CASE (I-CASE) tool. A CASE tool that encompasses the entire system life cycle. *See also* **Computer-aided software engineering.**

Integrated services digital network (ISDN). A data communications circuit that has the ability to transmit voice, data, text, and image signals at high speeds.

Integrity. The characteristic of a system, which enables it to accomplish what is intended.

Intelligence. Data and information obtained from the firm's environment.

Intelligence activity. The term used by Simon for the analysis phase.

Interactive mode. The status of a system when there is a two-way communication with the user.

Interexchange channel (IXC) circuit. The portion of a wide area network, which exists between the central offices of the common carriers.

Internal auditor. An employee whose main responsibility is to ensure the integrity of the firm's conceptual systems.

Internal control systems design. The participation of internal auditors in the SLC.

Interorganizational system (IOS). A cooperative effort between a firm and its suppliers and channel members to work together as one coordinated unit.

Intuitive style. The manager's decision making style that makes use of intuition. Contrast with **Systematic style.**

Inventory system. The accounting system that maintains a record of a firm's finished goods.

Inventory turnover. A performance ratio that captures the ability of a firm to maximize the return on its inventory investment.

Inverted file. An approach to establishing implicit relationships among data records through the use of an index.

Invoice. The document that is provided to a customer by the billing system as an official notice of the money owed to the firm for a purchase.

Job profile. The characteristics of a job in terms of the knowledge and skills that are required.

Job profile matching. The process of comparing job profiles for the purpose of identifying the degree of similarity.

Job reporting. The entry of data into the computer, which describes each step of the production process in detail, consisting of data such as job number, start time, stop time, operator number, and step number.

Joint application design (JAD). A formal approach to system development, which brings the participants together in a group setting.

Just-in-time (JIT). The approach to production control, which emphasizes very small lot sizes and the use of a physical signal, called a kanban, to signal the movement of materials from one production step to another.

Kanban. A signal issued by a production employee of a just-in-time manufacturing facility. The signal indicates that an employee is ready to perform processing on another unit.

Key. A data element that identifies a record.

Knowledge acquisition. The identification of the thought processes applied by an expert in solving a problem. Once acquired, the thought processes are incorporated in the knowledge base of an expert system.

Knowledge base. The portion of an expert system, which contains rules and other types of knowledge representation that describe a particular problem domain.

Knowledge engineer. The name used to describe a person who is capable of working with an expert in developing an expert system.

Knowledge worker. An employee whose contribution is primarily intellectual rather than physical. Managers and professionals are knowledge workers.

Knowledge-based system. *See* **Expert system.**

Laser disk. *See* **Optical disk.**

Lead time. The lapse in time from the point where a need to reorder is recognized until the materials arrive from the supplier.

Legacy system. A system that was implemented prior to structured techniques and represents a drain on resources, but is too important to scrap.

Leveled DFD. A group of data flow diagrams, which exists in a hierarchy of levels.

Line. *See* **Circuit.**

Line item. An entry in a listing. An example is a detail line on an invoice describing a product that the customer has purchased.

Linear programming (LP). A mathematical technique that determines the optimum mix or routing of resources in order to maximize a benefit or minimize a cost within the constraints. LP is the most common example of an optimizing model.

Linked list. An approach to achieving a logical organization of data that is different from its physical organization by incorporating implicit relationships in a file through data links. *See also* **Logical organization,** and **Physical organization.**

Local area network (LAN). A network of computers that are connected using circuitry owned by the firm. In most cases the network is restricted to a small area, such as a building.

Local loop. The portion of a data communication network, which extends from the firm's modem to the common carrier's central office.

Logical organization. The organization of the data in the database as viewed by the user. Contrast with **Physical organization.**

Lot size. The number of units in a production run.

Lower CASE tool. A software tool that is used in the lower levels of the hierarchy, as the firm follows a top-down system development approach. The best example is a code generator. Contrast with **Upper CASE tool.**

Machine readable. The characteristic of documentation that is easy to convert into computer code. For example, when pseudocode incorporates COBOL syntax, it is easy to convert the documentation into a COBOL program.

Magnetic ink character recognition (MICR). The means of entering data into a computer in the form of characters printed on paper documents using an ink that is easily magnetized.

Main memory. *See* **Primary storage.**

Maintenance cost. The expenses that are incurred when carrying inventory in stock.

Management by exception. A technique whereby a manager is concerned only with activities falling outside an area of acceptable performance.

Management control level. The term used by Anthony to describe managers on the middle level.

Management function. The basic tasks that all managers perform—plan, organize, staff, direct, and control—as specified by Henri Fayol.

Management information system (MIS). A system that provides the manager with information for decision making. The term was originally used to distinguish such a computer application from traditional accounting jobs. The text uses the term to describe information systems that are intended to meet the general information needs of all managers in the firm or of all managers in a specific organizational area.

Managerial role. A category of management activity, as viewed by Mintzberg.

Manufacturing information system. The functional information system that provides information concerning the firm's manufacturing activity.

Manufacturing resource planning (MRP-II). A software system that integrates all of the resources that are involved with the material flow through a manufacturing firm. The MRP-II system includes portions of the output subsystems of the manufacturing information system and interfaces with other subsystems within the CBIS.

Marketing information system (MKIS). The functional information system that provides information concerning the firm's marketing activity.

Marketing intelligence. Information that describes activities of the firm's competitors. Also called **competitive intelligence (CI),** and **business intelligence.**

Marketing research. The activity of gathering data and information that describe the firm's marketing operations. Most of the research is designed to gain a better understanding of customers.

Master file. A file containing data of a fairly permanent nature. Master files typically are maintained for a firm's customers, personnel, inventory, and so on. They form the conceptual resource.

Material requirements planning (MRP). A proactive approach to material procurement, which uses the master production schedule to anticipate future material needs.

Mathematical model. Any formula or set of formulas, which represents an object or activity.

Mental model. The term used by Rockart and DeLong to describe the image of the firm's activities in the executive's mind.

Menu. A list of choices displayed on a screen.

Menu-display technique. An approach to controlled dialog between a user and the computer, which makes use of menus of processes to perform. The computer displays a menu, and the user selects the choice that instructs the computer what to do next.

Menu-driven system. A system that relies primarily on menus to guide the user.

Message switching. Use of a computer to control the sending and receiving of messages in a network. The front-end processor can perform this task independently of the host.

Methodology. A recommended way of doing something.

Microform. Use of photographic film to store images in the form of reels (microfilm) or cards (microfiche).

Middle CASE tool. A CASE tool that is used to document processes and data during analysis and design. *See also* **Computer-aided software engineering.**

MIS steering committee. The group in an organization, which has responsibility for establishing policy concerning information resources, and overseeing the development of computer-based systems.

MIS strategy set. The collection of objectives, strategies, and so on that relate to the MIS.

Model. A representation of some phenomenon. Various types of models exist—physical, graphic, narrative, and mathematical.

Modeling language. A programming language that is especially tailored to the development of mathematical models.

Modem. The device in a data communications network, which transforms the digital impulses of computing equipment into the form used by communications equipment, and vice versa. A data communications channel usually includes a modem on each end.

Moderator. The person who coordinates the exchange of information during an audio conference.

Monitor. *See* **Supervisor.**

Multifunction drive. An optical disk drive that includes both WORM (write-once, read many) and rewritable disks.

Multiplexer. The data communications device that permits the transmission of multiple messages on a circuit at the same time.

Multiprogramming. The ability of a computer to concurrently process several programs.

Narrative model. A model that uses words to represent its entity.

Natural language. *See* **Fourth-generation language.**

Navigation. The movement up and down a hierarchy of menus.

Net present value (NPV). The discounted value of future benefits derived from a computer-based system, reflecting the time value of money.

Net requirements. The amount of new inventory that must be acquired for a production run, computed by subtracting the on-hand inventory from the gross requirements. *See also* **Gross requirements.**

Network. Most often used to describe an interconnection of computing equipment using data communications circuitry. Kotter uses the term to describe cooperative relationships among the people who accomplish the firm's objectives.

Network control program (NCP). The name often used for the data communications software contained in the front-end processor.

Network diagram. Either a critical path method (CPM) diagram or a program evaluation and review technique (PERT) chart that is used for planning and control.

Network management. The activity of planning, implementing, and operating a firm's data communications network or networks. The activity includes capacity planning, staff planning, and performance monitoring.

Network manager. The person who is responsible for network management. *See also* **Network management.**

Network server. The computer in a local area network, which controls the peripherals. *See also* **Local area network,** and **Peripheral.** Also called the **File server.**

Neural net. The network of neurons that give the brain a learning ability. Mathematical models that simulate the nets are called artificial neural systems. *See also* **Artificial neural system.**

Neurocomputer. A mechanical device that is designed to duplicate some of the processing of the brain.

New product committee. The group that decides which products the firm will manufacture and market.

Node. A circle in a network diagram. *See also* **Network diagram.** The term is also used to describe a point in a data communications network, which is occupied by a device such as a terminal.

Noneconomic justification. The approach for substantiating the worth of a computer without the use of monetary measures.

Nonhardware specific. The characteristic of a documentation tool to not reflect the technology that is used in the system. Data flow diagrams and Warnier-Orr diagrams both have this characteristic. System flowcharts do not.

Nonimpact printer. A printer that does not print by means of forcing an ink ribbon against the paper. Contrast with **Impact printer.**

Nonprocedural language. *See* **Fourth-generation language.**

Nonprogrammed decision. The term used by Simon to describe a decision that does not follow an established routine. Contrast with **Programmed decision.**

Normalization. The process of transforming the entities in a database into a form that stores the data in the most efficient way.

Objective. What a system is intended to accomplish, usually stated in broad terms. More specific standards are used to guide the system toward its objectives. *See also* **Standard.**

Observation. The gathering of data and information by viewing activity as it occurs, or by viewing evidence that the activity has occurred.

Office automation (OA). All of the electronic technologies used to facilitate the flow of communications within the firm and between the firm and its environment. Examples are word processing, electronic mail, and teleconferencing.

Online processing. One of two basic ways to process data, which requires the computer configuration to include some type of keyboard to enter transactions as they occur, plus direct access storage. The main advantage of online processing is that it enables the conceptual system to stay up-to-date with the physical system. Contrast with **Batch processing.**

Online transaction processing (OLTP). The online approach to processing accounting data. *See also* **Online processing.**

Open system. A system that interfaces with its environment.

Open Systems Interconnection (OSI) model. A set of data communications network standards that are being implemented on an international basis.

Open-loop system. A system without a feedback loop. *See also* **Feedback loop.**

Operating budget. The amount of money that is available to a unit to cover its expenses for a certain time period. It is often simply called the **budget.**

Operating sponsor. The manager who represents the executive sponsor in ensuring that the executive information system is implemented as planned. *See* **Executive sponsor.**

Operating system. The master program that controls the computer. In most cases, you cannot use the computer without following the instructions from the operating system. Early computers did not have operating systems and many system tasks had to be performed by the operator. The IBM System/360, introduced in 1964, was the first computer to offer an operating system furnished by the supplier.

Operational audit. An inspection of a conceptual system for purposes of improving it. The audit is normally conducted by internal auditors.

Operational control level. The name used by Anthony to describe managers on the lower level.

Optical character recognition (OCR). The means of entering data into a computer with an input unit that reads printed characters in much the same way as does the human eye.

Optical disk. A storage medium that represents data in the form of tiny pits or blemishes made in a disk by a laser beam. Also called **Laser disk, Compact disk,** and **CD-ROM.**

Optimizing model. A mathematical model that identifies the best solution in terms of achieving the specified objective. The objective is usually to minimize something, such as costs, or to maximize something, such as profit.

Order entry system. The accounting system that performs the initial processing on sales orders received from customers.

Order log. A record of sales orders received by the order entry system.

Order point. *See* **Reorder point.**

Organizational strategy set. The firm's objectives, strategy, and so on that serve as the basis for establishing the MIS strategy set.

Output subsystem. A subsystem of a functional information system, which transforms data from the database into information for the manager.

Outsourcing. The strategy of assigning certain of the firm's activities to outside organizations, called outsourcers, rather than performing the activities within the firm. The work is done in accordance with a long-term contract.

Packing slip. The document that is enclosed with products that are shipped to the customer.

Panel consensus. An approach to forecasting, which relies on a group such as a committee to jointly arrive at the projection.

Parallel communication. The simultaneous input of ideas, suggestions, and criticisms by participants in a group decision support system.

Parallel cutover. Operation of both the old and the new system until the performance of the new system is proven.

Parent. *See* **Hierarchical structure.**

Participative budgeting. The preparation of a budget through interaction between all management levels.

Payback analysis. An approach to economic justification, which compares the cumulative costs and benefits of a new system. *See also* **Economic justification.**

Peripheral. An input or output device that is a part of a computer configuration or a network.

Performance criteria. The standards of performance for the information services unit.

Performance ratio. A computed value used to portray some aspect of an organization's financial status.

Periodic report. A report prepared on a certain schedule, such as monthly. Also called a **repetitive report.**

Person month. The efforts of one person working for a month on a task. Used as a measure of the amount effort to accomplish a task, such as the implementation of a computer system.

Personal interview. The gathering of data and information through face-to-face questioning.

Phased cutover. The gradual introduction of a new system, one subsystem at a time.

Physical model. A model that uses physical objects, often in three-dimensional form, to represent its entity.

Physical organization. The organization of the data in the database as viewed by the computer. Contrast with **Logical organization.**

Physical resource. A resource that exists physically. Personnel, material, machines, and money are examples. Contrast with **Conceptual resource.**

Physical system. A system that exists physically. Examples are humans, computers, and firms. Contrast with **Conceptual system.**

Planning horizon. The future time period for which a manager has a planning responsibility.

Plotter. An output device that produces graphs.

Point of sale (POS) terminal. The keyboard terminal that is used in a retail store in lieu of a cash register.

Polling. The act performed by a network server or front-end processor of giving each terminal in the network an opportunity to send or receive a message. *See also* **Contention-based control,** and **Token-passing control.**

Port. The part of the front-end processor, which connects it with a data communications circuit. Multiple ports are common.

Postimplementation review. A formal evaluation of a system, which is conducted after it is implemented.

Preceptive style. An approach to gathering information whereby the manager screens out everything that does not fit within a particular area of interest. Contrast with **Receptive style.**

Preparation effort. The portion of the systems approach to problem solving, which involves taking a systems view of the problem area.

Preventive maintenance (PM). Repair work on a computer, which is intended to lessen the chances of a breakdown.

Primary data. Data that the firm gathers. Contrast with **Secondary data.**

Primary storage. The storage that is contained in the central processing unit. Also called **Main memory.**

Private line. A data communications circuit that the firm does not share with other users. Also called a **Dedicated line.**

Proactive environmental attitude. The view that a firm can influence its environment.

Probabilistic model. A mathematical model that incorporates probabilities.

Problem. A condition or event that damages or threatens to damage the organization in some negative way, or improves or threatens to improve the organization in some positive way.

Problem avoider. A manager who dislikes problems and will not attempt to solve them even when they become evident.

Problem domain. The problem area where an expert system is applied.

Problem identification. The point in the problem-solving process where the problem solver becomes aware of a problem or potential problem.

Problem seeker. A manager who enjoys the challenge of solving problems and seeks them out.

Problem solver. A manager who will not make a special effort to uncover problems, but will not back away when they become evident.

Problem solving. All of the activity that leads to the solution of a problem.

Problem trigger. Something that signals a problem or impending problem.

Problem-oriented language. A language designed to solve a particular class of problems. FORTRAN, COBOL, and BASIC are examples.

Problem-sensing style. The unique manner in which a manager responds to problem signals. *See also* **Problem avoider, Problem seeker,** and **Problem solver.**

Procedure-oriented language. A programming language that requires the programmer to code the statements in exactly the same sequence in which they will be processed. Contrast with **Fourth-generation language.**

Professional. A nonmanager who provides specialized knowledge and is usually compensated on a salary, rather than hourly, basis. The professionals and managers comprise the knowledge workers.

Program Evaluation and Review Technique (PERT). A type of network diagram, which includes a pessimistic, optimistic, and most likely estimate of the time required for each activity.

Program flowchart. *See* **Flowchart.**

Programmed decision. The term used by Simon to describe a decision that is made by following a prescribed routine. Contrast with **Nonprogrammed decision.**

Project dictionary. The package that contains all of the documentation prepared during the system development life cycle.

Project team. The group that has responsibility for developing a system.

Proposal. A suggestion that a particular action be taken. The systems analyst makes a study project proposal and an implementation project proposal. Suppliers of hardware and software make proposals that their products be selected. The proposal usually is in a written form but can be accompanied by an oral presentation.

Protected format. A means of reducing errors by designing an input screen in such a way that the user cannot enter data into certain areas.

Protocol. The standards that are used in interfacing data communications equipment and circuitry. It is commonly called "shaking hands."

Prototype. A system that is not developed with the intention of completely meeting a user's needs but of providing the user with an idea of how the system ultimately will appear and be used. The prototype is continually modified until it either serves as the blueprint of the operational system or becomes the operational system.

Prototyping. The act of using a series of prototypes as a means of defining users' needs.

Prototyping toolkit. Software that performs part of the prototyping task. Contrast with an **Integrated application generator.**

Pseudocode. Something that looks like computer code but is not. It is an informal way to document the logic of a computer program.

Purchasing system. A subsystem of the data processing system, which orders replenishment stock from a supplier.

Query language. A language that enables the user to query the database. The query language can exist alone or as a subset of a database management system.

Questions-and-answers technique. One of main ways to enter data and instructions into a computer from an online keydriven device. The computer asks a question and the user enters the answer.

Random access memory (RAM). Primary storage that permits both reading and writing. Contrast with **Read-only memory.**

Randomizing formula. The algorithm that is used to convert a record key into a DASD address. Also called a **Hashing scheme.**

Rapid application development (RAD). A structured approach to systems development, which begins with strategic planning and ends with prototyping.

Read-only memory. The primary storage that permits only reading, not writing. Contrast with **Random access memory.**

Realtime system. A conceptual system that responds to signals from a physical system in a sufficiently fast manner to control the physical system. The processing performed by an online credit-approval system in a department store is an example.

Receiving system. A subsystem of the data processing system, which performs the necessary processing when replenishment stock is obtained from a supplier.

Receptive style. An approach to gathering information whereby the manager is interested in everything. Contrast with **Preceptive style.**

Record. A collection of data elements that relate to a certain subject. Multiple records comprise a file.

Reengineering. An approach to systems maintenance, which calls for the entire system development life cycle to be repeated.

Regression analysis. A mathematical technique that is used in forecasting.

Relational structure. The database structure that uses implicit relationships. *See* **Implicit relationship.**

Remote journaling. The transmission of backup data to a remote site as transactions are processed. The data is not used to maintain a complete database as is the case with **Database shadowing.**

Reorder point (ROP). The balance-on-hand quantity that triggers a purchasing transaction. Also called **order point.**

Repetition construct. The structured programming construct that causes a sequence of processes to be repeated.

Repetitive report. *See* **Periodic report.**

Report writer. Software that prepares reports.

Request for proposal (RFP). The formal notification of prospective suppliers that a proposal is desired by the firm. *See also* **Proposal.**

Restructuring. An approach to systems maintenance, which calls for unstructured code to be recoded into a structured format without changing the functionality of the program.

Reverse engineering. The automatic generation of system documentation on a higher level. For example, computer code is used to generate data flow diagrams.

Reverse reasoning. One of the two basic approaches to the rule-based reasoning that an expert system uses, whereby the inference engine selects a rule that assigns a value to the goal variable and regards it as a problem to be solved. If another rule must be fired before the problem can be solved, the other rule becomes the problem. In this manner the inference engine backtracks through the rule set, attempting to fire rules that will produce a value for the goal variable. It is also called **backward chaining.** Contrast with **Forward reasoning.**

Review activity. The term used by Simon for follow-up after a decision is made.

Rewritable disk. An optical disk that permits new data to be recorded over old data. Contrast with **WORM (Write-once, read-many).**

Ring network. A data communications network that does not contain a central control point such as a network server.

Roll call polling. A way that a front-end processor or network server controls the network by asking each terminal in turn whether they want to use the channel.

Rule. The most popular knowledge representation technique used by an expert system. A rule consists of a condition and an action, and is fired when the condition is true.

Rule set. The group of rules in the knowledge base of an expert system, which represents a particular problem domain.

Safety stock. A extra quantity of an inventory item, which is carried to minimize the chance of a stockout.

Sales analysis. A study of the firm's sales in various ways, such as by product, by customer, and by salesperson.

Satisficing model. *See* **Suboptimizing model.**

Scenario. The specifications entered into a mathematical model to tailor it to a certain situation.

Scenario data element. A piece of data that is entered into a mathematical model to establish all or part of the scenario.

Schema. A description of all of the data elements in the database.

Secondary data. Data that someone else has gathered. Contrast with **Primary data.**

Secondary storage. Storage that supplements primary storage.

Selection construct. The structured programming construct that represents a logical choice between two or more alternatives.

Selective dissemination of information. Making information available to only those persons who should receive it.

Semistructured problem. A problem that includes some variables, which are identifiable and whose composition and relationships are understood. This is the type of problem that the DSS is intended to address.

Sequence construct. The structured programming construct that consists of a series of processes that are followed in order.

Sequential storage. A type of secondary storage in which records are arranged one after the other, and must be processed in the same order.

Session. A transmission of data over a data communications network beginning with an initialization (such as a telephone conversation's "hello"), and ends with a termination (such as "good-bye").

Simulation. The process of using a model to represent some phenomenon.

Simulator. The device, usually a computer, that is used to simulate some phenomenon.

Single-source data. Data that completely describes an activity, such as a sales transaction, and is collected from a single respondent, such as a customer.

Slack. Time on a noncritical path through a network diagram, which is in excess of the critical path time. *See also* **Critical path.**

Software library. All of a firm's software.

Solution criterion. The level of performance, which must be achieved in order to solve a particular problem.

Solution effort. The portion of the systems approach to problem solving, which includes the identification of the best solution, its implementation, and follow up. Also called **Design** and the **Synthesis phase.**

Source data automation (SDA). The design of a source document so that its data can be entered into a computer without the need for manual keying. Magnetic ink character recognition and optical character recognition are examples.

Source document. The document that contains input data to a system.

Speaker-dependent system. A speech recognition unit that is trained to recognize particular voices.

Speaker-independent system. A speech recognition unit that can recognize anyone's voice.

Special report. A report prepared in response to a special request or event as opposed to one prepared on a regular schedule.

Standard. A measure of the ability of a system to meet an objective.

Star network. A data communications network that contains a central control point, such as a network server.

Statement. This term has two meanings. First, a statement is the order that is given to the computer in a problem-oriented language. Programs written in such languages consist of multiple statements. Second, a statement is a document that is mailed to a customer as a reminder of a past-due receivable.

Static model. A mathematical model that reflects the condition of the entity at a single point in time. It is analogous to a snapshot.

Steering committee. An ongoing group that oversees some activity. *See also* **MIS steering committee.**

Stockout. The condition that exists when there is no inventory stock remaining for a particular item.

Store and forward. The action performed by a front-end processor when performing message switching, and the receiving terminal is busy or out of service. *See also* **Message switching.**

Strategic planning. The long-range planning performed by the firm's executives.

Strategic planning for information resources (SPIR). The development of long-range plans for the use of the firm's information resources.

Strategic planning level. The term used by Anthony to describe managers on the top level.

Strategy set transformation. The term coined by King to describe the technique of using a firm's business plan as a basis for the MIS plan.

Structured analysis. A top-down approach to studying an existing system by first analyzing the overall system, and then the subsytems on progressively lower levels.

Structured design. A method followed in systems design, which consists of initially specifying the system in general terms and gradually making the description more detailed.

Structured English. A relatively disciplined narrative description of a system or procedure. Only the three structured programming constructs are used. Names of conditions such as IF and WHILE and data names such as EMPLOYEE.NO are capitalized. Only data names in the data dictionary are used. Structured English is excellent for supplementing data flow diagrams.

Structured problem. A problem consisting of variables that are all identifiable and whose composition and relationships are understood. The problem of how much of an item to order (the economic order quantity) is an example.

Suboptimizing model. A mathematical model that does not necessarily produce the best solution, but is one that satisfies the user. Also called a **Satisficing model.**

Subschema. A subset of the schema, describing a particular user's data.

Subsystem. A system within a system.

Supersystem. The environment within which a system exists. The term **suprasystem** is also used.

Supervisor. When applied to computer software, the supervisor is the portion of the operating system, which remains in primary storage so that it can perform the major control functions and retrieve other routines from secondary storage when they are needed. Also called **Monitor** and **Executive routine.** The term is also used to describe a lower-level manager.

Supplier. An organization that provides the firm with needed machines or materials. Also called a **Vendor.**

Suprasystem. *See* **Supersystem.**

Survey. A study.

Symptom. A result of a problem rather than its root cause.

Synchronous exchange. Dialog between one or more senders and receivers, which requires messages to be received at the same time as they are sent. Audio and video conferencing have this characteristic. Contrast with **Asynchronous exchange.**

Synthesis phase. *See* **Solution effort.**

System. An integration of elements designed to accomplish some objective.

System development life cycle (SDLC). The phases of the system life cycle leading to cutover.

System flowchart. *See* **Flowchart.**

System life cycle (SLC). The phases of developing and using a computer-based system.

System software. Programs that are required to use a particular computer. Examples are operating systems, translators, and utility programs.

System study. The name often given to the analysis phase of the system life cycle.

Systematic style. The manager's decision making style that is based on the systems approach.

Systems analysis. The study of existing systems for the purpose of improving them.

Systems approach. A problem-solving methodology that consists of understanding the problem before a solution is attempted, and evaluating several alternate solutions.

Systems design. All of the activity that goes into determining the best structure of a new or improved system.

Systems integration (SI). A service performed by outsourcers of developing new systems for their clients. *See* **Outsourcing.**

Systems maintenance. The activity focused on operational systems for the purpose of correcting errors, keeping the systems current, and improving the level of user support.

Systems Network Architecture (SNA). The standards that IBM incorporates into its data communications hardware and software.

Systems view. A posture that regards phenomena, such as business organizations, as systems.

Telecom. *See* **Data communications.**

Telecommunications. *See* **Data communications.**

Telecommunications monitor (TCM). The name often used for the data communications software in the host.

Teleconferencing. The blanket term used to describe the office automation applications of audio conferencing, computer conferencing, and video conferencing.

Telephone tag. The "game" that you and another person play when you alternately call each other and the other person is unavailable or out.

Teleprinter terminal. *See* **Hard copy terminal.**

Teleprocessing. *See* **Data communications.**

Template. A pattern that is displayed on a screen to facilitate the form-filling approach to data entry.

Timesharing. The use of a computer by multiple users.

Token-passing control. An approach to network control, which consists of an electronic "token" being passed, in turn, to each terminal. The terminal with the token can use the channel.

Total-systems approach. The erroneous objective of early MIS designers who attmpted to meet all information needs of all managers.

Transaction file. A file containing descriptions of transactions, such as product sales, that are used to update a master file.

Transaction processing. *See* **Data processing.**

Translator. Any type of system program, which converts a source program into an object, machine-language program. Assemblers, compilers, and interpreters are translators.

Tree network. A data communications network that consists of multiple levels of devices arranged in a hierarchy. The use of a bus to connect devices in a LAN is an example. The term **hierarchical network** is also used.

Twisted pair. The traditional communications circuit technology that consists of four wires.

Unstructured problem. A problem consisting of variables and their relationships that cannot be identified.

Upper CASE tool A software tool that is intended to support the planning phase of the system life cycle.

User-friendly. Hardware or software that is easy to learn and use.

User interface. The portion of an expert system, which accepts inputs from the user and displays the results of the consultation.

Utility program. System software that performs tasks required by most users of a computer, such as formatting diskettes, copying files, erasing files, and so on.

Vendor. *See* **Supplier.**

Very high level language. An example of fourth-generation languages, which performs sophisticated processes from succinct code. APL is an example.

Video conferencing. The office automation application that uses both video and audio signals to link conference participants in geographically dispersed locations.

Video display terminal. *See* **Cathode-ray tube.**

Videotex. The office automation application that features the retrieval of stored textual and graphic information using a computer terminal.

Virus. An example of malicious software, which is transmitted from computer to computer by means of diskettes or electronic bulletin boards and causes harm to the user's programs or data.

Visual display terminal (VDT). *See* **Cathode-ray tube.**

Voice grade circuit. A communications circuit that is intended to provide only the level of quality needed to transmit human voices.

Voice mail. The office automation application that enables a person to send a message by speaking into an ordinary telephone. The message is stored in secondary storage. The other party retrieves the message at his or her convenience, using an ordinary telephone.

Voice mailbox. An area in the computer's storage, which is reserved for a certain person's voice messages stored in a digital form.

Warnier-Orr. A systems analysis and design tool that documents a system using a hierarchical arrangement of brackets.

WATS circuit. *See* **Wide Area Telecommunications Service.**

What-If game. A method of trying out alternate decision strategies using a mathematical model. The user asks, in effect: "What if I change this decision? What will the result be?"

Wide area network (WAN). A data communications network that covers a large geographic area such as a state, a nation, or the entire world. Contrast with **Local area network.**

Wide Area Telecommunications Service (WATS). A special billing arrangement offered by a common carrier, which provides data communications circuits at lower prices as the volume of calls increases.

WORM. The acronym that means "write-once, read-many," popularized by read-only optical disks.

WYSIWYG. The capability of a system, such as a desktop publishing system or a graphic word processor, to display output on the screen exactly as it will appear in hard copy form.

INDEX